HESPEROS

Hesperos

Studies in Ancient Greek Poetry
Presented to M. L. West
on his Seventieth Birthday

Edited by
P. J. FINGLASS
C. COLLARD
N. J. RICHARDSON

OXFORD
UNIVERSITY PRESS

OXFORD
UNIVERSITY PRESS

Great Clarendon Street, Oxford OX2 6DP

Oxford University Press is a department of the University of Oxford.
It furthers the University's objective of excellence in research, scholarship,
and education by publishing worldwide in

Oxford New York

Auckland Cape Town Dar es Salaam Hong Kong Karachi
Kuala Lumpur Madrid Melbourne Mexico City Nairobi
New Delhi Shanghai Taipei Toronto

With offices in

Argentina Austria Brazil Chile Czech Republic France Greece
Guatemala Hungary Italy Japan Poland Portugal Singapore
South Korea Switzerland Thailand Turkey Ukraine Vietnam

Oxford is a registered trade mark of Oxford University Press
in the UK and in certain other countries

Published in the United States
by Oxford University Press Inc., New York

First published 2007

British Library Cataloguing in Publication Data

Data available

Library of Congress Cataloging in Publication Data

Data available

Typeset by RefineCatch Limited, Bungay, Suffolk
Printed in Great Britain
on acid-free paper by
Biddles Ltd, King's Lynn, Norfolk

ISBN 978–0–19–928568–6

1 3 5 7 9 10 8 6 4 2

Preface

The Editors would like to thank: Hilary O'Shea and the Delegates of the Press for accepting and fostering this volume; the contributors, for their cooperation and timely papers; Ian McAuslan, for careful copy-editing; the Balzan Foundation, for graciously giving permission for the reprinting of Martin West's prize acceptance speech; Stephanie West, for wisdom and discretion; and Jim Adams, whose idea this all was.

All Souls College, Oxford / University of Nottingham P. J. F. F.
The Classics Centre, Oxford C. C.
Greyfriars Hall, Oxford N. J. R.

Contents

Abbreviations

A–B	C. F. L. Austin and G. Bastianini (eds.), *Posidippi Pellaei quae supersunt omnia* (Biblioteca Classica 3; Milan, 2002).
CA	J. U. Powell (ed.), *Collectanea Alexandrina* (Oxford, 1925).
CEG	P. A. Hansen (ed.), *Carmina Epigraphica Graeca* (Berlin, 1983–9).
CHD	H. G. Güterbock and H. A. Hoffner (eds.), *The Hittite Dictionary of the Oriental Institute of the University of Chicago* (Chicago, 1980–).
CPG	E. L. von Leutsch and F. H. Schneidewin (eds.), *Corpus Paroemiographorum Graecorum* (Göttingen, 1839–51). [reprinted Hildesheim 1958]
CPR	*Corpus papyrorum Raineri archiducis Austriae* (Vienna, 1895–).
CTH	E. Laroche (ed.), *Catalogue des textes hittites* (Études et commentaires 75; Paris).
DELG	P. Chantraine (O. Masson, J.-L. Perpillou, J. Taillardat), *Dictionnaire étymologique de la langue grecque: histoire des mots* (Paris, 1999^{2}). [1st ed. 1968–80]
D–K	H. Diels (ed.), *Die Fragmente der Vorsokratiker*^{6} (rev. W. Kranz; Berlin, 1951–2).
EGF	M. Davies (ed.), *Epicorum Graecorum Fragmenta* (Göttingen, 1988).
EGM	R. L. Fowler (ed.), *Early Greek Mythography* (Oxford, 2000–).
EM	K. Ranke and H. Bausinger (eds.), *Enzyklopädie des Märchens: Handwörterbuch zur historischen und vergleichenden Erzählforschung* (Berlin and New York, 1973–96).
FGE	D. L. Page (ed.), *Further Greek Epigrams* (revised and prepared for publication by R. D. Dawe and J. Diggle; Cambridge, 1981).
FGrHist	F. Jacoby *et al.* (eds.), *Die Fragmente der griechischen Historiker* (1923–).

GEF	M. L. West (ed.), *Greek Epic Fragments* (London and Cambridge, MA, 2003).
GGM	C. Müller (ed.), *Geographi Graeci Minores* (Paris, 1855–61).
GP	A. S. F. Gow and D. L. Page (eds.), *The Greek Anthology: The Garland of Philip, and Some Contemporary Epigrams* (Cambridge, 1968).
HE	A. S. F. Gow and D. L. Page (eds.), *The Greek Anthology: Hellenistic Epigrams* (Cambridge, 1965).
IEG	M. L. West (ed.), *Iambi et Elegi Graeci ante Alexandrum cantati*^{2} (Oxford, 1989–92). [1st ed. 1971–2]
IG i^{3}	D. M. Lewis *et al.* (eds.), *Inscriptiones Atticae Euclidis anno anteriores* (Berlin and New York, 1981–94).
IG ii–iii^{2}	J. Kirchner (ed.), *Inscriptiones Atticae Euclidis anno posteriores* (Berlin, 1913–40).
IGSK Ephesos	H. Wankel *et al.* (eds.), *Inschriften griechischer Städte aus Kleinasien. Die Inschriften von Ephesos* (Bonn, 1979–84).
K–G	R. Kühner, *Ausführliche Grammatik der griechischen Sprache. Zweiter Teil: Satzlehre*^{2} (rev. B. Gerth; Hanover and Leipzig, 1898–1904).
LfgrE	B. Snell *et al.* (eds.), *Lexikon des frühgriechischen Epos* (Göttingen, 1955–).
LIMC	*Lexicon Iconographicum Mythologiae Classicae* (Zürich, Munich, and Düsseldorf, 1981–99).
LSJ	H. G. Liddell and R. Scott, *A Greek-English Lexicon*^{9} (rev. H. Stuart-Jones *et al.*; Oxford, 1940).
M–W	R. Merkelbach and M. L. West (eds.), *Fragmenta Hesiodea* (Oxford, 1967).
PCC	J.-P. Migne (ed.), *Patrologiae Cursus Completus* (Paris, 1857–66).
PCG	R. Kassel and C. F. L. Austin (eds.), *Poetae Comici Graeci* (Berlin and New York, 1983–).
P.Colon.	B. Kramer *et al.*, *Kölner Papyri* (Opladen and Paderborn, 1967–).
PEG	A. Bernabé (ed.), *Poetae Epici Graeci. Testimonia et Fragmenta: Pars 1*^{2} (Stuttgart and Leipzig, 1996).
PLF	E. Lobel and D. L. Page (eds.), *Poetarum Lesbiorum Fragmenta*^{2} (Oxford, 1963). [1st ed. 1955]

PMG	D. L. Page (ed.), *Poetae Melici Graeci* (Oxford, 1962).
PMGF	M. Davies (ed.), *Poetarum Melicorum Graecorum Fragmenta* (Oxford, 1991–).
P.Oxy.	B. P. Grenfell, A. S. Hunt *et al.* (eds.), *The Oxyrhynchus Papyri* (London, 1898–).
RfAC	T. Klauser (ed.), *Reallexikon für Antike und Christentum* (Stuttgart, 1950–).
S–D	E. Schwyzer, *Griechische Grammatik. Auf der Grundlage von Karl Brugmanns griechischer Grammatik* (rev. A. Debrunner; Munich, 1934–71).
SEG	J. J. E. Hondius *et al.* (eds.), *Supplementum Epigraphicum Graecum* (Leiden, 1923–).
SGO	R. Merkelbach and J. Stauber (eds.), *Steinepigramme aus dem griechischen Osten* (Munich, Stuttgart and Leipzig, 1998–2004).
SH	P. H. J. Lloyd-Jones and P. J. Parsons (eds.), *Supplementum Hellenisticum* (Texte und Kommentare 11; Berlin and New York, 1983).
SLG	D. L. Page (ed.), *Supplementum Lyricis Graecis* (Oxford, 1974).
S–S	W. Schmid and O. Stählin, *Geschichte der griechischen Literatur* (Munich, 1929–48).
TL	E. Kalinka (ed.), *Tituli Asiae Minoris I. Tituli Lyciae lingua lycia conscripti* (Vienna, 1901).
TrGF	*Tragicorum Graecorum Fragmenta.* Vol. 1 *Didascaliae Tragicae, Catalogi Tragicorum et Tragoediarum, Testimonia et Fragmenta Tragicorum Minorum* (ed. B. Snell; Göttingen 1971[1], 1986[2]); vol. 2 *Fragmenta Adespota* (edd. R. Kannicht and B. Snell; 1981); vol. 3 *Aeschylus* (ed. S. L. Radt; 1977); vol. 4 *Sophocles* (ed. S. L. Radt; 1985[1], 1999[2]); vol. 5 *Euripides* (ed. R. Kannicht; 2004).
TrGFS	J. Diggle (ed.), *Tragicorum Graecorum Fragmenta Selecta* (Oxford, 1998).
W–D	J. Wackernagel and A. Debrunner, *Altindische Grammatik* (Göttingen, 1896–1957).

Notes on Contributors

David Bain was appointed Lecturer in Greek and Latin at the University of Manchester in 1971. He spent the next thirty years in the department, latterly as Professor of Greek, until his early retirement in 2001. He died very suddenly in 2004. His works include *Actors and Audience, a Study of Asides and Related Conventions in Greek Drama* (Oxford, 1977), and *Masters, Servants, and Orders in Greek Tragedy* (Manchester, 1981). He was an expert on what he called 'aischrologia' in Greek, and published a number of fundamental articles on the subject.

Winfried Bühler is Professor Emeritus of Classical Philology at the University of Hamburg. Since 1991 he has been living in Munich. His long-term project is an edition with commentary of the proverbs of Zenobius Athous, of which three volumes have been published to date. He got to know Martin West during a sabbatical year in Oxford in 1964–5, and has encountered him many times since, both in England and in Germany.

Walter Burkert is Professor Emeritus at the University of Zürich, where he has published widely on Greek religion. He holds honorary doctorates from Chicago, Fribourg, Oxford, and Toronto Universities, and in 1990 was awarded the Balzan Prize. He has been a friend of Martin West since 1959, and has worked with him on the Derveni Papyrus and on Oriental–Greek relations.

Paula da Cunha Corrêa has been a Lecturer in Greek Language and Literature at the University of São Paulo, Brazil since 1988. Martin West supervised her MA dissertation '*Harmonia* and *Nomoi*' at Royal Holloway and Bedford New College, University of London 1987 (published as *Harmonia; mito e música na Grécia antiga*, Humanitas, São Paulo, 2003), and informally co-supervised her Ph.D. thesis on Archilochus' war poems (*Armas e Varões; a guerra na lírica de Arquíloco*, Edunesp, São Paulo, 1998). Her postdoctoral research (Exeter and Oxford, 2000) was on Archilochus' fables and erotic poems, and she is now working on all other extant fragments in order to conclude a complete commentary on Archilochus.

Malcolm Davies is Fellow and Tutor in Classics at St John's College, Oxford, where his research interests lie in Greek poetry and folk tale. His doctoral thesis on Stesichorus was examined by Martin West.

James Diggle is Professor of Greek and Latin at Cambridge and a Fellow of Queens' College, and was University Orator from 1982 to 1993. He is the editor of the Oxford Classical Text of Euripides (1981–94). Among his other books are *Studies on the Text of Euripides* (1981), *Euripidea: Collected Essays* (1994), *Cambridge Orations* (1994), *Theophrastus:* Characters (2004), and (with F. R. D. Goodyear) an edition of *The Classical Papers of A. E. Housman* (1972).

Sir Kenneth Dover was Professor of Greek (1955–76) and Chancellor (1981–2005) of the University of St Andrews. He has also served as President of the British Academy (1978–81) and President of Corpus Christi College, Oxford (1976–86). His publications include commentaries on the *Clouds* and *Frogs* of Aristophanes (Oxford, 1968 and 1993), as well as numerous books and articles on Greek language, literature, and history. He was the Tutor for Admissions at Balliol College, Oxford who admitted Martin West in 1955.

Alex Garvie is Emeritus Professor of Greek and Honorary Professorial Research Fellow in the University of Glasgow. His research interests have been primarily in Greek tragedy, with his most recent publication being *The Plays of Sophocles*, a short introduction to Sophocles (London, 2005). At present he is preparing an edition of, and commentary on, Aeschylus' *Persae* for OUP. He first met Martin West in 1960 when they were both interviewed for a Research Fellowship in St John's College, Oxford.

Jasper Griffin was junior by one year to Martin West at Balliol College, Oxford; he was for many years a Fellow of Balliol, and latterly Professor of Classical Literature and Public Orator in the University. He is finishing a book on Greek tragedy in relation to history.

Eric Handley is Professor of Ancient Literature at the Royal Academy of Arts and a Fellow of Trinity College, Cambridge. He was Regius

Professor of Greek in Cambridge, 1984–94, and before that Professor of Greek at University College, London and Director of the Institute of Classical Studies. His main interests are in the ancient theatre, particularly in Greek and Roman comedy and in papyrus fragments of lost plays, on which he is a current contributor to *The Oxyrhynchus Papyri.*

W. B. Henry has research interests in Greek literary papyrology and the Greek lyric poets. He has held positions at Oriel College, Oxford, and the University of Texas at Austin. His doctoral thesis, written under Martin West's supervision, was published in revised form as *Pindar's Nemeans: A Selection* (Munich, 2005).

Adrian Hollis started teaching at St Andrews University. Since 1967 he has been a Fellow of Keble College, Oxford, also sharing with Martin West the teaching of Classics at University College, Oxford, until Martin moved to Bedford College, London. His interests lie in Late Republican and Augustan poetry (*Fragments of Roman Poetry c.60 BC–AD 20* is with the OUP), in particular Ovid (editions of *Metamorphoses* 8 and *Ars Amatoria* 1), and Hellenistic poetry (including Callimachus, *Hecale*) and numismatics. He has edited the *Classical Quarterly.*

Gregory Hutchinson is Professor of Greek and Latin Languages and Literature at the University of Oxford. He is equally interested in Greek and Latin, poetry and prose. His recent publications include *Greek Lyric Poetry: A Commentary on Selected Larger Pieces* (Oxford, 2001) and *Propertius,* Elegies *Book IV* (Cambridge, 2006). He is working at a volume on Hellenistic and Latin poetry books.

Stephen Instone was supervised by Martin West for his Ph.D. thesis 'Studies in Pindar' (Bedford College, University of London, 1983). Since 1988 he has been an Honorary Research Fellow at UCL, where his research interests include Pindar, Greek athletics, and Greek personal religion.

Kiichiro Itsumi is Professor of Greek and Latin Classics at the University of Tokyo. He has published papers on various aspects of Greek metre, and is currently finishing a book on Pindaric metre.

Rudolf Kassel is Professor Emeritus of Classics at the Institut für

Altertumskunde, University of Cologne. His major publications include editions of Aristotle's *Poetics* (Oxford, 1965) and *Rhetoric* (Oxford 1976), Menander's *Sicyonius* (Berlin, 1965), and (with Colin Austin) the eight-volume *Poetae Comici Graeci* (Berlin and New York, 1983–).

David Kovacs is Hugh H. Obear Professor of Classics at the University of Virginia. He has edited and translated Euripides in six volumes for the Loeb Classical Library and is the author of three companion volumes on the life of Euripides and problems in his text. In 1993 he held a Visiting Fellowship at All Souls. He was once invited by Martin West to teach a graduate course with him on *Iphigenia Aulidensis* and hopes their students benefited as much as he did.

J. L. Lightfoot is Sherwood Fellow and Tutor in Classics at New College, Oxford, to which she migrated after holding Prize and Post-Doctoral Fellowships at All Souls College. It was there, as her academic advisor, that M. L. West saw her through *Parthenius of Nicaea* (Oxford, 1999) and *Lucian: On the Syrian Goddess* (Oxford, 2003), and saw her embarked upon *The Sibylline Oracles* (Oxford, forthcoming); and where he helped foster her interests in the Ancient Near East, in Hellenistic and imperial prose and verse, and in hardcore textual scholarship.

Heinz-Günther Nesselrath is Full Professor of Classics (Greek Literature) at the Seminar für Klassische Philologie, Georg-August-Universität Göttingen. His research interests include Greek literature of the Roman Imperial period, classical Greek comedy, and Greek historiography, both classical and Christian. Among his recent major publications are: M. Ebner, H. Gzella, H.-G. Nesselrath, E. Ribbat, *Lukian: Die Lügenfreunde* (Darmstadt, 2001); *Platon und die Erfindung von Atlantis* (Munich and Leipzig, 2002); H.-G. Nesselrath, B. Bäbler, M. Forschner, A. de Jong, *Dion von Prusa, Borysthenes-Rede* (Darmstadt, 2003); *Platon,* Kritias*: Übersetzung und Kommentar* (Göttingen, 2006).

L. P. E. Parker is an Emeritus Fellow of St Hugh's College, Oxford. Before coming to Oxford, she lectured in the Universities of London and Newcastle upon Tyne. She has published a number of papers on metrical subjects, and a full-scale study of the lyric of Aristophanes (*The Songs of Aristophanes*, Oxford, 1997).

Christopher Pelling has been Regius Professor of Greek at Oxford University since 2003. Before that he was Martin West's successor as Fellow and Praelector in Classics at University College, Oxford. His most recent books are *Literary Texts and the Greek Historian* (2000) and *Plutarch and History* (2002). His current projects include a commentary on Plutarch's *Caesar*, a series of articles on Herodotus, and a study of historical explanation in Greek historiography.

Michael Reeve, once a colleague of Martin West at Oxford but from 1984 to 2006 Kennedy Professor of Latin at Cambridge, has edited for Teubner *Daphnis et Chloe* and Cicero's speech *Pro Quinctio* and for OUP Vegetius' *Epitoma rei militaris*, and has published many articles on the transmission of texts and some on the methodology of editing. Currently he is editing Geoffrey of Monmouth and studying the manuscripts of Pliny's *Natural History*.

Nicholas Richardson was a Fellow and Tutor in Classics at Merton College, Oxford from 1968 to 2004, and is at present Warden of Greyfriars Hall, Oxford. Martin West supervised his D.Phil. thesis on the *Homeric Hymn to Demeter*, which was published by OUP in 1964. He has also published a commentary on books 21 to 24 of the *Iliad* (Cambridge, 1993). His main research interests are in early Greek poetry, ancient literary criticism, Greek religion, and modern Greek poetry. He is currently preparing an edition and commentary on some of the other Homeric hymns.

Scott Scullion is Fellow and Tutor in Classics, Worcester College, and Faculty Lecturer in Classical Languages and Literature, University of Oxford. His primary research interests are Greek religion and Greek tragedy, and he has recently published papers on Euripides' alleged death in Macedon and on the fragments of his *Archelaus*, and a chapter on 'Herodotus and Greek religion' in the *Cambridge Companion to Herodotus.*

Calvert Watkins is Professor-in-Residence in Classics and Indo-European Studies at the University of California Los Angeles, and Victor S. Thomas Professor of Linguistics and the Classics, Emeritus, at Harvard University. His research interests include the cultural and literary interface between Hellas and Anatolia in the second and first millennia, Pindar's poetic grammar, and more generally the linguistics and poetics of all the older Indo-European languages. His most recent contribution (forthcoming) is 'The golden bowl: thoughts on the new Sappho and its Asianic background'.

Stephanie West is Fellow Emeritus of Hertford College, Oxford, and her main research interests are in Homer, Herodotus, and Lycophron. Since 1960 she has been married to Martin West.

Encomium

ΕΣΠΕΡΩΙ

ΣΟΦΙΑΙ

μελετᾶν ἄνδρ᾽ ἔμπειρον ἀκριβέων *στρ.*
ἔδοξε βουλᾷ συνετῶν ἐπαινέσαι
ἀφνειόν τ᾽ οὐ κατὰ δαμόταν θέμεν,
ἄξιον ὄντα χρέος πράσσειν μέγ᾽ ὀφειλόμενον·
τοσαῦτα κείνου μεμαθήκαμεν ἄμμες.

γενεὰς τὰς καθ᾽ Ἡσίοδον θεῶν *ἀντ.*
σαφανίσας κ᾽ Ἀρχίλοχον καὶ Θεόγνιδας,
τέτραπται πρὸς Διόνυσον ἠδ᾽ Ἄρη
ἁρμονίας τε λυρᾶν καὶ τέθμια Τερψιχόρας
ὥστ᾽ ἐξικέσθαι σοφίας ἐπ᾽ ἄωτον.

τολμᾷ δ᾽ ὑπερβαίνειν ὅρους ἐθνέων παλαιῶν· *ἐπ.*
ἀλλ᾽ οὐ γὰρ ἑλλανίδα μῆτιν ἐλέγξας
ἀπώσατ᾽, ἰχνεύει δ᾽ ἰδέας ἀοιδᾶν
φαίνων ἄρα μοῦνον ἐὸν Μοισᾶν γένος.

K. J. D.

'Forward into the Past'

Acceptance Speech for the Balzan Prize in Classical Antiquity, 2000

Martin Litchfield West

It might seem self-evident that someone who studies literature is engaged in literary studies. But one may distinguish at least three different approaches to the study of literature. The expression 'literary studies' is really applicable only to one of them, or at any rate there is one that is primarily suggested by it. My energies have been mainly devoted to the other two. The three approaches are, firstly, consideration of the intrinsic qualities of literary works, their beauties or infelicities, the author's imaginative universe, his compositional habits and techniques, and so on; secondly, inquiry into the work's relationship to the world outside itself, its dating, its authenticity, its debts to earlier models or more loosely to the tradition in which it stands, the intellectual and cultural influences operating on the author; and thirdly—an approach which may draw on both the other two, among others—the endeavour to resolve doubts at the verbal level about what exactly the author wrote and what exactly he meant. These three approaches may be summed up as literary criticism, literary history, and philology. I would categorize myself as a philologist and literary historian. My early training was almost wholly philological. At St Paul's School in London a legendary pair of teachers, W. W. Cruickshank and E. P. C. Cotter, concentrated on instilling in us a sense of Greek and Latin grammar and style. Week after week we translated passages of English prose and verse into Greek or Latin prose or verse, and our exercises were minutely and individually corrected and appraised. We also read authors, in class or by ourselves, but hardly saw beyond the meaning of the successive sentences and phrases.

At Oxford the emphasis was not at first very different. We read authors and did linguistic exercises, and seldom wrote essays. But we began to be aware of literary history, of the various lines of tradition, and of the interconnections between different authors. We became acquainted with real living scholars and saw what questions interested them and how they thought. The dominant figure was Eduard Fraenkel, whose monumental *Agamemnon* (1950) we had, with bemusement, sighted even at school. Some of us on our tutors' recommendation attended the famous but terrifying seminars which he used to hold each year, alternately on Greek and Latin texts. (Some of us indeed met our wives there.) Here we saw German philology in action; we felt it reverberate through us as Fraenkel patrolled the room behind our chairs, discoursing in forceful accents. As he spoke of his old teachers and past colleagues—Leo and Norden, Wilamowitz and Wackernagel—it was like an *apparition de l'Église éternelle*. We knew, and could not doubt, that this was what Classical Scholarship was, and that it was for us to learn to carry it on. 'The text must come first', Fraenkel used to say, and discussion of textual problems constituted a major element in his seminars. In his youth he had been mortified by Leo's surprise on discovering that Fraenkel was reading Aristophanes without an apparatus criticus. Indeed it is an evident truth that (as Bruno Snell once put it) 'Philologie ohne Textkritik ist eine nichtige Spielerei'. If one takes the text on trust from whatever edition lies to hand, or (even worse) from whatever translation, one runs great danger of drawing conclusions or building constructions that are easily shown to be unsound. The establishment of improved texts of ancient authors remains among our most important tasks, because it is on the texts that so much of our knowledge of antiquity rests. It is a mistake to suppose that scholars have long ago collated the manuscripts and made editions as good as can reasonably be hoped for. Five hundred years after the Renaissance huge numbers of manuscripts of even the most major authors still await collation and evaluation. And although hundreds of thousands of (usually erroneous) emendations have been proposed for corrupt or supposedly corrupt texts, the problems must continually be addressed afresh, and there is always the possibility of achieving convincing new solutions. As a young man I was advised (I think it was by E. R.

Dodds) that whereas there might still be opportunities of emending prose texts, in the poets significant advances were no longer feasible. I believe I may claim to have falsified that pronouncement, as emendations of mine in over forty Greek poets have been adopted by other editors in their texts. But the production of an improved text of an author does not depend only, or even mainly, on finding better manuscripts or making new emendations. It depends principally on unprejudiced reassessment of the whole of the available evidence for the text and the history of its transmission, and on the reconsideration of each question on the basis of this primary evidence, avoiding easy acquiescence in the choices of previous editors, which by palliating a difficulty may curtail the search before the truth is reached.

I encountered a capital example of this in editing Aeschylus. In the middle of his *Supplices* there is a famous choral ode that begins and ends with the praises of Zeus, 'Lord of Lords, most blessed of the Blessed Ones, most powerful of Powers'. The closing lines, as given by the tenth-century manuscript on which the tradition of this play depends, say:

He obeys the rule of no one seated above him; he is able to execute deed as soon as word of whatever his servile mind brings forth.

It is obvious that Aeschylus cannot have referred to Zeus' mind as 'servile'; it is a complete contradiction of all he has been saying about the god's being the supreme master of the universe, subject to no one else's will. The line must be corrupt. Franciscus Portus in the sixteenth century made it inoffensive by changing a single letter. With the substitution of a beta for a delta, making *δούλιος* into *βούλιος*, the line became

of whatever his counselling mind brings forth.

Editors were content with this, and it became the received text of Aeschylus for the next four hundred years. But it is wrong. Karl Heinrich Keck in 1851, by going back to what is transmitted and considering the problem anew, hit upon a far better solution. By repunctuating, redividing the words, and not replacing a whole letter but adding a single stroke to a letter so as to make an uncial lambda (*Λ*) into a delta (*Δ*), he arrived at:

he is able to execute deed as soon as word. What of these things is not brought forth by Zeus' mind?

This is certainly what Aeschylus wrote. It is superior to Portus' conjecture not because it is better to change half a letter than a whole letter, but because it transforms a limp ending into something much more pointed and absolutely characteristic of Aeschylus; both the form and the content of the rhetorical question are closely paralleled elsewhere in his work. Yet Keck's palmary emendation was scarcely noticed, and Portus' facile emollient continued to occupy editions. The reason is that scholars had ceased to think that there was a problem. Even after the truth was found, they preferred to stay with the reading that had become familiar rather than stir themselves to consider an alternative. I could wish it had been my own conjecture; but I am no less happy to have unearthed it and restored it to its proper place in the text. It perfects the ode.

A small matter, perhaps. But it serves to illustrate two greater things. One is the cumulative nature of Classical studies. For five hundred years scholars have been labouring to understand and where necessary correct the text of Aeschylus and other ancient authors. The modern editor has to look back over those labours and pick out what was profitable in them. The books of nineteenth-century or even sixteenth-century scholars are often still useful. The other thing is that one has to try to step outside the scholarly tradition of which one is a part. On the whole it has led us forward out of the mists to a clearer view of the objects of our study. But from time to time it may have taken a wrong turning, and a whole line of scholars has followed their leader along a false path. One must try to avoid tagging along behind them. It is not easy to question the beliefs in which one has been brought up, or the consensus of critics that a particular solution to a problem is the correct one, even if this consensus is the consequence of inertia rather than repeated independent evaluation.

My work on specific texts has included commentaries, especially on the poems of Hesiod, and translations, especially of Hesiod (in prose) and the lyric, elegiac, and iambic poets (in verse). The commentary remains one of the most useful types of work for the consumer and the most educative for the producer. It forces him to face up to questions of every kind: textual, interpretative, linguistic, stylistic, cultural, mythological, historical, and so on. When I was writing my first commentary (on Hesiod's *Theogony*) Stefan Weinstock asked me if it was to be 'insular' or 'continental'. He meant, would it be the sort of commentary that seeks only to elucidate the particular work which is its object, or the sort that reaches out in all directions and is full of material relevant to other authors in which related things occur. When he put the question, I was not familiar with the distinction, and not sure of my answer; but I think that in the event I leaned towards the continental, and find most value in those commentaries that have the ambition to build bridges out from the work under discussion to the rest of ancient literature. A note in such a commentary often becomes the classic statement of some observation relevant to many authors but prompted by the study of one. By making cross-references to commentators on other authors, scholars create a network of links across the exegetical corpus, and the seeker after insight on some point may find himself bounding happily from one volume to another.

In textual criticism the aim is to discern the truth behind the appearance—what the author actually wrote, as against what appears in the manuscripts. In deciding what is the truth, there are several criteria to be applied: sense, diction, metre, and the like, but also the plausibility, in the light of known processes of transmission, of the assumed relationship between the hypothetical original text and the text as actually preserved. In the case cited from Aeschylus, for example, the intrinsic excellence of the emended text combines with the ease of the assumption that the loss of one stroke from a delta in an ancient text without word division resulted in the transmitted reading. Analogous methodological considerations apply in some of the questions of literary history with which I have grappled. The literary history handed down from antiquity should be seen as having a status similar to that of an ancient text in a medieval manuscript. It is the end product of a process of transmission, in the course of which distortions and falsifications may have occurred. It cannot necessarily be taken at face value. The original truth may have come through the transmission process unscathed. But where different original truths might have come out with the same final appearance, we have to inquire which of them the appearance represents.

Just as there are editors of texts who are constitutionally disposed to believe in whatever the manuscripts offer, so in literary history there are some who will accept as creditworthy 'tradition' any proposition that seems to have documentary backing. Because we have a manuscript corpus of some 1,400 elegiac verses labelled as 'Theognis', there are those who insist on believing that Theognis wrote them all, despite compelling indications that he was only one of many poets represented in the collection. The great majority of scholars, to be sure, accept that it is some sort of anthology. By analysis of its contents I have tried to explain the process by which it came to appear in its present form. In some other areas I have found myself attacking much more firmly entrenched positions, for example, that a poet Homer wrote the *Iliad* and *Odyssey*, that the *Prometheus Vinctus* is by Aeschylus, and that a teenage girl called Erinna was the author of a much-admired poem called *The Distaff*. In each case I have not only argued that the received opinion is false, but endeavoured to explain the process by which history was falsified, and the relationship between the original truth and the eventual appearance. In my revisionist history, the *Iliad* and *Odyssey* are anonymous seventh-century epics propagated by rhapsodes who called themselves Homeridai and attributed their poems to their fictitious eponym 'Homer'. The *Prometheus*, and certain other plays anciently current under Aeschylus' name, were the work of Aeschylus' son Euphorion, who entered them in the competition claiming that his father had left them unperformed at his death. Erinna's poem was a brilliant, romantic pseudepigraphon composed by a male poet. I know that these views will continue to be resisted, chiefly because many people are too firmly attached to the conventional ones. But a scholar must hope that in the fullness of time the arguments will be considered on their merits and either countered with others equally rational or allowed to prevail.

A more complex essay in the field of literary history is represented by my book *The Orphic Poems* (1983). From the fifth century BC to the end of antiquity there are countless references to Orpheus and to 'Orphic' rituals, practices, and writings, and a few references to 'Orphics'. A collection of 'Orphic Hymns' has come down to us, as well as what pretends to be Orpheus' own account of the voyage of the Argo and numerous fragments of other poems. Modern scholars have often assumed the existence of some sort of religious movement describable as Orphism; but about its development there has been wide disagreement. What was evidently the most important of Orphic texts to the late Neoplatonists, the lengthy Rhapsodies, has been variously dated to the sixth century BC, to the Hellenistic period, or even later. Most scholars have felt so bewildered by the whole situation that they avoided taking up any position. I rejected the notion of any unified 'Orphism', and instead set out to establish, so far as might be possible, what different 'Orphic' poems were current in antiquity, what was the nature of their subject matter, at what periods and in what circles they were composed, and how (if at all) they related to one another. There was an abundance of evidence, but for progress to be made it required much analysis and synthesis, helped along by some boldness in speculation. It is a controversial area, and will remain so. But however much I may have gone astray in details, I believe that I followed the right path and that the edifice I constructed will prove to have a solid frame. Boldness in speculation is a quality that critics will find in most of my work. For some it is a term of censure: these are people who are always ready to denounce a speculation as 'mere' speculation. I should reserve the expression 'mere speculation' for cases where the hypothesis is not guided by particular indications, or has no special explanatory value. It will be found that many of the stones that I throw have the attractive property of killing two birds. These, I would claim, are something more than 'mere' speculations. Solid proof is hard to come by in our field, and the scholar who ventures nothing without it may be highly respected for soundness, but is unlikely to advance the subject very much. One must sometimes deploy one's imagination, while maintaining a critical (and self-critical) spirit. As Gottfried Hermann once wrote: 'nec temere hariolandum est in antiquitatis pervestigatione, neque carere divinationis adiumento possumus.'

The study of ancient music might be thought to be a field offering large scope for conjecture. But in fact, for the type of critical conjecture described in the previous paragraph, it offers very little scope. What is lost, is lost utterly. We fancy we have some notion of the constraints governing the music of Aeschylus. Anyone might compose melodies for the lyrics of the *Agamemnon* observing those constraints, but no such enterprise would deserve a place in a scholarly publication, because there is no possibility of reconstructing the lost music even conjecturally. Writing my book on ancient Greek music, therefore, was very largely a matter of gathering the mass of scattered evidence together and trying to explain each aspect of the subject in terms clear enough for my own understanding and for that of other untutored people. The most original part of the book is the analysis of the surviving melodies and fragments of melodies and the description of common features found in them. The other major strand in my work that deserves notice here is the investigation of oriental influences on Greek poetry and philosophy. I was led into this by my doctoral work on Hesiod's *Theogony*, a poem which shows such striking mythological parallels with Hittite and Babylonian texts that no one denies a historical connection. The interest thus stimulated subsequently found expression in several articles and in two books published twenty-six years apart. The first of these, *Early Greek Philosophy and the Orient* (1971), leaves a good deal to be desired, as others have noted. But it has aroused enthusiasm in some quarters, and I do not disown it entirely. The accounts of Pherecydes and Heraclitus are perhaps the most substantial contributions in it. I regret that the book has been almost totally ignored, *totgeschwiegen*, by the 'professional' historians of Greek philosophy, who remain absorbed in their own traditional agenda. The other book, *The East Face of Helicon*, published in 1997 (6,000 years to the day from the Creation of the World as calculated by Archbishop Ussher), is a different matter. This time I prepared myself for the task more thoroughly by studying the most relevant oriental languages—Akkadian, Ugaritic, Phoenician, Hebrew, Hittite—and reading the relevant texts in the original. The scope of the book is, broadly speaking, Greek poetry and myth from the beginnings down to 450 BC. It is not a new idea to explore cultural connections between archaic Greece and western Asia—Walter Burkert, the Balzan prizewinner of 1990, had published a valuable survey of the question—but my study is the most comprehensive to date, and its very bulk gives it a chance of making an impression on the general consciousness. The subject is of the highest importance for our appreciation of early Greek poetry and the influences that shaped it. Already in 1964 H. Petriconi, in a discussion of the *Epic of Gilgamesh* as a model for the *Iliad*, wrote that

> The days of an exclusively 'classical' scholarship are over. To write about Greek literature without knowing something of the West Asiatic has become as impossible as studying Roman literature without knowledge of the Greek.

I believe that the truth of this provocative assertion is increasingly being recognized. However, the West Asiatic contribution, pervasive as it appears, is only one ingredient in the rich compound that is Greek culture. In the years to come I hope to investigate another ingredient: the Indo-European heritage of mythology and of poetic language and form. It is all part of literary history. There is a view, fashionable in some quarters, that all interpretation of the past is necessarily subjective, that history is whatever you care to make of it, and that the very idea that there is such a thing as objective historical truth is a naive positivist error. If that were the case, scholarship would be little more than an intellectual game; and there are indeed those who seem to treat it as such. But such extreme relativism is nonsense. Of course many different types of equally valid history can be made by asking different sets of questions. But there are objective underlying facts, to which every construction must relate. They are not always attainable. But the scholar must try to attain them, or get as close to them as possible. That is far from being the only task. A fact is of little interest except in relation to other facts. Finding the most meaningful relationships is the great challenge, in scholarship as in life.

The Academic Publications of M. L. West

1960

1. 'Anaxagoras and the meteorite of 467 BC', *JBAA* 70 (1960): 368–9.

1961

2. 'An ancient reference to the Quadrantids', *JBAA* 71 (1961): 206.
3. 'Alleged apparitions of Halley's Comet in the eighteenth century BC and earlier', *JBAA* 71 (1961): 324–6.
4. 'Hesiodea', *CQ* NS 11 (1961): 130–45.
5. 'Lucretius, iii. 916–18', *CR* NS 11 (1961): 203–4.
6. 'Persius, i. 1–3', *CR* NS 11 (1961): 204.

1962

7. Review of J. Schwartz, *Pseudo-Hesiodeia* (Leiden, 1960), *CR* NS 12 (1962): 17–19.
8. Review of J. Martin (ed.), *Ménandre: L'Atrabilaire* (Paris, 1961), *Gnomon* 34 (1962): 251–3.
9. Review of J. D. P. Bolton, *Aristeas of Proconnesus* (Oxford, 1962), *The Oxford Magazine* NS 2 (1961–2): 374.
10. 'Konjekturen zu den orphischen Hymnen', *Philologus* 106 (1962): 121–2.
11. 'Empedocles on papyrus', *CR* NS 12 (1962): 120.
12. Review of G. S. Kirk, *The Songs of Homer* (Cambridge, 1962), *The Listener* vol. 68 (1962): 1019–20.
13. 'Zu Musaios', *Philologus* 106 (1962): 315.
14. 'More notes on the text of Hesiod', *CQ* NS 12 (1962): 177–81.
15. 'Nonniana', *CQ* NS 12 (1962): 223–34.
16. 'A latent fragment of Hecataeus' *Γενεαλογίαι*', *CR* NS 12 (1962): 200–1.

1963

17. Review of O. Reverdin (ed.), *Hésiode et son influence* (Geneva, 1960), *Gnomon* 35 (1963): 10–15.
18. 'Critical notes on Apollonius Rhodius', *CR* NS 13 (1963): 9–12.
19. 'On Nicander, Oppian, and Quintus of Smyrna', *CQ* NS 13 (1963): 57–62.
20. Review of H. Diller, *Die dichterische Form von Hesiods Erga* (Wiesbaden, 1962), *Gnomon* 35 (1963): 300–1.
21. Review of E. Heitsch (ed.), *Die griechischen Dichterfragmente der römischen Kaiserzeit* (Göttingen, 1961), *GGA* 215 (1963): 164–72.
22. 'Three Presocratic cosmologies', *CQ* NS 13 (1963): 154–76.
23. Review of *The Oxyrhynchus Papyri* 28, *Gnomon* 35 (1963): 752–9.
24. 'Iolkos in der griechischen Dichtung', *Glotta* 41 (1963): 278–82.
25. '*Γλωθρός*', *Glotta* 41 (1963): 282–5.

1964

26. 'The Muses buy a cow', *CR* NS 14 (1964): 141–2.
27. Review of P. I. Kakrides, *Κόϊντος Σμυρναῖος. Γενικὴ Μελέτη τῶν "Μεθ' Ὅμηρον" καὶ τοῦ ποιητῆ τους* (Athens 1962), *CR* NS 14 (1964): 213–14.
28. 'Two versions of *Jabberwocky*', *G&R* 2nd ser. 11 (1964): 185–7.
29. 'The medieval and renaissance manuscripts of Hesiod's *Theogony*', *CQ* NS 14 (1964): 165–89.
30. 'An epic fragment in Servius', *CR* NS 14 (1964): 242.
31. 'Megasthenes on the Astomi', *CR* NS 14 (1964): 242.
32. Review of F. Vian (ed.), *Quintus de Smyrne. La Suite d' Homère. Tome I* (Paris, 1963), *CR* NS 14 (1964): 257–9.
33. 'Miscellaneous notes on the Works and Days', *Philologus* 108 (1964): 157–73.

1965

34. Review of I. Löffler, *Die Melampodie. Versuch einer Rekonstruktion des Inhalts* (Meisenheim am Glan, 1963), *CR* NS 15 (1965): 110–11.

35. 'Haplology', *CR* NS 15 (1965): 139–42.
36. 'Euripides, *Hippolytus* 88', *CR* NS 15 (1965): 156.
37. Review of F. Krafft, *Vergleichende Untersuchungen zu Homer und Hesiod* (Göttingen, 1963), *CR* NS 15 (1965): 158–9.
38. Review of H. Maehler, *Die Auffassung des Dichterberufs im frühen Griechentum bis zur Zeit Pindars* (Göttingen, 1964), *CR* NS 15 (1965): 222.
39. Review of E. Heitsch (ed.), *Die griechischen Dichterfragmente der römischen Kaiserzeit. Band II* (Göttingen, 1964), *CR* NS 15 (1965): 224–5.
40. Review of H. Fränkel, *Einleitung zur kritischen Ausgabe der Argonautika des Apollonios* (Göttingen, 1964), *Erasmus* 17 (1965): 179–81.
41. 'Alcmanica', *CQ* NS 15 (1965): 188–202.
42. 'Tryphon *De Tropis*', *CQ* NS 15 (1965): 230–48.
43. 'The Dictaean Hymn to the Kouros', *JHS* 85 (1965): 149–59.
44. Review of N. A. Livadaras, *Ἱστορία τῆς παραδόσεως τοῦ κειμένου τοῦ Ἡσιόδου* (Athens, 1963), *Gnomon* 37 (1965): 650–5.
45. (with R. Merkelbach) 'The Wedding of Ceyx', *RhM* n.F. 108 (1965): 300–17.
46. Review of E. D. M. Fraenkel, *Kleine Beiträge zur klassischen Philologie* (Rome, 1964), *Erasmus* 17 (1965): 746–8.

1966

47. Review of *The Oxyrhynchus Papyri* 30, *CR* NS 16 (1966): 21–4.
48. '*Ζωρός* in Empedocles', *CR* NS 16 (1966): 135–6.
49. 'Theognostea', *Glotta* 44 (1966): 33–4.
50. Review of A. S. F. Gow (ed.), *Machon: The Fragments* (Cambridge, 1965), *JHS* 86 (1966): 200–1.
51. (with P. H. J. Lloyd-Jones) 'Oracles of Apollo Kareios', *Maia* 18 (1966): 263–4.
52. *Hesiod:* Theogony (Oxford, 1966). Pp. xiii + 459.
53. 'Three papyri of Hesiod', *Bulletin of the American Society of Papyrologists* 3 (1966): 65–78. [See no. 151]
54. 'Catching worms', *CR* NS 16 (1966): 274.
55. 'Euripides, *Hippolytus* 88 again', *CR* NS 16 (1966): 274–5.
56. 'Conjectures on 46 Greek poets', *Philologus* 110 (1966): 147–68.

1967

57. Review of K. Deichgräber, *Die Musen, Nereiden und Okeaninen in Hesiods Theogonie* (Wiesbaden, 1965), *CR* NS 17 (1967): 104.
58. 'Epica', *Glotta* 44 (1967): 135–48.
59. 'Fragments of Hesiod, *Theogony*', *The Oxyrhynchus Papyri* 32 (1967), 163–79.
60. 'Alcman and Pythagoras', *CQ* NS 17 (1967): 1–15.
61. 'A note on Theocritus' Aeolic poems', *CQ* NS 17 (1967): 82–4.
62. 'An epigram on Heraclitus', *CR* NS 17 (1967): 127–8.
63. 'Prose in Simonides', *CR* NS 17 (1967): 133.
64. 'Hesiod', in *The American Peoples Encyclopedia* (New York, 1967).
65. (with R. Merkelbach) *Fragmenta Hesiodea* (Oxford, 1967). Pp. xi + 236.
66. 'The contest of Homer and Hesiod', *CQ* NS 17 (1967): 433–50.
67. Review of P. Walcot, *Hesiod and the Near East* (Cardiff, 1966), *CR* NS 17 (1967): 268–9.
68. 'The Berlin Tyrtaeus', *ZPE* 1 (1967): 173–82.
69. 'Oracles of Apollo Kareios: a revised text', *ZPE* 1 (1967): 183–7.

1968

70. 'Two passages of Aristophanes', *CR* NS 18 (1968): 5–8.
71. Review of H. Schwabl, *Hesiods Theogonie: Eine unitarische Analyse* (Vienna, 1966), *CR* NS 18 (1968): 27–8.
72. (acting editor) Liddell-Scott-Jones, *Greek-English Lexicon: A Supplement.* Edited by E. A. Barber, with the assistance of P. Maas, M. Scheller, and M. L. West (Oxford, 1968). Pp. xi + 153.
73. Review of M. Platnauer (ed.), *Fifty Years (and Twelve) of Classical Scholarship* (Oxford, 1968), *The Oxford Magazine* (1968 Trinity 7): 390–1.
74. 'Two notes on Delphic inscriptions', *ZPE* 2 (1968): 176.
75. 'Notes on newly-discovered fragments of Greek authors', *Maia* 20 (1968): 195–205.
76. Review of R. Kassel (ed.), *Menandri Sicyonius* (Berlin, 1965), *JHS* 88 (1968): 162–3.
77. 'Notes on the Orphic Hymns', *CQ* NS 18 (1968): 288–96.

78. 'Near Eastern material in Hellenistic and Roman literature', *HSCP* 73 (1968): 113–34.
79. 'A pseudo-fragment of Heraclitus', *CR* NS 18 (1968): 257–8.

1969

80. Review of A. Colonna (ed.), *Esiodo. Le opere e i giorni* (Milan, 1968), *Gnomon* 41 (1969): 118–21.
81. 'The Sayings of Democritus', *CR* NS 19 (1969): 142.
82. 'Stesichorus redivivus', *ZPE* 4 (1969): 135–49.
83. Review of D. A. Campbell (ed.), *Greek Lyric Poetry* (London, Melbourne, New York 1967), *JHS* 89 (1969): 126–7.
84. Review of R. Führer, *Formproblem-Untersuchungen zu den Reden in der frühgriechischen Lyrik* (Munich, 1967), *JHS* 89 (1969): 127–8.
85. 'Echoes and imitations of the Hesiodic poems', *Philologus* 113 (1969): 1–9.
86. 'An atomist illustration in Aristotle', *Philologus* 113 (1969): 150–1.
87. 'The Achaean wall', *CR* NS 19 (1969): 255–60.
88. 'Three Greek baby-words', *Glotta* 47 (1969): 184–6.

1970

89–95. 'Athene', 'Cronus', 'Golden Age' (s.v. Time), 'Orpheus and Orphism', 'Poseidon', 'Prometheus', 'Uranus', *Man, Myth and Magic* (London, 1970–2).

96. Review of G.(I.) Tarditi (ed.), *Archilochus* (Rome, 1968) and C. Prato (ed.), *Tyrtaeus* (Rome, 1968), *CR* NS 20 (1970): 147–51.
97. Review of R. Hope Simpson and J. F. Lazenby, *The Catalogue of the Ships in Homer's* Iliad (Oxford, 1970), *The Oxford Magazine* (1970 Trinity 8), 322–3.
98. 'Hesiod, Erga 173a–e', *ZPE* 6 (1970): 54 and plate IVb.
99. (with R. Merkelbach) *Fragmenta Selecta*, in F. Solmsen, *Hesiodi Opera* (Oxford, 1970). [Cf. nos. 246, 322]

100–9. 'Certamen Homeri et Hesiodi', 'Choerilus', 'Cynaethus', 'Epic Cycle', 'Eumelus', 'Hesiod', 'Homeridae', 'Nonnus',

'Rhapsodes', 'Tryphiodorus', *The Oxford Classical Dictionary*[2] (Oxford, 1970).

110. 'Bemerkungen zu Versinschriften', *ZPE* 6 (1970): 171–4.
111. Review of E. Livrea (ed.), *Colluto: Il Ratto di Elena* (Bologna, 1968), *Gnomon* 42 (1970): 657–61.
112. 'Melica', *CQ* NS 20 (1970): 205–15.
113. 'Corinna', *CQ* NS 20 (1970): 277–87.
114. 'The Eighth Homeric Hymn and Proclus', *CQ* NS 20 (1970): 300–4.
115. 'A new approach to Greek prosody', *Glotta* 48 (1970): 185–94.
116. 'On Lesbian accentuation', *Glotta* 48 (1970): 194–8.
117. 'Hesiod, *Fragmenta*, again', *CR* NS 20 (1970): 416.
118. 'Burning Sappho', *Maia* 22 (1970): 307–30.

1971

119. Review of W. de Sousa Medeiros, *Hipponactea: Subsídios para uma nova edição crítica do iambógrafo de Éfeso* (Coimbra, 1969), *CR* NS 21 (1971): 12–13.
120. Review of G. L. Huxley, *Greek Epic Poetry from Eumelos to Panyassis* (London, 1969), *CR* NS 21 (1971): 67–9.
121. 'Aristophanes, *Acharnians* 1178–86', *CR* NS 21 (1971): 157–8.
122. 'Further light on Stesichorus' Iliu Persis', *ZPE* 7 (1971): 262–4.
123. *Early Greek Philosophy and the Orient* (Oxford, 1971). Pp. xv + 256. [Italian translation no. 358]
124. *Sing Me, Goddess* (London, 1971). Pp. 43. [Translation of *Iliad* Book 1]
125. *Iambi et Elegi Graeci ante Alexandrum cantati* I (Oxford, 1971). Pp. xvi + 256. [2nd edition no. 314]
126. 'Stesichorus', *CQ* NS 21 (1971): 302–14.
127. 'The cosmology of "Hippocrates", *De Hebdomadibus*', *CQ* NS 21 (1971): 365–88.
128. 'Callimachus on the Pythagoreans', *CR* NS 21 (1971): 330–1.

1972

129. *Iambi et Elegi Graeci ante Alexandrum cantati* II (Oxford, 1972). Pp. x + 246. [2nd edition no. 346]

130. Review of A. D. Nock, *Essays on Religion and the Ancient World* (Oxford, 1972), *The Spectator* 10th June 1972: 896–7.
131. Review of J. Rudhardt, *Le Thème de l'eau primordiale dans la mythologie grecque* (Bern, 1971), *JTS* 23 (1972): 581.
132. 'Lydian metre', *Kadmos* 11 (1972): 165–75.

1973

133. *Textual Criticism and Editorial Technique applicable to Greek and Latin Texts* (Stuttgart, 1973). Pp. 155. [Modern Greek translation no. 315, Italian no. 337, Hungarian no. 426, Portuguese no. 454]
134. 'Two unnoticed fragments of Polybius', *CR* NS 23 (1973): 9–10.
135. Review of G. P. Edwards, *The Language of Hesiod in its Traditional Context* (Oxford, 1971), *CR* NS 23 (1973): 19–20.
136. Review of C. Calame, *Etymologicum Genuinum: les citations de poètes lyriques* (Rome, 1970), *CR* NS 23 (1973): 99–100.
137. 'Indo-European metre', *Glotta* 51 (1973): 161–87. [Russian translation no. 308]
138. 'Greek poetry 2000–700 BC', *CQ* NS 23 (1973): 179–92.
139. 'Critical notes on Euripides' *Heracles*', *Philologus* 117 (1973): 145–51.

1974

140. 'Wartetext 12: Hexameters. P. Mich. Inv. 1261', *ZPE* 13 (1974): 282 and plate XIIIc.
141. (with R. Merkelbach) 'Ein Archilochos-Papyrus', *ZPE* 14 (1974): 97–112.
142. *Studies in Greek Elegy and Iambus* (Berlin and New York, 1974). Pp. ix + 198.
143. 'The medieval manuscripts of the *Works and Days*', *CQ* NS 24 (1974): 161–85.
144. 'Graeco-Oriental Orphism in the third century BC', *Sixth International Congress of Classical Studies* (Madrid, 1974), Summaries of Reports, 36–7. [See also no. 159]
145. 'Ein wiedergefundenes Archilochos-Gedicht?', *Poetica. Zeitschrift für Sprach- und Literaturwissenschaft* 6 (1974): 481–5.

146. Review of G. Nagy, *Comparative Studies in Greek and Indic Meter* (Cambridge, MA, 1974), *Phoenix* 28 (1974): 457–9.

1975

147. 'The metrical placing of small papyrus fragments', *Proceedings of the XIV International Congress of Papyrologists. Oxford, 24–31 July 1974* (Graeco-Roman Memoirs 61; London 1975), 341–7.
148. 'Archilochus ludens. Epilogue of the other editor', *ZPE* 16 (1975): 217–19.
149. *Immortal Helen* (London 1975). Pp. 18. [Inaugural Lecture, Bedford College]
150. 'The Lydian accent', *Kadmos* 13 (1974): 133–6.
151. 'Three papyri of Hesiod: corrigenda', *ZPE* 18 (1975): 191. [See no. 53]
152. 'Zum neuen Goldblättchen aus Hipponion', *ZPE* 18 (1975): 229–36.
153. Review of M. Hofinger, *Lexicon Hesiodeum: Index Inversus* (Leiden, 1973), *CR* NS 25 (1975): 320–1.
154. 'Cynaethus' Hymn to Apollo', *CQ* NS 25 (1975): 161–70.
155. 'Some lyric fragments reconsidered', *CQ* NS 25 (1975): 307–9.

1976

156. Review of W. S. Allen, *Accent and Rhythm* (Cambridge, 1973), *Gnomon* 48 (1976): 1–8.
157. Review of V. J. Matthews (ed.), *Panyassis of Halikarnassos* (Leiden, 1974), *CP* 71 (1976): 172–4.
158. Review of N. Austin, *Archery at the Dark of the Moon: Poetic Problems in Homer's* Odyssey (Berkeley and London, 1975), *TLS* 4 June 1976: 678.
159. 'Graeco-Oriental Orphism in the third century BC', in D. M. Pippidi (ed.), *Assimilation et résistance à la culture gréco-romaine dans le monde ancien: Travaux du VIe Congrès Internationale d'Etudes classiques (Madrid, Septembre 1974)* (Bucharest and Paris, 1976), 221–6. [See also no. 144]
160. 'The composition of the *Works and Days*' (Summary of paper read in 1974), *BICS* 23 (1976): 127.

161. 'The asigmatic Atlas', *ZPE* 22 (1976): 41–2.
162. '*θεόταυρος*', *Glotta* 54 (1976): 100–1.
163. Review of L. Bona Quaglia, *Gli 'Erga' di Esiodo* (Turin, 1973), *JHS* 96 (1976): 168–9.
164. Review of L. Di Gregorio (ed.), *Scholia vetera in Hesiodi Theogoniam* (Milan, 1975), *JHS* 96 (1976): 169.
165. Review of G. A. Privitera, *La Rete di Afrodite: Studi su Saffo* (Palermo, 1974), *JHS* 96 (1976): 170.
166. Review of B. Peabody, *The Winged Word: A Study in the Technique of Ancient Greek Oral Composition as seen principally through Hesiod's* Works and Days (Albany, NY, 1975), *Phoenix* 30 (1976): 382–6.

1977

167. Fragments of Hesiod, *Erga* and *Aspis*, *The Oxyrhynchus Papyri* 45 (1977): 40–62.
168. 'Erinna', *ZPE* 25 (1977): 95–119.
169. 'Balbilla did not save Memnon's soul', *ZPE* 25 (1977): 120.
170. 'Clues to the crossword from ancient Egyptians', *The Times* 9th July 1977: 12.
171. 'Four emendations in Aristophanes', *CQ* NS 27 (1977): 73–5.
172. Review of R. D. Dawe, *Studies on the Text of Sophocles* I–II (Leiden 1973), *CP* 72 (1977): 264–7.
173. 'Notes on papyri', *ZPE* 26 (1977): 37–43. [Followed by poem, 'Aus der Geschichte der Textüberlieferung']
174. 'Two notes on the Cologne Epode of Archilochus', *ZPE* 26 (1977): 44–8.
175. Review of E.-M. Voigt (ed.), *Sappho et Alcaeus* (Amsterdam 1971), *CR* NS 27 (1977): 161–3.
176. Review of M. Hofinger, *Lexicon Hesiodeum* I (Leiden, 1975), *CR* NS 27 (1977): 268.
177. 'Emendations in Plato, *Gorgias* and *Timaeus*', *CQ* NS 27 (1977): 300–2.
178. 'The tempo of Greek polysyllables', *Glotta* 55 (1977): 159–60.
179. 'Tragica I', *BICS* 24 (1977): 89–103.

1978

180. 'Die griechischen Dichterinnen der Kaiserzeit', in H. G. Beck, A. Kambylis, and P. Moraux (eds.), *Kyklos: Griechisches und Byzantinisches: Rudolf Keydell zum neunzigsten Geburtstag* (Berlin and New York, 1978), 101–15.
181. *Hesiod:* Works and Days (Oxford, 1978). Pp. xiii + 399.
182. Review of D. L. Page (ed.), *Epigrammata Graeca* (Oxford, 1975), *Gnomon* 50 (1978): 1–4.
183. 'Stesichorus at Lille', *ZPE* 29 (1978): 1–4.
184. Review of F. Vian (ed.), *Nonnos de Panopolis* I (Paris, 1976) and P. Chuvin (ed.), *Nonnos de Panopolis* II (Paris, 1976), *CR* NS 28 (1978): 8–10.
185. Review of L. L. Clader, *Helen: The Evolution from Divine to Heroic in Greek Epic Tradition* (Leiden, 1976), *CR* NS 28 (1978): 145.
186. Review of R. D. Dawe (ed.), *Sophocles. Tragoediae* I (Leipzig, 1975), *Gnomon* 50 (1978): 236–43.
187. 'Phocylides', *JHS* 98 (1978): 164–7.
188. 'La formazione culturale della *polis* e la poesia esiodca', in R. B. Bandinelli (ed.), *Storia e Civiltà dei Greci* I. *Origini e sviluppo della città. Il medioevo greco* (Milan, 1978), 254–90.
189. *Theognidis et Phocylidis Fragmenta et Adespota quaedam gnomica* (Kleine Texte 192; Berlin and New York 1978). Pp. iv + 49.
190. Review of W. W. Minton, *Concordance to the Hesiodic Corpus* (Leiden 1976), *CR* NS 28 (1978): 342.
191. 'Tragica II', *BICS* 25 (1978): 106–22.
192. 'An unrecognized fragment of Archilochus?' *ZPE* 32 (1978): 1–5.

1979

193. 'The Parodos of the *Agamemnon*', *CQ* NS 29 (1979): 1–6.
194. Review of J. Latacz, *Kampfparänese, Kampfdarstellung und Kampfwirklichkeit in der Iliad, bei Kallinos und Tyrtaios* (Munich, 1977), *CR* NS 29 (1979): 135–6.
195. Review of H. D. Rankin, *Archilochus of Paros* (Park Ridge, NJ, 1977), *CR* NS 29 (1979): 137.

196. 'The Prometheus trilogy', *JHS* 99 (1979): 130–48.
197. Obituary: E. R. Dodds. *University College* [Oxford] *Record* vol. 7 no. 5 (1979): 229–30.
198. Review of M. Hofinger, *Lexicon Hesiodeum cum indice inverso* II–IV (Leiden 1978), *CR* NS 29 (1979): 305–6.
199. 'Four Hellenistic first lines restored', *CQ* NS 29 (1979): 324–6.
200. 'Tragica III', *BICS* 26 (1979): 104–17.

1980

201. 'Iambics in Simonides, Bacchylides and Pindar', *ZPE* 37 (1980): 137–55.
202. 'Hésiode et la Grèce de l'époque géométrique' (Résumé), *Actes du Xe Congrès de l'Association Guillaume Budé (Toulouse, 1978)* (Paris, 1980), 117–18.
203. (ed. with K. J. Dover, J. Griffin, E. L. Bowie) *Ancient Greek Literature* (Oxford, 1980). [Italian translation no. 352; 2nd edition no. 409]
204. Review of P. W. van der Horst (ed.), *The Sentences of Pseudo-Phocylides* (Leiden, 1978), *CR* NS 30 (1980): 136–7.
205. Review of G. Nagy, *The Best of the Achaeans* (Baltimore, 1979), *TLS* 8th August 1980: 893.
206. 'The midnight planet', *JHS* 100 (1980): 206–8.
207. Review of E. Crespo, *Elementos antiguos y modernos en la prosodía homérica* (Salamanca, 1977), *JHS* 100 (1980): 215.
208. Review of M. Pintacuda, *La Musica nella tragedia greca* (Cefalù, 1978), *JHS* 100 (1980): 238.
209. Review of L. Berkowitz, *Canon of Greek Authors and Works from Homer to AD 200* (Costa Mesa, 1977), *JHS* 100 (1980): 238.
210. *Delectus ex Iambis et Elegis Graecis* (Oxford, 1980). Pp. ix + 295.
211. Review of E. Livrea (ed.), *Anonymi fortasse Olympiodori Thebani Blemyomachia (P. Berol. 5003)* (Meisenheim am Glan, 1978), *CR* NS 30 (1980): 276.
212. Review of R. D. Dawe, *Studies on the Text of Sophocles* III (Leiden, 1978), *CP* 75 (1980): 364–7.
213. Review of G. Paniagua, *Musique de la Grèce antique* [gramophone record], *Gnomon* 52 (1980): 697–700.
214. 'Tragica IV', *BICS* 27 (1980): 9–22.

1981

215. Review of B. Gentili and C. Prato (eds.), *Poetae Elegiaci* I (Leipzig, 1979), *CR* NS 31 (1981): 1–2.
216. Review of P. Radici Colace, *Choerili Samii Reliquiae* (Rome, 1979), *CR* NS 31 (1981): 104–5.
217. 'Girisha higeki-shijin niokeru uchuron' [Cosmology in the Greek tragedians] *Shiso* 7 (1981): 52–67. [Cf. no. 230]
218. 'Melos, Iambos, Elegie und Epigramm', in E. Vogt (ed.), *Griechische Literatur* (Neues Handbuch der Literatur 2; Wiesbaden 1981), 73–142.
219. 'The singing of Homer and the modes of early Greek music', *JHS* 101 (1981): 113–29.
220. Review of J. Chailley, *La Musique grecque antique* (Paris, 1979), *JHS* 101 (1981): 188.
221. 'Simonides' Danae fragment: a metrical analysis', *BICS* 28 (1981): 30–8.
222. 'Tragica V', *BICS* 28 (1981): 61–78.
223 Review of R. D. Dawe (ed.), *Sophoclis Tragoediae* II (Leipzig, 1979), *Gnomon* 53 (1981): 522–8.
224. 'Is the *Works and Days* an oral poem?', in C. Brillante, M. Cantilena, and C. O. Pavese (eds.), *I Poemi epici rapsodici non omerici e la tradizione orale: Atti del convegno di Venezia, 28–30 settembre 1977* (Padua, 1981), 53–73.

1982

225. 'Metrical analyses: Timotheos and others', *ZPE* 45 (1982): 1–13.
226. 'Disjunction of cola in iambic tetrameters', *ZPE* 45 (1982): 14–16.
227. 'The Orphics of Olbia', *ZPE* 45 (1982): 17–29.
228. 'Archilochus' fox and eagle: more echoes in later poetry', *ZPE* 45 (1982): 30–2.
229. Review of M. Vetta (ed.), *Theognis. Elegiarum Liber Secundus* (Rome, 1980), *CR* NS 32 (1982): 89.
230. 'Cosmology in the Greek tragedians', *Balkan and Asia Minor Studies* (Research Institute of Civilization, Tokai University, Tokyo) 8 (1982): 1–13. [See no. 217]

231. 'The metre of Arius' *Thalia*', *JTS* 33 (1982): 98–105.
232. 'Stesichorus' horse', *ZPE* 48 (1982): 86.
233. 'Three topics in Greek metre', *CQ* NS 32 (1982): 281–97.
234. 'Magnus and Marcellinus: unnoticed acrostics in the Cyranides', *CQ* NS 32 (1982): 480–1.
235. Review of J. F. Kindstrand (ed.), *Isaac Porphyrogenitus. Praefatio in Homerum* (Uppsala, 1979), *Proceedings of the African Classical Associations* 16 (1982): 67.
236. Review of A. M. Dale, *Metrical Analyses of Tragic Choruses* II (London, 1981), *JHS* 102 (1982): 255.
237. Review of F. R. Adrados (ed.), *Diccionario griego-español* I (α – ἀλλά) (Madrid, 1980), *JHS* 102 (1982): 256.
238. *Greek Metre* (Oxford, 1982). Pp. xiv + 208.

1983

239. 'Two lunatic notes', *ZPE* 50 (1983): 46.
240. 'Schwerlich Zufall', *ZPE* 50 (1983): 46.
241. Review of M. Campbell, *A Commentary on Quintus Smyrnaeus XII* (Leiden 1981), *CR* NS 33 (1983): 14–15.
242. Review of K. Alpers (ed.), *Das attizistische Lexikon des Oros* (Berlin, 1981), *CR* NS 33 (1983): 20–2.
243. Review of A. Casanova, *La Famiglia di Pandora* (Florence, 1979), *CR* NS 33 (1983): 126.
244. Review of M. Campbell, *Echoes and Imitations of Early Epic in Apollonius Rhodius* (Leiden, 1981), *CR* NS 33 (1983): 129.
245. 'Tragica VI', *BICS* 30 (1983): 63–82.
246. (with R. Merkelbach) 'Appendix nova fragmentorum', in *Hesiodi Opera*^{2} (Oxford, 1983), 227–32, 253. [Cf. nos. 99, 322]
247. Review of D. L. Page (ed.), *Further Greek Epigrams* (Cambridge, 1981), *JHS* 103 (1983): 186–7.
248. Review of B. Gerlaud (ed.), *Triphiodore* (Paris, 1982); H. (= E.) Livrea (ed.), *Triphiodorus* (Leipzig, 1982); H. Livrea (ed., adiuvante P. Eleuteri), *Musaeus* (Leipzig, 1982), *CR* NS 33 (1983): 184–7.
249. Review of D. A. Campbell (ed.), *Greek Lyric* I (Cambridge, MA and London, 1982), *CR* NS 33 (1983): 309.

250. Review of M. Brioso Sánchez (ed.), *Anacreónticas* (Madrid, 1981), *CR* NS 33 (1983): 310.
251. *The Orphic Poems* (Oxford, 1983). Pp. xii + 275. [Italian translation no. 364]
252. 'An Orphic scandal', *Omnibus* 6 (November 1983): 32–3.
253. 'The Hesiodic Catalogue: Xouthids and Aiolids', *ZPE* 53 (1983): 27–30.
254. Review of J. F. Kindstrand, *Anacharsis* (Uppsala, 1981), *Proceedings of the African Classical Associations* 17 (1983): 145–9.

1984

255. 'Music in archaic Greece', *Actes du VIIe Congrès de la F.I.E.C.* I (Budapest, 1983), 213–20. [Written 1979, appeared 1984]
256. Review of A. P. Burnett, *Three Archaic Poets* (London, 1983), *TLS* 13th January 1984: 30.
257. 'Problems in the Anacreontea', *CQ* NS 34 (1984): 206–21.
258. *Carmina Anacreontea* (Leipzig, 1984). Pp. xxvi + 65. [Reprinted with corrections Athens 1990]
259. Review of A. M. Dale, *Metrical Analyses of Tragic Choruses* III (London, 1983), *JHS* 104 (1984): 227–8.
260. Review of W. Burkert, *Structure and History in Greek Mythology and Ritual* (Berkeley and London, 1979), *JHS* 104 (1984): 232–3.
261. 'New fragments of Ibycus' love songs', *ZPE* 57 (1984): 23–32.
262. 'A new poem about Hesiod', *ZPE* 57 (1984): 33–6.
263. 'The ascription of fables to Aesop in archaic and classical Greece', in F. R. Adrados and O. Reverdin (eds.), *La Fable* (Entretiens sur l'Antiquité Classique 30; Geneva, 1984), 105–36.
264. 'Tragica VII', *BICS* 31 (1984): 171–96.

1985

265. *The Hesiodic Catalogue of Women* (Oxford, 1985). Pp. viii + 193.
266. Review of J. N. Bremmer, *The Early Greek Concept of the Soul* (Princeton, 1983), *CR* NS 35 (1985): 56–8.
267. Review of R. C. T. Parker, *Miasma* (Oxford, 1983), *CR* NS 35 (1985): 92–4.

268. 'Ieu!' *ZPE* 60 (1985): 10.
269. 'The lost opening of the *Choephoroi*', *LCM* 10.9 (November 1985): 130–1.
270. 'Hesiod's Titans', *JHS* 105 (1985): 174–5.
271. Review of D. Paquette, *L'Instrument de musique dans la céramique de la Grèce antique* (Paris, 1984), *JHS* 105 (1985): 209.
272. Review of A. Barker, *Greek Musical Writings* I (Cambridge, 1984), *CR* NS 35 (1985): 364–5.
273. Review of R. Glei (ed.), *Die Batrachomyomachie* (Frankfurt am Main and New York, 1984), *CR* NS 35 (1985): 379–80.
274. 'The Hesiodic Catalogue: new light on Apollo's love-life', *ZPE* 61 (1985): 1–7.
275. 'Archilochus: new fragments and readings', *ZPE* 61 (1985): 8–13.
276. 'Ion of Chios', *BICS* 32 (1985): 71–8.

1986

277. 'Early Greek philosophy', in J. Boardman, J. Griffin, and O. Murray (eds.), *The Oxford History of the Classical World* (Oxford, 1986), 113–23.
278. Review of A. W. Bulloch (ed.), *Callimachus: The Fifth Hymn* (Cambridge, 1985) and N. Hopkinson (ed.), *Callimachus: Hymn to Demeter* (Cambridge, 1984), *CR* NS 36 (1986): 27–31.
279. 'The singing of hexameters: evidence from Epidaurus', *ZPE* 63 (1986): 39–46.
280. 'Further echoes and imitations of the Hesiodic poems', *Philologus* 130 (1986): 1–7.
281. 'Last notes on Quintus of Smyrna', *Philologus* 130 (1986): 145–9.
282. Review of G. Chrétien (ed.), *Nonnos de Panopolis* IV (Paris, 1985), *CR* NS 36 (1986): 210–11.
283. Review of F. Vian and É. Battegay, *Lexique de Quintus de Smyrne* (Paris, 1984), *CR* NS 36 (1986): 310.
284. Review of E. Degani, *Studi su Ipponatte* (Bari, 1984), *JHS* 106 (1986): 206.

285. Review of G. A. Seeck, *Dramatische Strukturen der griechischen Tragödie* (Munich, 1984), *JHS* 106 (1986): 207.
286. Review of W. Burkert, *Die orientalisierende Epoche in der griechischen Religion und Literatur* (Heidelberg, 1984), *JHS* 106 (1986): 233–4.

1987

287–91. 'Apollo', 'Eros', 'Hesiod', 'Homer', 'Thesmophoria', in M. Eliade (ed.), *The Encyclopedia of Religion* (London and New York, 1986–7).
292. *Euripides:* Orestes (Warminster, 1987). Pp. ix + 297 [Pp. 1–25 by S. Barlow].
293. 'A new fragment of Heraclitus', *ZPE* 67 (1987): 16.
294. '*Ἀχνύς*' *ZPE* 67 (1987): 17–19.
295. 'Iaon', *ZPE* 67 (1987): 20.
296. *Introduction to Greek Metre* (Oxford, 1987). Pp. xi + 90. [Polish translation no. 468, Modern Greek no. 475]
297. Review of P. E. Easterling and B. M. W. Knox (eds.), *The Cambridge History of Classical Literature I: Greek Literature* (Cambridge, 1985), *Durham University Journal* 79 (1987): 374–5.
298. Review of A. F. Garvie (ed.), *Aeschylus:* Choephori (Oxford, 1986), *Gnomon* 59 (1987): 193–8.
299. Review of M. Hofinger and D. Pinte, *Lexicon Hesiodeum cum indice inverso: Supplementum* (Leiden, 1985), *CR* NS 37 (1987): 297.
300. 'Problems in Euripides' *Orestes*', *CQ* NS 37 (1987): 281–93.

1988

301. *Hesiod:* Theogony. Works and Days (Oxford, 1988). Pp. xxv + 79. [Translation]
302. Review of M. van Raalte, *Rhythm and Metre* (Assen and Wolfeboro, NH, 1986), *CR* NS 38 (1988): 78–80.
303. 'The rise of the Greek epic', *JHS* 108 (1988): 151–72.
304. Review of A. Belis, *Aristoxène de Tarente et Aristote* (Paris, 1986), *JHS* 108 (1988): 235–6.

305 Review of A. J. Neubecker (ed.), *Philodemus: Über die Musik, IV. Buch* (Naples, 1986), *JHS* 108 (1988): 236.

306. Review of G. Zuntz, *Drei Kapitel zur griechischen Metrik* (Vienna, 1984), *JHS* 108 (1988): 240.

307. 'P.Oxy. 3722 (Commentary on Anacreon): marginalia', *ZPE* 75 (1988): 1–2.

308. 'Indoevropejskaja Metrika', in V. V. Ivanov (ed.), *Novoe v zarubezhnoj lingvistike* 21 [Novoe v sovremennoj indoevropejstike] (Moscow, 1988), 474–506. [Translated from no. 137]

309. 'Conington's first emendation', *CQ* NS 38 (1988): 555.

1989

310. Review of J. M. Bremer *et al.*, *Some Recently Found Greek Poems* (Leiden and New York, 1987), *CR* NS 39 (1989): 9–11.

311. Review of J. Haudry, *La Religion cosmique des Indo-Européens* (Milan and Paris, 1987), *CR* NS 39 (1989): 144–5.

312. Review of K. J. Dover, *Greek and the Greeks. Collected Papers I: Language, Poetry, Drama* (Oxford, 1987), *Notes and Queries* 36 (1989): 88–9.

313. 'The early chronology of Greek tragedy', *CQ* NS 39 (1989): 251–4.

314. *Iambi et Elegi Graeci ante Alexandrum cantati* I^2 (Oxford, 1989). Pp. xvi + 258. [1st edition no. 125]

315. *Κριτικὴ τῶν κειμένων καὶ τεχνικὴ τῶν ἐκδοσέων* (Athens, 1989). [Translated from no. 133]

316. Review of J. M. van Ophuijsen (ed.), *Hephaestion:* On Metre (Leiden and New York, 1987), *JHS* 109 (1989): 237–8.

317. 'An unrecognized injunctive usage in Greek', *Glotta* 67 (1989): 135–8.

1990

318. 'Notes on Sappho and Alcaeus', *ZPE* 80 (1990): 1–8.

319. 'Colloquialism and naive style in Aeschylus', in E. M. Craik (ed.), *'Owls to Athens'. Essays on Classical Subjects presented to Sir Kenneth Dover* (Oxford, 1990): 3–12.

320. ‘Ringing welkins’, *CQ* NS 40 (1990): 286–7.
321. *Aeschyli Tragoediae cum incerti poetae Prometheo* (Stuttgart, 1990). Pp. lxxxv + 508. [Revised impression no. 410]
322. (with R. Merkelbach) ‘Fragmenta selecta’, in F. Solmsen *et al.*, *Hesiodi Opera*^{3} (Oxford, 1990), 109–246. [See no. 99 and no. 246]
323. ‘The Anacreontea’, in O. Murray (ed.), *Sympotica: A Symposium on the Symposion* (Oxford, 1990), 272–6.
324. Review of D. A. Campbell (ed.), *Greek Lyric* II (Cambridge, MA and London, 1988), *CR* NS 40 (1990): 214–16.
325. ‘Archaische Heldendichtung: Singen und Schreiben’, in W. Kullmann and M. Reichel (eds.), *Der Übergang von der Mündlichkeit zur Literatur bei den Griechen* (Tübingen, 1990), 33–50. [Cf. no. 493]
326. *Studies in Aeschylus* (Beiträge zur Altertumskunde 1; Stuttgart, 1990). Pp. x + 408.
327. ‘Dating Corinna’, *CQ* NS 40 (1990): 553–7.
328. Review of D. J. Mastronarde (ed.), *Euripides*: Phoenissae (Leipzig, 1988), *CP* 85 (1990): 311–17.

1991

329. Review of A. Barker, *Greek Musical Writings* II (Cambridge, 1989), *CR* NS 41 (1991): 45–6.
330. ‘The king’s ghost’s ghost kings’, in M. A. Flower and M. Toher (eds.), *Georgica. Greek Studies in Honour of George Cawkwell* (*BICS* Suppl. 58; London, 1991), 182–8.
331. Review of M. Maas and J. M. Snyder, *Stringed Instruments of Ancient Greece* (New Haven and London, 1987), *AJP* 112 (1991): 273–6.
332. *Aeschyli Persae* (Stuttgart, 1991). Pp. ix + 64.
333. *Aeschyli Agamemnon* (Stuttgart, 1991). Pp. vi + 97.
334. *Aeschyli Choephoroe* (Stuttgart, 1991). Pp. vi + 71.
335. *Aeschyli Eumenides* (Stuttgart, 1991). Pp. vi + 66.
336. Review of P. H. J. Lloyd-Jones and N. G. Wilson (eds.), *Sophoclis Fabulae* and *Sophoclea* (Oxford, 1990), *CR* NS 41 (1991): 299–301.
337. *Critica del testo e tecnica dell’edizione* (Palermo, 1991). [Translated from no. 133]

338. 'The religious interpretation of myth in Aeschylus', in Z. de Almeida Cardoso (ed.), *Mito, Religião e Sociedade: Atas do II Congresso Nacional de Estudos Clássicos* (São Paulo, 1991), 225–38.

1992

339. Review of F. Vian (ed.), *Nonnos de Panopolis* IX (Paris, 1990), *CR* NS 42 (1992): 19–20.
340. 'Alcman and the Spartan royalty', *ZPE* 91 (1992): 1–7.
341. '*ΣΟΝ ΤΟ ΚΡΑΤΟΣ ΙΕΡΑΞ*', *ZPE* 91 (1992): 8–9.
342. 'Analecta musica', *ZPE* 92 (1992): 1–54.
343. *Aeschyli Septem contra Thebas* (Stuttgart, 1992). Pp. ix + 72.
344. *Aeschyli Supplices* (Stuttgart, 1992). Pp. vi + 72.
345. *[Aeschyli] Prometheus* (Stuttgart, 1992). Pp. ix + 64.
346. *Iambi et Elegi ante Alexandrum cantati* II^2 (Oxford, 1992). Pp. 277. [1st edition no. 129]
347. *Ancient Greek Music* (Oxford, 1992). Pp. xiii + 410. [Modern Greek translation no. 418, Polish no. 474. Paperback reprint with minor corrections published in 1994]
348. 'An alleged musical inscription', *ZPE* 93 (1992): 27–8.
349. '*ΙΗΥ ΜΑΛ' ΑΥΘΙΣ*', *ZPE* 94 (1992): 230.
350. Review of D. A. Campbell (ed.), *Greek Lyric* III (Cambridge, MA and London, 1991), *CR* NS 42 (1992): 253–5.
351. 'Helen', *CA News* 6 (June 1992): 6. [Poem]
352. (ed. with K. J. Dover, J. Griffin, E. L. Bowie) *La Letteratura della Grecia antica* (Milan, 1992). [Translation of no. 203]
353. 'The eternal triangle. Reflections on the curious cosmology of Petron of Himera', in *Apodosis. Essays presented to Dr W. W. Cruickshank to mark his Eightieth Birthday* (St Paul's School, London, 1992), 105–10.
354. 'Notes on Dionysius Periegetes', *CQ* NS 42 (1992): 568–9.
355. 'The descent of the Greek epic: a reply', *JHS* 112 (1992): 173–5.
356. 'Iphigeneia', *CA News* 7 (December 1992), 2. [Poem]
357. 'Fragments of Homer, *Margites*', *The Oxyrhynchus Papyri* 59 (1992): 1–4.

1993

358. *La filosofia greca arcaica e l'Oriente* (Bologna, 1993). [Translated from no. 123, with minor corrections and additions]
359. *Greek Lyric Poetry: The Poems and Fragments of the Greek Iambic, Elegiac, and Melic Poets (excluding Pindar and Bacchylides) down to 450 BC*, translated with Introduction and Notes (Oxford, 1993). Pp. xxv + 213.
360. 'Teiresias', *CA News* 8 (June 1993): 7. [Poem]
361. *Carmina Anacreontea: Editio correctior editionis primae* (Teubner). Stuttgart and Leipzig 1993. Pp. xxvi + 66. [Corrected reprint of no. 258 with one page of Addenda]
362. 'Simonides redivivus', *ZPE* 98 (1993): 1–14.
363. 'Elephant', *Glotta* 70 (1992): 125–8.
364. *I poemi orfici* (Naples 1993). [Translated from no. 251, with minor corrections]
365. Review of D. A. Campbell (ed.), *Greek Lyric* IV (Cambridge, MA and London, 1992), *CR* NS 43 (1993): 236–8.

1994

366. 'The Babylonian musical notation and the Hurrian melodic texts', *Music and Letters* 75 (1993–4): 161–79.
367. 'Some oriental motifs in Archilochus', *ZPE* 102 (1994): 1–5.
368. 'Schwerlich Zufall (2)', *ZPE* 102 (1994): 6–7.
369. Review of G. Nagy, *Greek Mythology and Poetics* (Ithaca, NY 1990), *History of European Ideas* 18 (1994): 807–8.
370. Memoir: Reginald Pepys Winnington-Ingram (1904–1993). *Proceedings of the British Academy* 84. *Lectures and Memoirs* (1993), 579–97.
371. 'Thuc. V 23,6', *Eikasmos* 5 (1994): 137–8.
372. Review of C. M. J. Sicking, *Griechische Verslehre* (Munich, 1993), *GGA* 246 (1994): 183–97.
373. '*Ab Ovo:* Orpheus, Sanchuniathon, and the origins of the Ionian world model', *CQ* NS 44 (1994): 289–307.

1995

374. Review of D. A. Campbell (ed.), *Greek Lyric* V (Cambridge, MA and London, 1993), *CR* NS 45 (1995): 11–13.
375. Review of A. Allen (ed.), *The Fragments of Mimnermus* (Stuttgart, 1993), *CR* NS 45 (1995): 156–7.
376. '"Longinus" and the grandeur of God', in D. Innes, H. Hine, and C. B. R. Pelling (eds.), *Ethics and Rhetoric: Classical Essays for Donald Russell on his Seventy-Fifth Birthday* (Oxford, 1995), 335–42.
377. 'Ancient near eastern myths in classical Greek religious thought', in J. M. Sasson (ed.), *Civilizations of the Ancient Near East* (New York 1995), i. 33–42.
378. 'The date of the *Iliad*', *MH* 52 (1995): 203–19.
379. Review of N. Hopkinson and F. Vian (eds.), *Nonnos de Panopolis* VIII (Paris, 1994), *CR* NS 45 (1995): 434–5.
380. Review of A. Masaracchia (ed.), *Orfeo e l'Orfismo* (Rome, 1993), *CR* NS 45 (1995): 468–9.

1996

381. 'A criação do mundo helênico', *Folha de São Paulo*, 7 January 1996: section 5.12. [Newspaper interview]
382. Review of C. Penglase, *Mesopotamia and Greek Myth* (London, 1994), *Gnomon* 68 (1996): 657–62.

383–97. Articles in *The Oxford Classical Dictionary*[3] (Oxford, 1996): 'Anacreontea', 'Archilochus', 'Callinus', 'Dionysius (6) Chalcus', 'Elegiac Poetry (Greek)', 'Euenus of Paros', 'Hipponax', 'Iambic Poetry (Greek)', 'Margites', 'Mimnermus', 'Phocylides', 'Riddles', 'Semonides', 'Theognis (1)', 'Tyrtaeus'; light revision of 18 other entries.

398. *Die griechische Dichterin: Bild und Rolle* (Lectio Teubneriana, V). Pp. 48.
399. 'A fragment of *Prometheus Lyomenos*?', *ZPE* 113 (1996): 21.
400. 'The Berlin Corinna', *ZPE* 113 (1996): 22–3.

1997

401. Review of E. Pöhlmann, *Einführung in die Überlieferungsgeschichte und in die Textkritik der antiken Literatur* (Darmstadt, 1994), *Gnomon* 69 (1997): 1–5.
402. 'Homer's meter', in I. Morris and B. Powell (eds.), *A New Companion to Homer* (Leiden, 1997), 218–37.
403. 'Hocus-pocus east and west: theogony, ritual, and the tradition of esoteric commentary', in A. Laks and G. Most (eds.), *Studies on the Derveni Papyrus* (Oxford, 1997), 81–90.
404. Review of J. P. Brown, *Israel and Hellas* (Berlin and New York, 1995), *CR* NS 47 (1997): 111–12.
405. 'When is a harp a panpipe? The meanings of *πηκτίς*', *CQ* NS 47 (1997): 48–55.
406. *The East Face of Helicon. West Asiatic Elements in Greek Poetry and Myth* (Oxford, 1997). Pp. xxvi + 662.
407. Review of M. L. Gasparov, *A History of European Versification* (Oxford, 1995), *CR* NS 47 (1997): 431–2.
408. 'Akkadian poetry: metre and performance', *Iraq* 59 (1997): 175–87.
409. (ed. with K. J. Dover, J. Griffin, and E. L. Bowie) *Ancient Greek Literature*^{2} (Oxford, 1997). [1st edition no. 203]

1998

410. *Aeschyli Tragoediae cum incerti poetae Prometheo. Editio correctior editionis primae* (Stuttgart and Leipzig, 1998). Pp. lxxxv + 508. [See no. 321]
411. Review of H. van Thiel (ed.), *Homeri Ilias* (Hildesheim and New York, 1996), *CR* NS 48 (1998): 1–2.
412. Carmen gratulatorium, in F. Graf (ed.), *Ansichten griechischer Rituale: Geburtstags-Symposion für Walter Burkert, Castelen bei Basel, 15. bis 18. März 1996* (Stuttgart and Leipzig, 1998), 1.
413. 'Fragments with musical notation', *The Oxyrhynchus Papyri* 65 (1998): 81–102.
414. 'The textual criticism and editing of Homer', in G. W. Most (ed.), *Editing Texts / Texte edieren* (Aporemata 2; Gottingen, 1998), 94–110.

415. (with O. R. Gurney) 'Mesopotamian tonal systems: a reply' [to R. L. Crocker], *Iraq* 60 (1998): 223–7.
416. *Homeri Ilias. Volumen prius: Rhapsodiae I–XII* (Stuttgart and Leipzig, 1998). Pp. lxii + 372.
417. 'Grated cheese fit for heroes', *JHS* 118 (1998): 190–1.

1999

418. *Αρχαία Ελληνική Μουσική* (Athens, 1999). Pp. 551. [Translation of no. 347]
419. Review of J. Diggle (ed.), *Tragicorum Graecorum Fragmenta* (Oxford, 1998) and F. Jouan and H. van Looy (eds.), *Euripide. Fragments* I (Paris, 1998), *CR* NS 49 (1999): 8–10.
420. 'The end of Classics?', *Ad Familiares* 16 (Spring 1999), 12–13.
421. 'Frühe Interpolationen in der Ilias', *Nachrichten der Akademie der Wissenschaften in Göttingen I. Philologisch–Historische Klasse* Nr. 4 (Göttingen, 1999): 181–91.
422. 'Towards monotheism', in P. Athanassiadi and M. Frede (eds.), *Pagan Monotheism in Late Antiquity* (Oxford, 1999), 20–40.
423. 'Sophocles with music? Ptolemaic music fragments and remains of Sophocles (Junior?), *Achilleus*', *ZPE* 126 (1999): 43–65 with plates IX–XII.
424. (with S. R. West) 'Dividing Homer', *SO* 74 (1999): 68–73.
425. 'Ancestral curses', in J. Griffin (ed.), *Sophocles Revisited. Essays Presented to Sir Hugh Lloyd-Jones* (Oxford, 1999), 31–45.
426. *Szövegkritika és szövegkiadás* (Budapest, 1999). [Translation of no. 133]
427. 'The invention of Homer', *CQ* NS 49 (1999): 364–82.
428. Review of J. G. Younger, *Music in the Aegean Bronze Age* (Jonsered, 1998), *Bibliotheca Orientalis* 56 (1999), 750–3.
429–30. Articles 'Kolometrie' and 'Kolon', *Der Neue Pauly* 6 (Stuttgart and Weimar, 1999), 642–4.

2000

431. 'Music therapy in antiquity', in P. Horden (ed.), *Music as Medicine. The History of Music Therapy since Antiquity* (Aldershot, 2000), 51–68.

432. 'Heniochus and the shape of the Athenian orchestra', *ZPE* 130 (2000): 12.
433. 'Fable and disputation', in S. Aro and R. M. Whiting (eds.), *The Heirs of Assyria: Proceedings of the Opening Symposium of the Assyrian and Babylonian Intellectual Heritage Project held in Tvärminne, Finland, October 8–11, 1998* (Melammu Symposia 1; Helsinki, 2000), 93–7.
434. 'Metrik (griechisch)', *Der Neue Pauly* 8 (2000), 115–22.
435. 'Aeschylus, *Agamemnon* 104–59', *Lexis* 17 (1999), 41–56, 60–1; comments on others' Aeschylean colloquium papers, ibid. 38, 78, 104, 132–3, 148. [Appeared July 2000]
436. Review of G. Costa, *Le origini della lingua poetica indeuropea: voce, coscienza e transizione neolitica* (Florence, 1998), *Hermathena* 166 (1999): 123–5. [Appeared August 2000]
437. Review of J. Bottéro, C. Herrenschmidt, and J.-P. Vernant, *Ancestor of the West: Writing, Reasoning and Religion in Mesopotamia, Elam and Greece* (Chicago, 2000), *BMCR* 2000.09.22.
438. *Homeri Ilias. Volumen alterum: Rhapsodiae XIII–XXIV* (Munich and Leipzig, 2000). Pp. vii + 396.
439. Review of I. J. F. de Jong (ed.), *Homer: Critical Assessments* (London and New York, 1999), *G&R* 2nd ser. 47 (2000): 231–2.
440. Review of D. E. Gerber (ed.), *Greek Elegiac Poetry* and *Greek Iambic Poetry* (both Cambridge, MA and London 1999), *CR* NS 50 (2000): 402–3.
441. 'Geschichte des Textes', in J. Latacz (ed.), *Homers Ilias: Gesamtkommentar. Prolegomena* (Munich and Leipzig, 2000), 27–38.
442. Text and apparatus of *Iliad* A, in J. Latacz (ed.), *Homers Ilias. Gesamtkommentar* I/1 (Munich and Leipzig, 2000), 2–38; 'Orthographisches', ibid. x–xv.
443. *The All Souls Mallard: Song, Procession, and Legend* (All Souls College, Oxford 2000).

2001

444. 'The gardens of Alcinous and the oral dictated text theory', *Acta Antiqua Hungarica* 40 (2000): 479–88.

445. '*Iliad* and *Aethiopis* on the stage: Aeschylus & Son', *CQ* NS 50 (2000): 338–52.
446. 'Forward into the past', Fondazione Internazionale Balzan: Sintesi panoramiche redatte in occasione della cerimonia di consegna dei Premi Balzan 2000, 57–67. Speech of thanks: Cerimonia per la proclamazione dei Premi Balzan 2000, 50–5. [See pp. xx–xxviii above.]
447. 'Homer durch Jahrtausende. Wie die Ilias zu uns gelangte', *Troia—Traum und Wirklichkeit* (Begleitband zur Ausstellung), Stuttgart, 2001, 108–11.
448. Review of G. Liberman (ed.), *Alcée* (Paris, 1999), *CR* NS 51 (2001): 4–6.
449. 'The fragmentary Homeric Hymn to Dionysus', *ZPE* 134 (2001): 1–11.
450. (with E. Pohlmann) *Documents of Ancient Greek Music: the Extant Melodies and Fragments* (Oxford, 2001).
451. *Studies in the Text and Transmission of the Iliad* (Munich and Leipzig, 2001). [See no. 459]
452. 'West on Nagy and Nardelli on West', *BMCR* 2001.09.06.
453. '*Αρχαία Ελληνική Μουσική*', in A.-P. Chrestides (ed.), *Ιστορία της Ελληνικής Γλώσσας* (Athens(?), 2001): 1051–8.

2002

454. *Crítica textual e técnica editorial* (Lisbon, 2002). [Translation of no. 133]
455. 'Darius' ascent to Paradise', *Indo-Iranian Journal* 45 (2002): 51–7.
456. 'The name of Aphrodite', *Glotta* 76 (2000): 134–8. [Appeared May 2002]
457. 'Seventeen distorted mirrors in Plato', *CQ* NS 52 (2002): 380–1.
458. 'The view from Lesbos', in M. Reichel and A. Rengakos (eds.), *Epea pteroenta. Beiträge zur Homerforschung. Festschrift für Wolfgang Kullmann zum 75. Geburtstag* (Stuttgart, 2002): 207–19.
459. 'Zenodotus' text', in F. Montanari (ed.), *Omero tremila anni dopo: Atti del Congresso di Genova 6–8 Iuglio 2000* (Rome, 2002), 137–42. [Revised as chapter 2 of no. 451]

460. '"Eumelus": a Corinthian Epic Cycle?', *JHS* 122 (2002): 109–33.

2003

461. 'Some Homeric words', *Glotta* 77 (2001): 118–35. [Appeared February 2003]
462. *Homeric Hymns. Homeric Apocrypha. Lives of Homer* (Cambridge, MA and London, 2003). Pp. xii + 467.
463. *Greek Epic Fragments from the Seventh to the Fifth Centuries BC.* (Cambridge, MA and London, 2003). Pp. x + 316.
464. 'The only sensual pleasure without vice', *Ad familiares* 4 (2003): 12–14.
465. 'Dying one's own death: a footnote', *ZPE* 143 (2003): 70.
466. '*Iliad* and *Aethiopis*', *CQ* NS 53 (2003): 1–14.
467. 'Some problems in early epic texts', in D. Accorinti and P. Chuvin (eds.), *Des Géants à Dionysos: Mélanges de mythologie et de poésie grecques offerts à Francis Vian* (Alessandria, 2003), i. 147–54.
468. *Wprowadzenie do Metryki Greckiej* (Kraków, 2003). Pp. 127. [Translated from no. 296]
469. 'Atreus and Attarissiyas', *Glotta* 77 (2001): 262–6. [Appeared December 2003]
470. 'Musiche di cultura alta nell'antichità', *Enciclopedia della musica* III (Turin, 2003), 167–86.
471. Text and apparatus of *Iliad* B, in J. Latacz (ed.), *Homers Ilias: Gesamtkommentar.* II/1 (Munich and Leipzig, 2003), 2–57; 'Orthographisches', ibid. x–xv.
472. Article 'Colometry', in *Brill's New Pauly* 3 (Leiden and Boston, 2003), 537. [Translation of no. 429]
473. 'Alcaeus' brother', *ZPE* 145 (2003): 6.

2004

474. *Muzyka starozytnej Grecji* (Kraków, 2003). Pp. 447. [Translated from no. 347]
475. *Εισαγωγή στην αρχαία ελληνική μετρική* (Thessalonica, 2004). Pp. 109. [Translated from no. 296]
476. 'West on Rengakos (BMCR 2002.11.15) and Nagy (Gnomon 75, 2003, 481–501) on West', *BMCR* 2004.04.17.

477. 'Tuning up', *Archaeology Odyssey* 7.3 (May–June 2004): 6–7.
478. 'An Indo-European stylistic feature in Homer', in A. Bierl, A. Schmitt, and A. Willi (eds.), *Antike Literatur in neuer Deutung. Festschrift für Joachim Latacz anlässlich seines 70. Geburtstags* (Munich and Leipzig, 2004), 33–49.
479. 'The Flood Myth in Ovid, Lucian, and Nonnus', in J. A. López Férez (ed.), *Mitos en la literatura griega helenística e imperial* (Madrid, 2003), 245–59. [Submitted May 1995, appeared May 2004]
480. 'Phrygian metre', *Kadmos* 42 (2003): 77–86. [Appeared July 2004]
481. 'The death of Baldr', *JIES* 32 (2004): 1–9.
482. Review of B. Gentili and C. Prato (eds.), *Poetae Elegiaci*^{2} (Munich and Leipzig, 2002), *CR* NS 54 (2004): 299–300.
483. 'Monro, David Binning (1836–1905)', in R. B. Todd (ed.), *The Dictionary of British Classicists* (Bristol, 2004), ii. 668–9.
484. 'Geschichte und Vorgeschichte: Die Sage von Troia', *Studia Troica* 14 (2004): xiii–xx.

2005

485. 'The new Sappho', *ZPE* 151 (2005), 1–9.
486. '*Odyssey* and *Argonautica*', *CQ* NS 55 (2005): 39–64.
487. 'A new Sappho poem', *TLS* 24th June 2005: 8.
488. Review of D. Launderville, *Piety and Politics: the Dynamics of Royal Authority in Homeric Greece, Biblical Israel, and Old Babylonian Mesopotamia* (Grand Rapids, MI, 2003), *JSS* 50 (2005): 361–2.

489–92. Articles in *Die Musik in Geschichte und Gegenwart*^{2}, Personenteil 13 (Kassel and London, 2005): 'Philolaos' 521; 'Platon' 675–6; 'Porphyrios' 779; 'Ptolemaios, Klaudios' 1016–19.

493. 'Homero: a transição da oralidade à escrita', *Letras Clåssicas* (Universidade de São Paulo) 5 (2001): 11–28. [Lecture given in 1989; appeared 2005. Cf. no. 325]
494. Review of E. Rocconi, *Le parole delle Muse: la formulazione del lessico tecnico musicale nella Grecia antica* (Rome, 2003), *CR* NS 55 (2005): 487–8.

2006

495. ‘Archilochus and Telephus’, *ZPE* 156 (2006): 11–17.
496. Review of R. L. Hunter (ed.), *The Hesiodic Catalogue of Women: Constructions and Reconstructions* (Cambridge, 2005), *CR* NS 56 (2006): 275–6.

2007

497. *Indo-European Poetry and Myth* (Oxford, 2007). Pp. xiv + 530.

Part I

Epic

1

Terminal Problems

Stephanie West

In early summer 1623 John Donne, preaching on Psalm 6:8–10, considered why David defers his expression of thanks to the end, and appealed to what he saw as a general principle in poetic composition (Donne (1953), 41):

> Therefore might *David* be later and shorter here in expressing the duty of thanks, first, because being reserved to the end, and close of the Psalme, it leaves the best impression on the memory. And therefore it is easie to observe, that in all Metricall compositions . . . the force of the whole piece is, for the most part, left to the shutting up: the whole frame of the Poem is a beating out of a piece of gold, but the last clause is as the impression of the stamp, and that is it that makes it current.

This looks at first sight relatively uncontroversial; the modern reader expects a well-marked formal conclusion to any piece of writing, whether poetry or prose, claiming serious attention, so that the absence of this feature, in a work that cannot be suspected of having escaped its author's hands unfinished, is regarded as in itself a device of some sophistication. We are conditioned to apply to literature the counsel which Herodotus' Solon offers with regard to the evaluation of lives (1.32.9): σκοπέειν δὲ χρὴ παντὸς χρήματος τὴν τελευτὴν κῆι ἀποβήσεται. Yet when we are dealing with lengthy narratives

This essay explores a topic which first came to interest me in connection with the end of the *Odyssey*; its evolution has benefited from conversations with many colleagues over many years. I cannot now trace my intellectual obligations precisely enough to acknowledge all my creditors properly, but I am substantially indebted to the editors and take this opportunity to thank them.

this habit of mind perhaps reflects modern conditions of book production to a greater extent than seems to be generally admitted.

Closure has received greatly increased attention since the publication of Frank Kermode's *The Sense of an Ending* (1967) and Barbara Herrnstein Smith's *Poetic Closure* (1968); many classicists owe to Don Fowler's work (Fowler (1989), (1997) = (2000), 239–83, 284–307) a heightened awareness of the topic's importance. This has, understandably, led to some reluctance to acknowledge that quite a significant proportion of the major works of classical literature lack a marked conclusion. Particular instances of this apparent deficiency are thus treated in isolation, though the wish to discern subtle closural effect often results in rather strained interpretation.[1]

The desire for a formal conclusion, a recognizable epilogue or envoi, took time to develop.[2] 'Early hexameter poems, however well constructed overall, finish without ceremony. Their last lines, taken by themselves, could never be identified as last lines' (West (1985*a*), 121). 'The Homeric epics, as we have them, peter out' (Kenney (1977), 22). The absence of a formal coda is the more striking in view of the elaborate development of the prooemium in Homer and Hesiod. The *Iliad* and the *Odyssey*, the *Theogony*, and the *Works and Days* all display a strange uncertainty about their endings. The loose structure of Hesiod's works leads us to accept this indeterminacy quite easily. But with the *Iliad* and *Odyssey* modern readers find it hard to accept that the last lines simply conclude the last episode and have no further significance for the larger narrative. Yet the lay of Demodocus (*Od.* 8.266–366) illustrates clearly enough the acceptability of an abrupt ending without an explicit conclusion. The episode finishes with Aphrodite freshened up at Paphos, and that is enough. We have to reckon with the assumptions of a society where

[1] It is salutary to recall the discovery of the continuation of Theocritus 24 (see further Hunt and Johnson (1930), 23–4); the abruptness with which, in the mediaeval manuscripts, the poem breaks off at 140 had not seemed to Wilamowitz, among others, grounds for regarding the text as defective (Wilamowitz (1906), 241). Reeve (1984) warns us that we may not always know when endings have been lost; we should note the allegation in the ancient *Life* of Persius (8) that some lines have been removed from his incomplete last book so that it should appear finished.

[2] This topic is admirably treated by van Groningen (1960), 70–82 and Fränkel (1968*b*), especially 84–5, but their discussions are clearly not as widely familiar as they should be.

poetry is known only from performance, and what is related is part of a larger whole. The subject matter of epic is set in a distant past, and the outcome of the events narrated is, in broad outline, already known.

That the *Iliad* ends with a natural point of closure in human experience is in keeping with modern expectations of the conclusion of a literary work. We are the more inclined to attach to it a further significance, essential guidance for the interpretation of the whole, because this is a surprising place at which to end (see further Richardson (1993), 272–3). But that its last line might in antiquity be seen as simply concluding its last episode (24.609–803), allowing immediate continuation to the next event, is demonstrated by the alternative preserved in the T Scholia, introducing the *Aethiopis* with the arrival of Penthesileia: *ὣς οἵ γ' ἀμφίεπον τάφον Ἕκτορος, ἦλθε δ' Ἀμαζών | Ἄρηος θυγάτηρ μεγαλήτορος ἀνδροφόνοιο* (F1 *PEG*, *GEF*, *fr. spur. EGF*). Those who maintain the authenticity of *Odyssey* 24 on the grounds that it is essential for the interpretation of the epic as a whole (so Kullmann (1992); more subtly Lowe (2000), 151) play into the hands of those who find evidence of later addition in its stylistic and narrative awkwardnesses: their arguments convincingly present the considerations likely to have motivated a later continuator, but do nothing to mitigate the deficiencies of his work (see further S. R. West (1989)). In both *Iliad* and *Odyssey* we should beware of over-estimating the importance of echoes or inversions of Book 1 in Book 24. The episode was the norm, the part standing for the implied whole (as with readings from the Bible in church). Performance of the entire epic, over successive days (or nights? See Taplin (1992), 29–31, 39–41) must, at least until the establishment of the Panathenaic recitations, have been quite exceptional, if indeed, it ever occurred (see further Dowden (1996), 50–1, West (2001), 3–19).[3]

As the implications of Milman Parry's work were absorbed by Homerists (too many of whom had ignored Parry's predecessors), attention turned to the particular requirements of the literary

[3] I am not convinced that we are entitled to infer that both epics were recited *in their entirety* every four years; the ancient sources (Lycurg. *Contra Leocr.* 102, Pl. *Hipparch.* 228b, D.L. 1.57) stress that the recitation of episodes had to follow the order of the text and that only the *Iliad* and *Odyssey* were allowed, but would be consistent with performance of just a part at each celebration.

criticism of oral poetry. At first the result seemed to be little more than a plea for tolerance of inconsistency and occasional infelicities of expression (as with Penelope's χειρὶ παχείηι at *Od.* 21.6). More happily, increasing consideration has been given to the circumstances of performance, of some relevance to endings. By tone and tempo an experienced storyteller, whether in prose or verse, can warn his hearers that his tale nears its conclusion, though his words alone would not indicate this. A successful performer of oral narrative needs to master the art of stopping within a few minutes of observing some restiveness in his audience, while conveying the impression of having reached a natural break.[4] Lord (1960), 17 emphasizes that the ending of a song is particularly affected by indications that the singer is losing his hold on his hearers' attention: 'The length of the song depends upon the audience. One of the reasons why different singings of the same song by the same man vary most in their endings is that the end of a song is sung less often by the singer.' In a slightly more formal setting than the Balkan marketplace or coffee house of Albert Lord's researches we might consider Mark Griffith's suggestion (1983, 46–7) that a bard might sometimes end his recitation 'with a *sphragis*, in which he might establish his connection with the god whose festival it was or with the family at whose court he was singing, thus assuring his addressee of the mutual benefit derived from this song'. We see something of the sort in the Homeric *Hymn to Apollo* (165–78). Dowden (2004), 195 ingeniously suggests that the shorter Homeric hymns might sometimes have served to round off a performance, citing the first *Hymn to Dionysus* (D 8–9 in West (2003*b*)) οἵ δέ σ' ἀοιδοὶ | ἄιδομεν ἀρχόμενοι λήγοντές τ': 'This might be a factor in the otherwise poor closure of epic texts, the way they just peter out.' Such speculations serve to remind us how inadequately informed we are about the conventions of performance. If we find odd the lack of a marked conclusion we must bear in mind that our expectations rest on long experience of a fixed text, a definitive version. For the hexameter poets of archaic Greece the production of a written text must have been more a matter of

[4] See further Finnegan (1977), 54. A corollary is the technique of indicating that he could resume should his audience wish; Odysseus has clearly mastered this aspect of the bard's art (*Od.* 11.328–32).

making a fair copy of work in progress; it did not rule out continuous improvements and additions.[5]

Whatever Herodotus owed to lost works, Homer offered the only model for the organization of narrative on as grand a scale as his. The importance of his debt to Homer was recognized in antiquity. In the recently published Hellenistic inscription celebrating the glories of Halicarnassus *τὸν πεζὸν ἐν ἱστορίαισιν Ὅμηρον* heads the list of the city's writers (see Isager (1998), Lloyd-Jones (1999) = (2005), 211–32, *SGO* i. 39–44). *Μόνος Ἡρόδοτος Ὁμηρικώτατος ἐγένετο;* asks [Long.] (*Subl.* 13.3, *SEG* 48. 1330). The abrupt question (if the text is sound) implies that Herodotus' Homeric quality was a commonplace (cf. D.H. *Pomp.* 3), but the writer's view that Stesichorus, Archilochus, and above all Plato may equally be described as 'most Homeric' suggests caution in attempting to identify what specific Homeric qualities are meant. Herodotus' response to Homeric precedent, the affinities between Homeric epic and Herodotus, offer almost limitless scope for discussion (for a valuable survey see Boedeker (2002), 97–109). We need to distinguish between features common to both because characteristic of aural narrative, narrative intended to be heard by a group rather than studied by a reflective reader, and specific allusions to one or other epic; but this is easier said than done. At all events, epic precedent would not have suggested that the conclusion of the work was of particular importance.

Some weighty authorities have judged that the anecdote with which the *Histories* end (9.122) makes so unsatisfactory a conclusion as to indicate that the work is incomplete. Thus Wilamowitz (1893), 26 draws up his indictment: 'dass der jetzige abschluss des herodoteischen werkes nicht vom verfasser beabsichtigt ist, liegt auf der hand oder sollte es doch tun. mit der eroberung von Sestos möchte Herodot allenfalls schliessen: mit der geschichte von dem gepökelten heros Protesilaos und einer anekdote aus Kyros zeit konnte er es nicht. vor allem aber ist kein buch fertig das kein ende hat, sondern abreisst; das des Herodots aber hat seine einleitung und ordnung und

5 The problems presented by *Iliad* 9, and in particular by Phoenix's role, once seen as indications of multiple authorship, are better viewed as resulting from (incomplete) revision; see further Hainsworth (1993), 55–7, 81–2, S. R. West (2001).

will ein kunstwerk sein.'[6] Jacoby (1913, 372–9) elaborates, arguing that Herodotus died before finishing, a view supported by the notorious unfulfilled promises of *Assyrioi logoi* (1.106.2; 184) and of an account of the death of the traitor Ephialtes (7.213.3); he saw the foundation of the Delian League as the natural conclusion. Pohlenz, too, was troubled by the way in which the narrative 'im Sande verläuft'; he saw the Greek capture of Byzantium as the appropriate stopping point (1937, 163–77). Half a century later David Asheri expressed a similar unease (1988, xx–xxi): 'Il libro di Erodoto (ix 122) termina con una massima didattica di Ciro il grande. Termina o, meglio, si interrompe. Manca almeno un epilogo. Un'opera di questa mole non poteva chiudersi con un aneddotto occasionale, suggerito a sua volta da un altro aneddoto su un personaggio secondario. Erodoto è uno scrittore che, se e quando vuole, sa introdurre e riepilogare benissimo. L'ultima massima di Ciro non è un "messaggio" didattico che conclude ed unifichi tutta l'opera, né l'episodio di Sesto vuole simboleggiare il ripristino dei confini naturali tra Asia ed Europa, che Dario e Serse avevano tentato di cancellare: nulla nelle parole di Erodoto documenta simili intenzioni, né del resto messaggi segreti di questo tipo vennero mai decodificati dai lettori di Erodoto prima della fine del secolo scorso'.[7]

Among such decoders Asheri clearly had in mind the formidable Macan (1908), whose note on the last sentence runs thus: 'As argument, the conclusion looks, at first sight, oddly infelicitous for the

[6] 'That the present conclusion of Herodotus' work is not that intended by the author is obvious or should be. Herodotus could certainly have concluded with the capture of Sestos; he could not do so with the story of the pickled hero Protesilaos and an anecdote from the time of Cyrus. Above all no book is finished if it has no ending but breaks off; but Herodotus' book has its introduction and arrangement, and aims to be a work of art.'

[7] 'Herodotus' book ends (9.122) with an apophthegm uttered by Cyrus the Great. Ends, or rather breaks off. At any rate, an epilogue is lacking. A work on this scale could not close with a casual anecdote, suggested in its turn by another anecdote about a figure of secondary importance. Herodotus is a writer who, if and when he wishes, demonstrates very great skill in introductions and recapitulations. Cyrus' final maxim is not a didactic "message" concluding and unifying the whole work, nor is the Sestos episode meant to symbolize the restoration of the natural boundaries between Asia and Europe which Darius and Xerxes had tried to cancel. Nothing in Herodotus' words offers evidence of such intentions, nor, on the other hand, were secret messages of this type ever decoded by Herodotus' readers before the end of the last century.'

last word of a record, which has exhibited in unsparing colours the attempt of the Persians to extend their empire over Hellas, an attempt ending in failure and flight, the prelude to further loss and forfeiture. But something else is in Herodotus' mind. *Mutato nomine fabula narratur.* He is too delicate to dictate to the Greeks, or it may be to the Athenians; but the lesson is there for those who have ears to hear. It is at once the rationale of the Greek success, and a call to future expansion. The men λυπρὴν οἰκέοντες, the nurslings of poverty (7.102) and hard fare (9.82)—theirs is the victory, and theirs the empire, if they will: what the Persians had done in the days of Kyros, why should not the Greeks do in the days of Kimon, or of Perikles?'

Unfortunately, those with ears to hear might have discerned a different message, not an exhortation to expansion, but a warning. 'It should never have been doubted' (we read in what was to become the standard commentary, published only four years later) 'that this anecdote was deliberately chosen by the historian to close his work. It recalls the fact that the Persians, though now defeated, were a famous race of warriors; it perhaps is intended to warn the conquerors that they too may suffer decline and fail if they relax their discipline (cf. vii 102). No doubt the moral is a little obvious, the literary artifice somewhat naive, but is not all this characteristic of Herodotus?' (How and Wells (1912), ii. 331; see also Moles (1996), 275; (2002), 49). But while it would be easy to draw the moral that Persia had been ruined by luxurious living, the Persian Empire was still in good shape in Herodotus' time; the idea that its foundations had been rocked by the Greek victories at Salamis and Plataea belongs rather to Aeschylus' *Persae* than to Herodotus' world.

Recent discussions (see in particular Boedeker (1988), Herington (1991), Dewald (1997), Flower and Marincola (2002), 302–14) have favoured the view that this last chapter was indeed intended to be the conclusion of the *Histories*, though what Herodotus meant by it seems no clearer. Comparison with the *Iliad* suggests the most promising approach: just as Herodotus' elaborate proem conforms to epic practice, so too would an unmarked ending, leaving open the possibility of further continuation. (This interpretation, which is van Groningen's (1960, 70), in effect reverses Wilamowitz's.) As Macan (1895, i. 268) observes in his note on 6.1, 'It is characteristic of Herodotus to conclude a narrative, or gain a pause, by a biographical or anecdotal passage or appendix (cp. 4.143 f., 205; 6.137 ff.; 9.122).' We should thus resist the temptation to attach more weight to it than to many other anecdotes which serve to mark the end of an episode. The story of, for example, Darius' seminar on comparative funerary practice (3.38.3–4) or of Intaphernes' wife (3.118–19) can be related to important themes in the *Histories* and yield morals of wide-ranging significance; so much must be allowed to the final chapter. But what we may observe of narrative practice before Herodotus does not encourage us to seek matter of particular importance at the end. In so far as we see closural effect in Herodotus' last chapter it relates to the immediately preceding section, not to the work as a whole. Pausanias evidently admired this form of conclusion, since he ends his own work in a similar fashion (10.38.12–13) (see further Nörenberg (1973)).

For an historian the choice of a stopping point is not a simple matter;[8] the history of a war can hardly finish with the ceasefire, and we might regard as prudent a reluctance to identify a decisive end to the story of the Persian wars. 'All three of the extant monumental historians are beaten by the challenge of an ending' (Lowe (2000), 91) is a little unfair. Herodotus, we might guess, failed to see any such challenge. Having recorded a series of events falling under the general heading set out in his splendid opening sentence, connected within a chronological framework somewhat in the manner of the stages of a lengthy trade route, he had fulfilled his self-imposed task in saving from the iniquity of oblivion matter deserving commemoration; that would not have stopped him adding to what he had written, but did not entail an attempt to sum up what it all meant.

Thucydides cannot have intended to end where he does, in mid narrative, indeed in mid sentence (*pace* D.H. *Pomp.* 3),[9] even if he had changed his mind since writing his 'second preface', where (5.26.1) he envisages as his conclusion the defeat of Athens and the capture of the Long Walls and the Piraeus. Xenophon, having begun his *Hellenica* simply as a continuation of Thucydides, chose the battle

[8] For a survey of conclusions in ancient historiography see Marincola (2005); he well notes that Lucian has nothing to say about endings in *Quomodo historia conscribenda sit.*

[9] πρῶτον implies more to come. I hardly imagine that any reader will favour Konishi's argument to the contrary (1987).

of Mantineia as his terminus, while making it perfectly clear that it settled nothing (7.5.27). He did not avail himself of the opportunity to suggest the significance of the events related and thus simplify a confused continuum with a final assessment, or even to identify himself (having failed to follow the example of Herodotus and Thucydides at the outset) but offers simply the bare *ἐμοὶ μὲν δὴ μέχρι τούτου γραφέσθω· τὰ δὲ μετὰ ταῦτα ἴσως ἄλλωι μελήσει.*[10] We should at least be thankful to have this unambiguous indication that his narrative is complete. Since he can hardly have wished his work to circulate anonymously, he presumably relied on a colophon to identify it as his. It would of course be rash to suggest that the colophon as we find it later in literary papyri was already a feature of Greek book production; but the man who could devote to domestic detail the passion for orderliness evidenced in the *Oeconomicus* might have thought of it for himself or at any rate, if he had been aware of Near Eastern examples of the practice, would have been swift to see its advantages.[11]

Xenophon was not consistent in his treatment of the conclusions of his works. The *Anabasis* both begins abruptly and lacks an explicit ending; the arrival of Thibron to take over the remnant of the 10,000 is plainly the start of another story.[12] Xenophon himself appears to have been responsible for the postscript to the *Cyropaedia* which undercuts the magnificent and appropriate closure provided by Cyrus' death with a denunciation of Persian perfidy and decadence.[13] The *Memorabilia*, like the *Oeconomicus*, ends rather in the manner of a peroration. Speeches and philosophical discussion called for formal conclusion, but it is not so obvious that a writer who composes a record of interesting events ought to sum up when he reaches a good stopping point.[14]

[10] I doubt if we should see significance in the similarity of phraseology in his opening words (*μετὰ δὲ ταῦτα*) and his last.

[11] On features of oriental scribal practice adopted in Greek book production see West (1997), 26–7.

[12] Krüger's deletion of the last two paragraphs is generally accepted.

[13] Well discussed by Gera (1993), 299–300; see also Tatum (1989), 215–39.

[14] Most of the historical books of the Old Testament have low-key, unmarked endings. The writers perform their task of chronicling significant events within a certain period, but see no need to offer a summation. The theme throughout is God's purpose at work in His people, and an attempt to sum up would be premature.

A sense of the extensibility of a narrative, whether based on heroic legend or on events of the recent past, belonged very naturally to the oral/aural culture of archaic and early classical Greece. Hainsworth (1980), 45, considering the decline in quality manifest in the *Odyssey*'s present conclusion, well raises the question whether 'the art of the good ending does not imply a poet's assurance that his audience would allow his poem to run its full course. If so, the well-finished ending would be one of the late achievements of literature, and not likely to evolve until literary composition was undertaken in calmer circumstances than the noise of the princeling's court or the distractions of the marketplace'. It is no surprise that Apollonius provides the *Argonautica* with a marked conclusion (4.1773), to which there is rather more than at first sight meets the eye (see Hunter (1993), 119–20).

The old indeterminacy became artificial when the written text made the last line plain. Already with *Gilgamesh* we get a well-marked, clearly structural, ending; the epilogue takes us back to the walls of Uruk highlighted in the prologue (see George (2003), i. 47–54). But it was clearly wise for a writer to mark the conclusion as such if he was sure that he had reached it. The ends of rolls were physically vulnerable, while many texts have clearly suffered terminal accretion. Improved standards of book production, in particular the increased use of *coronis* and colophon, could counteract a reader's uncertainty as to whether his roll really extended to the conclusion intended by his author; such devices thus highlighted the ending. Polybius' epilogue (39.8.1–8) offers a model conclusion (even though a further book, wholly lost, is still in prospect), as he reviews the general plan and purpose of his work.

We are thus entitled to feel some surprise at the abrupt endings of Sallust's *Catiline* and *Jugurtha*; the latter leaves a particularly acute sense of incompleteness. 'The precise point at which the work ends seems arbitrary; the narrative simply stops rather than being properly rounded off' (Levene (1992), 54). Sallust might perhaps have invoked Thucydidean precedent (even if we find it impossible to believe that Thucydides meant his work to end as it does). The inconclusiveness of early Greek hexameter verse may be relevant to the strange ending of Lucretius' poem, where the death and destruction brought about by the plague at Athens mark the termination of a work which began with an elaborate celebration of life and light. 'Is the implication that the Athenians of this time lacked the wisdom of Epicurus, which alone would have enabled them to see their sufferings in a true light? Or is the point that the reader, as part of his training, needs to confront the worst and view it with open eyes, strengthened by the doctrines set out earlier in the poem? In either case, it is strange that the point is not made explicit.' Rutherford's reaction (2005, 248) will seem to many more natural than the view of G. E. R. Lloyd (2003, 218–19) that 'this is the perfect, or at least the most powerful, conclusion that there could be'. Perhaps we should fall back on the hypothesis that Lucretius died before he had completed his work.[15]

Latin hexameter poetry does not offer much in the way of well-finished endings. No such coda as the formal envoi of *Georgics* 4.559–66 concludes the *Aeneid*, and we are left to wonder whether Virgil really intended that his epic should end *vitaque cum gemitu fugit indignata sub umbras.* We do not look for anything more to happen after the death of Turnus; Aeneas will marry Lavinia, but if Dido's curse (4.618–20) is to be fulfilled he will not live happily ever after. The indeterminacy corresponding to the possibility of continuation natural in an oral tradition here prompts disturbing questions. But, whether or not we should rely on the information that had he lived Virgil intended to spend three years on polishing the epic, there are many indications apart from half-lines that it is unfinished, and we may leave open the possibility that a (brief)[16] epilogue was on his agenda. It would not be surprising if he postponed its composition.

Manilius did not follow the example set by *Georgic* 4; he produces good perorations to individual books, and the ending of Book 5 is certainly impressive, but it does not have the force of an epilogue. His unfulfilled promise to deal with planetary motion and influence (2.965; 3.156–8) may suggest that he died before completing his work, so it is hard to say whether his conclusion is a matter of accident or design. Of the surviving Latin epics only two were clearly

[15] Peta Fowler's revival of Bockemüller's transposition of 1247–51 to follow 1286 has much to recommend it, but does not wholly meet the difficulty (1997).

[16] 'Brief' since Book 12 is already the longest of the *Aeneid*'s books. Of course, as Maffeo Vegio demonstrated, there was no shortage of material for a thirteenth book (see further Graziosi (1990)).

finished when their authors died, Ovid's *Metamorphoses* and Statius' *Thebaid*; both end formally, with epilogues which provide closural effect while separating the author from his work. We may probably add Silius Italicus' *Punica*; at any rate, even if Silius might have wished to spend more time revising his epic, he could be well content with its conclusion in the triumphal procession of the godlike Scipio (see further Hardie (1993), 60).[17]

At all events we must be thankful that Roman writers evidently often felt that their works had reached a state of notional or partial completeness which allowed copies to be made for a limited circulation or to satisfy personal requests. The evidence of Cicero's correspondence on this point is familiar. It is also clear that books could pass into circulation without their authors' consent: thus Quintilian (1 *pr.* 7) includes among his motives for writing his work on oratorical training *quod duo iam sub nomine meo libri ferebantur artis rhetoricae neque editi a me neque in hoc comparati.* Galen similarly complains (*De libr. propr.* prooemium) that the working notes he gave his pupils for their private use circulated commercially in a distorted form (see further Hanson (1998)). We must guard against imposing on antiquity a model of publication and distribution derived from the routines of printing which rule out the fluidity still possible when the dissemination of a text depended on copying by hand. 'Print encourages a sense of closure, a sense that what is found in a text has been finalized, has reached a state of completion . . . Manuscripts remained closer to the give-and-take of oral expression' (Ong (1982), 136; see also Starr (1987)).

With Quintilian we have reached the period which saw the rise of the novel. It is appropriate to quote Mark Twain's (simplistic) conclusion to *The Adventures of Tom Sawyer* (1876): 'So endeth this chronicle. It being strictly the story of a boy, it must stop here; the story could not go much further without becoming the history of a man. When one writes a novel about grown people, he knows exactly where to stop—that is, with a marriage; but when he writes of juveniles, he must stop where he best can.' It is not literally true that all five of the surviving Greek novels end with a marriage. In Chariton and

[17] For valiant, and very different, attempts to establish that Lucan's epic is complete see Haffter (1957), Masters (1992), 216–59.

Xenophon of Ephesus the hero and heroine are married near the beginning, but their reunion is the narrative's goal. Chariton, probably the earliest, offers a well-prepared closure, directly addressed to the reading public. Xenophon and Longus give proleptic summaries of the happy future. Heliodorus, the last and greatest, finishes in a manner wholly consonant with the sophistication of his narrative (see further Morgan (1989)). The abrupt ending of Achilles Tatius' *Leucippe and Clitophon* is thus disconcerting. It is not just strangely rapid; it is inconsistent with the opening. The initial frame, involving conversation between the anonymous author and Clitophon, is not closed; at the start Clitophon was in Sidon, whereas at the end he is in Tyre, while Leucippe's whereabouts are quite obscure, though we may guess that her absence (or at any rate, the fact that she can be ignored) is connected with Clitophon's apparent unhappiness as indicated in the initial conversation (notwithstanding the conventional happy ending).

The problem has most recently been discussed by Repath (2005), who, developing the approach of Fusillo (1997), argues that this perplexing ending is to be seen as the culmination of Achilles' strategy of subverting the conventions of the 'ideal' Greek novel, frustrating the generic expectation of a happy ending. But this solution implies a reader more sophisticated than is likely to have been typical of the audience generally envisaged for this type of literature.[18] Moreover, our view of ancient fiction is partial and blinkered, and the isolation of the 'ideal' novel as a sub-genre reflects the circumstances of survival rather than a recognized literary category. Recent studies have emphasized that a long list may be compiled of narratives so closely akin to the five ideal novels as to make the demarcation of such a sub-genre unsatisfactory: it seems unnatural to treat them as a homogeneous group clearly to be distinguished from Antonius Diogenes' *Wonders beyond Thule*, the likely Greek prototype of *Apollonius King of Tyre*, and the *Apocryphal Acts*. Papyri have greatly enlarged our conception of the range of ancient prose fiction (see further Pervo (1987), Stephens and Winkler (1995)). I

[18] The readership of the Greek romance is of course controversial. But while the subtleties of quotation and allusion would be appreciated only by the well-educated minority, these narratives had plenty to entertain even an illiterate audience; see further Hägg (1994), S. R. West (2003).

should prefer to suppose that something is wrong with this novel's ending, whether the author got bored with his work and brought it to a premature conclusion, or planned a continuation which he failed to achieve or which did not survive. Perhaps, to put the matter more positively, his admirers were reluctant to wait till he had finished, and he was content to let what he had written pass into circulation while raising expectations of further instalments.

Whatever the explanation, the conclusion of Apuleius' *Metamorphoses* is hardly more satisfactory. The concentration of attention on the work's opening may make attractive the view that, as Andrew Laird puts it (2001, 267), 'The Prologue is a *coda*, if not an actual ending, to the story it heralds.' In this we might see imitation (or revival) of a feature highly characteristic of Homer and Hesiod. The prologue generates a sense of a narrator in full control of the story; this is quite absent from its final chapter. The last sentence offers a very unsatisfactory termination (11.31): 'Rursus denique quaqua raso capillo collegii vetustissimi et sub illis Sullae temporibus conditi munia non obumbrato vel obtecto calvitio sed quoquoversus obvio gaudens obibam.' The imperfect tense of *obibam*, highlighted by its final position, produces a sense of incompleteness. Even the reader who would like to see in this last book a sincere reflection of the faith which was Christianity's most serious rival, will find it hard to suppress a smile at Lucius' emphasis on his shaven head. This preoccupation with appearance is no way to commend the cult. The narrative of the latter half of the book (11.16–30) offers a series of false endings; our relief as Lucius finds an escape from his weird predicament through his encounter with Isis[19] turns to bewilderment as he faces not one but a succession of costly initiations, each of which is presented as if it will be the last. Lucius' own doubts about his third initiation (11.29) carry weight: just what is supposed to be going on?

Since Winkler's study (1985) it has been almost impossible to construe the last book as a straightforward document of religious experience. Winkler argued that the reader is meant to be left

[19] We should not forget that Lucius has known all along that he needs to eat roses to regain his human shape (3.25); Isis facilitates access (but we should not infer that otherwise it would have been impossible).

uncertain whether the novel's religious climax is to be taken seriously, but many will find this hermeneutic indeterminacy hard to accept. S. J. Harrison (2000, especially 235–59) persuasively stresses comic elements and incongruities, and argues that Apuleius' knowledge of Isiac religion 'is used for cultural and intellectual display and satirical entertainment rather than to assert any ideological or personal commitment'; his interpretation of the latter part of the book as a satire on religious mania and the avarice which exploited youthful religiosity is very attractive. But once we abandon the interpretation of the *Metamorphoses* as primarily a vehicle of religious edification (an interpretation which, advocated in its most thorough form by Merkelbach (1962), allowed the assumption that there might be rather more than met the uninitiated eye in much of the earlier narrative), we badly need a more marked conclusion to guide us in the work's overall interpretation. There is thus much to recommend the suggestion that the novel's original ending has not survived (see further van Mal-Maeder (1997), 112–14, Sandy (1999), 96).

From this survey of lengthy narratives of various types we can make a few general observations. The desirability of unambiguous closure was plainly not self-evident. Early hexameter poetry exemplifies the unmarked ending; its techniques for concluding episodes are also appropriate for transitions. A listening audience would have only a very approximate idea when the bard might be expected to end his performance, and an experienced performer would himself be guided by the response of his audience in deciding when to stop and how to bring his performance to a close in a manner which would stimulate a desire for a further instalment. A strongly marked conclusion to a long narrative, summing up the significance of a long series of heroic actions, did not fit the circumstances in which our epics took shape and Herodotus pioneered European historiography. Such indeterminacy and potential extensibility became less appropriate as writers came to envisage a reading public, though archaic precedent, above all that of Homeric epic, meant that the lack of a formal conclusion was unlikely to cause remark, while the roll format more easily allowed an author to postpone producing his final version than was possible with the codex.

Consideration of the evidence afforded by papyri for the relative popularity of the several books of Homer and Herodotus suggests that until the roll was superseded by the codex a complete text of either must have been a rarity. Correspondingly, the author of a work which might be expected to extend beyond a single roll would have been wise not to leave to the end matter of importance for the interpretation of the work as a whole, since readers must often have been frustrated by the difficulty of getting hold of the next instalment. Material which might make rather an effective conclusion would find a more secure home at the beginning, enhancing the author's chances of attracting an audience (as with the prologues of Roman comedy). An unmarked conclusion might leave the reader in doubt whether the last line of the text was indeed the ending intended by the author; Xenophon, the born organizer, demonstrated characteristic common sense with the unimpressive final sentence of his *Hellenica*. We should be wary of attempts to account for an unusually abrupt conclusion by the hypothesis that the writer chose an unconventional ending to stimulate reflection; such a tactic ran a serious risk of misconception on the part of readers who might suppose their texts to be incomplete. Locating another copy by which to check this suspicion would for many not have been feasible. Even under the Roman Empire the book trade was not well developed; literature was often disseminated through a network of friends.[20]

Bearing these circumstances in mind, we may briefly consider what must be the most discussed of all the problematic endings in ancient literature, that of the gospel of Mark, nowadays held by most scholars to be the earliest of the canonical gospels. Here we are dealing with a text rather shorter than most of my examples, and one not easily classifiable according to classical genres; though we are at liberty to speculate about its Aramaic antecedents, the concept of a gospel as a literary form cannot have been firmly established at the time of its composition, and it should not be supposed that it was self-evident where the narrative should stop. While with John, the last of the four canonical gospels, the final

[20] The well-known second-century letter P.Oxy. 2192 vividly illustrates the problems of getting hold of books; see further Starr (1987).

verse (21:25) offers a definitive *ne plus ultra*,[21] with Mark we meet a notorious problem. This is dangerous ground for the non-specialist, but the questions raised by the Gospel's abrupt ending are generally considered without regard to other works which now seem to lack a proper conclusion. I have profited particularly from the discussions of Wilamowitz (1926*a*), Nineham (1968), 439–53, Kermode (1979), Hooker (1991, especially 8–15 and 382–94), Donahue and Harrington (2002, especially 3–5) and Most (2005), 12–18 and 231–2.

In the oldest and best manuscripts Mark ends at 16:8, as the three women who have come to Jesus' tomb to anoint his body flee, apparently ignoring the instructions of a strange youth that they should report what they have found to the disciples, who will see Jesus again, as He had promised (14:28) in Galilee; ἐφοβοῦντο γάρ. The spuriousness of verses 9–20 has long been acknowledged, but it was generally supposed that the original ending had been lost, or that the evangelist had died before completing his work, until Wellhausen (1903) suggested that 16:8, the panic-stricken flight of the women from the empty tomb, was meant to be the end. Wilamowitz's study of the Gospel (1926*a*), which deserves to be better known, wholeheartedly responded to Wellhausen's suggestion, arguing that Mark's purpose was to relate what led those who had known Jesus to believe that He was the Messiah and emphasizing the importance of the Transfiguration (Mark 9:2–10): 'So lebt in diesem Buche der Glaube derer, die unmittelbar aus dem, was sie mit Jesus erlebt hatten, den Herrn in ihm erkannt hatten.' The leading Hellenist of his age did not judge worth considering the objection often raised that a book could not end ἐφοβοῦντο γάρ.

Still, Wilamowitz surely underestimated the disturbing quality of this enigmatic and inconclusive episode. 'The conclusion is either intolerably clumsy, or it is incredibly subtle' (Kermode (1979), 68); the latter alternative surely presupposes an inappropriate and

[21] The more remarkable in that we do not expect anything more after the last verse of the previous chapter (20:31). The writer of the Apocalypse similarly concludes his work in a manner which leaves no doubt that this is indeed the end. His concern for the integrity of his text (22:18–19) is to be noted; this is to be understood as a definitive version of his prophecy, not subject to modification.

anachronistic sophistication in the reader/listener.[22] The hypothesis, that the original ending was lost early, does not provide a straightforward solution. Of course the last leaf of a codex, the format fostered by the early Church, was peculiarly exposed to damage (as was the end of a roll if readers failed to rewind what they had finished reading), but if such an accident had occurred so early that there was still only a single copy it is hard to see why the evangelist himself, or one of his companions, did not make good the loss. While we could easily believe that the original copy might have been read and reread until the last page disintegrated, we should in that case expect the missing portion to have been replaced—whether transcribed from another copy or dictated *memoriter* by those who had taken its words to heart. The alternative hypothesis, that the writer died before completing his task, should not be lightly dismissed; a formally satisfying conclusion would have posed a peculiar challenge, and it would be natural for the evangelist to pause at this point, to review what he had written, and marshal his literary forces. That his work might have passed into circulation while still incomplete should not surprise us;[23] such, as we have seen, was the fate of a good deal of Latin hexameter verse.[24] In any case, the gospel was written mainly, if not exclusively, for fellow Christians and what happened next was known in broad outline to all believers. It is not surprising that Mark later seemed to need supplementation, once Matthew and Luke were in circulation; but terminal accretion, as with the conclusion of the *Odyssey*, was a regular hazard in antiquity for works with unmarked endings.

[22] We should envisage as the norm a group, one of whom reads to the others (cf. Apocal. 1:3), rather than solitary, reflective students.

[23] Hermas (*Vis.* 2.4.2–3) offers an interesting glimpse of the dissemination of literature in the early Church; such informal networking would tend to foster the premature circulation of material, in particular in response to personal requests.

[24] The ending of Acts, which has much higher literary pretensions, is also puzzling. 'Why does *Acts* stop at this point? Why does Luke not continue with an account of Paul's trial before the Emperor, culminating in either his release or his martyrdom? Either event would have made a most impressive close to the book' (C. K. Barrett (1998), 1236, cf. 1248–50). But Chrysostom saw considerable merit in this ending (*Hom.* 55 *In Acta Apostolorum* = lx. 382 *PCC*): *ὁρᾷς οἰκονομίαν θεοῦ; μέχρι τούτων τὸν λόγον ἵστησιν ὁ συγγραφεὺς καὶ ἀφίησι διψῶντα τὸν ἀκροατὴν ὥστε τὸ λοιπὸν ἀφ' ἑαυτοῦ συλλογίζεσθαι. τοῦτο καὶ οἱ ἔξω ποιοῦσι· τὸ γὰρ πάντα εἰδέναι νωθῆ ποιεῖ καὶ ἐκλελυμένον.*

Alcmaeon of Croton (D–K 24 B 2) enigmatically observed that men perish because they cannot join the beginning to the end. No contributor to this volume owes a greater intellectual debt than I do to its dedicatee, and joining beginning to end I may thus appropriately conclude with Donne's tribute to his long-suffering wife:

> Thy firmnes drawes my circle just,
> And makes me end, where I begunne.

2

The Monster and the Monologue: Polyphemus from Homer to Ovid

G. O. Hutchinson

The colourful career of the Cyclops in literary history strikingly exemplifies the complexities of Homeric reception. The aspects considered here will illustrate the value of narratological strategies, which have made such a vast contribution to our understanding of classical literature; but they will also suggest the value of extending narratology, and integrating it further with other types of criticism.

I

The blinded Polyphemus' speech to his ram (Hom. *Od.* 9.447–60) is remarkable for its narratological complexity, and for its imaginative explorations. We may start from listeners. To perceive the layering of the text, we should see speech and narrative alike as communicative acts. The intended addressee of Polyphemus' speech, the ram, does not understand it, and by nature cannot reply; the speech is actually heard by a different recipient, Odysseus, whom circumstances prevent from replying. As soon as he can, he vigorously and unwisely responds to the Cyclops' demeaning words (453, 460; 475–9, 502–5),

The massiveness of Martin West's achievements makes a Cyclopean piece not wholly inappropriate. It began life at a seminar run by Dr R. Armstrong at Balliol College, Oxford. It later made an appearance in Thessaloniki; I am grateful for the comments of Professors D. Iakov, S. Kyriakidis, Th. Papanghelis, and A. Rengakos.

almost as if the final οὐτιδανὸς ... Οὖτις had been an insult addressed to him. Odysseus is also the secondary (and internal) narrator; hence the Phaeacians, and then Homer's listeners, constitute further unintended and knowing audiences of Polyphemus' speech. The easy situation of Odysseus' intended listeners further contrasts with the peril of Polyphemus' unintended listener. All Polyphemus' unintended audiences heighten the irony and isolation of his utterance.[1]

Odysseus' role as narrator interacts with his role as character; he has indeed devised the plot, in competition with Polyphemus. Typical narratorial comments on Polyphemus' foolishness (442–3 τὸ δὲ νήπιος οὐκ ἐνόησεν, that the men were under the sheep) pick up their uneven battle of wits within the story (419: he thought I was so νήπιος that we would walk out with the animals). Polyphemus' ignorance of the real context to his monologue (Odysseus beneath the ram) is caused partly by his stupidity, but more by his pathetic limitation to the senses of feeling and hearing. For the outermost audience, Homer's listeners, pity for Polyphemus is in counterpoint with fear for Odysseus; the narratological set-up intensifies the fear (through the emotions of the secondary narrator) and makes the pity all the more surprising.[2]

The *Odyssey* is often thought more straightforward in its distribution of sympathies than the *Iliad*; but this moment shows otherwise. It is extraordinary to create sympathy for the man-eating violator of Zeus's laws, especially when his enemy is telling the story. The means is the monologue. It is partly that direct speech is the medium of emotion: the basis of epic pits a narrator, with maximum authority

[1] On speeches and narratology cf. de Jong (2004*b*), 8. It may often be helpful to approach narratology with an emphasis on communication (and so view non-narrative speeches as parallel to narration), as it may to approach it with an emphasis on content and the listener's reception (and so include dramas as wholes). For narratology in Homer cf. above all the fundamental work of de Jong (2001, 2004*a*, 2004*c*, etc.). 'Internal' (homodiegetic) means that Odysseus is a character in his own story. For the Cyclops episode, and this passage in particular, see among other works Reinhardt (1948), 79–91 = (1960), 64–73, Mondi (1983), Seaford (1984), 54, M. L. West (1997), 424–5, Nieto Hernández (2000), de Jong (2001), 233–49, Abry (2002), F. M. Schroeder (2002), J.-U. Schmidt (2003).

[2] For 9.442–3 (where ὡς οἱ should be preferred to ὥς οἱ) cf. especially the primary narrator's τὸ δὲ νήπιοι οὐκ ἐνόησαν, | ὡς δή σφιν καὶ πᾶσιν ὀλέθρου πείρατ' ἐφῆπτο at 22.32–3, and also his prominent comment on the companions at *Od.* 1.7–9.

and minimum emotion, against characters who have much emotion and less authority. The speech also shows us Polyphemus' own perspective on what has happened: just as the speech at the end of Horace's twelfth *Epode* makes it clear that the woman does not see herself as an 'old hag', so this speech reveals in the 'monster' a not unheroic outlook, where the only measures of value are strength and size (like Polyphemus' and the ram's). But there is much direct speech from Polyphemus in the episode, addressed to Odysseus or the other Cyclopes or Poseidon. This speech has a poignant isolation and intimacy. The Cyclopes live in detached families; Polyphemus has no family, and is close only to his animals (whom he organizes with unlooked-for care). His feeling for the ram displays more sensibility than we expected—almost the sensibility of the primary narrator in a simile. The ram's feeling for Polyphemus is perhaps partly a sad illusion, but partly at least Polyphemus' conscious fiction. This is shown by Polyphemus' hypothetical imaginings of a genuine communication and like-mindedness: *εἰ δὴ ὁμοφρονέοις ποτιφωνήεις τε γένοιο* (456). Precisely the actual absence of anyone to feel sorry for the Cyclops creates pity in the primary listener. The solitude of the Cyclops is contrasted, by the speech and its situation, with Odysseus' teamwork: the feeble man has blinded him *σὺν λυγροῖς ἑτάροισι* (454).[3]

The problematic communication with the animal generates the movements of the speech. The initial surprise at the ram's lateness, stressed by the enjambement of *ὕστατος* (448), leads to elaborate and touching rhetoric on the past: *πρῶτος . . . πρῶτος δὲ . . . πρῶτος δὲ . . . νῦν αὖτε πανύστατος* (447–53). That reaches a climax with the loss of sight (452–3); but the animal also leads to the bloodthirsty details

[3] For speeches in Homer to addressees that cannot answer see Pelliccia (1995), 161–8. That excellent general discussion unfortunately regards this speech as merely comic and rustic (164–7), partly through misinterpretation of *κακός* (453). Lines 452–5 (*ἦ σὺ ἄνακτος* | *ὀφθαλμὸν ποθέεις . . .*) could be taken as a question. For monologues in classical literature more widely see Schadewaldt (1926), J. Blundell (1980), Eigler (1988), Battezzato (1995), Auhagen (1999). Interesting for modern literature are e.g. Müller-Seidel (1980), 261–3, Ferrer (1990), Bennett (1998), 32–9, and Byron (2003), on the monologue poem (the precedent in Southey's 'Sappho', 'Lucretia', etc., is ignored). On the relation of Polyphemus to the other Cyclopes, cf. already Antisthenes fr. 53 Caizzi, *Σ*bT Hom. *Il.* 9.63*b* (ii. 412 Erbse). For Polyphemus' isolation, cf. the comparison with landscape at *Od.* 9.190–2.

of what the Cyclops would do to Odysseus if he caught him (458–9). Polyphemus is back to his old self, as regards the primary listener's response.[4]

Archaic art offers some context for the Homeric Cyclops, all the more if treatments of this popular episode are at first independent of the *Odyssey*, as archaeologists now often argue. The episode of the ram then becomes a pre-existing entity for Homer (cf. Middle Protoattic oinochoe fragments by the Ram Jug Painter, Aegina 566, 675–650BC). The contrast of Odysseus' team and the lone Polyphemus is a recurring feature of the art. On the neck of the Middle Protoattic amphora from Eleusis by the Polyphemus Painter the three men (the leader Odysseus marked out in white) encounter one Cyclops; on the body of the vase, by opposition, one man (with a goddess) encounters the three Gorgons. The truly strange Gorgons on that vase also provide a contrast with the huge but man-like Polyphemus. The slight emphasis on his single eye in Homer, not prepared in the narrative unlike the wine or the fire, seems to fit in with archaic depictions: there the assimilation to men is helped by the habitual profile (*not* employed with the Gorgons). There is special point in the *Odyssey*: for Polyphemus' violation of hospitality to have full force and suit the themes of the poem, he must be a man like his victims, and not a creature of a different species, without human δίκη (cf. Hes. *Op.* 276–80). But the art indicates that, in a stronger or weaker sense, even Homer will not be innocent of intertextuality.[5]

[4] For views in later antiquity that the address to the ram is rustic or absurd, cf. especially *Σ* Hom. *Od.* 9.456 (ii. 438 Dindorf) (argued against).

[5] Homer's technique on the eye is noted e.g. in Accius fr. 1 Funaioli, and seen as a sign of his following Hesiod; cf. also *Σ* Hom. *Od.* 9.106 (ii. 414–15 Dindorf). The Cyclopes appear as ἄνδρες, Hom. *Od.* 6.5 (cf. Garvie (1994), 82), 9.187, 494. Problems on Polyphemus' species: Arist. fr. 172 Rose. Vases of Polyphemus: see Touchefeu-Meynier (1992*a*), 156–7, (1992*b*), 954–60, Boardman (1998), 104–5, 116 (*Odyssey*), 119, 140; see also especially Snodgrass (1998). On the Polyphemus Painter's name vase (*LIMC* 'Kyklops' 17, Odysseus 94), see Osborne (1988), 1–6, (1998), 57–61, Whitley (1994), 63–5. The lament of the Gorgons in Pind. *Pyth.* 12.6–12 (cf. *Σ* 15b = ii. 265.10–20 Drachmann, Nonn. *Dion.* 25.42–7, 40.227–33), makes an interesting point of comparison with Polyphemus' monologue, especially in envisaging pathetic utterance from 'monsters'.

II

A responsive reading of Homer's scene is displayed in Aristophanes' *Wasps*—more so than in Euripides' *Cyclops*, where the grossness and blasphemy of Homer's figure are intensified, but the subtleties of the Homeric monologue are deliberately erased. A donkey has Philocleon beneath it; Bdelycleon shows sympathy for it, and a wondering incomprehension at its behaviour: κάνθων, τί κλαίεις; ὅτι πεπράσει τήμερον; (179). The sensible young man is taking, quite unsuitably, the role of the Homeric Polyphemus. Even more unsuitable is Philocleon's Odysseus: the name Οὖτις, whose point the dense Polyphemus continues not to grasp (Hom. *Od.* 9.455, 460), is used by the would-be Odysseus at the wrong point in the story, when he has been detected beneath the donkey.[6]

Fragments of Antisthenes and Aristotle indicate fifth- and fourth-century interest in the problems of Homer's account of the Cyclops. But the most spectacular turn in the Cyclops' fortunes comes when he is equipped with a love-object, Galatea: a turn which again centres on monologue.[7]

Ibycus is not given a strong claim to have initiated this change by P.Oxy. 4456. Although]κ̣λω̣π̣α̣[(line 4) is a probable reading, and although a commentary on Ibycus in second-century Oxyrhynchus is likelier than one on Philoxenus,]ε̣ρως̣ (11) need not refer to love, and ε̣πικλίειν τε[is unlikely to be part of the poetic text.[8]

Philoxenus' presentation of the amorous Cyclops' song was certainly the most famous treatment before Theocritus. It draws on the lyric tradition of the love song: in the dithyramb, the Cyclops' lyre-playing offers a lyric within lyric (and a solo monologue depicted within a choral performance). The idea of the unattractive lover's song goes back at least to Anacreon (*PMG* 358; 417, etc.?). The Cyclops in love is to be taken as a striking development of the

[6] Theology is of more concern to the *Cyclops* than subtlety. *Cyc.* 316–28 and 576–84 join Hom. *Od.* 9.275–6 and 359 into a grotesque rivalry with Zeus. Cf. Seaford (1984), 209.

[7] For Antisthenes and Aristotle, see n. 5 above, and cf. also Arist. *EN* 1180^{a}26–9.

[8] I have looked at the original of P.Oxy. 4456. ε̣πικλίειν τε here, preceded by comment and with a gap in the next line, will hardly be part of a lemma.

suggestions in Hom. *Od.* 9.230 οὐδ᾽ ἄρ᾽ ἔμελλ᾽ ἑτάροισι φανεὶς ἐρατεινὸς ἔσεσθαι; the music will be taken as a development of his Homeric whistling (315). Polyphemus' injunction to the dolphins to tell Galatea he is curing his love through the Muses (*Σ* Theocr. 11.1–3*b* = p. 241.8–17 Wendel; cf. *PMG* 822) develops the idea of animals as imagined speakers; the dolphins are to help Polyphemus with his chief concern Galatea as the ram is to help him with his chief concern Odysseus. But the physical distance from Galatea implied by the device contrasts with his (earlier? opening?) address to her (821); that address conveys both emotional contact and spatial separation.[9]

Philoxenus included the blinding (*Σ* Ar. *Plut.* 298b = p. 68 Chantry; *PMG* 820); but the course of his poem is unknown, and not to be reconstructed from Synesius (*Ep.* 121: Garzya (2000), iii. 252.1–2, 253.28–31). Synesius' story about Odysseus, Polyphemus, and Galatea is unlikely to allude to Philoxenus, by now obscure. It is perhaps most naturally seen as an autonomous creation.[10]

The success enjoyed by Philoxenus' conception is apparent in Theocritus. Poem 11 sets the amorous monologue of Polyphemus within a *dialogue* between Theocritus and Nicias: a dialogue that will grow with the production of answering poems (*SH* 566, Theocritus 13). While each, as a lover, is parallel to the forlorn Cyclops, they communicate as fellow sufferers and poets across the sea (between Sicily and Miletus). Callimachus picks this point up in his own address to Philippus on the Cyclops (*Ep.* 46 Pfeiffer = 1047–56 *HE*); unspoken dialogue with Theocritus, continuing that between Theocritus and Nicias, adds a further layer of complexity. Another layer is to be added to Theocritus 11, as his work accumulates, by poem 6.

[9] For Philoxenus, see Hordern (1999), (2004), Livrea (2004). The piece is earlier than 388, and could be from the late fifth century on; it cannot be proved earlier than Nicochares' *Galatea* in the 390s (fr. 4 *PCG*; J. K. Davies (1971), 422), though this seems probable. Association with Gauls (Timaeus *FGrHist* 566 F 69, etc.) is likely to come later. Ar. *Plut.* 290–301 (cf. L. P. E. Parker (1997), 554–6) as a whole look remarkably unlike new lyric or *PMG* 821; but the address to the animals (*PMG* 819) is of interest. For Timotheus' *Cyclops*, see Hordern (2002), 106–16. On Anacr. fr. 417, cf. Hutchinson (2001), 281.

[10] Cf. the improvisation in Polyb. 35.6. Synesius is not Aristaenetus, paraphrasing Callimachus. This extended narrative, which serves a specific purpose, does not accord with his manner of allusion; it is quite different from the sentence on history or mythology with which his letters often begin. On Synesius' letters cf. Hose (2003).

There Polyphemus, instead of repeating his monologue, answers another speaker with a denial of love; that poem is in dialogue with poem 11. The Cyclops' isolation in Theocritus 11 is heightened by the ironic parallel with his enemy Odysseus, gazing over the sea in solitude but not in love (Hom. *Od.* 5.156, 158).[11]

Polyphemus' looking (18, just before the speech) brings in the important motif of sight, thematized by the future blinding and the role of sight in love. He can still see; he cannot stop looking at Galatea (28–9, cf. 20, second line of speech). Seeing, and being heard, are more elusive in the present communication: Galatea is in the inaccessible sea (contrast Posidipp. 19.8 A–B). In poem 6 Polyphemus is accused of not seeing, in his lovelorn abstraction (8), but insists that he does see (21–4, with allusion to the future blinding); by not looking at Galatea, he will agitate her (25).[12]

The eye is in competition with Galatea: the word *κόρα* conjoins them (Galatea 11.25, 30, 60; other girls 11.77; eye 6.36). Polyphemus' love for his own eye eventually goes beyond affection (*τῶ μοι γλυκερώτερον οὐδέν* 11.53) to self-esteem for his own uniqueness. In 11 his eye is what prevents Galatea's love (31–3, just after sight and *χαρίεσσα κόρα*), and he is obliged to compensate it with other attractions. In 6, now out of love, his eye is still sweet to him (22), and he also admires its beauty, with the idiosyncratic judgement of a lover (cf. 18–19)—but a self-lover (34–8). This state of self-admiration had been suppressed and challenged by his love for Galatea and her disdain. Philoxenus and Homer and their rival conceptions of

[11] The Theocritus and Callimachus obviate any objection that intertextual 'dialogue' and 'dialogue' between characters are connected only through a word made important to criticism by Bakhtin. Callimachus' hexameter *Galateia* might also be relevant (cf. frr. 379–80, the work of the latter not certain). The popularity of Philoxenus is indicated by all the discussion of the poem and its origins (including Duris *FGrHist* 76 F 58), and by Nicochares frr. 3–5 *PCG* (probably), Antiphanes fr. 131, Alexis frr. 37–40 (cf. Arnott (1996), 139–49). On Posidipp. 19.5–8 A–B (read *οὐδ'* in 7?) see Petrain (2003) and Raimondi (2005). On Theocritus 6 and 11, see Hunter (1999), 215–61, and the works mentioned there; add Messi (2000), Fantuzzi and Hunter (2004), 149–51, 164–7.

[12] Cf. and contrast him *ἐρεθίζοντα* Galatea in Philoxenus, *Σ* Ar. *Plut.* 290c *a* = p. 65 Chantry, *PMG* 819). Com. Adesp. 1147.9–13 *PCG*, on love without sight as a complete paradox, exemplifies ancient presuppositions; Athen. 13.564e interestingly plays on the absence of Galatea's eyes from the song in Philoxenus as a sign of the Cyclops' future blindness.

Polyphemus interact across these poems. The Philoxenian conception predominates in 11, but is defeated in 6. Even in 11 Polyphemus ironically imagines being burned in his one eye, with the fire in his cave (50–3): an assertion of the greater importance of love, but also of the storyline which will really matter. The thinness his mother *sees* in Polyphemus (without *speaking* to Galatea) underlines again how alien this love is to the nature of the Cyclops (67–9); even within 11 he reverts to self-address and self-esteem (72–9, 79 in ironic interplay with Odysseus, cf. 38). If the reversion itself is actually taken from Philoxenus (cf. *PMG* 822), that only exemplifies the polarization of Philoxenus and Homer in this restaged intertextual dialogue.[13]

In 11, communication has advanced beyond that with the ram, but is still problematic; difficulties of species have added to the amatory problems. The life of a different type of being is the object of Polyphemus' frustration; the life of the ram had simply been the object of his sympathy. In 6 there is a more definite animal intermediary, the dog. He looks to the sea, as Polyphemus pretends not to, but does so in hostility commanded by his master; once he was a more amorous messenger. Communication is not a problem for the Cyclops freed from love; *he* will refuse embassies until Galatea meets his terms (31–3). The Cyclops is like an Achilles. Within the poem, and for now, he is free from subjection either to Galatea or to Odysseus (22–4).[14]

III

Theocritus' Polyphemus himself becomes simplified, and the object of a polarization with Homer. He is a significant figure for articulating the divisions of the Virgilian corpus. In the *Eclogues* he is an absent presence, a central figure of the Theocritean corpus edited out

[13] Important for the obvious play on *κόρη* is Empedocles fr. 103.7–8 Inwood (D–K 31 B 84.7–8) (Aphrodite) *ὣς δὲ τότ' ἐν μήνιγξιν ἐεργμένον ὠγύγιον πῦρ* | *λεπτῇισίν* <*τ'*> *ὀθόνῃσι λοχεύσατο* (Förster, for *λοχάζετο* or *ἐχεύατο*) *κύκλοπα κούρην*. Even in Theocr. 11.53 the idiom of loving as much as or more than one's eyes (Call. *H.* 3.210–11, etc.) makes the *οὐδέν* notable.

[14] The dog's and Polyphemus' seeing or otherwise relate to the reader's imaginative seeing, which the vivid description of the dog makes tantalizing. For comparison of the ram and Galatea, cf. Hunter (1999), 222.

of the Virgilian world. His words are heard, but mostly assigned to other speakers. *Eclogue* 2 elaborately reworks his monologue in Theocritus 11, for Corydon. 7.37–40 present the beginning of that monologue, addressed to the Nymph Galatea, but end by naming Corydon as the lover. 8.37–41 present the narrative of love that follows (Theocr. 11.25–9); the motif of the speaker *seeing* the beloved is brought out further (*Ecl.* 8.38, 41), but the speaker is not the Cyclops. Climactically, in 9.39–43 a song is heard which presents a later part of the monologue (Theocr. 11.42–9), addressed to the Nymph Galatea, but with no speaker; this can be taken as Polyphemus' own song. We hear it at multiple removes: Moeris' memory of a song by Menalcas which gives the song of Polyphemus. The lonely appeal of the Cyclops is diffracted through a world of poetic interaction, within the drama (orally) and beyond it (Theocritus and Virgil interacting textually, partly in the disguise of their characters).[15]

The reader's hearing of the unseen Cyclops is replaced in the *Aeneid* by seeing an unheard Cyclops. No speech is given in Achaemenides' retelling of the Odyssean narrative (*nec dictu adfabilis ulli* 3.621 reminds us of the speaking in Homer). Achaemenides' own seeing of the Cyclops is emphasized: | *uidi egomet* 623, *uidi* 626, cf. 648, 652); his seeing is then at once shared by the Trojans (*uidemus* 655, cf. 677), but again with no speech from Polyphemus, despite the *clamorem immensum* mentioned in the text (672). These acts of seeing are wrapped in numerous narratological layers: Aeneas' narration enwraps Achaemenides'; it is itself relayed to Dido, who can only hear not see the events (cf. 2.5, 11). But the vivid descriptions enable the reader in imagination to see seeing and unseeing Cyclopes and Polyphemus' eye (635–8, 658–64, 669, 677–81; 677 ***cernimus** astantis nequiquam **lumine** toruo*).[16]

[15] The scholiasts' identification of Simichidas with Theocritus in Theocritus 7 is doubtless implicit in *Ecl.* 9.32–6. The climactic movement of the *Eclogues* towards Arcadian song (so I would modify Jenkyns (1998), 157–69) is related to approaching Polyphemus. The name Galatea in the *Eclogues* gradually moves towards identification with the Nymph: not in 1.30–1, closer in 3.64–5 (and 72–3), cf. Theocr. 6.6–7, but note *puella* and *salices*; *Nerine* at last 7.37.

[16] The combination of sun, shield, and blinding in 635–8 has some connections with Laberius 89–92 Bonaria, cf. also Plaut. *Mil.* 1–4. The significance of the Cyclops as an object of seeing, not only a subject, is underlined at Virg. *Aen.* 11.263 *Aetnaeos uidit Cyclopas Vlixes* (in itself the misfortune, cf. Horsfall (2003), 172).

The indirectness of access in both Dido's and the reader's cases conveys Virgil's distance from his Greek models, but also intensifies the excitement of his recreating them. Seeing and not yet seeing the Cyclops has a metatextual dimension for the reader, as the Homeric episode is mirrored and the Homeric figure witnessed. The internal secondary narrator, Aeneas, again makes notable the sympathy which the text briefly arouses for Polyphemus, along with other responses. Virgil actually creates a kind of monologue without words. *ea sola uoluptas | solamenque mali* (3.660–1), of the sheep, connects to Hom. *Od.* 9.447–60, and especially to 459–60: *κὰδ δέ κ' ἐμὸν κῆρ | λωφήσειε κακῶν*. By a poignant irony, only the sheep, not revenge on Odysseus, are any kind of consolation. The phrase joins too with Evander's speech to his son, the pathos of which provides the impetus for the final action of the poem: Pallas is Evander's *sola et sera uoluptas* (8.581). However, the isolation of the Cyclops is here temporary; the other Cyclopes now come to his aid (3.675–6), not as in Homer. It is Achaemenides who has been in isolation (617–18): his enemies, not his *socii*, deliver him. But for all the turns on Homer, the depth of Virgil's reading is made clear.[17]

Roman art shows the popularity of the Theocritean conception: Polyphemus appears frequently at Pompeii and elsewhere, but usually in the company of Galatea. He is commonly playing to her or looking at her: song and sight, as in Theocritus. The Homeric future obtrudes: so at Pompeii I 7.7 (House of the Sacerdos Amandus) the prow of Odysseus' ship steals in at the right-hand edge as Polyphemus, looking in the other direction, relaxes with Galatea. In the Polyphemus Panel of the Mythological Room (19) at Boscotrecase (*c.*11 BC; New York, Metropolitan 20.192.17) Polyphemus and Galatea appear, but the Cyclops pelts Odysseus' ship in a second scene, subordinated to the first. This pair of scenes,

[17] Cic. *Tusc.* 5.115 illustrates a much less sympathetic attitude to Polyphemus' monologue, based on morality. The disjunction of the Polyphemus in *Aeneid* 3 from the Polyphemus in *Ecl.* 9.37–43 is stressed by his striding into the sea (*Aen.* 3.664–5, 670–1). Here tradition is realigned: he does not enter the sea in Homer, and is in the sea with or near Galatea in Posidipp. 19.7–8 A–B, and in the painting from the 'House of Livia' (Rome, Palatine; second half of 1st cent. BC), *LIMC* 'Galateia' 8. The idea of an unspoken monologue, seen in Polyphemus' body, calls to mind the novel of A. Stamatis, *Σαν τον κλέφτη μες στη νύχτα* (Athens, 2001), 234 (addressed to an actress) *Σαν το πρόσωπο, το σώμα σου να μονολογεί, χωρίς εσύ να μιλάς.*

Theocritean and Homeric, suggests a pictorial tradition too for double structures on the Cyclops. Ovid's Acis plays very little role in Roman painting; the traditions of visual art on Polyphemus, rather than deriving from Ovid, must have formed part of (in a broad sense) his intertextual material.[18]

Ovid's *Metamorphoses* confront (with complications) the Theocritean and Homeric Polyphemi, and two forms of Virgilian epos, across books 13 and 14. Intertextuality and narratology have reached an extreme of complexity. In 13 a conversation between Galatea and Scylla encloses the monologue of the primarily Theocritean Polyphemus. Galatea talks amicably to another female; Polyphemus addresses Galatea, in vain (870). The contrast is ironic: Scylla will herself turn into a monster, and attack Ulysses' men (14.70–1). Galatea's reciprocated love for Acis produces a setting for the monologue which creates another contrast: Galatea hears the monologue of unrequited passion while resting in Acis' lap. This position recreates the perilous placing in the *Odyssey* of Odysseus, an audience of Polyphemus. If the danger seems less immediate than Odysseus' (*procul* 787), the lovers' heedlessness and immobility will lead to the actual killing of Acis with a rock (cf. the play at 801, 869, contrast 805–7). While reverting to the Homeric scene, Ovid also invests the situation with contemporary point: Polyphemus is like a husband discovering the lovers in the act (cf. 873–5), and attacking the man. That scene is envisaged and encouraged by the *Lex Iulia de adulteriis coercendis*; it has a great impact on Ovidian narrative.[19]

In this situation, hearing and seeing are of great importance, especially seeing. Galatea both hears and sees the Cyclops: hearing is mentioned before the speech (783–8), seeing after (870 *nam cuncta*

[18] Acis seems to appear at Pompeii XI 6.d–e: Baldassarre and Pugliese Carratelli (1990–2003), ix. 725 (*LIMC* 'Galateia' 47). Pompeii I 7.7: Baldassarre and Pugliese Carratelli (1990–2003), i. 597–600 (*LIMC* 'Galateia' 13). Boscotrecase: Blanckenhagen and Alexander (1962), 38–43 and plates 40–3; *LIMC* 'Galateia' 22, add Leach (1988) 339–44. The 'House of Livia' (n. 17 above) offers an early depiction; *SEG* 30 (1980) no. 1141 (Assisi) probably dates from the 1st cent. AD rather than BC. In general see Montón Subias (1990), Touchefeu-Meynier (1997), 1016–17.

[19] For the *Lex Iulia*, cf. Crawford (1996), §60, *Dig.* 48.5.2.2, 25.*pr.*–1, and for this aspect Fayer (2005), 221–55. On the Cyclops in *Met.* 13, cf. among other works Nagle (1988), Solodow (1988), 31, Tissol (1990), Farrell (1992), Myers (1994), 101, Holzberg (1996), 149, Hopkinson (2000), 34–40, 211–31, Fantham (2004), 129–31, Subias-Konofal (2004).

uidebam). The disaster is that he, not yet blinded, sees them: *me uidet atque Acin, 'uideo'que exclamat* (874). His power of sight has been turned on himself as beautiful and large (840–1 . . . *placuitque mihi mea forma uidenti*; cf. 842 (to Galatea) *aspice sim quantus*); his eye, which he defends with rhetorical enthusiasm, is ominously likened to the all-seeing sun (851–3). It has been the alleged victim of love and Galatea (*altera iam rapuit* 775); but now causes real violence itself.[20]

In the *Eclogues*, the Cyclops' monologue was removed from him and broken into fragments; when at last he was permitted authorship, the 'song' condensed the Theocritean monologue into a few lines. Here Theocritus is swollen by Cyclopean excess: a swelling not so much of size as of style. The opening pastoral comparisons of Theocritus are comically extended in quite un-Ovidian fashion (13.789–807). The author's elaborate intertextual dialogue conflicts with the rude unsophistication of the speaker; the limited horizons of pastoral characters are pushed into a resolutely solipsistic outlook. The embarrassments of Polyphemus in Theocritus 11 are replaced by a self-confidence which recalls Theocritus 6, but also Homer and Euripides (842–4, cf. Eur. *Cyc.* 327?). Jupiter, the Sun, Neptune enlarge his magnificence. His size and strength make a preference for Acis incomprehensible (860–1 *sed cur Cyclope repulso | Acin amas praefersque meis complexibus Acin?*, with proud use of his race's name and scornful use of Acis'). His violent threats appear close to the end of the monologue, almost as in Homer (863–6; for the actual end, 869, cf. Theocr. 11.29). The subsequent action enables him to pull mountains apart (882–3), and show the Homeric force as enhanced by post-Homeric embellishment. He views Galatea as violent and savage in refusing him (798 *saeuior*, 801 *uiolentior*, 858 *tua fulmine saeuior ira est*), love as an Aetna (868–9). This partly displays the power of love (759–63); but it also displays the language into which the monster translates love, and the sphere in which he is really at home. The mixing of bodies in slaughter rather than love is what he really understands (865–6 *uiscera uiua traham* (with archaic alliteration) . . . *perque tuas spargam (sic se tibi misceat!) undis*). Aetna fears *him*

[20] On the eye in 851–3, cf. Tronchet (1998), 502, Hopkinson (2000), 225–6, Hardie (2002), 170 n. 54. The male gaze in the poem can mingle active and passive (subjection to love); interestingly, Tereus' predatory gaze (6.478, 515–18) is made passive by his own wilful agency (6.479–81, 490–3).

(877, cf. 868). The form of the monologue well conveys his uniqueness and self-obsession, his remoteness from reciprocated love.[21]

The Homeric monologue of book 14 contrasts with the Theocritean monologue of book 13 in its size (6 lines against 81). The relative size of the two basic intertexts is reflected (Homer 14 lines, Theocritus 61); but the difference also expresses how Polyphemus has been reduced to misery. Yet even in a short space he shows his gigantic excess of style, piling up relative clauses, especially with *cuius* (193–6). The content shows the bloodiness that appeared at the end of his first monologue, now directed against Ulysses or any companion he has left behind (192–3). The peril of the hearer Achaemenides is marked out with almost comic obviousness. The Homeric situation of listening evoked in book 13 (cf. *latitans* 13.786, 14.214) now comes close to its original form, and the Cyclops' true nature is restored. Whereas Virgil captured the sympathy of the Homeric monologue without the use of speech, Ovid uses monologue to disrupt the pity which Achaemenides' narrative had generated (188–90). The echo of the *beginning* of Evander's speech to Pallas (14.192 *o si quis referat mihi casus Vlixem*, cf. Virg. *Aen.* 8.560 *o mihi praeteritos referat si Iuppiter annos*) only brings out the obliteration of Virgilian complexity here. There is no Homeric ram. The Cyclops shortly becomes like an animal himself in his eating of men (14.207–9, cf. Hom. *Od.* 9.292–3). His hideous first-person description of cannibalism (194–6) goes beyond Homer and shows the ugly absorption of one body by another which is the antithesis of loving union.[22]

[21] Sil. 14.221–6 . . . *et tibi uictricem, Galatea, immiscuit undam* picks up the allusion to metamorphosis in 866, and triumphantly turns back the Cyclops' words. Mountains and rocks, constant accompaniments of the Cyclops' massive crudity (contrast Odysseus' crafted stick and pole), come together in the rock which he throws (*Met.* 13.882). Cf. Demetr. 115; note also Sen. Rh. *Suas.* 1.12 (Dorion in his *Metaphrasis of Homer*) ὄρους ὄρος ἀποσπᾶται. The repetition of Acis' name at Ov. *Met.* 13.861 also resembles the jealous repetition at Hor. *C.* 1.13.1–2. Farrell (1992) well brings out the non-Theocritean elements in the Cyclops of book 13; but when book 14 is brought into the discussion, the Theocritean basis in book 13 takes on an altered appearance, as one in a pair. Farrell's article also admirably relates narratology and intertextuality.

[22] The connections with metamorphosis are made clear at 15.88–95, with explicit mention of Cyclopes. The intertextuality will have been further complicated in antiquity not only by missing works but by the scholiastic tradition. P.Oxy. 3710 shows what rich commentaries would have been available to Ovid; and this part was particularly famous (cf. [Long.] 9.14) and much discussed. Cf. e.g. Philod. *Bon. Reg.* col. xxxvi.14–32, with Fish (2004), 112–14: of interest for Ov. *Met.* 13.841–3.

Again the intertextual complexity is matched by a narratological complexity. Achaemenides meets another refugee of Ulysses' travels; his narrative will be set against Macareus'. It has a further point in glorifying Aeneas, to whom ties of family and country are transferred: this has significance both in relation to Virgil's appropriation of Homer and in relation to the poem's shift from Greece to Rome. Instead of the contrast between Odyssean teamwork and Polyphemus' solitude, as in Homer, Achaemenides has been deserted by the Greeks. His constant seeing of the unseeing Cyclops is reversed, much as in Virgil, by the sight of Aeneas' ship (Virg. *Aen.* 3.651–2, Ov. *Met.* 14.218, after 178–9 (Greek ships seen leaving), 181 *uidi*, 183 | *uidi iterum*, at a later stage than *Aen.* 3.623, 626; 199). His seeing of the Cyclops recalls to his imagination the earlier seeing of his comrades being eaten (203–13). At the beginning of the speech he wishes to see Polyphemus again (*iterum*, with more play on intertextual repetition) if he is not grateful for seeing the sun; the sun is implicitly contrasted with the head and especially the sun-like eye of the Cyclops (172–5, cf. 13.852–3, Virg. *Aen.* 3.637).[23]

In the tradition of the Cyclops intertextuality, staging, imagery, communication, narratology combine to create a complex process of reception. Narratological form is of primary importance in the tradition; yet it is greatly enriched and complicated by other factors. Perception, with the Cyclops as subject and object of seeing and hearing, has been a particular concern. Form itself, in this tradition, has embraced intertextuality as well as narratology. Double, contrasting intertexts (Homer and Philoxenus or Theocritus) are employed in double, contrasting structures (two poems, two books of a poem, two parts of a corpus). The role of double textual form is notable in the tradition of a figure so stamped by oneness.

Important too for understanding the reception is the accumulating process of intertextual density which accompanies these neat forms. By contrast with the double forms, this process advances with

[23] For the Ovidian *Aeneid* and *Odyssey*, see among other works Ellsworth (1988), Döpp (1991), Baier (1999), Schade (2001), Tissol (2002), Papaioannou (2005) (ch. 3 for the Achaemenides episode). For mental seeing in Ovid, cf. e.g. *Tr.* 4.2.57–68, *Pont.* 1.8.33–8; *talia fingebam* in 14.213 turns the wishful musing of an elegiac lover (Tib. 1.5.20, 35 *haec mihi fingebam*) into epic terror.

the chronological succession of authors. It makes the latest text in some respects like the final image in Proust (*RTP* iii. 1047–8, Pléiade edn.): past texts gather beneath the present text like vast stilts. And yet Ovid contrives to make the walk of his text not 'difficile et périlleuse' but brisk and assured: the workings of intertextuality involve some simplification as well as complication. The elaborate and richly significant complexes we have been exploring are themselves derived from rich and elaborate complexes in Homer. One result of this little study in reception is to show that the Homer looks at least as subtle and sophisticated as any of the treatments that grow from it.

Appendix: Handel's *Acis and Galatea*

The bearing of these themes on the giant post-classical reception of Polyphemus may be illustrated from a single example, perhaps not unwelcome to our μουσικός honorand. In Handel's masque *Acis and Galatea* (first version 1718) the climax is formed by a trio (HWV 49a/17). The trio is a duet disrupted by an alien voice. The reciprocated love of Acis and Galatea is expressed by their shared motif and close counterpoint. The repeated quavers (Example 1 (a), bars 13–16) convey intense emotion, as for example in the duet 'Io t'abbraccio' from *Rodelinda* (HWV 19/24a, especially bar 15). The noisy interruption of the Cyclops (Example 1 (a), bars 17–22) conveys through a quite different musical language the violence he feels and will inflict, in his isolated and morally disastrous version of love: he has an argumentative as well as a comic function in the work. The detached descending octaves of his opening trochaic 'Torture, fury' contrast with Acis' and Galatea's rising iambic figure, and the growing intensity of its quavers. 'Torture, fury' forms a more extreme version of the detached 'Guerra, stragi' (HWV 10/10.8–10) with which the God in *Silla* urges the tyrant to try and be a bit more bloodthirsty (Example 1 (b)). The God's following run of semiquavers is seen in the Cyclops' part too (Example 1 (a) bars 20–1); these have been used in characterizing the Cyclops, from the announcement of his appearance by the chorus (HWV 49a/10.33–82), and his opening accompanied recitative (11.1–5). He is in agitated mental movement and causes disruptive movement in nature. His agitation here is heightened by the setting of the semi-quavers one syllable to a note (as in 10.33–56). The trio, then, displays a loving dialogue set against an isolated monologue—more visibly isolated than in the aria which comically reworks Ovid's own monologue ('Oh ruddier than the cherry', HWV 49a/12).[24]

Usually duets in Handel are formed like da capo arias, sometimes with an expansion of the A section (from A1 A2 to A1 A2 A3). Here the A section, unexpectedly ending in the dominant G minor, is followed by a B section; yet instead of a resumption, Polyphemus breaks in not just musically but physically, with action (whether or not visually represented). He hurls the rock that will slay Acis. He ends the trio singing alone; he has violently turned the trio into a solo. Handel has gone beyond the corresponding trio of his earlier *Aci, Galatea e Polifemo* (HWV 72/15 1st part), which is completed by Acis and Galatea before the recitative that contains the Cyclops' deed (HWV 72/15 2nd part). He has created a powerful fusion of form, drama, and moral point.[25]

[24] HWV numbers refer to Baselt (1978–86). The interpretation of the trio as interrupted duet appears already in Dean (1959), 165. Amorously close intervals are achieved in bars 15–16, although Acis is a tenor; *g″* for Galatea would have been within the singer's vocal range (cf. Beeks (1987), 213–14). The large intervals in bars 17–18 resemble Polifemo's characterization in *Aci, Galatea e Polifemo* (1708), cf. e.g. HWV 72/12. See also on *Acis and Galatea* Trowell (1987), R. Smith (1995), 15, 60–1, 78–9; best edition: Windszus (1991). Smith rightly implies a moral significance to the work; but its many differences from the religious oratorios would permit a more complex account. On the deity in *Silla*, originally female, see Dean and Knapp (1994), 263–4. Academic discussion of the Cyclops' modern reception is at least as early as Feder (1765).

[25] The semiquavers for the falling of the rock in *Aci, Galatea e Polifemo* (HWV 72/15 2nd part 14–20) have less of a broad significance than those used for the rock in *Acis and Galatea* (HWV 49a/17.32–43). The earlier work is not, like *Acis and Galatea*, abruptly quit by the Cyclops after his action. For possibilities that the rock in *Acis and Galatea* was depicted cf. Trowell (1987), 50.

Example 1

(a) Handel, *Acis and Galatea*, trio 'The flock shall leave the mountains' (HWV 49a/17) (instrumental parts other than continuo omitted)

(b) Handel, *Silla*, aria and recitative 'Guerra, stragi' (HWV 10/10)

3

Low Words in High Places: Sex, Bodily Functions, and Body Parts in Homeric Epic and Other Higher Genres

†*David Bain*

1. INTRODUCTION

> *δεξιτέρηι δὲ πελώριον ἔλλαβεν ἅρπην,*
> *μακρὴν καρχαρόδοντα, φίλου δ' ἀπὸ μήδεα πατρὸς*
> *ἐσσυμένως ἤμησε* (Hes. *Theog.* 179–81)

> *θῆρες δὲ φρίσσουσ' οὐρὰς δ' ὑπὸ μέζε' ἔθεντο,*
> *τῶν καὶ λάχνηι δέρμα κατάσκιον* (Hes. *Op.* 512–13)

To begin at the beginning, or at very least near the beginning (I do not wish to enter into a debate in which our honorand[1] has long been a lively participant): already in Hesiod (*Theog.* 180 and *Op.* 512) we see that a writer composing in what most would consider to be a higher genre (especially if we classify the writer as an epic poet, although 'wisdom literature' is undoubtedly a more appropriate designation for *Works and Days* than epic) is confronted by the need to

[The editors have kept as closely as possible to the text which David Bain left complete in essentials, but unrevised, at his sudden death in December 2004. Three additions by Christopher Collard, and one by Patrick Finglass, are marked with their initials.]

[1] To write about Greek epic poetry in a volume dedicated to Martin is a somewhat daunting task and, in my case at any rate, might appear to be presumptuous or like engaging in a demarcation dispute. Nevertheless, I hope he will find something of interest in what follows and excuse any areas of ignorance I may expose.

find a way of naming a body part which from the beginning was seen as 'shameful'.[2] In this particular case there is a long-standing debate about the words (or rather word) Hesiod does choose, μήδεα for the genitals of the founder of the dynasty of Olympian gods and μέζεα for the humble genital equipment of beasts, who hide their tails beneath them when they are shivering with cold. Martin West, if I am not mistaken, has discussed the words in question at least three times and displayed his usual learning, succinctness, and boldness.[3] This and the nature of the lemmata in question fit in well with the topic I am about to discuss: the manner in which epic poetry (and other higher genres) handles sexual material and words relating to bodily functions.

Two puzzles present themselves, with regard to μήδεα, most notably that of its etymology. First, the popular connection with the verb μήδομαι is denied in Chantraine's etymological dictionary.[4] Second, why does Hesiod use different forms in different works? I have no solution to these problems. I content myself with mentioning some of the more persuasive literature on them, since whether or not they provide satisfactory answers, they show their authors to be aware of two constant problems in the interpretation of Greek literature: how to assess the tone of words and how to evaluate the different demands made on authors writing within different genres.

Wackernagel in a brief but classic discussion of many terms relating to the more basic aspects of the Greek vocabulary notes the *Theogony* passage and 'dem noch unaufgeklärten μήδεα der Odyssee [*Od.* 6.129, 18.67]'.[5] Confessing himself puzzled by the other forms, the μέζεα of the *Works and Days* and the alleged μέδεα of

[2] This is a topic which will be discussed in a projected book of mine, to be entitled *Aischrologia*. [The editors have not been able to establish whether any work upon this book by David Bain will be published. CC]

[3] First in the dialectological section of his *Theogony* (pp. 85–6), then ad loc. in his *Works and Days*, and finally in West (1974*a*) (see n. 6).

[4] *DELG* s.v. μήδεα. See however now Perpillou in Blanc *et al.* (1997), 167: 'on notera cependant que la notion de "souci (majeur des hommes)" ferait partie du même ensemble de désignations indirectes que τὰ αἰδοῖα "(les parties) honorables" (et non pas "honteuses")'.

[5] Wackernagel (1916), 227.

Archilochus,[6] he suggests that August Nauck may have been correct to see in *μήδεα* a euphemistic term substituted in the epic tradition for something more coarse.[7] If I read him aright, this is a position acceptable to Martin West.[8] Later literature does not help with the question. In the Hellenistic period Callimachus[9] and Oppian use *μήδεα*, the latter somewhat obscurely, but clearly with reference to an animal, the gazelle.[10] The pharmacological writer Andromachus in a verse recipe refers to the *μήδεα* of the beaver, relating a well known piece of lore about the creature: *τά περ Ἴστριος ἔκβαλε κάστωρ μήδεα.*[11] After Hesiod *μέζεα* has left little trace, occurring in Nicander's *Theriaca* and Lycophron's *Alexandra* (of the genitals of Cronus), and being reflected in a Hesychian gloss.[12] None of these

[6] The vulgate of Archilochus fr. 222 is *ἶνας δὲ μεδέων ἀπέθρισεν*. West dissents (1974*a*, 136) and boldly eliminates any specific word for the genitals by reading *ἶνας δὲ μελέων*, which is a variant in the source, *Etymologicum Gudianum* 390. 42 ff. His conclusions are tentatively accepted by Gerber (1999) in the Loeb edition of early Greek iambus. Bossi (1990), 224–5 argues against.

[7] 'Es hängt natürlich mit dem *μέζεα* des Hesiod [*Op.* 512] und dem *μέδεα* des Archilochus [fr. 222 *IEG*] zusammen: aber wie? Nicht völlig abzuweisen ist der Gedanke Naucks, daß im Homertext *μέδεα* an stelle von *μέζεα* getreten sei; doch wäre dabei nicht so sehr an Textentstellung zu denken, als anzunehmen, daß man in züchtiger Rede den derben Ausdruck absichtlich umformte' (Wackernagel (1916), 227 n. 1).

[8] 'Nor is it likely that epic, with its avoidance of coarse words, would have tolerated *μέζεα* if such a similar form as *μέδεα*—no euphemism—had been in use in vernacular Ionic' (West (1974*a*), 136).

[9] Call. fr. 43.70 Pfeiffer, in his etymologizing of the town name Zancle from the weapon used in the castration of Uranus.

[10] Opp. *Cyn.* 4.439–44 *ἦν ποτ' ἐλῆις δόρκον δέ, φυλάσσεο μὴ μετὰ πολλὸν | ἐκτάδιον δολιχόν τε δρόμον καὶ τέρμα πόνοιο | τυτθὸν ὑποσταίη, λαγόνων ἀπὸ μήδεα χεύηι· | δόρκοι γὰρ περίαλλα δρόμοις ἐνὶ μεσσατίοισι | κυστίδα κυμαίνουσιν, ἀναγκαίοισιν ὑπ' ὄμβροις | βριθόμενοι λαγόνας, ποτὶ δ' ἰσχίον ὀκλάζουσιν.*

[11] Andromachus [no. 17 *RE*] *ap.* Galen 14.41 (lines 11–12 of second recipe: note that the word is used for *animal* testicles). On the beaver's sacrifice of his genitals in order to save himself compare Ael. *HA* 6. 34, Plin. *NH* 8. 109, Aesop 118 Perry, Apul. *Met.* 1.9, *Physiologus* 23, Horapollon 2. 65. These have great curative powers which are often mentioned in medical and pseudo-medical writers: see in addition *Cyranides* 2.19.3 Kaimakis *τούτου (τοῦ κυνοποτάμου ἢ κάστορος) οἱ ὄρχεις, τὸ καλούμενον καστόριον, εἰσὶν ὠφελιμοί.*

[12] Nic. *Ther.* 721–3 *αὐτίκα δὲ χρώς | μέζεα τ' ἀνδρὸς ὕπερθε τιταίνεται, ἐν δέ τε καυλὸς | φύρματι μυδαλέος προϊάπτεται* (of the effects on a man of the sting of a 'grape'-spider, an erection); Lyc. *Alex.* 761–2 *νῆσον δ' εἰς Κρόνωι στυγουμένην | Ἅρπην περάσας, μεζέων κρεάνομον.* Lycophron, here referring to Corcyra (= Drepane), alludes to a version of the myth of the overthrow of the Titans in which Zeus, like

instances refers to the animal kingdom. In prose there are two examples of μήδεα: in one of them the author, the mythographer Antoninus Liberalis, is possibly using a poetic source in referring to the change of sex granted the daughter of Galatea.[13] μέδεα appears to have left no trace.

Generic difference and the consequent differentiation of vocabulary are already apparent in the very early period of Greek literature. We are fortunate that in addition to epic we possess increasingly more of a contemporary genre, iambic, and are able even at the earliest stages of known Greek literature to make comparisons. *The locus classicus* on the 'Dezenz' of epic is to be found in a few rich pages of Wackernagel's *Sprachliche Untersuchungen zu Homer*,[14] in which he points out that epic has suppressed basic terms which had long existed in the Greek language and which must have been current at the time epic was taking the form in which we more or less know it today.[15] Confirmation, if confirmation were needed, is supplied by the occurrence of such words as βινῶ and κύσθος in Archilochus' iambic poetry and in Hipponax, taking us back into the seventh and sixth centuries BC.[16] These and

Cronus, castrates his father (Tim. *FGrHist* 566.79, Σ A.R. 4.983g = 302.3–5 Wendel). The Hesychian entry, which must presumably be poetic, has not been assigned to a provenance: Hsch. ε 6991 (ii. 230 Latte): εὐμεζέος [Meineke: εὐμάξεως cod.]· εὐφυοῦς [Latte: ἐφυεὶς cod., εὐφυῆς Musurus] τοῖς αἰδοίοις.

[13] Anton. Lib. 17.6. In the story of Leucippus, Antoninus appears to be offering an etymon for Leto Phytie who grants masculinity to Galatea's daughter: ἥτις ἔφυσε μήδεα τῆι κόρηι. If Nicander's ἑτεροιούμενα is here the source, one might be tempted to speculate that ἔφυσε<ν> μήδεα emanates from there (Martini, who was prodigal in finding Nicandrean echoes in Antoninus—see his 1896 Teubner p. xlvi—does not note this as one). Professor J.-M. Jacques, to whom I am grateful for correspondence on this matter, points out, however, that in general Antoninus' work gives the impression of being based on a mythological compendium rather than an allusive and elliptical Hellenistic poet, and that the suggested etymology is possibly too banal to be attributed to the poet. He notes Valckenaer's conjecture Φυσιμήδη and also draws attention to a further instance in prose from Artemidorus' dreambook which has not been taken into account by lexicographers: βουλεύμασι δὲ ἀπορρήτοις, ὅτι μήδεα καλεῖται τά τε βουλεύματα καὶ τὸ αἰδοῖον (Artem. 1.45 = p. 52.3–4 Pack).

[14] Wackernagel (1916), 224–9.

[15] 'Our *Iliad* took on its form as it was written down . . . the process of writing it down was intermittent and extended over many years': West (2001), 3.

[16] Cf. Bain (1991), 52 with n. 3 and 55–6.

other words mentioned by Wackernagel are all demonstrably very old.[17]

With iambic poetry there is no doubt about the level of language permitted at all stages of the development of the genre. The ancient literary tradition singled out iambic poetry as the prime source of obscene and unacceptable language and the ancestor in this respect of Old Comedy.[18] The greatest exponent of the genre, Archilochus, however, did not confine himself to the composition of iambo-trochaic poetry. He also wrote epodes, which are a kind of lyric (and of course a few poems which are indisputably full-blown lyric). Here we have a decisive instance of the strict generic rules having reached full development as soon as Greek literature started to be written down. Before Archilochus and no doubt in his lifetime there existed epic. There also must have existed the kind of popular verse and song that he presents. More precisely there must have been oral poetry in forms other than the hexameter which were never transmitted by writing, since for one thing it is inconceivable that Archilochus invented the sophisticated metrical forms of his epodic poetry.[19] It is quite clear that there already existed a generic distinction between the iambo-trochaic and the epodic works of Archilochus in terms of language. This point was succinctly made by Martin West with reference to the then recently discovered Cologne epode. He noted that although the subject matter of the epode was similar in character to much of what was already to be found in the erotic and scatological fragments of the iambo-trochaic Archilochus, the language dealing

[17] The words Wackernagel mentions and singles out for their age are πέρδομαι, χέζω, ὀμείχω, πέος, ὄρσος, ὄρχις, πυγή, πρωκτός (on ὄρχις see Watkins (1975)). ὄρσος and πυγή have left some trace in early dactylic poetry (for the former see Wackernagel (1916), 226 n. 1 and Neumann (1999), 202–5: on πυγόστολος at Hes. *Op.* 373 see West ad loc. and Vox (1980)). A word Wackernagel might have considered in addition is σκώρ, which also has a venerable ancestry (Oettinger (1999), 213–14 and Willi (2003), 65 n. 104). σκώρ and the compounds formed from its genitive σκατός figure in comedy, both Attic and West Greek, but not at all in medical writing.

[18] See, for example, Julian *Epist.* 89b p. 300cd (p. 140.23–6 Bidez and Cumont) (cited in Nesselrath's chapter in this volume, p. 139 n. 36). For recent literature on the free-spoken iambic tradition see Rosen (1988), Bowie (2002), who denies the link made in antiquity between Old Comedy and the 'iambic idea', and Cavarzere, Aloni, and Barchiesi (2001).

[19] On pre-Archilochean poetry see Dover (1964).

with this material was quite different: the language remains 'auf einer dezenter Ebene', and metaphor abounds.[20]

When confronted with vulgar language and the question of its relationship to genre, one must consider the question of whether certain topics were per se alien to certain genres. Mention of belching, masturbation, wet dreams, spitting, or farting, for example (although farting sometimes had religious significance to the extent of indicating a good omen[21]), might be thought scarcely conceivable in epic or tragedy, as distinct from comedy, satyr play, and mime.[22] The same might be said of hiccoughs, which are taken as characteristically comic by Plato in the *Symposium* when he makes the spokesman for Comedy, Aristophanes, subject to a sudden attack (Pl. *Symp.* 185c–d): *τυχεῖν δὲ αὐτῶι τινα ἢ ὑπὸ πλησμονῆς ἢ ὑπό τινος ἄλλου λύγγα ἐμπεπτωκυῖαν*. But there are some surprises. Snoring is found famously and terrifyingly depicted in Aeschylus' *Eumenides* (53; cf. 117–31). There is a constant confusion, starting in antiquity, which bedevils discussion of this area of vocabulary—that of sex and other bodily functions (sometimes taken wider)—between vulgar things and vulgar words for vulgar things.[23]

I now propose to examine six topics which, although they feature in higher literature, might be thought both beneath the dignity of their genres and to entail in consequence the use of indecorous vocabulary, for they involve passages in which cow dung, breasts, farting, animal sexuality, infantile incontinence, and urination are mentioned. I shall show that writers in the higher genres were capable of dealing with such apparently intractable topics while both preserving the dignity of the diction and without having to resort to

[20] 'In den Trimeter-Fragmenten werden die eindeutigsten Wörter ohne Zurückhaltung gebraucht, *σάθη, μύζειν, ἐπείσιον* ('männliches Glied', 'saugen', 'Schamgegend'). In der neu aufgefundenen Epode bleibt die Sprache auf einer dezenteren Ebene, *obwohl der Sinn auch hier deutlich genug ist* [my emphasis]. Metaphern werden an Stelle der eigentlichen Ausdrücke gebraucht. Nicht *ἐπείσιον*, sondern *θριγκός, πύλαι, ποηφόροι κῆποι* ('Firststein', 'Tor', 'grasige Gärten'), nicht das deutliche, physische *ἐπλήμυρα* ('ich hatte einen Samenerguß'), sondern *ἀφῆκα μένος* ('ich ließ Krafte ab')' (West (1974*b*), 484–5). Compare the discussion by Scherer (1963), writing before the discovery of the Cologne papyrus.

[21] See Radermacher (1931), 131–2; Katz (1999), 316 n. 3.

[22] This will turn out to be a precarious assumption (see below).

[23] See Bain (forthcoming) where reference is made to Russell's note on [Long.] *Subl.* 43.

vulgarisms. In addition, in the case of those passages where epic is involved, I shall scrutinize Wackernagel's suggestion that epic, or more particularly Homeric epic, shows more 'Dezenz' than other branches of high literature. In his view of Homer he had a predecessor in Athenaeus (or a source of Athenaeus).[24]

2. AN HOMERIC WORD FOR COW DUNG: *ὄνθος*

The nature and distribution of the rare word *ὄνθος* are puzzling. According to LSJ and its supplement the word is found three times in the *Iliad* in the same context, once in a play by Aeschylus, which may or may not be a satyr play (see below), once in a work of paradoxography, and once in a mythographer.[25] The alternative *κόπρος* is found twice in the *Iliad* with the meaning dung (22.414, 24.640), although neither of these applies specifically to cow dung. On the other hand, in *Il.* 18.575 as in *Od.* 10.411 the word is used by synecdoche for the stall occupied by cows. In *Od.* 9.329 the reference is to sheep's dung in the Cyclops' cave. The three references in *Od.* 17 are to the dung heap occupied by the dog, Argus (297, 299—the verb *κοπρίζειν*—and 306).

Surprisingly, *ὄνθος* re-emerges in late antiquity in the compound *ὀνθοφόρος*. There are two documentary instances: Wessely (1921),

[24] See below, section 7.

[25] *Il.* 23.775, 777, 781 (*ὀνθολόγοι* is Koechly's certain conjecture at Manetho 4.259 where the vulgate is *ἠδ' ἐπίμοχθοι* | *ἀνθολόγοι*: 'quod vix de *ῥιζοτόμοις* sive hominibus medicas aut veneficas herbas quaerentibus intelligi possit', Koechly). The prose examples are Antig. *Mir.* 140 [= Tim. *FGrHist* 566. 41] where it is stated that 'on Olympic days' the fountain Arethusa, instead of producing pure water, *ὄνθωι ῥεῖν*, and [Apollod.] *Bibl.* 2.5.5 (*bis*) where the noun is feminine and the reference is to the Augean stables. *ὄνθος* is also found (unnoticed by the lexica) in the famous passage of Polybius (12.4d) in which he criticizes Timaeus (presumably using some of Timaeus' own words). He notes, before refuting it, Timaeus' retailing of the lore that the Alpheus flows underground from Elis to Syracuse and affects the fountain of Arethusa: *ὄνθου τε πλῆθος ἀναβλύζειν τὴν Ἀρέθουσαν ἐκ τῶν κατὰ πανήγυριν θυομένων βοῶν*. He goes on to mention the *φιάλη* that allegedly having found its way from Olympia was cast up (*ἀναβαλεῖν*) by the fountain. Strabo uses less specific language in describing the dung, which he also ascribes to oxen (6.2.4): *καὶ θολοῦσθαι ἀπὸ τῶν ἐν Ὀλυμπίαι βουθυσιῶν*.

§108.4 (fourth century AD) and *CPR* 10.116.5 (AD 446), which looks like an official title.

In all of the literary instances, ὄνθος clearly refers to animal dung, in the majority of them to ox/cow dung. The Homeric occurrences come in the narrative of the foot race at the funeral games of Patroclus. In the Aeschylean example which is found in a fragment from the *Psychagogi*,[26] in which Tiresias in the underworld prophesies a bizarre death for Odysseus, the reference is to avian excrement:

> ἐρωιδιὸς γὰρ ὑψόθεν ποτώμενος
> ὄνθωι σε πλήξει νηδύος χαλώμασι·[27]
> ἐκ τοῦδ' ἄκανθα ποντίου βοσκήματος
> σήψει παλαιὸν βρέγμα καὶ τριχορρυές. (fr. 275 *TrGF*)

Animal dung may not seem an object fit to be mentioned in tragedy, and it has been suggested that the fragment emanates from a satyr play.[28] There is no evidence, however, that ὄνθος was a low word in antiquity. Nor is there, as we shall see, anything low about νηδύς: indeed νηδύος χαλώμασιν (or whatever the abstract noun is) might be considered a rather choice expression. It has to be admitted that the Homeric passage in which ὄνθος features is comic in tone, as Richardson points out in his commentary (on *Il.* 23.775–81). The arrogant lesser Ajax receives just punishment by being covered with dung after he has fallen in the foot race. Even so, the choice of words does not infringe the restraint of Homeric diction. Richardson sees here 'cruder language' prompted by the comic nature of the subject, and draws attention to the use of κόπρος elsewhere in the Homeric poems. I am not sure whether this is the correct way to interpret the use of ὄνθος here. It is by any standards a very rare word, and it is difficult to see that it should be regarded as cruder than κόπρος. The possibility should be raised that originally ὄνθος was specialized,

[26] The status of *Psychagogi* is disputed. The issue is complicated if the anapaests published first as P.Köln iii. 125 (now fr. 273a *TrGF*) belong to this play. They are certainly more redolent of tragedy than satyr drama.

[27] In the second line χαλώμασιν is Diels's conjecture for the manuscripts' χειλώμασιν. Nauck read κενώμασιν. This is a heavily emended line, but there can be no doubt that ὄνθος is present in it. In 24 I adopt Crusius' βρέγμα for transmitted δέρμα.

[28] Richardson speaks of the 'burlesque' nature of this fragment. [Cf. πέλεθος in the satyric Soph. *Ichn.* fr. 314.414. CC]

referring in particular to cow dung.[29] Alternatively, it may have been more refined than other, cruder words of the popular language current at the time the *Iliad* was put together.[30]

3. LA POITRINE DE LA BELLE HÉLÈNE

The third book of the *Iliad* describes the admiration and wonder felt at the sight of Aphrodite's breasts (3.396–8 καί ῥ' ὡς οὖν ἐνόησε θεᾶς περικαλλέα δειρὴν | στήθεά θ' ἱμεροέντα καὶ ὄμματα μαρμαίροντα | θάμβησέν τ' ἄρ' ἔπειτα: ironically the person who has this feeling is Helen herself). Wackernagel noted the avoidance of a familiar term for the female breast and the use of the neutral στῆθος.[31] Following his view that 'Homer' as distinct in this case from his epigoni observed a kind of 'Dezenz', he draws attention to one of the most famous examples in literature of a breast being exposed, asserting that this is not the kind of thing of which Homer would have been capable.[32]

[29] Adams (1982), 236 raises the possibility that Latin *fimus* was originally just such a specialized term. But in the equivalent narrative in the *Aeneid*, at the funeral games of Anchises, Nisus in the footrace undergoes humiliation similar to that of Ajax in the Homeric games, slipping on *fimus* and being covered with it (Virg. *Aen.* 5.333, 358). Adams (1982), 237 suggests that here, as distinct from the other two places where Virgil uses the word (*G.* 1.80, 2.347), 'its sense is probably more general = "filth".' It is clear, however, that, as in the corresponding games for Patroclus, there has been a preliminary sacrifice and that there is animal dung near and on the track (96–101: the sacrifice is more varied than that performed before the games for Patroclus where only βόες are slaughtered. Aeneas slaughters two sheep and two pigs, his allies *iuuenci*). When Virgil writes of a fall *in ipso | . . . immundoque fimo . . . sacroque cruore*, he must have in mind Ajax's fall (brought about by Athena answering Odysseus' prayer) τῆι ῥα βοῶν κέχυτ' ὄνθος ἀποκταμένων ἐριμύκων, | οὓς ἐπὶ Πατρόκλωι πέφνεν πόδας ὠκὺς Ἀχιλλεύς (*Il.* 23.775–6).

[30] e.g. *μόλος (see *DELG* s.v. μολύνω, Neumann (1999), 204, and Masson (1996), 95–9 = (2000), 251–5) or σκώρ.

[31] 'Vielleicht gehört es ebenfalls hierher, da der Dichter zwar die Frauenbrust erwähnt und die στήθεα ἱμεροέντα der Aphrodite gewundert (*Γ* 397), aber die alltäglichen, z. T. allerdings ursprünglich kindischen, Ausdrücke θηλή, μάμμη, τιτθός zu brauchen verschmäht' (Wackernagel (1916), 227).

[32] 'Dagegen wenn der Dichter der kleinen Ilias an einer den spätern Griechen eindrücklich gewordenen Stelle [fr. 19 *EGF*, *PEG* = 28 *GEF*] von der brückenden Wirkung des schönen Busens der Helena auf Menelaos spricht, geht er fühlbar über die Grenze hinaus, die sich der Dichter von *Γ* zieht' (Wackernagel (1916), 227 n. 2).

The earliest example of the story of Helen's winning over Menelaus and avoiding summary execution during the capture of Troy is in the *Little Iliad* (fr. 19 *EGF*, *PEG* = 28 *GEF*). For the information that Lesches told this story we are indebted to the scholia on Ar. *Lys.* 155–6:

> ὁ γῶν Μενέλαος τᾶς Ἑλένας τὰ μᾶλά πᾳ
> γυμνᾶς παραυιδὼν ἐξέβαλ', οἰῶ, τὸ ξίφος.

ἡ ἱστορία παρ' Ἰβύκωι, τὰ δὲ αὐτὰ καὶ Λέσχης ὁ Πυρραῖος ἐν τῆι μικρᾶι Ἰλιάδι καὶ Εὐριπίδης (*Andr.* 629–30): ἀλλ', ὡς ἐσεῖδες μαστόν, ἐκβαλὼν ξίφος | φίλημ' ἐδέξω (*Σ* Ar. *Lys.* 155a = p. 12 Hangard).

These give no information on the vocabulary the earlier poets used in describing the incident; and indeed it has been suggested that the exposure of the breasts came fairly late into the story, possibly under the influence of vase painting.[33] The first reference in high poetry available to us which explicitly names Helen's weapons of seduction is Eur. *Andr.* 629–30 (cited above), part of a passage in which Peleus is inveighing against Menelaus' uselessness and lack of moral fibre. There μαστός is the word used.

By any standards in English the words 'tit, tits' are frequently liable to the charge of being offensive terms. They are certainly not words a doctor would use when speaking to a female patient or, for that matter, any patient. In the modern world they are indeed used by women (especially young women) in what might be regarded as a postmodernist way of speaking (as with the recently evolved synonym 'boobs' and with a word for another part of the female anatomy, 'bum'), self-referentially and in an ironical or rebellious mode of discourse. These recent developments should not confuse the issue about the status of the words in polite conversation and 'polite' literature. No one in an academic exposition (no one except a ruthless exhibitionist) would, I take it, say, far less write, of the Amazons that they cut off their right 'tit/boob' (rather than 'breast') in order to be more adept at archery. The words for breast obviously belong in the discussion of Greek vocabulary I am undertaking. Is it the case that as with words for other bodily parts, the male penis, the female genitalia, the anus, there can be observed a distinction between

[33] See Ghali-Kalil (1955), 41–2, 97–8.

vulgar words (e.g., in the case of the penis, *πέος*) and respectable euphemisms (in medical writing, par excellence, *αἰδοῖον*[34])? Are there vulgar words for the female breast, words that are avoided in medical prose and would have certainly been avoided in discussion between physician and patient?

The female breast is a topic often exploited in erotic literature. It also occurs frequently in the context of breastfeeding of children, particularly of breastfeeding by mothers or wet nurses. Most memorably in this connection in literature it is mentioned when women, mothers, make appeals to their offspring reminding them that they have been fed, and allowed to live and prosper, because of the organ that the mother exposes. The *loci classici* are Hecuba's appeal to Hector in the *Iliad*,[35] reminding him that he was fed by her and begging him to reconsider a fatal conflict with Achilles, and Clytemnestra's appeal to her son and potential murderer, Orestes, in Aeschylus' *Choephori*.[36] In lyric, as one would expect, the language is predominantly decorous and metaphorical.[37]

Two different roots give rise to words denoting the breast in Greek. Originally there must have been a significant semantic distinction between the two, the *μα-* forms originally denoting the whole breast, whether female or male, the *τιτ-* form being used of the female breast and only that part of it that is in contact with the baby when it is being breastfed. Eventually, however, such distinctions do not obtain. Anatomical terms in Greek relating to adjacent parts or parts of the same unit tend to merge and lead to linguistic confusion

[34] See Bain (1999).

[35] See Richardson (1993) on *Il.* 22.79–81 (referring to Griffin (1980), 25 n. 66): *μήτηρ δ' αὖθ' ἑτέρωθεν ὀδύρετο δάκρυ χέουσα | κόλπον ἀνιεμένη, ἑτέρηφι δὲ μαζὸν ἀνέσχε.*

[36] Aesch. *Cho.* 896–8: *ἐπίσχες, ὦ παῖ, τόνδε δ' αἴδεσαι, τέκνον, | μαστόν, πρὸς ᾧ σὺ πολλὰ δὴ βρίζων ἅμα | οὔλοισιν ἐξήμελξας εὐτραφὲς γάλα*, where see Garvie.

[37] See Gerber (1978); on words for breast generally see Henderson (1991*b*), 148–9. The specialist word for the animal teat, *οὖθαρ*, a word of great antiquity and no doubt dignity when applied as it is in epic to animals, is twice used of humans in literature, once perhaps not surprisingly in Old Comedy (Teleclides fr. 33 *PCG*, an obscure fragment), and once by Clytemnestra in *Choephori* referring to her dream (532: she submits her breast to a snake which sucks it). Garvie ad loc. sees this as peculiarly appropriate to the character of Clytemnestra. Perhaps the word is appropriate because, for the purposes of the dream, we are in the animal kingdom. It may be that Aeschylus did not feel the normal word for the nipple was suitable for tragic diction.

or imprecision.[38] Lampito's μᾶλα (Ar. *Lys.* 155) is presumably poetic or colloquial, and certainly less crude than words beginning τιτ-. We find it, or rather its Ionic-Attic equivalent μῆλα, in poetry outside Old Comedy.

What conclusions should be drawn? I think that one cannot establish with this bodily part a clear distinction in the Greek vocabulary between basic and polite usage of the same level as one finds with, for example, words for the male organ.

4. THE BABY HERMES' FART

The author of the Homeric *Hymn to Hermes* apparently breaches the rules of epic by describing the infant Hermes' fart:

> σὺν δ' ἄρα φρασσάμενος τότε δὴ κρατὺς Ἀργειφόντης
> οἰωνὸν προέηκεν ἀειρόμενος μετὰ χερσίν,
> τλήμονα γαστρὸς ἔριθον, ἀτάσθαλον ἀγγελιώτην.
> (*H. Herm.* 294–6)

'Hier scheidet sich der bäurische Dichter scharf und deutlich vom adeligen Epos' says one commentator (Radermacher (1931), 131 ad loc.). But does he? The incident itself might be thought beneath the dignity of epic, but the mode of expression, whether or not the composer was a peasant, is not. The fart is expressed in the form of a kind of riddle by means of highly poetical, almost dithyrambic terms, as οἰωνὸν . . . τλήμονα γαστρὸς ἔριθον, ἀτάσθαλον ἀγγελιώτην. There is no hint of everyday language in this. The *vox propria* πέρδομαι is avoided, again a term mentioned by Wackernagel as alien to Homeric epic, but of undoubtedly aged pedigree.[39] Farting is a favoured topic of Old Comedy, whose poets do not hesitate to use more basic terms. In the little that we possess of satyr drama there is

[38] For vagueness and lack of precision in the naming of adjacent and constituent anatomical parts compare the interchangeable use of πυγή and πρωκτός (see Kock (1893), 219–20).

[39] Wackernagel (1916), 224 with n. 2. πέρδομαι and βδέω (words from the same root) are commonly used for farting in Old Comedy.

one certain, and two possible, references to farting.[40] This genre as well as containing subject matter that is sometimes beneath the usual level of tragedy, on occasions uses diction and verse technique that are alien to tragedy. While allowance has to be made for its poor state of preservation, its sexual vocabulary is fairly extensive; but it does not employ primary obscenities. Certainly in Eur. *Cycl.* the Cyclops refers to some sort of bodily function when boasting about his self-sufficiency. It is disputed whether the reference in πέπλον κρούω (327–8) is to masturbation or farting.[41] In either case, however, the expression is indirect. If the Cyclops is referring to a fart, he does not use πέρδομαι, the *vox propria.* κρούω is certainly a vulgar term in its metaphorical sexual use in Old Comedy,[42] but if it is applied to masturbation in the *Cyclops*, it is less vulgar than the terms from comedy specifically denoting masturbation such as στύομαι.

5. RAMPANT MULES IN PINDAR

In a previous discussion of the decorum of the higher genres, I stated that 'direct references to crepitation, defecation or erection would be out of place in lyric' (Bain (1991), 53). As long as one retains the adjective 'direct', this still seems to me to be true, but I ought to have emphasized that any of these topics could have been covered with perfect decorum by the adroit lyric poet in humorous or semi-serious mode if he had so desired. A case in point is Pind. *Pyth.* 10.36

[40] Soph. fr. dub. 1130.15–16 is an undoubted reference to farting in a satyr play. It has been suggested that Sophocles' *Ichneutae* contains a reference to farting (fr. 314.168 *TrGF*): see Bain (1995). Even if I am wrong to see in the word ψοφήσετε an allusion to death rather than farting, and Lloyd-Jones (1994), 140 = (2005), 126 is correct, one should note first of all the generic difference between satyr play and epic, and secondly that the language used also avoids the *vox propria.* The other possible reference is Eur. *Cycl.* 327–8, for which see below.

[41] For the former see Seaford ad loc.; for the latter, Radermacher (1953), 236.

[42] The distribution of κρούω in this sense is odd. It is found for certain in just one play of Aristophanes (*Eccl.* 989–90), where there is a 'running' pun on κρούω as a word for knocking on doors. Other examples of the verb and its compounds in comedy where the reference is said by Henderson (1991*b*), 171 to be sexual are for the most part highly doubtful. For a possible epigraphical instance (in a kind of sexual challenge?) see *SEG* 35 §915 κροῦε νικῶν με 'screw me if you can beat me!'

γελᾶι δ' ὁρῶν ὕβριν ὀρθίαν κνωδάλων. Pindar has in mind the erection (note ὁρῶν; Slater (1969) rightly takes ὀρθίαν to mean 'rampant'), not the braying of asses. I cannot agree here with Köhnken (1971), 161 (followed by Kurz (1974), 21–2) that Pindar intends the latter: the noun which the adjective qualifies, ὕβρις, scarcely leaves room for doubt.[43]

6. INFANTILE INCONTINENCE IN AESCHYLUS

Tragedy too for the most part avoids mention of bodily functions. The Nurse's speech in Aeschylus' *Choephori* is a notable exception. After stating that the care of the baby Orestes was a τριβή to her soul (749), she goes on to describe in intimate detail what it entailed (755–7):

> οὐ γάρ τι φωνεῖ παῖς ἔτ' ὢν ἐν σπαργάνοις
> εἰ λιμὸς ἢ δίψη τις ἢ λιψουρία
> ἔχει· νέα δὲ νηδὺς αὐτάρκης τέκνων.

It is not as though babies and infants do not figure in high genres like epic and tragedy,[44] but this passage is startlingly isolated in its allusion to infantile incontinence. The decorum of the vocabulary, however, should be noted. No direct vulgar term is employed. The hapax λιψουρία admittedly contains a reflection of οὐρῶ, but this essentially inoffensive word and its cognates are sometimes admitted by the higher genres. The first element of the unique compound is highly poetic: λίπτομαι is a fairly exotic verb.[45] LSJ finds a reference to the

[43] [The 'perfect decorum' of the phrase is aided by the enallage, which 'contributes obliqueness to a very refined obscenity' (Bers (1974), 45). PJFF]

[44] Cf. Kassel (1954), 44 = (1991), 39 'statim ab altera exclamatione incipit disciplina infantes fovendi copiose ita illustrata, ut cum rerum descriptio per humum repat, elocutio tragicum spirare non desinat; namque vides, quibus ampullis et sesquipedalibus verbis lactentis nocturnos clamores aut desiderium mingendi, nutricis officium pusillae alvi necessitates divinatione praecipiendi aut, si parum providentem se praestitit, lavando rem reficiendi poeta insignaverit'.

[45] Before the Hellenistic era it is only attested in Aeschylus' *Septem* (355, 380). After that it is found in Apollonius of Rhodes, Lycophron, and Nicander. λιψουρία is its only reflection. λίψ (C) in LSJ is a non-word: see Hesych. λ 1180 (ii. 604 Latte) where Latte accepts the deletion of ἐπιθυμία, which is based on the assumption that the word has intruded from above. The supplement to LSJ also accepts the deletion.

soiling of the nappy in the oblique phrase *νέα δὲ νηδὺς αὐτάρκης τέκνων*, but there is no need or warrant for category 3 ('bowels') in the entry under *νηδύς*. In Hippocr. *Aër.* 19.5 cited there *νηδὺν ἀναξηραίνεσθαι* refers to the stomach generally.[46] There is a significant generic difference between this passage and one in another genre which patently reflects it: the connection between them is marked by a verbal reminiscence in the word *ἐξέθρεψα*.[47] In Aristophanes' *Clouds* Strepsiades takes strong objection to the violence inflicted on him by his son, Pheidippides, and reminds him of what he had done to assist his early upbringing. One of his reminders concerns Pheidippides' infantile incontinence (1384–5):

> κακκᾶν δ' ἂν οὐκ ἔφθης φράσας, κἀγὼ λαβὼν θύραζε
> ἐξέφερον ἂν καὶ προυσχόμην σε.

This kind of vulgar baby talk[48] is quite absent from the parallel passage in Aeschylus.

7. URINATION AND CHAMBER POTS IN TRAGEDY AND SATYR PLAY

Mention of urination might be thought parallel to mention of defecation or to sexual activities and, given the general practice of the non-vulgar literary genres and the canons of the Greek rhetorical tradition, something one would not initially expect to meet, say, in tragedy or formal prose. This does not turn out to be the case. Wackernagel in his famous discussion of Greek basic vocabulary for

[46] Jouanna in the Budé edition translates 'que la ventre se dessèche' (p. 234; see also his note, pp. 331–2). The entry under *νηδύς* in Kühn and Fleischer (1989) has only two definitions, *venter* and *cavum*. On the other occasion when Aeschylus uses the word, it is clear that the reference is to the belly ('evacuations of the belly', fr. 275.2 *TrGF*: see below).

[47] Aesch. *Cho.* 750; Ar. *Nub.* 1380.

[48] See Dover on Ar. *Nub.* 1382, West (1969), Stephanopoulos (1983). Support is possibly given to Stephanopoulos against West by contemporary study of the language of infants: 'there seems good reason to believe that child language and baby talk represent the vocabulary of adult speakers, and that this vocabulary expresses ideas and attitudes towards children and childhood' (Golden (1995), 18; see further ibid. 12–18, with references).

bodily functions and body parts drew attention to the basic Ionic verb ὀμείχω and its virtual absence from epic.[49] Again, it is not immediately obvious why there should ever be occasion for urination to be mentioned in texts like the Homeric epics, rather than in a kind of wisdom book such as Hesiod's *Works and Days* where it is indeed to be found: μηδ' ἀντ' ἠελίου τετραμμένος ὀρθὸς ὀμείχειν (Hes. *Op.* 727).[50] The emergence of οὐρῶ 'urinate' must have been early in the development of the language since ὕω is already in Homer and Hesiod: Wackernagel (1916), 225 n. 1 points out that ὀμείχω is supplanted from the fifth century onwards by the 'sittsamere οὐρεῖν', which is metaphorical in origin, and cognate with an IE root meaning 'rain'. We find the verbs already in competition in Hesiod since ὀμείχειν in *Op.* 727 is followed by οὐρήσει in 729 and οὐρεῖν in 758. But the compound form ἐνομείχω is indeed found in epic, but in mock epic, *Margites* fr. 7.6 *IEG*. It may be significant that in this polymetric work it occurs in an iambic trimeter rather than a dactylic hexameter. The word for adulterer (μοιχός, which is derived from the former verb) and its derivatives proliferated in the language and indeed found their way into Latin.[51] It is questionable, however, whether native speakers would have made any connection between these terms (which were certainly disparaging, but scarcely obscene) and the venerable verb from which they derive. The presence of ὀμείχω in Hipponax[52] might be thought to suggest its vulgar character, but that can be counterbalanced by the noun ὀμείχματα in Aeschylus.[53] But since we know nothing of the provenance of this isolated word within the oeuvre of Aeschylus, it might be argued that its vulgar character indicated that it belonged to a satyr play.

[49] Wackernagel (1916), 225 with n. 1; (1888), 129 = (1953–79), i. 632.

[50] See West ad loc. and Watkins (1995), 14. This was later taken to be a Pythagorean injunction: Diogenes Laertius also uses the verb (8.17), while Iamblichus *Protr.* 107.16 substitutes the imperative of οὐρεῖν. No example of οὐρεῖν compounded with ἐπί, κατά, or πρός is given in Kühn and Fleischer (1989).

[51] See *DELG* s.v. μοιχός, Ernout and Meillet (1959) s.v. *moechus*, and Adams (1983), 350–3.

[52] Fr. 73.3 *IEG* = Degani. There it is found in company with τιλῶ, another low word (see Bain (1999), 274–5): ὤμειξε δ' αἷμα καὶ χολὴν ἐτίλησεν.

[53] Fr. 435. [ὀμείχματα, ἐνουρήθρα, and οὐράνη in satyr drama are discussed by Lopez Eire (2003), 389–90. CC]

οὐρῶ and its derivatives are common in medical writing,[54] attested in public notices,[55] and acceptable in oratory: one of the disreputable activities attributed to Conon and his companions was that they urinated on their fellow soldiers while on campaign (Dem. 54.4; the verb used is *προσουρῶ*). We twice meet in tragic authors a word for chamber pot, *οὐράνη*, but we cannot in either instance be absolutely certain whether we are not dealing with satyr plays. The word is found in Aesch. fr. 180.2 *TrGF* (*Ὀστολόγοι*) and Soph. fr. 565.1 (cited as from the *Ἀχαιῶν Σύνδειπνον* by Athenaeus: the play in question is more usually referred to as *Σύνδειπνοι*).[56] Both these passages are cited as examples of later impropriety in contrast to Homer's decorum,[57] but it is not specified what genre they came from:

> *Αἰσχύλος γοῦν ἀπρεπῶς που παράγει μεθύοντας τοὺς Ἕλληνας ὡς καὶ τὰς ἀμίδας ἀλλήλοις περικαταγνύναι . . . καὶ Σοφοκλῆς δὲ ἐν Ἀχαιῶν συνδείπνωι* (Athen. 1.17c) . . . *παρ' Ὁμήρωι δὲ οἱ ἀριστεῖς κοσμίως δειπνοῦσιν ἐν Ἀγαμέμνονος. εἰ δ' ἐν Ὀδυσσείαι*[58] *φιλονικοῦσιν Ἀχιλλεὺς καὶ Ὀδυσσεύς, καὶ Ἀγαμέμνων "χαῖρε νόωι",*[59] *ἀλλ' ὠφέλιμοι αἱ φιλοτιμίαι, ζητούντων εἰ λόγωι ἢ μάχηι αἱρεθῆναι δεῖ τὸ Ἴλιον. ἀλλ' οὐδ' ὅτε μνηστῆρας εἰσάγει μεθύοντας, οὐδὲ τότε τοιαύτην ἀκοσμίαν εἰσήγαγεν ὡς Σοφοκλῆς καὶ Αἰσχύλος πεποιήκασιν, ἀλλὰ πόδα βόειον ἐπὶ τὸν Ὀδυσσέα ῥιπτούμενον* (Athen. 1.17ef).

The majority view of scholars is that the *Ὀστολόγοι* was a satyr drama.[60] But Athenaeus in taking both Aeschylus and Sophocles to

[54] See Kühn and Fleischer (1989), s.vv. *οὐρήθρη, οὐρήθημα, οὔρησις, οὐρητήρ, οὐρητικός, οὖρον*, and *οὐρῶ*. Note also the LSJ entries for these words and for the desiderative form *οὐρηθριῶ*.

[55] e.g. *IGSK Ephesos* ii. 568, 568a, 569.

[56] This may well be the *Ἀχαιῶν Σύλλογος*: see Lloyd-Jones in the introduction to his 1996 Loeb edition of the fragments of Sophocles. He points out (p. 281) that 'it is hard to see how a chorus of satyrs could have figured in a play about this subject [the quarrel between Achilles and Agamemnon on Tenedos]', but goes on to suggest an explanation for their presence.

[57] Athen. 1.17c–f. Compare Eustathius *Od.* 1828.28.

[58] *Od.* 8.75. This dispute is otherwise unknown to epic: see Hainsworth ad loc. (in Heubeck, West, and Hainsworth (1988)), and Davies (1997), 106 n. 3, who points out that the anecdote is characteristically Odyssean.

[59] *Od.* 8.78. He could afford to do so, since he had received an oracle saying that a quarrel between the best of the chieftains was a prerequisite of the fall of Troy.

[60] See Radt's introduction to the fragments of the play (*TrGF* iii). Grossardt (2003) makes a good case for a satyrical *Ostologi*, but he is somewhat cavalier with the word 'obscene', and neglects to mentions that the generic status of the play he sees as providing a parallel, *Psychagogi*, is also disputed (see above).

task for impropriety might more naturally be thought to be referring specifically to tragedy, rather than a genre, satyr play, which although related to tragedy, was known not to have aspired to the dignity of tragedy.

Nevertheless, one should note that even if we are confronted by the language of the satyr play, this language chooses not to use the everyday Athenian expression for the object in question, *ἀμίς*.[61] On the other hand there is a secure reflection of *οὐρῶ* in tragedy in the form of the choice compound *λιψουρία* ('a desire to urinate', Aesch. *Cho.* 756, discussed above). Sommerstein points out that there was no sense of the verb being a taboo verb because, whereas it was regarded as improper to defecate or to have intercourse in public, 'public outdoor urination was evidently considered unobjectionable'.[62]

[61] An alternative word for chamber pot is found in what is certainly a satyr play: Sophocles, *Pandora* fr. 485 *TrGF* *ἐνουρήθρα*. For the *vox propria* *ἀμίς* see LSJ s.v.

[62] Sommerstein in the introduction to De Martino and Sommerstein (1999), 21 n. 17.

4

Smileumata Iliaka: Three Puzzling Verses

Walter Burkert

Martin West has rebuilt the foundations of Greek poetry from Homer and Hesiod through iambos and elegy to Aeschylus, not to mention his further contributions to some hundred other Greek authors. And since from more than forty-five years of personal friendship I know that the closest form of ὁμιλία one can achieve with Martin West is talking about very precise problems of Greek literature, I wish to present three suggestions for discussion from the *thesauroi* of his fundamental *Homerus: Ilias*.

I

Right at the beginning of the *Iliad*, in line 5, there is a textual problem which will strike even the casual reader of Homer: the disastrous wrath of Achilles has made many heroes prey for dogs and for all birds, οἰωνοῖσι τε πᾶσι. This is the text as edited by Martin West. Still one may wonder at πᾶσι: 'all' the birds, but just a few dogs? Or 'all the birds and dogs'? Not all birds are vultures, and some dogs at least are civilized.[1] In fact indirect tradition has a tempting alternative: οἰωνοῖσι τε δαῖτα, 'prey for dogs, for birds a meal', with an effective rhetorical chiasmus. This is the reading of Zenodotus, and

[1] Eustathius 256.8 (i. 390.24–5 van der Valk, on *Il.* 2.467–8), finds it necessary to defend πᾶσι as an hyperbole: οὐ τοῖς κατὰ κόσμον δηλαδή, ἀλλὰ τοῖς ἐκεῖ περὶ Τροίαν.

only of Zenodotus.[2] A conscientious editor can hardly avoid printing πᾶσι, the unanimous reading of papyri and manuscripts. An argument against Zenodotus, evidently raised by Aristarchus, is that δαίς should not be used of animals[3]—this is debatable for philologists and hardly convincing for the general reader. No doubt Zenodotus' version is the more appealing one, and it has found support through philology: three parallels in classical tragedy are nearly indisputable evidence that Aeschylus and his followers did read οἰωνοῖσι τε δαῖτα.[4] In the second half of the nineteenth century this became a hot spot of discussions about Aristarchus' reliability and method. The youthful Wilamowitz triumphantly proclaimed that 'the bad conjecture of Aristarchus' had been ousted 'from all unbiased heads'.[5]

This is *crambe repetita*. I still wish to present a suggestion of Alfred Heubeck which, as far as I can see, he never committed to writing. Heubeck's idea was that in this puzzling πᾶσιν another word was hidden, meaning something like 'meal'. An appropriate verbal root is not far to seek: 'eating' is πάσ(σ)ασθαι, mostly used in aorist forms; remember also ἄπαστος (*Il.* 19.346). The present πατέομαι is less frequently used, and probably secondary by word formation. The root should be *pat-*.[6] A noun from this root would be *πάστις.[7] This word is unattested, but we can confidently affirm that in a proper context no ancient Greek would have had difficulties in understanding it.

Following Heubeck's idea, we run into a metrical problem. The ν of *πάστιν is indispensable; so the conjecture involves further manipulation of Homeric verse. The simplest change is πάστιν τ' οἰωνοῖσι—though we may regret that this ruins the chiasmus.

[2] Athenaeus 12 f. For an original and startling study of Zenodotus' manuscript and method see West (2001), 33–45.

[3] Athenaeus 12 f.; *contra Il.* 24.43. Latacz (2000) prints West's text, but sides with Zenodotus in translation ('Bankett') and commentary (i/2 p. 19).

[4] Aesch. *Suppl.* 800–1, Soph. *Ant.* 29–30, Eur. *Ion* 504–5, see Pfeiffer (1968), 111–13; doubts, without argument, in Nickau (1977), 43 n. 32. A problem arises from Catullus 64.152 (Ariadne speaking): *dilaceranda feris dabor alitibusque / praeda*: did Zenodotus' reading survive until Catullus?

[5] Wilamowitz (1884), 20, referring to Nauck (1877), xi: 'die aristarchische schlechte conjektur . . . für alle nicht unfreien köpfe vertrieben'.

[6] Chantraine (1999), 863. See also *LfgrE* s.v. πάσσασθαι.

[7] On this suffix see S–D i. 504–5, ii. 356 n. 1; cf. μαίομαι, μάσσατο, μάστις, Risch (1974), 39–40.

Linguistically a transition from *πάστιν to *πάσσιν is impossible, but some misunderstanding of this kind in listening to recitation would easily happen; πᾶσιν is such a common word, while *πάστις was about to die out. Once understood as πᾶσιν, the change of word order could follow, as a skilled performer was prone to put that meaningless 'all' into the background. Hence ἑλώρια τεῦχε κύνεσσι οἰωνοῖσι τε πᾶσι. On the other hand, the replacement of *πάστιν by the more common word δαῖτα would enforce the same change of word order. All this remains toying with possibilities, across two stages of textual change. This may be the reason why Alfred Heubeck did not elaborate on his idea, nor publish it. I still think it worth consideration, even if it remains doubtful whether this refers to the history or to the prehistory of our text.

II

Now for another verse I have already had a chance to discuss with Martin West. The lines about Ajax of Salamis in the Catalogue of Ships (*Il.* 2.557–8) were hotly debated in antiquity, since the archaic epoch. They put Ajax side by side with the Athenians, which the Megarians were unwilling to accept. They claimed Salamis had been Megarian—but as far as we know, the final Athenian conquest came with Solon (1.1, 3.1 *IEG*); hence those verses must be a Solonian or post-Solonian interpolation. The controversy need not be documented here, nor will the question about historical facts of the sixth century be resumed.[8] It has also long been stated that in the rest of the *Iliad* no special proximity of Athenians and Ajax is to be found. A Megarian writer produced a variant to 557–8 which leaves out the Athenians; it has not found sympathy with modern scholarship.[9]

[8] The material is succinctly presented by West on verse 558 (1998–2000, i. 71), and by Latacz (2003), 179–80. See also Heitsch (1968), Visser (1997), 17–8, 447–54.

[9] Strabo 9.1.10:

> Αἴας δ' ἐκ Σαλαμῖνος ἄγεν νέας ἔκ τε Πολίχνης
> ἔκ τ' Αἰγειρούσσης Νισαίης τε Τριπόδων τε.

Modern criticism states that the number of ships is missing—but the quotation need not be complete; a verse such as τῶι δ' ἅμα νῆες ἕποντο δυώδεκα μιλτοπάρηοι (*Il.* 2.637) could have followed.

Hence verse 558, omitted by Aristarchus, is today normally athetized, as it is in Martin West's edition. He also assumes an Athenian interpolation of verses 547–51, a reference it seems to the Panathenaic festival. Incidentally, the controversy testifies to the relative age of these verses: they definitely are pre-Alexandrian.

But even an interpolated verse should still make sense. The wording of 558, as generally printed and translated, down to Latacz's new commentary, is odd. Ajax brought twelve ships from Salamis,

στῆσε δ' ἄγων, ἵν' Ἀθηναίων ἵσταντο φάλαγγες,

'he led and stood them where the Athenian lines were standing': 'leading' ships is a standard expression in the Catalogue of Ships, but how could Ajax place them in the Athenian battle line? 'Lines' were not yet standing at the shore.[10] *Φάλαγγες* clearly refers to the fighting unit, not to troops stowed away in ships. Latacz notes that the whole text is dealing with a disposition for battle rather than with a 'catalogue'.[11] Yet the transition from ships to phalanx, apparently stressed by the repetition of *ἄγεν—ἄγων*, is puzzling. Visser paraphrases 'daß Aias seine Truppen neben denen der Athener aufgestellt hätte';[12] yet these 'Truppen' of Ajax are not in the text.

Why not read the text in a different manner?

στῆσε δ' ἀγῶν', ἵν' Ἀθηναίων ἵσταντο φάλαγγες,

'he set up fight where the rows of the Athenians were standing'. This removes the reference to the ships and turns to Ajax's role in battle; the *φάλαγγες* fall into place. In oral performance the two texts would have differed, since accents were pronounced in hexameter recitation.[13] But in written form the two readings were, and are, indistinguishable, since *scriptio plena*, which would have marked *ἀγῶνα*, seems improbable, while the *ἄγεν* of verse 557 would suggest *ἄγων* for 558.

[10] Visser (1997), 451–2: 'Das achaiische Heer befindet sich . . . noch nicht in schlagbereiter Formation'.

[11] 'Aufstellungsplan', 'Aufmarschplan' (Latacz (1977), 51 with n. 12; cf. Latacz (2003), 180). In general, see Latacz (1977), 26–49. Visser (1997), 452 notes the missing caesura in 558 and concludes that this verse is not by the 'Iliasdichter'.

[12] Visser (1997), 17.

[13] It is only the German school tradition of reading verse by 'ictus' that obliterates the accents. F. H. Bothe, *Homeri Carmina* I (Leipzig, 1832), while athetizing 558, notes 'vereorque ne ponendum sit *στῆσε δ' ἀγῶν'*.'

The expression ἀγῶνα ἱστάναι, 'to set up a fight', is not Homeric: στῆσε does not recur for arranging ships,[14] but at least three times in battle arrangement (4.298, 6.433, 16.199); there is one parallel for the connection with ἀγῶνα, but with different meaning and context.[15] Yet the meaning of 'fight' or 'battle' is found in the famous Athenian epigram on the battle of Marathon, where even ὁ στήσας . . . τὸν ἀγῶνα has been proposed by Adolf Wilhelm. This may strengthen the hypothesis of a sixth-century interpolation: it perfectly fits Athenian ideology by the beginning of the fifth century.

If understood in the way proposed here, 'Ajax setting up fight in proximity to the Athenians', Ajax is performing his characteristic role as the great helper in battle. This probably is the basic function of this hero, with his huge protective shield. Von der Mühll (1930) = (1976), 435–72 has given a pertinent picture of such a 'Kampfhelfer'. Before the battle of Salamis, the Athenians expressly summoned Ajax and Telamon from Salamis (Hdt. 8.62). The Athenian reworking of the Iliadic verse, the intention to bring Ajax and Athenians together in the φάλαγγες, is all the more evident. This goes together with the reference to the festival of Erechtheus, i.e. the Panathenaea, some verses before.

It is still remarkable how restricted the Athenian reworking has evidently been. The Athenian representative in the *Iliad*, Menestheus, son of Peteos (2.552), does not even come from Athenian tradition—later Atthidographers had difficulties in inserting Menestheus between Theseus and his sons. Rather, he seems to be a joke at the expense of the Athenians: 'Resist the force' (Menestheus from Μενεσθένης), Son of the 'Flier' *Πετηός.[16] The main text of our *Iliad* is not Athenian-Peisistratean.

[14] 23.745 is different: 'they stopped in the harbour'.

[15] *Hymn. Apoll.* 150, the splendour of the Delian festival, ὅταν στήσωνται ἀγῶνα. Thucydides' quotation (3.104) has καθέσωνται ἀγῶνα, which those looking at Sophilos' picture of the 'Athla of Patroclus' (*LIMC* i. (1981), s.v. 'Achilleus' §951) may prefer; ἀγών as a festival also in Alcman 3.I.8 *PMGF*; epigram on Kallimachos the polemarch *IG* i³ 784 = *CEG* 256, with reference to Wilhelm and Shefton. *ΑΓΟΝΑ* is clearly legible, the supplement hὸ(ς) στέσας πολέ]μαρχος Ἀθεναίον τὸν ἀγôνα is judged 'fortasse brevius' by Hansen.

[16] See the remark of West (1998–2000), i. xxxiv on Πετεῶιο.

III

What shall we do with a drunken oxhide? It is the seventeenth book of the *Iliad* which confronts us with such a problem. Homer is great, of course, down to the last metaphor. But still—let us have a closer look. In the midst of the fighting after the death of Patroclus his unfortunate corpse is dragged to and fro; this is likened to a group of men 'stretching' an oxhide (βοείη) from all sides. The background of reality is clear, including the detail that one may use fat to make the hide more pliable. What is surprising is that the text calls the oxhide 'drunken with grease', μεθύουσαν ἀλοιφῆι (17.390). The manuscripts are unanimous. The scholia explain the process; best is Eustathius 1111.48 (iv. 69.70–1 van der Valk): 'as it (the hide) is made to lose moisture by the tension, the fat enters the pores and makes the hide more pliable'. 'Full of fat, like drunken people', the scholia (A) explain, ἀντὶ τοῦ πεπληρωμένην λίπει, ὡς οἱ μεθύοντες, with a variant recommending olive oil: ἐλαίωι διάβροχον (Schol. bT), τούτωι γὰρ μαλαττόμενα τὰ κατεσκληκότα ἀνίεται (*T*). Apollonius Sophista (p. 110.14 Bekker) too explains: 'this is metaphor, thoroughly moist with fat', μεταφορικῶς, διάβροχον τῶι λίπει. Thus Ameis and Hentze (1908), ii. 24 suggest the meaning 'stark durchtränkt', followed by Schadewaldt (1975): 'getränkt mit Fett'. Eustathius succeeds at least in bringing up metaphorical μεθύειν from Demosthenes (4.49): king Philip 'drunken' with success; Eustathius is anxious to state that Homer's expression was 'not too much harsher' (οὐκ ἂν εἴη πάνυ σκληρότερον) than Demosthenes' expression. The picture is 'adorned by impressiveness', ἐναργείαι κεκοσμημένη, the bT-Scholia say. Mark Edwards, in his excellent contribution to the Cambridge commentary (1991, 99), acknowledges 'a powerful and surprising metaphor'. Bewilderment does remain for ancients as for moderns, suppressed by admiration. Walter Leaf, in his earlier commentary, proved less impressed: 'an almost grotesquely violent metaphor, to which there is no parallel in Greek . . . *To be drunk* is the primitive and only sense of μεθύειν, coming from days older than the Greek language: it never meant *to drip* or *be soaked*' (1902, ii. 243). The problem is glossed over by translations into modern languages, and even by the arrangement of

LSJ.[17] As far as I can see, Leaf remains unrefuted: the text we read is violent, grotesque, impossible.

Conjectures on the *Iliad* should be forbidden, or, as Louis Robert once suggested for colleagues too fond of supplementing metrical epigrams, they should be relegated to special journals that provide a playground far from serious scholarship. Still it cannot be forbidden to react to bewilderment by groping for other possible readings. There is a Greek word resembling μεθύουσαν in sound, yet with a meaning that might fit: μυδόωσαν, from μυδάω. This verb, together with μυδαίνω (mostly causative) and the adjective μυδαλέος, has a wide range of meaning (cf. LSJ), from 'wet', 'damp', 'dripping' (*Il.* 11.54) through 'melting', 'disintegrating' (Soph. *Ant.* 1008) down to 'putrefaction' (Aeschylus fr. 53A *TrGF*, Soph. *Ant.* 410). It means 'soaked' by rain in Hesiod (*Op.* 556); it is glossed with διάβροχον in Archilochus (fr. 249 *IEG*, cf. ἐλαίωι διάβροχον Schol. bT *Iliad* 17.390). In Hippocrates it is used for a certain state of wounds and ulcers, translated 'fongueuse' ('spongy') by Littré;[18] it may refer to an untidy state of babies in Antimachos (63 Matthews = 90 Wyss, with Wyss's remarks). Medeia gives a certain drug to Jason with which to anoint himself, 'liquidizing' it (A.R. 3.1042–3; cf. 1247): μυδήνας τόδε φάρμακον ἠύτ' ἀλοιφῆι | γυμνωθεὶς φαίδρυνε τεὸν δέμας. Here the best translation for μυδήνας seems 'to soak' (so Gillies (1928)); this shows some association of a μυδῶν-state with ἀλοιφῆι, 'anointing'.

To come back to *Il.* 17.390: μυδόωσαν ἀλοιφῆι, 'soaked with fat', would clearly fit, not excluding the association of disintegration (μαλάττεται Schol.)—although I would not stress that they are fighting about a corpse.

[17] LSJ has two references for a metaphorical meaning of μεθύω, 'to be drenched, steeped in any liquid', in addition to *Il.* 17.390: μεθύων ἐλαίωι λύχνος, Babrius 114.1, and μεθύεις ὄμβροισι (a χείμαρρος), Antiphilos *A.P.* 9.277.3 = 823 *GP*. But in both cases the meaning is in fact 'to be drunk', i.e. 'to be crazy with arrogance', which is going to be refuted, as the context shows (cf. Dem. 4.49 used by Eustathius); there is nothing of this in *Il.* 17.390. Christopher Collard draws my attention to LSJ μεθύσκω I.2: 'moisten' (citing Philip *A.P.* 6.99.4 = 2730 *GP*)—but this too is a pointed expression: the herdsman uses milk instead of wine for libation, hence ἐν . . . γάλακτι βωμοὺς . . . μεθύσας. There remains Babrius 89.9, a lamb 'given a wonderful drink' by the ewe.

[18] [Hippocr.] *VC* 15 (iii. 242.21, 244.9 Littré); *VC* 21 (iii. 256.15 Littré); *Ulc.* 10 (vi. 408.6 Littré).

I would not dare to say I am presenting an 'emendation'; this is just a guess about the possible original intention of the text, which in this form probably was never committed to writing. A slip in the process of dictation seems more probable than an error in copying. Whether the dictating singer would have pronounced *μυδόωσαν* or *μυδάουσαν*, is impossible to say, but not very important in this case, even if *-οω-* would be closer in sound to *-υου*. Anyhow the writer's hand jumped to the more common word and produced *μεθύουσαν*, to be reluctantly admired by Homerists.

Whether for 'Homer' in general we prefer to think of a series of competent singers or of one uncommonly gifted genius, or even of both in succession, it is not a perfect and intangible text we have in our hands. Accidents must have happened in the complicated production of the first written text, which in a sense would have been the first Greek library—a collection of leather scrolls, in the possession of *Homeridai* or their unknown sponsor? All this remains desperately controversial; we are groping in a mist of fantasies. I am still afraid that for the first written text there was no reading of proofs. No wonder some lines seem to be ruined past recovery.[19] Faint indications of slips may be spotted here and there that reflect the enormous difficulties which were involved in bringing about this text which we are so happy to have.

[19] *Il.* 1.291 *τούνεκά οἱ προθέουσιν ὀνείδεα μυθήσασθαι* is such a case. The overall sense is fairly clear, but a satisfactory grammatical identification of the transmitted verb form *προθέουσιν* (*θε-* or *ἑ-* ?) seems impossible to achieve.

5

Hesiod's *Theogony* and the Folk Tale

Malcolm Davies

I

It is well known that Hesiod's *Theogony* contains a number of folk tale motifs.[1] West's 1966 commentary specifies Prometheus and Epimetheus, 'the pair of brothers, one clever and one stupid, or one good and the other bad' (p. 309) and the succession myth of lines 453–506, with 'the father who tries to dispose of his children in order to prevent the fulfilment of a prophecy that one of them will overthrow him; the child who is exposed, but who grows up in safety nevertheless and returns to claim his inheritance; the man who is swallowed by a monster or demon and afterwards rescued alive and whole from his belly; the ogre who cannot be defeated by strength, but can easily be outwitted by a trick' (p. 293). I shall be saying more about all these examples. But first I wish to suggest that a further folk tale motif is lurking in the aetiological account of how Prometheus tricked Zeus over sacrificial portions (555–616).[2] The story pattern I am looking to compare occurs in a circle of tales to which proper attention was first drawn by Alexander Haggerty Krappe,[3] 'that most

[1] J. Cobet's entry s.v. 'Hesiod' in *EM* (vi. 942 ff.) is disappointing.

[2] On this passage see, apart from West's commentary, the articles on the 'Prometheus–Pandora myth' by Aly (1913), von Fritz (1956), Wehrli (1956), and Heitsch (1963*a*) (all reprinted in Heitsch (1966) (ed.)).

[3] Krappe (1927), 154–7. The stories here listed constitute Type 1184 'The last leaf' in Aarne and Thompson (1961). Krappe cites them to illustrate the derivation from them of a detail in the medieval Welsh *Story of Tristan* (on which see now Bromwich (1991), with bibliography in 226 n. 62), where King Arthur gives Mark the choice of

learned and commonsensical of comparatists'.[4] God and the Devil reach an agreement over the establishing of some permanent state of affairs on a condition apparently favourable to the Devil. Paradoxically, this condition turns out to favour God, and the Devil retires discomfited.

So in a German tale from the Lower Rhine, 'the Devil wished to divide the rule over the world with God, his master. They came to an agreement to the effect that God was to rule when the trees are in foliage, the Devil, when they have shed their leaves. Unfortunately for the Devil, the decision was overheard and came to the knowledge of the trees. Thus it happened that, when autumn came, the fir-tree, the holly, and the juniper tree, as well as the mistletoe, the boxwood and the ivy, kept their leaves. Still other trees did not shed theirs until they got new foliage in May. Thus the Devil realized that he had no chance, and retired to his subterranean abode, cursing heartily, though ineffectually, all indiscretion and eavesdropping.'

This narrative shares a number of features with Hesiod's tale of Prometheus and Zeus:

1. Hesiod's narrative is *aetiological*,[5] explaining a curious feature of Greek sacrifice. The German tale explains how it is that certain trees are evergreen rather than deciduous. A Tyrolese tale likewise has God granting the Devil a boon to be fulfilled on the day when the oaks have lost all their leaves (which they never do). A thwarted Devil claws at that tree's leaves and tears them, which explains their peculiar shape.

2. That the relevant party's discomfiture is associated with *a benefit to mankind* does not emerge so clearly from the German tale as it does from Hesiod's. But the motif of human benefit is more explicit in other versions. An Austrian account pictures the Devil yearning to acquire the souls of ploughmen who swear excessively. God promises him them when the old leaves of all trees have dropped and the new

having Esyllt either when the leaves are on the trees or when they are off. By choosing the latter option and overlooking the holly, ivy and yew, he inadvertently ensures that his wife will remain with Tristan permanently.

[4] Anderson (2000), 162. For a brief introduction to Krappe's scholarly achievements see the article s.v. by A. Gier in *EM* (viii. 346–8).

[5] See West (1966*a*), 305 ('the Prometheus myth is aetiological through and through') and 308–9.

have not yet appeared. The Devil is thwarted because the oak keeps its old leaves after new foliage has sprouted. And in a Breton account, the devil is angry that all Bretons are getting into Paradise, none to Hell: God grants him the souls of all who die while the heath is not in bloom. The Devil's joy is short-lived as he observes that the heath of Brittany puts forth some flowers even in midwinter. In a variant from Mecklenburg, an impoverished man will give his soul to the Devil when all trees have lost their foliage. God hears the man's prayer and allows some to keep their leaves until others have put forth theirs.

3. Hesiod's narrative portrays benefit to mankind but also *longer-term misfortune* (the hard existence punitively imposed by Zeus), and such ambivalence occurs in the folk tales under examination. Our Breton version closes with the Devil planting vines and establishing public houses to open up a new path to perdition for mankind. This final complication evokes another story, about the Serbian Saint Sava (rather than God) and the Devil.[6] Its version of the misleadingly attractive option that turns out to be less rewarding is even closer to Hesiod: the Devil repeatedly blunders in his bargains with the saint, successively preferring the half of onions that is visible above the ground, the half of potatoes that is below, the half of wheat below, and finally, when it comes to planting vines, the thick mass of liquid to the clear 'soup'. At the last he brews brandy to be 'medicine to the old and madness to the young', and disappears in a fury.[7] Apart from its closing aetiology, this story shares with Hesiod the notion of the superficially tempting portion of food which transpires to be relatively disappointing.

In Hesiod, men and gods lived together in amity until Prometheus' ruse. In the circle of folk tales examined, especially the German version with which we began, a friendly relationship between God and the Devil seems presupposed by their bargain. 'It is usually a matter', says Krappe (1927, 156), 'of an amicable arrangement between God and the Devil'. One is reminded of the folk-tale concept of a primal friendship (Davies (2001), 208–9) between beings that later converts to estrangement. 'Freundschaft zwischen Tier und Mensch',

[6] For a translation of this tale see Ćurčija-Prodanović (1957), 165–9.

[7] For a similar tale, with St Cado outwitting the devil, see Soupault (1971), 175–8.

this phenomenon has been dubbed (Horn, *EM* v. 299), and our folk tales show 'Freundschaft zwischen Gott und Teufel'.

We may therefore infer a more general framework with God and Devil *collaborating* in various spheres of creation. Folk tale sometimes pictures the two powers combining to fashion the world (Davies (2001), 208–9), the Devil fetching mud from the sea floor, which God then uses to give the world form. Or the two together make man, with the Devil given responsibility for the less appealing areas of the anatomy. Occasionally, one of the two fashions an animal, and the other responds with an antithetical creature.[8]

All this is highly suggestive for the background to Hesiod's narrative. Since it begins with men and gods still consorting together, the recent creation of mankind, by Zeus or by Prometheus, is obviously presupposed. One scholar (Heitsch (1963*a*), 3 = (1966), 421) has plausibly suggested that Prometheus' fashioning of mankind directly preceded Hesiod's events. Or again, Zeus' fashioning of Pandora in Hesiod might be interpreted as analogous to the aforementioned folk-tale creation of an antithetical creature (woman) to match man. The folk tale ends with the Devil retiring permanently to a subterranean cavern. The long-term consequence of Prometheus' ruse (with the ban on mortals' use of fire and Prometheus' theft as intermediate stages) is also a punitive segregation—admittedly not quite so self-imposed—when Prometheus is bound to a rock in the remote Caucasus. 'Unter dem Sammelnamen des Teufels im modernen Märchen sich sehr Verschiedenartiges bergen kann', as Karl Meuli sagely observed some time ago.[9] The notion of punitive expulsion from Paradise or the company of the gods is both early and widespread.[10]

[8] So e.g. the Devil makes a mouse and God creates a cat to attack it (Röhrich (1974), 25–7 ≈ (1991), 29–31 and *EM* s.v. 'Adam und Eva' (i. 94)). For further examples of these 'créations dualistes' (sun / moon, cat / dog etc.) see Sebillot (1968), 114–15.

[9] Meuli (1921), 15 = (1975), ii. 604. Cf. Christiansen (1959), 163: 'the Devil may be a fool who is easily tricked or a clever lawyer constantly overruled . . . but there is never any religious sentiment in the stories in which he appears.'

[10] Kakridis (1930), 473 = (1971), 64 = Calder and Stern (1970), 185–6 (all with n. 41) illustrates this motif from Greek literature with the (mortal) cases of Ixion, Endymion (Hes. fr. 245 M–W), and Pelops (Pind. *Ol.* 1.65–6). Add Hephaestus and Prometheus (cf. below, n. 42) and Ate (*Il.* 19. 91 ff.). He also quotes the expulsion of Adam, Eve, and the Devil from the garden of Eden (Genesis 2–3). So, in the Hebrew legend, both mankind and the enemy of God are driven from the divine presence, which is similar to what we find in the *Theogony*.

There may seem to be a key difference in that the Devil is outwitted, while Prometheus was clearly envisaged in the original form of the story as outwitting Zeus.[11] But Zeus does win in the long run.

II

As we saw above, the numerous folk-tale features of Hesiod *Theogony* 453–506 were clearly identified by Martin West. A mode of approach building on his work might note the narrative's remarkable compliance with the patterns of a hero's quest as established in Vladimir Propp's famous *Morphology of the Folktale* (Propp (1968); cf. Davies (2002), 5 ff.). Probably the best-known and most influential aspect of this monograph is its observation that such quests regularly commence with a *lack* requiring to be liquidated (Davies (2002), 11). The lack in Hesiod is of Zeus' brothers and sisters, trapped in their father's maw, and the hero is Zeus himself, who, as youngest sibling, fits the role of questing hero to perfection.[12] Numerous folk tales open with a similar lack, the hero or heroine's siblings having been somehow abducted. Hesiod's tale thus represents Propp's first Function ((1968), 26; I.3): 'members of the younger generation absent themselves', combined with Function VIII: 'the villain causes harm or injury to a member of a family', especially subsection 7 (p. 32): 'the villain causes a sudden disappearance'. Even the detail (*Theog.* 464) that Cronus' consumption of his children was motivated by a prophecy of how he would be overthrown by his own son has a Proppian propriety, since such prophecies do feature in his scheme (Table I.8 (p. 120)). Note in particular p. 128: 'a nightingale

[11] West (1966*a*), 321 observes that 'it has long been recognised that in the original story Zeus did not see through the trick, but was thoroughly deceived . . . The statement that he was not . . . is manifestly inserted to save his omniscience', and Wehrli (1956), 31 = (1972), 51 = Heitsch (1966), 412 rightly detects 'fast ausdrückliche Polemik' in the insistent characterization of Zeus as ἄφθιτα μήδεα εἰδώς (545, 550, 561). We may compare the words πάντα ἴσαντι νόῳ of Apollo's omniscience at Pind. *Pyth.* 3.29. For analogous significant epithets in archaic poetry 'polemicizing' against tradition cf. Alcaeus fr. 42 *PLF*, Voigt, with Davies (1986), 261–2.

[12] See Davies (2003*b*), 34–5 for the youngest sibling motif (not restricted to the number three).

foretells the humiliation of the parents by the son . . . *This serves as the motivation for the villainy* [my italics]. The parents place the sleeping boy in a boat . . .'. Such disposing of the awkward offspring may seem a thousand miles removed from Cronus' cannibalism, but that motif is, in fact, very much at home in this part of Propp's scheme. See p. 144 on another instance of prophecy in a specific folk tale: 'the groom predicts the birth of a sister who . . . shall devour her father and mother and all people under their command'.[13] Perhaps we are dealing with the transference of the cannibalism motif?

One of the most interesting episodes in Propp's scheme is the hero's encounter with a helper figure or donor, who regularly supplies a 'magical agent' ensuring success (Davies (2002), 5 ff.). The figure is represented in Hesiod by Cronus' own mother Gaea[14] (her role is occupied by Metis in the corresponding part of Apollodorus' *Bibliotheca* (1.2.1)). This detail too is very appropriate to the values of folk tale. In the lair of his adversary, the hero often finds himself paradoxically aided and abetted by a female relative of the ogre—most frequently his wife or daughter (Davies (2003*a*), 139 ff.: cf. Crooke (1908), 169). Compare the giant's wife in Jack and the Beanstalk, or Persephone who helps Heracles against her husband Hades in the quest for Cerberus, or Ariadne, or Medea. Gaea is Cronus' mother, Metis his sister, but the pattern still holds.

As for the 'magical agent', is this not the emetic administered to Cronus? A beverage also features among Propp's 'magical agents' (p. 45), though the drink in question is more normally consumed by the hero himself (perhaps the original function of the moly plant in *Odyssey* 10, as I hope to discuss elsewhere). For its use against the adversary compare (from Wagner's *Die Walküre* Act I, ultimately deriving from Germany's Volsung Saga) the sleeping potion which

[13] Cf. the pregnant Hecabe's dream about Paris.

[14] I take *Γαίης ἐννεσίῃσι* at 494 to refer not (as West) back to the stone strategem of 468 ff., but forward (cf. *Γαίης φραδμοσύνῃσιν* at 626, 884, 891) to the emetic. 496, which West interprets as referring to that, I deem an interpolation (following Heyne) to clarify an obscure narrative. I suppose the role of Metis as helper to be original, not (as Söder (1939), 14) a later 'clarification' of Hesiod's narrative. To give his poem unity (cf. Solmsen (1949), 26) Hesiod has Gaea intervene periodically through the poem with advice (154, 459, 884, 891), rather like the warner figure of later Greek literature (see West (1978), 167), and he has replaced Metis with Gaea to fit this pattern.

Sieglinde administers to her husband Hunding, so as to expedite her plotting and escape with Siegmund.[15] Which reminds us that, with all siblings restored, Zeus marries his sister Hera and assumes control of the Universe; while the Proppian quest generally ends not merely with the initial lack liquidated, but (Function XXXI (pp. 63–4)) with 'the hero . . . married and ascend[ing] the throne'.

Another approach to this episode, one not at all incompatible with Propp's, would note that it combines two folk tale themes of long standing: (1) 'The exposed child', rightly identified, as we saw above, by West in his commentary;[16] and (2) 'The youngest brother who rescues his elder brothers'.

The first theme has been the subject of a detailed monograph, so less needs saying.[17] But we should stress (what was already apparent on Proppian principles) that the exposing of the child is regularly motivated by a prophecy of future events. There are so many instances among the stories assembled by Binder that one regrets the absence of the entry 'Prophezeiungen' from his Index.[18] I add here a

[15] For the related motif of the demon or ogre outwitted by having alcohol administered to him for the first time see Schröder (1968), 325 ff., Davies (2004), 684 ff. Cf. also West (1983*a*), 135.

[16] Zeus is not literally exposed (born in an isolated locale, etc.). But his infancy shows many features of literally exposed heroes—preservation unbeknown to the persecuting ruler, triumphant return upon reaching maturity etc.

[17] Binder (1964), summarized (with corrections) by the author in *EM* s.v. 'Aussetzung' (i. 1048–65). See more recently Huys (1995) with Binder (1997), 330–3; and for further bibliography see Bremmer in Bremmer and Horsfall (1987), 30 n. 27. On the generally stereotypical nature of heroes' birth and infancy in folk tale see e.g. Krappe (1927), 15, Bremmer (loc. cit.), 28–9.

[18] The following list (with Binder's page numbers in brackets) deliberately omits both Cyrus and Romulus and Remus. Greek myth: Aegisthus (p. 139), Oedipus (p. 142), Paris (p. 144), Perseus (p. 132), Telephus (pp. 130 ff.: Binder fails to make it clear that one source of his version (b) ('Alcidamas' *Odyssey* 14) has an oracle tell Aleos that his daughter and Telephus' mother-to-be Auge will bear a child who will kill Aleos' sons). 'Historical' individuals: Agathocles (p. 149), Gilgamos (p. 160). From non-Greek sources: Nimrod (p. 160), Moses (p. 169), Judas (pp. 173–4), Feridun (p. 176), Hormizd (p. 191), Aghata (p. 196), Campaka (p. 197), Krishna (p. 207), Vanaraja (p. 213), Florindo (p. 240), Constantine (p. 248). Feridun is particularly interesting since he features as the child of whose unwelcome succession to his throne the serpent king Zohak (in this instance *not* his grandfather) dreams in an Iranian narrative the similarity of which to Hesiod's account has been argued by Littleton (1970), 102 ff., especially 104–5. For context and Iranian background see Puhvel (1987), 117 ff., especially 120–1. For a Ugandan version of the 'Gilgamos' story see Krappe (1927), 27. On the story of Krishna's birth see now Matchett (2001), 53–4 and 126–7.

little-known example from Greek myth that escaped Binder's trawl,[19] the rare variant which claims exposure for one (or both) of Oedipus' sons. *Σ* Eur. *Phoen.* 13 (i. 249 Schwartz) = Lysimachus *FGrHist* 382 F 20: *Λυσίμαχος* (*Λιγύστιος*: *corr.* C. Müller) *δέ φησιν ὡς ἐκ χρησμοῦ τοὺς παῖδας ἀκούσας ἀλληλοκτονήσειν ἐξέθηκε τὸν Πολυνείκην* (*scil.* *Οἰδίπους*), *Κάστωρ* (*FGrHist* 250 F 18) *δὲ ἀμφοτέρους ἐκτεθῆναι.*

Another instance of the pattern which Binder might have adduced occurs in Matthew's Gospel.[20] A prophecy to King Herod seeming to threaten his rule (2:5) is the idiomatic incitement to a Proppian 'act of villainy' whereby he attempts to kill the child in question (2:16–18).[21] The child is then spirited out of the country to Egypt, from which he returns when Herod is dead (2:13–15 and 19–22). Only the birth of the child is slightly displaced within the narrative, coming before the actual prophecy.[22] The extra details in Luke's

[19] Of the various omissions of non-Greek or Roman material from Binder's monograph, perhaps the most serious is that of the Irish tale of 'Balor with the evil eye', handled by Krappe (1927), 1–43. Balor has been informed by a druid that he will be killed by his daughter's son and therefore imprisons her in a tall tower. When the hiding place is breached and the daughter bears three sons (dismissed by Krappe (1927), 16 as 'the late addition of a story-teller': but remember Zeus and his two brothers and Propp's folk-tale principle of 'trebling'(pp. 74–5)), he orders them to be drowned. A similar story is told of the Irish hero Finn: see O'Hogain (1988), 12–13 (Finn 'does not kill his grandfather, but in a somewhat moderated manner, takes his property instead').

[20] See Beare (1981), 72 ff. on 'a cycle of infancy legends', especially 72: 'variations on ancient themes of myth and legend which recur widely in the Near and Middle East. The discovery of the child and his miraculous escape from the enemies who threaten his life'. Cf. M. Frenschkowski s.v. 'Neues Testament' in *EM* (ix. 1386–7): 'dies Kindheitslegenden des Matthäus und Lukas übertragen in je unterschiedlicher Gestalt weitverbreitete Stoffe aus der Geburts- und Kindheitsgeschichte berühmter Männer auf Jesus'.

[21] See in particular Saintyves (1928) and cf. O'Hogain (1988), 277: 'in both Ireland and Scotland there is a tendency to assimilate Finn's tyrant grandfather, from whom he has to be spirited away as a baby, to . . . Herod. We are often told that the grandfather ordered the slaughter of all baby-boys.' He detects a conscious 'borrowing of the motif' from Matthew.

[22] Displaced because, as the story now stands, it is the Three Magi who first draw Herod's attention to Christ's birth. Brown (1993), 114–15 plausibly suggests that, in the original form of the story, Herod directly dreamed of the child's birth, and 'a once independent . . . story' involving the Magi 'has been introduced, displacing' that dream. On the possible sources of the Magi story see recently Frenschkowski (1998), 23 ff. The original story would then match other tales of a dream causing fear in a powerful ruler, not least the versions of the story of Moses and the Pharaoh (see n. 25) which are found outside Exodus.

Gospel[23] supply further idiomatic features: the child's birth in a lowly place, a manger according to Luke 2:7, a cave[24] (where Zeus and other comparable heroes are born, exposed, or reared) according to the Apocrypha; the child's speedy approach to maturity (Luke 2:48 ff.) etc.[25]

Classical scholars[26] have further cited from Suetonius' *Life of Augustus* (94.3) that emperor's freedman and keeper of records: *auctor est Iulius Marathus, ante paucos quam nasceretur menses prodigium Romae factum publice, quo denuntiabatur, regem populo Romano naturam parturire; Senatum exterritum censuisse ne quis illo anno genitus educaretur.* Once again, we have the revelation of the future which motivates both fear and an 'act of villainy' (on the Senate's part), here frustrated by a number of pregnant (and ambitious) Roman women who, hoping that the prophecy referred to their own as yet unborn offspring, *curasse ne senatus consultum ad aerarium deferretur.* For another parallel see Cassius Dio 45.1.5 (cf. Norden (1924), 158 n. 2): the astrologer Nigidius Figulus greeted Augustus' father, on the birth of his son, with the words δεσπότην ἡμῖν ἐγεννήσας. The father is not best pleased: αὐτὸν ἐκταραχθέντα ἐπὶ τούτῳ καὶ διαφθεῖραι τὸ παιδίον ἐθελησάντα . . . The occurrence here of practically the same verb (ἐκταραχθέντα ~ ἐταράσσετο) as Matthew uses of Herod's perturbation is striking, as (more relevantly for Hesiod) is the fact that this version, like Hesiod's, features son rather than grandson. Although Hesiodic gods can feel fear (see e.g. *Theog.* 167), Hesiod's account does not bring out this aspect as

[23] 'None of the four stories that make up the cycle [in Matthew] has any relationship to the cycle found in the Gospel of Luke, nor is it possible to work the two cycles into a common narrative framework' (Beare (1981), 73).

[24] 'A tradition which can be traced back to the second century located the birth of Jesus in a cave' (Marshall (1978), 107, citing sources).

[25] The absence of Christ from Binder's monograph jars, since Herod's infanticide recalls Pharaoh's in two accounts of the birth of Moses supplementary to the Old Testament's, which Binder does deal with (1964, 169). Cf. Beare (1981), 75 ('the Moses story is the immediate inspiration of the Gospel tale'), Allison (1993). Note, further, with e.g. Binder (1964), 170–1, that the probably early and original motif of a murder-inducing prophecy occurs only in sources other than Exodus: on these cf. Frenschkowski (1998), 23. The entry by D.-R. Moser in *EM* s.v. 'Christus', 2.2 'Geburt' (ii. 1414–15) likewise fails to touch on the all-important motif of prophecy.

[26] Bremner in Bremmer and Horsfall (1987), 30 cites this passage, whose potential relevance to Matthew was once much discussed: see Saintyves (1928), 269, Norden (1924), 158 (with bibliography in n. 2), Frenschkowski (1998), 25.

explicitly as Dionysius of Halicarnassus' later summary of events (*Rom. Ant.* 2.19.1 *Κρόνος ἀφανίζων τὰς ἑαυτοῦ γονὰς φόβῳ τῆς ἐξ αὐτῶν ἐπιθέσεως*). But that the story belongs in the above-mentioned cycle is beyond doubt.

One final instance confirms this statement, and allows us also to confirm our honorand's *aperçu* 'you can always find something in Hesychius' (West (1966*a*), 238: cf. Krappe (1927), 18). The motif of prophecy to a ruler followed by fear and resort to the 'act of villainy' that is infant exposure recurs in the story of Acrisius' enquiry of the Delphic oracle (Apollodorus *Bibliotheca* 2.4.1 = Zen. *Cent.* 1.41 (*CPG* i. 15–17); §156 Parke and Wormell (1956) = L23 Fontenrose (1978)). Given the similarity to Hesiod's story of Cronus' overthrow, cue Hesychius *α* 2575 (i. 91 Latte) *Ἀκρισίας· Κρόνος, παρὰ Φρυξίν*.

The second theme—'the younger brother who rescues his elder brothers'—needs more attention. We have seen that several folk tales presuppose absent siblings. More specifically, a widespread tale[27] relates how a varying plurality of brothers sally forth to find themselves brides. In this they are successful. But while returning they all fall foul of a giant or ogre who transforms both brides and brothers to stone, so that the youngest brother, left behind at home, has to go on a quest to rescue them by killing the adversary with the help of 'grateful animals' and of the giant's wife, whom he marries. Apart from the motif of petrification, note that the adversary is regularly implied to be a *cannibal*[28] ('fee, fie, fo, fum, I smell the blood of a Christian man!')[29] and the place in which he imprisons the brothers is easily identifiable as the Other- or Underworld.[30] I have shown

[27] The relevant group of tales is summarized and analysed by U. Masing s.v. 'Brüder suchen Schwestern' in *EM* (ii. 887 ff.).

[28] See, for instance, the related tale of 'Däumling und Menschenfresser' (cf. M. Meraklis' article s.v. in *EM* (iii. 360 ff.)) which has seven brothers encountering the seven daughters of a cannibal in the latter's home.

[29] From the Scottish 'Child Rowland' (Briggs (1970), i. 180–4) where the titular hero goes questing when first his sister Helen, and then the two elder brothers who went looking for her, have failed to return home. She has been abducted and all three imprisoned by the king of Elfland, utterer of the words in question, found also at e.g. Jones (1956), 20–3.

[30] For instance, the dragon occupying the adversary's role in one group of tales leads the brothers to the Underworld (Masing *EM* ii. 890), and the location in which Child Rowland (n. 29) discovers his siblings is clearly the Other- or Underworld, since it is a region of *twilight* (cf. Davies (1988), 279 n. 16) and he has been warned by a helper figure not to eat or drink there (cf. Davies (2004), 607 n. 9).

(Davies (2003*a*), 139–40) in connection with the story of Heracles and the Trojan sea-monster, how the belly of such a monster can stand for Hell or the Underworld, so that the fit with Hesiod's tale of the cannibalistic Cronus is remarkably close.

Folk-tale vestiges in the sequel to this episode in Hesiod will also bear closer comparative analysis. At 501 ff., once Zeus has overthrown Cronus, but before the Titanomachy, he releases the Cyclopes whom his father had bound, and they, in gratitude, bestow upon him the thunderbolts and lightning flashes which henceforth serve as the trademarks of his power.[31] With them he conquers the Titans. Not in his commentary on those lines, but in his later study of Oriental influences, West (1997, 295) drew attention to 'the motif that the god requires special weapons, . . . supplied to him by a divine craftsman', and cites the invocation (Walcot (1966), 31) of the Ugaritic epic of Baal, wherein that deity is helped to triumph in his duel with Yammu by Kothar, the 'Ugaritic Hephaestus' (Fontenrose (1959), 136), who supplies him with two turning clubs or magic maces.

Now a Norse expert[32] has independently detected 'a type which is readily paralleled in Indo-European myth and can be traced elsewhere in Old Norse literature. Its essential thematic structure is that there is a deity represented as a divine smith who has forged a supremely powerful weapon. Another deity obtains the weapon and kills the divine smith with it. Thereafter the conqueror becomes heroically powerful and the weapon becomes his characteristic instrument of aggression. The two deities are often represented as father and son.' These generalizations were inspired by Eilifr Godrunarson's *Thorsdrapa*, a poetic narrative from the late tenth century AD recounting how Thor engages the giant Geirrodr in combat: they both hurl red-hot, glowing iron bolts or bars at each other, until Thor kills the giant with his own weapon.[33] Doubtless, 'in the

[31] Apollodorus 1.2.1 claims that the Cyclopes also gave Poseidon and Hades their characteristic trident and helmet of invisibility for the Titanomachy. But etymologically, the Cyclopes' names (Argos, Brontes and Steropes) associate them only with Zeus' weapons.

[32] Clunies Ross (1981), 389. For the various sources of the tale see 370 n. 2.

[33] For the possibility that Thor was originally envisaged as castrating Geirrodr see Clunies Ross (1981), 388 (Saxo Grammaticus' *Gesta Danorum* has Thor drive red-hot iron through his opponent's vitals). In Hesiod, of course, it is Uranus who is castrated but for traditions that Cronus suffered the same fate see West (1983*a*), 134–8. Thor

original myth . . . Geirrodr is the giant smith who has forged what is to become Thor's characteristic weapon', Mjollnr, his famous giant-slaying hammer, to be identified with the aforementioned iron bar.

Two analogues are cited for the relevant pattern: Sigurd from German folk tale, who kills Fafnir the dragon and Reginn the cunning dwarf and smith, his own foster-father; and Indra (from the *Rgveda*) who kills Tvastr, divine smith and forger of his thunderbolt. The context of the first story[34] reveals further similarities with Zeus' position. Sigurd was exposed as a child and suckled by a hind, a frequent folk tale 'Aussetzung' motif (e.g. Romulus, Remus and the wolf: see Binder (1964), Index s.v. 'Tierabstammung') of which a vestige remains in those non-Hesiodic accounts of Zeus' rearing which mention Amalthea (cf. Frazer (1921), i. 7). Sigurd was brought up by 'a cunning smith, his tutor or fosterfather, Reginn or Mimir, who is at first his ally and helper, later his enemy' (Fontenrose (1959), 530). It is hard to read these words without recognizing that quintessential figure of folk tale, the ambivalent helper,[35] especially hard when the scholar quoted proceeds: 'this is a theme observed before, kinship and conflict between the champion and the artisan god, who is sometimes his father.' That formulation also reminds us that a paradoxical blood relationship frequently subsists between the hero's ambivalent helper and the climactic adversary. So the Graeae who grudgingly help Perseus are the sisters of Medusa whom he beheads (see Fontenrose (1959), 285–6 and Davies (1988), 286), and Gaea and Metis are wife or sister of Cronus. The characteristic weapon

nowhere features as son of Geirrodr, but for the lack of any tradition as to his birth (and even the possibility that Odin's paternity is a relatively late development) see Clunies Ross (1981), 388 n. 59. The Irish hero Lug, brought up by his uncle, a smith, as a smith, kills his grandfather Balor (above, n. 19) by driving a red-hot iron bar through his evil eye (Krappe (1927), 4). For the possible equivalence in such contexts of blinding and castration see e.g. Devereux (1973), 36 ff. and Buxton (1980), 25. For the significance of the smith figure see n. 34.

[34] A helpful introduction to the various traditions concerning Sigurd's infancy and youth in Fontenrose (1959), 534 ff. (especially 539 on the acquiring of the sword) and K. Düvel in *EM* xii. 673 ff. For the frequency of the pattern whereby the folk tale hero is brought up by a smith see D. A. Miller (2000), 261 ff., especially 266–8. Cf. in general E. Marold's article s.v. 'Schmied' in *EM* (xii. 105 ff., especially 106 on Reginn).

[35] On ambivalent helper figures in general see e.g. Davies (1988), 283–4. For smiths in particular as ambivalent helpers in folk tale see Marold (n. 34), 105 and 107.

which Sigurd obtains from the cunning smith and which he employs to despatch both foster-father and dragon is, of course, the famous sword Gram.[36]

As for Indra and Tvastr, it is now possible to give an accurate and concise account of similarities with Zeus and Thor, thanks to the two-volume boon that is Thomas Oberlies's monograph. Indra, then, is a close equivalent of Thor (and Heracles: Oberlies (1998–9), i. 249–50 and n. 485)[37] and is characteristically born 'outside of the world of chaos' ('Ausserhalb der Welt des Chaos': Oberlies Index s.v. 'Indra' (p. 574): we recall that Thor is 'above all that deity of the Norse pantheon who is concerned with the confirmation of order against the ever-present threat of disorder' (Clunies Ross (1981), 387). In a manner strongly reminiscent of Zeus' rearing, Indra is, in effect, exposed—being brought up outside his family home—and develops with supernatural speed (Oberlies 251–4 and nn. 498 and 593). To move back to features shared with Thor, Indra is brought up by Tvastr (Oberlies 253–4), a deity treated in some passages of the *Rgveda* as Indra's actual father (Oberlies 253 n. 504). Tvastr is a smith god comparable, for instance, to the Greek Hephaestus, the Norse or Germanic Volund or Wieland (Oberlies 255 ff., especially n. 505) and, like the smiths of folk tale in general, he commands demonic knowledge and magical powers (Oberlies 257). Tvastr forges Indra's characteristic weapon, the bolt,[38] after which Indra kills him (Oberlies 254 and 258),[39] an act whose folk-tale significance Oberlies perceptively identifies: it is a typical motif, he says, for the hero either to steal the smith's weapons or get them into his possession by killing the owner.[40] Zeus does neither as regards the Cyclopes—to return finally to the point from which this portion of the argument began—but it may be noted that he does later swallow Metis, his erstwhile helper, thereby permanently gaining her

[36] Fontenrose (1959), 536 convincingly shows that the *Thidrekssaga* and various south German sources indicate that 'originally Gram and Hrotti were one sword, the giant sword of the dragon's cave'.

[37] All references henceforth are to this first volume.

[38] For Tvastvr's role as smith see Oberlies 255–6, 254 with n. 505, 258.

[39] Cf. his Index s.v. 'Indra . . . erschlägt seinen Vater, den Himmelsgott'.

[40] For the alternative tradition that Indra steals Tvastvr's weapons (*Rgveda* 6.44.22) see Oberlies 254 n. 509.

wisdom,[41] which is how Oberlies (254 n. 509) interprets the significance of the folk-tale hero's theft of the weapons or murder of their owner.

III

Prometheus has been assimilated to the figures of Python and Typhoeus.[42] The assimilation initially staggers one, but Cronus' epithet ἀγκυλομήτης was probably taken by Hesiod to refer to his crooked cunning (cf. West (1966*a*), 158), and the folk tale's questing hero, when confronted either by ambivalent helper or climactic adversary, often has resort to the twin poles of force or cunning (Davies (2002), 14–15). The agon between hero and adversary can occasionally take the form of a combat of wits, and that would be one way of interpreting the outsmarting of Zeus by Prometheus with which this study began.

I have elsewhere[43] mentioned a Melanesian story 'of two brothers who fished the Earth out of the Ocean and made themselves wives from it to become the ancestors of mankind. One brother was clever, the other stupid, and mankind forfeited immortality when the clever brother received a message of immortality for men which his brother . . . conveyed to the snakes.' I found the pair of brothers 'reminiscent of Prometheus and Epimetheus', but added that 'the comparison is

[41] The Cyclopes can reasonably be regarded as, like the Titans, 'older and unsuccessful rivals of Zeus', and Cyclops as 'originally a sky-god like Zeus, his round eye being the sun and his weapon the thunderbolt', who 'was somehow related to Zeus': see Cook (1914), 317; also 320 for the tradition (Hellanicus *FGrHist* 4 F 88) that 'Cyclops' was the son of Uranus (cf. Hes. *Theog.* 502: the Cyclopes as Οὐρανίδαι). If this Cyclops were, like the Cyclopes, a smith (and, as son of Uranus, an equivalent of Cronus displaced by Zeus), there could be a very close match with the Indo-European pattern of a god extracting his characteristic weapons from a smith figure representing his father.

[42] Fontenrose (1959), 513. Prometheus, according to Euphorion fr. 99 *CA*, was the product of the giant Eurymedon's rape of Hera, which explained Zeus' expulsion and fettering of him, the theft of fire being a mere excuse. For Hera as 'mère d'un génie du feu', that is, Prometheus, Python or Typhoeus, see Vian (1952), 176–7.

[43] Davies (1987). The passage quoted occurs on p. 75. For the source of the Melanesian story see n. 52.

not very illuminating because no detail corresponding to the theft of fire is to be found in the Melanesian story'.

The issue cannot be discussed or decided in any satisfactory way without being placed in the far wider context of the phenomenon of 'twin culture heroes'. Of Jacob and Esau in Genesis 25:21–6 Gaster has observed[44] that 'many peoples throughout the world tell (or have told) stories about primeval twins or heroic pairs from whom they, and their nearest neighbours, derive their cultural and ethnic origins'. Siblings with symmetrically similar names differing either as regards *beginning*, as with Pro- / Epi-metheus, Romul- / Rem-us,[45] and, from Burma, Titha-Kumma and Dyaza-Kumma,[46] or *ending* are particularly relevant. The latter class, more numerous, is exemplified from non-Indo-European cultures by, for instance, Khulun and Khunlai, from whom the Ahom kingdom in Assam traced descent; Olo-sipa and Ola-sapa from Panope in the Caroline Islands; Kirimaikalu and Kirimaika (the Koita of New Guinea); Honsu and Honsi (the Dahomey: cf. Gaster). There is, rather surprisingly, an Indo-European parallel of sorts in lists of Italian saints, where we find, with differing endings, Sisinnius and Sissinidorus and, with divergent beginnings, Picumnus and Pilumnus, Mutunus and Tutunus, while from the French religious calendar can be culled Ferreolus and Ferretinus (Chakravarty (1997), 42).

We draw closer to the significance of Pro-metheus and Epimetheus and, indeed, to the significance of the whole story, when, as in the case of Cain and Abel or Jacob and Esau, 'the twins are . . .

[44] Gaster (1969), 163 and 366–7. For compendious general introductions to 'culture heroes', with bibliography, see e.g. the entries s.v. in *Encyclopedia of Religion and Ethics* 4.175 ff., *Religion in Gesch. und Gegenwart* 4.1836 and, in particular, *EM* viii. 593 ff. by Donald Ward (594–5 on the more specific question of culture heroes as twins). Further relevant bibliography in Liou-Gille (1980), 158 n. 76.

[45] A recent study of Romulus and Remus with up-to-date bibliography: Bannon (1997), 158 ff. Gaster merely assumes their status as culture heroes, but if, e.g., the division of Roman society into patricians and plebeians was traced back to the twins (cf. Cornell (1975), 28–9) the assumption may be valid. Cf. Liou-Gille (1980), 158 on the general pattern: 'si l'un des jumeaux, ou les deux, sont laissés en vie, ils acquièrent des pouvoirs particuliers, magiques et bénéfiques à la communauté.'

[46] For further remarks and bibliography on rival twins in folk tale see Davies (2003*b*), 33 and n. 9 and cf. n. 47 below. For a pair of twins whose contrasted nature is brought out by means other than variation of name see Halfdan the Black and Halfdan the White: cf. Chakravarty (1997), 41.

portrayed as rivals . . . one of them . . . of divine origin and therefore superior, or else of demonic origin and therefore inferior, to the other' (Gaster (1969)).[47] In this more specialized area, varied endings include, 'among the Hurons . . . "Good Creator" (*Hahgwediju*), and . . . "Bad Creator" (*Hahgwedaetgah*)', and from 'the Gwelle Peninsula . . . Tokumbinana the clever twin and his stupid brother Tokovoruru', while those whose names differ by prefix, like Prometheus and Epimetheus, include 'among the Ainu of Japan, Shi-acha . . . the "rough uncle" and Mi-acha the "good uncle"' (Gaster (1969)). However, the aforementioned Tokumbinana and Tokovoruru, by representing stupid and clever twin brothers, bring us closer to the Greek pair from a different angle, as does the analogous pairing, again from Ainu legend,[48] of Penanpe ('he who lives in the upper reaches of a river') and Pananpe ('he who lives in the lower reaches of a river'). In the relevant story, Penanpe gives to a crow which has requested salmon soup the biggest salmon he has caught and he carefully washes it first. He is therefore rewarded by the Crow God, who bestows on Penanpe's puppy the ability to drop gold coins. The dirty Pananpe, by contrast, grudgingly gives the smallest and dirtiest salmon he has caught. His puppy, consequently, drops piles of dung which befoul its owner.[49]

We must therefore ask whether Prometheus or Epimetheus can plausibly be presented as having at some stage of their development played the role of 'twin culture-heroes'. In the case of Prometheus the situation is clear: no character in Greek literature has a stronger claim:[50] note in particular *Prometheus Bound* 442 ff.[51] It has been

[47] For the phenomenon of twins or two brothers personifying qualities that produce antithesis or polarization cf. Max Luthi in *EM* s.v. 'Bruder, Brüder' (ii. 845 (1)), Ward on 'dualism', Watts (1963), especially pp. 47 ff. on 'the primordial pair' and 113 ff. on 'the two brothers', etc.

[48] For a general introduction to Ainu folk tales see the article s.v. 'Japan' by T. Ozawa in *EM* (vii. 480 ff.).

[49] For an English translation of this story see Kayano (1985), 26 ff. Dr Y. Sano, Tokyo, kindly procured me this reference from Professor Tomomi Sato, Ainu specialist at Hokkaido University.

[50] See especially Kleingünther (1933), 66 ff. on Prometheus 'der Kulturbringer'. Cf. Thraede, *RfAC* v. 1198–9, West (1997), 581–2 etc.

[51] Growing scepticism over Aeschylean authorship (e.g. West (1990), 51 ff.) might be thought relevant: if Prometheus' role of culture hero was invented by the play's author (so Wilamowitz (1914), 132: cf. Kleingünther (1933), 132, West (1997), 581

suggested that the name and therefore the function of Epimetheus is a later invention, artificially designed to contrast with that of Prometheus.[52] But the above-mentioned ubiquity of twin culture heroes who embody a dualistic polarity,[53] and in particular the widely attested principle of expressing this polarity through the brothers' nomenclature, sometimes in its prefix, seem to tell against this idea.

etc.) and that author is not Aeschylus, the possibility of influence from contemporary sophistic theories of culture arises. But the primeval nature of contrasting twin brothers as culture heroes supports an earlier date for the status of the Greek pair.

[52] Another pair of contrasting brothers that is relevant to Hesiod's poetry can be found in the *Works and Days* and comprises Hesiod himself and Perses. Walcot (1966), 98–9 has ingeniously suggested that a version of the folk-tale brothers Good and Bad (cf. n. 47 above) preserved in a Hurraian narrative may have influenced the poem.

[53] See n. 47 above.

6

The *Homeric Hymn to Hermes*

N. J. Richardson

In his very useful Loeb edition of the Homeric Hymns Martin West gives a verdict on the longer *Hymn to Hermes* (No. 4): 'Of all the earlier Greek hexameter poems, it is without doubt the most amusing'. He then goes on to qualify this praise: 'It is also the most untraditional in its language, with many late words and expressions, and many used in slapdash and inaccurate ways; and it is the most incompetent in construction, with many narrative inconsistencies and redundancies and no command of the even tempo appropriate to epic storytelling' (West (2003*b*), 12).

It is true that modern readers have found the hymn difficult to understand at various points, and there are places where we are not sure what is the correct reading of the text, or whether some lines have been lost. Some scholars in the past have argued that the last episode, in which Apollo gives Hermes the patronage over a minor prophetic cult near Delphi, is an addition to the poem's original composition. Sometimes there are elements in the narrative which seem at first sight inconsequential: for example, the mysterious old farmer whom Hermes meets as he is driving Apollo's cattle through Onchestus, and who later informs Apollo about this (87–93, 185–212). In another version the old man is called Battos (perhaps 'Blabberer'), and is punished by Hermes for betraying him, by being

It is a great pleasure to offer this article to my former supervisor, whose work has set so high a standard for us all. I should like to thank my fellow editors and also Oliver Thomas for their most helpful comments.

turned to stone: the story is an *aition* for a place called *Βάττου σκοπιαί* (cf. Hes. fr. 256 M–W, Ov. *Met.* 2.685–707, Antoninus Liberalis 23). It has been argued that this version predates the hymn, and that this would give more point to the story of the old man. On the other hand, it may well be later (so Holland (1926)), and the old man does in fact have a function. Not only does he give Apollo information, but also in the later trial scene before Zeus, where Apollo accuses Hermes of the theft, he is mentioned as the only witness to the crime (354–5), and this evidence counterbalances Hermes' argument from probability (265–73, 376–7).

In spite of such uncertainties, however, the main lines of the narrative are clear enough, as can be seen from the brief summary which West gives (2003*b*, 13). On the day of his birth Hermes leaves his cradle, finds a tortoise, and makes its shell into the first lyre, with which he sings of his own birth. He then steals fifty of Apollo's cattle and takes them to the river Alpheios, ingeniously disguising his tracks and driving them backwards. He slaughters and roasts two of them, and then returns to his cradle the same night. Apollo tracks him down and takes him off to be judged by Zeus, who orders them to be reconciled. Hermes gives back the cattle, and his music and song enchant Apollo, who is given the lyre by his younger brother. Hermes receives a share in Apollo's pastoral role, and various other functions and attributes, and the two brothers remain close friends thereafter.

Closer analysis reveals that the central theme, Hermes' cattle theft, is framed by the two episodes of the invention of the lyre, and his appeasement of Apollo by its music and gift of the instrument to him. Both include songs by Hermes, about his own birth (54–61), and the origin of the gods in general (424–33). Both of these evoke comparison with songs of young men at feasts (55–6, 453–4). This simple structure is complicated by the last episode, concerning the arts of prophecy (526–68), which looks like an addition. But, as we shall see, the themes of music and prophecy are closely interlinked.

Further elements of balance and parallelism can be identified: for example, between the two journeys of Hermes with the cattle, and Apollo in search of them; the two episodes at Onchestos (87–93, 185–212); the episodes at the river Alpheios (99–141, 397–416); and the two 'defence speeches' of Hermes to Apollo and Zeus

(260–81, 366–90). This kind of parallelism is not untypical of early Greek narrative technique in general (cf. for example Fenik (1974), 133–232).

Thus we have a narrative whose main storyline is well defined, but whose language and episodes are sometimes difficult to follow, or to interpret in detail. Many words, expressions or motifs seem untypical in terms of the early epic tradition. As a result, some scholars have even dated the hymn as late as the fifth century BC (cf. especially Görgemanns (1976), 113–28). At the same time, West's initial verdict on this hymn as 'without doubt the most amusing' of early hexameter poems would find general support. The story itself inspired Sophocles to write his satyr play *Ichneutai*, and Shelley was so delighted by the hymn that he made a fine verse translation of it.[1]

The resolution of this question of the poem's quality lies in its essentially comic character (cf. Radermacher (1931), 216–17, Janko (1982), 148–9). Down to the fifth century BC, types of poetry which might be broadly classified as comic tend to use a different register of style and language and follow different narrative conventions from more serious forms. The language is closer to contemporary or everyday speech, the characters are more like ordinary people (though sometimes exaggerated or caricatured), and plot construction (for example in Attic comedy) is much looser and more episodic. All of these features can be seen in the *Hymn to Hermes*. The supposed lateness of the language may be explicable in these terms. We do not have much evidence otherwise of more colloquial language from the archaic period, by which to assess this. What strikes one also about the hymn is the humanization of the two main gods, Hermes and Apollo. Hermes, it is true, performs supernatural exploits, given that he has only just been born. But much of the narrative of these is told in a human way, with the details of the making of the lyre, disguising his tracks, and so on. Of course in Homeric epic the society of the gods is generally portrayed in human terms, but this hymn goes further in this respect. It is significant that

[1] On the relationship of the *Ichneutai* to our hymn cf. Koettgen (1914) and Radermacher (1931), 183–4, 216. Steffen (1960), 9 expresses doubts about Sophocles' use of the hymn, but this is surely unjustified. For Shelley's admiration cf. Richardson (2003), xxvi and xxxiv n. 14.

neither Hermes nor Apollo is explicitly said to adopt any form of human disguise when meeting the old farmer (the only mortal character in the poem), as gods normally do both in the Homeric poems and in the other hymns.

Most striking of all is the way in which Apollo himself is cut down to size, and made to look ridiculous. He is baffled by Hermes' tricks, asks for information from the old man, and needs the help of a bird omen (213–14) to track him down, in spite of his supposed omniscience (of which Hermes later reminds him several times: 467, 474, 489). In a similar way in Pindar's *Ninth Pythian* Cheiron has to remind Apollo that he is omniscient, when he asks him for advice and information. A good deal is made of the theme of Apollo's acquisitiveness or greed for wealth, something about which he is himself sensitive to criticism (cf. 176–81, 330 and 335, 494–5, 546–9).

Above all, instead of being the god of the *kitharis*, who claims this as his own attribute after his birth in the *Hymn to Apollo* (131–2), he evidently knows nothing of such stringed instruments until introduced by Hermes to the lyre (cf. especially 450–5). The instrument which Hermes invents, the tortoise-shell lyre, is actually only once (423) called λύρη (unless the word occurred in a lacuna after 415, or in 418), whereas it is frequently equated with the κίθαρις or φόρμιγξ (cf. 64, 506, 509, 515, and (ἐγ)κιθαρίζειν at 17, 423, etc.). The tortoise-shell λύρη, first mentioned by Archilochus (fr. 93a.5 *IEG*), is considered by modern scholars to have been a smaller and lighter instrument than either of these, used by amateur musicians, as opposed to professionals. Yet in the hymn it is equated with the traditional instrument (or instruments) used to accompany epic song.[2] Moreover, although the subject matter of Hermes' own songs is that of traditional hymnic poetry, his own parentage and birth and the origin of all the gods (57–61, 427–33), their style is compared to that of the mocking songs of young men at feasts (cf. 55–6 and 453–4), a quite different type of poetry. This new music strikes Apollo as wonderfully original and somehow superior. Apollo also asks Hermes whether he was born with this skill, or learnt it from a god *or*

[2] This equation occurs in some other poets of the sixth and fifth centuries BC: cf. West (1992), 50–1. On the identity and uses of these various instruments see West (1992), 48–57, and Maas and Snyder (1989).

a mortal (440–2), an odd question to ask of a god. Hermes himself honours Mnemosyne, mother of the Muses, first of the gods, because she is his patron (429–30), which might even seem to put him on a higher plane than Apollo, who calls himself a companion (ὀπηδός) of her daughters, the Muses (450).

It is no coincidence that the story told in the hymn should have been the inspiration for a satyr play, the *Ichneutai.* Not only the comic theme, and the irreverent treatment of the gods, but also the inventiveness of Hermes, and the rustic setting, make it ideal for such treatment.[3]

It is surely also significant that this hymn is the only one in which we find an element of coarser humour typical of comic poetry. When Apollo picks up Hermes after accusing him of the theft he 'emitted an omen, an insolent servant of the belly, an unruly messenger' (295–6): in other words, a fart. (In theory, it could also refer to a burp, but this seems less probable.) The unusual language is elevated and riddling, in a mock-epic manner. In Aristophanes' *Clouds* (392–4) a fart is seen as a parody of the thunder of Zeus, and it is also comically treated as an omen in the *Knights* (638–42). Another parallel from Attic comedy is Eubulus fr. 106.1–10 *PCG*, where οἰκείων ἀνέμων ταμίας in a riddle is interpreted as πρωκτός.[4]

The relationship of the two brothers Apollo and Hermes is portrayed in a complex way. In some respects they are diametrically contrasted, in others (especially after their reconciliation) they closely resemble each other. The trickster Hermes is the archetypal 'baby brother' who undermines the seriousness of his much older sibling. Apollo is a god of light who operates in the daytime, whereas Hermes is a god of darkness and the night (cf. also Garvie (1986) on Aesch. *Cho.* 727–8, Sier (1988), 260–2, on Aesch. *Cho.* 816–18). He is also 'empowered as envoy to Hades' (572–3). Apollo is concerned with truth and justice, Hermes is a god of deception and 'prince of thieves' (292; cf. also Finglass (2007) on Soph. *El.* 1395–6). Apollo's speeches, when addressed to other gods, are straightforward and direct (cf. especially 334–64), whereas Hermes is the master of rhetorical tricks and persuasive falsehoods (260–80, 366–90). At the same

[3] On inventions as a feature of satyr drama cf. Seaford (1984), 36–7.
[4] On Hermes' fart and Attic comedy see also Bain's paper in this volume, pp. 51–2.

time, both are concerned with amassing wealth, and patrons of flocks and herds (and in Hermes' case, wild and tame animals in general (567–71); for Apollo as protector of flocks see Finglass (2007) on Soph. *El.* 6–7). Both are gods of music, and Hermes will receive from Apollo a minor share in divination as well. Both perform exploits immediately they are born, although Hermes' mercurial rapidity outdoes that of Apollo, as described in the *Hymn to Apollo* (127–39), where this god simply breaks the bonds which hold him, and begins to walk on the earth.

As musicians they complement each other. Hermes' style is mocking, light-hearted, more suited to the symposium and improvisatory amoebean song (54–6, 454), even when he is singing hymnic or theogonic songs, in contrast to the grander, public, and choral types of music which are described in the *Hymn to Apollo.* When Hermes first encounters the tortoise, he greets him with the words

> *χαῖρε, φυὴν ἐρόεσσα, χοροιτύπε δαιτὸς ἑταίρη,*
> *ἀσπασίη προφανεῖσα* (31–2)

> 'Hello, my lovely, my dance-beat dinner companion,
> welcome apparition!' (West's translation).

The language suggests comparison with a dancing girl (or *hetaira*). Later, when Hermes plays to Apollo, the language is again that of erotic love and desire (421–3 *ἐρατὴ δὲ διὰ φρένας ἤλυθ' ἰωή . . . καί μιν γλυκὺς ἵμερος ᾕρει . . . λύρῃ δ' ἐρατὸν κιθαρίζων . . .* 426 *ἐρατὴ δέ οἱ ἕσπετο φωνή*). Its effect on Apollo is described in the same way:

> *τὸν δ' ἔρος ἐν στήθεσσιν ἀμήχανος αἴνυτο θυμόν* (434)

and

> *ἀτρεκέως γὰρ ἅμα τρία πάντα πάρεστιν,*
> *εὐφροσύνην καὶ ἔρωτα καὶ ἥδυμον ὕπνον ἑλέσθαι* (448–9).

The idea of the *hetaira* is elaborated by Hermes (475–88). As West translates: 'Be a fine musician, fondling this clear-voiced girlfriend who knows how to talk fine and fittingly. Take her confidently to the banquet and the lovely dance and the bumptious revel, a source of good cheer day and night. If one questions her with skill and expertise, she speaks all kinds of lessons to charm the fancy, easily tickled with tender familiarity, avoiding tiresome effort. But if a novice questions her roughly, then she will utter useless, discordant rubbish'.

The Greek plays on words with both musical and erotic connotations: cf. especially 485–6

> ῥεῖα συνηθείῃσιν ἀθυρομένη μαλακῇσιν,
> ἐργασίην φεύγουσα δυήπαθον

where *συνηθεία* can mean 'intimacy' or 'intercourse', but is used of musical practice by Plato (*Leg.* 656d); *μαλακός* can be applied to musical harmony or pitch (LSJ s.v. III 2e); *ἀθύρειν* is used of music or song (*Hymn* 19.15, *Anacreontea* 41.11); and *ἐργασίη* can be applied to the trade of a courtesan (Hdt. 2.135.1, Dem. 18.129) or to sexual intercourse (Arist. *Problemata* 876^{a}39).

The emphasis on the ways in which the lyre responds to questioning well or badly, depending on how she is treated, is echoed in the final episode, on the theme of prophecy. Apollo describes how he will give helpful responses to those who come with divine favour, whereas others will have a wasted journey (541–9). The same theme recurs with the 'bee maidens', whose utterances can be truthful or deceptive, and who must be questioned accurately by Hermes for his own pleasure (558–66).

In this respect, music and prophecy resemble each other, and Apollo too, like Hermes, can lead mortals astray by his ambiguities. The ending of the hymn also, in a way, rehabilitates Apollo, restoring his proper dignity and status as the oracular god *par excellence*: not even Hermes can take this from him, as he alone can have full access to the mind of Zeus (533–40). The final section is thus on a more serious level than the rest of the poem, and the restoration of Apollo's status adds dignity to his brother by association (cf. Schwabl (1986), 154–6).

In the background to this review of the portrayal of Hermes and Apollo in the hymn is the more difficult question of whether there is a direct relationship to the *Hymn to Apollo*. Was the *Hymn to Hermes* composed with this poem in mind? One clue may possibly lie in the surprising introduction of Onchestos (in Boeotia) as the place where Hermes meets the farmer, since this is again singled out for special attention on Apollo's journey from Pieria in search of a site for his oracle, in the *Hymn to Apollo* (230–8). In the other version of the story of the old man, the encounter with Hermes takes place in Arcadia. If Hermes is travelling towards the Alpheios river in Elis, there is no obvious reason why Onchestos should be chosen as a landmark. It is described as λεχεποίη (88), and this epithet was also used at *H. Ap.* 224 of Teumessos, just before the passage about Onchestos. The epithet otherwise only recurs twice in Homer (*Il.* 2.697, 4.383); note also ποιήεντος of Onchestos at *H. Herm.* 190, used at *H. Ap.* 243. These are tenuous clues, but it is possible that our poet chose this place through association with the *Hymn to Apollo* (cf. Dornseiff (1938), 82, Janko (1982), 148–9, Schwabl (1986), 155–6).

There are other points of a more general kind which could suggest a relationship between the two poems.[5] The rapidity of Hermes' exploits after his birth might be viewed as 'upstaging' Apollo in his own hymn. After his appearance Apollo claims the *kitharis*, the bow, and the art of prophecy (131–2). In the *Hymn to Hermes*, it is Hermes who creates the lyre, and Apollo fears that he may also rob him of his bow, as well as stealing back the *kitharis* (514–15). Moreover he explicitly tells Hermes that he cannot lay claim to his own skill in prophecy (533–40). The more awe-inspiring aspects of Apollo's character in his hymn are deflated by Hermes: of course, in this respect the author of the *Hymn to Hermes* could have in mind the general portrayal of Apollo in the early Greek tradition, where, in contrast to Ares, Aphrodite, and Hephaestus, and even Zeus and Hera, he is almost always seen as a serious and imposing deity.

This question also raises the issue of the relative dating of these two hymns. West dates the *Hymn to Apollo* in its present form to 523 BC and regards *Hermes* as 'the latest of the major Hymns' (2003*b*, 11–12, 14). Not everyone will accept such a late dating for both works, and this question is notoriously hard to resolve. It does, however, seem reasonable to assume that the *Hymn to Apollo* (whose fame is attested already in the late fifth century by Thucydides, 3.104) was the earlier of the two poems, and that its prestige was such that it

[5] For earlier discussion of possible points of contact cf. Radermacher (1931), 110–11, 229, Dornseiff (1938), 81–3, Janko (1982), 127–8, 148–9, and Schwabl (1986), 154–6.

would have been familiar to the author of the *Hymn to Hermes*. In that case, it makes good sense to view the second of the two hymns as deliberately conceived to form a light-hearted, or even parodic, response to the grandeur and seriousness of the first.

Part II

Lyric, Elegiac, Iambic

7

Night Thoughts (Archilochus 23 and 196a West)

Eric Handley

Fragment 23 *IEG* of Archilochus is the end of an iambic poem preserved in P.Oxy. 2310 (vol. 22, 1954), first edited by Mr Edgar Lobel. From where it becomes comprehensible, at the end of line 7 of the surviving text, the speaker of the verses, ostensibly the poet representing himself, gives his reply to a woman whose words he has just finished quoting. He sets out to turn aside the bad things that she has heard people say. I am not (he then asserts) the feeble wretch you seem to take me for, but a man of some standing, capable alike of being friendly to my friends and unrelentingly active against my enemies. Finally, in a passage with a figurative force that has been well recognized, he presents himself as a city previously inviolate, but now captured and ready to be ruled by the woman in a dominance that many will envy.

The lines that concern us are those with which the speaker begins:

> . . . ἠ̣μειβόμ[ην·
> "γ̣ύνα[ι], φάτιν μὲν τὴν π̣ρ̣ὸς ἀνθρώπω̣[ν κακὴν
> μὴ τετραμήνηις μηδ̣έν· ἀμφὶ δ' εὐφ̣[ρόνηι
> ἐμοὶ μελήσει· [θ]υμὸν ἴλ[α]ον τίθεο . . ."

I am grateful for comments to Pat Easterling and Neil Hopkinson; and also to the Editors for (among other things) the reference to Housman (1888). A new discussion of Archilochus 23 *IEG* by Ewen Bowie is to appear in the Acta of the Conference held in Paros in October 2005.

Lobel stopped short of restoring 9, remarking in a note that *μέλει . . . ἀμφί* is unattested; Martin West (1974*a*), 119 sees no credible alternative to *εὐφ[ρόνηι*, unless it is the genitive or the accusative of the same noun: the meaning is (he says) 'And as for a (or the) night, I will take care of the matter'. Near enough, one might think, if there were doubts about *ἀμφί*, would be the *μέριμνα δ' ἀμφὶ πτόλιν* of Aesch. *Sept.* 843. None the less, as it stands, interjected between 'Have no fear' and 'Be kind to me' (or however we translate *ἵλαος*) such a reference to the (or a) night lacks context, and could only be intelligible to the person addressed, or to the poet's intended audience, if something had been said about it earlier. So it could have been; but a demonstrative or some other form of reference back would be helpful to verify the hypothesis. One can recall the man in Menander who said *σιωπᾶν βούλομαι τὴν νύκτα τὴν πολλῶν κακῶν ἀρχηγόν* (*Plokion* 296 *PCG*), 'The night that initiated so much trouble, I'd rather not talk about it': he, however, is speaking, and known to be speaking, as an unhappy husband.

Accordingly, there is some encouragement to look in other directions. One such is to take *εὐφρόνη* in the sense of *εὐφροσύνη*, even though the shorter form appears to be firmly established in its sense of 'night' (the kindly time) since Hesiod (*Op.* 560); there is some relevant discussion in an early paper by Housman ((1888) = (1972), i. 24–8), on which see Diggle, this volume. Alternatively, one can aim for a similar effect by restoring *εὔφ̣[ρονα* (Lasserre, in Lasserre and Bonnard (1958)) or another form of *εὔφρων* (perhaps *εὔφ̣ρ̣[*– can be read). The result seems odd in the context: thus, as translated by Anne Pippin Burnett (1983, 70) 'Madame, do not let this vulgar calumny distress you. Pleasure is my care so make your heart propitious. . .'; or by Bonnard, op. cit., 'Femme, les méchants propos des gens n'ont pas à te faire frissoner! Pour ma part, je ne veux retenir que ceux propres à me réjouir . . .'. In terms of rhetoric, this is hardly a winning preface to the claim that he is a man of standing with a firm attitude to friend and enemy alike.

Nearer the mark, Wolfgang Luppe (1995), 21–2 accepts the reference to night, and proposes that *ἀμφὶ εὐφρόνην* in the sense of 'overnight', 'during the night', or something similar, should go with *θυμὸν ἵλαον τίθεο*, the *ἐμοὶ μελήσει* being in parenthesis: thus 'die Nacht über—daran ist mir gelegen—mach gnädig deinen Sinn'. Parallels for ἀμφί in a temporal sense look good enough to make one wonder why such an interpretation was not considered from the first. It will perhaps do to mention Pind. *Ol.* 1.97 λοιπὸν ἀμφὶ βίοτον 'lifelong', like *Ol.* 2.30, τὸν ὅλον ἀμφὶ χρόνον; and of a more precise time, Xen. *Cyr.* 5.4.16 ἀμφὶ δείλην 'at evening', and similarly ἤδη ἀμφὶ ἡλίου δυσμὰς ἦν, *Anab.* 6.4.26; while for the dative we have Pindar again, with ἁλίωι ἀμφ' ἑνί 'in the course of a day' at *Ol.* 13.37. There is more in S–D ii. 439. Accordingly, one needs to ask whether the phrase ἀμφὶ δ' εὐφρόνηι (or -ην), if that is what Archilochus wrote, would need to be detached from ἐμοὶ μελήσει at all: could it not have meant 'I'll think about it overnight'? It would be tempting to be led to this straight away by the English colloquial idiom 'I'll think about it', with its interesting double significance, if it were not for another disputed passage of Archilochus which offers similar problems and may be open to a common solution.

In the Cologne Epode (196a *IEG*), first published by Merkelbach and West (1974), we again have the latter part of a conversation between the speaker, ostensibly the poet, and a woman on whom, after an initial rebuff, he is once again exercising his arts of persuasion. In reply to his advances, she reminds him that there is someone else at home that he should think of. There are, he replies, pleasures of Aphrodite that we can enjoy other than the supreme one . . . and this he proceeds to demonstrate, in what we might call coldly an act of non-penetrative intercourse, claiming that he is going to do as she asks him (i.e. set aside for now his total passion), and at the same time disparaging the girl at home. She is named as Neoboule, a woman not unknown to him (or as it was to prove, to posterity), who is presented here in the role, as it seems to be, of an elder sister in whom he professes no further interest. Lines 9–13 (13–19 *IEG*) read as follows:

τ]έρψιές εἰσι θεῆς πολλαὶ νέοισιν ἀνδ[ράσιν
παρὲξ τὸ θεῖον χρῆμα· τῶν τις ἀρκέσε[ι.
τ]αῦτα δ' ἐφ' ἡσυχίης εὖτ' ἂν μελανθη[
ἐ]γώ τε καὶ σὺ σὺν θεῶι βουλεύσομεν·
π]είσομαι ὥς με κέλεαι . . .

It is common ground that ταῦτα in 11 refers back to the earlier stages of the discussion, now largely lost, in which there was talk of a full and thence a lasting union: 'All that we will consider in peace and quiet, you and I, when . . .'. The suggestions for completing line 11 are remarkably diverse. So much appears from the discussion by Slings in Bremer *et al.* (1987), 37, and see some remarks by Günther (1996*b*), 64 n. 24: examples are μελανθῆ[ι μοι γένυς 'when my cheeks are bearded', or μελανθῆ[ι σοι τρύγη 'when your grape grows dark'. Both these afflict the argument with a certain lack of immediacy; and the man in particular has no interest in representing himself as immature, never mind the girl. What seems clear is that, as in fr. 23, major issues are being set aside in favour of a more immediate persuasion; and no one who has persisted this far with this discussion will be surprised if it turns to 'night' as the essential missing word, whether in the form of νύξ with another word (so νύξ, ὁμοῦ, *exempli gratia*, Page in *SLG*), or εὐφρόνη preceded by γ', as proposed, though not printed, in Degani and Burzacchini (1977), 14. In either case, the metrical pattern resulting would be anomalous in the early iambic writers as so far known (see Slings, quoted above), but not, I think, impossible to contemplate. Podlecki (1984), 48, translates as 'We shall take thought of this at our leisure, when it is dark, with God's help'. εὖτ' ἂν is just 'when', as in fr. 3.2; one could consider οὐρανός for εὐφρόνη, if there were any great advantage in doing so.

Thinking things over in peace and quiet, and thinking overnight are related concepts that can be spoken of in Greek idiomatically and with full sincerity. So at Thucydides 1.85.1, as mentioned by Degani and Burzacchini (above), the Spartan king Archidamus argues for caution: μηδὲ ἐπειχθέντες ἐν βραχεῖ μορίωι ἡμέρας . . . βουλεύσωμεν, ἀλλὰ καθ' ἡσυχίαν; at Herodotus 7.12, Xerxes has night thoughts, νυκτὶ δὲ βουλὴν διδούς, in the course of deciding whether or not to invade Greece. The notion of night thoughts, which this discussion is seeking to establish in the two passages of Archilochus, is encapsulated in proverbial form in the phrase ἐν νυκτὶ βουλή, amply documented in the lexica and the paroemiographers, from whom it may be sufficient to refer to Zenobius iii. 97 (*CPG* i. 82) and to quote the *Etymologicum Gudianum* (ii. 567 De Stefani, s.v. εὐφρόνη), where the passage of Menander that we at present know as *Epitrepontes* 252–3 is taken as a type example. The entry reads ἡ νύξ· παρὰ τὸ εὖ φρονεῖν ἐν αὐτῆι, ὡς Μένανδρος, ἐν νυκτὶ βουλήν, ὅπερ ἅπασι γίνεται, διδοὺς *ἐμαυτῶι*; commentators quote variations on the theme, including Phocylides 8, *νυκτὸς βουλεύειν, νυκτὸς δέ τοι ὀξυτέρη φρὴν* | *ἀνδράσιν· ἡσυχίη δ' ἀρετὴν διζημένωι ἐσθλή*.

Archilochus is by no means alone in playing variations on common *topoi*. One can think at once of 25 *IEG*, a trimeter poem that takes off from the Homeric tag *ἄλλος γάρ τ' ἄλλοισιν ἀνὴρ ἐπιτέρπεται ἔργοις* (*Od.* 14.228); as the scholiast ad loc. remarks, *τοῦτο Ἀρχίλοχος μεταφράσεως* <*ἠξίωσεν*>*· ἀλλ' ἄλλος ἄλλωι καρδίαν ἰαίνεται*; and Euripides duly followed with a line in his *Oeneus* (fr. 560 *TrGF*) *ἀλλ' ἄλλος ἄλλοις μᾶλλον ἥδεται τρόποις*. What matters so often in the case of such echoes is not just the fact but the flavour given by the echo in its new context; and context, in dealing with fragments, is what we so often lack, with as much loss to our understanding in Archilochus, one might suspect, as anywhere else.

What this discussion suggests is that in picking up the common topic of night thoughts, Archilochus is able to let the context (that is, speaker and occasion) give colour to the phraseology. It is intended to sound hollow, not to the person being addressed, but to the poem's audience—to reinforce, in other words, the compound reaction of disapproval and somewhat sneaking admiration one is liable to feel when witnessing a smooth talker at work. In our passages of Archilochus, such a suggestion, for lack of a fuller context, can only remain speculative, acceptable, perhaps, in a celebratory volume rather than in a learned editor's annotations.

To show the direction of the speculation, here are two passages of comedy where the context (partly because they are in comedy) is clearer as well as fuller, and where the speaker of an ordinarily straightforward expression undercuts himself with the audience in using it. Aristophanes, *Lysistrata*, Kinesias and Myrrhine: at the peak of the sequence of sexual teasing, 949: 'I will,' says Myrrhine, 'really truly I will—just undoing this; but, darling, do be sure to vote for peace'. Kinesias: *βουλεύσομαι* 'I'll think about it'. Then Menander, *Dyskolos* 129 ff., typically, something calling for a smile rather than a laugh. The audience knows, from the dramatic type he represents and his behaviour so far, that the young hero's boon companion Chaireas is likely to be much less effective in helping along the love affair than his pretensions suggest. 'Rather a sharp customer, your peasant farmer,' he says, 'not just him, pretty well all of them. I'll go, just me alone, and see him first thing in the morning', *ἕωθεν αὔριον*. Coming from him, in that situation, we all know what that means: he is opting out. As if we didn't, young Sostratos' reaction 'Glad of an excuse, he was' (135–6) makes quite sure that we do.

8

A Human Fable and the Justice of Beasts in Archilochus

Paula da Cunha Corrêa

The following notes are on fragments (174 and 177 *IEG*) belonging to one of the most important and well-known epodes of Archilochus (172–81), in which 'The Fable of the Fox and the Eagle' is narrated. They are extracts from a larger study in which all fragments of Archilochus that contain fables and animal metaphors will be examined, with an emphasis on the particular *ethos* of each animal.[1]

1. A HUMAN FABLE (174 *IEG*)

Verses of two of Archilochus' epodes (174 and 185 *IEG*) that narrate fables, respectively 'The Fox and the Eagle' and 'The Fox and the Monkey', are quoted by [Ammonius] in order to exemplify the differences between *ainos* and proverb. However, owing to the nature of

[1] I am most obliged to Martin West, who supervised my MA dissertation on *Harmonia* and *Nomoi* (RHBNC, University of London 1987), co-supervised my thesis on Archilochus' war poems (1995) and read my postdoctoral research on Archilochus' epodes and erotic poems (2000), for his very helpful comments on my work throughout these years. I am especially grateful to Martin and Stephanie for their friendly hospitality and for facilitating my stays in Oxford. I also thank Patrick Finglass, Nicholas Richardson, and Christopher Collard for their suggestions on this paper. The investigation of the ἤθη of the two animals in this fable, the fox and the eagle, not included in this paper, has been developed in a larger study on Archilochus' epodes (forthcoming).

what has been collected in ancient anthologies of proverbs and fables, this distinction remains, to this date, controversial. For example, Sumerian scribes of the second millennium BC and their Assyrian successors (8th–7th centuries BC) frequently included under the category of 'proverbs' narratives which we would call 'fables'. Gordon (1958), 2 notes that in *Collection IV* of Sumerian proverbs and fables, four proverbs are classified as 'fables, parables or anecdotes', and that 38 of the 125 so-called 'animal proverbs' contained in *Collection V* are in fact very similar to the fables of Aesop.

Unfortunately, [Ammonius] (*De adfin. vocab. diff.* 18, p. 5 Nickau) quotes only the very beginning of Archilochus' epode:[2]

αἶνος καὶ παροιμία διαφέρει. ὁ μὲν γὰρ αἶνός ἐστι λόγος κατ' ἀναπόλησιν μυθικὴν ἀπὸ ἀλόγων ζῴων ἢ φυτῶν πρὸς ἀνθρώπους εἰρημένος, ὥς φησι Λούκιος Ταρραῖος ἐν τῷ πρώτῳ περὶ παροιμιῶν· οἷον ἀπὸ μὲν ἀλόγων ζῴων ὡς παρ' Ἀρχιλόχῳ,

174 *IEG* *αἶνός τις ἀνθρώπων ὅδε,*
ὡς ἆρ' ἀλώπηξ καἰετὸς ξυνεωνίην
ἔμειξαν,

Fable and proverb differ. For the fable is a mythical story told by animals or plants to men, as says Lucius of Tarrha in his first book *On Proverbs*. As, for example, a [fable] of animals in Archilochus (174 *IEG*): 'This is a fable of men: how a fox and an eagle joined in partnership.'[3]

In spite of their textual divergences, the majority of editors agree that these verses introduced a version of 'The Fable of the Fox and the Eagle' (Aesop 1 Perry):

An eagle and a fox became friends and decided to live near each other to strengthen their friendship by cohabitation. Thus, as one flying up in a very high tree made her nest, the other, going into the underlying shrubbery, gave

[2] This is a work of Herennius, the Greek grammarian and historian from Biblos (1st–2nd c. AD). Cf. also *Et. Gud.* i. 48.15–19 De Stefani, Herennius Philo 32 (Palmieri 174–81), Eusthathius in Hom. *Od.* 1768.62 (= ii. 83.45–6 Stallbaum), *Σ* Hom. *Od.* 14.508 (ii. 600.12–14 Dindorf); *An. Par.* iii. 371.13 Cramer, Choeroboscus iii. 114.25–31 Gaisford, Diogenianus *Praefatio* (*CPG* i. 178.6–12), Apostolius *praefatio* (*CPG* ii. 236.2–5). Apoll. Dysc. ii. 1.224.3 Schneider and Uhlig quotes only the second verse.

[3] All translations are mine, unless otherwise stated.

birth. One day, when the fox went out for pasturage, the eagle, in lack of provisions, flew down into the shrubbery, snatched the cubs and then, along with her own offspring, feasted on them. When the fox, on her return, realized what had happened, she was more distressed by the difficulty of avenging herself than with the death of her young; for as a land animal, she was incapable of pursuing a winged one. Therefore, standing apart, she cursed her enemy—the only alternative left for the powerless and weak. But soon the eagle happened to pay the penalty for her impiety with regards to friendship. For when a goat was sacrificed in the country, she flew down and took from the altar a burning entrail. When this had been taken to the nest, a strong wind kindled a bright flame from a thin and old straw. Therefore, the eagle's offspring were burnt, since they were not yet fully fledged. They fell to the ground and the fox, running up to them, devoured them all within the eagle's sight.

The fable shows that those who break a vow of friendship, even if they escape the punishment by the hands of the wronged who are weak, certainly do not escape god's vengeance.

Although this text is late, written probably between the first and third centuries AD, Aristophanes (*Av.* 652–4) identified this fable as being Aesopic as early as the fifth century BC. A scholium on this passage notes, however, the existence of an earlier version of the fable in Archilochus. Therefore, either Aristophanes did not know Archilochus' epode—a difficult hypothesis, owing to the number of references and quotations of Archilochus' verses in Aristophanic comedy, besides the fact that this epode, in particular, was well known by later authors—or Aristophanes does what became a common practice in the Classical and Hellenistic periods: any Greek fable, regardless of its origins or earlier versions, is attributed to Aesop.

Both fragments quoted by [Ammonius] (174 and 185 *IEG*) announce the beginning of an *αἶνος* by means of a formulaic expression.[4] The narrator of fragment 185 *IEG* says he will tell Cerycides and others an *αἶνος*. In this epode, however, the narrator declares more impersonally 'this is a fable of men' (174 *IEG*).[5] What can this mean?

Although some fables have human beings, seasons, and gods as

[4] Cf. Van Dijk (1997), 140 for the formular *incipit* of fables.

[5] 174.1 *IEG*: the single divergent text is that of Brunck (1772), *αἶνός τις ἔστ᾽ ἀρχαῖος ἀνθρώπων ὅδε*. Diehl (1926) quotes an imitation in Moschio (*TrGF* i. 97 F 8.1): *ἦν ἆρα τρανὸς αἶνος ἀνθρώπων ὅδε* . . .

characters, according to [Ammonius] (*De adfin. vocab. diff.* 18, p. 5 Nickau), it is more typical of the genre to present 'animals and plants'. With this verse, however, Archilochus creates an amusing ambiguity, since 'a fable of men' can be either one that men tell (subjective genitive), or one that is *about* men (objective genitive). According to the latter reading, the poet relates human activities. Besides, the expression 'a fable of men' may suggest, through the comparison of humans with beasts, that the behaviour of rational and irrational beings is not very different, or it simply reminds us that the function of the *αἶνος*, as its etymology indicates, is to present human deeds through enigmas.

The other alternative is that the phrase 'a fable of men' indicates that this was a well-known fable of wide circulation, *told by men*. One interpretation along these lines, suggested by Kallós (1951–2), 68, is that Archilochus desired to make clear the distance between this *αἶνος* and other narratives that had their origins in the Muses. The poet would have heard this tale from men: it was neither his 'invention' nor the fruit of 'divine inspiration'.[6]

The suggestion that this *αἶνος* could have come from 'other sources' is interesting, because five years later, Williams (1956) compared 'The Fable of the Fox and the Eagle' of Aesop and 'The Fable of the Serpent and the Eagle' narrated in the Assyrian-Babylonian *Myth of Etana*, and Trencsényi-Waldapfel (1959) was the first[7] to draw parallels between the fable in the *Myth of Etana* and Archilochus' version of 'The Fable of the Fox and the Eagle'. As in the case of the comparisons made between *Gilgamesh* and the *Iliad*, the problem is to know how and when the Assyrian fable could have been brought to Greece.

There are three texts of the *Myth of Etana*, respectively in old Babylonian, Middle, and New Assyrian, and the oldest version dates back to the seventeenth century BC. Etana, the first king, has no heirs and therefore the sun god Shamash, who is also the god of justice, gives him the following instructions: Etana must save an eagle that has been plucked and imprisoned in a well, and care for her until she

[6] See also Nøjgaard (1984), 77, for whom Archilochus' fable has popular sources.

[7] Cf. later Baldi (1961), La Penna (1964) and Adrados (1964), among others. For the *Myth of Etana*, cf. Langdon (1931), J. V. K. Wilson (1985), Dalley (1989) and Foster (2005).

is strong enough to transport him up to the heavens in order to obtain the flower of birth. 'The Fable of the Serpent and the Eagle', which must be very ancient and, originally, independent of the myth, was inserted in this narrative to explain why the eagle is captive.

This fable tells us how once an eagle and a serpent made a pact of friendship sealed by oaths and witnessed by the god Shamash. They built their nests respectively on the top and at the foot of a tree and, in the two older versions of the fable, the serpent provided food for both families, while according to the neo-Assyrian version the eagle and the serpent went out hunting together and then divided their prey. One day, however, the eagle decided to feed her young the serpent's offspring, in spite of the warnings she received from one of her fledglings that reminded her of the vows of friendship. When the serpent, on her return, found her nest empty, she invoked Shamash, recalling the oaths sworn. Shamash heard the serpent's appeal and instructed her how to avenge her stolen young: the serpent should lie in ambush in an ox's corpse and when the eagle came for the meat, she would capture, pluck, and throw the eagle in a hole from which there was no escape. Williams (1956), 73 claims that the Akkadian fable contains no moral. However, on the contrary, the perjurers in the Akkadian fable and in that of Archilochus are both punished by gods (Zeus / Shamash) who are related to the heavens and exact justice.

Besides the 'Fox and Eagle' fable narrated in Archilochus' epode, Williams (1956) comments on the versions of the fable in Aesop (6th c. BC), Phaedrus (1st c. AD), Babrius (2nd–3rd c. AD), an Egyptian fable of a cat and vulture contained in the *Myth of the Sun's Eye* (1st–2nd c. AD), two stories from the *Pañcatantra* he believes to have been inspired by this fable,[8] the eleventh-century retranslation of Aesop into Greek (Syntipas collection), two fables contained in a medieval Armenian collection and two twelfth-century versions, one in Old French by Marie de France, and one in Hebrew by Berechiah ben Natronai han-Naqdān. Later, in 1959, Baldi indicated the existence of echoes of the *Myth of Etana* in *The Eumenides* and *Libation Bearers* of

[8] Trencsényi-Waldapfel (1959), 319 erroneously searches for influences of the *Pañcatantra* stories, which are more recent, in Archilochus.

Aeschylus, and Adrados (1964) was the first to note that the simile in the parodos (55–9) of the *Agamemnon* contains the same motif.

In Archilochus' fable (174 *IEG*), the narrator begins by telling us how the fox and eagle 'joined in partnership' (2–3).[9] The verb μείγνυμι[10] (to join, mingle) allows for a double entendre: for besides meaning to *mix* or *unite* in a bond, it is also used with reference to the meeting of adversaries at the beginning of a battle or dispute,[11] and this hostile connotation of the verb may forebode the sinister outcome of this partnership or community (ξυνεωνίη).[12]

Eagles and foxes are not enemies in nature, for eagle eggs are generally out of the fox's reach, while eagles feed rather on rodents and smaller birds than on fox cubs. However, in the Assyrian version of the fable, the two partners are the eagle and the serpent, the former being the latter's natural predator. Archilochus may have known the *Myth of Etana* by means of a paraphrase or translation of the neo-Assyrian version.[13] But in case Archilochus had this fable as his model, why would he have replaced the serpent with a fox?

Baldi (1961), 381 and Adrados (1964), 282 believe the serpent was replaced because it is a dangerous and evil creature in the fables of Greek tradition. Since animal traits are conventional, it is evident that in the process of translating a fable from one culture to another the original characters may be replaced by local ones that share the

[9] ὡς ἄρ' ἀλώπηξ κερδαλῆ τε κᾳετὸς ξυνωνίην ἔθεντο Brunck (1772), ὡς ἄρ' ἀλώπηξ κᾳετὸς ξυνωνίην ἔθεντο Liebel (1812), Gaisford (1814–20), i. 307 (fr. 38). West's text (*IEG*) is identical to that found in Fick (1888) and Hoffmann (1898).

[10] ἔθεντο in Ammonius, Herennius; ἔμιξαν in other sources. ἔμειξαν is Fick's correction (1888).

[11] *Il.* 15.510, Callinus 1.11 *IEG*, Alcaeus 330 *PLF* = Voigt, Pind. *P.* 4.213, Ar. *Ran.* 278 and Soph. *OC* 1047.

[12] Cf. Ar. *Av.* 651–3 ὡς ἐν Αἰσώπου λόγοις | ἐστὶν λεγόμενον δή τι, τὴν ἀλώπεχ' ὡς | φλαύρως ἐκοινώνησεν αἰετῷ ποτε. Manuscripts A and P (*CPG* i. 178) present the form ξυνωνίην or -αν. Fick's correction (1888) ξυνεωνίην was adopted by Hoffmann (1898) and West, *IEG*. Baldi (1961), 382 notes that there is a perfect correspondence between the terms ξυνεωνίη and 'šulmânu' in the oaths proffered respectively in the fables in Archilochus' epode and in the *Myth of Etana.*

[13] According to Burkert (1984), 112–13 ≈ (1992), 122–3, we cannot be certain Archilochus was familiar with the *Etana* text, although the chances are good, given the presence of a proverb in the Cologne papyrus fr. 196^a.39–41 *IEG* attested 1,000 years earlier in royal correspondence from Mari, and the knowledge of the Phoenician-Aramaic leather roll in 185 *IEG*.

same qualities. The Aztec version of the fables of Aesop, for instance, replaces the fox by the coyote.[14] However, one may argue that the serpent has negative traits in only three of the five fables of Aesop in which she figures and, in these cases, she is only really perverse in fable 196 and 221 Perry, for in fable 197 she is simply querulous and a natural predator. In fables 362 and 268 the serpent is neither good nor evil, and in 198 she is a victim who complains to Zeus of always being crushed under men's feet.

In other fables narrated by Babrius and Phaedrus, vipers and serpents tend to bear more negative connotations, but even these later collections do not present coherent representations of the animals. The snake is a victim of men and wasps respectively in fables 573 / 573a and 463.216 (Perry's Appendix), a predator overpowered by her adversary's ruse (Perotti's Appendix 407 in Perry), and the snake called Dipsas is not particularly wicked (515.458 Perry's Appendix). Vicious snakes and vipers figure in Babrius 143 (= Phaedrus 120), Phaedrus 18, and in fables 438.90 and 440.96 (Perry's Appendix), the more sinister connotations having become naturally prevalent with the wide spread of Christian beliefs, but perhaps not yet firmly established in archaic and classical Greece.

On the other hand, the change of animals in narratives, whether these are fables or anecdotes, is quite common and generally due to their oral transmission. One example is the case of an Assyrian anecdote written on a tablet from 716 BC, of which we have three Greek versions from the Roman period in the Augustan Collection, Babrius, and Mesomedes. For eight or nine centuries, the narrative was preserved in a perfectly recognizable form, although the characters were not always the same.[15] There are also cases in which versions of the very same fable present characters that are different but equivalent and the insignificant alterations seem fortuitous.

It is possible that Archilochus was familiar with a version of the fable in which the eagle and fox were already the main characters

[14] This is a translation, made by sixteenth-century Jesuits in Mexico, of Aesopic fables into the native language of the Aztecs: cf. Brotherson and Vollmer (1987).

[15] Diels (1910), col. 993 ff., Ebeling (1927), 49, Williams (1956), 70, Gordon (1958), 1 and West (2000), 95 quote many similar cases. See also Ebeling (1927) for the representation of animals with different traits in Sumerian fables.

(Baldi (1961), 381). Eagles were trained in ancient India to hunt foxes and rabbits, and we have evidence that such a practice was maintained at least until the 1960s in certain parts of Asia.[16] The most ancient Greek source quoted for the training of eagles for fox-hunting is Ktesias, but it is possible that this custom was older and more widespread. If Babylonians and Assyrians also used eagles in fox hunts, Archilochus might have heard an oriental version of the fable in which these two animals were the leading characters.

Another hypothesis is that Archilochus replaced the serpent by a fox in order to confer on his narrator or 'lyric I' that which, according to Philostratus, was the 'principal role' in Graeco-roman fables. For this is the same role 'he' plays in 'The Fable of the Fox and the Monkey' (185–7 *IEG*) and, most probably, in the 'Fox and Hedgehog' proverb (201 *IEG*).[17] This may have been the principal factor in the choice of a fox for the central character. And it is therefore only reasonable to agree with all those who, since Buchholtz (1886), 130, believe that in this fable, in the context of iambic satire and vituperation, the poet hides behind the fox's mask, while the eagle represents his present political adversary and former friend who, outside of the fable's framework, received the name Lycambes.[18]

[16] Keller (1963), 5–6.

[17] The fox's most characteristic traits are her cunning (she is κερδαλέος, ποικίλος) and practical intelligence (μῆτις). In Aesopic fables, she frequently searches for powerful allies. For Archilochus 201 cf. Bowra (1940*b*), 28 and Corrêa (2001). In Hesiod's fable (*Op.* 203–12), since the hawk usually has doves, not nightingales as its prey, the choice of the nightingale may be due to the fact that this bird, like the poet, is musical (West (1978), 206, Nelson (1997), 236; *contra* Livrea (1970), 13, Dalfen (1994–5), 163). Likewise, in the Etana myth, the main character is the eagle that convinces Shamash to release her with the kind of argumentation typical of poets: if she dies, nobody will hear of Shamash's justice; therefore, she begs to be set free in order to praise Shamash ('I will si[ng] your [pra]ises for all time'; 'Let me cause your name to be heard for all time'. Translation from Foster (2005).

[18] It is most probable that Archilochus used the significant names (Lycambes, Neobula, Charilaus, Leophilos . . .) to attack historical political enemies or adversaries.

2. THE JUSTICE OF BEASTS (177 *IEG*)

ὦ Ζεῦ, πάτερ Ζεῦ, σὸν μὲν οὐρανοῦ κράτος,
σὺ δ' ἔργ' ἐπ' ἀνθρώπων ὁρᾶις
λεωργὰ καὶ θεμιστά, σοὶ δὲ θηρίων
ὕβρις τε καὶ δίκη μέλει.

Zeus, father Zeus, yours is the power in heaven, you oversee men's deeds, wicked and lawful, and the violence and the justice of beasts are your concern.

These verses are attributed to Aeschylus (FP) or to Antilochus (F) in the manuscripts of Stobaeus (1.3.34 = i. 58.11 Wachsmuth and Hense).[19] In the case of Aeschylus, it is an interesting error, since today many critics believe he had this epode of Archilochus in mind while composing the parodos of the *Agamemnon*.[20]

According to Eusebius (*Praep. ev.* 13.13.54), Clement (*Strom.* 5.127.1 = ii. 412.3 Stählin) attributed the verses to Archilochus and reproduced them along with other quotations in order to demonstrate similarities between pagan and Hebrew beliefs. The context is relevant, because Clement quotes these verses of Archilochus as an example of the Greek belief in an all-mighty God (παντοκράτωρ) and concludes from the texts he lists that 'the Lord will save populous

[19] Liebel (1812) believed it was a poem in iambic tetrameters. Lasserre and Bonnard (1958) united fragments 177 and 176 *IEG* in this order; *contra* Rivier (1952), 465 and Bond (1960), 599.

[20] Kallós (1951–2), 68–9 compared Archilochus 177 *IEG* with Soph. *El.* 175 and suggested that Aeschylus had Archilochus' verses in mind when he composed the beginning of *Prometheus Bound* 5, while Baldi (1959) and (1961) believed in the existence of 'strange analogies' between the *Myth of Etana*, Archilochus 177 *IEG* and Aesch. *Cho.* 247–51, 492, 985–6, 997–1000 and *Eum.* 127–8, 130–2, 145–7, 246–7, 230–1. Cavarzere (1989), 117 traced similarities between the beginning of this fragment of Archilochus and Hor. *Epod.* 5: *at o deorum quidquid in caelo regit | terras et humanum genus*, pointing to the correspondence between λεωργὰ καὶ θεμιστά and *fas nefasque* 5.87. However, as Cavarzere notes, the context in Horace is different and Zeus, as a god who oversees everything (παντόπτης), is to be found in various passages of Greek poetry and prose (see n. 30).

cities and, with his hand, he will take hold of all <the> inhabited earth, as if it were a nest'.[21]

Because the fox is the weaker party, and is now impotent in view of the eagle's inaccessibility, she can do no more than to invoke Zeus.[22] This is done with vehemence[23] and, as is customary in prayers, she proclaims the god's prerogatives: his is the power of the universe.[24] The fox's language imitates the elevated diction characteristic of prayers. However, the larger context of the prayer—that of a fable within an iambic poem—excludes the possibility of considering this 'solemn poetry'.[25] A parallel may be found in the beginning of a verse of an iambic poem of Hipponax (38 *IEG*):

ὦ Ζεῦ, πάτερ <Ζεῦ>, θεῶν Ὀλυμπίων πάλμυ,
τί μοὐκ ἔδωκας χρυσόν . . .

Zeus, father Zeus, sultan of the Olympian gods, why have you not given me gold . . . ?[26]

West (1997), 504 compares the first verse of the fox's prayer in Archilochus (177.1 *IEG*: 'yours is the power of heaven') to the Lord's Prayer, but notes that the expression is already found in the Old Testament (1 Chron. 29:11) and, following Williams (1956), 72, Trencsényi-Waldapfel (1959) and Baldi (1961), 383, points to an even older parallel in the Assyrian tradition. The serpent also makes a

[21] Clem. *Strom.* 5.127.3 (= ii. 412.10–11 Stählin): *ὁ κύριος σώσει πόλεις κατοικουμένας, καὶ τὴν οἰκουμένην ὅλην καταλήψεται τῇ χειρὶ ὡς νεοσσιάν*. However, the verb *σώσει* ('will save') present in the manuscripts of Clement and Eusebius is, according to Des Places (1983), 385, n. 2, evidently a copyist's error for *σείσει*. We should then read: 'the Lord will *shake* populous cities and, with his hand, he will take hold of all the inhabited earth, as if it were a nest'. The image is that of a world destroyed by the hands of a supreme god, just as Zeus will (indirectly) destroy the eagles' nest in Archilochus' 'Fox and Eagle' fable.

[22] Adrados (1964), 269 supposes the eagle pronounces this prayer.

[23] *πάτερ Ζεὺς μὲν* Stobaeus (FP). The second vocative, *πάτερ Ζεῦ*, is not present in Clement and Eusebius (Brunck (1772)). All other editions follow Stobaeus. Gerber (1970), 39 notes the emphatic polyptoton (*σόν, σύ, σοί*). Cf. *σὸν μὲν* in Clement.

[24] According to Page (1964), 143, the influence of epic diction in this fragment is very strong, and *Ζεῦ πάτερ* is a traditional verse beginning. Cf. Hom. *Il.* 1.503, 3.365, 5.421, 757, 762, 872, *Od* 1.45 = 1.81, 20.11, Hes. *Theog.* 71, *Hym. Herm.* 368, Aesch. *Eum.* 618, Soph. *Trach.* 275, Lyc. 691, Besantinus *AP* 15.25.7, and for Zeus as the father of the Olympian gods in Archilochus see also fragments 25.6, 98.13 and 122.2 *IEG.*

[25] *Contra* Carey (1986), 64–5.

[26] Translated by Gerber (1999).

similar prayer to the god Shamash in the 'Fox and Serpent' fable narrated in the *Etana* epic (Old Version 1 46–51):

> 'You know, O Shamash, the evil he did!
> Your net is the wi[de] meadow,
> Your trap [is the distant heaven]:
> May the eagle not [escape] from your net,
> Th(at) perpetrator of ev[il and ab]omination,
> Who harbored e[vi]l against his friend!'[27]

In both fables, that narrated in Archilochus' epode and in the *Etana*, the gods fulfil the supplicants' requests.[28]

The concept of a god who sees all things, who *oversees* (all) *men's deeds* (2: *ἐπ' ἀνθρώπων ὁρᾷς*), fits Clement's purpose well.[29] And Stobaeus quoted Archilochus' fragment in the chapter on 'The justice of god which is appointed to observe all of men's deeds on earth and which punishes the unjust'.[30] In this sense, as Pettazzoni (1956), 145, 119, 132 noted, it is significant that the omniscience of Zeus should be related to sight, as is the omniscience of Varuna and Ahura Mazda, and that the notion of divine punishment is to be found in Greek literature since Homer.[31] It is also particularly pertinent, considering Archilochus' fragment 177 *IEG*, that the vengeance of Zeus falls 'especially on those who break oaths', and that it is for this

[27] Translated by Foster (2005), 537.

[28] According to West (1997), 504–5, the whole structure of the fox's prayer in Archilochus is 'in accord with Near Eastern tradition'. One may add that the majority of the characteristics pointed out (an apostrophe to the god, the affirmation of his power and the censure directed towards the aggressor) are typical of Greek prayers in general.

[29] *ἐπ' ἀνθρώπους ῥεῖς* Clem., Eusebius (Brunck). Page (1964), 143 notes that this second verse recalls *Od.* 13.213–14: *Ζεὺς . . . ἀνθρώπους ἐφορᾷ*. Cf. n. 20.

[30] Stobaeus (L) 1.3.34 (IV Heer) *περὶ δίκης τοῦ θεοῦ τεταγμένης ἐποπτεύειν τὰ ἐπὶ γῆς γιγνόμενα ὑπὸ τῶν ἀνθρώπων, τιμωροῦ οὔσης τῶν ἁμαρτανόντων*. Cf. Pettazzoni (1956), 147–51 and Hom. *Il.* 16.386–7, *Od.* 14.82–4, Hes. *Op.* 238–42, 251, 267–9, 276–9, 706, *Theog.* 217, 220–2, *Theognidea* 375, Aesch. *Suppl.* 139, *Eum.* 1045, Soph. *Ant.* 184, *El.* 174–5, 696–7, *OT* 551–2, *OC* 1086, *Aj.* 758–61, Eur. fr. 404, 508 *TrGF*, *Ion* 440–1, *El.* 953–6, 1177, *Andromeda* fr. 134a *TrGF*, Ar. *Ach.* 435, Eubul. fr. 9, 1–2a / 4b–5 *PCG*; and in prose: Hdt. 5.56, Pl. *Leg.* 4.715e–16b, 905d–6b, 906d–7b, Plut. *Mor.* 161e and Porphyrius *ἐκ τοῦ Περὶ Στυγός* 148. Cf. also Hesych. *π* 372 = p. 19 Hansen, s.v. *πανόπτης*.

[31] *Od.* 20.75, 15.523 ff., *Il.* 16.385–8.

reason that Zeus is invoked when oaths are either made or broken (Hom. *Il.* 3.276, 19.257, 8.411; Pind. *Pyth.* 4.166–7).[32]

In the prayer Archilochus' fox makes, human deeds are mentioned first and qualified as λεωργὰ καὶ θεμιστά (3: 'wicked and lawful').[33] The adjective λεωργός ('wicked') is derived from λεῖος which means 'smooth', that which has been 'flattened out', 'reduced to dust' and, consequently, 'destroyed'. According to Chantraine (1954), this is an 'important and difficult term', glossed by Hesychius (λ 791 = ii. 590 Latte) as κακοῦργος, πανοῦργος, ἀνδροφόνος ('evil doing', 'knavish', 'homicidal'). When Chantraine quotes Archilochus (177), he translates λεωργός by 'criminal' and recalls the beginning of the *Prometheus Bound* where Kratos uses the adjective for the Titan (lines 4–5).[34] In Pollux (3.134 = i. 196.29–30 Bethe, *ap.* Xen. *Mem.* 1.3.9), λεωργός is said to be a rude and vulgar term: it is 'one of the many substitutes for κακοῦργος' that, according to its model, designates the 'evildoer' who is capable of everything. The older form κακοεργός[35] was replaced by πανοῦργος[36] in the Attic dialect and by λεωργός in the Ionic (Chantraine (1954), 32–3).

But Archilochus amuses himself—for this is a fox speaking of human acts—when he adds that not only the doings of men, but also

[32] Cf. Pausanias 5.24.9 for Zeus *horkios* at Olympia.

[33] καὶ ἃ θέμις Stobaeus (L), Clement; καθέμι[σ]τας οἵ Stobaeus (FP); καθέμιστας (A) Stobaeus; τε καὶ ἀθέμιστα Eusebius; κἀθέμιστα Gaisford (1814–20), i. 297 (fr. 17), Hoffmann (1898), Treu (1959), and Lasserre and Bonnard (1958); καὶ θεμιστά is the correction made by Liebel (1812: κᾀθέμιστα) and adopted by the majority of editors. As Masson (1952), 37–8 noted, Liebel's correction is to be preferred in view of the parallelism between λεωργὰ καὶ θεμιστά and ὕβρις τε καὶ δίκη; and it is also confirmed, according to West (1974*a*), 134, by *Od.* 17.487. Page (1964), 143 points out cognates of θεμιστά in epic, but believes that λεωργά is a 'new' term.

[34] Cf. also Kallós (1951–2), 68–9. This 'transgressive' Prometheus is fixed to high crags (τόνδε πρὸς πέτραις | ὑψηλοκρήμνοις τὸν λεωργὸν ὀχμάσαι), as the eagle in Archilochus 176 makes little of her former friend from a 'high crag' (ὁρᾷς ἵν' ἐστὶ κεῖνος ὑψηλὸς πάγος, | τρηχύς τε καὶ παλίγκοτος;). The passage (*PV* 4–5) is also quoted in the *Suda* with the observation that Prometheus is λεωργός because he endures all, or attempts all things (πάντολμος): he 'dies for the people's sake' (ὁ ὑπὲρ τοῦ λεῶ ἀποθνήσκων).

[35] Cf. κακοεργός (*Od.* 18.54) and κακοῦργος as an adjective in Herodotus (1.41) and Antiphon (2.4.2).

[36] πανοῦργος is also an injurious term without juridical value in tragedy (Aesch. *Cho.* 384) and comedy (Ar. *Ach.* 311).

the δίκη and ὕβρις of animals are Zeus' concern.[37] The construction is perfectly symmetrical, the ὕβρις and δίκη[38] (violence and justice) of beasts corresponding to human actions that are λεωργά and θεμιστά (wicked and lawful), but it operates an inversion. For if we may admit that beasts are capable of 'wicked' (λεωργά) or 'correct' (θεμιστά) deeds, that is, actions that are destructive or lawful in that they abide by custom or habit, δίκη and ὕβρις belong to the human sphere of action and are punished by the avenging Zeus who, as the 'Eye of Δίκη',[39] is related to the heavens and can therefore see all things on earth.

West (1997), 505 noted that there are no parallels to be found in archaic Greek literature for a Zeus who is concerned with justice among animals, except in Aeschylus' simile (*Ag.* 55–9), which depends on this fable of Archilochus.[40] For this is precisely a generic characteristic of the αἶνος or fable: to transmute that which is human into the animal domain.[41] In fables and αἶνοι beasts speak, think and act just as we do. Therefore, if Zeus 'witnesses' all human acts in Archilochus' αἶνος, it is only natural that the δίκη and ὕβρις of animals should be his concern. Were this not an αἶνος, the terms would probably be reversed.

A scholium on the *Iliad* (19.407c = iv. 647–8 Erbse) indicates that since antiquity this αἶνος of Archilochus has been compared to that of 'The Nightingale and the Hawk' in Hesiod (*Op.* 202–11).[42] This is the oldest record of a fable in European literature. Unlike the

[37] Cf. *Od.* 17.485 θεοὶ . . . | ἀνθρώπων ὕβριν τε καὶ εὐνομίην ἐφορῶντες, Hes. *Op.* 238: οἷς ὕβρις τε μέμηλε . . . | τοῖς δὲ δίκην Κρονίδης τεκμαίρεται.

[38] For the antithesis ὕβρις / δίκη cf. also *Od.* 6.120, Hes. *Op.* 190, 217, 225, 238, Theognis 291, 378, 751 and Xenophon D–K 21 B 1.15–17 (i. 127.10–12) = B 1.15–17 *IEG.*

[39] Cf. Pettazzoni (1956), 147.

[40] The usual and contrary notion begins with Hesiod (*Op.* 276–80, on which see below).

[41] According to La Penna (1964), 31 n. 2, the fox's prayer is similar to that which Muwatallis, the Hittite king, addresses to the solar god (cf. Gurney (1990)) and the prayer of an animal to the god of justice is a *topos* of fables already in Sumerian literature. Cf. the wolf's prayer in Gordon (1958), 53.

[42] Both αἶνοι, that of Archilochus and of Hesiod, are also quoted together by Stobaeus (see above). For further discussion of these passages, cf. Daly (1961), Puelma (1972), Fränkel (1975), 146, West (1978), Nøjgaard (1984), 102, and Nelson (1997).

majority of fables in which, according to Daly (1961), 47, there is first a preparation of the scene, then the narration of an action and lastly a commentary on its results, Hesiod's fable plunges *in medias res.* After describing the Iron Age men and their lifestyle (*Op.* 174–201) the narrator tells an *αἶνος* for the kings. The *αἶνος* is by definition enigmatic and, therefore, this narrative is not for all kings, but only for those who are capable of grasping it (202 *φρονέουσι*):

> *ὧδ' ἴρηξ προσέειπεν ἀηδόνα ποικιλόδειρον,*
> *ὕψι μάλ' ἐν νεφέεσσι φέρων, ὀνύχεσσι μεμαρπώς·*
> *ἣ δ' ἐλεόν, γναμπτοῖσι πεπαρμένη ἀμφ' ὀνύχεσσιν,*
> *μύρετο· τὴν δ' ὅ γ' ἐπικρατέως πρὸς μῦθον ἔειπεν·*
> *"δαιμονίη, τί λέληκας; ἔχει νύ σε πολλὸν ἀρείων·*
> *τῇ δ' εἶς ᾗ σ' ἂν ἐγώ περ ἄγω καὶ ἀοιδὸν ἐοῦσαν·*
> *δεῖπνον δ' αἴ κ' ἐθέλω ποιήσομαι ἠὲ μεθήσω.*
> *ἄφρων δ' ὅς κ' ἐθέλῃ πρὸς κρείσσονας ἀντιφερίζειν·*
> *νίκης τε στέρεται πρός τ' αἴσχεσιν ἄλγεα πάσχει."*
> *ὣς ἔφατ' ὠκυπέτης ἴρηξ, τανυσίπτερος ὄρνις.*

So said the hawk to the dappled-necked nightingale, carrying her up high in the clouds, held fast in his talons. She wept piteously, pierced by his curved talons, while he, with overwhelming might, told her the following: 'Miserable one, why do you cry? You are held by one far better than you. You will go wherever I take you, even though you are a songstress. If I so wish, I will have you for supper, or let you free. Foolish is he who wishes to confront the stronger: he is deprived of victory and adds pains to shame.' Thus spoke the swift-flying hawk, the long-winged bird.

In this case, the predator is not an eagle, as in Archilochus, but a hawk whose speech concludes the *αἶνος* with a moral that celebrates the law of the mighty. Many critics since Aristarchus found this moral bizarre, and the more so for being directed at the kings. Aristarchus consequently expunged verses 210–11 which contain the moral, claiming that it is not fit for an animal (*ἄλογον*) to enunciate moral sentences.[43] Aristarchus' opinion reflects the practice of his own times, when the morals of older fables, such as this one, originally pronounced in dialogues by the characters, were now formulated by an external narrator and placed at the end of the narrative as a

[43] Aristarchus is followed in modern times by Göttling and Rzach, as Daly (1961), 46 notes.

'golden key'. However, in spite of the reason declared by Aristarchus for deleting the verses, perhaps his real motivation was the content of the moral, and not so much the fact that it is a hawk that delivers it.

Hesiod's narrative presents difficulties that have been explained by some critics as resulting from the insertion of a pre-existent fable in the poem. This is possible, in view of the manner in which the fable launches *in medias res.*[44] The problem is that although the narrator declares at first that the αἶνος is directed towards the kings, the narrative itself and the moral stated by the hawk do not seem to apply to kings, who are the strongest, but to Perses. Does the fable evince the dangers faced by the weaker who, partaking of ὕβρις, contest the stronger, or is it a critique of the kings' conduct, as Erasmus may have understood?[45]

Immediately after the fable, the narrator addresses Perses who is advised to heed δίκη ('justice') and to avoid ὕβρις ('violence'). According to Dalfen (1994–5), 177, this is the nightingale's ὕβρις, for which she is rightfully punished.[46] Since the impious hawk is not chastised for his acts, where then is the promised lesson for the kings? If not in the fable, it is certainly in the commentary of the narrator who proclaims that even kings must submit to divine justice (214–16), and that the entire earth and human population pay for the injustice of kings whose laws are crooked (262: δίκας σκολιῶς ἐνέποντες). Because Zeus is all-seeing,[47] these gift-devourers (263–4: βασιλῆς . . . δωροφάγοι)—an epithet that recalls the hawk that devours the weaker—must be righteous.[48]

[44] Cf. Verdenius (1985) and Jedrkiewicz (1989). Contrariwise, Dalfen (1994–5), 161 indicates similarities between the beginning of this αἶνος and that of 'The Fox and the Monkey' in (Archilochus 185–7).

[45] Cf. Erasmus, *Scarabeus Aquilam quaerit* 145–50: 'Porro si quis recentiorum temporum príncipes expendat, vereor ne non ita passim reperiat, in quem non quadret foedissimum illud convitium, quod apud Homerum Achilles torquet in Agamemnonem, δημοβόρος βασιλεύς. Nam Hesiodus δωροφάγους appellat, rectius tamen παμφάγους appellaturus.' Cf. Hes. *Op.* 39 and 264.

[46] That one should not fight against the stronger is also the moral of other Aesopic fables: cf. Puelma (1972), 87.

[47] *Op.* 267: πάντα ἰδὼν Διὸς ὀφθαλμὸς καὶ πάντα νοήσας.

[48] According to Livrea (1970), 19 n. 4, the moral is to be found in verses 276–80. In fact, with these verses Hesiod may have intended to balance the fable's moral in order that it may be directed towards the kings. Nelson (1997), 239 offers a difficult interpretation: the nightingale represents the kings that, for their injustice, die in the

At the end of this 'Ode to Justice', there is a curious remark. Perhaps in order to justify the differences between both morals, that proclaimed by the hawk and that of the narrator, unlike Archilochus' fox who declares that (177.3–4 *IEG*) 'the violence and the justice of beasts are your concern', Hesiod's narrator says that Zeus bestows laws only upon human beings (276–9):

> ἰχθύσι μὲν καὶ θηρσὶ καὶ οἰωνοῖς πετεηνοῖς
> ἔσθειν ἀλλήλους, ἐπεὶ οὐ δίκη ἐστὶ μετ' αὐτοῖς·
> ἀνθρώποισι δ' ἔδωκε δίκην, ἣ πολλὸν ἀρίστη
> γίγνεται·

[Zeus ordained that] fish, beasts and winged birds should devour each other, for there is no justice among them. But Zeus gave men justice, which is by far the best.

If with these verses Hesiod denies 'the parallelism between the animal and the human world' (West (1984), 244–5), we must then ask ourselves what is the function of his αἶνος. For of what use is a fable if it cannot be translated into human terms? With these verses, perhaps the poet seeks to avoid contradiction between the hawk's moral and the narrator's admonitions that are external to the fable and predict the punishment of the stronger but unjust kings. By asserting that in the animal world there is no divine justice and that the law of the mighty rules, but that among humans the wicked will be punished by Zeus, Hesiod completes the fable's moral which, otherwise, would serve only for Perses. And this moral addressed to the kings, which warns them that even if animals may do as they please, they must heed the justice of Zeus, in no way differs from the lesson present in Archilochus (177 *IEG*) and Aeschylus' 'Hymn to Zeus' (*Ag.* 160–83): the powerful crush the weaker, but these have their divine protectors who in time exact retribution.[49]

In the epode of Archilochus, as in the oriental versions of the fable, what is emphasized is the punishment of perjury, not the rights of the weak against the mighty. But the simple fact that the last notion

talons of the hawk (= Zeus): '. . . Hesiod's fable is uniquely suited to lead us, as it does, from the injustice of the Iron Age (180–201), a situation which seems first mirrored in the fable, to Zeus' punishment of such injustice (213–83), the situation the fable finally settles upon'.

[49] Cf. West (1979), 5.

should be attested in archaic Greek literature is significant. La Penna (1964), 35, criticizing distinctions usually made between the West and the East respectively as universes of rational and irrational attitudes and spirits, stresses the fact that the fable—and, we may add specifically in this case, that of Archilochus—because it is derived from the Babylonian, presents 'problems and moral tendencies that come, in part, from there [from the orient]'. For the 'search for an objective *Díke* that protects the humble against the mighty and that is guaranteed by the divinity, a search that is at the heart of the Greek ethics of Hesiod's *Erga*'—and also of Archilochus' epode—'is spurred on by the oriental ethic that has its roots in that of Babylon', contrary to what is usually supposed.[50]

The need to obtain vengeance for wrongs suffered and, in the 'Fox and Eagle' fable, to punish the perjurers, more than a fundamental trait for the concept of masculinity in the archaic and classical periods,[51] is an important aspect of Greek morality. Originally, an oath was a 'curse which a man lays upon himself, to take effect if what he declares is false' (West (1966*a*), on *Op.* 231). In this sense, the later comment made by Cicero (*Nat. Deor.* 2.91) is pertinent. In a discussion of the vengeance of the gods, he says that the adversaries of Archilochus and Hipponax did not suffer injury from the iambic poems as part of a divine plan: the victims brought such evils upon themselves.

In some versions of the Lycambid saga, not only 'Father Lycambes', but also his whole family, destroyed by the iambic poems of Archilochus, paid the price for the betrayal of an old friendship and a broken oath. Therefore, according to the saga and its critical fortune, these poems were not 'ineffectual as abuse'[52] nor 'rather mild',[53] but they may also have been, themselves, a means for the weaker to punish mighty perjurers.

[50] La Penna (1964), 35–9 quotes other examples in Sumerian literature of protests of the weaker against the unjust mighty, and a dialogue between a slave and his master that he compares to the *Life of Aesop*. For the struggle of the weak against the mighty, see also *Il.* 21.184, 485, Pind. *Ol.* 10.39, *Nem.* 10.72, Soph. *El.* 219, *Ant.* 63.

[51] Cf. Carey (1986), 67 who quotes Archilochus 23.15, 126 *IEG*, Solon 13.6, Theognis 337 ff., 872, Eur. *Her.* 585 ff. and Pl. *Men.* 71e in this respect.

[52] A. P. Burnett (1983), 63.

[53] Podlecki (1984), 49.

9

Hipponactea quaedam

Calvert Watkins

Hesiod, Homer, and Aeschylus aside, few authors have been as well served by Martin West as Hipponax, in edition (*IEG*) and commentary (1974*a*) alike. With considerable trepidation I venture to offer him herewith these *quaestiunculae* as a token of friendship and admiration.

37 *IEG*

ἐκέλευε βάλλειν καὶ λεύειν Ἱππώνακτα. Choeroboscus on Hephaestion (Consbruch (1906), 195.15–22) cites this and two further instances where Hipponax treats the diphthong *ευ* before vowel as short (i.e. with correption): fragments 43 *μάκαρ ὅτις* < > *θηρεύει* †*πρήσας* and 44 *καί τοί γ' εὔωνον αὐτὸν εἰ θέλεις δώσω.* Gerber (1999), 383 n. 1 notes that while Choeroboscus refers to the *λευ* of *λεύειν*, the same correption may occur in *ἐκέλευε*, 'since initial tribrach [as in 43 *IEG*, C.W.] is much commoner than an anapaest'. I defer to the *Jubilar* on the metrics, but another argument for the correption here might be the repeated phonetic figure in *ἐΚεΛΕΥΕ* . . . *ΚαιΛΕΥΕιν*.

25 *IEG*

“*ἀπό σ’ ὀλέσειεν Ἄρτεμις.*”—“*σὲ δὲ κὠπόλλων.*” A pretty example of sixth-century colloquial Ionic tmesis. The restriction to single intervening enclitic or particle (cf. 47 *IEG πρὸς μὲν κυνήσεις*) reminds us of the probably roughly contemporary Latin *prae tet tremonti* (Carmen Saliare) and *sub uos placo* etc. (Festus 190, 307). As Wackernagel (1892), 406 = (1953–79), i. 74 rightly saw in the article which gave his name to the first law of Indo-European syntax, we observe the preconditions for the Celtic infixed pronoun. Note also that the pragmatic sequence of unstressed and contrastively stressed *σ(ε)* and *σέ* is echoed unchanged in the English equivalent two and a half millennia later: ‘God damn you.’ ‘God damn YOU.’

28 *IEG*

Hipponax rails at the painter Mimnes, calling him a *κατωμόχανε*, which is Greek, and *νικύρτα καὶ σάβαννι*, which are not. The second is corrupt in the citation of Tzetzes and basically unknown; but *νικύρτας* is glossed by Hesychius as *δουλέκδουλος*, ‘slave born of a slave’. In the spirit of fun that runs like a *Leitfaden* through Martin’s work I offer the following modest proposal, one unsusceptible of demonstration but which I have not yet succeeded in falsifying.

Masson in his commentary calls Lydian an ‘hypothèse gratuite’ for the original language of *νικύρτας*. But as a foreign-language insult presumably familiar both to the East Ionian poet speaker and the East Ionian addressee Mimnes, Lydian as the source language would seem more like a ‘default’ suggestion. Can one construct out of known Lydian morphemes a tolerably well-formed string with a meaning somehow paraphrasable as *δουλέκδουλος*?

Lydian *ni-* is the negative prefix (Gusmani (1964), 172), from IE **nē-* (Melchert (1994), 340). Lydian *-τα-* (<*τ*> = [ts$^{(\prime)}$]) is an adjectival suffix, from IE **-tyo-* (Shevoroshkin (1967), 43, Gusmani (1969), 143, Melchert (1994), 334). And *kud* (<d> = [đ]) is relative adverb ‘as, where’ (Gusmani (1964), 155) from Proto-Anatolian

$^{*}k^{(w)}udV$ (Melchert (1994), 332). Sommer (1930) had already compared Old Church Slavonic *kъde* ‘where’, and with the negative prefix one can compare OCS *nikъde(že)* ‘nowhere’ for the sense and *někъde* ‘somewhere’, for the form. I conclude that a Lydian *nikud(V-) could exist with the meaning ‘nowhere’.

If we allow the possibility of forming a relational adjective in -*τa*- to this adverb (compare the inherited use of *-tyo- with local adverbs [W–D II.2.697–9], Hitt. *appizziya*- ‘rear’ < *opi-tyo-, Greek ὀπισσο-, and later Sanskrit formations [Pāṇini 4.2.104] like *kutas-tya*- ‘coming from where?’, (with *api*) ‘of unknown origin’, both from Monier-Williams citing the Uttararāmacaritā as source), then there could have existed a Lydian *nikudτa- [nikuđtsa-] ‘belonging to nowhere’, ‘coming from nowhere’. In a sixth-century BC class society with a sense that birth conveyed status, the much later term δουλέκδουλος would seem a fair periphrasis of such a term. ‘He’s a real nowhere man.’ My Croatian student Ana Galjanić, from Zagreb, notes the Serbian expression *Nikogović* ‘Mr Nobody’, which she glosses as ‘no one, of no significance, without pedigree, a “lowlife” ’. The parallelism with the putative Lydian construct and its semantics is evident.

Phonologically the replacement of the cluster [đts], interdental spirant or apico-alveolar approximant + dental affricate by [rt], apical rhotic + dental stop, seems well within the realm of possibility in the Greek treatment of foreign words and names.

42 *IEG*

τέαρε[. . . . .]δεύειε† τὴν ἐπὶ Σμύρνης
ἰθὺ διὰ Λυδῶν παρὰ τὸν Ἀττάλεω τύμβον
καὶ σῆμα Γύγεω καὶ [Σεσώ]στρ[ιος] στήλην
καὶ μνῆμα Τῶτος, Μυτάλιδι πάλμυδος,
πρὸς ἥλιον δύνοντα γαστέρα τρέψας.

At first sight this looks like a versified Baedeker of points of interest on the road to Smyrna from the interior of sixth-century Lydia. Yet it is not just an itinerary, but also a versified synonymikon of words for funerary or commemorative monuments. These are precisely presented as a poetic list; and such lists, enumerations or catalogues, widespread in early Indo-European literatures, repay close attention. As I wrote (Watkins (1995), 47): 'What seem . . . to be simple lists . . . may turn out to be artistically elaborated merisms . . .'. In a forthcoming monograph while discussing the Aśvin hymns RV 1.116 and 117 which consist of a 'catalogue' of the Aśvins' deeds, Stephanie Jamison writes, 'A list derives its power not from the identity of the individual items upon it, but from the piling up of one after the other, their multiplicity. In this case the multiplicity is emphasized by the otherwise obscure personal names of the beneficiaries (or occasionally victims) of the Aśvins' activity.'

Hipponax's list is just so, as art: an enumeration of four monuments linked by repetition, *παρὰ τὸν* W *καὶ* X *καὶ* Y *καὶ* Z, but embellished by variation, the first with definite article and the remainder without it, word order PN_{gen} N, N PN_{gen}, PN_{gen} N, N PN_{gen}, and the last the most complex by Behaghel's 'law of increasing members', for which see Watkins (1995), 24. The list of those memorialized would sound exotic to a Greek speaker from anywhere else in Hellas—three Anatolians and an Egyptian (on whom see Herodotus 2.106), with the final Anatolian Τώς, syntactically the most complex, the least well known.

Yet it is possible to 'deconstruct' Hipponax's four-member poetic list, and to show that it is in fact composed of two dyads interwoven: the Homeric formula *τύμβωι τε στήληι τε* (*Il.* 16.456–7 = 674–5) with *τε* replaced by *καί*, and the rhyming pair *καὶ σῆμα . . . καὶ μνῆμα . . .* The case is instructive on how such poetic lists may be created or expanded.

See on the pair *τύμβωι τε στήληι τε* Watkins (forthcoming). For the pair *κασίγνητοί τε* (Ϝ)*έται τε* in the Lycian context of *Il.*16.456 = 674 (death of Sarpedon) compare the Asianic 'four quadrants of social appurtenance' along two parameters: *blood – alliance* and *close – distant* which I saw in *Il.* 5.473–4 (Sarpedon to Hektor) and the Hittite set enumerated in the Proclamation of Telepinus §1 (*CTH* 19), as argued in Watkins (1998), reprinted for a different audience in Watkins (2002). In the strict Asianic context of *Il.* 16.456 = 674 (Ϝ)*έται* should designate either close male relatives by marriage, or else partisans by birth, depending on the parameter—whatever else it might mean elsewhere.

40 *IEG*

{*Ἀθηνᾶ*} *Μαλίς*, a local, presumably Lydian divinity invoked (*λίσσομαί σε*) by the poet or speaker. Hesych. *Μαλίς· Ἀθηνᾶ* (*μ* 190 = ii. 626 Latte). The gloss was removed by Bergk. Classical and Byzantine tradition beginning with Hipponax and his eventual commentators clearly places the goddess *Μαλίς* in various locales in Western Anatolia. These include Lydia (Hippon. fr. 40 *IEG*; cf. also Hellanicus *FGrHist* 4 F 112 = fr. 112 *EGM*, who says that the hero Akeles was the son of Herakles and Malis, a slave of the Lydian queen Omphale), Isauria (according to St Basil, *Vita S. Theclae* 2.15 = lxxxv. 592 *PCC*, Dalisandos was the city of Malis and the god Sandas) and possibly Lesbos (*PLF* fr. incert. utrius auct. 17 (p. 295): '*Μᾶλις* (or *Μάλις* with Masson) was spinning. . .' (see below)). These texts were gathered by Höfer (1909–10), and their relevance to Hipponax first noted by Masson (1962), 128–9.

Höfer and later Laroche (1973) called attention to the syncretism of Herakles with the Anatolian warrior god Sandas, known in Cuneiform Luvian texts like the Zarpiya ritual since the second millennium. Masson, after presenting the above dossier involving Malis, concluded that Malis was related to Omphale and either a heroine or native divinity in Lydia and a *parhedra* of the local Herakles, i.e. of Sandas. 'One wonders if the hellenized myth of Herakles and Omphale has taken the place of a Lydian myth of Sandas and Malis' (1962, 129). The myth was perhaps more widely distributed in Southern and Western Anatolia.

Neumann (1979), 269 with n. 37 added Theocr. 13.45: when the Argonauts stopped at the Propontis, *Μᾶλις* was one of the three water nymphs who for love pulled the beautiful boy Hylas into their spring, to the despair of the enamoured Herakles, causing him to desert the expedition.

Neumann (1967), (1970) and Laroche (1967), 53–4 had earlier pointed to the well-attested divine name Maliya in Lycian texts, 'the native equivalent of Athena' in Melchert (2004), 36. Melchert (2002) made compelling arguments for seeing the hitherto unrecognized Lycian reflex of the warrior god Sanda in Lycian *hãtahe* (gen. sg.), *passim* in the Xanthos stele, *TL* 44. Note the simile *ãka Herikle* 'like

Herakles' in 44 a 50 (Schürr (1998)), reinforced by Melchert's reading (2002, 250 n. 38) of the numeral in the preceding passage not as CII '7' but OII '12', 'referring to the twelve deeds of Heracles'.

Neumann (1967), 34–5 noted that the clearest evidence for syncretism of Maliya with Athena was *TL* 149, 150 *Maliya wedrẽñni* 'M. (protectress) of the city' (Rhodiapolis) beside Greek inscriptions from the same findspot *Ἀθαναία ἁ Πολιάς* and *ἡ Ῥοδιαπολειτῶν θεὰ Ἀθηνᾶ*. Note also the Lycian phrase in *TL* 44 a 43 as interpreted by Melchert: (*nelede* . . .) *pttara* : *maliyehi* : *hãtahe*: '(He laid down [trophies]) in Patara (sacred to) Maliya for Sanda'. Both are directly comparable to the information of St Basil of Isauria about the city Dalisandos cited above.

The Lycian goddess Maliya was assumed since Neumann (1967) to be the first-millennium reflex of the second-millennium Hittite goddess ᵈMăliya; Neumann himself (1979) was later more cautious in view of her status as a river goddess.[1] But it is still asserted by Hutter (2003), 231: 'Maliya is another great goddess whose origin is not to be sought with the Luvians, but she was highly esteemed among them too'. Yet this ᵈMaliya belonged to the old pantheon of Kaneš/Nešaš (Otten (1971), 32 with references to Goetze), and was apparently both a divinized river ᶠᴰMaliya and a vegetation deity *ŠA* ᴳᴵŠKIRI$_6$ ᵈMaliya GEŠTIN-*aš ḫalki* AMA-*ni* 'for ᵈMaliya of the garden, mother of wine and grain' KUB 43.23 Rs. 49′–51′ ed. V. Haas, cf. Haas (1994), 156 n. 18. These are not attributes of Lycian Maliya or *Μαλίς*. ᵈMaliya has finally no known connection with the second-millennium Luvian ᵈSantas (or with Marduk/ᵈAMAR.UD).

These facts would suggest that the link between second-millennium Hittite-Luvian ᵈMaliya and first-millennium Lycian Maliya is rather tenuous, and rests largely just on homophony. We can as easily imagine a local Western and Southwestern Anatolian female divinity Maliya, perhaps a *parhedra* of and sharing some features with the more widely attested warrior god Santa in the second millennium, and persisting in that region in the first millennium, as Sandas and Malis the protectors of Dalisandos (Isauria), and eventually partly or fully hellenized in the couples Herakles and Omphale,

[1] For the documentation see van Gessel (1998), i. 294–7, with references.

or Herakles and Malis the slave of Omphale (Lydia).[2] Rather than (with Hutter (2003), 232) seeing the water nymph Malis of the Hylas legend as a continuity of the 'river Maliya', I would suggest that Malis is there in Theocritus because of Herakles, not because she is a river. But the evidence for the nymph Malis here is slim.

It is notable that where Malis is or will be syncretized with Athena she does not appear linked to Sanda (or Herakles): Lycian *Pttara Maliyehi* 'Patara belonging to Maliya', *Μᾶλις* the spinner of Lesbos, and *Μαλίς* of Hipponax. Neumann (1979) noted that E. Simon (1967), 125 n. 146 identified the spinner Malis as Athena Ergane (Delphi *Αθαναι Ϝαργαναι* Schw. 319, s. vi/v). An ivory statuette of a spinning woman in Lydian headdress with distaff, spindle, and slender thread was found in the temple of Artemis in Ephesus, *c.*600 BC. She looks remarkably like an illustration of *PLF* fr. incert. utrius auct. 17, and is perhaps relevant to the Lesbian poet and to Hipponax as well: see Akurgal (1962), 376, especially with pl. 99, fig. 18.

If this Western Anatolian goddess Mali(ya) is only tenuously connected with the (Ka)nesite ^{d}Maliya, shares some attributes with the martial Sandas, and is ultimately identified or syncretized with Athena, we might consider a Western Anatolian etymology. Over twenty years ago (Watkins (1985)) I proposed to see a root noun **mon-* in the Hittite and Luvian neuter *māl* (with Anatolian nasal dissimilation) 'inner strength, mental force' (*CHD* iii. 124 'a quality desirable for men in combat, such as boldness, ferocity, skill', which one can 'know' for oneself (*šakk-*), just as one can 'remember' or 'forget' one's own *μένος* in Greek). A derivative of this etymon[3] could furnish our divine name, and one eminently suitable for syncretism with the Greek Athena. Recall only Athena in the role of Mentor.

I close with the full text of the Lesbian poet's fragment (cf. the ivory statuette mentioned above) and an elemental parallel:

Μᾶλις μὲν ἔννη λέπτον ἔχοισ' ἐπ' ἀτράκτωι λίνον

PLF fr. incert. utrius auct. 17

Malis was spinning with a slender thread on the spindle

[2] Fauth (1969) cited by Neumann (1979) relates the name Omphale to an Anatolian DN *Ουπις*, but the phonetic similarity is not compelling.

[3] For others in Luvian see Melchert (1994), 131–3, and for further and more speculative Western Anatolian connections of this root see now Melchert (2004), s.v. *mle-*. I remain unconvinced by Rieken (1999), 51.

Tri cóil ata ferr fo-longat in mbith:
cóil srithide hi foildeirb,
cóil foichne for tuinn,
cóil snáithe tar dorn dagmná.

The Triads of Ireland 75 (in K. Meyer (1906))

Three slender things that best support the world:
the slender stream of milk from the cow's dug into the pail,
the slender blade of green corn upon the ground,
the slender thread over the hand of a skilled woman.

10

Pindaric Accompaniments

W. B. Henry

The performance of Pindar's epinician odes has been much discussed of late, in particular the question whether the odes were composed for a vocal soloist or for a choir.[1] But the instrumental accompaniments have received comparatively little attention.[2] In this article I shall consider the evidence to be found in the texts of the odes themselves concerning the instruments used, and finish by suggesting that a metrical observation may enable us to make some progress.

In a number of the odes, it is made clear that both lyre and aulos were used in the accompaniment. So at *Ol.* 3.8–9, the poet's task is *φόρμιγγά τε ποικιλόγαρυν καὶ βοὰν αὐλῶν ἐπέων τε θέσιν | Αἰνησιδάμου παιδὶ συμμεῖξαι πρεπόντως*. In *Ol.* 10, Pindar says to the victor Hagesidamus (93–4) *τὶν δ' ἁδυεπής τε λύρα | γλυκύς τ' αὐλὸς ἀναπάσσει χάριν*, and at *Nem.* 9.8 we find the exhortation *ἀλλ' ἀνὰ μὲν βρομίαν φόρμιγγ', ἀνὰ δ' αὐλὸν . . . ὄρσομεν*. In *Nem.* 3, the poet states near the beginning that he will communicate the ode provided by the Muse to the voices of the choral performers and to his lyre (11–12 *ἐγὼ δὲ κείνων τέ νιν ὀάροις | λύρᾳ τε κοινάσομαι*), but it is implied towards the end by a metaphorical reference to the song as *πόμ' ἀοίδιμον Αἰολίσσιν ἐν πνοαῖσιν αὐλῶν* (79) that the aulos was

[1] I shall assume choral performance, but this is not of fundamental importance for my argument. See e.g. West (1992), 346, Hutchinson (2001), 366.

[2] See however Herington (1985), 28–9, 181–2, West (1992), 346 (also for Bacchylides, for whom the evidence is too slight to justify a fresh examination), Hutchinson (2001), 367. There is an extended discussion in Graf (1889), 37–47.

also used in the accompaniment. Finally, in *Ol.* 7.11–13 we read ἄλλοτε δ' ἄλλον ἐποπτεύει Χάρις ζωθάλμιος ἁδυμελεῖ | θαμὰ μὲν φόρμιγγι παμφώνοισί τ' ἐν ἔντεσιν αὐλῶν. | καί νυν ὑπ' ἀμφοτέρων σὺν Διαγόρᾳ κατέβαν: the combination is not then an unusual one, but one used 'frequently' (θαμά).

'Frequently', but not, as it seems, invariably.[3] Pindar does not, of course, ever have occasion to say that a particular instrument was *not* used in the performance of any one of his odes, but there are enough odes in which only the lyre is mentioned to make it a reasonable assumption that an aulos-player was not always involved.[4] For example, at *Ol.* 9.13 Pindar refers to himself as ἀνδρὸς ἀμφὶ παλαίσμασιν φόρμιγγ' ἐλελίζων: no reference to the aulos. If an aulos-player was an essential part of the proceedings, we should have expected the instrument to be mentioned, whether alongside the lyre or, as in the case of *Nem.* 3, separately. So at *Pyth.* 8.29–31, Pindar states that he does not have the time ἀναθέμεν | πᾶσαν μακραγορίαν | λύρᾳ τε καὶ φθέγματι μαλθακῷ: the same comment applies. At *Ol.* 1.17–18, Pindar tells himself to take down his lyre, at *Nem.* 10.21 to rouse the lyre; at *Nem.* 4.44–5 the lyre is asked to weave a song.[5] Theron deserves ἐγκωμίων τε μελέων λυρᾶν τε τυγχανέμεν (*Ol.* 2.47), a curious remark if Pindar's epinician odes consistently called for both lyre and aulos.[6]

Some of the odes, then, were accompanied by both instruments, but the aulos was not always required, and in some poems, only the lyre is mentioned. Can any more be said? I believe so, but first I must sketch briefly some aspects of what I take to have been the typical performance conditions for Pindaric epinicians.[7]

The chorus performing an ode would have required training and

[3] Graf (1889), 40 goes astray in finding evidence in this last passage for Pindar's universal practice. Martin (2003), 163, writes that '*aulos* and stringed instruments . . . together emblematize the ideal musical celebration for a victor', but it is not clear whether he would wish to argue that the aulos was always used.

[4] In *Ol.* 5, only the aulos is mentioned (19), but this ode is spurious (cf. e.g. Henry (2003), 11 n. 2).

[5] Cf. at line 5 of the same poem εὐλογία φόρμιγγι συνάορος, a category that we should expect to include the ode being performed.

[6] Cf. also *Ol.* 2.1, 4.2. The relevance of *Pyth.* 2.69–71 (on the Καστόρειον) is uncertain.

[7] Here I am in general agreement with Croiset (1880), 96–8.

direction. These functions will have been performed either by Pindar himself (cf. *Nem.* 3.11–12, quoted above) or by a substitute instructed by the poet: Aeneas, named at *Ol.* 6.88, and Nicasippus, named at *Isth.* 2.47, seem to be substitutes of this kind,[8] and there were no doubt others. It is natural to suppose that the person who trained and directed the chorus would accompany them on the lyre while performing these duties: *Nem.* 3.11–12 seems to imply this for the poet, and of course Pindar commonly refers to himself as playing the lyre. No purpose would have been served by bringing in an additional performer simply to provide lyre accompaniment. I should assume that such accompaniment was provided for all the odes, even when no instruments are mentioned.

When the aulos was employed, a player would have had to be engaged, probably a professional in most cases. Such a player could not reasonably be expected or required to commit the entire text of an ode to memory. In order to perform his task, he needed to know only the music for the strophe and (when an ode was triadic in form) the epode, the number of repetitions, and, if the responsion within the ode was not strict, the places where freedoms of responsion were to be found within the stanza, and the form that they took. This last requirement is of some importance. Except in the case of resolution,[9] any freedom of responsion of which the aulos-player was not aware in advance would cause him to become out of step with the other performers for a time. The result would be a disastrous cacophony, to which we may expect Pindar to have been particularly sensitive: for example, it has been plausibly argued on the basis of a new interpretation of the opening of *Dith.* 2 that the arrangement of the dithyrambic chorus in a circle rather than in a line, as previously, gained his approval precisely because it resulted in improved coordination.[10]

It is, I suggest, in this requirement that the aulos-player should have at his disposal some indication of where freedoms of responsion were to be expected, and what form they would take, that we should find the explanation of what has hitherto seemed a puzzling

[8] Cf. e.g. Hutchinson (2001), 414.

[9] I do not mention contraction, since I believe that Pindar can be shown not to have admitted this liberty: see Henry (2003).

[10] See D'Angour (1997).

feature of Pindar's metrical practice in his odes in dactylo-epitrite: three of the five odes for which aulos accompaniment is attested belong to this category *(Ol.* 3, 7, *Nem.* 9).[11] It has been observed[12] that the link-anceps in Pindar's dactylo-epitrite stanzas is generally long, but that if a link-anceps at any position within the stanza is to be short in any instance of that position, then it must be short in the first instance (first strophe or epode), or at least in the first triad. Exceptions are only admitted in association with proper names. As West says, 'the first triad sets the standard of strictness for the rest. More often than not, however, a short anceps in the first triad is not reproduced in the later ones'.

Now it cannot plausibly be argued that the audience would be disturbed by a short anceps in one of the later stanzas that had not been anticipated in the first instance of the position concerned: one may doubt whether they would even notice the distinction between short ancipitia that had and those that had not been duly anticipated in accordance with the rule. Nor would any such freedom pose a difficulty for the chorus or for their trainer, accompanying them on the lyre: both had the text to guide them. But for the aulos-player a procedure such as Pindar adopts would be extremely helpful. It would enable him to predict on the basis of a single memorized musical pattern the positions in which irregularities might be found in later stanzas: provided that he took particular care over those few positions and had sufficient warning prior to the performance of any isolated irregularities involving proper names, there would be no danger of his getting out of step with the other performers.

If this explanation of Pindar's practice in the dactylo-epitrite odes is correct, we should expect to find a similar strictness in the two aeolic odes for which aulos accompaniment is attested. *Nem.* 3 is indeed metrically very strict. Only twice do we find an isolated 'long' in a position elsewhere occupied by a 'short', and in one of the two anomalous passages, precise correspondence can easily be restored

[11] The dactylo-epitrite *Pyth.* 12 may well also have had aulos accompaniment. It was composed in honour of a victorious aulos-player, and much of it is concerned with the instrument.

[12] See West (1982), 74, referring to an unpublished treatment by W. S. Barrett.

by conjecture.[13] The number of free responsions of this kind in *Ol.* 10 is only slightly greater, and each occurs at the beginning of a verse in the strophe. The first position of verse 2 is short at 8 and 50 (*Κρόνου*), long elsewhere. The first position of verse 3 is short in the first three instances and the last two, otherwise long. The first position of verse 5 is generally short, but long at 68 for a proper name. The first position of verse 6 is long in the third and fifth strophes (48, 90), otherwise short. Such a restricted number of irregularities, all verse-initial, would not create any serious difficulty for the aulos-player.

If we turn now to one of the aeolic odes in which the only instrument named is the lyre, we find a very different situation. Five of the eight verses of the stanza of *Nem.* 4 contain theoretically anceps positions not consistently represented by either a 'short' or a 'long'; four of the five have two such positions.[14] An aulos-player, if one was engaged, could not hope to stay together with the other performers unless he laboriously memorized the text of the whole ode. The same is to be said of *Ol.* 9 and *Pyth.* 8, as a glance at Snell's metrical schemes at once makes clear;[15] and although we have no evidence concerning the instrumental forces employed in the first performance of *Pyth.* 10, for example, considerations of the same kind may well lead one to doubt whether Pindar can have expected the aulos to be used, unless it is supposed that he had not yet learnt how best to accommodate the aulos-player's needs at the time of his earliest compositions.

Parth. 2, a composition in simple aeolic metre for which aulos accompaniment is attested at line 14 (*αὐλίσ̣κων ὑπὸ λωτίνων* seems unavoidable), may appear to count against my hypothesis. Ancipitia not consistently represented by either a 'short' or a 'long' are found in the strophe in verses 1 (four examples, or five if *ἐνῆκεν* is accepted

[13] At 59, *ὄφρα θαλασσίαις ἀνέμων ῥιπαῖσι πεμφθείς*, strict responsion could be produced by replacing *ῥιπαῖσι* with *πνοαῖσι*. The phrase *ἀνέμων ῥιπαῖσι* may be due to the influence of *Pyth.* 9.48 or fr. 33d.2–3; cf. also fr. **140c. For *πνοαί* of winds, cf. *Ol.* 3.31, *Pyth.* 3.104, 5.121, *Parth.* 2.16. The freedom at *Nem.* 3.48, *Κένταυρον ἀσθμαίνοντα κόμιζεν*, is not so easily removed, however.

[14] See the metrical scheme in Henry (2005), 26.

[15] To the ancipitia marked as such by Snell in *Pyth.* 8 there is to be added the first position of epode 2, short at 36 (*Ὀλυμπίᾳ̣* is to be retained: see O. Schroeder (1900), 12) and 76, long elsewhere.

at line 61[16]) and 2 (one example) and in the epode in verses 1 and 2 (one example each). But the performance conditions for a composition of this kind will have been quite different from those for an epinician ode. In particular, I should have thought it very unlikely indeed that a professional aulos-player was engaged. I would suppose rather that one of the girls of the chorus played. Some support for this view may be found in the use of the diminutive *αὐλίσκ̣ων* which occurs nowhere else in Pindar: here perhaps it indicates a miniature form of the instrument specially adapted for use by a child. If I am right, the girl playing the aulos will no doubt have been involved in preparations for the performance from the beginning, if only so that she could participate in the dancing. She will have been no less familiar with the text of the ode than the other girls of the chorus.

Our evidence, then, so far as it goes, is consistent with the hypothesis that Pindar set strict limits on his use of ancipitia in his epinician odes in order to ensure that the aulos-player could with only a little effort remain in time with the other performers throughout the performance of any ode in which his services were called upon. Where the aulos was not to be used, Pindar's practice could be freer, as we see in a number of the aeolic odes. It is striking, however, that there are no such exceptions among the odes in dactylo-epitrite. One may well wonder whether aulos accompaniment was universal in the case of the epinicians belonging to that category: admittedly, the lyre is mentioned without the aulos in *Nem.* 10 (21), but such references need not be exclusive. I should prefer a different explanation. Pindar is not particularly likely always to have known in advance the precise forces to be used in performing odes commissioned from him. He may well have thought it advisable to allow for the possibility of aulos accompaniment in the first or a subsequent planned performance even when no definite information on the subject was available to him at the time of composition. Only when he knew for certain that no aulos-player was to be engaged could he safely allow himself greater freedom.

16 Against, see Henry (2003), 14 n. 28.

11

Lucian and Archilochus, or: How to Make Use of the Ancient Iambographers in the Context of the Second Sophistic

Heinz-Günther Nesselrath

Lucian's pamphlet 'The Mistaken Critic, or: On the nefarious day' is one of the most vitriolic pieces of invective in ancient Greek literature, easily rivalling the repeated spoutings of acid comments that Demosthenes and Aeschines directed against each other. The enemy that Lucian demolishes in this pamphlet apparently made the mistake of taking Lucian to task on a topic where the versatile Greek satirist hailing from Syrian Samosata was most sensitive: he dared question Lucian's competence in the subtleties of Greek style and expression, contending that Lucian had used the word *ἀποφράς* (meaning 'unlucky / ill-omened') in an inappropriate and 'barbarous' way. Being called a 'barbaros' in matters of language was one of the things Lucian liked least, and in 'The Mistaken Critic' he pounced upon his adversary with savage delight, insulting every bit of his opponent's character and life and demonstrating his own mastery of Greek prose style at the same time. What interests me here is how Lucian starts his rhetorical demolition work, namely by invoking Archilochus:

I now say to you what Archilochus said, that you have caught a cicada by the wing—just in case you should have heard of an iambic poet Archilochus, a Parian by birth, a man who was quite independent, outspoken and not at all reluctant to be abusive, even if he was going to inflict the greatest pain on those who would encounter the bitterness of his iambics. Well, when one such person spoke ill of him, Archilochus said that the man had caught a cicada by the wing, likening himself to the cicada which is by nature vociferous even without any compulsion and which cries out more loudly whenever it is caught by the wing. 'Ill-starred fellow,' he said, 'what reason do you have for provoking against you a vociferous poet who is in search of ... subject matter for his iambics?'[1]

As Archilochus in this excursus likens himself to a cicada, Lucian likens himself to Archilochus, even though he then hastens to expressly deny that: 'These same threats I make to you, not, by Zeus, likening myself to Archilochus (how could I? I am far from doing that!) ...'.[2] This denial, however, is wholly perfunctory; Lucian is not even content with just the one Archilochus, but invokes all the rest of the famous old iambographers: 'Not even Archilochus, I think, could have responded adequately, even if he had invited both Semonides and Hipponax to help him in dealing with just one of your evil traits, such children in every kind of abominable behaviour did you make Orodocides and Lycambes and Bupalus, who were the butts of their iambics'.[3] According to this description, Lucian's enemy surpasses all the famous opponents of the three iambographers, and Archilochus

[1] Luc. *Pseudol.* 1: *τὸ δὲ τοῦ Ἀρχιλόχου ἐκεῖνο ἤδη σοι λέγω, ὅτι τέττιγα τοῦ πτεροῦ συνείληφας, εἴπερ τινὰ ποιητὴν ἰάμβων ἀκούεις Ἀρχίλοχον, Πάριον τὸ γένος, ἄνδρα κομιδῇ ἐλεύθερον καὶ παρρησίᾳ συνόντα, μηδὲν ὀκνοῦντα ὀνειδίζειν, εἰ καὶ ὅτι μάλιστα λυπήσειν ἔμελλε τοὺς περιπετεῖς ἐσομένους τῇ χολῇ τῶν ἰάμβων αὐτοῦ. ἐκεῖνος τοίνυν πρός τινος τῶν τοιούτων ἀκούσας κακῶς τέττιγα ἔφη τὸν ἄνδρα εἰληφέναι τοῦ πτεροῦ, εἰκάζων ἑαυτὸν τῷ τέττιγι ὁ Ἀρχίλοχος φύσει μὲν λάλῳ ὄντι καὶ ἄνευ τινὸς ἀνάγκης, ὁπόταν δὲ καὶ τοῦ πτεροῦ ληφθῇ, γεγωνότερον βοῶντι. "Καὶ σὺ δή," ἔφη, "ὦ κακόδαιμον ἄνθρωπε, τί βουλόμενος ποιητὴν λάλον παροξύνεις ἐπὶ σεαυτὸν ... ζητοῦντα ... ὑποθέσεις τοῖς ἰάμβοις;"* The Archilochus passage is fr. 223 *IEG*. English translations of Archilochus' fragments and testimonia are taken (sometimes slightly modified) from Gerber (1999).

[2] Luc. *Pseudol.* 2: *Ταῦτά σοι καὶ αὐτὸς ἀπειλῶ, οὐ μὰ τὸν Δία τῷ Ἀρχιλόχῳ εἰκάζων ἐμαυτόν—πόθεν; πολλοῦ γε καὶ δέω.* In a similar way Horace warns an adversary not to provoke his wrath, *namque in malos asperrimus* | *parata tollo cornua,* | *qualis Lycambae spretus infido gener* | *aut acer hostis Bupalo* (*Epod.* 6.11–14 = Archil. test. 25 Gerber). Likewise Ovid: *postmodo, si perges, in te mihi liber iambus / tincta Lycambeo sanguine tela dabit* (*Ibis* 53–4 = Archil. test. 28 Gerber; cf. also lines 521–2 = Archil. test. 30 Gerber).

[3] Luc. *Pseudol.* 2: *σοὶ δὲ μυρία συνειδὼς ἰάμβων ἄξια βεβιωμένα, πρὸς ἅ μοι δοκεῖ οὐδ' ἂν ὁ Ἀρχίλοχος αὐτὸς διαρκέσαι, προσπαρακαλέσας καὶ τὸν Σιμωνίδην καὶ τὸν Ἱππώνακτα συμποιεῖν μετ' αὐτοῦ κἂν ἕν τι τῶν προσόντων σοι κακῶν, οὕτω σύ γε παῖδας ἀπέφηνας ἐν πάσῃ βδελυρίᾳ τὸν Ὀροδοκίδην καὶ τὸν Λυκάμβην καὶ τὸν Βούπαλον, τοὺς ἐκείνων ἰάμβους.*

and Semonides and Hipponax taken together would not be sufficient to castigate the many vices of this monster. In spite of this declaration, however, Lucian himself by no means desists from attacking this enemy (after all, his invective has only just started), though he had proclaimed himself markedly inferior to Archilochus only two sentences ago. If we follow this train of thought to its logical conclusion, it would mean that Lucian—despite his explicit counterclaim—apparently regards himself as not only equal but even better than the iambic poets of old: at the end of this pamphlet his adversary will be utterly destroyed.

Did Lucian, then, consider himself a worthy (and maybe even superior) successor to the iambic poets of old? Although these poets have not much of a presence in other Lucianic writings,[4] Lucian indeed seems to have considered them a not unimportant part of his literary heritage. This is suggested by a famous passage in 'The Twice-accused', where a personified Dialogue enumerates all the components that Lucian forced him to put up with: 'he took away from me the respectable tragic mask that I had, and put another upon me that is comic, satyrlike, and almost ridiculous. Then he . . . penned me up with Jest and Iambos and Cynicism and Eupolis and Aristophanes . . . At last he even dug up and thrust upon me Menippus, a prehistoric dog . . . '.[5] Here, 'Iambos' surely means not just 'invective', but harks back to the famous poets who are expressly mentioned at the beginning of 'The Mistaken Critic'.

By Lucian's time various images of Archilochus were current in the Graeco-Roman world. On the one hand, he ranked as a truly great poet and could be mentioned side by side with Homer:[6] in a

[4] There is a fleeting mention of Archilochus and Hipponax in *Adv. Ind.* 27: *Ἡδέως δ' ἂν καὶ ἐροίμην σε, τὰ τοσαῦτα βιβλία ἔχων τί μάλιστα ἀναγιγνώσκεις αὐτῶν; τὰ Πλάτωνος; τὰ Ἀντισθένους; τὰ Ἀρχιλόχου; τὰ Ἱππώνακτος; ἢ τούτων μὲν ὑπερφρονεῖς, ῥήτορες δὲ μάλιστά σοι διὰ χειρός; . . . ἢ ἐκεῖνά γε πάντα οἶσθα καὶ γιγνώσκεις αὐτῶν ἕκαστον, τὸν δὲ Ἀριστοφάνην καὶ τὸν Εὔπολιν ὑποδέδυκας;*

[5] *Bis Acc.* 33 (translation by A. M. Harmon, who, however, translates *τὸν ἴαμβον* with 'Satire'): *τὸ μὲν τραγικὸν ἐκεῖνο καὶ σωφρονικὸν προσωπεῖον ἀφεῖλέ μου, κωμικὸν δὲ καὶ σατυρικὸν ἄλλο ἐπέθηκέ μοι καὶ μικροῦ δεῖν γελοῖον. εἶτά μοι εἰς τὸ αὐτὸ . . . συγκαθεῖρξεν τὸ σκῶμμα καὶ τὸν ἴαμβον καὶ κυνισμὸν καὶ τὸν Εὔπολιν καὶ τὸν Ἀριστοφάνη . . . τελευταῖον δὲ καὶ Μένιππόν τινα τῶν παλαιῶν κυνῶν . . . ἀνορύξας, καὶ τοῦτον ἐπεισήγαγεν μοι . . .* On this passage, see Braun (1994), 326–7.

[6] The first one (known to us) to do this—though under negative auspices—was the Presocratic philosopher Heraclitus: *τόν τε Ὅμηρον ἔφασκεν ἄξιον ἐκ τῶν ἀγώνων*

passage cited by Aristotle,[7] already the orator and sophist Alcidamas (a contemporary of Isocrates) puts both together as the first examples of *σοφοί* whom everyone honoured; just a few decades before Lucian, Dio of Prusa adduces them as a pair of poets, 'with whom no other is worth comparing';[8] according to Philostratus, the sophist Hippodromus called Homer the 'voice of sophists' and Archilochus their 'spirit/inspiration'.[9] Among the Alexandrian philologists, Aristophanes of Byzantium seems to have been especially fond of Archilochus;[10] further favourable judgements of Archilochus' poetic qualities are found in Horace,[11] Pseudo-Longinus[12] and Quintilian.[13] Moreover, a vivid reflection of Archilochus' status as a great poet is presented by the anecdote in which the god Apollo

ἐκβάλλεσθαι καὶ ῥαπίζεσθαι καὶ Ἀρχίλοχον ὁμοίως (D–K 22 B 42 (i. 160.9–10) = Archil. test. 34 Gerber).

[7] Arist. *Rhet.* 2.23 p. 1398^b10–13: *καὶ ὡς Ἀλκιδάμας, ὅτι πάντες τοὺς σοφοὺς τιμῶσιν· "Πάριοι γοῦν Ἀρχίλοχον καίπερ βλάσφημον ὄντα τετιμήκασι, καὶ Χῖοι Ὅμηρον οὐκ ὄντα πολίτην . . .".* In Aristotle's times Heraclides Ponticus already wrote what in view of its title could have been an extended comparison between Homer and Archilochus in two books (Heraclid. fr. 178 Wehrli = Archil. test. 63 Gerber).

[8] Dio *Or.* 33 [16 von Arnim].11 (= Archil. test. 16 Gerber): *δύο γὰρ ποιητῶν γεγονότων ἐξ ἅπαντος τοῦ αἰῶνος, οἷς οὐδένα τῶν ἄλλων ξυμβάλλειν ἄξιον, Ὁμήρου τε καὶ Ἀρχιλόχου . . .* On the Latin side, see Velleius 1.5.1–2: *clarissimum deinde Homeri illuxit ingenium . . .* (2) *. . .neque quemquam alium, cuius operis primus auctor fuerit, in eo perfectissimum praeter Homerum et Archilochum reperiemus.*

[9] Philostr. *V.Soph.* 2 p. 620.5–10 (= Archil. test. 41 Gerber): *ὁ Ἱππόδρομος . . . ἐσπούδαζε . . . καλῶν τὸν μὲν Ὅμηρον φωνὴν σοφιστῶν, τὸν δὲ Ἀρχίλοχον πνεῦμα.* See also Antipater of Thessalonica *AP* 11.20.5 = 189 *GP*. The comparison of Homer and Archilochus takes an interesting turn in a short epigram by the Emperor Hadrian, presented as an inscription for Archilochus' tomb, in which his 'raving iambics' are said to have been caused by the Muse herself, 'in order to do Homer a favour' (*AP* 7.674 = 2122–3 *FGE*: *Ἀρχιλόχου τόδε σῆμα, τὸν ἐς λυσσῶντας ἰάμβους | ἤγαγε Μαιονίδῃ Μοῦσα χαριζομένη*). According to these lines the Muse deflected Archilochus' poetic genius into iambics to preserve Homer's status as the greatest of Greek poets; see Page ad loc.

[10] See Cic. *Att.* 16.11.2 (apparently not in Slater (1986), but see Nauck (1848), 249, where this passage is given as 'fr. II' of Aristophanes' 'Comm. in Callimachi *Πίνακας*'): *quod vereris ne ἀδόλεσχος mihi tu, quis minus? cui, ut Aristophani Archilochi iambus, sic epistula* <*tua*> *longissima quaeque optima videtur.* On the great Alexandrian scholars' treatment of Archilochus, see von Blumenthal (1922), 25–31.

[11] Hor. *Epist.* 1.19.23–31 = Archil. test. 27 Gerber. At about the same time, Valerius Maximus (6.3[ext.].1) called Archilochus *maximum poetam aut certe summo proximum.*

[12] [Long.] 13.3 = Archil. test. 38 Gerber, and 33.5 = Archil. test. 39 Gerber.

[13] Quint. 10.1.60 = Archil. test. 45 Gerber.

himself ejects the man who had killed Archilochus in battle from his temple, citing as his crime that he had slain a 'servant of the Muses'. This story is told or alluded to by the second-century BC scholar Heraclides Lembus,[14] Plutarch,[15] Dio of Prusa,[16] Aelius Aristides,[17] Galen,[18] and Aelian.[19] Already the bucolic poet Theocritus praised Archilochus as beloved by Apollo and the Muses.[20] By Lucian's time, then, many competent voices had held Archilochus in high esteem.

The second image of Archilochus developed until Lucian's times was that of the harsh but justified (and therefore helpful) critic, who directed his darts against those who really deserved it. This image is most fully developed by Dio of Prusa in his first speech to the citizens of Tarsus (*Or.* 33 [16 von Arnim]): Dio puts Archilochus next to Homer himself in poetic rank (see above), but sees both in contrast with each other where themes and their treatment are concerned: 'Homer praised practically everything . . . But Archilochus went to the other extreme, toward censure—seeing, I imagine, that men have greater need of that—and first of all he censures himself . . . Thus he who is good at rebuking and upbraiding, and at revealing by his words the sins of men, is evidently superior and preferred above those who praise'.[21] For Dio, then, Archilochus' poetry is valuable especially because it aims at revealing and correcting the faults of human beings. This attitude might have appealed very much to Lucian, and perhaps he even took a clue from Dio's treatment of

[14] Heracl. Lemb. *π. πολιτειῶν* 25 (p. 22.18–21 Dilts) = Archil. test. 15 Gerber.

[15] Plut. *De sera num. vind.* 17. 560e = Archil. test. 13 Gerber.

[16] Dio *Or.* 33[16 von Arnim].12 = Archil. test. 16 Gerber.

[17] Aristid. 3.610 Lenz–Behr = Archil. test. 17 Gerber.

[18] Galen. *Protr.* 22 (p. 118.3–4 Marquardt) = Archil. test. 14 Gerber. Galen even cites the verse by which Archilochus' killer was ejected: *Μουσάων θεράποντα κατέκτανες· ἔξιθι νηοῦ.*

[19] Aelian fr. 83 Domingo-Forasté = Archil. test. 12 Gerber. On Archilochus' death as part of the 'Archilochus legend' see C. W. Müller (1985).

[20] Theocr. *Epigr.* 21 Gow = *AP* 7.664 = 3434–9 *HE* = Archil. test. 37 Gerber.

[21] Dio. *Or.* 33[16 von Arnim].11–13 = Archil. test. 16 Gerber (where, however, §13 is not included): *Ὅμηρος μὲν σχεδὸν πάντα ἐνεκωμίασε . . .* (12) *Ἀρχίλοχος δὲ ἐπὶ τὴν ἐναντίαν ἧκε, τὸ ψέγειν, ὁρῶν οἶμαι τούτου μᾶλλον δεομένους τοὺς ἀνθρώπους, καὶ πρῶτον αὑτὸν ψέγει . . .* (13) *ὥσθ' ὁ λοιδορεῖν ἱκανὸς καὶ καθάπτεσθαι καὶ φανερὰ τῷ λόγῳ ποιεῖν τὰ ἁμαρτήματα δῆλον ὅτι κρείττων ἐστὶ καὶ προκέκριται τῶν ἐπαινούντων* (translation above by Lamar Crosby, in Cohoon and Lamar Crosby (1951), slightly modified). See also §§17–19 in the same speech.

Archilochus;[22] one reason to think so is provided by the fact that the image of Archilochus as the sharp but constructive critic is nowhere else drawn on such clear lines.[23]

There is, however, yet a third image of Archilochus, and it is probably the one with the widest currency in antiquity: that of the unbearable mocker and blasphemer.[24] Its earliest preserved witness is Pindar, who already talks of 'fault-finding Archilochus many times in helplessness fattening himself on harsh words of hatred'.[25] Next there is the already mentioned Alcidamas[26] (cited by Aristotle), calling Archilochus directly βλάσφημος, a word which—together with its cognate βλασφημία[27]—would stick to him for ever. Callimachus compared Archilochus' violent attacks with 'the dog's pungent bile and the wasp's sharp sting, and he has his mouth's venom from both'.[28] Plutarch censures Archilochus several times for being ἀκόλαστος[29]

[22] The relationship between Lucian and Dio has been discussed by Pernot (1994), who detects a number of interesting similarities between the two, but cautiously refrains from postulating a direct influence by Dio upon Lucian. See also Swain (1994), Georgiadou and Larmour (1997).

[23] There are some hints of it in authors later than Lucian: Men. Rhet. p. 393.9–12 Spengel = p. 122 Russell and Wilson: καὶ Ἀρχιλόχου δὲ οὐκ ἀμελήσεις, ἱκανῶς κολάσαντος τοὺς ἐχθροὺς τῇ ποιήσει . . . ; Julian, *Misopogon* 1 p. 337ab (p. 155 Lacombrade): Ἀλκαίῳ δ' οὐκέτι οὐδ' Ἀρχιλόχῳ τῷ Παρίῳ τὴν μοῦσαν ἔδωκεν ὁ θεὸς εἰς εὐφροσύνας καὶ ἡδονὰς τρέψαι· μοχθεῖν γὰρ ἄλλοτε ἄλλως ἀναγκαζόμενοι τῇ μουσικῇ πρὸς τοῦτο ἐχρῶντο, κουφότερα ποιοῦντες αὑτοῖς ὅσα ὁ δαίμων ἐδίδου τῇ εἰς τοὺς ἀδικοῦντας λοιδορίᾳ.

[24] According to Aelian, the Athenian nobleman Critias (later to become the leader of the infamous Thirty Tyrants) had already taken Archilochus to task for slandering even himself (Aelian, *VH* 10.13 = Critias D–K 88 B 44 (ii. 396.6–18) = Archil. fr. 295 *IEG* = Archil. test. 33 Gerber); this, however, is not so much an indictment of Archilochus' general inclination to slander as rather of a kind of 'confessional urge' which the aristocratic Critias found rather inappropriate.

[25] Pind. *Pyth.* 2.55–6: τὰ πόλλ' ἐν ἀμαχανίᾳ ψογερὸν Ἀρχίλοχον βαρυλόγοις ἔχθεσιν πιαινόμενον . . .

[26] See above n. 7.

[27] See e.g. Plut. fr. 40 Sandbach (τὸν μὲν γὰρ Ἀρχίλοχον καὶ τὸν Ἱππώνακτα βλασφημίας συγγράψαι κατὰ τῶν λυπησάντων); Aristid. 3.611 Lenz–Behr = Archil. test. 17 Gerber: Ἀρχίλοχος περὶ τὰς βλασφημίας οὕτω διατρίβων.

[28] Callim. fr. 380 Pf. = Archil. test. 36 Gerber.

[29] Plut. *Cato min.* 7.2: ὁ δὲ Κάτων . . . πολλὰ τὸν Σκιπίωνα καθύβρισε, τῷ πικρῷ προσχρησάμενος τοῦ Ἀρχιλόχου, τὸ δ' ἀκόλαστον ἀφεὶς καὶ παιδαριῶδες; *De curios.* 10.520ab: τῶν ὑπ' Ἀρχιλόχου πρὸς τὰς γυναῖκας ἀπρεπῶς καὶ ἀκολάστως εἰρημένων.

and *βλάσφημος*[30] as well as for choosing very inappropriate subject matter for his poetry.[31]

In Lucian's own times, the Cynic Oenomaus sarcastically takes the god Apollo to task for declaring Archilochus a poet worthy of heaven: 'What, then, was the reason, for which you considered Archilochus worthy of heaven? Don't begrudge, you biggest philanthropist of all the gods, this way upward to others either! What do you command us to do? Obviously that which Archilochus did, if we should want to seem worthy of your hearth, namely to harshly insult the women who don't want to marry us and to consort with catamites—for they are by far worse than other bad people—using metres, because that is the form of communication of gods as well as of divine men like Archilochus?'[32] Aelius Aristides defends Archilochus as a worthy poet, yet calls his iambi a 'rather disagreeable' form of poetry;[33] similarly Aelian, though he explicitly and extensively narrates how Apollo honoured Archilochus after his death (see above), nevertheless mentions his 'foul mouth and slanderous speech'.[34] Maximus of Tyre simply dismisses Archilochus as a *ὑβριστής*.[35] In the

[30] See fr. 40 Sandbach, cited in n. 27.

[31] Plut. *De recta ratione audiendi* 45a: *μέμψαιτο δ' ἄν τις Ἀρχιλόχου μὲν τὴν ὑπόθεσιν.*

[32] Oenomaus fr. 1.5–6 (pp. 71.19–72.28 Hammerstaedt; see also his commentary on pp. 109–115): *Τί ποτ' οὖν ἦν τοῦτο, δι' ὅ σοι Ἀρχίλοχος ἔδοξεν ἄξιος εἶναι τοῦ οὐρανοῦ; Μὴ φθονήσῃς, ὦ φιλανθρωπότατε θεῶν, μηδ' ἄλλοις ἀνθρώποις τῆς ἄνω ὁδοῦ. Τί πράττειν κελεύεις ἡμᾶς; Ἢ δηλαδὴ τὰ Ἀρχιλόχου, εἰ μέλλοιμεν ἄξιοι φανεῖσθαι τῆς ὑμετέρας ἑστίας; Λοιδορῆσαι μὲν πικρῶς τὰς οὐκ ἐθελούσας ἡμῖν γαμεῖσθαι, ἅψασθαι δὲ καὶ τῶν κιναίδων, ἐπειδὴ τῶν ἄλλων πονηρῶν πολὺ πονηρότεροί εἰσι· οὐχὶ δίχα μέτρου, αὕτη γὰρ διάλεκτος καὶ θεῶν, ὥσπερ οὖν καὶ θείων ἀνδρῶν, ὥσπερ Ἀρχιλόχου.*

[33] Aristid. *Or.* 3.610 = Archil. test. 17 Gerber: *τὸ . . . δυσχερέστερον εἶδος τῆς ποιήσεως.*

[34] Aelian fr. 83 Domingo-Forasté = Archil.test. 12 Gerber: *τὸ αἰσχροεπὲς καὶ τὸ κακόρρημον.*

[35] Max. *Dial.* 18.9b: *Τὸν δὲ Ἀρχιλόχου ἔρωτα, ὑβριστὴς γάρ, χαίρειν ἐῶ.* See also Sext. *Adv. Math.* 1.298, where the iambographers Hipponax and Archilochus are classified as models for irascible (*ὀργίλοι*) people. In classical Latin literature, too, the image of an Archilochus full of rage and lashing out at others is predominant, see Cic. *Nat. Deor.* 3.91 (*qui erat Archilochi versu volneratus*); Hor. *Epist.* 1.19.23–5 (*Parios ego primus iambos | ostendi Latio, numeros animosque secutus | Archilochi, non res et agentia verba Lycamben*; see also lines 26–31), Hor. *AP* 79 (*Archilochum proprio rabies armavit iambo*); Quintilian however (10.1.59–60) presents a more positive picture of Archilochus' poetical powers (*ex tribus receptis Aristarchi iudicio scriptoribus iamborum ad hexin maxime pertinebit unus Archilochus. Summa in hoc uis elocutionis, cum ualidae tum breues uibrantesque sententiae, plurimum sanguinis atque neruorum, adeo ut uideatur quibusdam quod quoquam minor est materiae esse, non ingeni uitium*).

fourth century, the Emperor Julian, when trying to create an ideal new pagan priesthood, emphatically forbids these priests to read the old iambographers (or their kindred spirits, i.e. the poets of Old Comedy);[36] even in the sixth century AD, the orator Choricius still regards Archilochus as being second to none 'in thoughts and speech of utmost dissoluteness'.[37] Christian writers were only too happy to take up this tune and condemn—by indicting Archilochus—one of the outstanding exemplars of pagan Greek poetry: Origen called him 'a man who displayed his poetry in the worst and most wanton subject matter and showed his outrageous and filthy character';[38] similarly Eusebius, taking his clue from Oenomaus,[39] denounced Archilochus as 'a man who used every kind of foul language and unspeakable words, which a moral man would not bear listening to, against women in his poems';[40] and Theodoretus simplified this by labelling Archilochus 'a most shameful poet'.[41]

A remarkable development of Archilochus' image can also be found in the epigrams collected in the *Anthologia Palatina*. Some of the earlier ones (from the third century BC until the times of the early

[36] Julian *Epist.* 89b p. 300cd (p. 140.23–6 Bidez and Cumont): *ἱερωμένος τις μήτε Ἀρχίλοχον ἀναγινωσκέτω μήτε Ἱππώνακτα μήτε ἄλλον τινὰ τῶν τὰ τοιαῦτα γραφόντων. Ἀποκλινέτω καὶ τῆς παλαιᾶς κωμῳδίας ὅσα τῆς τοιαύτης ἰδέας· ἄμεινον μὲν γὰρ καὶ πάντα.* Earlier, Valerius Maximus had asserted that the Spartans banned Archilochus' writings from their community because of its impudent language, not wanting their children to be influenced by these kinds of texts (Val. Max. VI 3(ext.),1 (*Lacedaemonii libros Archilochi e ciuitate sua exportari iusserunt, quod eorum parum uerecundam ac pudicam lectionem arbitrabantur: noluerunt enim ea liberorum suorum animos imbui, ne plus moribus noceret quam ingeniis prodesset. itaque maximum poetam aut certe summo proximum, quia domum sibi inuisam obscenis maledictis lacerauerat, carminum exilio multarunt*).

[37] Choric. 32.2.38: *Ἀρχίλοχον γὰρ οὐδὲ παραβάλλειν ἔνεστιν ὅλως ἑτέρῳ μηδὲν εἰς ἔννοιάν τε καὶ λέξιν ἐσχάτης ἀκοσμίας ἐκλελοιπότα.*

[38] Orig. *Contra Cels.* 3.25: . . . *τὸν Ἀρχίλοχον, ἄνδρα ἐν κακίστῃ καὶ ἀσελγεστάτῃ ὑποθέσει ἐπιδειξάμενον τὴν ἑαυτοῦ ποιητικὴν καὶ ἦθος ἀσελγὲς καὶ ἀκάθαρτον παραστήσαντα* . . .

[39] Oenomaus fr. 1 Hammerstaedt, as cited above in n. 32, is preserved in Euseb. *PE* 5.33.5–6.

[40] Euseb. *PE* 5.32.2: *Ἀρχίλοχον, ἄνδρα παντοίαις κατὰ γυναικῶν αἰσχρορρημοσύναις καὶ ἀρρητολογίαις, ἃς οὐδ' ἀκοῦσαί τις σώφρων ἀνὴρ ὑπομείνειεν, ἐν τοῖς οἰκείοις ποιήμασι κεχρημένον.*

[41] Theodoretus, *Graec. Cur. Aff.* 10.36: *Ἀρχίλοχον, αἰσχρότατον γενόμενον ποιητήν.*

Empire) sing his praise as a poet,[42] but already in the third century BC we find a sympathetic treatment of the daughters of Lycambes, whom Archilochus is supposed to have driven to suicide by his venomous verses: the epigrammatist Dioscorides puts into their mouth—but after their death—a very effective plea of defence against Archilochus' slanderous attacks.[43] About 150 years later Meleager of Gadara seems to have written a similar piece;[44] but while in Dioscorides the poor women concentrated on proving Archilochus' claims as false, branding them as 'frightful reproach and a hateful report against our family' (*καθ' ἡμετέρης γενεῆς ῥιγηλὸν ὄνειδος φήμην τε στυγερήν*), in Meleager they move on to attack their accuser: 'bitter Archilochus spewed forth much that is shameful against our virginity . . . Muses, why did you direct his violent iambics against girls, favouring an impious man?'[45] Later, the tide turns ever more decisively against Archilochus. Possibly in the first century AD, Gaetulicus[46] wrote a fictitious verse inscription for Archilochus' tomb, in which the Parian poet is described as 'the first to dip a bitter Muse in Echidna's gall and to stain mild Helicon with blood' and the wayfarer is exhorted to 'pass by quietly, lest you stir up the wasps that settle on this tomb'.[47] Finally, in the sixth century AD, Julian of Egypt in two epigrams predicts dire consequences from Archilochus' death

[42] *AP* 7.664 = 3434–9 *HE* = Archil. test. 37 Gerber, ascribed to either Leonidas of Tarentum or to Theocritus (*Epigr.* 21 Gow): *Ἀρχίλοχον καὶ στᾶθι καὶ εἴσιδε τὸν πάλαι ποιητὰν | τὸν τῶν ἰάμβων, οὗ τὸ μυρίον κλέος | διῆλθε κἠπὶ νύκτα καὶ ποτ' ἀῶ. | ἦ ῥά νιν αἱ Μοῖσαι καὶ ὁ Δάλιος ἠγάπευν Ἀπόλλων, | ὡς ἐμμελής τ' ἐγένετο κἠπιδέξιος | ἔπεά τε ποιεῖν πρὸς λύραν τ' ἀείδειν.* *AP* 11.20 = 185–90 *GP* (Antipater of Thessalonica, of Augustan times): *Φεύγεθ', ὅσοι λόκκας ἢ λοφνίδας ἢ καμασῆνας | ᾄδετε, ποιητῶν φῦλον ἀκανθολόγων, | οἵ τ' ἐπέων κόσμον λελυγισμένον ἀσκήσαντες | κρήνης ἐξ ἱερῆς πίνετε λιτὸν ὕδωρ. | (5) σήμερον Ἀρχιλόχοιο καὶ ἄρσενος ἦμαρ Ὁμήρου | σπένδομεν· ὁ κρητὴρ οὐ δέχεθ' ὑδροπότας.*

[43] *AP* 7.351 = 1555–64 *HE* = Archil. test. 20 Gerber.

[44] *AP* 7.352 = 4742–9 *HE* = Archil. test. 21 Gerber. This epigram—two lines shorter than Dioscorides'—is inscribed as *ΑΔΕΣΠΟΤΟΝ, οἱ δὲ ΜΕΛΕΑΓΡΟΥ.*

[45] *πολλὰ δ' ὁ πικρὸς | αἰσχρὰ καθ' ἡμετέρης ἔβλυσε παρθενίης | Ἀρχίλοχος· . . . | Πιερίδες, τί κόρῃσιν ἐφ' ὑβριστῆρας ἰάμβους | ἐτράπετ', οὐχ ὁσίῳ φωτὶ χαριζόμεναι;*

[46] If he is to be identified with Cn. Cornelius Lentulus Gaetulicus, who was put to death by Caligula in AD 39.

[47] *AP* 7.71 = 197–202 *FGE* = Archil. test. 22 Gerber: *Σῆμα τόδ' Ἀρχιλόχου παραπόντιον, ὅς ποτε πικρὴν | μοῦσαν ἐχιδναίῳ πρῶτος ἔβαψε χόλῳ | αἱμάξας Ἑλικῶνα τὸν ἥμερον. . . . | (5) ἠρέμα δὴ παράμειψον, ὁδοιπόρε, μή ποτε τοῦδε | κινήσῃς τύμβῳ σφῆκας ἐφεζομένους.*

even for Hades: in the first he warns no less than the dreadful Cerberus himself to beware of the now dead Archilochus ('now even you must fear a horrifying shade: Archilochus is dead. Be on your guard against the pungent iambic wrath engendered by the bitter anger of his tongue'[48]); in the second he voices the fear that all the dead may now try to flee from Hades because of Archilochus' fearful presence, which once drove Lycambes' daughters into Hades.[49] Thus, over the centuries, the character of Archilochus' poetry has been reduced to pure verbal venom, which threatens to wreak havoc even in the underworld.

In Lucian's times, this development is only in the making, and our satirist (as shown above) was able to choose from a more extended range of images of Archilochus; what apparently most appealed to him was an image combining the traits of the remarkable poet and of the harsh but helpful social critic, as Dio had depicted him. There is, however, still something else: the very fluidity still present in Archilochus' image in Lucian's time (when it had not yet been reduced to the venom-spouting persecutor of personal enemies) made it possible for Lucian to present an image of Archilochus that in important aspects reflects other heroes in Lucian's satiric writings and even the portrait Lucian sometimes—in the guise of certain personages within his own works—likes to draw of himself. Calling Archilochus *ἄνδρα κομιδῇ ἐλεύθερον καὶ παρρησίᾳ συνόντα* (*Pseudol.* 1), he stresses two key concepts found in many positive characters (or phenomena) of his other writings, namely *ἐλευθερία* and *παρρησία*.[50] Thus, the idealized Athens of Lucian's *Nigrinus* is an *ἐλευθέρα πόλις* (*Nigr.* 13, 14, 17); Lucian's most revered philosopher, Demonax, combines both *ἐλευθερία* and *παρρησία* in an exceptional degree (*Demon.* 3, 11); the god Momus is a great friend of *παρρησία* as well (*J. Trag.* 19,

[48] *AP* 7.69 = Archil. test. 23 Gerber: *Κέρβερε . . . | ἤδη φρικαλέον δείδιθι καὶ σὺ νέκυν· | Ἀρχίλοχος τέθνηκε· φυλάσσεο θυμὸν ἰάμβων | δριμὺν πικροχόλου τικτόμενον στόματος . . .*

[49] *AP* 7.70: . . . *εἰ γὰρ φέγγος ἔλειπον ἀλυσκάζουσαι ἰάμβων | ἄγριον Ἀρχιλόχου φλέγμα Λυκαμβιάδες,* | (5) *πῶς οὐκ ἂν προλίποι σκοτίων πυλεῶνας ἐναύλων | νεκρὸς ἅπας φεύγων τάρβος ἐπεσβολίης;*

[50] Both are, of course, also typically Cynic virtues: for *ἐλευθερία*, see Luc. *Symp.* 16, *Catapl.* 13, *V. Auct.* 7, *Peregr.* 18, *D. Mort.* 2.3, 20.9, 21.3; for *παρρησία*, see *Demon.* 50, *J. Conf.* 5, *V.Auct.* 8, *Peregr.* 18, *D. Mort.* 20.9, 21.3.

Deor. Conc. 2, 6, 14), as is the hero of *Zeus Tragodos*, the Epicurean Damis (*J. Trag.* 44). As for Lucian himself, both ἐλευθερία and παρρησία become patron goddesses of his namesake Parrhesiades ('Son of free speech') in *Pisc.* 17, who is, of course, the purest embodiment of that which his name denotes; in *Merc. Cond.* 4 Lucian (being the 'I' in this pamphlet) ascribes παρρησία to himself, while in *Apol.* 1, ἐλευθερία is ascribed to him by others.

In this way, Lucian consciously chooses a certain image of Archilochus (among those then in existence), which he then develops further in order to adapt it to the persona he wants to present of himself. One might almost say that he fuses his own literary image with that of Archilochus so as to be able to pounce on his enemy with greater authority and effect. And though Archilochus is not mentioned explicitly again in *Pseudologista* after the first two chapters, he remains a background presence throughout. When in the last chapter Lucian warns his adversary that he may still—after having been clobbered with wagonloads of outrageous insult—not yet have fully realized what kind of ἀνὴρ ... μελάμπυγος he has offended, that word again belongs to the literary heritage of Archilochus (fr. 178 *IEG*).[51] Despite his denial in *Pseudol.* 2, Lucian appropriates Archilochus' persona very effectively in this invective, giving the Parian poet's afterlife in antiquity a new and interesting twist.

[51] The Archilochus quotation (μή τευ μελαμπύγου τύχῃς) became a proverbial expression (Zenob. *Cent.* 5.10; Zenob. Athous 2.85; Michael Apost. *Cent.* 11.19; Macar. *Cent.* 5.82) and was then connected with Heracles, where μελάμπυγος was explained with his δασύτης περὶ τὴν πυγὴν (Zenob. *Cent.* 5.10). In *Pseudol.* 32, μελάμπυγος and δασύς are likewise combined.

Part III

Tragedy

12

Housman's Greek

James Diggle

'The scene is a police court, and it is a case of stealing spoons. The accused, a well-dressed man of gentlemanly appearance, is described in the charge sheet as Sir Richard Jebb, M.P., Regius Professor of Greek in the University of Cambridge, D.Litt., Hon. DCL Oxon., Hon. LLD Edinburgh Harvard Dublin & Glasgow, Hon. Doct. Philosoph. Bologna.[1] The magistrate remarks that it is sad to see a person of his antecedents in such a position. A constable met him in the small hours of the morning not far from the House of Commons; thinking that he looked bulky, and feeling sure in his own mind that this appearance was caused by silver spoons, he took him to the police station. Sir Richard has entrusted his defence to a disreputable-looking attorney with the same Christian name; a Mr Porson. Mr Porson represents to the magistrate that his client is a gentleman of good position and hitherto blameless life; he is a fellow of Trinity, a college possessing a large amount of silver plate; and the butler is in court, prepared to testify that no missing spoons have ever been traced to Sir Richard Jebb. Moreover, when his pockets were turned out at the police station, no spoon was found there.'

I am indebted to Dr R. D. Dawe, Mr P. G. Naiditch, Prof. R. Renehan, and Dr C. A. Stray for helpful comments, and to The Society of Authors and the Syndics of Cambridge University Library for permission to cite Housman's unpublished lecture notes.

[1] Housman is copying the list of degrees which Jebb advertised on the title page of his editions of Sophocles. This explains why he does not include a more signal honour, the Order of Merit, to which Jebb was appointed in 1905. Housman himself declined the Order in 1929 (H. Maas (1971), 277, Naiditch (1988*a*), 28).

This is Housman, in a course of lectures entitled 'The Application of Thought to Textual Criticism', which he gave to undergraduates at Cambridge in 1913 and 1921.[2] He used the same title and some of the same material in 1921 for his celebrated lecture to the Classical Association (*Classical Papers* (1972), 1058–69), but he did not use this passage, which has never before been printed. We shall return later to Jebb and the police court and see how the lecture and the trial proceed.

Before his election to the Chair of Latin at University College, London, in 1892, Housman wrote as much on Greek as on Latin. In his candidature for the Latin Chair he offered himself, if he were unsuccessful, as a candidate for the Chair of Greek, which was also vacant.[3] After 1892 he wrote little on Greek, and, when asked why, he replied 'I found that I could not attain to excellence in both' (Gow (1936), 15). But the little that he did write fostered in the minds of some of his contemporaries a belief in the continued excellence of his Greek. His review of Pearson's Sophocles in 1925 'might well have caused the uninstructed to wonder which of the two men was professor of Greek' (Gow (1936), 16). Wilamowitz is reported to have said in 1926 'Although we Germans know that Housman is a rabid Germanophobe, we are unanimous in regarding him as the greatest authority both on Greek and Latin amongst the English-speaking peoples.'[4] Housman retreated behind a veil of ironic self-depreciation. 'Unfortunately he is almost as wrong about my Greek at any rate as he is about my Germanophobia.' To Pearson he wrote

[2] The text of the lectures is in the Cambridge University Library (Add. Ms. 6874). This is evidently the passage alluded to by Gow (1936), 42. The passage is summarized by Naiditch (1988*a*), 186.

[3] For the text of Housman's application see Naiditch (1988*a*), 14.

[4] Housman, quoting an unnamed former pupil, in a letter to Sir James Frazer (1927), published by Ackerman (1974), 362. The pupil was Annette M. B. Meakin, who published a slightly different version of Wilamowitz's remark in *The Times*, 7 May 1936. See Richards (1941), 83 n. 1, N. Page (1983), 162, Brink (1986), 230 n. 74, Naiditch (1988*a*), 128. And yet only two years earlier Wilamowitz revealed that he had been unaware of Housman's Sophoclean conjectures until he saw them in Pearson's edition ('Dankbar bekenne ich, drei vortreffliche Emendationen kennen gelehrnt zu haben, zwei von Housman' (Wilamowitz (1924*b*), 2318 = (1935–72), i. 463; cf. Naiditch (1988*a*), 247)). Nor does he mention any of Housman's conjectures in his edition of Aeschylus (1914). The letter of Wilamowitz to E. H. Blakeney (to which Richards refers) is now published by Bierl, Calder, and Fowler (1991), 123–6.

in the same year, 'Hunt has sent me some new Callimachus from the next Oxyrhynchus volume, and I am making a manful pretence of knowing the language.' And when (we may assume) Pearson demurred, Housman re-echoed 'The number of good Greek scholars whom I have deceived into thinking that I know Greek is mounting up, and I add your scalp to Platt's and Headlam's' (H. Maas (1971), 422–3). D. S. Robertson, Pearson's successor as Regius Professor of Greek at Cambridge, asserted that Housman 'knew far more Greek than most Grecians' (1936, 113).[5] When H. D. Jocelyn went further and asserted that 'Housman knew Greek more widely and more profoundly than any man in England between 1887 and 1936' ((1987*a*), 108 = (1988), 27), heads were shaken.[6] I do not intend to compare Housman with his contemporaries. My aim is less ambitious: to examine what Housman wrote on Greek and to estimate its value.

Almost all of the early Greek work was on tragedy.[7] 'All this work is learned and clever, but very little of it is right' (Lloyd-Jones (1973), 137 = (1982), 183). And yet Lloyd-Jones and Wilson praise 'a number of brilliant suggestions' in the papers on Sophocles (1990, 5). Let us see how much of this work is right, and how much is brilliant.

First (in 1887) comes the paper 'On Soph. *Electr.* 564, and Eur. *I.T.* 15 and 35' (*Classical Papers* 10–13), in which Housman emends three passages, diagnosing in each a type of corruption which he was to illustrate on many later occasions, transposition of letters. I shall examine this paper in detail. If we wish to measure the stature of the finished warrior, it will be useful to see the raw recruit, when his weapons are still untried.

His first two proposals are misconceived, and the third, though not misconceived, is not acceptable. He begins by attacking the text of Soph. *El.* 563–4: ἐροῦ δὲ τὴν κυναγὸν Ἄρτεμιν τίνος | ποινὰς τὰ πολλὰ πνεύματ' ἔσχ' ἐν Αὐλίδι ('Ask the huntress Artemis what sin she punished when she stayed the frequent winds at Aulis' Jebb). He claims that the fleet was held back at Aulis not by a windless calm but by adverse winds, as in Aesch. *Ag.* 192 ff. and 'fifty other sources'. He

[5] See also Robertson (1949), 450.

[6] See Hooker (1987), Jocelyn (1987*b*), Watt (1987), Lloyd-Jones (1988), Naiditch (1988*b*) (≈ (1995), 64–7), Calder (1988), Mayer (1989), Pinsent (1990), 1.

[7] The exceptions are conjectures in Isoc. *Pan.* 40 and *Σ PV* 472 (*Classical Papers* 22–3). On the latter see Herington (1972), 146.

dismisses as evidence Ov. *Met.* 13.183–4 *nulla aut contraria classi | flamina erant*, for no better reason than that, by Ovid's own admission, the *Metamorphoses* lacked final revision. We cannot blame him for not knowing that a scholiast on Eur. *Orestes* and Tzetzes on Lycophron (both later quoted by Jebb) say explictly that Artemis held back the winds, but we can blame him for overlooking *IA* 9–11, where the waters and the winds in the Euripus are described as silent. He bolsters an unfounded assertion with a tone of jaunty banter: 'Artemis did not restrain the winds at Aulis: had she done so, Agamemnon might have laughed her to scorn and Iphigenia would never have been sacrificed. To the ships of the heroic age and the age of Sophocles alike, a calm was no hindrance: they were equipped with oars.' A robust practical answer was offered by Jebb (1894): that the rowers were men under arms, and the ships were heavily laden. 'It is intelligible, then, that they should await the aid of wind before attempting the passage of the Aegean.' It is not only intelligible, but fully in accord with Greek practice: you use the oars to get out from the shore, then you hoist sail and use the winds. If the winds fall, and you are obliged to resort to the oars again, that is bad luck. No prudent commander entrusts an army to a windless sea.[8]

And so Housman's attack on the transmitted text is based on imperfect knowledge and faulty reasoning. His remedy for a problem which does not exist is to emend πολλὰ to πλοῖα: 'ask Artemis why winds detained the ships at Aulis'. This emendation has received more respect than it deserves. It is reported by Pearson (1924), Kells (1973), Kamerbeek (1974), and Lloyd-Jones and Wilson (1992); and Jebb politely says that it 'would be an attractive remedy, if the idea of a *calm* were not admissible' (1894, 82).[9] The conjecture is detrimental to the sense. Housman translates '(Ask Artemis) why gales detained the fleet'. But τίνος ποινᾶς means more than 'why?' It means 'in requital for what?' (in Jebb's translation, 'Ask . . . Artemis what sin she punished when . . . '). So the meaning is 'Ask Artemis *in requital for what* (or *to punish what sin*) winds detained the fleet.' The requital was demanded by Artemis, not by the winds, and Artemis,

[8] See Diggle (1994*a*), 430–6, 439–41.

[9] This is Jebb's only reference to Housman in his commentaries (Naiditch (1988*a*), 178).

not the winds, is the proper subject for the verb. If one were to plead that the winds are envisaged as agents of Artemis, and so may be described as exacting punishment for a sin committed against the goddess, I should answer that recourse to such a plea is an admission that the emended text is, in this respect, less natural than the text unemended. Further, while the article with τὰ πολλὰ πνεύματα is apt (as Jebb shows), the noun πνεύματα, once it is deprived of both article and epithet, limps lamely in the wake of τὰ πλοῖα, and cries out for a defining epithet, such as 'adverse'.[10]

Housman turns to Eur. *IT* 15, where Agamemnon is described as δεινῆς τ' ἀπλοίας πνευμάτων τ' οὐ τυγχάνων, of which the best sense we can make (and it is nonsense) is 'and not finding a dreadful impossibility of sailing and (not finding) winds'. Here the most appealing solution is δεινῆι δ' ἀπλοίαι, 'but because of dreadful impossibility of sailing and through not finding winds'. This solution (δ' for τ' Barnes, the datives Rauchenstein and Madvig)[11] Housman praises frigidly as 'the only one which seems to deserve mention'. But he rejects it because 'the assumed error is not easily explicable'. The emended text assumes two separate corruptions: of δ' to τ' and of the dative terminations to genitives. Housman claims that 'we can hardly postulate with prudence the occurrence of both mistakes together'. But δέ and τε are constantly confused, as he admits.[12] And the idiomatic asymmetry of causal dative and causal participle[13] was an open invitation to corruption—the apparently constructionless dative was changed to genitive, so that, like πνευμάτων, it might be constructed with τυγχάνω. To postulate the occurrence of both mistakes together, when each of them separately is a simple explicable error, requires no effort of imagination. We must accept the δέ, reasons Housman; therefore we cannot with prudence accept the datives. What sort of reasoning is this? The mature Housman later censured the 'anxious adherence to the ductus litterarum' which 'made Porson spoil his

[10] Unknown to Housman, Fröhlich had already proposed τὰ πλοῖ' ἀπνεύματ', 'why she kept the ships windless', which has at least the merit of leaving Artemis as subject, but introduces an adjective attested only in later prose. This conjecture is mentioned by Pearson and Dawe and is accepted by Kells.

[11] For the attribution to Rauchenstein see Diggle (1994*a*), 521.

[12] See Diggle (1981), 59, (1974), 3 = (1994*a*), 91.

[13] See Diggle (1972), 242 = (1994*a*), 53, (1974), 3 = (1994*a*), 91, (1996*a*), 194.

famous correction of Eur. Ion 1115 by omitting a necessary particle' (1930, xxxiv–xxxv). Would Housman, in his earlier years, have argued that Porson, after correcting one explicable mistake, ἐγνώσμεθ' ἐξ ἴσου· κἐν ὑστάτοις κακοῖς for ἔγνως· μεθέξεις οὐκ ἐν ὑστάτοις κακοῦ, was not entitled to add the particle δ' after μεθέξεις, because 'we can hardly postulate with prudence the occurrence of both mistakes together'?[14]

Housman is championing a cause which he ought never to have championed: that the fleet may not be described as becalmed at Aulis. His argument leads him to dismiss the testimony of Ovid. That was wilful. It leads him to emend Sophocles. That was rash. It leads him to deploy a feeble and faulty logic against a plausible conjecture in Euripides. As if this were not bad enough, he next impugns the epithet δεινῆς, whose 'flatness', he says tendentiously, 'might be tolerated by an indulgent schoolmaster in the verses of a beginner'. By shuffling the letters of δεινῆς τ' he creates νήστει δ' (with ἀπλοίαι), 'through a famine-causing ἄπλοια', taking the adjective from Aesch. *Ag.* 193, where the winds which held back the fleet are described with a string of imaginative epithets, of which one is νήστιδες. Housman is not troubled, as he should have been, that an epithet which is so boldly picturesque in Aeschylus' lyrics stands out, like a patch of purple, in the penny-plain verses of this iambic prologue.

His third conjecture is at *IT* 35, where he shuffles the letters of ὅθεν νόμοισι τοῖσιν into νόμοις ἵν' ὀθνείοισιν. I have commented on this elsewhere ((1969), 57–8 = (1994*a*), 31).

In the following year (1888) he published two papers on Aeschylus. In one (*Classical Papers* 14–21) he proposed ten emendations in the *Persae.*[15] Along with the generality of editors, I pass over six of these in silence. Three have received, and deserve, consideration.[16] One stands out, bold and brilliant. At 814–15 the MSS have κοὐδέπω κακῶν | κρηπὶς ὕπεστιν ἀλλ' ἔτ' ἐκπαιδεύεται, 'no foundation of evils

[14] In fact, it is likely that Porson did add the δ' and that his conjecture has been misreported: see my app. crit., Clarke (1937), 100–1, Brink (1986), 213 n. 22.

[15] A conjecture of Housman's on *Pers.* 674 ff. was published by Tyrrell in 1887 (*Classical Papers* 1253).

[16] 63 πέδοι for ποδί ('highly probable', Broadhead (1960); recorded in app. crit. by West (1998)), 451 ἐξωθοίατο for ἐκσωιζοίατο (recorded by Murray (1937, 1955), Page (1972), and Broadhead), 664 γᾶι for τε (accepted by Page; recorded by West).

is yet laid, but still . . . '. Taking as his starting point Schütz's ἐκπιδύεται ('there gushes forth') for the nonsensical ἐκπαιδεύεται, Housman argues that the line requires a further change, for two reasons: first, the clash of metaphors ('the laying of a foundation and the welling forth of a spring are two images which refuse to be made one'), and, second, the absurdity of 'no foundation of evils is yet laid' (which means that the evils have not yet begun), 'but they are still gushing forth' (which means that they must have begun some time ago). For κρηπὶς ὕπεστιν he proposes κρηνὶς ἀπέσβηκ', 'the spring of evils is not yet dried up but still gushes forth'. This conjecture was accepted by Headlam (1900), Sidgwick (1900), and Broadhead (1960). But it is now in danger of being eclipsed by a conjecture published four years later by T. G. Tucker (1892),[17] ἐκπλινθεύεται for ἐκπαιδεύεται, or by Page's modification of it εἰσπλινθεύεται. Consider which of these two is the choicer image: 'the spring of evils is not yet dried up but still gushes forth', and 'the foundation of evils is not yet laid but is still being built up (*or* built on to)'. The compound ἐκπλινθεύομαι is attested once in classical prose, but not in this sense; εἰσπλινθεύομαι is not attested at all. Nor is the simple verb πλινθεύομαι found in tragedy: the tragic poets ignore this verb and leave it to comedy and prose. It reeks of bricks and mortar.[18]

Housman's conjecture relies on no juggling with the order of the letters. It comes from an instinctive apprehension of what sense and style require. Housman, as if he is stunned by his boldness, as if he realizes obscurely, yet still does not wholly believe, that he has done something new and remarkable, asks the reader, in almost apologetic tones, 'not to take fright at what may strike the first glance as a violent change',[19] and he proceeds to show how the change may be accounted for.[20] 'The best emendations of all', he wrote much later,

[17] The conjecture was revived by Lawson (1934), and is accepted by Belloni (1988).

[18] The root πλινθ- is attested in tragedy once in the adjective πλινθυφής (*PV* 450), twice in the noun πλίνθευμα (*TrGF* adesp. 269a, date unknown, *TrGF* 128 Ezechiel 9, post-classical).

[19] Against the charge of violence his tone turned later from apology to defiance. 'There is an industriously propagated legend that many of my own corrections are "violent" or "palaeographically improbable", by which is merely meant that they alter a good number of letters' (1930, xxxiv).

[20] The rare κρηνίς (Eur. *Hipp.* 208, Call. fr. 751, Theoc. 1.22) was readily corruptible to the much commoner κρηπίς. To Housman's examples of -εσβ- corrupted to

'are those which are both true and difficult, emendations which no fool could find' (1930, xxxiv). This is one of them.

I shall say less of the much longer paper on the *Agamemnon* (*Classical Papers* 55–90), in which he proposed about thirty emendations. Of these only one has ever gained widespread approval, πειθήμονες for πενθήμονες at 420. This was accepted by Wecklein (1888), Verrall (1889), and Headlam (1910). Of modern editors, Martin West (1998) reports though he does not accept it. It had already been proposed tentatively by Karsten. Of the other conjectures, West reports one more (ὀνειρόφοιτοι for ὀνειρόφαντοι in the same line), and Page, too, reports one (παμονᾶς for πημονάς at 1012). The tally is not impressive.[21]

Also in 1888 appeared a paper entitled '*ΣΩΦΡΟΝΗ*' (*Classical Papers* 24–8), in which Housman proposed to restore, in several passages of tragedy, the unattested form σωφρόνη as an equivalent to σωφροσύνη, and εὐφρόνη (attested only in the sense 'night') as an equivalent to εὐφροσύνη, and the unattested ἀφρόνη as an equivalent to ἀφροσύνη. His attempt fails completely. He begins by claiming that, if the form δυσφρόνη exists as an equivalent of δυσφροσύνη, there is no reason to deny the existence of these other shorter forms. 'In our salvage from the wreck of Greek literature the word δυσφρόνη = δυσφροσύνη is found at one place, Hes. *Theog.* 102 δυσφρονέων, and a certain emendation of W. Dindorf's restores it at one more, Pind. *Ol.* II. 95 ⟦52 Snell⟧ δυσφρονᾶν'. The facts are less favourable than he supposes. We now have the evidence of a papyrus in both places. In the first the papyrus (as well as several manuscripts) offers δυσφροσυνέων, and this is certainly right. In the second a papyrus offers αφροσυν[, and although the truth remains uncertain this reading throws the gravest doubt on Dindorf's emendation. In all of the passages in which Housman restores the shorter forms either the text is sound or better remedies are available.[22]

Two years later (in 1890) came a paper on Euripides' *Medea*

-εστ- add Eur. fr. 971.2 ἀπέσβη] ἀπέστη Plut. *Mor.* 1090c pars codd., Hdt. 4.5.4 κατασβῆναι] καταστῆναι pars codd. See also Cobet (1878), 279.

[21] There followed in 1890 (the final contribution on Aeschylus) a review of Tucker's edition of *Supplices* (*Classical Papers* 120–7).

[22] See (for example) Fraenkel on Aesch. *Ag.* 264 and 584, and West on Hes. *Theog.* 102, and compare Housman's discussion of Eur. *Hipp.* 1034 with Barrett's.

(*Classical Papers* 112–19). Housman proposed emendations in nine passages. Like Page (1938), I have reported two of these in my apparatus criticus: at 339 δαὶ for δ' αὖ and at 382 ὑπεσβαίνουσα for ὑπερβαίνουσα. These are simple changes, slightly modifying the sense; and both could be right. In a third passage Housman shows a truer perception than many of what is faulty, but his remedy is not acceptable.[23] His other emendations are best forgotten. I mention only one of them, which displays a strange want of taste. At 25 Medea is described as τὸν πάντα συντήκουσα δακρύοις χρόνον, 'melting away the whole of her lifetime in tears'. Page explains, what Housman fails to comprehend, why τὸν πάντα χρόνον is an acceptable object for 'melting away'. Housman emends χρόνον to χρόα, 'melting away the whole of her flesh with tears', insensitive to the banality of 'the whole of' as a qualification for 'her flesh'.[24]

Housman sent other conjectures in Euripides to Murray. Murray (1902, 1904) reported four, of which three are implausible (*Heracl.* 1050, *Andr.* 1065, *Hec.* 460), and the fourth is possible but is not demonstrably preferable to an older conjecture (*IT* 335 τε] ἐς Valckenaer, πρὸς Housman).[25] But there are three more Euripidean conjectures, again not published by Housman himself, which I regard as certain, and two of which I regard as palmary. One was published by Tyrrell in his edition of *Bacchae* in 1892,[26] the other two were published by Platnauer in his edition of *IT* in 1938 from the margin of Housman's copy of England's edition.[27] The simple κακοῖς σε for κακοῖσι at *IT* 483 I have commended elsewhere.[28] The simple

[23] At 319–20, on which see Diggle (1994*a*), 260–2.

[24] 'He never wrote a more characteristic, nor in many ways a finer article than the emendations in the *Medea*' (Marlow (1955), 184). This is an extraordinary judgement.

[25] The conjecture had been anticipated by Fritzsche (Diggle (1994*a*), 521).

[26] Tyrrell published two conjectures by Housman (not four, as stated by Naiditch (1988*a*), 218). For the conjecture at 837 see *Classical Papers* 1256.

[27] Platnauer also reports conjectures at 1246 and 1259 (I mention the latter in my app. crit.). Housman's review (in 1890) of a commentary on *IT* by I. Flagg (*Classical Papers* 128–30) contains some uncharacteristic but not uninteresting comments on Euripidean plot construction. His remarks on the improper use of rough breathing for coronis fell on deaf ears, and, even though he amplified them in his review of Pearson in 1925 (*Classical Papers* 1097–8), they continue to do so.

[28] Diggle (1981), 81–2. *Phoen.* 437 supplies another instance of 'the reflexive use of σε'.

and brilliant ἔπειτ' ἀντίπαλον for ἐπὶ τἀντίπαλον at *Ba.* 278 has been accepted by Murray (1909) and others. I offer a brief comment on the third. Orestes, as yet uncleansed of matricide, describes how the Athenians made him eat at a separate table and refused to speak to him, ὅπως | δαιτὸς γενοίμην πώματός τ' αὐτῶν (Scaliger: αὐτοῦ L) δίχα (*IT* 951–2), 'so that *I might be* apart from their food and drink'. For γενοίμην, joined in an insufferably feeble construction with the prepositional phrase, Housman proposed τ' ὀναίμην, a choice verb, echoing Homer (*Od.* 19.68 δαιτὸς ὄνησο), and affording a more satisfactory role for the prepositional phrase, 'so that I might have the benefit of food and drink apart from them'.[29]

Housman became a member of the Cambridge Philological Society in 1889, and in 1890 he read to it a paper on fragments of Euripides (*Classical Papers* 1254–5). Of the eight emendations proposed two may be right. First, fr. 860, an entry from the Etymologicum Magnum on the Red Sea, παρ' Εὐριπίδηι Φοινίσσαις "ἅλμη" εἴρηται. Since Euripides does not use the word ἅλμη in the *Phoenissae*, and even if he had done so the remark would not suit the entry, Housman proposed "Φοίνισσα ἅλμη", anticipating Martin West, who has made a similar proposal.[30] Second, fr. 897.1–2 παίδευμα δ' Ἔρως σοφίας ἀρετῆς | πλεῖστον ὑπάρχει (Casaubon: -ειν Athen.), contorted words of uncertain meaning, variously emended, but never more neatly than by Housman's ἐρατῆς for ἀρετῆς ('so that love is said to lesson men in lovely wisdom').[31]

In *The Classical Review* of March 1891 W. G. Rutherford and Lewis Campbell contributed emendations and supplements in the newly published papyrus fragments of Euripides' *Antiope*. On 14 March in a brief note in the weekly journal *Academy* (*Classical Papers* 173) Housman took them to task for failing to emend the easily emendable corruption ὁλκοῖς γε ταυρεοίοισιν διαφερουμένη, for which he

[29] Even the situation is comparable to a degree. Melantho orders the beggar Odysseus out of the house (ἀλλ' ἔξελθε θύραζε, τάλαν, καὶ δαιτὸς ὄνησο), so that he will stop annoying the occupants.

[30] Φοίνισσαν ἅλμην (1983*b*, 78), the accusative so that (I infer) the words may stand together. Kannicht in *TrGF* v. prints φοίνισσα(ν) ἅλμη(ν), a prudent compromise.

[31] The conjecture is accepted by Diggle (*TrGFS*), by Jouan and Van Looy (2003), and by Kannicht (*TrGF*). For παίδευμα in this sense see fr. 54.1–2; for σοφίας ἐρατῆς, Sol. 13.52 *IEG* ἱμερτῆς σοφίης.

restored ταυρείοισι διαφορουμένη. What Housman restored is the reading of the papyrus, which its first editor had misreported.[32] 'It surprised me', he wrote, 'that the first editor did not correct this obvious blunder, and I looked to see it removed by the first critic who took the fragment in hand.'

The interest of this note lies not in the correction, which anyone could have made. It lies in the tone which Housman adopts towards Rutherford and Campbell. He calls them 'two distinguished Grecians', whose emendations are 'numerous and intrepid'. 'Dr Rutherford "would restore" to Euripides the senarius σὺ μὲν χερῶν τὸ πνεῦμ' ἐκ πολεμίων λαβών, which Euripides, I think, would restore to Dr Rutherford', while 'Prof. Campbell proposes to enrich the tragic vocabulary by the importation of ἄχρι, in accordance with his opinion that it is not yet "time to cease from guessing and to begin the sober work of criticism"'. And Housman proceeds to make his own correction 'at the risk of incurring Prof. Campbell's censure for premature sobriety'.

Campbell responded disingenuously, a week later, that some corrections are 'too much a matter of course to be worth mentioning'. In the following week (*Classical Papers* 173–4) Housman calmly exploded this response, and added that 'The further fragments of Prof. Campbell's *Antiope* (a drama which I much admire and hope to see completed), published in last week's *Academy*, have been slightly corrupted by the scribes', and castigated Campbell for several errors of accentuation.[33]

Housman had entered the lists not with any constructive purpose. The fragments, if he had wished to study them more attentively, offered ample scope. His purpose is negative and destructive. Masking his indignation with a look of incredulity, and his sarcasm with a veneer of good-humoured wit, the neophyte makes fun of established scholars. It may be that he was irritated by Campbell's recent criticism of some of his emendations in the *Agamemnon*.[34] What he was at the risk of incurring was not 'censure for premature

[32] The papyrus has not only διαφορ- (as its editor quickly acknowledged) but also -σι (Diggle (1996*b*), 119).

[33] Campbell chose not to take offence and 'gracefully concluded the correspondence with a final epistle' (Naiditch (1988*a*), 238, who quotes part of it).

[34] I owe this suggestion to Naiditch (1988*a*), 237 n. 76–2.

sobriety' but the loss of a supporter in his application for the Chair at University College next year. We may admire the magnanimity of Campbell, now in nearly his thirtieth year as Professsor of Greek at St Andrews, who, so far from taking offence at a young man's impertinence, wrote of Housman in his testimonial: 'Though often differing from his conclusions, I cannot withhold my admiration from his style of reasoning.'[35]

It is on the two long articles on Sophocles which follow next and on the much later review of the Oxford text of Sophocles in 1925 (*Classical Papers* 1093–8) that Housman's reputation as a Greek scholar was held, in his own lifetime, and perhaps is still held in ours, to hinge. The first of them, 'Sophoclea', was published at the end of 1891 (*Classical Papers* 209–26),[36] the second, 'The *Oedipus Coloneus* of Sophocles', in July 1892 (*Classical Papers* 181–208).[37]

Housman proposed about seventy emendations. Of these Pearson (1924) accepts eight and reports a further sixteen,[38] Lloyd-Jones and Wilson (1992) accept seven and report a further eleven, while Dawe (1996) accepts only three and reports only a further four.[39] I shall mention those which either have gained most favour or appear to me to be the most meritorious.

I begin with some fairly simple changes. First, a change of punctuation, *OC* 980–1 οὐ γὰρ οὖν σιγήσομαι, | σοῦ γ' ἐς τόδ' ἐξελθόντος ἀνόσιον στόμα ('when thou hast gone so far in impious speech', Jebb's translation), where Housman saw that ἀνόσιον στόμα is a vocative ('when you have gone to this length, you foul mouth', my translation). John Jackson expressed astonishment that, over sixty years later, 'Housman's vocative . . . still knocks at a barred and bolted

[35] For the whole testimonial see Naiditch (1988*a*), 17–18.

[36] The article is wrongly assigned to 1892 in *Classical Papers* (Naiditch (1984), 137 = (1995), 149; cf. (1998), 648).

[37] I treat this article here, although it had not been published by the time of his election (it was completed in February): see Naiditch (1988*a*), 105, 236, 245. There is a supplementary note on *OC* 527 in 1893 (*Classical Papers* 231).

[38] The figures given by Naiditch (1988*a*), 178 n. 60–8, and the remarks on Tyrrell and Dawe, need correction.

[39] I have included in these totals some emendations which were anticipated by others. To the four which I mention below add *OT* 602 (Foerster) and 1494–5 (Hertel), but not *El.* 541 ('Hermann' Pearson, apparently a slip for 'Housman').

door' (1955, 194).[40] In fact it had been accepted by Tyrrell (1897) and Radermacher (1909). It has now been accepted by Dawe, who printed it silently without attribution in his first two editions, and by Lloyd-Jones and Wilson, who record that it was anticipated by Maehly, to whom Dawe ascribes it in his third edition.

At *OT* 866–7 *οὐρανίαι 'ν αἰθέρι* convincingly remedies the metre and the inept preposition in the transmitted *οὐρανίαν δι' αἰθέρα*, and is accepted by Pearson and by Lloyd-Jones and Wilson, but not by Dawe.[41] It proves to have been anticipated by Enger. At *Ant.* 439–40 *ἀλλὰ πάντα ταῦθ'* (or *ταῦτα πάνθ'*) *ἥσσω λαβεῖν* | *ἐμοὶ πέφυκε τῆς ἐμῆς σωτηρίας* Blaydes proposed *πάντα τἄλλ'*, which Housman improved to *τἄλλα πάνθ'*. It is accepted by Pearson, reported by Dawe and by Lloyd-Jones and Wilson. It proves to have been anticipated by Herwerden.[42]

At *Aj.* 1378–80 *τόνδε συνθάπτειν θέλω* | *καὶ ξυμπονεῖν καὶ μηδὲν ἐλλείπειν ὅσων* | *χρὴ τοῖς ἀρίστοις ἀνδράσιν πονεῖν βροτούς*, 'I wish to share in burying this man and to share in the toil and leave out none of the things that mortals should toil over for noblest men', *πορεῖν* for *πονεῖν* ('that mortals should provide') neatly relieves us of a feeble repetition of the verb 'toil'. Pearson ignores this, Lloyd-Jones and Wilson report it, and Dawe, having reported it in his first two editions, has at last, in his third edition, put it in the text.

At *Phil.* 606–8 *ὃν οὗτος νυκτὸς ἐξελθὼν μόνος* | *ὁ πάντ' ἀκούων αἰσχρὰ καὶ λωβήτ' ἔπη* | *δόλιος 'Οδυσσεὺς εἷλε*, 'whom (*sc.* Helenus) this man, going forth alone at night, the man of whom all shameful and dishonouring words are spoken, *cunning* Odysseus captured', the epithet 'cunning' is a limp and pallid appendage to the vigorous and colourful obloquy which goes before. Housman's *δόλοις*, 'he captured by cunning', gives the word some useful work to do: to supply apt detail to an otherwise bare and unqualified verb. The emendation

40 Cf. Diggle (1981), 66, 120.

41 *δι' αἰθέρα ταθέντες* (Dawe (1982)) is not acceptable, since it entails split resolution (L. P. E. Parker (1968), 253). For the prodelision *οὐρανίαι 'ν* (which troubled Lloyd-Jones and Wilson (1990), 100) see Diggle (1981), 33.

42 Dawe rightly attributes it to Herwerden, Lloyd-Jones and Wilson wrongly to Blaydes. Blaydes in 1859 proposed *πάντα τἄλλ'*, Herwerden (1868), 14 both this and *τἄλλα πάνθ'*. For further commendation see Diggle (1994*a*), 51–2. See also Lloyd-Jones and Wilson (1997), 72.

is accepted by Pearson (with the approval of Wilamowitz),[43] and by Lloyd-Jones and Wilson, but not by Dawe.[44]

Next, four emendations in *OC* which are rather more adventurous. In the lengthiest of all his notes, on 266–7 ἐπεὶ τά γ' ἔργα μου | πεπονθότ' ἐστὶ μᾶλλον ἢ δεδρακότα, Housman argues that 'my deeds are sufferers rather than doers' is no way to say 'I am the sufferer rather than the doer', and demolishes with scornful panache the attempts of Jebb and others to establish that 'my deeds' means no more than 'I' or that the active participles may stand for passives. His ἐπεὶ τά γ' ἔργα με | πεπονθότ' ἴσθι μᾶλλον ἢ δεδρακότα, 'know that I am the sufferer rather than the doer of those deeds', restores normality with neatness and economy. It is not reported by Pearson. It is accepted by Lloyd-Jones and Wilson, who comment that 'the infuriating superiority of the rhetoric should not blind one to the cogency of the reasoning' (1990, 225), and record that it was anticipated by Hertel in 1876. Dawe, having ignored it in his first two editions, has now accepted it in his third.

At 359–60 ἥκεις γὰρ οὐ κενή γε, τοῦτ' ἐγὼ σαφῶς | ἔξοιδα, μὴ οὐχὶ δεῖμ' ἐμοὶ φέρουσά τι, a syntactical difficulty is elegantly removed by ἔξοιδα· μή που δεῖμ' ἐμοὶ φέρουσά τι; Lloyd-Jones and Wilson find this 'not easy to resist' and accept it. Pearson and Dawe ignore it. And Lloyd-Jones and Wilson again stand alone in accepting the transposition of 1028–33 after 1019,[45] and at 1514 Δῖαί τε βρονταί for αἱ πολλὰ βρονταί. Pearson mentions the former, Dawe ignores both. At 1358–9 ἐν πόνωι | ταὐτῶι βεβηκὼς τυγχάνεις κακῶν ἐμοί, to remove the impossible πόνωι . . . κακῶν ('trouble of evils') Housman proposed ἴσων for κακῶν ('standing in the same trouble, you gain a lot equal to mine'). This was accepted by Pearson and approved by

[43] See n. 4 above.

[44] Dawe, having reported δόλοις in his first two editions, suppresses it in his third, preferring to make Odysseus the dispenser instead of the recipient of obloquy, by writing ἀπακουῶν for ἀκούων. 'He captured him, not with the sword or spear, but with words' (Dawe (1998), 122). Who says so?

[45] See also Lloyd-Jones and Wilson (1997), 129–30, Günther (1996*a*), 53. Housman explained in 1918 why transposition is 'the most unpopular of all methods of emendation' (*Classical Papers* 969). Naiditch (1984), 138 = (1995), 150, claims that this paper should be dated 1917, but later acknowledges that it should not (1998, 648 n. 7).

Wilamowitz,[46] but Dawe and Lloyd-Jones and Wilson relegate it to the apparatus criticus, the former preferring the obelus, the latter Martin's *κλόνωι* for *πόνωι* ('turmoil of evils'), an expression quite without appeal.

Finally, Housman's most brilliant Sophoclean emendation, accepted by Pearson, but not even reported by Dawe or by Lloyd-Jones and Wilson. At *OT* 1275–6 the messenger says that Oedipus *πολλάκις τε κοὐχ ἅπαξ | ἤρασσ' ἐπαίρων βλέφαρα*, which Jebb translated 'not once alone but oft struck he his eyes with lifted hand'. It is impossible to supply 'hand' as an object for the participle *ἐπαίρων*. It is equally impossible to supply 'brooches', as others have suggested. The only possible object is *βλέφαρα*, 'he struck his eyes as he raised them'. Lloyd-Jones and Wilson (1990, 5) believe that this gives acceptable sense, and, prompted by F. Ferrari (1983), 35–6, cite in support Sen. *Oed.* 962–4 *manus in ora torsit. at contra truces | oculi steterunt et suam intenti manum | ultro insecuntur, uulneri occurrunt suo* ('He thrust his hands against his face. But his fierce eyes stood firm to meet them, and, straining, they voluntarily follow their hand and rush upon their wound'). No connection exists between Sophocles and Seneca. The Senecan eyes commit suicide in Roman fashion: they stand firm to meet the oncoming stroke and then fall eagerly upon it. That is comprehensible. The Sophoclean Oedipus kept striking his eyes as he was raising them. Why Oedipus should be raising his eyes all the time that he was striking them is not comprehensible.[47]

Nauck proposed *ἤρασσε πείρων βλέφαρα*, 'he struck his eyes as he pierced them', and this is the only conjecture admitted into their apparatus criticus by Lloyd-Jones and Wilson. The expression is topsy-turvy. If one of these verbs is to be a participle, it must be the other verb: 'he pierced his eyes as he struck them'.[48] Page[49] proposed *ἤρασσ' ἔπειρε βλέφαρα*, 'he struck, he pierced his eyes', and this is accepted by Dawe. It is admirable. But is it preferable to

[46] See n. 4 above.

[47] 'Edipo leva perentoriamente gli occhi' (Ferrari), 'he lifted up his eyes and . . . struck them' (Lloyd-Jones (1994*b*)). This is to translate not *ἐπαίρων* but *ἐπάρας*.

[48] Rightly, on this point at least, Broadhead (1968), 95.

[49] In Broadhead (1968), 95. Broadhead and Dawe report Page's conjecture as *ἔπειρεν*. Page would not have warranted the *ν*.

Housman's *ἤρασσε περόναις βλέφαρα*, 'he struck his eyes with the brooches'?

Two arguments, one metrical, the other palaeographical, have been adduced against Housman's conjecture. Neither is valid. It has been claimed[50] that 'the only example of a tribrach in the second foot followed by a "dactyl" in the third' is *Phil.* 1232 *παρ' οὗπερ ἔλαβον τάδε τὰ τόξ' αὖθις πάλιν*. But there is a second example at *OC* 284 *ἀλλ' ὥσπερ ἔλαβες τὸν ἱκέτην ἐχέγγυον*. Further, 'conjunctions of trisyllabic feet are extremely rare in Sophocles'. But there are six or seven other examples.[51] Finally, 'it seems doubtful whether at the time Sophocles composed the *OT* he would have admitted a line such as that given by Housman's emendation'. This, perhaps, is prompted by the false notion that Sophocles admitted resolution with increasing frequency, like Euripides. Frequency of resolution scarcely varies from play to play, except in *Philoctetes*, which exceeds the norm.[52] At all events, a sufficient answer is provided by *OT* 967 *κτανεῖν ἔμελλον πατέρα τὸν ἐμόν; ὁ δὲ θανών*, an example, unique in Sophocles, of three consecutive resolutions.

In terms of palaeography the change of *ἐπαίρων* to *-ε περόναις* is at least as plausible as the change of *ἐπαίρων* to *ἔπειρε*. Phonetic confusion of *αι* and *ε* and of *ω* and *ο* is very common. So, as Housman puts it, 'if the termination *-αις* were represented by one or other of its abbreviations and so lost, the resultant *ηρασσεπερον* would be really the same thing as *ηρασσεπαιρων*; or this corruption may have taken place first and extruded *αις*'. By contrast, while *επειρ* might easily be corrupted to *επαιρ*, there is no obvious reason why a finite verb terminating in *-ε* should have been corrupted into a participle terminating in *-ων*. Housman's dative supplies an appropriate qualification to the verb *ἤρασσε*, much as did his *δόλοις* to the verb *εἷλε* at *Phil.* 608.

[50] This and the following claims are made by Broadhead. He has persuaded Dawe (1973), 259 n. 2.

[51] *Aj.* [854], *Trach.* 1096, *Phil.* 796, 932 (three resolutions, two consecutive), 1029, 1420, **OC* 1414. Two resolutions which are not consecutive occur in at least eight other lines: *Aj.* *575, *1302, **El.* 326, 433 (?), *Phil.* *605, [*794], 815, 923, 1018, 1327. I have used brackets to indicate that the line is deleted by Dawe and/or Lloyd-Jones and Wilson, an asterisk to indicate that one or both of the resolutions occurs in a proper name.

[52] See Schein (1979), 77.

And so we come to the election of 1892. Housman mustered an impressive set of sponsors. Among the others, besides Campbell, who were competent to commend his Greek were Tyrrell, from Trinity College, Dublin, Verrall and Henry Jackson, both of Trinity College, Cambridge, Gildersleeve, editor of the *American Journal of Philology*, which had published the paper on *Persae* and was to publish the paper on *OC* later in this year, and Wecklein from Munich, who recorded that he had adopted two of the Aeschylean emendations.[53]

Hereafter, on his election to the London Chair, Housman wrote little on Greek authors. What he did write was mainly prompted by the publication of new papyrus texts:[54] Bacchylides in 1898 and 1906 (*Classical Papers* 442–69, 657), Menander in 1908 (*Classical Papers* 758–9), the *Paeans* of Pindar in 1908 (*Classical Papers* 763–9), Callimachus in 1910 (*Classical Papers* 798, 801–8), the *Pirithous* of either Euripides or Critias in 1928 (*Classical Papers* 1147). The rest is largely astrology: astrological epigrams from Oxyrhynchus in 1903 (*Classical Papers* 598–601), newly discovered verses of Dorotheus of Sidon in 1908, 1911, 1922 (*Classical Papers* 740–57, 840–3, 1070–2), identification of the ἀστὴρ σείριος in the prologue to *IA* in 1914 (*Classical Papers* 886), an astrological papyrus from Michigan in 1927 (*Classical Papers* 1109–13). He also contributed to several volumes of *Oxyrhynchus Papyri*.[55]

Housman's knowledge of what the ancients said of the stars was second to none. H. Stuart Jones, editor of the ninth edition of Liddell and Scott's *Greek-English Lexicon* (1940), wrote that 'in this thorny subject [astrology] difficulties frequently arise, for which Professor

[53] For Tyrrell see Naiditch (1988*a*), 216–20; for Verrall, 211–14; for Jackson, 165–71; for Gildersleeve, 244–6; for Wecklein, 246–7 (there are errors in n. 83–4). Wecklein had adopted emendations at *Sept.* 948 (no one would now accept this) and *Ag.* 429 (πειθήμονες: see above, p. 152).

[54] Housman's earliest response to a new papyrus was a conjecture in the *Ath. Pol.*, published (not by him) in *CR* 5 (1891), 110. The editors of *Classical Papers* do not 'suppress' this item 'without warning' (Naiditch (1988*a*), 30). See their Preface.

[55] XIII (1919) 1604 (Pindar, *Dithyrambs*); XV (1922) 1790 (Ibycus), 1793 (Callimachus), 1794 (*Epica Adespota* 4 *CA*; 122 Page (1942)), 1796 (124 Page; LX Heitsch (1963*b*)); XVII (1927) 2079, 2080 (Callimachus). The supplement in Ibycus (*PMG* 282.31 = S151.31) is accepted by Page (*PMG*) and Davies (*PMGF*), who wrongly attribute it to ed. pr. The supplement in 1794.3 is accepted by Powell (*CA*) and Page (1942).

A. E. Housman, when appealed to, never fails to provide a solution'.[56] Since this is a subject in which I have no knowledge,[57] I shall say nothing on this part of his papers. I shall speak only of the papers on the new literary texts.

Modern editors of Bacchylides accept or report a fair number of Housman's supplements or corrections. Some of these were proposed independently by others in or about the same year (1898). Snell (1961) accepts eleven of them, giving Housman joint credit for nine[58] and sole credit for two.[59] Maehler (1982) accepts a further four, for which he gives Housman sole credit.[60] But, as Housman said, in observing that Palmer had contributed more to the text of Bacchylides than to Ovid's *Heroides*, 'skimming the first cream off a new-found author is only child's-play beside gleaning after Bentley over a stubble where Heinsius has reaped' (*Classical Papers* 471).[61]

In one of the Bacchylides papers Housman strikes a note reminiscent of the paper on *Antiope*. 'It surprised me' (he had written then) 'that the first editor did not correct this obvious blunder, and I looked to see it removed by the first critic who took the fragment in hand.' There his target was Rutherford and Campbell. Here he aims higher, at Jebb. The papyrus of Bacchylides had been edited by Kenyon, and 'one cannot fairly expect a palaeographical expert to be

[56] p. vii. It was not only on astrology that Housman was able to instruct Jones: see Housman's letter to him on *λαικάζειν* published by Jocelyn (1980), 37. See also N. Page (1983), 125.

[57] 'Housman's mastery of astrological intricacies is caviare to the gourmet' (Shackleton Bailey (1962), 110 = (1982), 111).

[58] At 1.145, 5.184, 193, 194, 9.10, 10.51, 13.103, 229, 17.7. At 3.67 the supplement *εὖ λέ]γειν*, which has now been confirmed by a scholium (P.Oxy. 2367), was proposed not by Platt (as Jebb reports) but by Housman *ap.* Platt (1898), 59. Similarly the supplement at 13.112–13, which editors ascribe to Desrousseaux, should be jointly ascribed to Housman (ibid. 62). A few other proposals which Snell ascribes to others should probably be ascribed to Housman, since he first published many of his proposals 'without explanation in the *Athenaeum* for Dec. 25th 1897 and Jan. 15th 1898' (*Classical Papers* 442). See Fletcher (1946), 92.

[59] At 5.193, 13.95.

[60] At 13.94, 130 (*πνοᾶι*, attributed to Housman by Maehler, by Snell to Jebb, who had proposed *πνοῆι*), 150 (attributed to Blass by Snell), 177.

[61] Cf. the Preface to Juvenal (1931), xxxviii: 'he [Leo] could restore with ease and felicity a new-found remnant of Menander which had only been edited by a Frenchman, but a much-laboured field like the text of Juvenal would yield no harvest to his husbandry.'

a metrical expert as well . . . But there must be quite half a dozen scholars in England who understand these matters, and it surprises me that Mr Kenyon could get none of them to help him. The consequence is that his text contains at present a good many metrical solecisms: some of these are introduced by his own conjecture, and three or four supplementary violations of metre are proposed in the notes by Professor Jebb' (*Classical Papers* 443). Jebb, unlike Campbell, was stung by the rebuke. He protested, in a blustering and testy reply, that, if there are only half a dozen who understand metre, 'no one of any modesty could feel hurt at being left out of such a group' (Jebb (1898), 132). Housman had phrased his insult carefully, and Jebb, through incomprehension or wilfulness, did not take his meaning. When Housman says that 'there must be quite half a dozen scholars in England who understand these matters', he does not mean that there are very few who understand them, but that there are quite a few, and it is therefore all the more insulting to Jebb to say that he is not one of them. Kenyon had applied to Jebb for help where he needed it, in metrical knowledge, where quite half a dozen other scholars could have given it, and Jebb failed him.[62] In the case of *Antiope*, it was the amateur teaching the professionals how to do their job. In the case of Bacchylides, the Professor of Latin in London was teaching the Regius Professor of Greek in Cambridge.

The Cairo papyrus of Menander was published in 1907, and when Housman published his own proposals in the following year he ruefully observed that over a hundred which had occurred to him at a first reading had been anticipated in the meantime by Leo and Wilamowitz and others. 'The remainder, and the fruits of a second perusal' still amounted to about fifty. Some of these were to be proved false by more accurate reporting of the papyrus or by further

[62] Naiditch (1988*a*), 180–6 has a useful discussion of the issues. But he should not have cited Housman's definition of a literary critic ('a man who has things to say about literature which are both true and new') in order to define what Housman may have meant by the term 'metrical expert' ('a man who has things to say about metrics which are both true and new' Naiditch). Housman would have regarded the ability to say things about metre which are both true *and new* as rare indeed. His concern here is not with novelty (Kenyon's advisers did not need the ability to say anything new about metre) but with understanding (they needed to understand the fundamental metrical rules), which, since half a dozen possess it, is not all that rare. The point is rightly understood by Jocelyn (1990), 62.

papyrus finds, and the rest have left scarcely a trace on the modern apparatus criticus.[63] But there is one which is now known to be right, although editors give Housman no credit for it. At *Perik.* 532 (Sandbach) the first editor printed πολλῶν γεγονότων <δὴ> [ξ]ένων, and alternative remedies for the metre were at once devised (<γε> γεγονότων [ξ]ένων Leo, γεγονότων <τῶν > Wilamowitz). Housman saw that [ξ]ένων does not suit the context and proposed γεγονότων [ἀ]θλίων. This was at first ignored, then, a few years later, was discovered to be the reading of the papyrus. From this hangs the cautionary tale which he was to tell in the Preface to his Lucan (1926, xxx). 'Though my name was still absent from the note [in the editions next published], ἀθλίων was present in the text; not however because it was true and necessary and certain, but for a very different reason. . . . But if the papyrus had been lost in the meantime, or had proved indecipherable, editors would have gone on for years and centuries printing either <γε> or <τῶν> and never mentioning ἀθλίων, because of the false but ineradicable opinion that the probability of a conjecture depends on its nearness to the text.'

Housman's contribution to the papyrus fragments of Pindar is impressive. Thirteen of his supplements, far the larger part, are accepted by Snell and Maehler (1975).[64] More impressive still is the contribution in Callimachus. Pfeiffer (1949) accepts fourteen proposals, again the larger part.[65] One is exceptionally clever: at fr. 75.7, where Hunt printed ἐξενέπειν (εξανεπει corrected to εξενέπειν the papyrus) καὶ τῶν ἤρυγες ἱστορίην, Housman's ἐξ ἂν ἐπεὶ adroitly restores two Callimachean mannerisms, tmesis and postponement of the conjunction. Two supplements have been confirmed by later examination of the papyrus.[66]

In 1928 he supplied the missing second halves of fourteen successive trimeters in a fragment of the *Pirithous* of either Euripides or (more probably) Critias (*TrGF* 43 Critias F 5.7–20 = *TrGFS*

[63] One supplement (*Perik.* 321) is accepted by Sandbach. If Sandbach ever spoke of the Menandrean corrections in the terms imputed to him by Graves (1979), 203 (285 n. 14), I should be surprised.

[64] I include fr. 70b.9 (Housman, not Bury). He also contributed a conjecture at *Pyth.* 10.69 to Sandys' Loeb edition (1915, p. xlii); it is reported by Snell and Maehler.

[65] I include fr. 192.6–7: not Platt but Housman *ap.* Platt (1910).

[66] At fr. 75.33 and 194.58.

II(b).7–20). The supplements are faultless and imaginative, but, in a context as fragmentary as this, no supplement can be convincing, and, like Snell, I prefer to print none.[67] But I follow Housman in expelling the solecistic future infinitive with ἄν in another of the fragments (F 7.14 = *TrGFS* III.10), by adopting his λέγειν for λέξειν, a proposal which Snell does not even record.[68]

The only paper which it remains to mention is on a passage in the second *Mime* of Herodas in 1922 (*Classical Papers* 1056–7),[69] where Housman, who had a taste for such things, explains a *risqué* joke.

And so Housman's work on Greek texts divides into two distinct parts. In the eleven years up to his election to the London Chair in 1892 he devoted as much attention to Greek authors as to Latin. Thirteen papers on Latin authors (amounting to 108 pages in the *Classical Papers*) were matched by twelve papers and two reviews on Greek authors (125 pages).[70] With only two insignificant exceptions, all the Greek papers and reviews were devoted to the tragic poets. Between 1893 and 1936, during which time he published his editions of Juvenal, Lucan, and Manilius, he published a further 148 papers or reviews, of which only seventeen were devoted exclusively to Greek,[71] and these were for the most part devoted to astrological texts or were immediate responses to the first publication of new papyri. Only the review of Pearson's Sophocles in 1925 recalls the earlier work on tragedy.

It is time to return to Jebb and the police court. There is a well-known problem at Soph. *OT* 1505, where the manuscripts offer μή σφε παρίδῃς, which is unmetrical. Dawes had proposed μή σφε περιίδῃς. Against this Porson had observed that the tragedians never

[67] In line 10 Θεσσαλούς (both in the original publication and in *Classical Papers* 1147) should be corrected to Θε[σσαλούς.

[68] Snell refers to Kannicht on *Hel.* 448 for parallels for the transmitted construction. What Housman would have said about these parallels may be inferred from *Classical Papers* 1067–8.

[69] In *Classical Papers* 1056 the initials of A. D. Knox are wrongly printed as A. G.

[70] I include in these figures the note on *OC* 527 published in 1893 (see n. 37 above), since it belongs with the earlier papers, and item 2 (on fragments of Euripides) from the Appendix to *Classical Papers.*

[71] This figure does not include the (dozen or so) brief items in the Appendix to *Classical Papers.*

allow the prefix περι before a vowel in iambics. And so Porson proposed μὴ παρά σφ' ἴδῃς, while Housman in 1892 proposed μή σφε δὴ παρῇς. In his commentary Jebb had argued in favour of Dawes's conjecture and against Porson's. Housman, in his lecture, begins by examining the four arguments which Jebb used against Porson. He shows that each of them is based on faulty logic.

First, Jebb argues that such an example of tmesis as μὴ παρά σφ' ἴδῃς 'is alien from the style of ordinary tragic dialogue'. This, Housman observes, is simply untrue: there are several examples of tmesis in Sophoclean iambics. But, even if it were true, it would have no relevance to the question whether the tragedians admitted περι before a vowel. Jebb is arguing as if he believed that, by casting a doubt on the conjecture of Porson, he has strengthened the case for the conjecture of Dawes. This, says Housman, is the behaviour of a defence attorney who is said to have handed to the barrister his brief marked, 'no case; abuse plaintiff's attorney'.

Second, Jebb argues that 'the extant remains of Attic Tragedy justify Porson's remark that compounds of περί were avoided, but are too small to warrant a rule absolutely excluding them'. Housman observes that if the remains of tragedy are too small to warrant this rule they are also too small to warrant the rule known as Porson's law; and that, in fact, the remains of tragedy contain a dozen violations of the latter rule, but none of the rule about περί.

Third, Jebb argues that 'the probability of such a rule, intrinsically slight, is further lessened by the περίαλλα of the Euripidean anapaest' (he is referring to fr. 115). On the contrary, says Housman, its probability is increased thereby. For the number of anapaests in tragedy is a mere handful compared with the number of iambic trimeters. If there were no rule against περί followed by a vowel in iambics, we should expect the iambics to contain a dozen examples. Further, when Jebb says that the probability of the rule is intrinsically slight, 'What he means is that he would never have guessed the existence of such a rule himself, and it was only found out by the acute and accurate and unprejudiced observation of Porson . . . When I began to learn Latin the probability of the rule that *mensa* is feminine struck me as intrinsically slight; but I have not yet come across a passage in Latin literature where *mensa* is neuter, as I expected it to be, so I accept the rule.'

Fourth, Jebb argues that 'one *reason* why περί before a vowel should be usually avoided is evident: a compound with ἀμφί would in most cases express the same notion, without resolving the foot: *e.g.* ἀμπέχω, ἀμφίστημι dispensed with the need for περιέχω, περιΐστημι. A single example like our passage goes far to break down the assumed universality of the exclusion.' What, Housman asks, is this single example? 'Jebb has so lost his way that the very facts of the case have escaped his memory, and he has forgotten that the περιίδηις which he is defending is not the reading of any MS but merely of the editions which he learnt by heart at school.'

Next follows the introduction to the scene in the police court. I shall quote the whole of the remaining narrative, in which Housman appears as the prosecuting counsel and attempts to prove Jebb's guilt by using the same four fallacious arguments against him which Jebb had used against Porson.

'I am prosecuting for the police, and I mean to discharge my painful duty without fear or favour. I begin by observing, "Your worship will notice that Mr Porson has a very red nose." That is the first of the four arguments by which I hope to deprive Sir Richard Jebb of his liberty. Mr Porson buries his face in his handkerchief, whether to conceal his nose or to conceal his opinion of my intellect I do not know; and I proceed to my second argument: it is quite true, as Mr Porson says, that Sir Richard Jebb has always avoided stealing spoons when people were looking; but that is no sufficient reason for supposing that he does not steal them now and then when he is unobserved. Third argument: the probability of Sir Richard Jebb's innocence, intrinsically slight, is further lessened by the fact that a silver spoon has been found in the pocket of an Irish Home Ruler. Now comes the fourth argument; and this is a thunderbolt. One reason why Sir Richard Jebb has hitherto avoided stealing spoons is evident: he is fairly well-to-do, and until he stood for Parliament, and incurred that heavy expenditure on bribery and treating of electors which is involved in contesting a University seat, he was able to pay his way honestly; but a single fact like this goes far to show the sort of man he really is. By this time the combined power of my logic and eloquence, coming on the top of last night's potations, has reduced Mr Porson to a maudlin condition; but at these words he does manage to hiccup out "What fact are you referring to?" "I am referring", I reply, "to the indisputable and incriminating fact, that Sir Richard Jebb's pockets were found to contain no spoon." '[72]

Housman described Bentley as 'highly and equally eminent in Greek and Latin', and allowed the same title to Markland alone among English scholars (*Classical Papers* 1005). He had stuck to Latin himself, he said, because he could not attain to excellence in both languages. For him the attainment of excellence (to apply what he said in his memoir of Arthur Platt) was the building of a monument. And 'a scholar who means to build himself a monument must spend much of his life in acquiring knowledge which for its own sake is not worth having and in reading books which do not in themselves deserve to be read'. Thus were Housman's studies, unlike Platt's, 'warped and narrowed by ambition' (*Classical Papers* 1272).[73]

Manilius was his monument. If he had chosen Greek, was there a monument there to be built? Scholars of good judgement have remarked that he did well to abandon the tragic poets, where 'the certainty and finality which distinguish scores of Housman's Latin emendations are hardly to be achieved' (Gow (1936), 15).[74] Of Aeschylus and Sophocles that is true. It is not true of Euripides, who,

[72] I append as a melancholy postscript Kamerbeek's note on *OT* 1505: 'Porson's objection . . ., ably contested by Jebb . . ., is now much invalidated by the certain reading of Eur. *Hyps.* 32.5 πε]ριέχουσ' ἐν ἀγκάλ[αις.' Even Dawe (1982) adduces this passage. This is not a reading but a supplement by the first editors, and we now know that it is wrong (see *TrGF* v/2. 767).

[73] This striking expression ('"Warped and narrowed" are strong words': Kenney (1989), 622) does not originate with Housman. I find it in F. M. Cornford, *Microcosmographia Academica* (1908) (Ch. IV 'one whose mind has not been warped and narrowed by merely intellectual interests'), G. Gissing, *Workers in the Dawn* (1880) (Ch. XI 'those whose brains have not been warped and narrowed by the hereditary burden of a crown'), and in an essay by H. D. Thoreau, *Life without Principle* (1863) (= Glick (1973), 174–5) ('we are warped and narrowed by an exclusive devotion to trade and commerce'). Dr Stray adds Matthew Arnold, *Johnson's Lives of the Poets* (1878) (= Super (1972), 318) ('we are to conceive of Johnson and his century . . . as capable of being warped and narrowed in their judgements of poetry by this exclusive task'), apparently (so 'exclusive' suggests) echoing Thoreau. And he observes an earlier example in an American popular periodical of 1836 (accessible via Google Book Search: http://books.google.com). Here is another unnoticed echo: 'Philology was tame, and dull, and flat: | God said "Let there be larks," and there was Platt' (A. Burnett (1997), 251; cf. 537) ~ 'Nature and Nature's laws lay hid in night: | God said, *Let Newton be!* and all was light' (Pope).

[74] Similarly Robertson (1936), 113, (1949), 452; Lloyd-Jones (1973), 137 = (1982), 183.

after Murray's edition, remained, as he still remains, a fertile field of soluble problems. Housman told Murray in 1900 that 'The Bacchae, Iph. Taur., and Medea are the only three plays I have really studied' (H. Maas (1971), 52). I, for one, regret that he found no more time for Euripides.

13

Greek Tragedy: Text and Context

A. F. Garvie

Recent scholarship has insisted that, if we are to understand Greek tragedy correctly, we must get behind our own modern cultural assumptions, and recognize that it was written for an audience with a very different cultural background. That means that the proper way to study it is in the context of fifth-century Athenian civic democratic ideology. Few indeed have seriously questioned the 'historicist' approach to Greek tragedy.[1] Conversely, the idea that it means almost as much to us in the twenty-first century as it did to the original audience, because human nature does not radically change from one generation to another, tends to be seen as old-fashioned, and 'universalist' has become almost a derogatory label.[2] I do not intend to argue that the 'historicist' approach is wrong. Historians are entitled to use tragedy as a source for the understanding of fifth-century society,[3] and, conversely, there is much in tragedy that can be fully appreciated only by those who are familiar with the nature of the society for which it was written. Aeschylus' *Persae* is a legitimate historical source for the Battle of Salamis, his *Eumenides* for attitudes to the Areopagus in the early 450s. A reader's appreciation of Euripides' *Troades* is enhanced by the knowledge that in the year

[1] Griffin (1998) is a notable exception (but see also the response of Seaford (2000)); also Taplin (1986). For Rhodes (2003) Athenian drama reflects 'the *polis* in general rather than the democratic *polis* in particular' (119).

[2] See for example Hall (1997), 94, and, for a different view of 'universality', Macleod (1982), 131, 144 = (1983), 27, 40.

[3] See for example Pelling (1997*b*).

before its first production the Athenians had treated the Melians in the same way as the Trojans are treated in the play. When we see or read the many plays in which powerful women are presented, it is helpful to know how real women were treated in fifth-century Athens—their exclusion from the political process and from much of public life. In the sphere of ethics the theme of 'friends' and 'enemies'[4] is one that requires explanation for a modern reader.

The purpose of this paper, however, is to show that there is still something to be said for the 'universalist' approach, and that the 'historicist' approach, if it is carried too far, can lead to wrong interpretations of a play. The two approaches can be combined, and the question is really one of priority. To put it crudely, is it better to begin with the text of a play, and to form our own judgement before we consider how far it needs to be modified in the light of our knowledge of ancient attitudes and presuppositions, or should we from the beginning consciously subordinate our own aesthetic response to our knowledge of the context in which the work was produced? In many cases it may not make much difference, but in others the two approaches can produce different results. I remain to be convinced that the 'historicist' approach is *a priori* more reliable. If we 'know' what the Athenians were thinking at the time of a play's first production, there is a danger that we shall read that into the text even when it is not there, and, conversely, that we shall miss what *is* there. If we know in advance what we are looking for, it is not difficult to find it. At the time when we 'knew', for example that *Supplices* was a very early play of Aeschylus, it was not hard to interpret it in terms of the political situation in the 490s.[5] Now that we know that the play belongs to Aeschylus' maturity, it is just as easy to produce an interpretation that fits that period.[6] My concern in this paper, however, is not with the question of how far, or in what sense, Greek tragedy is political, but with the more general problem of how we should read a play.[7]

One problem with the 'historicist' approach is that, when tragedy is used as source material for the study of fifth-century Athenian

[4] See especially Dover (1974), 180–4, Blundell (1989).

[5] See Garvie (1969), 146–50.

[6] Forrest (1960), Sommerstein (1997).

[7] Gellrich (1995) provides helpful discussion of the relationship between text and context in interpreting tragedy.

culture, it is all too easy to find undue dramatic significance in matters that the ancient audience took for granted. The playwright's purpose was not to inform *us* but to entertain his audience, and, if possible, to win the prize.[8] He may at the same time hope to make his audience think about the nature of its society, whether to confirm it in its cultural assumptions or to question, and even subvert them, but it cannot be taken for granted that this is his main purpose in writing his play. If, in *Supplices*, Aeschylus presents Argos as having a democratic constitution combined with monarchy, there is a satisfactory dramatic reason for his doing so: it is the best way for him to create sympathy for both Pelasgus in his terrible dilemma, and for the city itself. He cannot be presented as a tyrant; the Athenian audience (or most of it) was in favour of democracy.[9] Similarly, in *Ajax* Sophocles portrays Menelaus as a typical Spartan, not because he wishes to encourage anti-Spartan feeling, but because he wants us to disapprove of him and to see through his apparently sound words on the need for discipline in a city (1073–6).[10] The dramatist draws on accepted wisdom and common belief, but only as a starting point for the presentation of ideas which may be original and disturbing. It is not enough to identify the ideas and attitudes of the playwright's contemporaries; much more important is to study what the dramatist makes of them as he constructs his play. I can see no good *a priori* reason to suppose that political or ideological, rather than dramatic, considerations determine that structure.

A second problem with the 'historicist' approach is that its practitioners tend to underestimate the fact that a Greek tragedy was performed in front of an audience which, if the play is to succeed, must to a greater or lesser degree identify or at least empathize with some, if not all, of the characters.[11] For Aristotle in his *Poetics* the

[8] 'The tragedian's primary concern is to satisfy an audience that looked for emotional stimulus and aesthetic satisfaction' (Heath (1987), 46–7).

[9] This is no doubt an over-simplification. For the ability of the Athenian audience to experience different perspectives in the same play, and for Greek tragedy to affirm elite as well as democratic values see Griffith (1995), especially 72–5, 107–24.

[10] On *Supplices* see Garvie (1969), 150–4, on *Ajax* Garvie (1998), 216 and nn. on 1073–6, 1091.

[11] For my purposes it matters little whether we talk of identification or sympathy or empathy or engagement or involvement. On the subtle differences among the terms see Lada (1993), 101–3.

combination of pity and fear is closely associated with the *οἰκεία ἡδονή* of tragedy. Whether his contemporaries, or indeed the contemporaries of the three great tragedians, shared his view is not something to be discussed here.[12] My own view is that Aristotle is to be trusted, as is, more recently, Heath (1987), who may have underestimated the importance of our intellectual reaction to the problems presented by tragedy,[13] but who is certainly right to highlight the emotional effect upon an audience. Our reaction to the characters is produced in various ways—by what we see them doing or hear them saying, or by what other characters, or the Chorus, say about, or to, them. Unlike the epic poet, however, the dramatist cannot present characters through his own authorial voice. It is above all through the construction of his plot that the playwright is able to manipulate our emotional response to the characters.[14] He can juxtapose contrasting scenes, or he can build up slowly to an emotional climax. By emphasizing now this, and now that, aspect of the situation he can make us almost forget what we really know is going to happen, so that, when it does happen, it comes as a surprise.[15] He can make us look at people and situations in ways that, if we had been left to ourselves, it would never have occurred to us to do. The three tragedians may differ from one another in their dramatic technique. We identify perhaps more closely with Aeschylus' principal characters than with those of Sophocles. In Aeschylus the characters, or some of them, are generally anxious from the beginning, and, the more we hear them expressing their fears for the future, the more anxious we too become. Sophocles' celebrated dramatic irony depends on a certain detachment on the part of the audience, particularly in *Oedipus Tyrannus*. The characters, or some of them,

[12] Hall (1996*b*), 304, argues that 'the *Poetics*' near-total displacement of the *polis* from tragedy' is 'an astonishingly original innovation' (394); *contra* Rhodes (2003), 105, 'the view that the only legitimate way to study drama is to study it in its civic context is one for which it is hard to claim ancient support'.

[13] He concedes (especially 88, 157–8) that tragedy has an intellectual and moral content, but denies that this is its purpose. Lada (1993) is surely right to insist on the inextricability of intellect and feeling in the audience's response. For the question of how far emotions are themselves culturally determined see Lada 95, 112.

[14] 'Manipulating the sympathies of the audience to achieve the desired tragic effect is an important part of the dramatist's art' (Stinton (1975), 239 = (1990), 166).

[15] Garvie (1978).

may think that everything is going well, but the audience, which is in the position of the gods themselves, shudders as it knows how wrong they are. For all three tragedians, however, the essentials remain true. Aristotle, again, in his insistence on plot as the most important element in tragedy (*Poet.* 1450^{a}15, etc.), got it right.

With these considerations in mind I shall look briefly at three specific plays, *Persae*, *Antigone*, and *Medea*. In all of them the critic who starts from the dramatic text will interpret it differently from the one whose starting point is the context of the play. I shall try to show that the former approach is more satisfactory.

If any play may be thought to cry out for the 'historicist' approach it is Aeschylus' *Persae*, the only surviving tragedy to deal with an event from recent history. Obviously both Aeschylus and every member of his audience in 472 BC, only eight years after the battle of Salamis, a battle in which Aeschylus himself may have participated, were delighted at the Greek victory over the hated Persian invader. We might, therefore, expect the play to be a triumphant celebration of a national victory. So perhaps did the original audience, which may have known in advance at least the subject of the play, from gossip if not from the announcement in the *proagon*.[16] But was it at the same time puzzled as to how a play with such a subject could be made appropriate to a *tragic* competition? A satisfactory definition of 'tragedy' and the 'tragic' remains elusive,[17] but probably most ancient audiences would share the view of most modern audiences or readers, that tragedy should deal with suffering and take it seriously. How does a patriotic celebration square with this? In the nineteenth and the first half of the twentieth centuries, in which the celebration idea was widely held, the Persians were often seen as figures of fun, especially in the final scene.[18] Against this view Broadhead (1960),

[16] It is, however, uncertain whether the *proagon* was part of the festival before the building of the Periclean Odeum in the late 440s. For the little that is known about it see Pickard-Cambridge (1988), 63–4, 67–8, Goldhill (1987), 59, Csapo and Slater (1994), 105, 109–10.

[17] See the papers and responses in Silk (1996) (ed.); also Most (2000).

[18] So Prickard (1879), while accepting that the play is 'a true tragedy', writes (on 906–end) that the final scene 'must have been nothing but ludicrous to any spectator'. Murray (1940), 121, who thought that the play might have been presented as part of an annual series of such celebrations at the Great Dionysia in the 470s, tried hard to explain how it could be 'a great tragedy' when 'it was apparently a

xv–xxxii, argued strongly, and correctly, that *Persae* is in every sense a tragedy. His interpretation of that tragedy is, I think, unduly simple, but that is another matter.

In recent years the pendulum has swung back again, but now in a more sophisticated way, with the influential work of Hall (1989, 1993, 1996*a*) and T. Harrison (2000). All of these are an invaluable source of information about the Persian background to the play, and, more important, about Athenian attitudes to the Persians in the fifth century BC. Hall argues that *Persae* itself was largely responsible for forming those attitudes, and for establishing the notion of the Persians as irredeemably the 'Other', the polar opposites who help the Athenians to establish and define their own identity. There is, for example, much stress in the play on the luxurious oriental lifestyle of the Persians, with ἁβρο- words making a frequent appearance. Hall shows conclusively ((1989), (1993), 120–1, (1996*a*), on 41) that in the sixth century such, and other, words denoting luxury are normally laudatory in their context, while in Attic literature of the fifth century, from the Persian Wars onwards, they are regularly pejorative when applied to men. I have no doubt that this is true, but the question is whether Aeschylus himself intended the words to bear this connotation.[19] Hall herself does not deny the presence of tragic pathos in the play. Harrison goes further, in arguing that the entire play presents a 'concerted strategy of patriotic stimulation' (53).

If we adopt the other approach, and start from the assumption that this is a play in which the audience is expected to identify or empathize with the characters, we find something different. It presents Aristotle's favourite type of tragedy (*Poet.* 1453^{a}7–10), that in which a man (or in this case a whole country and a man, Xerxes) falls from a position of high reputation and great prosperity into ruin because of some error (ἁμαρτία), the same simple pattern that Aristotle found, and we find, for example, in Sophocles' *Oedipus Tyrannus.* The difference is that Oedipus thought that all was well

performance written to order for a public celebration'. As late as 1965 Haldane (35 n. 18) can write 'there is an element of burlesque in this caricature of Xerxes [tearing his clothes]'. T. Harrison (2000), 135 n. 1 provides a useful bibliography.

[19] See also Kurke (1992). For Griffith (1998), 44–8, on the other hand, the differences between the Persians and at least the aristocratic members of the audience were not so very great.

with him, and only the audience, and Teiresias, knew better, whereas here from the very beginning the Chorus, followed by Atossa, fear the worst. The success of the play must be judged on Aeschylus' success in persuading us to identify or sympathize with them in their fears, and that is a matter for dramatic criticism, rather than for political or ideological commentary. *Persae* has always been an underrated play, studied mainly as a curiosity, the only surviving specimen of historical drama, or as the earliest surviving tragedy, and therefore as evidence for the early evolution of the genre. Not enough attention has been paid to its qualities as a drama, to its plot construction, or to the complexity of the tragic situation. Just as Oedipus, at the beginning of Sophocles' play, is at the height of his powers and success, addressed by the Priest almost as a god (31–4), the best of men and the saviour of his people (46–8), so in *Persae* the Chorus in its parodos lays much stress on the Persians' wealth and luxury and success, and on their divinely appointed destiny to win wars by both land and sea.[20] The dramatic point is that the greater their initial prosperity, the harder will be their fall. At the same time the Chorus is anxious. Prosperity is dangerous; it can so easily turn into excessive prosperity, and success cannot last for ever. Alternations are the norm in human life. As in Sophocles, human beings fall into error. So for most of the play the emphasis is on Xerxes' errors of judgement, and not until the Darius scene will the catastrophe be interpreted in terms of punishment for *hybris*.

Atossa adds to the foreboding. She too is worried about the possible loss of Persian wealth and the failure of the expedition. She narrates to the Chorus her nightmare and the unfavourable omen which she has seen. In the dream the two women whom Xerxes tries to yoke to his chariot represent Persia and Greece respectively, but we are explicitly told (185–6) that they are sisters of the same family. Here at least there is no suggestion that the Persians are the 'Other'. The only difference between them is that the Persian horse is submissive, while the Greek horse rebels and upsets the chariot.

[20] Müller's transposition of 93–100 to follow 113 is certainly correct: see Garvie (1999), 21–6.

Atossa (211–14) takes comfort from the fact that, whether Xerxes has won or lost, he is not responsible to the city, and is still the ruler of the land. The implied contrast is with Athenian democratic magistrates. Hahn (1981), 182, remarks that, since these lines have no dramatic function, they must have a political or ideological function. But they do have a dramatic function. Atossa is indulging in mere wishful thinking, whose futility will be demonstrated by the Chorus at 584–97. She questions the Chorus leader about the geographical location of distant Athens, about the size of the army and its resources, and about its form of government. She is astonished to learn that the Athenians are said to be no man's slaves or subjects (242), in other words that their constitution is democratic. The whole passage is, not surprisingly, a favourite with those who adopt the historicist approach, and even those who maintain that *Persae* is a genuine tragedy have to admit that patriotic touches are not entirely absent. Broadhead (1960), xix–xx, is one of the few scholars to consider it anything other than a digression, but his interpretation is the wrong one. In his view the dialogue is inserted by the poet to allow Atossa to enjoy the reassurance of the Chorus leader for a little while before the arrival of the Messenger confirms that all the forebodings have come true. But there is no reassurance in the dialogue. The Chorus leader describes the small forces of the Athenians and their reliance on the silver mines of Laurion. After all that we have heard in the parodos about Persian gold, the symbolism of the inferior metal, silver, should be obvious. Moreover, the Athenian army, or state, is not subject to proper discipline. How could so poor and weak a country defeat the rich and mighty Persian empire? So Atossa seeks reassurance, but she does not obtain it. She knows that in the omen a hawk attacked and defeated a more powerful eagle, the symbol of Persian royalty. And now, in a clear reference to Marathon (244; cf. 236), the Chorus leader points out that the weak has already defeated the stronger. Where Atossa desperately tries to find reassurance, the audience can see only the culmination of the initial stage of foreboding, and we are now ready for the Messenger's account of the battle. It would be foolish to deny that Aeschylus' audience took pride in the superiority of Athenian democratic institutions, or at least of the Greek *polis*, over Persian despotism, but that does not mean that his principal aim was to gratify that pride.[21] Rather, he uses it to demonstrate the incomprehension of Atossa and to confirm that her attempts at optimism are doomed to failure.[22]

If we think that there is no room for further foreboding, we are wrong. With the departure of the Messenger, Atossa retires to her palace to bring offerings for the gods. She complains that the Chorus's advice to do so earlier has now proved singularly unhelpful, and yet she is still prepared to do it in the hope that things may get better in future (520–6). This again is wishful thinking of the kind that Aeschylus will employ so often in the *Oresteia*, whose audience will shudder every time that it hears a character say, 'let us hope that things will turn out well'. Here the audience is well aware that what lies ahead for the Persians is not (Broadhead on 840–2) 'a brighter future', but Plataea, and, when the ghost of the dead Darius emerges from his tomb at the summons of the Chorus, one of his functions will be to predict that defeat. The foreboding carries on, remarkably, beyond the end of the play.

The final scene is the lyric lamentation shared between Xerxes and the Chorus, which caused so much embarrassment to Victorian critics, unfamiliar as they were with the conventions of formal Greek lamentation, the *mirológia* of more modern Greeks.[23] Far from being an awkward coda, this scene marks the emotional climax of the play, as the double tragedies of Xerxes and of Persia come together in an antiphonal, and increasingly exciting, lyric exchange.[24] Unfortunately, we can only imagine the effect of the music and the choreography. Finally language breaks down altogether, and to the accompaniment of incoherent cries and sounds the Chorus and

[21] In the Messenger's reports the only reference to the Athenian army is at 355. At 362 Themistocles is a Greek, not an Athenian, man, at 409–10 the Athenian ship which was the first to engage the enemy is a Greek ship, while at 454–5 it is to the Greeks that god gave the glory. The patriotism is panhellenic rather than narrowly Athenian. Aeschylus seems to have gone out of his way to understate the latter.

[22] 'If there is praise of Athens [in *Persae*], it is designed to intensify the bewilderment and gloom of the characters on the stage' (Macleod (1982), 131 = (1983), 27).

[23] On this subject Alexiou (1974) is still the standard work.

[24] At 1034 λυπρά· χάρματα δ' ἐχθροῖς the joy of the Persians' enemies serves as a natural polarization. In this context all the stress is on the pain. Quite different is the Athenian *epitaphios*, in which the lamentations of the enemy are part of a hymn to the greatness of Athens (Loraux (1986), 50).

Xerxes leave the theatre. It is an emotional conclusion almost unparalleled in Greek tragedy. T. Harrison (2000), 111 (cf. 105), contends that, 'to measure the authenticity or the quality of a tragedy by the degree of sympathy elicited by the suffering of its protagonists is simply a random and futile exercise'. This comes close to saying that because it cannot be objectively measured it cannot be there at all.[25] Rather, if we do not feel pity here for the Persians, something has gone badly wrong with the production. Segal is right to talk about the 'expansion of our sensibilities in compassion for others', and Cartledge right (though I would put it more strongly) to declare that 'tragic pathos is achieved by requiring the Athenian audience to sympathise somewhat, if not empathise, with their former—but also very much present—Persian enemies'.[26] As the audience leaves the theatre, it is surely not with the smug satisfaction that Athenians are not like oriental barbarians, and that this kind of thing could never happen to them. Rather, it is astonished to find that the Persians are human beings like themselves, and that they share the same propensity to seek prosperity which may turn out to be excessive, and to make mistakes, or, if we prefer the moralizing interpretation which Darius alone in the play propounds, inadvertently to commit acts of *hybris*, which turned out to be *hybris* only in retrospect;[27] how could Xerxes know in advance that Poseidon would take offence at his building of a bridge (749–51), even as important a bridge as this one?[28] That Aeschylus could use the great victory of Salamis to make his audience pity the enemy and fear for themselves, is a remarkable achievement.

The 'historicist' approach to Sophocles' *Antigone* is presented uncompromisingly by Sourvinou-Inwood (1989), 134: 'If we wish to read a text such as the *Antigone* as closely as possible to the ways in

[25] Similarly, A. M. Bowie (1981), 158 criticized Jasper Griffin for finding pathos in Homer, where its existence cannot be objectively demonstrated; but see Heath (1987), 31–2.

[26] C. P. Segal (1996), 165, Cartledge (1997), 25 (quoted by T. Harrison (2000), 161 n. 16, as 'a judicious fudge'). See also Goldhill (1988), Pelling (1997*a*), 13–18. Contrast Harrison 115: 'the *Persians* then is not a work with which we can, or should, identify too readily'.

[27] For Harrison 110–11 *Pers.* does not fit Aristotle's criteria for tragedy because Xerxes deserved to suffer. The tragedy, I believe, is more profound than that.

[28] See Garvie (1999), 25.

which its contemporary audience did, we must reconstruct in detail their cultural assumptions, by means of which meaning was created, and try to read through perceptual filters created by those assumptions; otherwise we will inevitably read through our own assumptions by default, and as these are very different from those of the Athenians of the late 440s, they will inevitably produce very different meanings from theirs.' From the point of view of a fifth-century male audience,[29] Antigone might seem to have everything against her. Unlike Ismene, the ordinary person who represents conventional morality and attitudes, Antigone does not know how to behave as a woman should.[30] By symbolically burying her brother she deliberately breaks the law. To the original audience it would not seem self-evident from the beginning that Creon was wrong to put the interests of the *polis* before those of the family, Antigone's sole concern. While women had their part to play in funerals, it was restricted under Solon's legislation, and was perhaps particularly limited in the case of public funerals of those who died in war.[31] It was the state that controlled the procedure, and it was certainly not a woman's duty to organize a funeral. Her role was to leave her natal family, to accept the *kyrieia* of her husband, and to procreate children. Although she was still expected to remain loyal to her natal, as well as to her married, family,[32] Antigone's loyalty to Polyneices makes it impossible for her to marry at all, and so fulfil the role of wife and mother. In a sense, she will after all marry Haemon in Hades (1240–1), but at 898–9 those whom she longs to see there are her parents and her brother. Underlying all this, some scholars have traced male fears of

[29] Whether women were present in the audience is still disputed. Henderson (1991*a*) argues strongly for their participation, but distinguishes usefully between the actual and the notional audience, the males to whom the playwright by convention addresses his play; see also Gould (1980), 39 n. 2 = (2001), 113 n. 2, Csapo and Slater (1994), 286–7.

[30] The case against her is comprehensively set out by Sourvinou-Inwood (1989) and (1990). See also Pomeroy (1975), 93–119 on Antigone and other tragic women who adopt male characteristics to achieve their goals; Hester (1971), 22–3, Sorum (1982).

[31] Sourvinou-Inwood (1989), 137, (1990), 30, Alexiou (1974), 4–23, Pomeroy (1975), 80, Humphreys (1983), 83–8, Loraux (1986), 24–5, 45, Just (1989), 110–11, Rehm (1994), 7–8, 21–9.

[32] Gould (1980), 43 = (2001), 123–4, Griffith (1999), 51–2.

what would happen if women, the emotional, irrational, disorderly gender, were allowed to get out of control.[33]

We should certainly be on our guard against our own cultural conditioning, before we simply dismiss the male chauvinism of Creon and his prejudice against young men, who were generally believed to be unfit for rule (Just (1989), 178). There are, however, aspects of Antigone's character which we, no less than an ancient audience, might criticize. She claims apparently to be a loving sort of person (523), but she treats her sister abominably. When Ismene, showing courage of which we had thought her incapable, claims in front of Creon to have shared in the burial, she is bitterly rejected by Antigone (549).[34] According to the Greek ethical code one should help one's friends and harm one's enemies.[35] But tragedy can arise when the two categories become confused. So Creon treats his nephew as an enemy, while Antigone treats him as a friend, because he is her brother. But this leads her to treat, not only her uncle Creon, but also Ismene her sister as enemies.[36] From the beginning she is intent on a martyr's death. It is not enough for her to bury her brother; she wants the glory for having done so (86–7). This may be one of the reasons for Antigone's, very variously interpreted, repetition of the symbolic burial: she wants to be caught, so that everyone may know about, and praise her for, her deed.

We may not like Antigone, and we may feel that Ismene is the more attractive character. Yet, against all these odds, Sophocles contrives to arouse our admiration for her, by showing that she is the one who does what is right. We do not have to like the Sophoclean hero, but, as Nussbaum (1986), 63 (cf. also 66), remarks,[37] criticism of Antigone is 'not incompatible with the judgment that she is morally superior to Creon'. Antigone is right to bury Polyneices, and Creon wrong to forbid it. By the end of the play there can be no

[33] Sourvinou-Inwood (1989), 140, Gould (1980), 55–7 = (2001), 147–53, Segal (1981), 192, (1995), 119, Loraux (1986), 146–8, Just (1989).

[34] Her sarcastic *Κρέοντ᾽ ἐρώτα· τοῦδε γὰρ σὺ κηδέμων* tells strongly against the alternative view that her concern is to save Ismene from sharing her fate.

[35] See n. 4 above.

[36] It is this tangle which gives rise to the notorious ambiguity at 523, *οὔτοι συνέχθειν, ἀλλὰ συμφιλεῖν ἔφυν.*

[37] See also Winnington-Ingram (1980), 323.

doubt about this, because Creon is warned by the prophet Teiresias that he has angered the gods by refusing burial to the dead and by burying the living (i.e. Antigone in her rock-cut tomb). He sets out, too late, to undo the harm that he has done. But at the end of the play, having lost both his son Haemon and his wife Eurydice through suicide, he will admit that he was wrong and that it was all his fault (1261–9). The rationality on which he prides himself is defeated by the *δυσβουλία* of the woman, and he who forbade lamentation for Polyneices (28, 204) ends up by lamenting emotionally himself (Segal (1995), 126–31). If, then, Creon was wrong, in a conflict in which there is no possibility of compromise, Antigone must have been right. Some have unconvincingly attempted to evade this conclusion by arguing that, although Creon was punished by the gods for forbidding the burial, at the same time they disapproved of Antigone for carrying it out.[38] It is true that we are never explicitly told that the gods approve of Antigone's action, but neither are we told the contrary. She is not rewarded for her deed, and she goes to her death bewildered that the gods have abandoned her (921–8). Why the gods let it happen is an unanswerable question. Yet Antigone herself never wavers in her conviction that she has acted rightly. That is her tragedy, a more profound tragedy than Creon's. He suffers for doing what was wrong, Antigone for doing what was right. The final third of the play belongs to Creon, not Antigone, but his recognition of his error shows that Antigone was right.

At what stage in the play we reach this conclusion is open to debate.[39] Heath (1987), 73–7, is confident that at no stage can the issue have been in doubt for the audience. But this is to ignore the disadvantages under which Antigone labours in the eyes of a male

[38] Brown (1987), 9; for Sourvinou-Inwood, the gods approve of the result of Antigone's deed, but not of her subversive action nor of Antigone as a character.

[39] Not all members of the audience may have done so at the same time. Bennett and Tyrrell (1990) argue that in the subtext of the play Antigone represents the Athenians as the traditional upholders of the customary rights of burial in mythic times. On the diametrical opposition between this view and that of Sourvinou-Inwood, Foley (1995), 142 remarks that arguments based solely on democratic ideology do not in themselves support the view that either Antigone or Creon is right; in Athens there might be different opinions as to how best to serve the *polis*. For Lefkowitz (1986), 81–4, as for Heath, the audience would from the beginning have seen Antigone's action as 'within the bounds of accepted female behaviour'.

audience. At the other extreme, Sourvinou-Inwood argues ((1989), 144, (1990), 24–6) that the audience is not alienated from Creon until the Haemon scene, and that only in the Teiresias scene is it revealed that Antigone was right to claim that she had served the unwritten customs of the gods. Rather, Sophocles begins his gradual manipulation of the audience's sympathies early in the play. Creon's refusal of burial must have caused it at least some unease. At Athens in the fifth century it seems to have been normal to deny a traitor burial in Attica, but there was nothing to prevent his corpse from being buried in a neighbouring country.[40] The bodies of criminals thrown into the *barathron* were regularly left unburied, but they were at least hidden from public view, so that pollution was avoided. Heath (1987), 75, rightly remarks that 'whenever the refusal of burial becomes an issue in tragedy, it is seen as an emotive wrong.' The audience might already have seen *Ajax*. If so, when Creon appears on stage and explains the apparently sound principles on which he intends to rule, the audience might again recall that play, in which similar principles are put into the mouth of the villain Menelaus. The rhetorical structure of Creon's speech already suggests that he is excessively concerned with his own position as the new king, and we may well wonder, as apparently does the notably unenthusiastic Chorus leader (211–14), how the edict forbidding the burial follows from these excellent principles. As the play goes on it becomes increasingly clear that Creon has all the characteristics of the traditional tyrant, his intolerance of opposition, his assumption that the motivation of any opponent must be materialistic (222, 293–303, 310–14), his view of his subjects as slaves or animals to be broken in (289–92, 477–9), his conviction that the city belongs to him (738). None of this would be lost on the tyrant-hating members of the Athenian audience.

As Creon progressively loses the audience's sympathy, we might expect that Antigone gains in its sympathy. But it is not quite as easy as that. Sophocles requires that she should remain an isolated figure. This is part of her tragedy. So the male Chorus is distinctly

[40] As far as the play is concerned this possibility is nowhere suggested (see Easterling (1997*a*), 26–8; also Hester (1971), 19–21, 55). The issue is presented at its starkest—burial or non-burial, with nothing in between.

unsympathetic when it discovers that she has performed the burial, and, although it unbends to some extent in the scene before she is led out to her death, a note of disapproval is still strongly present at 853–5. What impresses it most is not that she has been proved to be right, but that she is as stubborn as her father Oedipus (471–2). The audience's sympathy for Antigone builds up more subtly. Ismene loves her sister (99), the Messenger is, at least superficially, sorry for her (436–9), and Haemon reports that the common people are on her side (692–700, 733).[41] There is little trace of romantic love in this play, but one function of the Chorus's ode on the power of Eros (781–800) is to suggest how much Antigone's decision has cost her.[42] When she is finally led off to her death, to be the bride of Hades,[43] bewildered by what she sees as the Chorus's incomprehension (839–52), and by her abandonment by the gods, unable even to give a rational explanation of her action, but still convinced that she was right, it would be very hard to withhold our pity from her. She may be isolated within the play, but Sophocles contrives that for that isolation we pity her. 'Like most literary works the *Antigone* manipulates the cultural assumptions of its time. The play itself both uses them and goes beyond them' (Just (1989), 207).

Euripides' Medea starts off with even more disadvantages than Antigone. She is not only a woman, but a barbarian woman, and one who, in the traditional story of Jason and the Argonauts, was versed in sorcery. We might expect her to validate the theory that the presentation of such powerful and dangerous women in tragedy served to reflect male fears of what might happen if they were not controlled. 'Because she was a foreigner', says Page (1938), xxi, 'she could kill her children; because she was a witch she could escape in a magic chariot.' Euripides, however, will surprise us. He hints at Medea's

[41] Sourvinou-Inwood (1989), 144 and 146, (1990), 15–16, dismisses Haemon's claim as an unsubstantiated assertion. Since, however, Creon's reply to Haemon at 734 implicitly accepts its truth, we must, I think, take it at face value. At 907 Antigone's βίᾳ πολιτῶν might seem to contradict it, but she has not heard Haemon's report of public opinion.

[42] For the power of Eros as one of the central themes of the play see Winnington-Ingram (1980), 92–8.

[43] For Antigone as the bride of death see Rehm (1994), 59–71 (with earlier literature on the theme).

powers of sorcery only at 395–7 when she swears an oath by Hecate. Any woman might be skilled in the use of *φάρμακα*, whether medicines or poisons (384–5, 718, 789).[44] Medea will certainly escape at the end of the play on the chariot of the Sun, but till then she knows of no magical way to escape. Her foreignness *is* emphasized from the first lines of the play, but always in a way that evokes not contempt but pity—pity for a poor woman who is far from home and family in Colchis (253–8), and who will never again pass through the Symplegades to return to that home. The Symplegades (1–2, 433–4, 1263–4; cf. 211–12) serve as a kind of recurring symbol for her loneliness and helplessness. We see her first through the eyes of other, ordinary people, the Nurse, the Paidagogos, and the Chorus of Corinthian women (quite unlike the male Chorus of *Antigone*), all of whom are sympathetic to her and hostile to her husband. There are in the prologue some hints of danger to the children. But if, as seems probable,[45] Euripides was the first to introduce into the story Medea's deliberate killing of her children, the original audience would hardly be prepared by the prologue for the later development of the plot. We hear Medea's emotional offstage cries, but when she finally comes out of the house her entrance is a deliberate anticlimax; this is no monster, but a very reasonable woman, one indeed who in her famous complaint about the wretched plight of women in Greek society (230–51) can identify herself with the Greek women of the Chorus (231 *γυναῖκές ἐσμεν*; cf. 407–8).

It will be some time before we are reminded of the danger to the children. Euripides will employ the same technique for much of the rest of the play. A scene or passage in which our sympathy may seem to weaken is regularly followed by one in which it is restored, as our attention is directed to some other concern. Before (260–3) and after Medea's successful manipulation of the weak Creon she announces her intention to take revenge (for a fifth-century audience a morally acceptable course of conduct), but says nothing about the children.

[44] See Knox (1977), 211–18 = (1979), 306–11, Easterling (1977*b*), 179, Barlow (1989), 158–9, R. Friedrich (1993), 220–3. Just too (1989), 264–76, finds Euripides' treatment of Medea consistent with the stereotypical view of women in general.

[45] See Diggle (2004). For Manuwald (1983), 40–56 and Michelini (1989), 115–16, Neophron anticipated Euripides in making Medea the murderess of her children; see also Harrauer (2000), 31–2.

The Chorus leader in female solidarity approves. Her triumph over Creon (368–75) is unpleasant, but our thoughts are soon turned to the problem of where she will find a refuge, and the episode is followed by the first stasimon, whose theme is the unfortunate position of women in society. After all this, when the self-satisfied, insensitive Jason enters, a man and a Greek, even the most hardened chauvinist in the audience would find it hard to sympathize with him. His claim to have done Medea a favour by bringing her from her barbarian homeland to enjoy the benefits of Greek civilization (534–41) might in another context have made good sense to the Athenian audience, but here it is entirely discredited by the character of the speaker.[46] The Chorus leader is not impressed (576–8), and neither is the audience. Throughout the scene, as we hear of Jason's attitude to his children, we forget the danger from their mother.

The problem of Medea's refuge is solved by the arrival of Aegeus.[47] We may have some misgivings about her manipulation of this second, decent, man, more indeed than we did for Creon, and we may even begin to suspect that Euripides, through Medea, is manipulating us too in the audience, but on the whole we are pleased that she has found her refuge. Even circumstances, and perhaps the gods themselves,[48] seem to be working on Medea's side. The first real jolt to our sympathy[49] comes immediately after Aegeus' departure, when Medea reveals to the Chorus her plan to kill her children (791–6). For the first time (811–13) the Chorus leader expresses disapproval. Yet our sympathy is not entirely lost; even as she tells us of her plan she makes it clear that she loves the children (791, 795). In the scene in which Jason falls victim to Medea's third manipulation the pathos begins to increase (899–905, 922–3), but so do our fears. As the children leave with the fatal wedding gift, the Chorus assumes that they are as good as dead, and for the first time shows some sympathy for Jason (989–95). We too are sure that we shall never see the

[46] Saïd (2002), 85 ≈ (1984), 42 remarks that in Euripides 'anti-Barbarian talk, whose spokesmen are very suspect, is always invalidated by the context.'

[47] On the Aegeus scene see Grethlein (2003), 331–52. For the relationship between it and the end of the play see Worthington (1990).

[48] For the appearance of Aegeus as part of a coherent theological design see Kovacs (1993), 45, 48–50, 58–60.

[49] See Rehm (1994), 100 with n. 17.

children again, so that their reappearance at 1002 comes as a complete and pleasant surprise. For many critics her speech at 1019–80 is the emotional highlight of the play.[50] As she agonizes over whether to kill her beloved children, or to spare them, it becomes ever clearer that she is as much a victim as is Jason, and our sympathy is again strengthened. Our fears are forgotten during the long messenger speech, which concentrates entirely on the deaths of Glauce and Creon. Then once more our thoughts return to the children as Medea steels herself for the last time to kill them.

In the final scene Euripides, having for much of the play built up our sympathy for Medea, suddenly and deliberately shatters it. As Jason demands entrance to the house, seeking revenge, all eyes are on the door, waiting for it to open. Instead, Medea appears high above, as a kind of *dea ex machina* on the chariot sent by her grandfather the Sun to convey her safely to Athens. We welcomed gladly the coincidence of Aegeus' arrival. Much less welcome is the intervention of the gods to secure the triumph and the safety of a woman who has murdered her children. How can the gods approve of it? Even if A. P. Burnett (1973) and (1998), 192–224 and Kovacs (1993) are right that all along Zeus has been concerned to punish Jason for breaking his oaths,[51] and that the punishment necessitates the total destruction of his family, it is the horror, not a sense of righteous satisfaction, that is surely uppermost in the audience's mind. That the gods did not reward Antigone did not prove that she was wrong; that they *do* reward Medea does not show that she was right to kill her children.

[50] See, for example, Friedrich (1993), 229 ('it contains the conflict of the play. Up to this point there has been no real dramatic conflict'), Easterling (1977*b*), 188–9 (we need the speech 'in order to achieve the full depth of tragic seriousness'), J.-U. Schmidt (1999), 257–64. According to Seidensticker (1990), 91, 'since Reeve's [1972] paper lines 1056–80 have become the most discussed problem of authenticity in Greek tragedy'. Seidensticker himself, in defending the lines, gives a full history of the controversy. Manuwald (1983), 46–50, 56–61, and Diggle, in the 1984 OCT, follow Reeve in deletion, while others (e.g. Lloyd-Jones (1980), Kovacs (1986), Rehm (1994), 143–5) prefer a less drastic excision. Those who, with varying interpretations, retain the whole speech include Foley (1989), especially 66–73, 83–5, Michelini (1989), A. P. Burnett (1998), 209–14, 273–87.

[51] Kovacs himself (1993), 68, describes the portrayal of the gods' justice as repellent. He argues that in using Medea to punish Jason they are also punishing Medea for the murder of her brother. For the importance of oaths in *Medea* see also Vickers (1973), 282–6, Schein (1990), 60–1 with n. 14.

This is the kind of world in which we live, one in which the attitude of the gods is unfathomable. It is a most disturbing play. We sympathized with Antigone, whom we did not greatly like, in her determination to do what was *right*. We have come to sympathize with the downtrodden Medea, but she does what, by the standards of any age and culture, is clearly *wrong*. Our sympathy has obviously shifted to the shattered husband, who as we now know (1397, 1399–1400; we were misinformed at 76–7, 88), loved his children too, the children whom Medea will not even allow him to touch. But Medea herself, although she has her refuge in Athens, cannot look forward to a happy life there. There is no joy for anyone at the end, and ultimately we sympathize with both Jason and Medea.

In all three plays it would be a mistake to assume that the playwright's intention is to make some kind of political statement or to help the audience to define its identity as citizens of a democracy. He may invite them to question their conventional assumptions, and, by playing upon their emotions, to change their minds about many things that, before they entered the theatre, they had taken for granted. Fifth-century Athenian culture is indeed the background for all our surviving tragedies. We need to understand it, but what matters is how the playwrights used it. The tragic problems that they present are, despite all the differences between cultures, the tragic problems of every age.

14

Desperate Straits and the Tragic Stage

Jasper Griffin

Tragedy implies intensity. Its experience demands an intensity of suffering, emotion, atmosphere, and situation, exceeding that of ordinary existence. The poets can be seen to have a repertoire of devices to escape the humdrum daily round and to present life as more than just One Damn Thing After Another: to enliven and ennoble it with acute suffering, extreme situations, and agonizing decisions. All of that, of course, must be presented and experienced in the Grand Style.

Those situations are, let us insist (in opposition to those scholars who overemphasize their literary and conventional aspect), intimately linked to events in real, recent, and contemporary life. The same scenes and the same pressures occur on the tragic stage and in the history of the sixth and fifth centuries BC. It cannot be doubted that influence flowed both ways. The tragedians echoed spectacular events of history; agents in that history behaved in ways influenced, perhaps dictated, by patterns familiar in poetry.

We can take first the kind of episode, which is the subject of a classic article by John Gould.[1] This is the motif of 'supplication', first visible to us with the prayer of Thetis to Zeus in *Iliad* 1, and that of Priam to Achilles in *Iliad* 24. Person A, *in extremis*, makes a desperate request of person B for succour, placing himself ostentatiously at B's

It is a pleasure to offer this paper to an old friend, whose work has illuminated Attic Tragedy, among many other areas of ancient literature.

[1] (1973) = (2001), 22–77.

mercy, ideally by the gesture of crouching at his feet and embracing his knees. B is thus put under great pressure to redress the balance, and to restore more normal human relations, by granting A's prayer and giving him protection. The person to whom the appeal is addressed feels a loss of the normal freedom of action, an inhibiting sense of constraint.

Away from the tragic stage and in our ordinary world, a partial analogy might perhaps be the situation in which A and B are talking together, and A suddenly says to B, 'I love you'. To that utterance, which has the effect of placing A at B's mercy and risking a wounding rebuff and rejection, only one response can be acceptable, and B is, of course, under immediate and intense pressure to give it. The Greek word for that pressure is αἰδώς, *aidôs*: conventionally translated 'shame', but meaning, rather, that acute sense of constraint and inhibition.

Another scene, closely akin, is that of a desperate person taking refuge and claiming sanctuary from pursuit at an altar or some other sacred place. In both cases, the situation normally involves the moment of decision between life and death. 'The agents of the tyrant are close on our heels!' *(Heraclidae)*; 'This altar is my sole hope of deliverance from instant death!' (*Heracles, Andromache, Ion* . . .); 'Our hateful cousins are pursuing us, to force us into a marriage worse than death!' (Aeschylus, *Suppliants*).

In tragedy, for obvious reasons of spectacle, the place of refuge is usually an altar, and so in the open air, rather than (say) a closed room at a temple, in real history the refuge of the regent Pausanias of Sparta (Thuc. 1.134.1). We shall return to his situation. The consecrated place, too, possesses the power to impose *aidôs*, restraint, on the violent. The weaker party claims against the stronger the protection of the divine.

No scenario is commoner in tragedy. We can easily see a reason why. Tragedy needs, above all, to escape from the dull round of the ordinary world and to set its action in another sphere, not identical with this world but related to it and closely resembling it. In that world it seems natural, on the one hand, that there should be constant interludes of music, singing, and dancing; and, on the other, that there should occur scenes of the greatest possible emotional intensity. Ideally, such scenes should also involve some important moral choice or some human disaster, and—above all—they should bring in the agency and participation of the gods. It is an incidental advantage for Attic tragedy that altar scenes preserve the unity of place by remaining in one fixed setting.

The aim in all this is to pierce the dull carapace of routine and indifference, and to touch the deep springs of emotion. The characters on the stage face fearful choices. Must I avenge my father by killing his murderer, my own adulterous mother? (*Choephori,* both *Electra* plays). Must I accept these refugees clustered at the altar, at the risk of bringing war on my people? (both *Supplices* plays, *Heraclidae*). Must I defy the tyrant's edict and obey the divine law, by burying my brother's body at the risk of death? (*Antigone*). To punish my unfaithful husband, can I bring myself to kill my own children? (*Medea*). Such acute and agonizing decisions are the stuff of tragedy: engrossing as theatre, and also rich in material for serious reflection.

We find a revealing precedent and parallel in the culminating episode of the *Iliad.* Achilles, having killed Hector, defies the divine law by refusing to give up his corpse for burial. Guided by a god, old Priam, the bereaved father, comes through the night to plead for the body of his son. Achilles is eating and drinking with his companions, and—suddenly—the atmosphere is transformed. There at Achilles' feet is the great king Priam, begging for the body and reduced to kissing the hand that slew him. The scene is frozen. All eyes turn to Achilles: he must decide, and he must decide now, what he will do.

The poet compares the scene to that when a homicide, on the run, arrives unexpectedly, in search of protection: will he be taken in, or will his plea for asylum be rejected? (*Il.* 24.468–570). The tableau, and the moment, are of supreme intensity and involve a momentous decision, and we already know that Zeus himself is intently watching. Achilles finds that he must weep before he brings himself to comply with the old man's appeal.

Aeschylus, too, evidently attached great value to such moments. The high point of *Septem* is the decision of Eteocles to go out and fight in single combat with his own brother (653–719), a duel in which both will be killed; of *Supplices,* the forcing of the king to accept the suppliant refugees at the risk of war, a war in which he will lose his life (340–489). The *Oresteia* opens with a passionate meditation on Agamemnon's forced decision at Aulis: should he sacrifice his daughter Iphigenia, or should he abandon his Zeus-sent mission to punish the guilty city of Troy (*Ag.* 104–267)?

That decision is symbolically re-enacted on his return to Argos, when he finds himself, after expressing his most anxious reservations, nevertheless trampling underfoot the precious stuffs, the rich store of his house, which in colour resemble a stream of blood issuing from its door (*Ag.* 905–57). It finds a second climax with the agonized decision of Orestes to obey the oracle and kill his guilty mother (*Cho.* 892–930).

The same can be said of such plays as Sophocles' *Electra* and *Philoctetes*, and of Euripides' *Medea* and *Bacchae*. In each of them we watch the central characters taking momentous and painful decisions, of the sort which are by no means everyday occurrences, but which can and do come up in life.

Certain more or less stock situations established themselves early in Attic tragedy as typical scenes. They continued to command attention and emotion throughout the fifth century. They include various forms of the demand for revenge; suppliants pleading for asylum and bringing with them the risk of war; the demand of a god for sacrifice, which (to interest tragedy) must be human sacrifice; killing, especially within the family; the discovery of some life-destroying mistake (*Ajax*, *Oedipus Tyrannus*, Deianeira in *Trachiniae*, Theseus in *Hippolytus*, Agave in *Bacchae*); and extreme anguish, whether physical or mental.

Physical anguish is something of a Sophoclean speciality—Oedipus in *Oedipus Tyrannus*, Heracles in *Trachiniae*, Philoctetes; but there is also Prometheus in *Prometheus Vinctus*, Polymestor in Euripides' *Hecuba*, and even Hippolytus at the end of his play; though indeed his physical agony (his injuries will be fatal) is far less vividly depicted, and really seems less intensely felt, than most of those we have mentioned.

It is striking that in two of the extant plays (*Oedipus Tyrannus, Hecuba*) a character is blinded during the action and appears before us in that mutilated condition, while Hippolytus is fatally injured in a chariot crash and brought in dying. Another fatal crash is described in gruesomely vivid detail in Soph. *El.* 680–763, but that one is a fiction. Heracles is brought in, tortured by the envenomed robe which is killing him (Soph. *Trach.* 983–1278). Pentheus in

Bacchae is actually dismembered, and his body is brought on in pieces.

The situation of a desperate person, forced to risk everything in the role of refugee and suppliant, is of its nature intense, strongly enlisting the sympathies of the audience. It also produces a striking tableau, and—another advantage for the stage—one which stays still and does not move about. This is indeed so obviously true that we are tempted to write off the motifs of suppliant and sanctuary as merely melodramatic, 'theatrical' in the bad sense. The poets, we may incline to say, repeat over and over again a scenario which belongs all too clearly to the theatre, rather than to real life.[2]

That would be a grave mistake. What we know of the real history of the period (and we must remember that we know only a fraction of that history) is full of instances, both of *hiketeia* and of the claiming of sanctuary at sacred places. The austere Thucydides describes how Themistocles of Athens, on the run from his enemies, finds himself forced to take refuge with the king of the Molossians, his enemy. In the fortunate absence of the king, he squats by the hearth, the most sacred spot in the house, and (on the advice of the queen) holds the royal baby in his arms. 'And that' (the grave historian assures us) 'was the supreme gesture of supplication.'[3] It worked. The king took him in and gave him protection. Euripides' tragedy *Telephus* famously showed the Mysian prince performing the same gesture, holding the child Orestes at the hearth in the house of Agamemnon, to force the father to help him—a man, again, whom Agamemnon naturally regarded as an enemy.

Thucydides also describes Pausanias of Sparta, pursued by the ephors on a charge of treason, running into a temple and being starved out by his pursuers (Thuc. 1.134): a situation closely analogous to that of a play like Euripides' *Heracles*, in which the family of

[2] Shakespeare makes use of the motif, when the Duchess of York and her children try to claim sanctuary from Richard III, but the scene is short and understated: 'Much have I heard of sanctuary men, But sanctuary children ne'er till now!'—and the scene passes off in scornful laughter (3.1.55–6).

[3] *καὶ μέγιστον ἦν ἱκέτευμα τοῦτο*, Thuc. 1.137.1. Cf. Griffin (1998), 57 n. 64, on the regular omission of such characteristic details by the moderns: 'Clio, the austere Muse of serious modern historiography, draws her skirts aside. She prefers, she says, a diet of very dry bread.'

the absent Heracles, proscribed by the usurper Lycus, take refuge at an altar, while the tyrant blockades them there and finally forces them to leave for execution.

In Athens itself we read that Ephialtes, in the course of his struggle to cut down the powers of the Areopagus, was alarmed by the sight of its prominent supporters coming towards him, and that he 'took refuge at the altar',[4] 'wearing only his *chiton*'—perhaps to heighten the pathos of his position? Perhaps just a joke? Such scenes, to our jaded palate savouring rather of melodrama, were in the real history of the period both common and powerful.

The pages of Herodotus and Thucydides are as full as those of the tragedians of similar episodes. As the Argive king in Aeschylus' *Supplices* refused to give up the Danaids to their pursuers, so the Molossian king refused to give up Themistocles to his; as the Athenians in *Heraclidae* refused to give up the children of Heracles to the Argives, so the Samians refused to surrender the boys from Corcyra to the Corinthians who intended to take them to Lydia for castration (Hdt. 3.48).

So, too, the people of Zacynthus refused to surrender the exiled King Demaratus to the Spartans (Hdt. 6.70), and King Alyattes of Lydia refused to give up some Scythians, although they were charged with a hideous crime, to Cyaxares the Mede (Hdt. 1.74). That meant war; as it did, in myth, for the Argive protectors of the Danaids, and for the Athenians when they protected the children of Heracles. Nor was the fifth century the end. In 382, for example, we find the Spartans demanding that the Athenians expel the Theban exiles who have found sanctuary there; and so on.[5]

As for taking refuge at altars, the instances are countless; both in tragedy, as Aesch. *Sept.* 98–9, *Supplices*, Soph. *OT*, Eur. *Heraclidae, Andromache, Supplices, Heracles, Ion, Alcmena, Alope, Danae, Dictys, Telephus* ... and also, as we should expect, in history. A classic instance, discussed at length by Herodotus, is that of Pactyes, the Lydian who stole the Lydian treasure from the Persians and was pursued by them. After anxious thought, the Cymeans handed him

[4] [Arist.] *Ath. Pol.* 25.3–4. It is not made clear what altar, perhaps as a result of compression of the source.

[5] Plut. *Agesilaus* 23.7; 37 at end.

on to the Milesians, and they to the Chians, who tore him from the temple of Athena Poliouchos and gave him up.[6] It was long remembered against them.

We find Plataeans sitting in supplication at the altar of the twelve gods in Athens, to press the Athenians into accepting Plataea as an ally (Hdt. 6.108). In 480 the Athenian envoys, coming to ask for Apollo's help against the invading Persians, sat as suppliants in the *adyton* of Delphi, to press the god into giving a less discouraging oracle than his negative first response (Hdt. 7.141). There were *hiketai* on the Athenian Acropolis, when the Persians took it; they were put to the sword (Hdt. 7.53.2).

In the later fifth century, the motif is still no mere archaism. In 428, some Mityleneans took refuge at altars to avoid the vengeance of Athens (Thuc. 3.28). Corcyreans claimed sanctuary similarly in their civil war (Thuc. 3.70, 75). Late in the war, a Spartan officer was forced to take refuge at an altar from the violence of his own mutinous soldiers (Thuc. 8.84.3).

The altars often failed to protect, as they failed at Corcyra, in the violence of *stasis*. Elsewhere, we find Euryleon, tyrant of Selinus, killed at the altar of Zeus Agoraios (Hdt. 5.46), and Aristotimus, tyrant of Elis, killed at the altar of Zeus the Saviour (Paus. 5.5.1). An Aeginetan who managed to cling to the door of the temple of Demeter Thesmophoros had his hands hacked off, an act which caused long-lasting divine displeasure (*ἄγος*, Hdt. 6.91). In tragedy, the family of Heracles are forced away from the altars by the tyrant Lycus with the threat of fire (Eur. *Her.* 238–347), and Andromache is tricked into leaving sanctuary by a particularly heartless device of the Spartan Menelaus (Eur. *Andr.* 411–63).

Lysias reports, describing the terrible period of the ascendancy of the Thirty at Athens, that people were dragged away from shrines to their death.[7] Most memorably, Theramenes was dragged from the altar to execution on the orders of the tyrant Critias: he shouted to the intimidated Councillors who were looking on, 'Of course, I knew that this altar would not protect me; but I want to show to gods and

[6] Hdt. 1.157–60: a story very interesting in this connection.

[7] Lysias 12.96: *τοὺς μὲν ἐκ τῆς ἀγορᾶς, τοὺς δ' ἐκ τῶν ἱερῶν συναρπάζοντες βιαίως ἀπέκτειναν* . . . Cf. ibid. 98: neither *ἱερά* nor *βωμοί* were any defence.

men that these people are not only murderers but also guilty of sacrilege against the gods . . .'.[8]

Such transactions sometimes left behind a lasting sense of unease. The people of Chios, Herodotus tells us, accepted a piece of land as blood money for surrendering Pactyes to his pursuers, but for a long time they chose not to make any use of its produce (1.160). The Spartans, according to the sober testimony of Thucydides (1.128), having massacred a number of revolted Helots who had taken sanctuary in the precinct of Poseidon at Taenarus, thought the great earthquake that followed was a punishment of this sacrilegious action.

Memories for this sort of thing were very long. In 431 the Spartans thought it worth while to make propaganda against Athens by raking up the case of the Cylonian conspirators, who, more than a hundred years earlier, had been killed by the Athenians after claiming sanctuary (Thuc. 1.125). The Athenians hit back by bringing up against Sparta two episodes, both some fifty years in the past: that at Taenarus which we have discussed, and also the dubious affair of the death of Pausanias the regent (1.128), the circumstances of whose death were such that Delphi ruled that there was indeed a religious fault to be atoned.

The word is, again, ἄγος; one is tempted to call it a breach of the rules of the game, but clearly it was also more than that. It comes as no surprise that in the Corcyra *stasis*, the epitome for Thucydides of all the horrors of civil strife in the Peloponnesian War, the claiming and violation of sanctuary figure prominently (Thuc. 3.81).

There are many more references in the sources to similar episodes in the turbulent history of the fifth century. Their resemblance to tragedy is clear and close. It is worth emphasizing that many of these episodes were extremely sensational. Demaratus, Themistocles, Pausanias: these were among the most famous men of their times, and their stories must have been much repeated, discussed, varied, and ruminated upon. Before deciding what conclusion to draw, let us consider a couple of other motifs, if so they may be called, both in tragedy and in life. Two which were extremely prominent in that disordered age are the theme of exile, and that of large military expeditions and their military discipline.

[8] Xen. *Hell.* 2.3.52–3.

The figure of the exile, the man on the run, is already familiar in Homer. Usually he has killed a man: *φύγεν ἄνδρα κατακτάς* is a formulaic expression. That is a thing (apparently) that might happen to anyone. He then just makes himself scarce, to avoid blood feud with the victim's relatives.[9] When Priam suddenly appears, crouching at the feet of Achilles, Homer compares the silence and tension in the room to the atmosphere—apparently familiar to his audience—when a homicide arrives on the run, begging for reception and countenance (*Il.* 24.480–4). Occasionally a man takes to flight because of some other unpleasantness. Phoenix had seduced his father's mistress, and the old man had cursed him (*Il.* 9.447–80); he got out and did not come back.

Among archaic poets, exile looms large in the life and work both of Alcaeus and of Theognis. But the late sixth and fifth centuries seem to have seen more men in exile than any previous time. That is asserted explicitly of his own period by Thucydides.[10] We hear some names of exiled men, though of course very many others have not come down to us. We might start perhaps with Hippias of Athens, who attempted to return with the Persians in 490, and Demaratus of Sparta. He, too, in 480, accompanied the King against Hellas and his own people; as did Dicaeus of Athens (Hdt. 8.64).

Aristides, called the Just, was ostracized; Themistocles, his great opponent, fled into exile. Into exile went the prominent Delphian Cobon, who influenced the oracle in favour of Cleomenes and was detected (Hdt. 6.66), and Plistoanax, king of Sparta, and two Spartan polemarchs (Thuc. 5.72), and the great Hermocrates of Syracuse (Thuc. 8.85.3), and the great and notorious Alcibiades of Athens, and the historian Thucydides, and the historian Xenophon, and (it seems) the historian Herodotus, who apparently could not go back to Halicarnassus. Nor should we forget Chrysis, priestess of Hera at Argos, who fled to Phlius after accidentally burning down the temple (Thuc. 4.133).

It is hard to know how frequent the incidence of exile really was.[11]

[9] More rarely, a boy has killed a boy, as happened to Patroclus (*Il.* 23.85–6).

[10] *οὔτε φυγαὶ τοσαίδε ἀνθρώπων καὶ φόνος*, 1.23.2.

[11] Even so celebrated a poet as Ovid is known to have been exiled only because he tells us so in his own poems, *Tristia* and *Ex Ponto*.

A possible test case offers itself: not wholly reliable, but at least indicative. A group of men about whom some biographical information survives is that of the philosophers. In their biographies, exile is a regular theme. Xenophon has been mentioned already. Theodorus, called 'the godless', ὁ ἄθεος, was exiled, first from Athens (D.L. 2.102), and then from Cyrene (2.103). Theophrastus and 'the philosophers' were exiled from Athens (5.77). 'Some said' that Pythagoras died in exile (8.40); some said it also of Empedocles (8.52).

In the biography of many philosophers we also find it recorded that they had a taste of being enslaved: thus Phaedo (D.L. 2.105), Plato (3.19), Xenocrates (4.14), and Diogenes, who is—suggestively—reported to have compared himself to a typical sufferer in tragedy (6.29). Both Bion (4.50) and Aristippus (2.77) fell in with pirate ships. The striking thing, perhaps, is that, whether or not they were historical (for that, of course, we usually cannot know), these episodes were evidently what people expected to find in the biography of a prominent or interesting person.

Tragedy is no less interested in the theme of exile. We find the traditional exiles of heroic myth, Orestes and Polynices and Alcmaeon. Amphitryon and Oeneus and Hippolytus, in turn, are driven out on their wanderings. Danaus takes to flight with his daughters, and their return to Argos is the theme of the *Supplices* of Aeschylus. Oedipus, who in the epic died and had his funeral at Thebes (*Il.* 23.679), is made by the Attic playwrights to wander in exile and die in Attica (*Oedipus Coloneus*). So must Heracles, at the end of the *Heracles* of Euripides, where it seems that, by a most daring stroke, the whole story of his pyre on Mount Oeta and subsequent immortality is silently denied, and that the broken hero will end his days as an exile—where else?—in Athens.

Medea carefully prepares her retreat to Athens, in flight from her crimes in Corinth, and, after trying to kill the young Theseus there, must go on her travels again (Euripides *Medea, Aegeus*). To Athens come Iolaus and the children of Heracles, in flight from Eurystheus (*Heraclidae*). For Attic tragedy, it was at Athens that the wanderer Orestes found deliverance from his divine tormentors (*Eumenides*), despite the many rival versions that laid his confrontation with them at one or other place in the Peloponnese.

The depiction of exile can come at the beginning of the play, as in *Oedipus Coloneus* or *Heraclidae*, or at the end, as in *Choephori* or *Hippolytus* or *Heracles*. It can be developed with painful details, as by Oedipus' resentful memories at the opening of *Oedipus Coloneus* and at ibid. 1354–69, or by those of Orestes at Eur. *El.* 232–7, or—more fully—at *Phoen.* 388–407.

In that play, Jocasta starts by asking her exiled son Polynices whether the loss of one's country is very grievous:

τί τὸ στερέσθαι πατρίδος; ἦ κακὸν μέγα;

In reply, he lists the miseries of exile. Jocasta draws the conclusion that one's country does seem to be the dearest thing of all. 'You could not begin to express', replies her son, 'how dear it is!'

– ἡ πατρίς, ὡς ἔοικε, φίλτατον βροτοῖς.
– οὐδ' ὀνομάσαι δύναι' ἂν ὡς ἐστὶν φίλον.

We recall that the exile of Hippolytus was meant by his angry father as a harsher punishment than death (*Hipp.* 1045–9).

The man in exile needs friends, *xenoi*, like Orestes' loyal Pylades (Eur. *El.* 82–5). He may make a foreign marriage and count on that dynastic connection to get him back home, like Polynices (*Phoen.* 408–34). He may be supported and strengthened by an oracle, as in myth Orestes relies on Delphi (*Eumenides*); in history, the oracle was exploited for propaganda and return by the exiled Alcmaeonids (Hdt. 5.62–5).

He may have some trusty retainer, like the Paedagogus who assists Orestes; but exiles feed on hopes, they say (*Phoen.* 396), and an exile is but weak (Eur. *El.* 236). An exile's friends are soon out of breath (*Her.* 301–6): we can say, in fact, that misfortune has no friends (*Her.* 561). It is even hard for an exile to find a wife (*Andr.* 972–6). As for those who wait for the exile's return, Sophocles' Electra can speak for the hope deferred that makes the heart sick: 'As I have waited for him', she says, 'I have seen all my hopes wither; I am fading away' (Soph. *El.* 303–6; cf. Aesch. *Cho.* 164–201; Eur. *El.* 201–12, 275).

We find in the tragedians some striking passages of explicit instruction to immigrants on the way to behave in a host city, with warnings that they are not likely to be over-popular and must watch their step.[12] The reception of 'suppliants' (in modern parlance, refugees or asylum seekers) is a central theme in such plays as Aeschylus' *Supplices* and Euripides' *Heraclidae.* At *Oedipus Coloneus* 198, 258–9, we hear that so god-fearing a city as Athens really should receive suppliants.[13]

As these exiles crowd the tragic stage, Hellas itself is full of refugees, defeated partisans, resentful exiles, hoping and plotting for return. Everywhere there are broken men, intriguing with political allies and against political opponents. During the Peloponnesian War, especially, Hellas resembles the Europe of the 1930s. The words for exile, φυγάς, φεύγω, come constantly in Thucydides, who seems to take for granted that every city has its hungry exiles, nameless and collective, hoping and scheming to return.[14]

The exiles of tragedy thus reflect the real world. The suppliants and the refugees who throng the tragic altars interact revealingly with democracy. By the last decade of the fifth century, it is apparently quite natural to ask a mythical hero whether he is in exile because of a decision of the *demos* or of the king (Eur. *Or.* 766). We may compare the question immediately asked, when Odysseus is reported to be at the head of those at Aulis who demand the death of Iphigenia: is he acting on his own, or has the army appointed him? Both elected and volunteering, αἱρεθεὶς ἑκών, comes the reply (Eur. *IA* 1363–4).

These questions reflect the contemporary world and are anachronistic for the heroic period, when king Odysseus, single-handed, could crush a mutiny (*Il.* 2.164–210) or silence a popular movement to punish an unpopular Ithacan aristocrat with death:

ἀλλ' Ὀδυσεὺς κατέρυκε καὶ ἔσχεθεν ἱεμένους περ (*Od.* 16.430)

In *Troades* King Menelaus declares proudly that the doom of his unfaithful wife Helen, recovered from Troy, is up to him—but (unheroically enough) only because it has been left to him by decision of the troops:

[12] Aesch. *Suppl.* 191–233 and *passim*, Soph. *OC* 171–87, Eur. *Med.* 11–12, *Ion* 289–90, 578–607.

[13] See also *Med.* 386 ff., 511 ff., 613, 642 ff.

[14] We can mention Epidamnus, 1.24; Ithome, 1.103; Lesbos, 4.52; Megarians, 4.66; Locrians, 5.4; Samians, 8.21; Thasians, 8.64; Athenians, 8.70.

ἅπας στρατὸς
κτανεῖν ἐμοί σ᾽ ἔδωκεν, ὅνπερ ἠδίκεις (901–2)

'The whole army has given you to me to execute: to the man whom you wronged.' Democracy in action, indeed!

Popular intervention and control can thus often be seen invading tragedy; but we notice that it is by no means always—not even usually—for the best. The relation of all this to real democracy is far from simple, and what we might think to recognize as democratic touches are often, within the plays, rather bad than good.

Exiles may be isolated men, like Orestes; they may be accompanied by a crowd of dependent refugees, women and children, like Danaus in Aeschylus' *Supplices*, or Iolaus in *Heraclidae*. So, too, in the Pentekontaetia, the Messenians who had been besieged on Ithome finally capitulated to the Spartans—there was an old oracle, Thucydides tells us, bidding Sparta 'spare the suppliant of Zeus of Ithome'—and they left with their wives and children and were settled by the Athenians, from hatred of the Spartans, at a strategically important place: Naupactus (Thuc. 1.103.1–3).

This is, in fact, what the world is like. It is not a world to raise the spirits and to warm the heart. It is indeed, in the full sense, a tragic world. It is also a world in which oracles, gestures of supplication, the expulsion, reception, and rejection of refugees, all play a prominent part. That is why it fits so naturally with the tragic stage.

Tragedy as a performance is set in a ritual, and it is itself very hospitable to rituals of many kinds. The music and dancing brought a certain solemnity and ritual atmosphere. But since, in the context of fifth-century Greece, all these things, ritual, music, and dancing, were more natural and less isolated from normal life than they can easily be to a modern audience,[15] the evocation of such music added extra poignancy to moments of dramatic intensity. Their set forms and regular rhythms are powerful devices to arouse and govern emotion, and to give shape to events. They also reinforce the message that the world of tragedy is pervaded by the relations of the human and

[15] In the dithyrambic contest every year at the Dionysia twenty choruses competed, each fifty members strong: a thousand performers every year, quite apart from all the other occasions when *choroi* danced and sang.

the divine; that it is full of the action, both of the gods and, often, of the dead.

Now, the fact of exile need not of itself necessarily have anything religious or ritualized about it. Sometimes it may be a mere act of running away, as when young Phoenix, having antagonized his father, simply gets out and does not come back (*Il.* 9.447–80). We can observe how the tragic poets often bridge the gap, by invoking as the occasion of exile some point of religious *miasma*: the hero must leave because, like Oedipus or Orestes or Heracles,[16] he has committed a dreadful action and is too defiled to stay in the community. Or they may use the motif, equally religious in colouring, of successful *hiketeia*: when, as in the *Supplices* of Aeschylus, the exile finds, somewhere, countenance and a resting place.

The motif can also be turned in other ways, as when, in a terrible scene, the supplication of Polynices is rejected by his injured and unforgiving father (Soph. *OC* 1154–466), or—in a rather frivolous development—when in *Helen* the heroine, who is camping out, and claiming sanctuary, at the tomb of the father of the Egyptian king who wants to force her into marriage, is apparently free to come and go at will.

A coda to these forms of desperation shall be the last and most desperate of all ways out: suicide. Most people in the fifth century seem not to have thought it religiously or unambiguously wrong, although we shall find that view strongly represented in Plato.[17] Like physical torment, it is something of a Sophoclean speciality. In the seven extant plays six people—Ajax, Deianira, Jocasta, Antigone and Eurydice and Haemon—make away with themselves, while Polynices goes off to certain and foreknown death.[18]

Suicide may accompany recognition of some fearful fact or deadly mistake, as it does with Ajax, Jocasta, and Deianira. It may be an escape from unbearable shame or grief, as with Euripides' Phaedra and Evadne (Eur. *Suppl.* 990–1071). It may be a threat, as it is on

[16] *Θήβας μὲν οὖν ἔκλειπε τοῦ νόμου χάριν*, Eur. *Her.* 1322.

[17] *Phaedo* 61c ff.; *Leg.* 873c ff.

[18] Cf. Hirzel (1907), Fraenkel (1932), 470–3 = (1964), i. 465–9, Dover (1974), 168–9. Dover notes the Athenians' 'high regard for the man who faces the instrument of death unflinchingly, no matter whether the hand that wields it is another's or his own'.

the lips of the chorus at Aesch. *Suppl.* 455–73, or an intention, not followed up, in a situation of disaster (Eur. *Her.* 1241–352), or a punishment imposed by a community (*Or.* 946–56). In a play like *Helen* it may even be a threat which we cannot take very seriously.[19]

In the history of the time we find plenty of suicides recorded: not all of them, doubtless, with truth or beyond doubt. Some people said that Themistocles committed suicide (Thuc. 1.138.4). King Cleomenes of Sparta is said to have killed himself, and (which shows how much people hated his memory) in a peculiarly horrid way (Hdt. 6.75). The only disagreement was for which of several acts of sacrilege heaven brought such a death upon him.

The people of Xanthus, beset by Harpagus, set fire to the town with their women and children (Hdt. 1.176). The Athenians whom Xerxes trapped on the Acropolis threw themselves down to their death (Hdt. 8.53). Some Corcyreans, trapped by their enemies in civil war, destroyed themselves (Thuc. 3.48; cf. 3.81.3). Xerxes, we read, honoured highly the memory of Boges, the Persian governor of Eion: besieged by Cimon, he had immolated on a great pyre his children, his wife, his concubines, his servants, and himself (Hdt. 7.107)—as Croesus had intended to do, in the version of his story which we read in Bacchylides 3.

This conspectus shows again something which was, after all, to be expected: the great similarity between mythical drama and contemporary history. In both, the same kinds of intense moment, spectacular action, and eye-catching gesture and situation, commanded immediate attention and lived in lasting remembrance. Even in these extremely 'dramatic' episodes, the theatre did not lose touch with reality. And reality (we might say) was often highly theatrical.

To end on a note of mild polemic, very little of all this can be seen to have any resonance as Athenian party political propaganda. The Muse of Tragedy does not very often condescend to that level, much as some of our politically minded contemporaries would like her to settle down and live on it. She has concerns that are far more terrible: more painful, more haunting—in a word, more tragic.

[19] Lines 348–85, partly because of the dithyrambic language Helen uses.

15

Sophocles' Learning Curve

Christopher Pelling

ὁ Σοφοκλῆς ἔλεγε τὸν Αἰσχύλου διαπεπαιχὼς ὄγκον, εἶτα τὸ πικρὸν καὶ κατάτεχνον τῆς αὑτοῦ κατασκευῆς, τρίτον ἤδη τὸ τῆς λέξεως μεταβάλλειν εἶδος, ὅπερ ἠθικώτατόν ἐστι καὶ βέλτιστον

διαπεπαιχὼς: *διαπεπαλαιχὼς* Webster; *διεπεπλακὼς* Bergk; *διαπεπαικὼς* Herwerden; *διαπεπλιχὼς* Bernhardy; *διαπεπλοχὼς* Schoene; *διαπεφευγὼς* Schöll. *αὑτοῦ* E. Müller, Bergk: *αὐτοῦ* editores antiquiores, Festa, Babbitt. *μεταβάλλειν*: *μεταλαβεῖν* Bernhardy.

(Sophocles, T 100 *TrGF* = Plutarch, *How to Observe one's Progress in Virtue* 79b)

Sophocles' remark, put into *oratio recta*, means this: 'After practising to the full the bigness of Aeschylus, then the painful ingenuity of my own invention, now in the third stage I am changing to the kind of diction which is most expressive of character and best.'

(Bowra (1940*a*), 401 = (1953), 125)

Sophocles used to say that he first lightened Aeschylus' heaviness, then the austerity and affectedness of his own style, and only then did he, as a third step, try to change the actual nature of the language, which has the most bearing on morality and virtue.

(Waterfield's translation in Waterfield and Kidd (1992), 131)

Sophocles' dictum may be hard to interpret, as those two very different renderings suggest:[1] but it is certainly important. Two of the

[1] Waterfield's translation takes it in much the same way as Babbitt's 1927 Loeb: 'For as Sophocles said, that only after handling with a light touch the turgidity of Aeschylus and next his [Babbitt reads *αὐτοῦ*] harshness and artificiality in composition, did he, as a third step, change the character of the language, which has the

most influential mid-twentieth-century discussions of Sophocles' style operated by trying to fit the surviving plays to the threefold scheme;[2] the most recent, and very thorough, discussion of *The Language of Sophocles* (Budelmann (2000)), cites it in the third sentence of the first page. If authentic, it would be a rare case where we can see a great practitioner reflecting on his own technique, no less illuminating—perhaps even more illuminating because less jokey—than Aristophanes' remarks in several *parabaseis* on the various stages of *his* early development.[3] (That is a comparison to which we will return.) And, despite the scepticism that such literary anecdotes normally excite among sober scholars,[4] there may be good reason why they suspect that this one is indeed authentic, or at least has its origin in an authentic comment even if it is not a verbatim quotation: it is 'so strange it must be genuine' (Reinhardt (1979), 7 ≈ (1933), 15); 'das zweite [i.e. the remark on 'bitterness', τὸ πικρόν] würde kein Fremder zu sagen gewagt haben' (Wilamowitz in a letter of 1904 = Calder (1979), 56–7). We can even see how an authentic remark could have survived in some form, for it is a guess, but a plausible one, that the remark could come from Sophocles' contemporary Ion of Chios.[5] Ion was himself a tragic poet, enjoyed

most to do with moral character and goodness'. Not that Waterfield and Kidd are unaware of the discussions since Babbitt: a footnote gives a full bibliography. The issues concerning this sentence are by no means settled, then, and a further contribution may not be out of place. Philippon in the Budé (Klaerr, Philippon, and Sirinelli (1989)) has 'Ainsi Sophocle disait qu'après avoir été peu sérieux en imitant l'art grandiose d'Eschyle, puis en pratiquant un art personnel des effets violents et recherchés, il s'occupait désormais, dans un troisième temps, de modifier les traits de son style, parce que c'est la qui peint le mieux les caractères et a le plus de valeur.'

[2] Webster (1936), 143–62, Earp (1944), 11–13 and *passim*. That implies what is not at all likely, that these three phases refer to periods of Sophocles' mature career rather than his earlier formation. Reinhardt (1979), 7 ≈ (1933), 15 sees that this is implausible but still defends the approach, suggesting that further development on the same trajectory might still be traced even after the third stage had been reached. I share the scepticism of Perrotta (1935), 8 and Long (1968), 4–5 about this approach. Its most usual application has been in detecting Aeschylean ὄγκος in the *Ajax*, but perhaps we should see this as plot-determined rather than a sign of immaturity.

[3] *Eq.* 541–4, *Nub.* 528–32, and especially *Vesp.* 1016–28: see Mastromarco (1979) and Halliwell (1980).

[4] The classic statement of this sceptical approach is Lefkowitz (1981).

[5] That is not the only possibility. Webster (1936), 143 thought it came from the prose work *On the Chorus* attested for Sophocles himself; De Martino (2003), 446 still thinks that possible, in the course of a rather optimistic reconstruction of the περὶ

gossiping about his meetings with the great and what they had said, and we know that he wrote about Sophocles;[6] we know too that Plutarch knew Ion's work well, and used it thoughtfully and tellingly.[7] If Ion is the intermediary, then Plutarch's version will be only that one step away from Sophocles' original remark, despite the five-hundred-year time lag. This, then, may be a fitting topic for a tribute to Martin West, who has written with such distinction on Ion[8] as well as on Sophocles—and on so much more.

I

Bowra's discussion of the passage (1940*a*) is the most thorough and still the most quoted, and it will be helpful to summarize the main points that he tried to establish. We may distinguish eleven.

(a) Despite the specifying of *lexis* in the third and 'best' phase of Sophocles' development, the remark refers not just to diction but to 'more general aspects of his art' ((1940*a*), 385, cf. 392 = (1953), 108, cf. 115).

(b) There is no reason to think that Plutarch has transposed Sophocles' words into the literary language of his own time; most of the crucial terms (ὄγκος, πικρόν, κατασκευή, ἠθικώτατον) can be traced plausibly to fifth-century or at least to

χόρου. Pinnoy (1984), 163–4 prefers to think of initial oral transmission, then inclusion in a rhetorical textbook, probably Peripatetic and 'probably from the circle of Dionysius of Halicarnassus'. The case for Ion is stated most fully by Bowra (1940*a*), 386 = (1953), 108–9—indeed, overstated, for Bowra should not have said that 'the word ἔλεγε implies that Sophocles' statement was made in conversation; it means "said" or "used to say"'. In fact ἔλεγε can readily be used of 'saying' in a text, as in the next chapter (79f) in citing Thucydides' text (1.18), and at e.g. *Sol.* 2.2, *Cor.* 15.4, *How a Young Man should Listen to Poetry* 14d, 36c, *On the Decline of the Oracles* 416f, 430a, etc. Nor should we press the imperfect to suggest a repeated remark, as in Bowra's suggested 'used to say', adopted by Waterfield: ἔλεγε is often used of one-off statements, as at e.g. *Them.* 5.7, *Cam.* 10.4, *Pomp.* 59.7, and in many other cases. Still, transmission through Ion does remain the most likely possibility. Cf. also n. 25 below.

[6] *FGrHist* 392 T 5(b), frr. 6 and perhaps 23 (if e.g. Ἴωνα τὸν Χῖον (Bergk) is read for †Ἰωνικόν τινα at *Life of Sophocles* 20).

[7] I discuss Plutarch's use of Ion in Pelling (forthcoming).

[8] West (1985*b*).

Aristotelian terminology, and even *κατάτεχνον* cannot be securely regarded as belonging to the 'Roman period'.

(c) *διαπεπαιχώς* must govern not only *τὸν Αἰσχύλου ὄγκον* but also *τὸ πικρὸν καὶ κατάτεχνον τῆς αὐτοῦ κατασκευῆς*, and we should not understand a further word to mean 'adopted' with the second group.

(d) If this is so, *διαπεπαιχώς* is best taken as 'play through', as Plato spoke at *Leg.* 769a of a 'game well played out' as *παιδία καλῶς διαπεπαισμένη*.[9] Here it will be equivalent to 'practise to the limits'. If taken in that sense, it can apply to both the first two phases, and emendation is unnecessary.[10]

(e) *ὄγκος* should here be non-pejorative: Bowra suggests 'bigness', an impartial sense that could extend to positive grandeur as much as to anything pompous or bombastic.

(f) *κατασκευή* should be 'fabrication' or 'invention'—a general term for constructing a poetic drama. This second stage 'was at least of his own fabrication' whereas the first practised 'an art which belonged to Aeschylus, and that is why *Αἰσχύλου* is so soon followed by *αὑτοῦ*' ((1940*a*), 394 = (1953), 118): in other words, the *αὑτοῦ* is subjective genitive, 'his' fabrication in the sense that he, Sophocles, is doing the fabricating.

(g) *τὸ πικρὸν καὶ κατάτεχνον* should be taken closely together as a single concept (otherwise it should be *τὸ πικρὸν καὶ* <u>*τὸ*</u> *κατάτεχνον*), and means a 'painful ingenuity'—painful in the sense that it conveys to the audience a sense of pain at what is happening on stage, for instance in their response to Athena's mocking of Ajax or Niobe's killing of her children.

(h) The third phase is depicted as one that is still in progress: if Sophocles said *ἤδη*, he meant 'I am now. . .' (changing to this style).[11] It follows that the present *μεταβάλλειν* is the appropriate tense, and Bernhardy's change to the aorist *μεταλαβεῖν* did not deserve the approval it had received from Schoene and Wilamowitz.

[9] A parallel already adduced by Perrotta (1935), 8 n. 1.

[10] For the various emendations see n. 40 below.

[11] That was also stressed by Perrotta (1935), 8 n.1.

(i) μεταβάλλειν is best taken as 'change to', 'change and adopt', as for instance at Eur. *IA* 343–4 κᾆτ', ἐπεὶ κατέσχες ἀρχάς, μεταβαλὼν ἄλλους τρόπους | τοῖς φίλοισιν οὐκέτ' ἦσθα τοῖς πρὶν ὡς πρόσθεν φίλος.[12]

(j) ὅπερ . . . βέλτιστον could grammatically be taken either as referring to the 'the type of style' or to the act of changing: the first is preferable, as the relevant comparison is of different states rather than different changes, and it is hard to see how the act of changing rather than the changed style could be described as ἠθικώτατον. 'Sophocles after mentioning his third stage says what it is and praises it' ((1940*a*), 398 = (1953), 121).[13]

(k) ἠθικώτατον is to be taken in a sense familiar from Aristotle, 'concerned with character', and more precisely here 'expressive of character': Sophocles is priding himself on finding the style which allows his figures to 'talk in character'.

There is one missing person in this discussion, and that is Plutarch. Bowra does not even give much attention to the rest of the sentence in which the dictum is embedded, even though, as we shall see, and as another commentator remarks,[14] no fewer than four of the same or similar words recur in it, in several cases with a rather different sense from that which Bowra suggests for the words of 'Sophocles' himself. But even that is insufficient context to see the use to which Plutarch is putting Sophocles' remark. One reason why commentators, not only Bowra, may be less sensitive than they might to Plutarch's interests here is the simple way they name the treatise:

[12] This parallel too was already adduced by Perrotta. Bowra adds some further cases.

[13] Oddly, Bowra does not discuss the further possible way of taking ὅπερ . . . βέλτιστον, which is not to define Sophocles' new style, but style in general, as the aspect which is ἠθικώτατον καὶ βέλτιστον: that, as we saw, is the way Babbitt, Philippon, and Waterfield took it (n. 1): 'try to change the actual nature of the language, which has the most bearing on morality and virtue' (Waterfield). This goes with Bowra's construal of μεταβάλλειν as 'change to' rather than simply 'change', point (i) above. I agree with Bowra here, though for different reasons: if, as I think but Bowra did not, Plutarch/Sophocles is referring primarily to style and language throughout, it does not make sense to suggest that it is only at this third stage that he addresses this particularly crucial aspect.

[14] Pinnoy (1984), 160: λέξεως–λόγον, μεταβάλλειν–καταβῶσιν, κατάτεχνον–κατατέχνων, ἠθικώτατον–ἤθους.

nearly all use the Latin *De Profectibus* (or *-u*) *in Virtute*.[15] The fuller and more correct title is *Πῶς ἄν τις αἴσθοιτο ἑαυτοῦ προκόπτοντος ἐπ' ἀρετῇ* (or perhaps *πρὸς ἀρετήν*[16]), literally 'How one might observe oneself making progress in (or 'to') virtue', or the Latin *Quomodo quis suos in virtute sentiat profectus*. That title should alert us to the way that Sophocles' dictum is likely to fit Plutarch's themes very closely indeed. This is not merely something about development, but about one's own alertness to that development; and not just any development, but development in virtue, ethical development. Those words *ἠθικώτατον καὶ βέλτιστον* are likely to be working rather harder than Bowra suggested, and in a different way: and not only those.

II

How to Observe one's Progress in Virtue has a clear agenda. It is attacking the (extreme) Stoic view that any deficiency in virtue is as bad as any other: 'a miss is as bad as a mile'.[17] If pressed, that view implies that anyone who manages to become virtuous does so all at once—that, prior to shedding the last vice, someone would be as non-virtuous as ever at 5 o'clock in the evening, then fully virtuous at 9 o'clock the next morning. Not merely does Plutarch reject this as counter-intuitive,[18] he also—typically, and as the title suggests—provides some practical advice on how one can track one's own gradual progress.

[15] So also Wilamowitz, Schmid, Perrotta, Webster, Post, Long, Pinnoy, Budelmann, De Martino. Some, e.g. Earp and Reinhardt, give the reference as simply to '*Moralia*'. The honourable exception is Jebb (1892), xlvi n. 1, who gives the full Greek title.

[16] *πρὸς ἀρετήν* is the version of the Lamprias catalogue (§87), *ἐπ' ἀρετῇ* that found in the codices. The difference is not without its interest, for *πρὸς ἀρετήν* is supported by the first sentence of the text, *ἐπ' ἀρετῇ* more closely represents Plutarch's own position that 'virtue' does not come all at once at the end of the process. Cf. Philippon (n. 1), 149–50.

[17] Long (1986), 204. For a good discussion see Rist (1969), ch. 5, especially 90–3 on the suddenness of virtue. Many Stoics eschewed the extreme position: cf. especially Sen. *Ep. ad Lucil.* 72.9–11, 75.8–14 with Philippon (n. 1), 148–9.

[18] On Plutarch's anti-Stoic argument, see Babut (1969), 47–50 (observing that Plutarch's allusiveness implies a reader already familiar with the Stoic background), 53–4, 319–20; Philippon (n. 1), 145–59.

At this point of the essay he has been discussing the value of learning how not to envy the trappings of worldly success, but to give more weight to virtue.[19]

7. Once you can weigh matters of virtue against externals and shed your envies and your jealousies and those things that needle and bring down many beginners in philosophy, this too is a substantial indication that you are making progress. Something else that matters a good deal is the change in the matter of *logoi*. For almost all beginners go in pursuit of the *logoi* that bring reputation: some are like birds, drawn by lightness and ambition to swoop on to the sparkling heights of science; others, 'like puppies' (in Plato's words) 'who delight in dragging and tearing', move towards heated arguments and bewildering paradoxes and sophistic casuistry; most, as they embark on dialectic, immediately load themselves up for sophistry; some of them go around picking up pointed anecdotes and stories from history, so that it is a little like Anacharsis' remark about the way he saw Greeks using their money for no purpose other than for counting it—in the same way these people use *logoi* to be counted by and to do their counting,[20] and get no other benefit from them at all. Antiphanes' remark is relevant too, in the use made of it by one of Plato's followers.[21] For Antiphanes jokingly said that there was a city where it was so cold that the words froze immediately on utterance, and then later when they thawed out people would listen in summer to what was said in winter. In the same way (he remarked) most

[19] On that section of the argument see van der Stockt (1999*a*), who analyses Plutarch's use of quotations closely and suggests that this, *On Self-Praise* 545e–546b, and *On Peace of Mind* 472b–473b are all drawn from an original passage in Plutarch's own notes (the *ὑπομνήματα* mentioned in *On Peace of Mind* 464f), in this case notes on 'a theme that included self-confidence, ethical priorities, strivings, and jealousy'. On these *ὑπομνήματα* see also the other papers of van der Stockt and van Meirvenne cited in n. 48 below, especially van der Stockt (1999*b*). The use of such notes is likely for our passage too: notice in particular the sequence of parallels with *How to Listen to Lectures* 41e–42d (below, nn. 32, 36, 40, 46, and 47; also the Simonides quotation, 79c ~ 41f, and other parallels of phrasing and thought—*φιλότεχνον, πανηγυρικά, θέατρον, ἐπανορθωσόμενος, κουφότερον, περιττόν*). But this does not affect the current argument. Whatever Plutarch's preparatory methods, we shall see how carefully he adapts this Sophoclean quotation to his thematic development.

[20] Text and translation uncertain.

[21] Reading *ὅ τις εἶπεν τῶν Πλάτωνος συνήθων* and rejecting Madvig's <*ἐπὶ*> before *συνήθων*: cf. Wilamowitz (1905), 149–59 = (1935–72), iv. 202–3, arguing that the subject of *ἔφη* four lines later (the bracketed '(he remarked)' in my translation) should be the same as this *τις*, and not Antiphanes himself. <*ἐπὶ*> is however still read in the Teubner, Loeb, and Budé texts. In the 1974 second edition of the Teubner Gärtner notes that the <*ἐπὶ*> is uncertain (p. 380).

people found that they only understood in their old age what Plato had said to them when they were young. People experience the same thing with philosophy as a whole, until such time as their judgement takes a fixed, healthy form (κατάστασιν ὑγιεινήν) and begins to spend time with those *logoi* that can instil character and magnitude (ἦθος καὶ μέγεθος) and to go looking for *logoi* whose tracks, as in Aesop's tale, turn inwards rather than outwards. For just as Sophocles said that, after having had his fun with the pomp of Aeschylus, then the harsh and technical phase of his own construction, he was now as a third step changing to the type of diction which is most characterful and best, so it is also with those who practise philosophy:[22] when they come down (or 'come home', καταβῶσιν: see n. 42) from the showy (πανηγυρικῶν) and the technical (κατατέχνων) to the *logos* that fastens on character and emotion (τὸν ἁπτόμενον ἤθους καὶ πάθους λόγον), they are beginning to make genuine, unpretentious (ἄτυφον) progress.

8. Be careful, indeed, when reading philosophers' writings and listening to their *logoi*, to make sure that you are not paying more attention to the words alone than to the content, nor leaping more on something that is uncongenial and excessive than on what is useful, substantial, and helpful; and that is not all—keep on your guard too when you are spending time with poetry and history-books, making sure that nothing escapes you that is deftly said and contributes to correction of character or lightening of emotion (τῶν πρὸς ἐπανόρθωσιν ἤθους ἢ πάθους κουφισμὸν ἐμμελῶς λεγομένων). Simonides says that the bee 'has a care for yellow honey' in flowers, while humans like and take nothing from them but colour and smell; in the same way the person who is himself finding and collecting something important when others are engaging with poetry just for pleasure and play (ἡδονῆς ἕνεκα καὶ παιδιᾶς) is the person who seems already to be coming to know what is beautiful and close to home (τοῦ καλοῦ καὶ οἰκείου) by becoming familiar with and affectionate towards it. As for those who use Plato and Xenophon just for their diction (λέξις), culling from them nothing other than what is pure and Attic as if it were the dew and moisture, what would you say they were doing if not enjoying the nice smell and bouquet of a drug but not welcoming or recognizing its capacity to ease pain or bring purgation?

(*How to Observe one's Progress in Virtue* 78d–79d)

And Plutarch goes on to explain that one can similarly get moral

[22] The crucial sentence is here translated as far as possible without prejudice to the interpretation, but some parts of that translation will have to be defended by the later discussion.

insight from all sorts of other experiences—watching boxers (there is a tale here of Aeschylus watching in the company of Ion of Chios), being bitten by a mouse, seeing someone drinking from their hands for want of a cup. 'Thus it is that paying attention, and keeping one's training alert and active, makes one sensitive and receptive to whatever conduces to virtue, wherever it comes from' (79e). Those beginners who go prancing 'into the *agora* or to where the young men are gathering or into a king's symposium' and roll out their new-found sophisms are not real philosophers, any more than drug sellers are real doctors (80a).

So the person with real philosophical aptitude has to work through several stages. In the first it is easy to go wrong, if one gets carried away and shows off; then there must be a period of sustained training, where one needs to be constantly alert for what is improving; then finally one may get to a period of settled virtue, one which—there is a strong implication—is also closest to the person's own truest nature (note οἰκείου, 'close to home' near the end of the quoted passage). Sophocles' dictum is all too relevant. Let us take each of these stages in turn.

The rest of the sentence in which Sophocles' words are embedded is evidently closely parallel: aspiring philosophers may 'come down' (or 'come home', and if that rendering of καταβαίνειν is correct it develops further the idea that this style is truer to their nature: see n. 42) 'from the showy (πανηγυρικῶν) and the technical (κατατέχνων) to the *logos* that fastens on character and emotion (τὸν ἁπτόμενον ἤθους καὶ πάθους λόγον)'. 'The showy and the technical' seems to represent two phases rather than one, for κατάτεχνον, 'technical' is one of the words Plutarch has just used to describe Sophocles' second phase. The showy or 'panegyrical' will in that case correspond to the first, Aeschylean period, and ὄγκος, with its suggestions of building up for impressiveness and display, fits that well enough: the world of the *Frogs*, especially 939–40, is not too far away.[23] Other parts too of the surrounding passage refer to the taste for show that typically attends that first phase: the philosophical beginners who, one way or

[23] Close enough indeed for Lessing (1790) to have suggested that Plutarch either should have written (Lessing's p. 322) or did write (p. 324) Εὐριπίδης for Σοφοκλῆς, on the assumption that this is a reference to *Ran.* 939–43: but the other stages do not fit Aristophanes' phrasing at all.

another, go for the *logoi* which bring reputation, including the puppy-like who love their heated arguments and casuistry, wanting 'to be counted by' such big talk, or those who go prancing into the *agora* or the king's symposium to roll out their sophisms. True, they are the people who are getting it wrong, whereas Sophocles got it right; if this is all about 'going in search of *logoi*', he found the *logoi*—those of Aeschylus—that could be valuable. Bowra is correct (point (e) above) to draw attention to the way that ὄγκος can have a favourable as well as a negative connotation;[24] nor will it be coincidence that Aeschylus crops up only a page later, when he is watching the boxers along with Ion of Chios,[25] and knows the right way of learning a lesson and passing it on. But it is still reasonable to see the Aeschylean qualities as a positive *counterpart* of the more distasteful showiness shown by less gifted beginners, which aspiring philosophers need to abandon if they are to make genuine, 'unpretentious' (ἄτυφον) progress. The wording is closely echoed a few pages later in ch. 10, when Plutarch turns to the corresponding development in actions rather than *logoi*: there too the good student needs to avoid 'the panegyrical and the showy' (τὸ πανηγυρικὸν καὶ πρὸς ἐπίδειξιν, 80e), and if one is too concerned with making a display of one's merits one is clearly 'still looking outwards' (ἔξω βλέπων ἔτι), rather than 'inwards' like Aesop's tracks here at 79a, and still concerned with reputation. That 'still' conveys a point which Plutarch then develops, the way that good students outgrow that showiness in a course of arduous self-improvement (81b–c) until they finally shed that 'pretention' (τῦφον, 81f).

One reason why Sophocles gets it right may be that for him, but not for those bad philosophers, this first phase is only 'play', διαπαίζειν—or so he could later, with the wisdom of retrospect, present

[24] Cf. also Post (1947), and already Wyttenbach ad loc.

[25] That apparently tangential mention of Ion may suggest delicately that Ion is the source for that story: similar cases might be e.g. *Phil.* 21.5 (Polybius), *Caes.* 32 (Pollio), and *Ant.* 25.3 (Dellius). If so, it is even more tempting to identify Ion as the source for the Sophocles anecdote too: cf. *Per.* 28.5–7, where two anecdotes may well come from Ion (Pelling (forthcoming), n. 93) but only the second is attributed to him. Interestingly, the Aeschylus-Ion incident happens at a festival, and that may also pick up πανηγυρικῶν here.

it (and if he can present it with a lightness of touch, smiling at his own expense, that too is playful). Bowra is probably right to regard Plato's παιδιὰ καλῶς διαπεπαισμένη, a 'game well played out', as the most illuminating parallel, but it remains true that the sense of 'play' is stronger in Greek than in that English translation: one can 'play out' a role in English when it is all deeply serious and unpleasurable, but διαπαίζειν does convey something light and gamesome. The ὄγκον is then best taken as internal accusative, characterizing the content of this 'play'. Perhaps, in that case, Bowra is too swift to reject the renderings 'imitate playfully' (LSJ s.v. 3)[26] or 'handle with a light touch' (Babbitt (1927)),[27] for that is what having ὄγκος as the content of the 'play' will amount to. This will be the case even if Bowra is right, as he probably is, to resist the suggestion that this playfulness amounted to *mockery* of Aeschylus:[28] '[w]e can hardly believe that Sophocles regarded his own first works as making fun of Aeschylus. If there was a joke, it was surely against himself for imitating the master with too great devotion' ((1940*a*), 387 = (1953), 111). My translation 'having had his fun with' tries to capture that nuance.[29] As in other cases, too, when Plutarch uses παιδ- or παιζ-words in a context of development, there is in the background a

[26] LSJ qualifies with a cautious 'perh.'. Neither the 1968 nor the 1996 Supplement revises the entry.

[27] Bowra (1940*a*), 387 = (1953), 110. His main reason is that neither rendering is appropriate for the accusatives of the second phase as well as that of the first (his point (c) above): but if my argument below is correct, that point no longer holds, as any extension to the second phase has to be taken as a zeugma. Waterfield's 'lighten', however, seems impossibly far from the way διαπαίζειν is used elsewhere.

[28] Such mockery is implied by Pinnoy (1984), 161–2, who takes the phrase as parallel to Demetrius *On Style* 3.147, τοὺς Τρῶας διαπαίζουσα ὥσπερ παῖδας, where Innes (1972), 200 rightly translates 'make fun of'. In that case the accusative would be one of direct object, not internal. It is true that this sense of διαπαίζειν would be in line with most other uses of the word, where the point is regularly humour where someone else is the butt (LSJ s.v. 2), and there is a separate anecdotal tradition of a Sophoclean joke at Aeschylus' expense (*TrGF* iv. T 52a–d). But it was more regular to think of Sophocles as deeply respectful of Aeschylus (cf. especially Ar. *Ran.* 788–93, and also *Life* 4), and it fits Plutarch's argument better to have Sophocles as a positive exemplum throughout, picking the best model and using it properly in the way outlined at the end of the essay at 84b–85b, rather than making him parallel to Plato's pups of 78e–f, snapping disrespectfully at the heels of the great.

[29] Philippon's 'avoir été peu sérieux en imitant . . .' (n. 1) captures it too.

suggestion of παιδεία, education, as well as παιδιά, play.[30] In that first phase, the two genuinely went together.

What of the second stage? That seems to be anything but 'play', for the whole context—indeed, the whole essay[31]—makes it clear that this period of development is very hard work. In ch. 8, it is *others* who spend time with their texts 'just for pleasure and play', ἡδονῆς ἕνεκα καὶ παιδιᾶς. The person who is making the right sort of development will have his eye on other things. The picture here is closely parallel to *How a Young Man should Listen to Poetry* 30e, where again the comparison of παιδιά and παιδεία is in point: 'the young man who is a true lover of honour and beauty and who fastens on (ἁπτόμενον) poetry not for play but for education (μὴ παιγνίας ἀλλὰ παιδείας ἕνεκα) will not listen idly or carelessly to things uttered with an eye to bravery or self-control or justice.'

That should affect the way we take τὸ πικρόν here. The run of the argument suggests that this should at least primarily refer to the bitterness and pain *caused to Sophocles himself* rather than to his audiences. (That 'at least primarily' raises a point to which we will return.) In the same way, the equivalent progress in actions in ch. 10 will require a phase of 'using the biting and the bitter particularly on oneself' (τῷ δηκτικῷ καὶ πικρῷ χρῶνται πρὸς ἑαυτοὺς μάλιστα, 81c).[32] An elegant paradox underlies the language here, for two of the favourite words for Sophocles were ἡδύς, 'pleasant', and γλυκύς, 'sweet', the classic antonyms of πικρός: Radt in his Testimonia has a whole section under the heading 'Sophocles suavis' (*TrGF* iv. TT

[30] Compare *Lyc.* 16.8–9, where Spartan παιδεία involves learning obedience, something especially visible when boys are at play (παίζοντας: the point then recurs at *Comp. Lyc. Num.* 4.4); *Ant.* 29.1, where Cleopatra's playfulness (παιδιά) is one way in which she 'trained' (διεπαιδαγώγει) Antony; *Socrates' Sign* 579c; and especially *How a Young Man should Listen to Poetry* 30e, quoted in the next paragraph. Of course, the words are toyed with in this way long before Plutarch: cf. Pl. *Leg.* 803d.

[31] Earlier, for instance, ch. 3 had dwelt on the 'hard work and training' (πόνος καὶ ἄσκησις) needed to drive out indolence, 76e–f; but the path gets easier in the final stages (ch. 4, 77c–d). Later ch. 11 shows the painfulness of grappling with one's own deficiencies: it is best to cause oneself pain (ἀλγύνειν), but otherwise one should accept the discomfort (ἐγκαρτεροῦντα) of constructive criticism from others (82b–c).

[32] And notice how in the parallel passage in *How to Listen to Lectures* (above, n. 19) Simonides' bees pass over the most attractive flowers to settle on the 'harshest and sharpest' (τραχύτατον καὶ δριμύτατον), 41f: it is the effect on them, again there a 'useful' one, that matters.

108–14). If Aeschylus was the 'loudest-voiced' (μεγαλοφωνότατος) and Euripides the 'all-wise' (πάνσοφος), Sophocles was simply the 'sweet' (γλυκύς: T 133 = Phot. *Bibl.* 101b4), so sweet that the comic poets and others called him the 'honey-bee' (TT 108–12).[33] There are frequent suggestions too that not merely Sophocles' style but also the man himself was 'pleasant'—'his character was so attractive that he was loved everywhere and by everyone' (*Life* 7), this man who was so εὔκολος, so 'easy to get on with' (Ar. *Ran.* 82)—and the two suggestions can be brought together: 'Sophocles was the most pleasant of people, and inclined to his own character (ἐπὶ τὸ ἴδιον ἦθος ἔκλινεν) in his lyrics: that is why he was called the honey-bee' (T 111 = *Σ Ajax* 1199), and one notices again that suggestion that Sophocles' own character was reflected in his mature style. At least part of that paradox turns on this 'bitterness' that Sophocles has earlier had to endure. It is a painful process to become Mr Pleasant.[34]

In that case, too, κατάτεχνον in both its occurrences in the crucial sentence is best taken with literal reference to the τέχνη, the skill or craft, that the poet or philosopher is learning. This is when playtime is over, and they settle to learning the tools of their trade, acquiring their 'technical' proficiency.[35] And it is relevant that κατασκευή too

[33] Such parallels between poets and bees are collected and discussed by Waszink (1974): unsurprisingly, it is the seductive 'sweetness' that is usually in point.

[34] Therefore 'pungent', the translation favoured by Jebb (1892), xlvi, Pinnoy (1984), 162, and Budelmann (2000), 1 is not satisfactory, even though in other contexts πικρός can be used in an approving way of literary style: the more negative 'bitter' or 'harsh' is required both by the implied paradox, with the pleasurable Sophocles in this phase characterized by the opposite quality, and by the 'pain' implied by the run of Plutarch's general argument. Waterfield's 'austerity' does not quite capture πικρόν, but is at least right in suggesting that the word conveys the way the style felt to Sophocles himself, not (or not just) his audiences. If I am 'austere', I am the one who feels it most.

[35] LSJ has veered between taking κατάτεχνον as 'artificial' and 'full of art': the ninth edition has 'artificial', corrected to 'full of art' in the 1968 Supplement, corrected back to 'artificial' in the 1996 Revised Supplement. Both renderings are sensitive to some aspect of the word. This is the phase where indeed the 'skill' or 'art' is developed, but it is in the final phase rather than this one that the poet is truest to his own nature, and in that sense it is at this stage 'artificial'. In other instances too κατάτεχνον conveys accomplishment and skill (e.g. Philodemus *AP* 5.132.5 = 3232 *GP*, *Σ* Ar. *Av.* 919c = p. 144 Holwerda), but also sometimes over-elaboration or pedantry (e.g. Greg. Naz. *On the Holy Spirit* 20). The word is rare (Plutarch's only two uses are in this passage) and late, and here in particular Bowra's conviction (point (b) above) that it goes back to Sophocles' own phrasing seems over-optimistic.

can readily be used of rhetorical 'constructions' of different sorts, especially where *lexis* is concerned,[36] for the harsh and technical phase will indeed be defined by the development of rhetorical technique. But this is one of several double meanings in the sentence, for an even more pertinent κατασκευή is the construction of or working on *the person himself*, moving the 'judgement' along (in the terms of the previous sentence in the text) until it takes that fixed, healthy form (κατάστασιν ὑγιεινήν): as Plutarch puts it in Aristotelian terms in *On Moral Virtue*, a 'disposition (*hexis*) is a strengthening and κατασκευή of an irrational potentiality which comes about through habituation' (443d).[37] It follows here that τῆς αὑτοῦ κατασκευῆς is unlikely to be only 'his formation' in the sense of 'his doing the forming', with αὑτοῦ as only a subjective genitive: it will also be an objective genitive, 'the formation of him'. Both nuances matter: he is forming himself. And it is hard work.

Where does that leave Bowra's argument (point (c)) that διαπεπαιχώς should grammatically continue to govern the accusatives τὸ πικρὸν καὶ κατάτεχνον τῆς αὑτοῦ κατασκευῆς? Perhaps this is simply wrong; we can understand a μεταβαλεῖν, or perhaps infer a less specialized 'adopted', from what follows rather than a διαπεπαιχώς from what precedes.[38] But if Bowra is right in continuing to understand διαπεπαιχώς, we have what E. J. Kenney calls a 'true zeugma', like Pope's 'See Pan with flocks, with fruits Pomona crowned', or Sophocles' own καὶ μή μ' ἄτιμον τῆσδ' ἀποστείλητε γῆς, | ἀλλ'

[36] LSJ s.v. κατασκευή VI; s.v. κατασκευάζω 6–8 and especially 10. The terminology is especially frequent in Dionysius of Halicarnassus, and was one of the reasons why Pinnoy (1984) suggested a source in Dionysius' circle (above, n. 5). Within Plutarch notice the parallel passage (n. 19) at *How to Listen to Lectures* 41c, where λέξις can be deceptive when it is added with a certain ὄγκος καὶ κατασκευή to the subject matter; also e.g. *On the Pythian Oracles* 396f, poets write in a way which is austere and φιλοσόφως in substance but similar to Homer and Hesiod 'in power, grace, and κατασκευῇ τῇ περὶ λέξιν'; *How a Young Man should Listen to Poetry* 16c and 30d; *Lyc.* 19.2.

[37] Cf. *Per.* 8.1, Pericles' περὶ τὸν βίον κατασκευή ('way of life', Stadter): partly how he 'fitted himself out' (cf. *C.min.* 35.5, *On Socrates' Sign* 578e), partly how he 'constructed' his life. Such moral training is parallel to the τῶν σωμάτων κατασκευαί that are a feature of early childhood (*On Love of one's Offspring* 495c).

[38] See Fraenkel on Aesch. *Ag.* 797f., quoting with approval K–G ii. 566–8, 'in antitheses often something must be supplied out of one element to supplement the other', and 'from a following verb of a specialized meaning a verb of a generalized meaning must be understood'.

ἀρχέπλουτον καὶ καταστάτην δόμων ('do not cast me out of this land dishonoured, but [keep me here] rich in ancestral wealth and restorer of my house', *El.* 71–2) or *ἀλλ' ἢ πνοαῖσιν ἢ βαθυσκαφεῖ κόνει | κρύψον νιν* ('But either [consign them to] the breezes or with deep dust bury them', *El.* 435–6), or Lucretius' *quod si immortalis nostra foret mens, | non tam se moriens dissolui conquereretur | sed magis ire foras uestemque relinquere, ut anguis* (sc. *gauderet*) ('if our mind was immortal, it would not so much complain at being dissolved on death but rather [rejoice] at going out and leaving its clothing like a snake', 3.612–14).[39] The Lucretian and the first Sophoclean examples are especially pertinent, as the verb to be understood is the opposite of the word that has figured in the previous clause. So we may still agree with Bowra that emendation is not required.[40]

[39] Where Kenney (1971), ad loc. quotes also Livy 45.20.9 *orantes ne noua falsaque crimina plus obesse Rhodiis aequum censerent quam antiqua merita, quorum ipsi testes essent* (sc. *prodesse*). Kenney distinguishes this 'true zeugma', where a word of different or contrary meaning needs to be understood, from syllepsis (also now often called zeugma) where the same word changes its meaning or nuance: examples of the second would be 'he put out the cat and the light', or Flanders and Swann's Madeira-drinker 'raising her glass, her courage, her eyes and his hopes'. Similar 'true zeugmas' are Pind. *Pyth.* 4.1856, *οὔτε ἔργον οὔτ' ἔπος ἐκτράπελον κείνοισιν εἰπών*, Eur. *Ion* 1064–5, *ἢ θηκτὸν ξίφος ἢ λαιμῶν ἐξάψει βρόχον ἀμφὶ δειρήν* (both cited by Housman (1901), 405 = (1972), 545): '[t]he idiom is commoner than one might expect' (Dawe (1982), on Soph. *OT* 117). Other examples from Homer, Pindar, and tragedy are collected by Bruhn (1899), 113–14 §198, I and II and by Dawe.

[40] Bowra had good further arguments for rejecting Webster's *διαπεπαλαιχώς* (= 'fought his way through'): as he says, that would more naturally take a dative than an accusative ((1940*a*), 387 = (1953), 110). Bergk's *διεπεπλακώς* would mean 'thoroughly moulding', from *διαπλάττω*. That is a good Plutarchan word (*On the Pythian Oracles* 401e, *On the Decline of the Oracles* 427b) and one that can be used of literary composition (cf. LSJ s.v. I); but if so it should refer to fiction, the 'making up' of a whole story or explanation, rather than to the construction of particular stylistic features. So, with the simple word *πλάττω* / *-ομαι* or other compounds, *C.min.* 63.7, *On the Pythian Oracles* 408d, *Table Talk* 732a, and e.g. Diod. Sic. 3.11.2, 17.41.8, Iambl. *Life of Pythagoras* 35.258. Herwerden's *διαπεπαικώς* implies a verb **διαπαίω* which does not seem attested elsewhere, and any sense of 'smiting thoroughly' would be just as inappropriate for the second limb while not particularly suited even to the first. Bernhardy (1869), 305 intended his *διαπεπλιχώς* (from *διαπλίσσομαι*) to mean 'überschreitend', but LSJ seems right in taking the word to mean 'with legs apart'. Better would be Schoene's *διαπεπλοχώς* from *διαπλέκω*, 'weave together': the simple verb *πλέκω* is often used of literary composition, and Pind. *Pyth.* 12.8 shows that the compound can be too. It may be important that Plutarch himself uses the word in a literary simile in the parallel passage (n. 19) at *How to listen to Lectures* 41e; it also comes in a metaphor of playfully 'putting together' riddles at *Banquet of the Seven*

Let us move on to the third phase: what is meant by this 'type of diction that is ἠθικώτατον καὶ βέλτιστον'? If we base interpretation on what has come before in Plutarch's argument, then the crucial indicator would be the previous sentence, where the philosopher of mature judgement consorts 'with those *logoi* that can instil character and magnitude (ἦθος καὶ μέγεθος)'—a different sort of bigness, clearly, from that Aeschylean ὄγκος—and 'whose tracks ... turn inwards rather than outwards'. That was still talking about the final phase of *self*-formation, so we might expect the most relevant 'character and magnitude' to be that which the philosopher or poet has developed and is still developing *for himself*: it would be 'characterful' in the sense that it is both best for and truest to Sophocles' own character, just as the 'bitterness' was primarily the pain caused to Sophocles himself. 'Truest to', in the sense that well-played music should be ἠθική, 'expressive of character', just as a statesman's speech should convey his own genuine self (*Precepts on Public Life* 802f); and in the sense in which Brutus accepts his fate by making a remark ἠθικῶς, 'in character' (*Brut.* 51.4). And adopting this style generates in Sophocles something ἠθικόν too, in the sense that the word is used in the work *On Moral Virtue*, περὶ ἠθικῆς ἀρετῆς: correct habituation fosters *in one's own soul* the morally 'characterful', τὸ ἠθικόν, with the development of reasonableness and moderation (ἐπιείκεια καὶ μετριότης, 451f). The 'characterful', then, is full of not just any character, but good character: that good character may always have been there—it indeed needed to be there if it was to seek and sustain the right sort of habituation—but it paradoxically emerges at its clearest when it has acquired all the technical artifice that is also required. This is close to being a serious equivalent of Aristophanes' claim that it was at the height of his skill, once he too had passed through several phases of development, that his own moral goodness as well as his professional technique emerged at their clearest.[41]

Wise Men 154b. But the perfect form, though good Attic (Herodian περὶ παθῶν 2.356), is very rare: in this compound it is found only in [Hippocr.] *On the Nature of Bones* 16 (ix. 190.7 Littré). Schöll's διαπεφευγώς is also possible, though weaker and palaeographically less plausible. In all these suggestions it is a pity to lose the sense of 'play', and if I am right in positing a zeugma no change is required.

[41] This is particularly clear at *Vesp.* 1015–50: after several preliminary phases (1018–22) he now produces the best comedy Dionysus has ever heard (1046–7); but

Yet, if we go on to the second half of the crucial sentence and beyond, we see that there must be another aspect to this too. The equivalent stage of the philosophers' development is to move[42] to 'the *logos* that fastens on character and emotion', τὸν ἁπτόμενον ἤθους καὶ πάθους λόγον. In itself that *could*, just, correspond to the *logos* that 'fastens on' Sophocles' own character and emotion, and brings them out in his artistic production; but just as, read against what precedes, the ἦθος in ἠθικώτατον would most readily be Sophocles' own, so now the ἦθος in ἤθους καὶ πάθους would most readily refer to the way a *logos* can fasten on the character of others, of the people who are so affected by Sophocles' poetry when they read or hear it. In *On Talkativeness* (504b) Sophocles' own character Nestor is said to have spoken ἠθικῶς when trying to calm the angry Ajax, 'I do not blame you, because you are acting well but speaking badly' (= fr. 855 *TrGF*): that is 'morally' effective, characterful in that it is geared to the *hearer*'s character, 'in words which show his knowledge of character' (as Helmbold translates it) or 'with understanding of character' (Russell).[43]

he has not let success go to his head, and makes sure the targets of his attacks remain the proper ones (1023 ff.). That is because he retains a γνώμην ἐπιεικῆ (1027): no ὄγκος (!) has crept into his φρόνημα (1023). Compare the claim in *Nub.* 537 that, after his early successes had led him to put such trust in his audience, his comedy is appropriately σώφρων (537): highly jokey, of course, but a joke that works on similar assumptions. *Eq.* 541–4 has some parallel to our passage in a different way, in the three phases that have been necessary before the poet has come to be his own, independent self.

[42] καταβαίνειν gives an interesting metaphor, especially as it serves as the counterpart of the less charged μεταβάλλειν, 'change to'. Perhaps there is a sense of 'coming down' to the coast, a more comfortable environment, or even 'coming home'? That would fit the important nuance that the final phase is also the one where poets or philosophers are truest to their own nature. Cf. καταπλεῖν at 81f, where the equivalent phases of action are in point.—There is an editorial curiosity here, as many modern editions print μεταβῶσιν: thus Babbitt in the Loeb (1927) and Klaerr, Philippon, and Sirinelli in the Budé (1989). That reading goes back through Wyttenbach and Reiske at least as far as Xylander. Paton, Wegehaupt, and Pohlenz read καταβῶσιν in their 1925 Teubner (correcting Bernardakis' μεταβῶσιν in the earlier Teubner), and καταβῶσιν is kept by Gärtner in his 1974 second edition. Of these only Reiske notes that there is any textual problem. I have been unable to check all the relevant manuscripts, but Luigi Ferrari has kindly consulted those in Rome, K (= Vat. 1309), p (= Palat. (Vat.) 178), and S (= Vat. 264), and Barbara Kowalzig those in Paris, A (= Par. 1671), C (= Par. 1955), and E (1672): they confirm that all six read κατα-. I am most grateful to both, and also to Chris Collard for alerting me to the problem.

[43] The word is used of similarly tactful advice at *Alex.* 52.4, *Precepts on Public Life* 809e, and *How to Tell a Flatterer from a Friend* 72b and 73f.

That certainly seems to fit better with the way the argument develops in the next chapter, for that concerns precisely what poetry does for others: how one should read, how poetry can, if written properly and read properly, do one so much good. This doubleness in ἠθικός is not even quite an ambiguity, for it captures the deeper insight that morally correct behaviour is the best thing both for the doer and the recipient. Thus when the good wife abandons any forward or shameless or showy (πανηγυρικόν) behaviour and concentrates on developing her skills (φιλοτεχνεῖν) in the 'characterful and life-based' acts of rapport (ἐν ταῖς ἠθικαῖς καὶ βιωτικαῖς χάρισι) with her husband, that suits both the 'characters' involved just as it involves both their 'lives' (*Advice on Married Life* 142b). (Notice the similarity of language there to our present passage: these are the ways Plutarch thinks when he talks of ethical development.) Compare too *Comp. Lyc. Num.* 4.2, where Plutarch suggests that the Romans prefer their girls to marry young because that is ἠθικώτερον for living together: the husbands can then mould their young characters. Once again, ἠθικώτερον for *everyone*—for the wives, for the husbands (this is a matter of living *together*), for Rome as a whole. When things are got morally right, one can no longer separate out a single person to be the gainer.

If ἠθικός has a doubleness in this way, then we should go back to the second phase, and particularly to τὸ πικρόν. Just as it is unlikely to be coincidence there that κατασκευή can so readily be used of rhetorical constructions as well as of self-formation, so it is unlikely to be coincidence that πικρόν can so naturally apply to the effect on others, even if the primary application has to be to the effect on the poet himself. So the paradox we noticed earlier will have the further aspect that Sophocles had to cause pain to others, as well as to himself, before he could give them so much pleasure: that was all necessary in the course of finding his technical feet and developing his distinctive voice.

The Sophocles sentence, then, is not merely deeply integrated into the argument, it is fulcral to it, with careful choice of vocabulary moving the focus gradually from something more self-centred—the formation of the poet—to the impact on others of what the poet produces. This is the central move within a wider drift of meaning in the whole passage, one to which the ambiguity of that initial ζητεῖν λόγους, 'go in search of *logoi*', is important. Is this a search for *logoi* to read and listen to, or for *logoi* to deliver? For aspiring philosophers the very first stage would normally require the first of those two senses: you need to find the right oral or written texts to absorb. This suits the way that some take off for works of science, with their heads in the air: presumably they will be studying such books and listening to such discussions rather than writing or delivering them themselves. It also fits the Anacharsis remark, on the benefit that one can gain from the *logoi* one has heard, and it certainly fits the effect of Plato's conversation on his disciples. But every philosopher, then as now, finds it difficult to be merely a passive recipient of *logoi*, and there comes a stage where they start spreading the word to others. One of the signs of the unsatisfactory aspirant is that they start spreading it prematurely and in the wrong way, tearing at their subject matter puppy-like, throwing their sophisms around, rolling out what they have discovered to the public, the youth, or the kingly symposium. The good students, on the other hand, will be closer to the model of Sophocles, and more discriminating in what they 'roll out'.

Bowra took ἠθικώτατον differently, as 'expressive of character' (point (k)), the character not of Sophocles himself nor of his audience, but of the figures he puts on stage. Others translate similarly.[44] This may be what the real-life Sophocles meant, if he genuinely used the word: it certainly fits one strand in the way Sophocles' art was praised by others, for the *Life* notes the way that he could use 'a single half-line or a single λέξις' to convey character (ἠθοποιεῖν, *Life* 21). Yet, if we concentrate on Plutarch, on this textual 'Sophocles' rather than the real-life equivalent, it will be plain that this fits the argument much less straightforwardly. In particular, the move in the rest of the sentence to the impact on other people's ἦθος would be jarring. True, one could fill in the steps of an argument that would make the jump a comprehensible one, for Plutarch of all people would understand

[44] e.g. Wilamowitz (1905), 150–1 = (1935–72), iv. 203–4, Perrotta (1935), 8, Earp (1944), 12, Pinnoy (1984), 160, 163, Philippon in his translation (n. 1) and at 303 n. 9, Budelmann (2000), 1; and already Bernhardy (1869), 305, 'bis er endlich das Geheimnis der *Ethopoïe* fand'. Webster (1936), 143 (cf. 153) has 'adapted to the temper of the particular speech'.

how characterizing others could have a salutary impact on readers, and indeed on himself. That is what his *Parallel Lives* are all about; in several proems he theorizes that process,[45] and a certain amount of that theory is already implicit at the end of this very essay, in the famous passage where he encourages his readers when faced with a dilemma to ponder what Epaminondas would have done, or Lycurgus, or Agesilaus: that is a way of self-fashioning which is like looking in a mirror, he says (85a–b), using an image that again he uses for his own biographical writing (*Aem.* 1.1).[46] Nor is that alien to some of the anecdotes told about Sophocles: this was the man, famously, who portrayed people 'as they ought to be' (Aristotle, *Poetics* 1460^b32 = T 53a), and that was rightly or wrongly taken to mean 'as they ought to be *morally*' (TT 53b, 172, cf. 120), the sort of characters who could become role models. Nor, once again, is it far from the *Frogs*, where Aeschylus' portrayals are more likely to be morally uplifting than those degenerate characters of Euripides. So the argument could indeed be supplemented in some such way. But what is hard to believe is that any first-time reader, following Plutarch's argument closely, would immediately have filled in all those steps of the argument, and would have tied down the general 'characterful' to this much more specific 'characterizing'. At most that can be only one possible sense among several that are felt, and not the most dominant.

Where does this leave Bowra's most general point, that Sophocles should be taken as speaking about 'more general aspects of his art' and not about mere 'diction'? At least in terms of Plutarch's use of the story, that requires rephrasing. Mere diction is certainly in the air: notice how the next chapter begins, specifically attacking those who are interested only in 'the words alone', quick to take offence at anything that grates, culling Plato or Xenophon only in search of pure Atticism. We are there close to the world of the Second Sophistic, for instance of Lucian's *Lexiphanes* or his *On a Slip of the Tongue*, where a non-Attic solecism would make pedantic purists turn up

45 Esp. *Per.* 1–2, *Aem.* 1, *Demetr.* 1, *Alex.* 1, *Nicias* 1, *Cimon* 2.

46 Cf. also *How to Listen to Lectures* 42b, *On Controlling one's Anger* 456a–b, *Apophthegmata of Kings* 172d: these passages are discussed illuminatingly by Alexei Zadorojnyi in a forthcoming paper.

their noses.[47] Diction, λέξις, is specifically what those unsatisfactory readers of Plato and Xenophon concentrate on; quite evidently, it is still the point. It is still the point a chapter later, where Plutarch continues to urge the value of substance ahead of λέξις (80c–d). Yet once again the Sophocles sentence is here fulcral, for ἠθικώτατον moves the emphasis to 'more general aspects of his art' just as surely as λέξις still focuses on 'diction'. The point is that *even in matters of diction* Sophocles, by this stage of perfection, was choosing a style that was good for character and virtue. Bowra quotes Aristophanes' *Frogs* to indicate that fifth-century criticism could naturally be concerned with the larger aspects of drama and not just with style; he would have done better to use the play to suggest that matters of style could themselves be felt to have a larger, ethical dimension. The poet who stimulates virtue uses different words, just as he uses different music, from the poet who stands for decline. If that were not the case, several parts of the *agon* between Aeschylus and Euripides would fall very flat.

To summarize: of the eleven points we separated out in Bowra's interpretation, we have not yet directly discussed (b), the possibility that Plutarch rephrased Sophocles' dictum in his own language. Of the others only three, (h)–(j), can be accepted as they stand, all concerning the final change as one that is still in progress and that moves to a style that is immediately praised. There is also some force in a fourth, (e), on ὄγκος as non-pejorative, though it is also relevant that such ὄγκος has points in comparison with a more pejorative 'showiness'. Point (a), on the 'more general aspects of his art', needs to be put in a different way. The others need revision if a rendering is to suit the carefully modulated run of Plutarch's argument.

[47] On this linguistic fastidiousness cf. recently Swain (1996), ch. 2, Schmitz (1997), ch. 3, Whitmarsh (2005), ch. 3. Plutarch's distaste for such carping purism is again clear at *How to Listen to Lectures* 42e, where again he criticizes young men who praise a lecturer's diction, words, and fine delivery (λέξεις καὶ ῥήματα καὶ τὸ καλῶς ἀπαγγέλλειν) but do not trouble about his content.

III

That is all very well: this explication of Plutarch's twists and turns may be of interest to the increasing number of Plutarch buffs, and most of these will not be surprised to hear that Plutarch's rhetorical virtuosity is more subtle and devious than scholars used to assume. But what of those more interested in Sophocles? Does any of this indicate, not merely the use Plutarch puts the dictum to, but what the real-life Sophocles might actually have said and meant?

What one might call the naive and hopeful view would go like this. Plutarch is an author of Good Faith (it is hard to put this in any but old-fashioned terms). He knew his Ion well (and that is true), and also had enough feeling both for Sophocles and for fifth-century culture to have a good idea of what Sophocles would have meant (that too is true). He can therefore be relied upon to have accurately construed and conveyed what Sophocles meant. If that view is right, then the argument of this paper has been as relevant to Sophocles as to Plutarch.

That view, or a version of it, is not as naive as all that, though it is useful to focus on Plutarch's readers as well as Plutarch himself, for they would presumably take this as something that made sense both for the real-life Sophocles to have said and for Plutarch to use in this way. It is reasonable, then, to infer that those readers would not tie down the meaning of the dictum as specifically as Bowra suggests. If, for instance, they had taken *ἠθικώτατον* as *only* meaning 'characterizing' or *κατασκευῆς* as *only* a term of poetic construction, they would have found the development of the argument bewildering. An audience in the second century AD is not the same as a group of fellow banqueters in Sophocles' own day, but not every aspect of the two worlds is so different, and the approach is not irrelevant.

Still, it really is too hopeful to assume that Plutarch gives us a direct filter on to Sophocles' own meaning. Plutarch's capacity to remould and impose his own stamp on his material is increasingly recognized, and that extends to his use of quotations. In particular, recent research in Leuven has focussed on Plutarch's nests of quotation, analysing cases where identical clusters of citations and anecdotes are found in different essays, and showing how the point of those citations and anecdotes is often reshaped to suit the context.[48] The immediately preceding citation from Aesop is itself an example of how the original point of a quotation can be retooled to its new setting. In the original fable, the story was one of a lion who waited for animals to come to him in his cave, and the wary fox noticed that every track led inwards and none led outwards: it requires some mental gyrations to fit that story as a whole to the context here, rather than just the inwards-outwards contrast, and it is hard to think that an audience that made those gyrations would be anything but distracted.[49] So it is very possible that Plutarch has somehow repointed Sophocles' words, taking what he needed and only what he needed for his context.

That is likely enough. What is not at all likely is that Sophocles just happened to phrase himself in terms that turned out so apposite to Plutarch's ethical and argumentative concerns. It would be very convenient if Sophocles had used words that were ambiguous in precisely the right way, or with exactly the right breadth and vagueness to embrace the various nuances, both stylistic and ethical, that Plutarch needed. It would be even more convenient if Sophocles had used nothing but such terms, and had not used a single word which was appropriate only to style and not to advance in self-knowledge, or if he had used so few words that would apply only to his own development or to its impact on others and not to both. Surely that is too convenient to be plausible. A little tweak or variation of phrasing here, a dropping of an inapposite word there—that is exactly what we would expect Plutarch to have done. Plutarch 'has rephrased the original',[50] thoroughly and deftly, even if we cannot tell exactly how;[51] he 'is

[48] In particular van der Stockt (1999*a*), (1999*b*), especially 584, 591, (2002), and van Meirvenne (1999), especially 535–6, and (2002).

[49] Perhaps one could say that a philosopher or a poet who always absorbs and never gives anything out is deficient or even dangerous; but the point would be a weak, wayward, and confusing one.

[50] Lloyd-Jones (1955), 158 = (1990*b*), 364. So also Pinnoy (1984), 160–1.

[51] The only attempt (I think) to guess the detail of the adaptation is that of Schmid in S–S i/2. 313 n. 5, who suggested that ὅπερ . . . βέλτιστον was an addition of Plutarch himself. That in fact is implausible, at least as stated: it would be tantalizing of Sophocles, even this textual 'Sophocles', to say only that he 'was now changing to a third style' without saying any more about it. One can indeed understand why even

wresting the scripture for his own purpose'.[52] It may well still be that Plutarch retains important aspects of what Sophocles did say, for it would not be like him to travesty or fabricate completely. But what is least likely of all is that Plutarch gives us the dictum, the whole dictum, and nothing but the dictum. Anyone making use of this passage should visualize a large warning sign, 'Danger: Plutarch at work'.

those who include the 'most characterful and best' in Sophocles' remark feel that further definition might be called for: thus Post (1947), 251 suggested emendation to (*exempli gratia*) ἐς τρίτον ἔτι τὸ ἡδὺ μεταβάλλειν. That precise wording is implausible for Plutarch's text, for it would not fit his argument; but Post may be right in sensing that the real-life Sophocles would have said something more.

[52] Post (1947), 250.

16

'Darkness, my Light': Enigmatic Ajax

S. J. Instone

I start with a hypothesis, the ancient narrative hypothesis (or introduction) to the *Ajax*. After 27 lines (in Pearson (1924)), we have, with ἑαυτὸν διαχρῆται ('he kills himself'), reached line 865 of the play. The hypothesis takes only two more lines to account for the remaining 555 lines of the play: εἰσὶ δὲ καὶ ἐπὶ τῷ τέλει τοῦ δράματος λόγοι τινὲς Τεύκρου πρὸς Μενέλαον, οὐκ ἐῶντα θάπτειν τὸ σῶμα. τὸ δὲ πέρας, θάψας αὐτὸν Τεῦκρος ἀπολοφύρεται ('In the end part of the play, there is a debate between Teucer and Menelaus, who won't allow Ajax's body to be buried. At the end, having buried him Teucer laments him.'). In fact the summary of the last third of the play is so summary that Teucer's second debate, with Agamemnon, and the critical intervention of Odysseus who ensures that Ajax is buried, are passed over.

This imbalance in the hypothesis draws attention to the curious fact that the protagonist is dead after little more than three-fifths of the drama. And there are a number of other oddities in the play, such as Ajax's probable violent death on stage (though this is not necessarily a unique type of event in Greek tragedy: cf. Soph. *Niobe* fr. 441a *TrGF*), and the scenes of wrangling over his burial between Teucer and Menelaus and subsequently Teucer and Agamemnon. These latter scenes are sometimes held to be the key to the play's cohesion: 'According to the traditional heroic code, one's merit must be recognised also by other people. The question of his burial becomes the symbol of that recognition . . . The final part of the play is no mere coda, but an indispensable development of the drama as a whole'

(Garvie (1998), 10–11). But the scenes, notwithstanding their dramatic function, degenerate into abuse and alter the tone of the second part of the play. Where Teucer (1123) jokes to Menelaus that even Menelaus in armour would be no match for him in his light armour, a scholiast commented, 'Such witticisms do not belong to tragedy; wanting to spin out the drama after Ajax's death, he wrote in bad taste and dispelled the proper tragic feeling' (*τὰ τοιαῦτα σοφίσματα οὐκ οἰκεῖα τραγῳδίας· μετὰ γὰρ τὴν ἀναίρεσιν, ἐπεκτεῖναι τὸ δρᾶμα θελήσας, ἐψυχρεύσατο, καὶ ἔλυσε τὸ τραγικὸν πάθος*, Christodoulou (1977), 227). It was this remark that led to Waldock categorizing the play as a diptych (1951, 49–79). A further oddity is Ajax's 'deception' speech (646–92), where his decision to die is couched in language suggesting that he will live. This is a strange type of speech from an otherwise blunt hero and one whose meaning(s) continues to be disputed—a thorough survey and evaluation of different interpretations of the speech is in Hesk (2003), ch. 5. *Alii alia*: for some the play is unified because it is emotionally charged throughout (Heath (1987), 207–8), for others the second half of the play is an invitation to consider the play in political terms, to consider the pros and cons of different types of leadership (cf. Rose (1995); for a persuasive rebuttal of this view see Griffin (1999*a*)). Tycho von Wilamowitz (1917), 51 called the play 'primitive', though its date is uncertain and it would be rash to state that it was certainly an early work of Sophocles. Its eccentricities fascinate, and consensus of opinion is conspicuous by its absence.

But there is another dimension to the play which I wish to explore briefly. The oddities of the play mentioned above revolve around two central themes of the play, life and death, or, more particularly, the value of being alive and the value of being dead. The cohesion of the play becomes more apparent, and some of the oddities mentioned above less odd, if one sees Sophocles' depiction of Ajax as intending to suggest that a certain type of life is no better than death and that in some circumstances death can create a sort of 'life'. Seen in this light, the apparently sharp distinction between life and death becomes less sharp, and Ajax's death becomes less of a dividing point in the play. In what follows I shall attempt to show how the text both of the *Ajax* and (briefly) of other plays of Sophocles draws attention to this blurring of life and death.

The play opens with Athene telling Odysseus what Ajax has been doing. Angered at losing to Odysseus in the competition for the arms of Achilles, he thought he would kill Odysseus and the other Greek leaders, but Athene deluded him, so he killed flocks of animals thinking they were the Greeks. Ajax is suffering from a divinely inflicted illness (66 *νόσον*); he is so mad that Odysseus does not want to see him (88) and pities him in his plight. Ajax is alive but, as indicated in Odysseus' profound and memorable lines, like all of us tantamount to a phantom or shadow (125–6 *ὁρῶ γὰρ ἡμᾶς οὐδὲν ὄντας ἄλλο πλὴν* | *εἴδωλ' ὅσοιπερ ζῶμεν ἢ κούφην σκιάν*, comparable to Pindar, *Pyth.* 8.95–6 *σκιᾶς ὄναρ ἄνθρωπος* and picked up at the end of the play (1257 *τἀνδρὸς οὐκέτ' ὄντος, ἀλλ' ἤδη σκιᾶς*) when, though dead, he continues to exert power. What sort of life is this, we ask. 'Even in his delusion he is a splendid figure' declares Garvie (1998), 123. Hardly. He has been reduced to ignominy and to a life that is but a shadow of its former self. An important line here is Athene's *ἐγὼ σκοτώσω βλέφαρα καὶ δεδορκότα* (85), 'I shall darken his eyes even though they shall still see', which subliminally suggests that she will inflict on him the darkness of death though he is still seeing the light of day and alive. In the parodos that follows, the chorus of Ajax's sailors do not concentrate simply on the greatness of Ajax and his heroic status, but highlight in addition and in Pindaric manner the problems that greatness brings in its wake and the special vulnerability of the great to the abuse of others. Speaking of the malicious rumours they believe Odysseus to have circulated about who was responsible for the slaughter of the cattle, they say: 'One who targets great souls could not miss; but saying such things about me, he would not be effective at all, for jealousy creeps against the powerful man' (154–6 *τῶν γὰρ μεγάλων ψυχῶν ἱεὶς* | *οὐκ ἂν ἁμάρτοι· κατὰ δ' ἄν τις ἐμοῦ* | *τοιαῦτα λέγων οὐκ ἂν πείθοι·* | *πρὸς γὰρ τὸν ἔχονθ' ὁ φθόνος ἕρπει*), similar to Pindar *Pyth.* 11.29–30. We are further encouraged to question the downside to Ajax's life as a hero.

Enter Tecmessa. She sums up the double-sided picture so far presented: 'For now the terrible, great, raw-powered Ajax lies sick in a raging storm' (205–7, *νῦν γὰρ ὁ δεινὸς μέγας ὠμοκρατὴς* | *Αἴας θολερῷ* | *κεῖται χειμῶνι νοσήσας*). What she means is that he *was* terrible, great and powerful, but now he is reduced to the status of the sick and, subliminally again, dead (*κεῖται*: 'he lies (dead)', anticipating its use with this meaning at 899 and 913). This last innuendo is made explicit in 215, *θανάτῳ γὰρ ἴσον πάθος ἐκπεύσῃ* ('You will learn of a suffering equal to death'). So much for Ajax's state when he is mad; when he has recovered his sanity it is even worse. When he was mad his deathly feebleness was apparent only to others, but when he recovers his senses, not only others but now he too is aware of it. This is Tecmessa's point at 271–7 (277 *ἆρ' ἔστι ταῦτα δὶς τόσ' ἐξ ἁπλῶν κακά;* 'Aren't these woes double the single ones of before?'). When Ajax comes to his senses and realizes his humiliating condition, 'I die' he cries (343 *ἐγὼ δ' ἀπόλλυμαι*). And more cryptically and emotionally, in dochmiacs, 'Darkness, my light, o darkness of the underworld most bright' (394–5 *σκότος, ἐμὸν φάος, | ἔρεβος ὦ φαεννότατον*). His present life is not worth living: it is not a life at all. It is a life tantamount to death, and must entail death because only death will yield him any sort of life: death and darkness will be life for him, and the second part of the play will show how this can be so. As the ancient *Life* of Sophocles said (paragraph 21 Pearson), and as Easterling has reminded us (1977*a*, 128–9), Sophocles had the happy knack of capturing the essence of one of his characters in a half-line or single expression. Ajax makes clear how for him death will be life at the end of his first long speech: honour is what is valuable for a man of good birth like himself, whether he is alive or dead (479–80, *ἀλλ' ἢ καλῶς ζῆν ἢ καλῶς τεθνηκέναι | τὸν εὐγενῆ χρή*). If he gets it when dead, and not when alive, then he is better off dead. The presence and sight of his son play a crucial role here. For on seeing and addressing him, Ajax comes to realize that the only time of life worth living is when one is incapable of thought, i.e. when one is either an infant or dead. This is brought out when he says to his son that he envies his son's state because he is unaware of his father's woes: 'For the pleasantest life consists in being aware of nothing' (554 *ἐν τῷ φρονεῖν γὰρ μηδὲν ἥδιστος βίος*). In the first stasimon that follows, the chorus take up the idea that a life of pain is not worth living, saying that his former deeds of valour are now despised by the Atreidae (616–20), and imagining his mother mourning him as if with a funeral lamentation when she hears of his insufferable plight: 'For a mad person is better off hidden in Hades' (635 *κρείσσων γὰρ Ἅιδᾳ κεύθων ὁ νοσῶν μάταν*). Here the chorus conflate the idea that his sickness has made his life no life with the implication that he will indeed have no life and be dead and lamented by his mother. The ode as a whole foreshadows a major theme of the second half of the play, namely that only after his death will his *great* deeds (as opposed to his mad deeds) be remembered and looked back on, and his status revived.

To sum up so far: Ajax's life is a life of death. Death is the only life he can contemplate, because then his recent madness, humiliation, and dishonour will be forgotten, and his great deeds of the past will be remembered and his honour thereby restored.

So to the notoriously problematic 'deception' speech (646–92). The main problem has traditionally been taken to be that if, as seems to be the case, Ajax is intent on death in order to escape a life that is no life, why does he describe his plans to kill himself in terms that can be interpreted to suggest that he has contemplated a change of mind and is intent on life? Why, in other words, does he attempt either to deceive Tecmessa (and, perhaps, the chorus), or to persuade himself, into believing that he will live? Various more or less plausible answers to this question have been offered. Reinhardt even went so far as to say that Ajax is the victim of self-deception to such an extent that he 'involuntarily veils his meaning' (Reinhardt (1979), 26 ≈ (1947), 34), as if the subtlety of the language was an accident on Ajax's part and Sophocles did not wish us to believe that Ajax himself was conscious of it. But most critics have tended to take one of two lines. Either Ajax, out of pity for Tecmessa, wants to deceive her (and perhaps the chorus and audience) into thinking that he intends to live (though by making him the dispenser of false hopes, this motive would seem to make him cruel rather than pitying); or (e.g. Knox (1961), 14 = (1979), 137–8, Garvie (1998), 186) he expresses himself ambiguously to convey his recognition of the value of changing his mind and living even though he cannot bring himself to carry out such a change (though this would be unexpected, since so far the change that he has recognized to be of value is the change from life to death, not from contemplation of death to life).

But in the light of what I have suggested so far about how for Ajax life is tantamount to death and death life, there is possibly a more plausible way of understanding the speech. Ajax expresses himself in terms that may suggest to us (and do suggest to Tecmessa and the chorus) that he has changed his mind, and describes his plan to kill himself in terms suggesting a plan to live, because for him (though not for Tecmessa or the chorus) death *is* life (394–5 'Darkness, my light, o darkness of the underworld most bright').

When he says 'Everything changes, and so do I', he still intends to kill himself but wants to get across that for him his death will be a change to life because he will be moving from a state of life tantamount to non-existence to a state, albeit dead, where he will regain honour and 'life'. He can therefore present his death in a positive light. This is what 651 (ἐθηλύνθην στόμα, 'my speech has been softened') implies: not that Tecmessa has made him change his mind, but that he is no longer going to present his death as something negative and frightening (as he did to Tecmessa and the chorus earlier). In dying he will yield to the gods (contrast his earlier rebuff of them reported in the messenger's speech 767–75) and give honour to the Atreidae (666–7: they can interpret his death as a victory for themselves and a show of respect). Lines 669–70, 'Both things terrible and things most strong yield to honour (τιμαῖς ὑπείκει)', take up the last point but suggest also, when applied to his own situation, that the terrible strength he had when he was alive performing great deeds now yields to posthumous honours. The next lines, 670–6, are particularly revealing: snowy winters give way to summer, and night (in this context the darkness of death) gives way for the light (φέγγος) of day to shine, i.e. bright glory will return to him. And then, 'All-conquering sleep binds and sets free, and does not hold forever', i.e. the sleep of death is a release for him, releasing honour. So when at 677 he says, 'And we, how shall we not learn good sense?', he means not 'How shall I not learn to be sensible and renege on my decision to die', but 'How can I fail to recognize that it is sensible for me to die, since, as I have shown, one thing gives way to another, and the gloom of my death will give way to my being gloriously honoured?'

He then explains how this can happen: 'For I realize that our enemy must be hated only to the extent that he will later become our friend', i.e. even the Atreidae will eventually yield me honour (679–80, as indeed they do, albeit grudgingly, later in the play). The next lines are: 'Towards my friend I shall want, while serving him, to be of help only so far, believing that he will not always remain so. For in the eyes of most mortals the harbour of friendship is untrustworthy' (680–3). Here, in the context of his own situation, he is providing a justification for his intended death: he will respect the Atreidae only to the extent of yielding to them by dying, not to the extent of being a living friend to them. He ends his speech with words to Tecmessa: 'Pray that what my heart wants will be accomplished' (686), i.e. 'Be at one with me in my desire for death'; then to the chorus, 'Honour (τιμᾶτε) for my sake these same things as she' (687–8), and 'If you do what I say, you may perhaps learn that, even if now I am unhappy, I have been saved', i.e. death is not a bleak nothingness but, if honour is given its rightful place, it can constitute for me when dead a change from misery to safety.

There is nothing radically new in this reading of the 'deception' speech: 'for him death *is* his salvation, the only means of preserving his *arete*' (Garvie (1998) on 691–2). I merely wish to emphasize that the speech is understandable in terms of Ajax's paradoxical outlook expressed in what he said at 394–5 ('Darkness, my light' etc.) that underlies the whole speech and is the main reason for his describing his forthcoming death in terms of life.

In the second stasimon that follows the 'deception' speech the chorus sing to Pan in rapturous joy: 'I would say that there is nothing that cannot be said, since Ajax has beyond hope repented of his anger and great quarrels with the Atreidae' (715–18); and with similar optimism when Tecmessa, roused by the chorus after they have heard the messenger reporting that Ajax had to be kept indoors for a day if he was to escape Athene's wrath, rebukes them for disturbing her now that she is 'recently rested from unceasing woes' (787–9 ἀρτίως πεπαυμένην | κακῶν ἀτρύτων). But later, after hearing from the messenger, the truth dawns on Tecmessa: 807–8, 'I now realize I have been deceived by the man, and that I have been cast out from my former position of favour with him' (ἔγνωκα γὰρ δὴ φωτὸς ἠπατημένη | καὶ τῆς παλαιᾶς χάριτος ἐκβεβλημένη). For Tecmessa and the chorus, the only life Ajax should live is life as normally understood. Posthumous honour and remembrance, which Ajax regards as preferable to being alive, mean nothing to the chorus as friends (483) or to Tecmessa as a wife who will go into slavery regardless of what honours he receives (496–9). But it does not follow that Ajax intended to deceive the chorus and Tecmessa into believing that he had changed his mind and was now determined to live. Not every consequence is intended. The chorus had taken in only the surface meaning of Ajax's speech; moreover, in typical Sophoclean manner, they are wont to jump to conclusions. Earlier, in the parodos, in order to extol Ajax's greatness all the more, they had maligned Odysseus and claimed that he was slandering Ajax (148–51), when Odysseus himself had stated his position rather differently (23 *ἴσμεν γὰρ οὐδὲν τρανές, ἀλλ' ἀλώμεθα*, 'for we know nothing sure, but are confused'; and 121–2 *ἐποικτίρω δέ νιν | δύστηνον ἔμπας, καίπερ ὄντα δυσμενῆ*, 'but I pity him in his misery nonetheless, although he is my enemy'). R. C. T. Parker (1999), 15 points out that there is another similar distortion when an emotional Tecmessa blames Ajax's death on Athene's favouritism for Odysseus (952–4). It is a common Sophoclean dramatic device to highlight the forthcoming tragedy with a misleading joyous ode. So at *Antigone* 1108–243 Creon says he will release Antigone, the chorus leap to conclusions and sing a joyous song to Bacchus, and immediately afterwards the messenger announces the death of Haemon and then Antigone. In the *Oedipus Tyrannus*, after Oedipus has told Jocasta he intends to summon the servant of Laius, and we fear the worst because Jocasta has just rushed off stage, the chorus suggest that Oedipus might be the child of a mountain nymph and foresee joyous dances on Mount Cithaeron (1086–109). And the *Philoctetes* provides perhaps the closest parallel when, after the arrival of the disguised merchant urging Neoptolemus to sail away, the chorus, believing that Philoctetes will be saved and taken home (not realizing that at this stage Neoptolemus still intends to take Philoctetes back to Troy: cf. 639–42) sing of how he will return home to Oeta (719–29). Sophocles liked to create and exploit a gap between on the one hand the expectations of a naive chorus and the hopes of some of the characters in the play and on the other hand the harshness of reality as it inexorably turns out.

But just how does Ajax suppose that death will bring him life and honour? Three main ways are emphasized in the play. Firstly, after his death the focus, albeit diffuse, is not only on the consequences of his recent acts done in madness, but on his reputation overall and his great, truly heroic, deeds of the more distant past: the memory of them survives. Secondly, his son lives on. And thirdly, the significance of being alive per se is diminished when we are confronted with the despicable figures of the still living Menelaus and Agamemnon.

The first way in which when dead he is alive is because when dead his earlier great deeds are recalled in detail, resuming the theme of his general greatness that has intermittently surfaced before (216, 364–6, 502, 613–19; more on his greatness in March (1991–3), 11–18). The chorus remind us what a comfort his presence was to them at night (1211–13), while Teucer recalls his *arete* to Agamemnon at 1273–88. Who thwarted Hector's assault on the Greek ships? Ajax. Who faced Hector in single combat? Ajax. And, again, Odysseus (1338–41): 'I would not dishonour such a man by denying that I saw in him alone the best of us Argives, apart from Achilles, who came to Troy.' His very death causes his great deeds of the past, which honour him, to be remembered and his true worth to become apparent.

Secondly, the significance of his son Eurysaces. Before dying, Ajax gives his son his great shield after which his son is named (574–6). Through this shield, in name and substance, his son lives on. His famous words to Eurysaces make it particularly clear that he lives on through his son (550–1): ὦ παῖ, γένοιο πατρὸς εὐτυχέστερος, | τὰ δ' ἄλλ' ὅμοιος· καὶ γένοι' ἂν οὐ κακός, 'O son, may you become more fortunate than your father, but in other respects like him; and then you would not become bad'). And when Ajax is dead, his son stands by his father and holds on to him, holding both a lock of hair and his father's body itself (1180–1), a vivid manifestation on stage of the common Pindaric idea that a son can revive a glorious father's honour by inheriting his father's abilities and following in his footsteps. This seems to me a more plausible interpretation of this scene than that of Burian, who believes that Eurysaces' supplication of his father's body makes it tantamount to a sacred hero's tomb, and that the play thereby ends with Ajax transformed into a sacred hero and allusions to his contemporary cult (Burian (1972), 154; cf. March (1991–3), 33–4). And right at the end of the play, Teucer in anapaests tells Eurysaces, 'Child, lovingly take hold of your father, and as strongly as you can with me lift his torso' (1409–11 παῖ, σὺ δὲ πατρός γ', ὅσον ἰσχεύεις, | φιλότητι θιγὼν πλεύρας σὺν ἐμοὶ | τάσδ' ἐπικούφιζ'). So the play ends with Eurysaces demonstrably inheriting his father's strength and showing that it lives on, and, by literally raising Ajax's body, metaphorically raising his status (for more on the significance of the onstage attention to the body and burial see Easterling (1988), 91–8).

But in contrast, and this is the third point, others who literally live on are petty and nonentities. The chorus had prepared us for this idea in the parodos with their distinction between great and small men (154–61); and Odysseus in his famous words to Athene had reduced everyone who lives to phantoms or insubstantial shadows (125–6). When we come to hear Menelaus and Agamemnon themselves, as they attempt to argue against the burial of Ajax, we see the truth of this. Teucer sums up Menelaus as a 'foolish man speaking petty words' (1162 *ἀνδρὸς ματαίου φλαῦρ' ἔπη μυθουμένου*). Agamemnon cuts an equally contemptible figure. What contrasts them most with Ajax is that they are represented not as being, like Ajax, the doers of great and effective deeds, but as all words, insulting and ineffective words. They also contrast with Ajax in the way they speak: Ajax does not enjoy stichomythia (apart from, briefly, 529–45), preferring monologues in old-fashioned epic style, whereas Menelaus (1120–41) and Agamemnon (1346–69) like the cut and thrust of fifth-century debate. And they are shamed losers: they lose their arguments vetoing Ajax's burial, and slink away dishonoured, because they have achieved nothing, like one of Pindar's defeated athletes (*Ol.* 8.68–9, *Pyth.* 8.81–7). Whereas Ajax lives on through the memory of his great deeds and his son, Menelaus and Agamemnon leave the stage ignominiously and leave nothing behind. The breath of life, represented by the words breathed out by Menelaus and Agamemnon, is shown by the end of the play to be a feeble and inglorious substitute for deeds of strength.

The idea that death can be preferable to life that we find in the *Ajax* is not unique to that play of Sophocles. Antigone says she will bury Polynices and 'It will be a glory for me to die doing this' (72). By contrast, at the end of the play Creon lives on but is as good as dead with no glory to his credit: 'When men lose their joys of life, I do not count such a person as being alive, but I reckon him to be a living corpse (*ἔμψυχον νεκρόν*)', says the messenger (1165–7). Creon has nothing at the end of the play except a miserable life. By contrast, Antigone looks forward to meeting her family in Hades (897–9): she honoured her family, and because of that has a future beyond the grave. Philoctetes, and Heracles in the *Trachiniae*, show how life with physical pain, not just life with mental pain, can be unliveable. For the dying Heracles death is better than an ignoble, tormented life (1173), and when his end comes and Hyllus asks how Heracles can possibly ask him to set fire to his pyre and kill him, Heracles cries out, 'I am not asking you this, but I call upon you that I might have you as a healer and the only cure of my woes' (1208–9). For Philoctetes peace of mind comes only when he is asleep, 'controlling neither hand nor foot nor anything, but like someone lying dead in Hades' (860–1). And above all Oedipus. When he is alive and has come to see the truth, normal life is unliveable. Only in death will he regain his status. He will not die in the normal sense. The end for Oedipus is something special: 'When I am no longer, then I am a man' (*OC* 393 ὅτ' οὐκέτ' εἰμί, τηνικαῦτ' ἄρ' εἴμ' ἀνήρ). When the end does come for Oedipus, he is θαυμαστός (1665), someone who lives on as an object of awe. We are back to Ajax. As 'the arrogant Theban' (West (1980), 44) Pindar says, 'If someone has been supremely successful . . . he journeys to an end that is better than the blackness of death' (*Pyth.* 11.55–7 . . . μέλανος . . . ἐσχατίαν καλλίονα θανάτου).[1]

[1] I would like to take this opportunity to thank Martin for having supervised my PhD and for his good advice over many years.

17

Problems in the Prologue and Parodos of *Bacchae*

Scott Scullion

It is a great pleasure to be able to offer these notes to Martin West, to whom I am indebted personally for his encouragement and friendship, and in common with all other Hellenists for the fabulous learning and constant stimulus of his work. I hope that one or other of the discussions that follow may seem to him not unworthy—and regret that under the circumstances I could not ask him in advance where the others go astray.[1]

I give the text of Diggle's Oxford Classical Text as lemmata, with apparatus of my own.

PROLOGUE: VERSES 13–25

Δι. *λιπὼν δὲ Λυδῶν τοὺς πολυχρύσους γύας*
Φρυγῶν τε, Περσῶν ἡλιοβλήτους πλάκας
Βάκτριά τε τείχη τήν τε δύσχιμον χθόνα
Μήδων ἐπελθὼν Ἀραβίαν τ' εὐδαίμονα
Ἀσίαν τε πᾶσαν ἣ παρ' ἁλμυρὰν ἅλα
κεῖται μιγάσιν Ἕλλησι βαρβάροις θ' ὁμοῦ
πλήρεις ἔχουσα καλλιπυργώτους πόλεις,
ἐς τήνδε πρώτην ἦλθον Ἑλλήνων πόλιν,

[1] I am very grateful to the editors for a number of helpful suggestions.

τἀκεῖ χορεύσας καὶ καταστήσας ἐμὰς
τελετάς, ἵν' εἴην ἐμφανὴς δαίμων βροτοῖς.
πρώτας δὲ Θήβας τάσδε γῆς Ἑλληνίδος
ἀνωλόλυξα, νεβρίδ' ἐξάψας χροὸς
θύρσον τε δοὺς ἐς χεῖρα, κίσσινον βέλος·

16 ἐπελθὼν LP, Strabo 1.2.20: ἐπῆλθον Strabo 15.1.7 17–26 hoc ordine habet P.Berol. 21235 20 damn. Bernhardy, Bock: post 22 trai. Pierson πρώτην *Chr. Pat.* 1595 cod. A, coni. Cobet: πρῶτον LP, *Chr. Pat.* cod. C πόλιν LP: χθόνα *Chr. Pat.*, coni. Schenkl 21 τἀκεῖ Wilamowitz: κἀκεῖ LP: [. .]κ̣ει P.Berol. 21235 23 τάσδε P.Berol. 21235, coni. Pierson: τῆσδε LP

The intense controversy that raged over this passage until recently has abated; Kovacs's text in his Loeb edition differs from Diggle's only in verse 20, where he accepts πρῶτον from LP and χθόνα from *Christus Patiens.* I shall try to stir a little flame from the ashes of the controversy, arguing for four alterations in Diggle's text.

Let us begin with what was long felt to be the intractable problem of verses 20–2. The difficulties of these lines arise from their connection both with what precedes and with what follows. Firstly, verses 21–2 specify what Dionysus did while in Asia, his route round which was laid out in 13–19, after 20 has gone on to mention his arrival in Greece, which is rather awkward.[2] Secondly, though one might claim truly enough with Diggle (1994*a*), 452 n. 50 that 20 'refers to Dionysus' arrival' whereas 23 'specifies what he did on his arrival', it is nevertheless the case that 23–4 as expressed not only imply the content of 20—Dionysus must have arrived in Thebes in order to make it cry the *ololuge*—but repeat the notion of priority (πρώτην . . . πρώτας), and that 20 is therefore, despite Diggle's fine distinction,

[2] Scholars have sometimes defended the manuscript text. Gottfried Hermann (1823), 10 translated 'peragratis multis Asiae regionibus, nunc primum ad hanc Graecorum urbem accessi, illic quoque [κἀκεῖ] sacris meis introductis', which Oranje (1984), 34–5 n. 85 interprets, in Hermann's intended sense, thus: 'Only after I had left Lydia and Phrygia, and had visited Persia . . . and Asia, did I come on here to Greece (i.e. in order to dance and establish my rites), after I had danced there too, and established my rites there, so that (by doing so) I might be manifest to mankind as a god.' See also Rijksbaron (1991), 9–10. The difficulties are that 'after I had danced there *too*' would be expressed as though 'i.e. in order to dance and establish my rites' were explicit in what precedes, and that even understood thus the sentence is still a pointlessly awkward way of expressing what might have been put simply and clearly. Hence this line of defence has remained very much a minority view. My own suggestion (below) involves taking κἀκεῖ in a sense similar to Hermann's.

tautologous of 23–4. Moreover, 20 and 23 are very similar verbally as well as in sense, and 'what Dionysus did' is not specified until 24, so that the effect of pointless and inelegant repetition is pronounced. To solve the first problem, Pierson suggested transposing 20 after 21–2, and this was still accepted by Dodds (1960), 66 on 20–2 and by Kopff (1982) in his text. But the juxtaposition of 20 and 23 produced by the transposition exacerbates the second problem by bringing the tautologous lines into immediate proximity. Conscious of this, both Dodds and Kopff also replace *πόλιν* in 20 with *χθόνα*, which appears in *Christus Patiens* 1595 and was conjectured by Schenkl, and retain LP *πρῶτον*. This produces a narrowing focus from 'first came to Greek soil' to 'first city in the Greek land', and so Dodds (on 20–2) claims that with *χθόνα* 'the tautology vanishes'. But even with this change 20 says nothing that is not implied by 23–4, and the effect of plodding repetition is still heightened by the transposition of 20 before 23. Pierson's transposition has now gone out of favour, partly because of the evidence of P.Berol. 21235 of the first century BC or first AD, published by Brashear (1975), which contains 17–26 in the same order as in the manuscripts. The evidence of the papyrus, unknown to Dodds, was known to Kopff, but no subsequent editor has been tempted to maintain Pierson's transposition in the face of it (cf. Diggle (1994*a*), 451–2). The counter-evidence of the papyrus is not of course decisive (see below, n. 8), but in combination with the other objection it reduces the appeal of the transposition to the vanishing point. Whether or not verse 20 is transposed, the amelioration of the tautology and verbal repetition that is effected by retaining *πρῶτον* and by replacing *πόλιν* with *χθόνα* is very slight, and the latter is moreover justified on illusory grounds. Recent scholars (contrast Dodds (1960), 66 n. 1) have failed to take into consideration the context of the adaptation of the line in *Christus Patiens*. The author employs *Ba.* 13–20 when his narrator addresses Christ and says that, having passed over (*παρελθὼν* in *Chr. Pat.* 1590 for *ἐπελθὼν* in *Ba.* 16) a series of other places, *ἐς τήνδε πρῶτον ἦλθες Ἑβραίων χθόνα* (*Chr. Pat.* 1595). Seven lines later the narrator speaks of the women who have accompanied him from the Galilee (*Ἀλλ' ὦ λιποῦσαι Γαλιλαίας χωρίον, | ἐμὸς θίασος*, *Chr. Pat.* 1602–3), Christ's homeland in the north, to the tomb in Jerusalem, and such a narrator must speak of Christ as appearing at first in the *land* of the

Hebrews, that is in Bethlehem and the Galilee, not in the *city* of the Hebrews, Jerusalem. There is no justification for assuming that the author of *Christus Patiens* had before him a manuscript of *Bacchae* which just happened, in contrast to the tradition as we know it, to contain as text or variant precisely the word χθόνα which he required instead of πόλιν in his own context. Scholars who read χθόνα ought to be clear that they are adopting Schenkl's conjecture rather than preferring a variant in the tradition, and most of us will feel that the claim of χθόνα, as a conjectural emendation, is very weak.

Wilamowitz thought to address the first problem differently, by leaving 20 where it is in all our witnesses but emending κἀκεῖ in 21 to τἀκεῖ. This has been widely accepted, as by Diggle and Kovacs, but cannot, I think, be right. The τά in this locution always has the sense of 'matters/events/affairs' (LSJ s.v. ἐκεῖ translate τἀκεῖ 'What is *or* happens there, events there'), as in *Ba.* 49, τἀνθένδε θέμενος εὖ, 'having settled matters here well'. This is true of all of the *comparanda* offered by Diggle (1994*a*), 451 n. 47 in commendation of Wilamowitz's emendation:

Andr. 737:	ὅταν δὲ τἀκεῖ θῶ κατὰ γνώμην ἐμήν.
IT 540–2:	Ορ. τίς εἶ ποτ'; ὡς εὖ πυνθάνῃ τἀφ' Ἑλλάδος.
	Ιφ. ἐκεῖθέν εἰμι· παῖς ἔτ' οὖσ' ἀπωλόμην.
	Ορ. ὀρθῶς ποθεῖς ἄρ' εἰδέναι τἀκεῖ, γύναι.
Ion 645:	κρείσσω νομίζω τἀνθάδ' ἢ τἀκεῖ, πάτερ.
IA 672:	σπεῦδ' ἐκ Φρυγῶν μοι, θέμενος εὖ τἀκεῖ, πάτερ.
fr. 578.5 *TrGF*:	τἀκεῖ κατ' οἴκους πάντ' ἐπίστασθαι καλῶς

It is also true of other instances in Euripides of τά used in this way, for example *Ba.* 669 φράσω τὰ κεῖθεν, *Med.* 1117 καραδοκῶ τἀκεῖθεν οἷ προβήσεται, *Hec.* 1291–2 εὖ δὲ τἀν δόμοις | ἔχοντ' ἴδοιμεν, *El.* 76 ἡδὺ τἄνδον εὑρίσκειν καλῶς, *El.* 422 τἄνδον ἐξάρτυε, *IT* 726 παρευτρεπίζετε | τἄνδον μολόντες τοῖς ἐφεστῶσι σφαγῇ, *Heracl.* 279 καραδοκῶν τἀνθένδε, *Heracl.* 436–7 αἰνέσαι δ' ἔχω | καὶ τἀνθάδ', *Her.* 617 ἵν' ἐλθὼν τἀνθάδ' εἰδείην πάρος, *Or.* [1368], *IA* 740 ἐλθὼν δὲ τἄξω πρᾶσσε, τἀν δόμοις δ' ἐγώ (cf. Soph. *El.* 1424–5, reading Ηλ. Ὀρέστα, πῶς κυρεῖτε; Ορ. τἀν δόμοισι μὲν | καλῶς). 'Having set matters there a-dancing and established my rites' is the only legitimate way to understand the phrase as emended by Wilamowitz, and that is clearly unacceptable sense. Kovacs (2002*b*), 15 translates 'having set everything in Asia a-dancing', which camouflages the strange Greek in an English idiom to which it does not correspond. Wilamowitz himself offered no translation or justification of his original suggestion ((1879), 179 = (1935–72), iv. 15), and the version in his later translation of the play skirts the problem: 'Nun bin ich in der ersten Stadt von Hellas, | der Osten ist schon meinem Dienst gewonnen'[3] (Wilamowitz (1923), 162). I suspect that simple 'there' or 'over there' is the sense he meant τἀκεῖ to have. There is a small group of idiomatic phrases composed of τά and a directional adverb (τἀνθένδε, 'on this side', *Ba.* 938, *Or.* 1278; τἀκεῖθεν, 'on that side', *Med.* 1004; τἀντεῦθεν, 'henceforth', *El.* 1247; τἄνδον, 'inwardly', *Or.* 1514) which have been 'lexicalized', that is, have become words independent of their original composition and sense ('things on this side', and so on), but τἀκεῖ does not number among these, in Euripides or elsewhere. Granting the sense Wilamowitz must have intended, 'having danced and established my rites (over) there'—which is the only sense that would work—involves attributing to τἀκεῖ a lexicalized status and meaning that is not attested.

The passage needs reconsideration. Verse 20 creates both the problems we have identified: it interrupts the flow of description of what happened in Asia, and is both verbally similar to and tautologous of 23–4. There are two further objections that can be made to the verse. We have observed its inelegant similarity in sense and expression to 23–4, but we can make the further objection that precisely on that ground it undercuts what ought to be the climactic effect of 23–4. Πρώτας δὲ Θήβας κτλ. is surely intended as a sharp refocusing—not weakened by an anticipatory narrowing of focus—on Greece itself, and on Thebes in particular, after the lengthy catalogue of barbarian and Helleno-barbarian lands. A second objection has to do with the notional itinerary with which Euripides was operating. Thebes may well be the first city in Greece that Dionysus has set to celebrate maenadic rites (23–5), but it can hardly be the first place in Greece that he has come to (20). The god himself could simply make an epiphany in Thebes, but that cannot be true of his flesh-and-blood Lydian maenads, who say 'I rush dancing from the land of Asia'

[3] 'Now I am in the first city of Greece; the East is already won to my worship.'

(64–5) and speak of themselves as 'escorting Bromius down (κατάγουσαι) from the mountains of Phrygia into the broad streets of Greece' (83–7), from which it is plain enough that Euripides was thinking of a land journey by the route from Asia Minor through Thrace, Macedon, and Thessaly. So similarly at 565–75 the chorus speak of Dionysus on his way to Pieria as leading his bacchants across the Axius and Lydias rivers in Macedon. This may seem a narrowly logical objection to verse 20, but the other passages show that Euripides had a land route to Thebes in mind, and it is therefore odd that he should write a line inconsistent with this. In the absence of verse 20 the inconsistency and the whole question of the route would simply not arise, as they need not and would better not in this context. By contrast, the statement 'But Thebes first in Greece have I set to ecstatic cries' (23–4) is not subject to this objection.

From every point of view, then, verse 20 is the heart of the problem, and it is tempting to revive the forgotten suggestions of Bernhardy and Bock and delete it.[4] That would leave 13–22 without a main verb, but Strabo, who at 1.2.20 quotes 13–16 with ἐπελθών in 16, quotes 13–17 at 15.1.7 with ἐπῆλθον, and this may well reflect a variation in the ancient textual tradition of *Bacchae*—though one would not wish to put very much weight on this evidence as such.

If we delete 20 and accept Strabo's ἐπῆλθον in 16 we are left with a longish catalogue of places governed by a single main verb in the middle with preliminary and pendent participles. For similarly structured sentences one must look in the main to Euripidean lyric rather than iambic, but there are two strong justifications for doing so. Our passage is of the type 'catalogue of a journey', and it just so happens that such passages occur elsewhere in Euripides only in lyric, though

[4] Bernhardy (1857) proposed the deletion of 20 as part of a general rearrangement of the passage, with 23 transposed after 25 and a lacuna marked after 23. The proposal closest to that advocated here is that of Bock (1871), who deleted 20 and accepted Kirchhoff's ἐδείχθην for ἵν' εἴην in 22. ἐδείχθην (based on *Christus Patiens* 1564) is in some ways an attractive conjecture (cf. *Ba.* 47, 50; Ar. *Thesm.* 629), but the effect of finality it would produce would lessen the impact of 23. By contrast, the final clause following upon the participles of 21 reinforces the 'preamble' quality of 13–22 and produces anticipation of the main verb of the next sentence (ἀνωλόλυξα), i.e. of the linguistic and thematic culmination of the god's first action in Greece. I know of Bernhardy's and Bock's conjectures only from the appendix 'Adnotationis Criticae Supplementum' in Kopff (1982).

there is a good iambic parallel in the 'catalogue of things seen' at *Suppl.* 653–63. The second reason is more subtle. What Dionysus says in the prologue, from its opening Ἥκω Διὸς παῖς τήνδε Θηβαίαν χθόνα onward, corresponds to the catalogues of places where the god might be, and the anticipation of epiphany, which are regular features of Greek hymns.[5] In *Bacchae* Dionysus appears, on his own angry initiative, to the Thebans who have signally failed to invoke him, and describes his own advent in hieratic language, which reaches its preliminary culmination in the phrase ἵν' εἴην ἐμφανὴς δαίμων βροτοῖς (22). The kind of hymnic invocation the prologue speech alludes to often involves a single main verb extended by participles.[6] Catalogues of places visited or things seen in non-hymnic contexts often also employ a single verb, but there is a clear and ironic allusion here to divine epiphany as invoked in hymns. The syntactical style in question, with a single main verb governing an extensive itinerary (*vel sim.*), occurs in iambics at *Suppl.* 653–63 (main verb ὁρῶ at the very beginning) and in a number of Euripidean lyrics: (verb at or near beginning) *IT* 218–28, 422–38, *Phoen.* 202–13; (verb in middle) *Tro.* 122–37, *IT* 126–36. The last is a good example of both the syntactical structure and the hieratic tone with which Euripides seems to be eliciting associations in our passage:

> ὦ παῖ τᾶς Λατοῦς,
> Δίκτυνν' οὐρεία,
> πρὸς σὰν αὐλάν, εὐστύλων
> ναῶν χρυσήρεις θριγκούς,
> ὁσίας ὅσιον πόδα παρθένιον
> κληδούχου δούλα πέμπω,
> Ἑλλάδος εὐίππου πύργους
> καὶ τείχη χόρτων τ' εὐδένδρων
> ἐξαλλάξασ' Εὐρώπαν,
> πατρῴων οἴκων ἕδρας.

More needs to be said about the syntax of 13–22 as emended in the way I am advocating. In the first line, ἥκω has its usual force 'I have arrived', and the aorist ἐπῆλθον in 16, like ἥκω and like the aorist

[5] The classic account is Norden (1913), 143–77.
[6] See Norden (1913), 166–8, 'Der Partizipialstil der Prädikation'.

ἀνωλόλυξα that follows in 24, would be perfective in sense ('I have traversed' . . . 'I have caused to cry ecstatically'), as the aorist of ἔρχομαι often is in tragedy, the perfect being relatively rare. The pendent aorist participles then mean 'having danced and established my rites', antecedent to the present-perfective sense of ἐπῆλθον just as, if verse 20 is retained, they are antecedent to ἦλθον: Seaford (1996), 69 translates 'I come to this city first of the Greeks, after having there (in Asia) set them dancing and established my initiations', and likewise Wilamowitz (quoted above) and Kovacs (2002*b*), 15 ('I have now for the first time returned to Greece, having set everything in Asia a-dancing'). κἀκεῖ will mean 'even there', as at *Alc.* 744 and *Heracl.* 594. In both these cases κἀκεῖ refers to the underworld, which is a special sense of ἐκεῖ, but there is no reason why an ἐκεῖ that does not refer to the underworld should not likewise be combined with καί in the sense 'even' (which Euripides uses also e.g. at *Alc.* 356 and *Ion* 1608[7]). Dionysus has established his ecstatic rites and manifested his divinity *even* in barbarian and Helleno-barbarian lands, with the implication that his doing so among his fellow Greeks is natural and inevitable. This sets up the culminating effect of the specification of Thebes against a general Greek background in 23. The long sentence we get as a result is parallel in structure and in the tense of main verb and participles to what follows in 23–5: 'I have traversed various places in Asia, having danced and established my rites even there, but Thebes is the first place in Greece I have made to cry ecstatically, having put the fawnskin on them and given them a thyrsus.' That is good syntax and sense, and the passage is better without verse 20.

One is cautious about secluding a verse attested in a relatively early

[7] For καί . . . καί . . . where the first is adverbial and the second copulative a good parallel to our passage is Xen. *Hell.* 4.8.5 ἐννοουμένους ὅτι καὶ ἐν τῇ Ἀσίᾳ, ἡ ἐξ ἀρχῆς βασιλέως ἐστί, καὶ Τμῆνος, οὐ μεγάλη πόλις, καὶ Αἰγαί εἰσι καὶ ἄλλα γε χωρία ἃ δύνανται οἰκεῖν οὐχ ὑπήκοοι ὄντες βασιλέως with Denniston (1954), 293 (II.A.1); cf. also *Il.* 13.636–7 with Denniston (1954), 323–4. As Dover says in his addenda to Denniston (1954), 585 on p. 324, 'καί . . . καί couple disparate ideas' (which is a firm ground for accepting Toup's conjecture at Aesch. *Ag.* 677), and it is therefore unnatural to take them as corresponsive in *Ba.* 21. Further examples of καί 'even' in Allen and Italie (1954), 309 s.v. II. On *Ion* 1608, where καί is followed by δέ, see Denniston (1954), 200, who dissociates the two in this and five other tragic passages, taking καί as 'even' or 'also' and δέ as the connective, and allows that this analysis may be correct in other cases of the combination.

papyrus, but of course interpolation begins early. Thus, for example, Diggle, Mastronarde (1994), and Kovacs (2002*a*) agree in secluding *Phoen.* 11, 51, and 1017–18, which are attested in papyri—11 in two papyri, indeed, and 51 in three—that are not significantly later in date than P.Berol. 21235.[8] The interpolation of 20 can readily be explained. The participles χορεύσας and καταστήσας in 21 are antecedent to ἐπῆλθον in the present-perfective sense or, perhaps, 'coincident' with ἐπῆλθον ('I have traversed Asia and danced and established my rites even there'), but a reader failing to register either usage would take them as antecedent to ἐπῆλθον in past sense, that is as indicating that dancing and establishment preceded traversal, and so find them strange. Hence some enterprising person (before the first century BC or first AD, the date of P.Berol. 21235) composed a line, doubtless inspired by verse 23, containing an event to which χορεύσας and καταστήσας could be antecedent. The interpolation of 20 would require and so account for the alteration of ἐπῆλθον to ἐπελθών in 16.

In verse 23 P.Berol. 21235 has τάσδε rather than τῆσδε of the medieval manuscripts; Pierson had conjectured τάσδε, and this is now regarded as certainly correct. Kassel (1976), 35 = (1991), 187–8, commended by Diggle (1994*a*), 452, favours τάσδε, noting (with reference to Barrett (1964), 157 on *Hipp.* 12) that in prologues a deictic pronoun will go with the place name identifying the precise setting of the play, and claiming in addition that a deictic should not be used of the wider area: 'In der Tat erwartet man, zumal im Prolog, das Pronomen nicht bei dem geographischen Begriff, der den weiteren Rahmen bezeichnet, sondern bei dem Ortsnamen, der den Schauplatz des Dramas angibt.'[9] Against this claim however are the following passages:

Andr. 16–17: Φθίας δὲ τῆσδε καὶ πόλεως Φαρσαλίας
σύγχορτα ναίω πέδια

[8] *Phoen.* 11, attested in P.Oxy. 3321 (2nd–3rd c. AD) and P.Oxy. 3322 (1st–2nd c. AD); 51, attested in the same two papyri and in P.Oxy. 3712 (2nd c. AD); and 1017–18, attested in P.Oxy. 224 (2nd–3rd c. AD.). Diggle and Mastronarde agree, Kovacs dissenting, in damning also 558, attested in P.Oxy. 3153 (2nd–3rd c. AD).

[9] 'Indeed one expects the pronoun, especially in the prologue, not with the geographical term that indicates the wider setting but with the place name that gives the scene of the drama.'

Here it is the plains *neighbouring* Phthia and Pharsalia that are the most specific location, and since, as M. A. Lloyd (1994), 9 notes, 'Phthia is apparently a region, not a *polis*, . . . Pharsalus, on the other hand, is a *polis*', the deictic occurs here with the least specific of three locations (cf. Eur. *Antiope* fr. 179 *TrGF*).

Hec. 8–9: (Polydorus says he was sent to the house of Polymestor:)
ὃς τήνδ' ἀρίστην Χερσονησίαν πλάκα
σπείρει

33–6: ὅσονπερ ἐν γῇ τῇδε Χερσονησίᾳ
μήτηρ ἐμὴ δύστηνος ἐκ Τροίας πάρα.
πάντες δ' Ἀχαιοὶ ναῦς ἔχοντες ἥσυχοι
θάσσουσ' ἐπ' ἀκταῖς τῆσδε Θρῃκίας χθονός.

The Chersonese is the more specific location, and twice has a deictic, but the less specific 'this land of Thrace' also has one.

Heracl. 34–5: πεδία γὰρ τῆσδε χθονὸς
δισσοὺς κατοικεῖν Θησέως παῖδας λόγος

'This land' must here mean Athens/Attica, as both recent editors conclude (Wilkins (1993), 53 on 34–7 *sub fin.*, Allan (2001), 135 on 34–5; cf. verse 38 and see Wilkins's note), but the specific location of the play is Marathon (verse 32), which does not itself have a deictic.

One might also cite *Hel.* 1–4, where 'the Nile here' (Νείλου μὲν αἵδε καλλιπάρθενοι ῥοαί) is in the context a much more specific location than 'this land' (Πρωτεὺς δ' ὅτ' ἔζη τῆσδε γῆς τύραννος ἦν). One should also bear in mind such a contrast of very specific and more general location, each accompanied by a deictic, as *Suppl.* 29–31:

ἐκ δόμων ἐλθοῦσ' ἐμῶν
πρὸς τόνδε σηκόν, ἔνθα πρῶτα φαίνεται
φρίξας ὑπὲρ γῆς τῆσδε κάρπιμος στάχυς.

The general principle that deictics in prologues identify the setting is sound, but these passages show that Kassel's claim that deictics are not also used of the more general area cannot hold. In *Bacchae*, a 'locating' deictic has already established the setting as Thebes in the first verse of the play. A single deictic serves to set the scene in *Alc.* (8), *Med.* (10), and *Or.* (46), and the location of the myth of

Pentheus was in any case well known to the audience. In the absence of any compelling criterion such as Kassel suggested, we are thrown back on the merits of the individual case.

We observe first that in the examples I have given of deictics used in prologues of general as well as specific locations the phrases τῆσδε χθονός and τῆσδε γῆς figure very prominently, and that what the medieval manuscripts offer in our passage is πρώτας δὲ Θήβας τῆσδε γῆς Ἑλληνίδος. Line endings of the form τῆσδε – × – χθονός or τῆσδ' ⏑ – × – χθονός (twice τῆσδε ⏑⏑ × – χθονός with proper names, *Hec.* 771 and *Pho.* 76) are very common in Euripidean iambics (32 instances[10]), functioning practically as a formula, and as with epic formulae there is a metrical variant for managing words of the shape ⏑ – ⏑ – that begin with consonants and those shaped – – ⏑ – : *Med.* 702 and 916 τῆσδε γῆς Κορινθίας, *Hipp.* 12 τῆσδε γῆς Τροζηνίας. The χθών formula appears also in the accusative (*Med.* 604 τήνδε φευξ-οῦμαι χθόνα, *Hipp.* 29, and often elsewhere), and for this too there is a γῆ variant: *Med.* 10 τήνδε γῆν Κορινθίαν, *Hipp.* 29 τήνδε γῆν Τρο-ζηνίαν. The obvious way to say 'of this land of Greece here' in this position in the line is τῆσδε γῆς Ἑλληνίδος, and all these facts indicate that the reading τῆσδε should not lightly be given up, perhaps indeed that there is at least a slight presumption in favour of the formulaic form of words.

There is on the other hand *Ba.* 1247 (Cadmus to Agave) ἐπὶ δαῖτα Θήβας τάσδε κἀμὲ παρακαλεῖς, where we find the papyrus reading in the same metrical position in the line (compare also *Ba.* 450, *Her.* 4, 271). There is also the consideration that, however widespread the occurrence of τῆσδε – × – χθονός or τῆσδε γῆς × – ⏑ – at line end, still the only ready way of adding the sense 'in Greece' to a line beginning πρώτας δὲ Θήβας τάσδε is with the phrase γῆς Ἑλληνίδος (χθών and γῆ very often appearing without the article in such locutions).

The choice is between repeating the deictic with Θήβας (as in verse 1) to emphasize the specific location, and perhaps to mark the sharp focus on Thebes within Greece, and placing a deictic with γῆς Ἑλλη-νίδος to mark the significant transition in the narration from barbarian and Helleno-barbarian lands to Greece itself. Verdenius (1980), 6,

[10] *Cycl.* 468, *Alc.* 477, 507, *Med.* 71, 353, 1237, 1357, *Heracl.* 206, 397, 515, *Hipp.* 12, *Hec.* 36, 771, *Her.* 138, *Tro.* 300, 457, *IT* 1080, 1422, *Ion* 1345, *Hel.* 538, [780], *Phoen.* 76, 476, 485, 591, 635, 972, 998, 1244, 1630, *Ba.* 215, 660, 1043.

defending the medieval manuscript reading, observes that '*τῆσδε* marks the contrast between *ἐκεῖ* (21) and *γῆς Ἑλληνίδος*', and that seems both the most obvious—and a thematically pointed—contrast and one which scarcely registers without the deictic. Compare perhaps *Heracl.* 303–6 *ἡμεῖς γὰρ κακῶν* | *ἐς τοὔσχατον πέσοντες ηὕρομεν φίλους* | *καὶ ξυγγενεῖς τούσδ᾽, οἳ τοσῆσδ᾽ οἰκουμένης* | *Ἑλληνίδος γῆς τῶνδε προύστησαν μόνοι*. The elaborate deictic phrase here stresses the notion 'in the whole of Greece' very emphatically, but keeping the simple deictic with *γῆς Ἑλληνίδος* brings out the contrast: 'having established my rites even there. Here in Greece, it is Thebes first of all that I have caused to cry.' To my mind, the deictic with *Θήβας* seems by contrast rather fussy, locationally superfluous and thematically needless. Choice is difficult, but given these considerations of sense and (mindful of the cautions in the previous paragraph) the formulaic quality of the phrase *τῆσδε γῆς Ἑλληνίδος* I am inclined to plump for the reading of the medieval manuscript, which should at any rate not be despised.

Thus I would print verses 13–25 as follows:

λιπὼν δὲ Λυδῶν τοὺς πολυχρύσους γύας
Φρυγῶν τε, Περσῶν ἡλιοβλήτους πλάκας
Βάκτριά τε τείχη τήν τε δύσχιμον χθόνα
Μήδων ἐπῆλθον Ἀραβίαν τ᾽ εὐδαίμονα
Ἀσίαν τε πᾶσαν ἣ παρ᾽ ἁλμυρὰν ἅλα
κεῖται μιγάσιν Ἕλλησι βαρβάροις θ᾽ ὁμοῦ
πλήρεις ἔχουσα καλλιπυργώτους πόλεις,
[ἐς τήνδε πρῶτον ἦλθον Ἑλλήνων πόλιν,]
κἀκεῖ χορεύσας καὶ καταστήσας ἐμὰς
τελετάς, ἵν᾽ εἴην ἐμφανὴς δαίμων βροτοῖς.
πρώτας δὲ Θήβας τῆσδε γῆς Ἑλληνίδος
ἀνωλόλυξα, νεβρίδ᾽ ἐξάψας χροὸς
θύρσον τε δοὺς ἐς χεῖρα, κίσσινον βέλος·

PARODOS: VERSES 68–70

τίς ὁδῷ, τίς ὁδῷ; τίς
μελάθροις; ἔκτοπος ἔστω,
στόμα τ᾽ εὔφημον ἅπας ἐξοσιούσθω·

The difficulty in this vexed passage, the text of which is not in doubt, is deciding quite what these apparently straightforward words mean. ἔκτοπος and ἐκτόπιος normally mean 'out of the way', as at Soph. *OT* 1340 ἀπάγετ' ἐκτόπιον ὅτι τάχιστά με, *Trach.* 32 ἄρουραν ἔκτοπον, *OC* 119 ποῦ κυρεῖ ἐκτόπιος συθείς . . .; Hence commentators have often taken our passage as an example of the formulaic request by those performing ritual that the crowd give way for the performers of the rite and observe 'sacred silence'. Good parallels for the giving way are Carm. Pop. 851a *PMG* ἀνάγετ', εὐρυχωρίαν | τῷ θεῷ ποιεῖτε· | θέλει γὰρ ὁ θεὸς . . . | διὰ μέσου βαδίζειν (compare *Ran.* 354–71); for the 'sacred silence' *IT* 123–5 εὐφαμεῖτ' ὦ | πόντου δισσὰς συγχωρούσας | πέτρας ἀξείνου ναίοντες and also Aesch. *Eum.* 1035, Ar. *Ach.* 237–8, *Eq.* 1316; and for the combination of both Ar. *Ach.* 238–40 σῖγα πᾶς. ἠκούσατ', ἄνδρες, ἆρα τῆς εὐφημίας; | . . . ἀλλὰ δεῦρο πᾶς | ἐκποδών· θύσων γὰρ ἁνήρ, ὡς ἔοικ', ἐξέρχεται. Diggle (1967), 261 = (1994*a*), 3 translates the traditional interpretation thus: 'Who is in the road? Who is in the road? Who is in the house? Let him make way; and let every man hush his lips to holy silence.' This, he points out, cannot be right:

> That bystanders should be requested to make way or depart is in itself not unreasonable; that a man who is inside his house should make way or depart is a request at which common sense stands aghast. Evasiveness will not content us: 'Those who are in the street (ὁδῶι) are to make way for the procession (ἔκτοπος ἔστω); *all*, including those indoors (μελάθροις), are to "hush their tongues to reverence"' (Dodds). Which is to say: ἔκτοπος ἔστω refers back only to the question τίς ὁδῶι;, while the persons alluded to in the question τίς μελάθροις; sit uncomfortably in between, waiting until στόμα . . . ἐξοσιούσθω reveals the reason for their invocation.
>
> (Diggle (1994*a*) 3–4)

Diggle's own conclusion is that ἔκτοπος ἔστω refers to τίς μελάθροις; and that these words mean 'Who is in the house? Let him be outside.'[11] To justify this sense of ἔκτοπος he points to *Pha.* fr. 773.68–9 *TrGF* = 111–12 Diggle, where a herald summons the people to hear the king's speech: ἐκτόπιοί τε δόμων ἐπαείρετε· ὦ ἴτε λαοί, 'rouse yourselves out of your houses', and to four other passages. There are

[11] As Diggle discovered after the original publication of his note, he had been anticipated by Jeanne Roux; see Diggle (1994*a*), 3 n. 1.

two objections to this, each in my view fatal. The first is that the ablatival genitive lacking in *Bacchae* but present in the *Phaethon* passage (in the latter assisted by the sense of the verb) is necessary to make ἐκτόπιος mean 'out of (the way of) the house', as it is too in all of the parallels Diggle offers: 'S. *O.T.* 193 f. πάτρας ἄπουρον, *O.C.* 233 ἑδράνων . . . ἔκτοπος, E. *I.T.* 80 ἔξεδροι χθονός, *I.A.* 419 δωμάτων ἔκδημος' (Diggle (1970), 118, on 111). Given the rarity of this sense, it would be strained to suggest that in *Bacchae* one could 'supply' such a construction from μελάθροις. The second objection is that on Diggle's interpretation ἔκτοπος ἔστω does not refer to τίς ὁδῶι; This makes the whole phrase intolerably awkward, or in other words invites the decisive criticism, precisely parallel to that Diggle himself makes of Dodds, that the symmetry of the passage is destroyed: 'Who is in the road? Who is in the road? Who is in the house? Let the latter come out of it, and everybody be quiet.' What is the point of mentioning those in the road, twice, if they are merely to be subsumed under ἅπας in a general injunction to silence?

If these are the words Euripides wrote, as no one doubts, it is as incredible that the imperative phrase ἔκτοπος ἔστω should apply to the third τίς and not to the first two (Diggle) as it is that it should apply to the first two and not to the third (Dodds). The solution to this problem lies in the sense of the locative dative, which need not mean 'in'. As S–D ii. 154 rightly observe: 'Der präpositionslose Lokalis hat im ältesten Griechischen in allen Numeri nicht nur die Bedeutung von nhd. "in", sondern auch von nhd. "an, bei, auf" u. a., griech. ἐν und ἐπί, ὑπέρ usw.' At *Od.* 17.530 the suitors sit θύρῃσι . . . ἢ αὐτοῦ κατὰ δώματ', 'at the doors (i.e. in the courtyard) . . . or here in the house'; compare *Od.* 21.35: Odysseus and Iphitus never knew one another τραπέζῃ, 'at the table'; *Il.* 21.389 ἥμενος Οὐλύμπῳ. The same usage is still found in tragedy. At Soph. *OC* 411 Thebans will stand 'at' Oedipus' tomb: σοῖς ὅταν στῶσιν τάφοις (Lloyd-Jones and Wilson (1990), 230–1, mentioning 'the awkwardness of the somewhat vague locative', restate the case for Lloyd-Jones's to my mind very unlikely emendation σοῖς ὅτ' ἀντῶσιν τάφοις). At Eur. *El.* 435–6 a dolphin gambols πρῴραις, 'at the prows'; Denniston (1939), 102, on 435–7 suggests 'for the prows', *dativus commodi*, but in an addition to his note gives a reference to the *OC* parallel; Kovacs in his Loeb edition accepts Willink's emendation of εἱλισσόμενος to <συν>ειλισσόμενος to govern πρῴραις. At *Her.* 906–8, when Athena sends confusion ἐς δόμους, 'into the house', she is μελάθρωι, which must therefore mean not 'in' but 'at' or 'by' the house (see Bond (1981), 304–5, on 906–9). (On this basis we probably ought to accept the manuscript reading at *Ba.* 38, according to which the maenads sit ἀνορόφοις . . . πέτραις, 'on' or 'among' roofless rocks.) The Homeric-Hesiodic usage and these few tragic parallels suffice to establish this sense of the locative dative against the general assumption that in fifth-century texts it must always mean 'in'. Its precise sense in a given case is in fact determined contextually. Here τίς μελάθροις; must mean 'Who is by the palace?' The chorus are fulfilling the god's command to come βασίλεια ἀμφὶ δώματα τάδε (60), that is to the orchestra/acting area in front of the *skene* (whose doorway represents the entrance to the inner courtyard of the palace), just where Pentheus later describes Dionysus appearing, πρὸς οἴκοις τοῖς ἐμοῖς, 'in front of my house' (645). The chorus enter along an *eisodos* towards this location, and as they do so they exhort anyone in their path (notional persons, or perhaps a few silent 'extras') to make way for them, both along the ὁδός by which they are approaching and round the gateway of the palace, where they will perform. They employ locative datives from their own point of view, to be understood in that context: 'Who is on the road? Who is on the road? Who is by the palace? Let him be out of the way, and let everyone sanctify his mouth to holy silence.' The aim is that the rite should be seen and heard clearly, as Dionysus has ordered (61): those standing in the chorus's way should fall back to watch its performance; everyone, including bystanders who are not in the way, should be silent.

PARODOS: VERSES 135–41

I have something new to say only about verses 135–41 (with which I give in the lemma some relevant wider context), but, partly because of the fundamental discussion of both passages by Henrichs (1984), these verses must be considered alongside 114–16 of the parodos:

αὐτίκα γᾶ πᾶσα χορεύσει,
Βρόμιος εὖτ' ἂν ἄγῃ θιάσους
εἰς ὄρος εἰς ὄρος, κτλ.

115 εὖτ' ἂν Elmsley: ὅτ' LP: ὅστις (et ἄγει) Triclinius

(The satyrs received the tympanon . . .)
ἐς δὲ χορεύματα
συνῆψαν τριετηρίδων,
αἷς χαίρει Διόνυσος.

ἡδὺς ἐν ὄρεσσιν ὅταν [ἐπωιδ.
ἐκ θιάσων δρομαίων
πέσῃ πεδόσε, νεβρίδος ἔχων
ἱερὸν ἐνδυτόν, ἀγρεύων
αἷμα τραγοκτόνον, ὠμοφάγον χάριν,
ἱέμενος ἐς ὄρεα Φρύγια Λύδι',
†ὁ δ' ἔξαρχος† Βρόμιος·
εὐοἷ.
ῥεῖ δὲ γάλακτι πέδον, ῥεῖ δ' οἴνῳ,
ῥεῖ δὲ μελισσᾶν νέκταρι.
Συρίας δ' ὡς λιβάνου κα-
  πνὸν ὁ Βακχεὺς ἀνέχων
πυρσώδη φλόγα πεύκας
ἐκ νάρθηκος ἀίσσει
δρόμῳ καὶ χοροῖσιν
πλανάτας ἐρεθίζων
ἰαχαῖς τ' ἀναπάλλων κτλ.

135 ὄρεσιν LP: corr. Elmsley ὅταν LP: ὃς ἂν Gompf, ὅς τ' ἂν iam Hermann
141 ὁ δ' P: ὅδ' L

The reading εὖτ' ἂν in 115 is Elmsley's convincing and now generally accepted emendation of ὅτ', which fails to respond metrically with the first two syllables of μαινόμενοι in verse 130. Triclinius' ὅστις, doubtless his own emendation, must be meant to stand for simple ὅς ('it is Bromius who leads'). In his Oxford Classical Text Murray accepted ὅστις, but translated the verse (in his apparatus ad loc.) *Bacchus fit quicumque ducit thiasos*, 'whoever leads the *thiasoi* becomes Bromius', understanding a reference to a male official who led the maenads in their ritual (as Dionysus *qua* missionary might be regarded as doing in the play) and who was identified during the ritual with the god, a figure later dubbed by Dodds (1940), 170 n. 71 the 'male celebrant'. In his commentary on the play, Dodds (1960), 82–3, on 115 (and already in the first edition of 1944) favoured Elmsley's reading at 115, but he detected the male celebrant and his identification with the god in verse 141, which he took to mean 'the Leader, i.e. the celebrant, is Bromius', and in ὁ Βακχεύς in 145, and in general took the celebrant's existence very much for granted (see Dodds (1960), 82–3 on 115, 86 on 135, 87 on 136, 87 on 141, 87 on 144–50, 88–9 on 151). The 'male celebrant' haunted subsequent scholarship both on the play and on Dionysiac cult until Henrichs (1984) wrote him out of existence, demonstrating that there is no genuine trace of such an official either in *Bacchae* or in our cultic evidence.

Henrichs (1984), 77–80 discusses what text of verse 135 we should accept and who the subject of 135–40 is. His aim is to combat Dodds's view that verse 141 means 'and the ἔξαρχος is, that is becomes, Bromius', and he does so partly by arguing that the subject of 135–40 is Dionysus himself, with ὅταν in 135, rather than a worshipper, with ὃς ἄν. Henrichs appears to have succeeded in convincing everyone that Dionysus is the subject and ὅταν the right text; in his article he reported that Diggle then preferred ὃς ἄν (Henrichs (1984), 91 n. 92), but Diggle would eventually print ὅταν in his text, with a reference to Henrichs's article in the apparatus (1994*b*). Henrichs's elimination of the 'male celebrant' is a milestone in the study of *Bacchae* and of the cult of Dionysus, but one can, without any implication for the central argument of his paper, venture to differ with him over the text and interpretation of *Ba.* 135–40.

Scholars' views on the question of the subject of 135–41 have generally determined which text they prefer in 135. If the subject is to be Dionysus—understood from the end of the preceding antistrophe—then we must have LP's ὅταν. If the subject is to be any worshipper, 'whoever', Gompf's ὃς ἄν, based on Hermann's ὅς τ' ἄν, is required.[12] We ought to reckon with the possibility that there is something seriously wrong with the text, as the difficulty of recognizing known metres in precisely this passage suggests, but if we must choose between ὅταν and ὃς ἄν it seems clear that we should prefer the latter.

There are two considerations that favour ὅταν and Dionysus as subject: ὅταν is the manuscript reading, and the application of ἡδύς

[12] No one has been able to discover a publication by Gompf of his conjecture; see Henrichs (1984), 79 with n. 37.

(135) to a worshipper would be unexpected, whereas it is commonly applied to the god (see Roux (1972), 290 on 135). There is however very little in the difference between the paradosis and the emendation, and though ἡδύς is unexpected it is perfectly comprehensible as a predicate of the worshipper. Sophocles uses ἡδύς of persons in the sense 'welcome' (*OT* 82, *El.* 929, *Phil.* 530, cf. Xen. *Hiero* 4.1), and the basic meaning of the word is that something or someone is 'pleasing' to someone. In the Theocritean version of the Pentheus story we find the verse αὐτὸς δ' εὐαγέοιμι καὶ εὐαγέεσσιν ἅδοιμι, 'may I be pure myself and be pleasing to the pure' (26.30), which is probably sacral language. Our passage may be conceptually similar, ἡδύς corresponding to εὐαγέεσσιν ἅδοιμι and ἡδομένα, applied to the Bacchant at the end of the epode (164–5), to αὐτὸς εὐαγέοιμι. At 64–7 (Ἀσίας ἀπὸ γαίας | ἱερὸν Τμῶλον ἀμείψασα θοάζω | Βρομίῳ πόνον ἡδὺν | κάματόν τ' εὐκάματον, Βάκ- | χιον εὐαζομένα), the πόνος ἡδύς of the Lydian maenad's dancing must be pleasing not only to herself but to the god (as is doubtless implied, and indeed Βρομίῳ is sometimes taken with πόνον ἡδύν). So in verse 135 the worshipper and his or her participation in the rite would be described in pleasing-to-other rather than pleasing-to-self terms, the other or others being the god or the god and other participants in the rite. So far I merely elaborate the suggestion of K. J. Dover accepted by Dodds (1960), 86 n. 2, but we can go a little further. The end of the antistrophe—τριετηρίδων, αἷς χαίρει Διόνυσος—plays a central role in the case for ὅταν, as it is thence that Dionysus is said to be understood as subject of ἡδὺς ἐν ὄρεσσιν ὅταν κτλ. This is very difficult (as I will argue in the next paragraph), but by contrast, if ἡδύς refers to the worshipper, the transition from antistrophe to epode would be natural, and would illuminate the sense in which ἡδύς is used. The beginning of the epode would give an example of the sort of thing Dionysus delights in at the trieteric festivals: 'Pleasing to him (at such festivals, which take place) in the mountains, is the person who . . . '.

Other considerations too favour Gompf's conjecture. There is no expressed subject in the manuscript text, and the view of some scholars that Dionysus is to be understood as subject from the end of the previous strophe is very difficult to accept in the absence of an ἐστί. There were standard methods of grammatically bridging strophes, especially in hymns, one of which Euripides uses at 87–8. This is what Norden (1913), 168–76 called 'der Relativstil der Prädikation', a relative pronoun beginning the new unit: [*βάκχαι*] ... *Διόνυσον κατάγουσαι* | [87] *Φρυγίων ἐξ ὀρέων Ἑλλάδος εἰς εὐρυχόρους ἀγυιάς, τὸν Βρόμιον·* | [*ἀντ. α*, 88] *ὅν ποτ' ἔχουσ' ἐν ὠδίνων λοχίαις κτλ.* It is, then, unnatural to understand Dionysus as the subject of the new sentence at 135, which ought to have its own expressed subject. Accepting this, scholars such as Wilamowitz (1921), 577–80 and Willink (1966), 31 proposed quite drastic transposition and rewriting in order to produce the necessary subject; Wilamowitz wanted to transpose 141 before 135.

A second major obstacle to understanding Dionysus as subject is that the sentence ends with the clause *ὁ δ' ἔξαρχος Βρόμιος* (141). This problem is not solved by taking the *δέ* as continuative (Henrichs (1984), 77 with n. 31) or as explanatory (Dodds (1960), 86, on 135, citing Denniston (1954), 169). If Dionysus is the subject, the sentence 'he is pleasing in the mountain when he does this and that, and the leader is Dionysus' or 'for the leader is Dionysus' is as objectionable as if it ends 'but the leader is Dionysus'. It is presumably recognition of this problem that led Diggle, while accepting Henrichs's argument that Dionysus must be the subject of 135–40, to put cruces round the otherwise unobjectionable words *ὁ δ' ἔξαρχος Βρόμιος* in 141. Reading L's *ὅδ' ἔξαρχος* (Kamerbeek (1953), 192, followed most recently by Kovacs in the Loeb) is no solution either; as Dodds (1960), 86 n. 1 rightly says, 'the deictic pronoun is hardly intelligible in this context'. Verdenius (1981) proposed the articulation *ὁ δ' ἔξαρχος, Βρόμιος*, which he renders 'and he is the leader, Bromius', a suggestion endorsed by Rijksbaron (1991), 19. This is a desperate measure; the sense would just about do, but the Greek cannot mean, and cannot be made by a comma to mean, 'and he is the leader, Bromius that is'. Verdenius (1962), 340 had earlier referred, as does Seaford (1996), 165 on 141, to K–G i. 657–8, who collect examples of the unambiguous subject of successive clauses being specified again by a *pronoun* in the second clause, but that is a quite different phenomenon from, and so no justification for, the use of the *name* here. Not only, then, does it seem impossible, without the aid of an *ἐστί*, to understand Dionysus as subject of 135–40, but to do so is also and independently ruled out by the *δέ*-clause that follows in 141. Each of these objections is very powerful, and it seems impossible to resist the force of the two together.

This passage should be compared with 72–82, a description of a series of ritual activities undertaken by 'anyone' (ὅστις) which culminates in mention of the god whom the worshipper serves, or who is the worshipper's leader (*Διόνυσον θεραπεύει*). Certainly one of the ritual activities described in our passage seems much more appropriate to a worshipper than to the god himself. 'Falling to the ground' (137), whether in delirium or from exhaustion (Henrichs (1984), 78 n. 33 assumes the latter), is surely an activity of the worshipper. Maenads are repeatedly depicted lying on the ground, or falling (for example the delirious maenad on the Derveni krater in the Thessalonike museum, well illustrated in Barr-Sharrar (1982), 15–16), but the god is not. On the contrary, his role is to urge on stragglers in the running and dancing (*Ba.* 147–8, reproduced above) with the exhortation *ὦ ἴτε Βάκχαι* (152–3). Henrichs (1984), 78 n. 33 replies to the objection of Dodds (1960), 87 on 136 that 'gods are not fatigued' by citing *Il.* 14.352–3, where Zeus falls asleep after making love to Hera on Mt Ida, but that is hardly an apt parallel for the notion that Dionysus might himself succumb to the exhaustion that overtakes his maenads. It is a potential objection to making the worshipper the subject that in actual cult it is Dionysus himself rather than the maenads who does the 'raw-eating' (138–9), as Henrichs (1978), 150 has shown. However, as Henrichs (1978), 151 n. 96 also observes, Euripides has the chorus in the parodos of *Cretans* (fr. 472.12 *TrGF*) describe itself as *τὰς ὠμοφάγους δαῖτας τελέσας* in an initiatory cult of Zagreus, whom the poet doubtless equated with Dionysus. This proves, what the bloody sequel in *Bacchae* strongly suggests, that Euripides could conceive his mythical maenads as engaging in *ὠμοφαγία*.

There is, then, abundant reason to prefer Gompf's ὃς ἄν—or another plausible emendation that would make the subject of 135–40 a representative participant in maenadic ritual—to the manuscript reading ὅταν.

18

Tragic Interpolation and Philip II: Pylades' Forgotten Exile and Other Problems in Euripides' *Orestes*

David Kovacs

This paper will argue that several passages in *Orestes* that have hitherto escaped suspicion are spurious, and further that in two of them (and perhaps in a third) there are allusions to fourth-century history, particularly to the Third Sacred War. It will be suggested that for once these interpolations are not anonymous: the chief suspect is the actor Neoptolemus.[1]

Orestes was a popular play in antiquity: τὸ δρᾶμα τῶν ἐπὶ σκηνῆς εὐδοκιμούντων, says the second hypothesis. We know of one revival[2] at the City Dionysia in 340 BC and another in the third century (*TrGF* i. 14–16). The large number of scholia discussing how the play was staged suggest that it was frequently performed. Revival often produces *aggiornamento* as actors or others connected with the production add lines or otherwise alter the play to suit the taste of its

This essay in purifying the text of *Orestes* is offered to Martin West as a small token of my admiration and affection and as an expression of gratitude for the many hours he spent discussing Euripidean textual problems with me during my visits to Oxford.

[1] Throughout I refer by author's name alone (or, in my own case, with first-person pronouns) to the following editions: Chapouthier (1973), Diggle (1994*b*), Kovacs (2002*a*), Schwartz (1887–91), Wecklein (1900), Weil (1879), West (1987), and Willink (1989). I record here my thanks to Elizabeth Meyer, Christopher Collard, and Patrick Finglass for their comments and suggestions.

[2] Not two, as Revermann (1999–2000), 463 n. 54 claims: the *Orestes* of 341 was that of Astydamas.

new audience. But surprisingly few lines in *Orestes* have been identified as interpolations. Diggle, for example, deletes some 112 verses, most of the deletions being of single trimeters.[3] I do not accept all of Diggle's deletions (nor does our honorand in his Aris & Phillips edition of the play), but I bring forward as new suspects six passages from the scene where Orestes and Pylades, having returned from the assembly that condemned Orestes and his sister to death, deliberate with Electra about what to do. The first two of these discussions concern the problem of Pylades' on-again-off-again exile.

IS PYLADES UNDER SENTENCE OF EXILE OR NOT?

Earlier in the play, in the course of the first tetrameter scene, Pylades announces (763–7) that he is is under sentence of exile, his father Strophios having banished him from Phocis:[4]

Πυ. κἀμὲ νῦν ὅρα τί πάσχω· καὶ γὰρ αὐτὸς οἴχομαι.
Ορ. πρὸς τίνος; τοῦτ' ἂν προσείη τοῖς ἐμοῖς κακοῖς κακόν.
Πυ. Στρόφιος ἤλασέν μ' ἀπ' οἴκων φυγάδα θυμωθεὶς πατήρ.
Ορ. ἴδιον ἢ κοινὸν πολίταις ἐπιφέρων ἔγκλημα τί;
Πυ. ὅτι συνηράμην φόνον σοι μητρός, ἀνόσιον λέγων.

Yet in the scene that follows the assembly, when Pylades has proposed to join Orestes and Electra in death, Orestes urges him not to do so on the grounds that he has a city and a father's house and a 'great harbour of wealth'. I give the wider context.

Πυ. ἐπίσχες. ἓν μὲν πρῶτά σοι μομφὴν ἔχω,
εἰ ζῆν με χρῄζειν σοῦ θανόντος ἤλπισας.
Ορ. τί γὰρ προσήκει κατθανεῖν σ' ἐμοῦ μέτα;
Πυ. ἤρου; τί δὲ ζῆν σῆς ἑταιρίας ἄτερ;
Ορ. οὐκ ἔκτανες σὺ μητέρ', ὡς ἐγὼ τάλας.
Πυ. σὺν σοί γε κοινῇ· ταὐτὰ καὶ πάσχειν με δεῖ.

[3] There are 36 deletions of single lines and 24 other deletions, most of two to five lines. Histrionic interpolations among these deleted lines are perhaps only 554–6, 644–5 (see scholia), 852, 904–13, 1049–51, 1227–30, 1564–6, 1598, and 1691–3. In addition I judge that the whole couplet 625–6 ought to be retained but its duplication at 536–7 deleted as a histrionic anticipation.

[4] Here and elsewhere I cite my own text. In the passages cited my text differs from Diggle's only at 766.

Ορ. ἀπόδος τὸ σῶμα πατρί, μὴ σύνθνῃσκέ μοι.
σοὶ μὲν γάρ ἐστι πόλις, ἐμοὶ δ' οὐκ ἔστι δή,
καὶ δῶμα πατρὸς καὶ μέγας πλούτου λιμήν.
γάμων δὲ τῆς μὲν δυσπότμου τῆσδ' ἐσφάλης,
ἥν σοι κατηγγύησ' ἑταιρίαν σέβων·
σὺ δ' ἄλλο λέκτρον παιδοποίησαι λαβών,
κῆδος δὲ τοὐμὸν καὶ σὸν οὐκέτ' ἔστι δή.

The scholiast (on *Or.* 1075, Schwartz i. 203) notes the contradiction and says ἰδίως ταῦτα ὁ Εὐριπίδης τοῦ Πυλάδου ἔμπροσθεν εἰρηκότος ὅτι ἐκβέβληται ὑπὸ τοῦ πατρός, εἰ μὴ ἄρα αἰνίττεται ὡς μετὰ θάνατον τοῦ πατρὸς δυνήσεται κατελθεῖν. The idea that the banishment need not be permanent was suggested in modern times by both Weil and Chapouthier, and Chapouthier follows the scholiast in saying that Pylades might return after Strophius' death. But this means interpreting 'You have a city' as 'You might in the future have a city if Strophius dies and his decree is deemed a dead letter.' And it is hard to see why Orestes says ἀπόδος τὸ σῶμα πατρί if he means to suggest that Pylades' return will be possible only after the death of his father.

Another possible approach is what we might call Tychoism. Tycho von Wilamowitz pointed out that in Sophocles the 'facts' of the plot are elastic and are often changed to heighten the drama of the individual scene.[5] We could argue that in 763–7 Pylades has no home because it heightens Orestes' misery that his troubles have involved his friend, whereas in 1075–7 Pylades has one so that his bravery and loyalty may be seen clearly in his decision to stay with Orestes. But this seems a stretch. Euripides is much less prone to this kind of looseness with the facts than Sophocles, and even in Sophocles it is hard to think of a contradiction this glaring.

A further approach would be to consider the passage a characterization of Orestes as thoughtless and egotistical: this is what Willink seems to sugggest in his notes on 1075 and 1054–5. (He also adopts Tychoism—the exile is 'relevant only to that earlier scene'—as a supplementary explanation.) But this seems an ineffective way to characterize since no one comments on the memory lapse. Lastly, characterization of Orestes fails to explain why Pylades himself

[5] See T. von Wilamowitz (1917) and Lloyd-Jones (1972) = (1982), 219–37 = (1990*a*), 401–18.

should be afflicted with a similar forgetfulness in 1093–4, a second passage contradicting the exile, to which we will return below.

Instead, I suggest that Euripides was not responsible for this contradiction and that a second hand introduced 1075–7.[6] If we remove these three lines, Pylades' assertion that because of their comradeship and their cooperation in the murder of Clytemnestra he deserves to suffer the same fate as Orestes is answered, in a slightly brutal but effective way, when Orestes says that Pylades' betrothal to Electra and his marriage tie to Orestes are now at an end: he can only say *χαῖρε*. Orestes' words are designedly harsh: only if he can persuade Pylades that their friendship is over can he prevent his friend from sacrificing his life for friendship's sake. There may be a further suggestion that a wife and children will furnish Pylades with a reason to live, and that their company may compensate Pylades for the loss of Orestes and Electra. So 1075–7 are better away. Another reason is provided by Willink, who notes that the line ends *οὐκ ἔστι δή* in 1076 and *οὐκέτ' ἔστι δή* in 1081 are nearly identical and uncomfortably close together. He proposes deleting 1081, but since 1081 is blameless, the repetition furnishes a further reason to delete 1075–7.

In a second passage Pylades rejects Orestes' advice and declares that he means to die with his friend:

Πυ. *ἦ πολὺ λέλειψαι τῶν ἐμῶν βουλευμάτων.*
μήθ' αἷμά μου δέξαιτο κάρπιμον πέδον,
μὴ λαμπρὸς αἰθήρ, εἴ σ' ἐγὼ προδούς ποτε
ἐλευθερώσας τοὐμὸν ἀπολίποιμι σέ.
καὶ συγκατέκτανον γάρ, οὐκ ἀρνήσομαι,
καὶ πάντ' ἐβούλευσ' ὧν σὺ νῦν τίνεις δίκας·
καὶ ξυνθανεῖν οὖν δεῖ με σοὶ καὶ τῇδ' ὁμοῦ.
ἐμὴν γὰρ αὐτήν, ἧς <γε> λέχος ἐπῄνεσα,
κρίνω δάμαρτα· τί γὰρ ἐρῶ καλόν ποτε
γῆν Δελφίδ' ἐλθών, Φωκέων ἀκρόπτολιν,

[6] Grüninger (1898), 38–40 grasps the other horn of the dilemma and deletes 763–71. But that passage, to me, looks perfectly Euripidean. Grüninger's deletion is part of an ambitious renovation scheme that would remove every mention of Pylades from the first half of the play and deny him a role in the murder of Clytemnestra. Such wholesale interpolation might have happened, of course, but I do not think he has proved his case.

ὃς πρὶν μὲν ὑμᾶς δυστυχεῖν φίλος παρῆ,
νῦν δ' οὐκέτ' εἰμὶ δυστυχοῦντί σοι φίλος;
οὐκ ἔστιν· ἀλλὰ ταῦτα μὲν κἀμοὶ μέλει·
ἐπεὶ δὲ κατθανούμεθ', ἐς κοινοὺς λόγους
ἔλθωμεν, ὡς ἂν Μενέλεως συνδυστυχῇ.

Here it is Pylades who forgets about the exile: only if he has not been exiled and has the option of going home does his emphatic refusal (1093–7) to go back to Phocis make sense, for it is pointless to refuse on moral grounds to do what is impossible on practical ones. These lines, therefore, like 1075–7, contradict 763–7. But that is not their only incongruity. Pylades begins by invoking a terrible post-mortem curse on himself if he should ever betray Orestes in order to seek safety for himself. It would be wrong, he explains, for him to leave Orestes and Electra to their fate since he is fully as guilty as they are (1089–91). So far, so good: his complicity in the death of Clytemnestra explains his decision to kill himself along with them. But then Electra, who had only been mentioned in passing (τῆδ', 1091), becomes the centre of the argument, and in order to explain (γὰρ, 1092) something that has already been adequately explained (his refusal to abandon them since he was involved in their actions), he adds that he regards Electra, who was betrothed to him, as fully his wife. This is obliquely relevant at best. Then he goes on: 'What good argument can I make when I return to Delphi if I stood by you two before your troubles but abandon you when you are in trouble? It cannot be: I too care about these things.' The last phrase, ἀλλὰ ταῦτα μὲν κἀμοὶ μέλει, could have been clearer than it is since 'these things' is vague and we can't tell who else it is that cares about them. Thereafter two genuine lines (1098–9) lead into the discussion of killing Helen as a way to hurt Menelaus. Lines 1092–7 could be excised without any loss. Furthermore, we get in ἐπεὶ δὲ κατθανούμεθ' (1098) a far more logical continuation of καὶ ξυνθανεῖν οὖν δεῖ με σοὶ καὶ τῆδ' ὁμοῦ (1091) than is 1092–7: the reference to impending death as motive for revenge connects up well with the announcement that their death is unavoidable. I thus propose deletion of 1092–7.[7]

[7] There is one other passage that envisages the return of Pylades to Phocis, 1209–10, where Pylades, moved by Orestes' admiration for the inventiveness of Electra, expresses the wish that he may be able to marry her after all. We could delete these

Why were these interpolations made? For we must remember the principle so trenchantly enunciated by Jackson (1955), 2:

> An interpolation, however, though the fact is occasionally forgotten, presupposes an interpolator—a man of like passions with ourselves, and therefore acting from motives, often foolish and not rarely discreditable, but always discernible to a seeing eye.

What was the motive for these interpolations? So far all we have noticed is that they introduce a gratuitous inconsistency into the plot. But there is other evidence. In 1094 there is a phrase that Euripides is unlikely to have written in 408 BC and which helps to date the interpolator and also to unmask his motive, Pylades' reference to his city of origin as 'Delphi, the acropolis of the Phocians'. In terms of mythical geography this description is wide of the mark. To be sure, in the Catalogue of Ships (*Il.* 2.519) the Phocians are said to control, among other sites, *Πυθὼ πετρήεσσα*, but there is no indication that it is their central gathering place or citadel. In the Homeric Hymn to Apollo (378–485) it is made clear that the servants of Apollo, who are brought in from Crete to administer the sanctuary, are a different population from the one that dwells around Delphi. It is the Delphians, not their Phocian neighbors, who will serve Apollo. This state of affairs is presupposed by the *Oresteia*, where Pylades is no Delphian but a Phocian and where Orestes claims (*Cho.* 674) to be a Daulian from Phocis, i.e. someone who inhabits one of the towns the Phocians controlled. That is, he pretends to have the same ethnic origin as Pylades actually has.

But tragedy sometimes reflects a contemporary state of affairs. What about the possibility that Euripides may have been describing Delphi as it was in his own day? There was a brief period at mid century when the Phocians were in control: in the 450s, after Oinophyta, Athens was briefly master of Boeotia and Phocis, and with Athenian support the Phocians took control of Delphi. The Spartans restored Delphi to the control of the Delphians in 448 (the Second Sacred War), and although the Athenians shortly thereafter

lines without loss, but I am not sure that it is necessary. Pylades may mean merely that he wishes he might marry Electra, and the reference to the act of bringing the bride to his ancestral home may not imply that he fails to recognize that under the present circumstances returning to Phocis is impossible.

handed it back to the Phocians, from the Thirty Years' Peace of 446/5 onwards the Delphians themselves were in charge, and the city and sanctuary, under the nominal control of the Amphictyony, were autonomous. Unless we imagine Euripides in 408 putting in Pylades' mouth a reference to that brief period forty years earlier in which the Phocians controlled the sanctuary, 'the acropolis of the Phocians' seems an unlikely description for Delphi either in mythical or contemporary historical terms. Furthermore, in the passages cited in LSJ 'acropolis' means 'citadel', 'castle', or 'stronghold', with the implication of fortifications, but during the entire archaic and classical period, to judge from the archaeological record, Delphi, as a pan-Hellenic sanctuary open to everyone, had none. With the exception, that is, of a brief period in the fourth century.

Fast forward about fifty years and things look different. In 356 the Phocians, previously convicted by the Amphictyonic Council for cultivating sacred land, had been ordered to pay a huge fine. A prominent Phocian named Philomelus persuaded his countrymen that the only way to avoid having their territory turned over to the god as sacred land was to elect him as general with full powers. His plan, it turned out, was to take over Delphi (D.S. 16.23–4). With the secret help of the Spartans he hired mercenaries, seized the sanctuary, and liquidated Delphian opposition. It was not long thereafter that the Phocians appropriated Delphi's store of coined money and, in the course of time, proceeded to melt down silver and gold from the temple offerings. With these funds they hired an army of mercenaries and became for a time the pre-eminent land power in Greece. What is more, they threw a wall around the shrine (D.S. 16.25), parts of which are visible today.[8] This state of affairs continued until Philip II, coming over the pass at Thermopylae, defeated the Phocians and forced them to agree to repay what they had taken. Phocian control of Delphi was over by 346.[9]

It was during this period, perhaps for the first time in history, that both halves of the phrase 'the acropolis of the Phocians' really describe Delphi. The interpolations, we may conclude, were made

[8] Bommelaer (1991), 217 says that the 'fortifications of Philomelos' were more limited in extent than Diodorus represents but does not seriously doubt ('il n'est donc pas invraisemblable') that these walls date from the Third Sacred War.

[9] For the chronology of the Third Sacred War see Hammond (1937).

during this time or in its immediate aftermath. The same story is told by the phrase *μέγας πλούτου λιμήν* in 1077. The wealth of Delphi, of course, was famous in all periods, but at 1077 the audience have not yet heard that Pylades lives in Delphi, and it is as a Phocian that he possesses 'a great harbour of wealth'. The Phocians were famous for their wealth only when they had taken over the Delphic treasures.

We now have good reason, I suggest, to suspect that these lines are interpolated and some idea when. What was the interpolator's motive? Unfortunately there is more than one possibility. One motive might be to influence Athenian foreign policy. The Athenians in the fifth century intervened on the Phocian side and in the fourth there must have been some in Athens who were favourably disposed to Phocian occupation of Delphi. When Philip intervened against the Phocians after refusing for a long time to tip his hand, it was a nasty shock to Demosthenes (9.11) and probably to many other Athenians as well. It could be that an actor, seeking to appeal to the pro-Phocian sympathies of some portion of his audience, insinuated into the play lines that retrojected into the mythical period both Phocian control of the shrine and Phocian appropriation of its wealth. There would be little point in doing this, however, at any time after the Phocians had been decisively defeated by Philip: such a claim would ring hollow after the Phocians had been forced to agree to a repayment of the treasures they had taken and deprived of their vote on the Amphictyonic Council. A revival in which interpolations were made with this motive would have to have occurred *c.*356–346.

References to the Phocians' wealth and to their fortifying of Delphi might equally have been intended to suggest the impiety and self-aggrandizement of the Phocians, most likely when it was a thing of the past. The Phocians as Phocians can have a 'great harbour of wealth' and have Delphi as their acropolis only by forcibly taking over Delphi. The phrases *μέγας πλούτου λιμήν* and *γῆν Δελφίδ' ἐλθών, Φωκέων ἀκρόπτολιν* might be intended to allude to Phocian expropriation of temple treasure and fortification of the sanctuary, actions recently discredited by events. The effect might be to appeal to any anti-Phocian sentiment that could be aroused and to commend retrospectively the actions of Philip in putting an end to Phocian impiety.

Another motive must be mentioned: interpolation can also serve to create a more emotionally rich, hence more successful, play. Actors, like the tragic playwrights themselves, not infrequently shape their plays in such a way as to borrow resonance from contemporary events, thereby increasing the emotional connection of the audience to the play. Euripides' lines on the duplicity of the Spartans, for example (*Andr.* 445–52) and the lines of an unknown actor on demagoguery (*Or.* 904–13) both in effect attach to the play some of the emotional valence of agents in the audience's contemporary world. Thus if the Phocian Pylades is in some way identified with the Phocians of the audience's own day, some of the resonances of Athens' connexion with the Phocians are transferred to the relation between Orestes and Pylades.

The play as it came from Euripides' hand already gave prominence to the theme of loyalty to friends in distress. No matter what attitude a member of the audience took toward the contemporary Phocian situation (and Athenian ambivalence is suggested by, e.g., Dem. 18.18), the idea of reciprocal loyalty in the contemporary world would add resonance to the play. On one side of the question, some of the Athenian audience would have felt that, in view of the long history of Athenian support for Phocian control of Delphi and in view of the alliance between Phocis and Athens made in 355 (see D.S. 16.25.7), continued support of them was the duty of friends. On the other side, recent events had shown the Phocians to be less than completely loyal to Athens and her interests: the Phocian leader Phalaecus, the third after Philomelus to command the Phocian state, sent mercenaries to Euboea to aid the Euboeans in driving Athenian influence out of the island (*Σ* Aeschin. 3.190 = p. 124 Dilts). Good relations with Athens were restored by the three generals who replaced Phalaecus: these men offered the Athenians the forts of Alponon, Thronion, and Nicaea near Thermopylae. But by the time the Athenian general Proxenus arrived to take possession of them, the triumvirate had been driven out by Phalaecus, and the Athenians did not get the forts (Aeschin. 2.132–5). Pylades' loyalty unto death might thus act as a foil to set off the instability of contemporary Phocis.

We do not have sufficient evidence to decide on internal grounds just what effect the interpolator intended his additions to have. But external evidence points to a man who must be our chief suspect, a man who had, as prosecuting attorneys say, both opportunity and motive. A fragmentary inscription of the didascalic record (*IG* ii–iii^2 2320.12–13: see *TrGF* i. 25–6 and Pickard-Cambridge (1988), 107–20) informs us that there was a revival of Euripides' *Orestes* in 340 and that the principal actor was Neoptolemus.[10] The didascalic record is incomplete, and it is possible to argue that the performance that gave us the interpolations we are discussing occurred in some other year between 356, the earliest date at which 'the acropolis of the Phocians' makes sense as a description of Delphi, and 340. But with so many tragedies of Euripides available for revival at the Dionysia, it does not seem all that likely that *Orestes* would have been revived twice in a decade and a half. Chances are good that this performance is the only one at the Dionysia in the period we are considering.

We know quite a bit about Neoptolemus from Demosthenes, who describes him as enormously popular and a friend of Philip II.[11] Demosthenes regarded Neoptolemus' influence as injurious to Athens' interests since he was a highly popular actor who several times addressed the Athenians on Philip's behalf and put the best construction on Philip's actions. It is a hypothesis worth considering that it was he who put the two passages ignoring Pylades' exile into the play, the one describing Pylades' home as 'a great harbour of wealth', the other making Delphi the Phocian acropolis.[12] The purpose of these references might well have been to remind the Athenians of the Phocians' recent occupation of Delphi and to commend Philip by implication for putting an end to it. Whether or not the political motive was as I have described, it is certainly likely that the added emotional resonances of the play, won at the cost of a contradiction

[10] The inscription is discussed in detail by Easterling (1997*b*), 214–17.

[11] The testimonia are collected in Csapo and Slater (1994), 232–5, 266, and 383. Since he came from the island of Scyros (*Σ* Dem. 5.22 = p. 123.1 Dilts), it is reasonable to conclude, as does Easterling (1997*b*), 217, that 'Neoptolemus' was a stage name, connecting him with Scyros' most famous mythical son. He might nevertheless have been an Athenian citizen and might be identical with Neoptolemus son of Antikles of the deme Melite: see MacDowell (2000), 210–11. Political use of tragedy, by Macedonians including Philip II, is well documented by Revermann (1999–2000).

[12] The second, of course, would have been spoken not by Neoptolemus himself but by the actor who played Pylades.

in the plot, were intended to contribute to the effectiveness of the play on the stage.[13]

The rest of this paper will discuss other passages in this same scene that deserve a suspicious glance. They may be by the same hand, though only in one case is there positive reason to think so. I have one line (1152) to delete *meo Marte* from Pylades' next *rhesis*, a speech in which I also mark a lacuna, two passages of five lines each (1158–62 and 1167–71) from Orestes' reply, and a further five lines (1195–9) from Electra's.

PYLADES' *RHESIS* (1131–52)

Pylades' first entrance at 729 had stirred Orestes to decisive action, and in this later scene too his intervention brings a change in what had up to that point been all lamentation and thoughts of death. First, he disabuses Orestes (1085–99) of the idea that he will agree to bury Orestes and his sister after they commit suicide: Pylades means to share their death even though he is under no legal compulsion to do so. Second, he suggests in a lively stichomythia (1100–30) that before they die they should get back at Menelaus by killing Helen, and he produces a plan for carrying this out. The concluding *rhesis* with which we are here concerned justifies murdering Helen and proposes a backup plan, burning down the house of Agamemnon and preventing Menelaus from taking it over.

Pylades' *rhesis* begins with a justification for killing Helen. Things would be different, he says, if we were proposing to murder a virtuous woman, but as it is, Helen will be paying the penalty to all of

[13] A similar method of proceeding is visible in *Iphigenia Aulidensis*. As I tried to show in Kovacs (2003*b*), in Euripides' original play, put on shortly after his death, the oracle requiring the sacrifice of Iphigenia was known, as one would expect, to the entire army. In the text that has come down to us, this version of the oracle is combined with one in which it is known only to Agamemnon's Privy Council. Accepting the contradiction allows for certain emotional effects the reviser found congenial. It is possible that the author of this much more extensive revision was also Neoptolemus. He is named in the didascalic record as the actor in the revival of one of Euripides' *Iphigenia* plays in 341. For further speculation on this question see Kovacs (2005), 392 n. 1.

Greece for the death of men and the bereavement of their parents, children, and wives:

> *νῦν δ᾽ ὑπὲρ ἁπάσης Ἑλλάδος δώσει δίκην*
> *ὧν πατέρας ἔκτειν᾽, ὧν δ᾽ ἀπώλεσεν τέκνα,*
> *νύμφας τ᾽ ἔθηκεν ὀρφανὰς ξυναόρων.*

So far, so good.[14] The next line, however, has a suspicious asyndeton.

> *ὀλολυγμὸς ἔσται, πῦρ τ᾽ ἀνάψουσιν θεοῖς,* 1137
> *σοὶ πολλὰ κἀμοὶ κέδν᾽ ἀρώμενοι τυχεῖν,*
> *κακῆς γυναικὸς οὕνεχ᾽ αἷμ᾽ ἐπράξαμεν.*

In my edition I quieted my suspicions by punctuating 1136 with a raised period, not wishing to clutter the small Loeb page with all my dark imaginings, but the connection between 1134–6 and 1137 is a lot looser and less evidently causal than asyndeton usually expresses.[15] Perhaps 1137 was originally preceded by something like <*ὀλέθρου δὲ τῆσδε κατὰ πόλιν θρυλουμένου*>, omission being caused by homoearcton.

Pylades continues: the Argives will invoke blessings on his and Orestes' head for this, and Orestes will henceforth be called 'the slayer of deadly Helen' instead of 'the matricide'. We must note here that although logically the change in Orestes' reputation among the Argives ought to mean an improvement in his chances for survival, neither Pylades nor Orestes draws this conclusion, and both regard death as virtually inevitable: cf. 1098 and 1163–4. It is only Electra's later intervention (1177–8) that promises the survival Orestes had faintly hoped for in 1173–4, a survival made possible only if they take Hermione hostage. The suggestion to kill Helen and also to burn down the house are presented by Pylades and accepted by Orestes as

[14] I am not at all sure that the translations, my Loeb translation included, have correctly rendered 1134–6. In particular *ὑπέρ*, 'on behalf of, in the name of', is hard to construe with *δώσει δίκην*, since that would imply, absurdly, that Helen is taking Hellas' place and is being punished in its stead. I am now inclined, as suggested by Wedd, to take *ὧν* as referring to an omitted dative antecedent and construing 'in the name of all Hellas' with that: 'But as things stand those whose fathers and sons she killed and whose wives she widowed, acting in the name of all Hellas, will punish her'.

[15] For some reason Bussler (1887) does not discuss this asyndeton.

a way to achieve some kind of κλέος *before their inevitable death*. In light of this we should consider 1143–52:

> οὐ δεῖ ποτ᾽, οὐ δεῖ Μενέλεων μὲν εὐτυχεῖν,
> τὸν σὸν δὲ πατέρα καὶ σὲ κἀδελφὴν θανεῖν,
> μητέρα τ᾽ . . . ἐῶ τοῦτ᾽· οὐ γὰρ εὐπρεπὲς λέγειν·
> δόμους δ᾽ ἔχειν σοὺς δι᾽ Ἀγαμέμνονος δόρυ
> λαβόντα νύμφην· μὴ γὰρ οὖν ζῴην ἔτι,
> εἰ μὴ ᾽π᾽ ἐκείνῃ φάσγανον σπάσω μέλαν.
> ἢν δ᾽ οὖν τὸν Ἑλένης μὴ κατάσχωμεν φόνον,
> πρήσαντες οἴκους τούσδε κατθανούμεθα.
> ἑνὸς γὰρ οὐ σφαλέντες ἕξομεν κλέος,
> καλῶς θανόντες ἢ καλῶς σεσωμένοι.

Pylades' point is that it is simply wrong[16] for Menelaus to prosper when his brother and his brother's family have perished or are soon to perish. He does not, it seems, deny that the living persons on the list in 1144–5 will soon be dead but merely says that since all are either dead or shortly to die it is wrong for Menelaus to prosper and possess Orestes' house.[17] The point about the house then leads naturally into Pylades' Plan B: burning down the palace before perishing will also have a certain rightness about it.[18] The last line of the speech, however, is suspicious. Hitherto Pylades has been speaking of final acts of revenge committed before Orestes' inevitable death, and Orestes in 1163–6 takes the same view: ἐγὼ δὲ πάντως ἐκπνέων ψυχὴν ἐμὴν | δράσας τι χρῄζω τοὺς ἐμοὺς ἐχθροὺς θανεῖν, κτλ. In 1173–6 he touches on the possibility of survival but in such a way as to make it clear that this is the merest of daydreams. It is only Electra who offers a plan for turning this daydream into reality. It is hard, in view of

[16] The asyndeton in 1143 is a bit difficult but not impossible: 1143–7 give the grounds for the moral satisfaction Pylades says everyone will feel at this murder.

[17] Broadhead (1968), 170–2 proposes deleting 1145–8 on the grounds that the reference to Clytemnestra is rhetorically awkward and to understand 'sc. Μενέλεων' with ἔχειν in 1146 is difficult with three other persons having been mentioned in between. But if we delete 1145, as Hartung was inclined to do, the rhetorical awkwardness is eliminated and the difficulty of subjects much reduced. It could be argued that the aposiopesis with regard to Clytemnestra is a typical Euripidean touch, seen in 27, but equally an actor could have been inspired by this earlier passage to introduce another (in my judgement much less successful) example here.

[18] The idea that Menelaus must be prevented from taking over the Argive kingship and palace is one that becomes important later in the play (see 1594–6) and has been anticipated (see 1058–9).

this, to see why Euripides would have allowed Pylades with 1152 to steal Electra's thunder. I suggest that the line is an interpolation designed to give the speech a sonorous finish.[19] The meaning of 1149–51 then is 'But if we fail to kill Helen, we will then burn down this house and perish. For we will achieve one of these goals and win renown.'

ORESTES' REPLY (1155–76)

Orestes' speech in reply also has lines that have raised suspicion, though the preferred solution for some of them has been emendation rather than athetesis. I propose deleting 1158–62. Here are 1155–64:

φεῦ·
οὐκ ἔστιν οὐδὲν κρεῖσσον ἢ φίλος σαφής,
οὐ πλοῦτος, οὐ τυραννίς· ἀλόγιστον δέ τοι
τὸ πλῆθος ἀντάλλαγμα γενναίου φίλου.
σὺ γὰρ τά τ' εἰς Αἴγισθον ἐξηῦρες κακὰ
καὶ πλησίον παρῆσθα κινδύνων ἐμοί,
νῦν τ' αὖ δίδως μοι πολεμίων τιμωρίαν
κοὐκ ἐκποδὼν εἶ· παύσομαί σ' αἰνῶν, ἐπεὶ
βάρος τι κἀν τῷδ' ἐστίν, αἰνεῖσθαι λίαν.
ἐγὼ δὲ πάντως ἐκπνέων ψυχὴν ἐμὴν
δράσας τι χρῄζω τοὺς ἐμοὺς ἐχθροὺς θανεῖν, κτλ.

(1) At 1158 West notes Herwerden's *καλῶς* for *κακά*, and Wecklein in his appendix says 'fort. *σοφά*'. West's suspicion is justified. I have examined every instance of *εἰς* (*ἐς*) in Aeschylus, Sophocles, and Euripides without coming up with a parallel to *τὰ εἰς Αἴγισθον κακά*. Yet since there is also no parallel to *τὰ εἰς Αἴγισθον* without a noun (Herwerden's conjecture) or *τὰ εἰς Αἴγισθον σοφά* (Wecklein), athetesis may be preferable to emendation. (2) *πλησίον παρῆσθα κινδύνων ἐμοί* is a remarkable combination. Its two components may be separately paralleled (*παρεῖναι* + dat. is common for giving help

[19] Cf. 1245, clearly designed for the same purpose. Wecklein's appendix notes that Nauck was once inclined to delete 1151–2, but I see no reason to touch 1151.

and support, and for πλησίον κινδύνων Willink cites Diggle's emendation of *Ion* 711, πέλας δεινῶν for δείπνων, which is probably right), but 'you stood by me in the vicinity of danger' does not seem quite Euripidean.[20] (3) There is an unwanted asyndeton in 1161.[21] Porson proposed fixing this by writing παύσομαι δ' αἰνῶν σ', and if the lines are genuine this seems necessary. But interpolators in the fourth century seem to like abruptness and asyndeton,[22] so it is possible that we have 1161 exactly as it was written. (4) Lastly, from the emphatic ἐγὼ δὲ in 1163 we would naturally conclude that Orestes' own actions had hitherto not come in for mention, but in fact they do in 1161–2. If we omit 1158–62, the connection with what precedes is clearer: Orestes says that *for his part* he means to take the advice his excellent friend had offered him.

When we come to 1167–71 there are once again difficulties.

> Ἀγαμέμνονός τοι παῖς πέφυχ', ὃς Ἑλλάδος
> ἦρξ' ἀξιωθείς, οὐ τύραννος, ἀλλ' ὅμως
> ῥώμην θεοῦ τιν' ἔσχ'· ὃν οὐ καταισχυνῶ
> δοῦλον παρασχὼν θάνατον, ἀλλ' ἐλευθέρως
> ψυχὴν ἀφήσω, Μενέλεων δὲ τείσομαι.
> ἑνὸς γὰρ εἰ λαβοίμεθ', εὐτυχοῖμεν ἄν·
> κεἴ ποθεν ἄελπτος παραπέσοι σωτηρία, κτλ.

Lines 1167–9 contain qualifications and restrictions that are irrelevant to the argument. It would be sufficient for Orestes to say 'I am the son of Agamemnon, who once led all of Greece on the great expedition against Troy', but instead of this simple statement, which would explain well why Orestes feels he has a reputation to defend, we are told that Agamemnon 'commanded Hellas, having been deemed worthy, not (being) a king, but nevertheless he had some power of a god (= god-given power?)'. If the point is that Agamemnon, though commander of the Greek forces, was not king of all Greece, that seems fussy since no one would think he was. Yet he was

[20] Christopher Collard points me to *Phoen.* 159–60, ἐκεῖνος ἑπτὰ παρθένων τάφου πέλας | Νιόβης Ἀδράστῳ πλησίον παραστατεῖ, but this sorts itself out with comparative ease, πέλας + gen. showing location near the (quite concrete) tomb of Niobe's daughters and πλησίον παραστατεῖ cooperation with Adrastus.

[21] Bussler (1887), 36 classifies it as causal, but Pylades' loyalty and goodness is not the cause of Orestes' ceasing to praise him.

[22] See Page (1934), 96–7.

king of Argos/Mycenae, and he had the full measure of kingly authority, not just 'some' divine power. It is hard to see why Euripides should have made Orestes speak so lamely at this moment of high emotion. Note further that 1172 joins up nicely with 1166. Orestes has just spoken of causing his enemies pain, and in this context it means the two plans enunciated by Pylades. If he can succeed at one of them (ἑνός), all will be well. The reference back to the ἑνὸς of 1151 is unmistakable.[23] The passage as a whole is improved considerably by the deletion of these lines, the motive for whose interpolation is not entirely clear. Might there be some connection between this passage and the sympathies of Neoptolemus? Philip too was proposing to lead a pan-Hellenic expedition to fight the barbarian. Could this interpolation be intended to suggest that Philip, though not leader by right of Greece, possessed 'a certain god-given power' and thus should be 'deemed worthy'?

ELECTRA'S PROPOSAL

If I am right about the spuriousness of 1152, no one in the play so far has suggested that there is any way Orestes and Electra can escape with their lives, and only Orestes has expressed this wish. But Electra thinks she has a way, and after a brief stichomythia she enunciates it as follows:

Ηλ. Ἑλένης θανούσης ἤν τι Μενέλεώς σε δρᾷ
ἢ τόνδε κἀμέ (πᾶν γὰρ ἓν φίλον τόδε),
λέγ' ὡς φονεύσεις Ἑρμιόνην· ξίφος δὲ χρὴ
δέρῃ πρὸς αὐτῇ παρθένου σπάσαντ' ἔχειν.
κἂν μέν σε σῴζῃ μὴ θανεῖν χρῄζων κόρην
[Μενέλαος Ἑλένης πτῶμ' ἰδὼν ἐν αἵματι],
μέθες πεπᾶσθαι πατρὶ παρθένου δέμας·
ἢν δ' ὀξυθύμου μὴ κρατῶν φρονήματος
κτείνῃ σε, καὶ σὺ σφάζε παρθένου δέρην.

[23] What follows is Orestes' daydream, and Diggle is right to segregate the next four lines decisively from what precedes by adopting Willink's κεἰ for εἰ in 1173.

καί νιν δοκῶ, τὸ πρῶτον ἢν πολὺς παρῇ,
χρόνῳ μαλάξειν σπλάγχνον· οὔτε γὰρ θρασὺς
οὔτ᾽ ἄλκιμος πέφυκε. τήνδ᾽ ἡμῖν ἔχω
σωτηρίας ἔπαλξιν· εἴρηται λόγος.

1196 del. Nauck

I suggest that Nauck's deletion of 1196 be extended to cover 1195–9. The passage spells out what is meant by taking Hermione hostage and holding a sword at her neck. It distinguishes two possible outcomes, treating them as equally likely, yet it handles neither in a way that is above suspicion and leaves things at a point where 1200 becomes awkward. The first outcome is this: 'If he helps to save you because he doesn't want his daughter to die, after seeing Helen lying in her own blood, release the girl into her father's possession.' West notes that the present *σῴζῃ* cannot mean 'saves you' but rather 'acts in a way tending towards saving'. Yet the lines suggest handing over Hermione before the result is certain. The second possibility is that Menelaus, unable to control his pride and hot temper, will keep on trying to bring about Orestes' death, and in that case *καὶ σὺ σφάζε παρθένου δέρην*. West translates 'make as if to cut the girl's throat', which is what the context calls for, but 'try to cut the girl's throat' would be a less indulgent rendering, and most natural of all would be 'proceed to cut the girl's throat'. In itself this imperative is both idiomatic in tense and possible as an order.[24] But it puts the situation at a juncture where it seems awkward to say 'and I think that even if he blusters at first, in time his angry feelings will soften: he's not brave or tough by nature'. By contrast if 1200 follows on 1194, it explains the extortion simply and economically. The motive for the interpolation is roughly analogous to that at *Hel.* 892–3: in both cases an order to take a drastic and irrevocable action is interpolated into the text, probably to cause the audience to draw in their breath sharply.

[24] See Bakker (1966), 43–9 for instances where the present imperative marks a go-ahead signal to perform an action the hearer has already been told about.

19

Some Poetic Connections of Lycophron's *Alexandra*

Adrian Hollis

It is not surprising that, of all the issues raised by the *Alexandra*, scholars should have devoted most time and effort to historical and geographical problems—to the identification of kings and political leaders lying behind the poet's riddles (e.g. 1441 'the Thesprotian and Chalastrean lion', 1444 'the wolf of Galadra'), to Lycophron's account of the West and its relation to Timaeus,[1] and, above all, his prophecy of Rome's future greatness (1226–30). All of these have been vigorously disputed, and three positions maintained: (a) the work should be ascribed in its entirety to Lycophron of Chalcis (first half of the third century BC), said by external evidence to have been a member of the Pleiad, who came to Alexandria and helped to arrange the comic poets for the Library; (b) because of the historical references and the political understanding which it displays, the *Alexandra* could not have been composed before the second century BC, and therefore must come from the pen of 'another Lycophron',[2] or else have been mistakenly ascribed to the famous Lycophron, so that we do not know the real author's name; (c) the main part of the *Alexandra* does indeed belong to the third century and Lycophron of Chalcis, but at least

[1] See the valuable note of Fraser (1972), ii. 1065–7, n. 331.

[2] Σ 1226 *Λυκόφρονος ἑτέρου νομιστέον εἶναι τὸ ποίημα, οὐ τοῦ γράψαντος τὴν τραγωιδίαν.*

two passages (1226–80 and 1446–50) were added in the second century BC.[3]

On the above matters our honorand has *propiora consilia*.[4] My purpose here is less ambitious: to place the *Alexandra* in the context of other Hellenistic poetry. Attempts to do this have been less full and systematic—or at least the results are less easily available.[5] Perhaps the most crucial are the links between Lycophron and his fellow townsman Euphorion of Chalcis.[6] The reason is that upholders of the *Alexandra*'s traditional date (first half of the third century) need not agonize over the question of priority between Lycophron and Callimachus or Lycophron and Apollonius,[7] but anyone who believes in the priority of Euphorion (born between 275 and 268 BC)[8] over the *Alexandra* can hardly ascribe the latter to the

[3] Although claiming no authority or originality, perhaps I should say briefly what seems most plausible to me. That the *general* picture of the West in Lycophron belongs to a type prevalent *c.*280–250 BC but disappearing thereafter, I accept from Fraser (1972, ii. 1066). On the other hand I am more sympathetic than he is (ibid.) to Momigliano's interpretation (1942) of γῆς καὶ θαλάσσης σκῆπτρα καὶ μοναρχίαν (1229) in an attenuated sense which need not imply more prescience than was reasonable for the early-mid third century. Exaggeration both in glorifying past achievements and predicting future ones seems equally typical of Hellenistic and Roman poetry and may scarcely have raised an eyebrow. As to the possible interpolation of 1226–80 and 1446–50, I am moved by the argument of L. Schmidt (1848), to which Fraser draws attention (see also Stephanie West (1983), 122 with n. 29), that lines 1281–2 do not naturally follow the passage on Aeneas and the foundation of Rome. But it seems hard to point to anything in general style, vocabulary, metre, or poetic connections (see my discussion of Lycophron and Euphorion *ad fin.*) which sets 1226–80 apart from the rest of the poem.

[4] Stephanie West (1983) and (1984). For a recent discussion of Lycophron, see Richard Hunter in Fantuzzi and Hunter (2004), 437–43.

[5] As several scholars have observed, the Index to Pfeiffer (1953) s.v. Lycophro, p. 134, contains only a fraction of the material spread through his commentary in vol. i.

[6] I tend to agree with Magnelli (who plans a complete edition of Euphorion) in favouring the priority of Lycophron; see Hunter in Fantuzzi and Hunter (2004), 438 n. 106.

[7] For links between A.R. and Lycophron, see my paragraph on Argonautic legends. Although I myself suspect that Apollonius is the earlier, a straight comparison between the two hardly enables one to solve the problem. To judge from his comments on ἄγχουρος (*Arg.* 3.1386, also Lyc. 418) and on μυδαίνω (*Arg.* 3.1042, also Lyc. 1008), Vian, who inclines to date the *Argonautica* in the decade 250–240 BC (1974–81, vol. i. p. xiii) believes in the priority of Apollonius, while Fraser (1972), from his comment on γατομέω (i. 636 and ii. 897 n. 158) upholds that of Lycophron.

[8] See van Groningen (1977), 249–50.

famous tragedian, Lycophron of Chalcis. My own concern is simply to show how extensive are the links between Lycophron and other major Hellenistic poets, notwithstanding the fact that he wrote in iambics and they largely in hexameters or elegiacs. Recent additions to Hellenistic poetry continue to increase the store of available material; I have found in Lycophron some ninety points of contact with Callimachus which seemed to me not negligible, and about forty with the much scantier fragments of Euphorion.

It is worth categorizing the various types of connection which we shall find. In the first place there is the shared use of exceptionally rare words, but with no resemblance of context.[9] Secondly there are myths, cult-titles, or geographical allusions common to Lycophron and one or more of the other Hellenistic poets which may be of interest either for the mere fact of their occurrence or for particular variants, e.g. when they show Lycophron to agree with one of his fellow poets against another—in this class, references to the Argonautic legend are most valuable. Finally come those cases where a verbal resemblance is linked to a similarity in the context, so that on occasion one may venture to decide which poet wrote second, by unravelling the thought processes of one author and suggesting how the presence in his mind of the other's words would have led him to write as he did. No secure general rules can be laid down for this exercise;[10] each case must be argued on its own merits. In selecting the authors with whom to compare Lycophron, I concentrate on those who are of particular significance in the world of Hellenistic poetry. For the present purpose I have ignored Lycophron's huge debt to fifth-century tragedy.

Nonetheless, let us start by considering two pre-Hellenistic poets, Hipponax and Antimachus of Colophon, whose work was alive, discussed, and imitated in the third century. We can see the mark of Hipponax upon Callimachus' *Iambi*—in the first of which (fr. 191 Pfeiffer) Callimachus actually pretends to be the old poet returned

[9] According to Fraser (1972), ii. 1073 n. 358, 'The surviving coincidences between Lyc. and Call. consist almost entirely of rare words, irrespective of context, and not of episodes: see the list given by Pf., s.v. Lycophro.' But Pfeiffer wrote elsewhere (1953, xliii) 'si respicias quot *res et* vocabula . . . '; as noted above, his index s.v. Lycophro contains only a fraction of the parallels.

[10] One cannot expect to find incompetent or ill-harmonized borrowing (such as sometimes happens in the *Appendix Vergiliana*) which betrays the later writer.

from the dead—and on the *Mimiambi* of Herodas.[11] His presence in the *Alexandra* was observed by Tzetzes (on 855), ὦ Λύκοφρον, γίνωσκε ὅτι τὰς μὲν λέξεις ἀπὸ Αἰσχύλου κλέπτεις, ἐξ Ἱππώνακτος δὲ πλέον, and is signalled by the rare words ἀσκέρα (855, 1322, Hipp. fr. 34.3 *IEG*, cf. fr. 32.5), ἔρπις[12] (579, Hipp. fr. 79.18), πάλμυς (691, Hipp. fr. 38), and others which at least have a Hipponactean flavour: παμφαλάω (1433 παμφαλώμενος, Hipp. fr. 164 παμφαλῆσαι, cf. Tzetzes on Lyc. 1162 παπταλώμεναι), ὀφελτρεύω (1165, Tz. quotes Hipp. fr. 79.17–20 including ὀφέλλοντα (19) and ὄφελμα (20)), κασωρεύω and κασωρίς (772 and 1385, cf. Hipp. fr. 135c κασωρῖτις).

The merits and demerits of Antimachus of Colophon aroused fierce controversy in the third century; even Callimachus, whose adverse judgement on the *Lyde* was most celebrated (fr. 398 Pf.), elsewhere shows signs of his influence.[13] The most interesting point of contact between Antimachus and Lycophron concerns *Alexandra* 20–1 οἱ δ' <u>οὖσα</u> γρώνης εὐγάληνα χερμάδος | ναῦται λίαζον and an emendation[14] in our longest fragment of the *Lyde* (68 Matthews = 57 Wyss), preserved on a third-century BC ostrakon now in Berlin. Antimachus was describing the part played by Athena in the construction and equipment of the Argo; according to the ostrakon he wrote (line 2) <u>σοῦσ'</u> ἐτίθει παντοῖα θεά, πόδας ἠδὲ κάλωας. Now σοῦσον was only known as an Asiatic name of the lily, which (Powell argued)[15] would have fibres too brittle to produce ropes. Therefore he proposed οὖσ' for σοῦσ', relying on Hesychius' entry οὖσα· σχοινία, νεὼς ὅπλα (ο 1871 = ii. 798 Latte), and on Alexander of Aetolia, fr. 3.21 *CA*, Magnelli[16] διὰ μὲν καλὸν ἤρικεν <u>οὖσον</u>. Emendation of σοῦσ'

[11] Dated to the 270s and 260s BC by Cunningham (1971), 2. A striking parallel between the *Iambi* of Callimachus (fr. 197.3) and Lycophron (930) lies in the compound ἱπποτέκτων (not attested elsewhere), applied to Epeius.

[12] Said by Schol. ad loc. to be an Egyptian word. von Holzinger (1895) ad loc. and Intr. p. 21) wonders whether πέρρα = sun (1428), likewise said to be Egyptian, might also be Hipponactean.

[13] e.g. in Call. fr. 10 we find, in a single line, two of the nouns in -τύς (μαστύς and ἀλητύς) for which Antimachus was notorious. See Matthews (1996), 188, on his fr. 54 = 48 Wyss.

[14] Emended first by Powell (1919) and later independently by Wilamowitz ((1924*a*), 273 = (1935–72), iv. 367). See Stephanie West (1967), 260–3 for discussion and bibliography.

[15] Powell (1919), 91.

[16] Magnelli (1999).

to οὖσ' in the *Lyde* is not certain, but highly plausible; Antimachus may have read οὖσον or σοῦσον for the vulgate ὅπλον in *Odyssey* 21.390.[17] I remark in passing how well all this fits with the traditional date and authorship of the *Alexandra*: we would have two poets, Lycophron and Alexander of Aetolia, who were close contemporaries, fellow members of the Pleiad and scholarly collaborators in the service of Ptolemy Philadelphus,[18] making common use of a work celebrated and notorious at the time, Antimachus' *Lyde*.[19]

More than one very rare myth from Antimachus recurs in Lycophron, e.g. the spring which gushes forth when Achilles alights on Trojan sand (*Alex.* 245–8):[20]

ὅταν Πελασγὸν ἅλμα λαιψηροῦ ποδός
εἰς θῖν' ἐρείσας λοισθίαν αἴθων λύκος
κρηναῖον ἐξ ἄμμοιο ῥοιβδήσηι γάνος,
πηγὰς ἀνοίξας τὰς πάλαι κεκρυμμένας.

Schol. ad loc. quotes Antimachus fr. 136 Matthews:

ῥίμφα δ' ἀπ' ἠπείροιο μελαίνης ὑψόσ' ἀερθείς
Πηλείδης ἀνόρουσεν ἐλαφρῶς ἠύτε κίρκος.
τοῦ δ' ἔμπροσθε ποδῶν κρήνη γένετ' ἀενάουσα.

An obscure cult shared by these two poets is that of Demeter-Erinys (Antim. fr. 33 M.):

ἐγγύθι δὲ προχοαὶ ποταμοῦ Λάδωνος ἔασιν
Δήμητρος τόθι φασὶν Ἐρινύος εἶναι ἕδεθλον.

The joining of these two lines (quoted separately) was first suggested by Meineke, and gains some colour from *Alexandra* 1040–1 Δίκης ἑάσει τάρροθος Τελφουσία | Λάδωνος ἀμφὶ ῥεῖθρα ναίουσα σκύλαξ.[21] I have also found the following rare words and forms common to Antimachus and Lycophron: ὄστριμον (Ant. fr. 55, Lyc. 94),

[17] See Matthews (1996), 208–9.

[18] See Pfeiffer (1968), 119.

[19] In one of his scholarly works Lycophron commented with apparent approval on a line of Antimachus (see Matthews (1996), 158, on his fr. 39).

[20] For discussion of the context, see Martin West (1966*b*), 157, and Matthews (1996), 329–31. It remains unclear to which poem of Antimachus the fragment should be ascribed.

[21] A briefer reference to the same cult in *Alexandra* 153 Ἐρινύς. Note also Callimachus fr. 652 Ἐρινύι Τιλφωσαίηι.

ἀνακυπόω (Ant. fr. 150, Lyc. 137, cf. Nicander, *Ther.* 705),[22] παός (Doric form of Homeric πηός), noted by Schol. Nic., *Ther.* 3 as Antimachean (fr. 159), also Lyc. 416, δέπαστρον (see Matthews on fr. 19).

Two poets who seem to have been elder contemporaries of Callimachus and whose writings can be taken to precede the *Alexandra* (even on the earliest dating of Lycophron) are Philetas[23] and Alexander of Aetolia. Very little of Philetas survives; our failure so far to add anything substantial to his work from papyri is both puzzling and disappointing. But, from among these meagre remnants, alongside Lyc. 814 (of Odysseus) γαληνὸν ἦμαρ οὔποτ' ἐν ζωῆι δρακών one can set fr. 7.2 *CA* = fr. 4.2 Spanoudakis θυμέ, γαληναίηι δ' ἐπιμίσγεαι οὐδ' ὅσον ὅσσον. This fragment probably belongs to the *Hermes*, which involved Odysseus (fr. 5 *CA* = 1 Spanoudakis, from Parthenius, *Narr. Amat.* 2);[24] the propensity of that hero to address his θυμός in Homer, coupled with the *Alexandra* parallel, increases the likelihood that he is the speaker in Philetas too. The adjective ὄμπνιος, which Philetas noticed ἐν Ἀτάκτοις Γλώσσαις[25] and may have popularized among Hellenistic poets,[26] occurs twice in Lycophron (621, 1264).

As to Alexander of Aetolia, I have already talked about οὖσον, which he (fr. 3.21 *CA*, Magnelli) and Lycophron (20) may have taken from Antimachus. Two uncommon, though by no means unparalleled, mythical variants which Alexander shares with Lycophron regard Helen as mother of Iphigenia (Lyc. 103, Alex. Aet. fr. 12 *CA* = 11 Magnelli) and Hector as a son of Apollo (Alex. Aet. fr. 13 *CA* = 12 M., Lyc. 265); in both cases Stesichorus and Euphorion concurred. One might argue for a more subtle kind of influence from Alexander fr. 3.14–16 to Lycophron 133–5. The story in this fragment of Alexander (quoted by Parthenius, *Narr. Amat.* 14) conforms to a familiar type: Cleoboea, wife of Phobius, tries to seduce her husband's young guest, Antheus—

[22] The simple κυπόω, previously unique in Lyc. 1442, now has a companion (unrecognized by the LSJ Revised Supplement) in Call. *SH* 257.8 κυπωθείς.

[23] Who now has two recent editors, Sbardella (2000) and Spanoudakis (2002).

[24] See the discussion in Lightfoot (1999), 380–1.

[25] Dettori (2000), 113–24, Spanoudakis fr. 44.

[26] I strongly suspect that Callimachus, fr. 1.10 ὄμπνια Θεσμοφόρος is a verbatim quotation from Philetas' *Demeter* (perhaps even the first words of that poem).

ὁ δὲ Ζῆνα Ξείνιον αἰδόμενος
σπονδάς τ' ἐν Φοβίου καὶ ἅλα ξυνέωνα τραπέζης
κρήναις καὶ ποταμοῖς νίψετ' ἀεικὲς ἔπος.[27]

In Lycophron 133–5 the subject is Paris, who, by abducting Helen, 'showed no regard for the love of Antheus, nor for the purifying salt of Aegaeon [Poseidon] shared between guest and host':

οὐκ αἰδούμενος
οὐδ' Ἀνθέως ἔρωτας οὐδὲ τὸν ξένοις
σύνδορπον Αἰγαίωνος ἁγνίτην πάγον.

According to the scholia, Menelaus had stayed with Paris in Troy, and, when the latter had accidentally killed his favourite Antheus, son of Antenor, Menelaus saved Paris from any consequences by taking him back to Sparta. Several similarities between the passages strike one: the pattern αἰδόμενος—οὐκ αἰδούμενος, the reverence (or lack of it) for the shared salt of hospitality, and a young man (not the same young man) called Antheus who is loved and killed. While Alexander's Antheus—to judge from the 'manchette'[28] in the manuscript of Parthenius—appeared in Aristotle[29] as well as the *Milesian Tales*,[30] no other source mentions Lycophron's Antheus. It would be rash to conclude that Lycophron invented him, but I suspect that the association of name and wording in Alexander has been partly responsible for what we read in Lycophron.

Undoubtedly the closest links with the *Alexandra* are to be found in Dosiadas' *Βωμός* (*CA* p. 175). The two poems are mentioned in the same breath by Lucian, *Lexiphanes* 25 καθάπερ ὁ Δωσιάδα Βωμὸς ἂν εἴη καὶ ἡ τοῦ Λυκόφρονος Ἀλεξάνδρα, καὶ εἴ τις ἔτι τούτων τὴν φωνὴν κακοδαιμονέστερος. Apart from the riddling manner, we meet the same kind of extravagant compounds, and striking verbal similarities: e.g. Lyc. 33 τριεσπέρου λέοντος, Dos. 11 Τριεσπέροιο (both of Heracles); Lyc. 63 γιγαντοραίστοις ἄρδισιν, Dos. 17–18 Ἰλοραιστᾶν |

[27] I print τραπέζης, the conjecture of Brunck and others (see Lightfoot (1999), 465). Magnelli retains the manuscript's θαλάσσης, which is hard to defend.

[28] For these short notices, naming authors in whom the story is allegedly found, see Lightfoot (1999), 246 ff. They are clearly not due to Parthenius himself, and there is no guarantee that they have hit upon the actual sources used by P.; in some cases there is reason to think otherwise.

[29] Probably from a *Constitution of Miletus*.

[30] Or 'Milesian writers' (see Lightfoot (1999), 454).

... ἀρδίων (both of the arrows which passed from Heracles to Philoctetes);[31] Lyc. 1066 κρατοβρῶτος, Dos. 17 ἀνδροβρῶτος (both of Tydeus); Lyc. 461 ἀίτα, Dos. 5 ἀίτας.[32] In fact most of the themes in Dosiadas' *Βωμός* can be paralleled in Lycophron: Achilles married to Medea in Elysium (L. 174–5 and 798, D. 3), Thetis putting her children into the fire (L. 178, D. 3), the rejuvenation of Jason (L. 1315, D. 2 and 5), Philoctetes cremating Heracles (L. 916 ff., D. 11) and killing Paris (L. 64 and 912, D. 10), Odysseus stealing the Palladium (L. 658, D. 16) and going a second time to Hades (L. 813, D. 17), Troy thrice sacked (L. 31–2, 52, 69–71, D. 18). One of the few exceptions is Talos, the bronze guardian of Crete (Dos. 6 ff.); it may be significant that he appears prominently in Apollonius Rhodius (*Arg.* 4.1638 ff.).

Another near relative of the *Βωμός* is the Theocritean *Syrinx* (see the introduction and commentary in Gow (1950))—note above all στήτας (Dos. 1, *Syr.* 14) and Penelope as mother of Pan (Dos. 16, *Syr.* 1–2).[33] Most scholars have gladly denied this poem to Theocritus, but Gow found no more compelling reason to do so than an archaeological point (the shape of the instrument) on which the last word may not have been spoken. There has been a tendency to date the *Βωμός* of Dosiadas and other similar technopaegnia early in the third century BC, but our evidence is slender—more substantial in the case of Simmias[34] (see *CA* pp. 116–20 for his shaped poems entitled *Wings*, *Axe*, and *Egg*). It is worth mentioning here a recently discovered riddling epigram on the Oyster (*SH* 983), which came together with a voluminously learned commentary (*SH* 984); the papyrus itself is of the second century BC, the poem perhaps earlier. I am somewhat reminded of Philetas fr. 16 *CA* = 20 Spanoudakis, on the Flute.[35] If one could prove that all these works belong to the first half of the third century, they would provide a congenial environment for the *Alexandra*.

Among the poems of Callimachus, it is easiest to establish links between Lycophron and the *Hecale*, and there may even be

[31] For ἄρδις, see Pfeiffer on Callimachus, fr. 70.2.

[32] See Gow on [Theocritus] 12.14 for this very rare gloss.

[33] Also in Euphorion, fr. 109 *CA*.

[34] Said by Hephaestion, *Encheiridion* p. 31.4 Consbruch to have written before Philicus.

[35] Peter Parsons originally compared Philetas fr. 10 *CA* = 25 Spanoudakis.

indications that Callimachus wrote first.[36] The last man to possess a complete copy of the *Hecale* (*c.* AD 1200) was probably Michael Choniates.[37] In his summary of the main plot[38] Michael wrote *καταλῦσαί φασι καὶ ἐπιξενωθῆναι* [sc. *τὸν Θησέα*] *παρά τινι γυναικί* (*Ἑκάλη τῆι γυναικὶ τὸ ὄνομα ἦν*), *γραΐ μὲν πεμπέλωι καὶ πενιχρᾶι, ξενοδόχωι δ' ἄλλως ἀγαθῆι καὶ τοῖς παροδεύουσιν ἄκλειστον ἀεὶ προβαλλομένηι τὸ οἴκημα*. It is obvious that the concluding words of the summary are meant to be a paraphrase of *Hecale* fr. 2 Hollis *τίον δέ ἑ πάντες ὁδῖται | ἦρα φιλοξενίης· ἔχε γὰρ τέγος ἀκλήιστον*. This should turn our attention towards the preceding description of Hecale, *γραΐ μὲν πεμπέλωι*. The epithet *πέμπελος*, 'extremely old', is exceptionally rare, and not likely to have been in Michael's everyday vocabulary. The most plausible explanation for its presence in Michael is that Callimachus had used it in the initial description of his heroine,[39] not long after what we know to have been the poem's first line, *Ἀκταίη τις ἔναιεν Ἐρεχθέος ἔν ποτε γουνῶι* (fr. 1 Hollis = Call. fr. 230 Pfeiffer). Otherwise the earliest occurrences of *πέμπελος* are in Lycophron (682 and 826); the latter (*πέμπελον γραῦν*), though in quite a different context, could well have recalled Callimachus' epyllion.

In *Hecale* fr. 74.10 ff. H. (= fr. 260.51 ff. Pf.) an aged crow (*κορώνη*) swears by its wrinkled skin (10–11 *ναὶ μὰ τὸ ῥικνόν | σῦφαρ ἐμόν*) that one day the raven (14 ff. *δείελος ἀλλ' ἢ νὺξ ἢ ἔνδιος ἢ ἔσετ' ἠώς | εὖτε κόραξ* . . .) will offend Apollo and have its plumage changed from brilliant white to pitch black. Now *σῦφαρ*, a very rare word, is also found in Lycophron (793),[40] denoting Odysseus in his wrinkled old age; the very next line describes him as a *κόραξ*, to which bird Lycophron (unusually) transfers the fabled longevity of the *κορώνη*:

σῦφαρ θανεῖται πόντιον φυγὼν σκέπας
κόραξ σὺν ὅπλοις Νηρίτων δρυμῶν πέλας.

I doubt whether this can be a coincidence, and, if one poet is consciously or subconsciously recalling the context of the other (a

[36] Unfortunately we have no firm evidence which would give an absolute date for Callimachus' epyllion—it seems to be earlier than his Fourth Iambus (fr. 194).

[37] N. G. Wilson (1983), 204–6, Hollis (1990), 38–40.

[38] Test. 15 Hollis (cf. 36 Pf.).

[39] Suggested in Hollis (1997), 55–6.

[40] Where it should be regarded as a noun used predicatively (Lloyd-Jones) rather than an adjective (LSJ).

wrinked hide and a prophecy about a raven), it seems much more likely that Lycophron, in whom the association of *σῦφαρ* and *κόραξ* is only fleeting, recollects Callimachus than vice versa. Still on the subject of birds, and the same passage of the *Hecale* (some ten lines earlier), *Alexandra* 609–10 tells how the companions of Diomedes, changed into birds, would become tame and eat from the hand:

> καὶ κρῖμνα χειρῶν κἀπιδόρπιον τρύφος
> μάζης σπάσονται.

A scholiast on 609 is moved to quote Call. *Hecale* fr. 74.5 καὶ κρῖμνον κυκεῶνος ἀποστάξαντος ἔραζε. The context in Callimachus is not entirely clear, but Pfeiffer had already noted a possible similarity to that in Lycophron: perhaps the crow remembers how old Hecale (now dead) used to feed her. Again, if the link is a real one, it seems more likely that Lycophron is the borrower. The two attested occurrences of στόρνη both involve Theseus—in Call. *Hecale* fr. 69.15 he is crowned by women's girdles after overcoming the Marathonian bull, while in Lyc. 1330 he steals the girdle of Hippolyte. Beyond doubt there is a deliberate connection between *Hecale* fr. 62 ἧχι <u>κονίστραι</u> | <u>ἄξεινοι</u> λύθρωι τε καὶ εἴαρι πεπλήθασι and Lyc. 866–7 γυμνάδας <u>κακοξένους</u> | πάλης <u>κονίστρας</u> (respectively on Cercyon and Eryx, both of whom compelled passing strangers to wrestle with them), though from this comparison alone one could not deduce which poet wrote first.

A legend of some significance for the *Hecale* (though well enough known before Callimachus' time) concerned the recognition by Aegeus of his son Theseus through the sword and sandals left under a hollow rock in Troezen; this is mentioned twice by Lycophron (494, 1322), and the scholia on 494 quote *Hecale* fr. 9 to illustrate ἐκ κοίλης πέτρας with κολουραίηι ὑπὸ πέτρηι. The reference in Lyc. 111 Ἀκτῆς, διμόρφου γηγενοῦς σκηπτουχίας is more obscure. Pfeiffer on Call. fr. 194.68 ἀνὴρ ὄφις τὰ νέρθεν ἀμφὶ τῆς Ἀκτῆς naturally took the δίμορφος γηγενής to be Cecrops. But an alternative explanation offered by Tzetzes makes Lycophron allude to Erichthonius, who was in a more spectacular sense γηγενής, according to the very rare legend which formed a digression in the *Hecale* (fr. 70.8 ὡς δῆθεν ὑφ' Ἡφαίστωι τέκε Γαῖα). And Erichthonius equally had serpentine connections (cf. Ov. *Met.* 2.561 *infantemque vident adporrectumque draconem*). It would be very much in Lycophron's manner to tease his audience by a more oblique reference instead of a more obvious one.

The *Aetia* too provides material for comparison with Lycophron. Shared myths include child sacrifice to Palaemon on Tenedos (Call. frr. 91–2,[41] Lyc. 229 *Παλαίμων . . . βρεφοκτόνος*) and the feeding of the Greek army by the daughters of Anius (fr. 188, Lyc. 570–83). Often (as in this case) we are handicapped through knowing that Callimachus mentioned a certain legend, but not precisely which part of that legend. This is particularly true of Call. fr. 35, where the testimonium embraces the sin of the lesser Ajax, his death and the consequent sending of Locrian girls to serve Athena in Troy as an expiation. All parts of this story are prominent in Lycophron; if we could be sure that Callimachus dealt with the tribute of the Locrian maidens (the most obviously aetiological element), a possibility would arise of comparing three Hellenistic poets on the same theme: Callimachus, Lycophron, and Euphorion.[42]

Argonautic legends, of course, precede the Trojan War and the prophecies of Cassandra/Alexandra. Thus Lycophron is under no obligation to introduce them; he can follow his own fancy, and is all the more likely to choose stories of which other treatments would be familiar to a learned audience. Interestingly, we can sometimes set his version alongside both Callimachus' *Aetia* and Apollonius' *Argonautica*. More than once Lycophron seems to accord with Callimachus against Apollonius; on the other hand Lycophron follows the fortunes of the Argonauts in Libya, as did Apollonius but not (as far as we can tell) Callimachus.[43] Consider the case of Tiphys, helmsman of the Argo. Lycophron has him still directing operations around the dangerous coast of Libya (889–90):

ᾗι διὰ στενῶν
μύρμων ἐνήσει Τῖφυς ἄθραυστον σκάφος.

[41] In fr. 92 Callimachus seems to cite one Leander or Leandrius as a source.

[42] Euphorion would contribute fr. 53 *CA*. Pfeiffer (on Call. fr. 35) and van Groningen (his Euphorion fr. 192) doubt the ascription to Euphorion. For this legend as a problem of Hellenistic history, see Momigliano (1945), 49–53; Stephanie West (1984), 148–9 makes a more literary evaluation.

[43] Although Callimachus mentioned some of the Libyan place names which Lycophron connects with the Argonauts: Ausigda (fr. 706, cf. Lyc. 885), possibly Taucheira (Pf. on fr. 484, cf. Lyc. 877), these may rather reflect Callimachus' interest in his homeland of Cyrene (see Pfeiffer on fr. 602).

Apollonius, however, records his death much earlier, among the Mariandyni, at the site of Heraclea Pontica (2.854 ff.), and such was the general view;[44] thereafter he is commonly replaced by Ancaeus (A.R. 2.894 ff.). Mere carelessness on the part of Lycophron? The scholia on 890 duly reprehend him.[45] But it is worth bearing in mind that Tiphys' name can be read in a damaged papyrus of Call. fr. 17.9, in the middle of a narrative covering the final stages of the return voyage.[46] One could think up ways for Callimachus to introduce the name of a dead Tiphys—e.g. his absence might be regretted—but it is more natural to infer that he is still alive (even later than in Lycophron) and preparing to guide the Argo through the terrible darkness to be described in fr. 18.

A myth not Argonautic but with Argonautic connections is the burying of a sickle in Corcyra which accounted for the island's former name of Drepane. According to Lycophron (761–2) this was the sickle of Zeus, with which he mutilated Cronos, while the better-known sickle of Cronos lies in Sicily. Callimachus too (fr. 43.69–71) locates the sickle of Cronos in Sicily;[47] presumably, therefore, it is the sickle of Zeus[48] which explains the name Drepane in Call. fr. 14. That being so, Callimachus and Lycophron would agree together against Apollonius, who buries the sickle of Cronos in Corcyra (4.985–6). In both Callimachus and Apollonius the Colchians who, in their attempt to recapture Medea, pursue the Argonauts, split into two parties.[49] One sails down the Ister without finding the Argonauts, and, fearing to return home without Medea, founds the city of Polae[50] and other cities on the Illyrian coast;[51] the second comes through the Bosporus, and eventually arrives at Corcyra, where they do indeed encounter the Argonauts, but (not being able to bring back Medea) they too choose to stay on and settle.

[44] Σ A.R. 2.854 (p. 192.11-14 Wendel) records the variant opinion of Herodorus that he died (? at Heraclea) on the return rather than the outward journey.

[45] ii. 288 Scheer.

[46] Pfeiffer estimated that there may not have been more than six lines between fr. 12.6 and fr. 17.1.

[47] Twice in Pfeiffer's note on Call. fr. 14 (second line and two lines from the end) '*Iovis* falce' is a slip for 'Saturni'.

[48] It might possibly, however, be the sickle of Demeter (cf. A.R. 4.986 ff.).

[49] Pfeiffer on Call. fr. 9; cf. Fraser (1972), ii. 887–8 n. 86.

[50] See Fraser (1972), ii. 902, n. 191.

[51] A.R. 4.563 ff., Call. fr. 11 with Pfeiffer's note on line 7.

In Lycophron as well as the two other poets we find passages referring to this pursuit marked by the verb μαστεύω (or a cognate word). Pfeiffer, for once, fails to note the parallels, though he does cite the much later Dionysius Periegetes, who joins in the same game (490 ἴχνια μαστεύοντες ἀλήμονος Αἰητίνης). Callimachus (almost certainly) and Lycophron (certainly) speak of the party which founded Polae, but Apollonius of those who came to Corcyra. It is worth setting out the passages:

(a) μαστύος ἀλλ' ὅτ' ἔκαμνον ἀλητύι (Call. fr. 10[52])
(b) μαστῆρες ἀριστήων (A.R. 4.1003)
(c) μαστῆρας οὓς θυγατρὸς ἔστειλεν βαρὺς
Αἴας Κορίνθου τ' ἀρχός, Εἰδυίας πόσις. (Lyc. *Alex.* 1022–3)

The most striking Argonautic episode common to Apollonius (4.654 ff.) and Lycophron (874–6) but, as far as we know, unrecorded by Callimachus[53] concerns the pebbles on the beach of Aethalia (Elba) which, in their colour, replicate the oily scrapings from the bodies of the sailors. Also there is the encounter in Libya of the Argonauts with a divine figure, and the exchange of a gift for a service.[54] Apollonius (4.1537 ff.) makes Triton, who claims to be Eurypulus, receive a tripod, give a clod of earth, and show the Argonauts their safe exit. In Lycophron (886 ff.) Medea presents Triton with a golden mixing bowl in return for guidance, and then Triton predicts Greek rule over the land. One might detect a deliberate verbal link between A.R. 4.1550 (κτέρας of the tripod) and Lycophron 895 (the more recherché κτέαρ of the mixing bowl).

As mentioned earlier, the points of contact between Lycophron and Euphorion, though not appearing to us so numerous as those between Lycophron and Callimachus (perhaps because of the smaller amount of Euphorion which has been preserved), are even more striking,[55] and the relationship more crucial, in that the priority of

[52] Pfeiffer raised a possibility that this might be identified as the first line of fr. 11, which goes on to speak of Polae.

[53] One may wonder whether this aetion might yet find a place in Callimachus.

[54] The background lies in Pindar (*Pythian* 4) and Herodotus (4.179).

[55] As well as cases to be discussed later, note particularly Lyc. 887 ὤπασεν δάνος with Euph. fr. 42 δάνος ὤπασεν, the passages on Mopsus and Amphilochus (Lyc. 439 ff., Euph. fr. 98 *CA*), and, among single words, πόποι = gods (Lyc. 943, Euph. fr. 136). See further n. 60 below.

Lycophron, if established, would sit comfortably with the *Alexandra*'s traditional date and authorship, while the reverse would come close to demolishing these. I doubt whether one can prove either position to a determined sceptic by a straight comparison of passages from the two poets, but am fairly confident that the parallels with Euphorion provide no strong argument against the earlier dating of the *Alexandra*. Skutsch (1909), 1184–7 did attempt to establish the priority of Euphorion on literary grounds, but (even cumulatively) his arguments amount to little. For example, he contends that, as between obscure poets, the more obscure (Lycophron) should follow the less obscure (Euphorion) rather than vice versa. In the abstract this has a certain plausibility, but, once a myth had been handled in the riddling manner of Lycophron, later poets could not be debarred from giving it a fuller and less cryptic treatment. P.Oxy. 2812 includes a hexameter piece, probably by Nicander,[56] which, within the space of a few lines, covers in a simple enough style several topics familiar from Lycophron: building on the Hill of Ate (cf. Lyc. 29); a sea monster punishing the perjury of Laomedon (cf. Lyc. 34 ff.); the names of the snakes which came from Calydnae (cf. Lyc. 347). Skutsch's criterion would incline us to make Lycophron the later of these two poets, but if the author of the hexameters is indeed Nicander (*SH* 562), few would deny the priority of the *Alexandra*.[57] As far as we can tell, parallels with Lycophron are not confined to a single poem of Euphorion, but spread throughout the latter's works. This Skutsch took as a sign of Euphorion's priority; the greater likelihood lies the other way.[58] Finally, Skutsch's attempt to discredit any thought of Lycophron's priority on the ground that the elliptical references in the *Alexandra* would not provide enough information

[56] *SH* 562. The ancient commentator cites the poet's name, of which .ανδρος can be read.

[57] The matter has become somewhat more complicated owing to increasing recognition that there were two poets called Nicander—possibly grandfather and grandson. I tend to agree with Cameron (1995), 198–205, in ascribing *Theriaca* and *Alexipharmaca* to the older Nicander, but Jacques (2002), xiii, takes the opposite view. Links between the didactic poems and Lycophron include the words ἀρδηθμός, ῥόχθος, τράμπις, which are not found elsewhere.

[58] To take an example almost at random: Virgil absorbed Varius Rufus, *De Morte* in his youth, and imitated it throughout his poetic career (*Ecl.* 8.88, *Georgics* 2.506, *Aen.* 6.621).

for fuller references in Euphorion[59] must fail, depending as it does on the assumption that there were no other resources available for such myths. Even if Euphorion did not have to hand a commentary on the *Alexandra* (an idea which Skutsch seems to view with unnecessary scorn), I cannot imagine one of the most learned men of his day reading the *Alexandra* in a fog of uncomprehension.

Parallels between these two poets were listed and discussed by G. Knaack.[60] Pieces of Euphorion discovered since 1888 provide further material: Lyc. 223 τόμουρε, cf. Euph. *SH* 418.28 τόμουροι; Lyc. 629 ἄνδηρα, cf. Euph. *SH* 418.36 ἀνδήροισι; Lyc. 934, cf. Euph. *SH* 415 col. ii.14 ff. (rare myth of Comaetho). Much the most illuminating new comparison arises from the anonymous hexameter disinterred by Wilamowitz[61] from Didymus, and ascribed to Euphorion (*SH* 453):

ἔνθα Τρώϊον ἄλμα καὶ ἠρία Μουνίπποιο.

ἄλμα = 'grove' is elsewhere attested only at Lycophron 319.[62] The latter spoke of the Trojan princess Laodice, in her attempt to escape from the victorious Greeks, being swallowed by the earth at a spot 'where is the grove of her ancestor, and where the corpse of the prostitute heifer [Cilla] of secret wedlock lies united with her whelp [Munippus], before he eagerly drew her milk, and before she washed her limbs with water after the birth' (319–22):

ἵν' ἄλμα πάππου καὶ χαμευνάδος μόροι
τῆς λαθρονύμφου πόρτιος μεμιγμένοι
σκύμνωι κέχυνται, πρὶν λαφύξασθαι γάνος,
πρὶν ἐκ λοχείας γυῖα χυτλῶσαι δρόσωι.

A common interest of Lycophron and Euphorion in the luckless

[59] If Euphorion wrote second, he was not defeated by the phrase ἄλμα πάππου (319), but correctly identified the πάππος (not named by Lycophron) as Tros. See below.

[60] Knaack (1888); incidentally he believed in the priority of Lycophron. If one discounts bits of Euphorion which have come to light since then, Knaack could also have noted: Helen as mother of Iphigenia (Lyc. 103, Euph. fr. 90 *CA*); Odysseus and Sinon as cousins (Lyc. 345, Euph. fr. 69); πέμφιξ = 'ghost' (Lyc. 686 and 1106, and the most plausible meaning in Euph. fr. 134); Lyc. 1177 ταρμύσσουσαν, cf. Euph. fr. 124 ἀτάρμυκτον.

[61] (1926*b*), 290 = (1935–72), iv. 417–18.

[62] *Et. Mag.* quoted Lycophron to illustrate the word.

Munippus could already have been deduced from *Alexandra* 224 ff. and Euph. fr. 55 (the 'filius vates' of Servius on *Aeneid* 2.32 is the Aesacus of *Alex.* 224); an apparent difference is that Euphorion made him the legitimate child of Thymoetes and Cilla instead of Priam's offspring by Cilla (Lyc. 319–22 above) but the Latin commentator may be speaking imprecisely. As for 'the grove of her ancestor' (Lyc. 319), most commentators have identified the *πάππος* as Ilus, whose tomb Homer mentions (e.g. *Il.* 11.166). But the scholia on Lyc. 319 declare the *πάππος* to be Tros, and we can now see that this agrees with Euphorion. Since no other reference to the 'grove of Tros' has survived, it may be that some fuller ancient commentary on Lycophron, from which our scholia are drawn, actually quoted the line of Euphorion.

We do not know the context of Euphorion's hexameter, but the linking of the same otherwise unattested noun (*ἅλμα*) with the same two geographical indications (grove of Tros and tomb of Munippus) in both Lycophron and Euphorion suggests strongly that Euphorion too was describing Laodice's death. The only point to remember is that Euphorion (fr. 72) said something abut Laodice which Pausanias (10.26.8) was at pains to refute. It is not clear, however, to what exactly Pausanias objected—perhaps to Euphorion's account of her fate (on the ground that Agamemnon and Menelaus would not have allowed anything unpleasant to happen to the daughter-in-law of Antenor who had entertained Menelaus and Odysseus), perhaps to the tale of Laodice's love for Acamas—though that was not confined to Euphorion.[63] Pausanias' remark does not enable us to say definitely to what extent Euphorion's account of Laodice's end agreed[64] or disagreed with that of Lycophron.

The love affair of Laodice and Acamas itself provides no less instructive a comparison between these two poets:[65]

[63] According to the manchette attached to Parthenius, *Narr. Amat.* 16, the story was to be found in the *Palleniaca* of Hegesippus. See Lightfoot (1999), 478 ff.

[64] As Wilamowitz thought (n. 61).

[65] The whole myth of Laodice was discussed by Cazzaniga (1959), without reference, however, to Wilamowitz's line of Euphorion (*SH* 453). Tzetzes on 497 reprehends Lycophron for inconsistency in his account of Laodice, in a manner that is not altogether fair but somewhat amusing: *τὴν γὰρ θανοῦσαν πρὶν πεσοῦσαν χαράδραι* [he has in mind 316–18] *αὖθις ἀνιστᾶις καὶ νεκροῖς αὐτὴν πάλιν θνήσκουσαν, ὡς φής, συμφοραῖς τοῦ Μουνίτου Θρήσσης ἐχίδνης προσβολῆι τεθνηκότος.* But *θρήνοισιν*

(a) Lyc. 495–500

τοῦ [sc. of Acamas] *ποτ' εἰς λέχος*
λαθραῖον αὐτόκλητος Ἰδαία πόρις [sc. Laodice]
ἡ ζῶσ' ἐς Αἵδην ἵξεται καταιβάτις
θρήνοισιν ἐκτακεῖσα, Μουνίτου τοκάς·
ὃν δή ποτ' <u>ἀγρώσσοντα</u> Κρηστώνης ἔχις
κτενεῖ, πατάξας πτέρναν ἀγρίωι βέλει.

(b) Euph. fr. 58

ἡ [sc. Laodice] *οἱ* [sc. to Acamas] *Μούνιτον υἷα τέκε πλομένωι ἐνὶ ὥρωι*
ἀλλά ἑ Σιθονίηι τε καὶ ἐν κνημοῖσιν Ὀλύνθου
<u>ἀγρώσσονθ'</u> ἅμα πατρὶ πελώριος ἔκτανεν ὕδρος.[66]

The line of Euphorion recovered by Wilamowitz (*SH* 453) perhaps belongs not far from fr. 58 *CA*. It strengthens his verbal links with Lycophron (*ἅλμα*), illustrates an associated myth common to the two poets (Munippus) and suggests, if it does not prove, that Euphorion made Laodice die in the same spot as did Lycophron.

Among other parallels between these poets, I will draw attention to just one: *Alex.* 1278 *Ζωστηρίου τε κλιτύν* with fr. 95b *ἠδ' ἐπαπειλήσας Ζωστηρίωι Ἀπόλλωνι.*[67] The significant point is that this occurs in the passage of the *Alexandra* (1226–80) which is most strongly suspected of interpolation. Stephanie West recorded her impression that the doubtful lines make somewhat easier reading than the main body of the text. I have a similar feeling about links with the learned poets who provide the main subject matter of this investigation. This would be consistent with an interpolator who

ἐκτακεῖσα (Lyc. 498) need not imply that Laodice died from grief for Munitus; at the earlier time when Lycophron depicts her as swallowed up by the earth (316–18), there were many things for her to lament (e.g. the capture of Troy, besides her personal danger).

[66] Euphorion's wording is quite close to that in Parthenius 16 *ad fin.*, *χρόνου δὲ προϊόντος γίνεται τῶι Ἀκάμαντι υἱὸς Μούνιτος, ὃν ὑπ' Αἴθρας τραφέντα μετὰ Τροίας ἅλωσιν διεκόμισεν ἐπ' οἴκου καὶ αὐτὸν θηρεύοντα ἐν Ὀλύνθωι τῆς Θράικης ὄφις ἀνεῖλεν.* It looks as though Parthenius, unlike the compiler of his manchette (see n. 63 above), may have had Euphorion in mind. See Lightfoot (1999), 478–9.

[67] In fact this line (unlike fr. 95a *οὗτος μὲν Ζωστὴρ Φοίβου πέδον*) is not explicitly ascribed to Euphorion, but it illustrates the rare cult-title as in *Alex.* 1278. Euphorion has a liking for four-word hexameters.

knows what the game is, but does not play it with quite the same enthusiasm as the original author.[68]

What can we conclude, however tentatively, from this survey of Lycophron's poetical connections? Although one might think that Lycophron, because of his metre and matter, stands somewhat apart from mainstream Hellenistic poetry, I hope to have illustrated that the opposite is the case. In subject matter as well as vocabulary he has many links with Callimachus, Apollonius, and Euphorion (not to mention others about whom we know less, such as Alexander of Aetolia). He is interested in two earlier poets, Hipponax and Antimachus, whom we know to have been figures of influence and controversy in the first half of the third century BC. Concerning his riddling style, we have only slight justification for dating the *Ara* of Dosiadas (which has much the greatest affinity with the *Alexandra*) in this period, but the figured poems of Simmias can be placed here more securely. Other examples of riddling obscurity can be found in the epigram on the Oyster (*SH* 983) and in Philetas (fr. 16 *CA*). Obviously the *Alexandra* was composed as a challenge to the learned, in rather the same spirit as Philicus, himself a member of the Pleiad, wrote his hymn to Demeter, *καινογράφου συνθέσεως τῆς Φιλίκου, γραμματικοί, δῶρα φέρω πρὸς ὑμᾶς* (*SH* 677).

[68] Other words in this passage which are suggestive of learned Hellenistic poetry (but mostly not quite so rare) include *ἄμναμοι* (1227), *Καστνίας* (1234), *Ἀλμωπίαι* (1238), *δείκηλον* (1259), *σηκόν* (1261), *ὀμπνίαν* (1264), *τύρσιν* (1273).

Part IV

Metre and Textual Criticism

20

Dionysius' Ear

L. P. E. Parker

ἀλλ' ὅτε μέλλοι
ἄκρον ὑπερβαλέειν, τότ' ἀποστρέψασκε κραταιΐς·
αὖτις ἔπειτα πέδονδε κυλίνδετο λᾶας ἀναιδής.

(*Od.* 11.596–8)

Is not the arrangement of the words rolled down together with the weight of the stone, or rather does not the speed of the narrative outrun the rush of the stone? It certainly seems so to *me*.

(Dionysius of Halicarnassus, *De Comp. Verb.* 20)

On the whole, the poets seem to have been content to let their verses turn out as best they might. It cannot be proved that they deliberately sought special metrical effects to match the sense, though if not, lines like *H* 238 . . . or the whole passage λ 593–600 . . . are the most felicitous of accidents. Such cases are, however, exceptional.

(M. L. West, *Greek Metre* (1982), 39)

West is surely right. The formulaic language of the early hexameter poets grew up over time designed to produce good hexameters, verses that sounded agreeable. A poet composing with these preformed blocks would be unlikely to strive after special effects.[1] Yet the temptation to detect deliberate onomatopoeia in 598 is strong, as West concedes. Dionysius subjects the verse to close scrutiny in order

[1] It is worth noting that *Od.* 11.598 occurs in a section of the book which many, beginning with Aristarchus, have regarded as a relatively late insertion. If that is true, we may be considering the work of a poet who had begun to develop 'literate' habits of composition.

to define how the rhythmic effect that he feels has been produced. He observes that there are no monosyllables and only two disyllables. No long vowel or diphthong is followed by more than one consonant, and pairs of consonants appear only where needed to 'make position' following a short vowel. In fact, to his way of thinking, all the syllables are as short as possible. Then, the words are nowhere 'forced apart' by (apparent) hiatus, or final semivowel meeting initial semivowel.[2] But finally, and 'most surprising of all' (*μάλιστα τῶν ἄλλων θαυμάζειν ἄξιον*), all the 'feet', except the last, are dactylic. Unlike most ancient theorists, Dionysius shows himself genuinely interested in the sound of verse, but his surprise here does no credit to the sensitivity of his ear. Nearly one fifth of Homeric hexameters are holodactylic.[3] Moreover, he failed to notice one really remarkable fact about the verse in question: all the bicipitia except one are split by word-end:

–⏑|⏑ –⏑|⏑ –⏑|⏑ –⏑⏑| –⏑|⏑ ––

In the 640 verses of *Od.* 11 there is just one other such, 433:

–⏑|⏑ –⏑|⏑ –⏑|⏑ –⏑⏑ –⏑|⏑ ––

οἵ τε κατ᾽ αἶσχος ἔχευε καὶ ἐσσομένῃσιν ὀπίσσω

There are three with three split bicipitia:

223 –⏑|⏑ –⏑|⏑ –⏑|⏑ –⏑⏑| –⏑⏑| ––

ἀλλὰ φόωσδε τάχιστα λιλαίεο· ταῦτα δὲ πάντα

(where the break after *ἀλλά* is weak)

587 –⏑|⏑ –⏑|⏑ –⏑|⏑ –– –⏑⏑| ––

γαῖα μέλαινα φάνεσκε, καταζήνασκε δὲ δαίμων

and, with one elision:

82 –⏑|⏑ –⏑|⏑ –⏑|⏑ –⏑⏑| –⏑⏑| ––

ἥμεθ᾽, ἐγὼ μὲν ἄνευθεν ἐφ᾽ αἵματι φάσγανον ἴσχων

Four more verses have two split bicipitia, preceding penthemimeral caesura (–⏑|⏑ –⏑|⏑ –|): 71 and 353 (each with one elision), 220 (*ἀλλά* again) and 143.

[2] Dionysius' 'semivowels' are: *λ, μ, ν, ρ, σ, ζ, ξ, ψ*. See *De Comp. Verb.* 14.

[3] Van Raalte (1986), 36 gives the percentage of holodactylic verses for the Homeric poems as 19·91 for the *Iliad* and 18·62 for the *Odyssey*.

It will be noted, however, that in all these verses one biceps is never split: the fourth. That is in keeping with Hermann's Law, which, in so far as it is observed, eliminates words of the form ⏑–⏑ from the post-caesural section of the hexameter.[4] Lines composed *κατὰ στίχον* are always stricter in rhythm towards the end. According to West (1982), 37–8, Hermann's Law is broken in Homer about once in 550 lines, on average. According to van Raalte (1986), 98, the Law is observed with equal strictness after trochaic and penthemimeral caesura, although it produces consecutive split biceps only after the first (. . . ⏑|⏑ –⏑|⏑ –⏑⏑ ––). This may seem surprising at first sight, but it is a matter of the difference between formulaic and fully literate composition. The formulaic composer's building blocks have been developed over time to produce a pleasing result after the most common caesura, the trochaic, which means avoiding final 'blocks' of the form ⏑–⏑⏑––. He does not have an alternative set to follow penthemimeral caesura.

Callimachus observes Hermann's Law strictly, and shows a marked reluctance to divide consecutive bicipitia even in the pre-caesural part of the hexameter. In the *Hymns*, there is only one line with three consecutive divisions, 2.41:

–⏑|⏑ –⏑|⏑ –⏑|⏑ –⏑⏑| –|⏑⏑ –⏑
πρῶκες ἔραζε πέσωσιν, ἀκήρια πάντ' ἐγένοντο

There is only one other example in the *Hymns* of divided first and second biceps, 6.91:

–⏑|⏑ –⏑|⏑ –|– –⏑⏑ –⏑⏑| ––
ὡς δὲ Μίμαντι χιών, ὡς ἀελίῳ ἔνι πλαγγών

In fact, the only place where Callimachus is willing to accommodate amphibrachic words (⏑–⏑) is immediately before the trochaic

[4] See Parker (1958), 88–9. For a thorough investigation of the conditions under which split fourth biceps is commonly found, see van Leeuwen (1890), 265–76. From his lists it emerges that fourth biceps is most often divided: (1) by monosyllables, in which case there is often elision as well, e.g. . . . *σὺ δ'* | *ἀληθὲς ἐνίσπες*; (2) by phrases which tend to run together, like *περ* | *ἐών*, *περ* | *ἐόντα*; (3) by phrases that tend to coalesce with what follows, like *ἐπεί κε* |, *ἐπεί με* |, some of which also feature elision, as in *οὐκ ἄρ'*|, *ὅπως ἄμ'*|; (4) in a few other miscellaneous cases with elision; (5) by verses ending in a word of five syllables with spondaic fifth metron, e.g. . . . *στέρνον δὲ* | *Ποσειδάωνι*.

caesura (–⏑⏑ –⏑|⏑ –⏑|⏑ . . .), and he is not generous with them even there. In the 1,012 hexameters of the *Hymns*, there are, at most, 34 amphibrachic words. Six of these are preceded by a monosyllable either produced or accompanied by elision and a further six by very weak breaks.[5] That leaves just 22 clear cases. Yet amphibrachic words are not rare in Greek. It is only necessary to go through the first 66 trimeters of Aeschylus' *Agamemnon* to find 22 such words, with that value in the metrical context and without any attenuating factor (such as elision). Nor, indeed, does Callimachus avoid them at verse end, where there can be no question of split bicipitia: in the *Hymns*, 173 hexameters end with amphibrachic words.

Students of Greek metre and of Callimachus will immediately have perceived a connexion between the findings reported here and two of the laws regulating word end in the Callimachean hexameter formulated by Wilhelm Meyer (1885, n. 980):[6]

1. A trochee or dactyl in the second metron (–⏑⏑ –⏑|⏑| . . .) may not be produced by the end of a word of three or more syllables beginning in the first metron. [Lines beginning with monosyllables are not very common, so, although the rule eliminates –|⏖ –⏑|⏑ . . . and –|⏖ –⏑⏑| . . . , the embargos on –⏑|⏑ –⏑|⏑ . . . and –⏑|⏑ –⏑⏑| . . . are more significant.]

2. The penthemimeral caesura may not be preceded by a word of the form ⏑–. Thus, 6.91 *ὥς δὲ Μίμαντι χιών* (–⏑|⏑ –⏑|⏑ –| . . .) infringes both (1) and (2). The wish to avoid the rhythmic phrasing

[5] Monosyllables and elision: 1.69 *ἅ τ' ἐμοῖσι*, 2.94 *τόσ' ἔνειμεν*, 3.203 *ὅτ' ἔφευγεν*, 4.151 *σύ γ' ἐμεῖο*, 201 *τάδ' ἔλεξας*, 221 *σὺ δ', ἄνασσα*. Other weak breaks: 3.109 *ὄφρα γένοιτο*, 144 *ὅττι φέρῃσθα*, 4.53 *οὐκέτ' ἄδηλος*, 88 *τίπτε τάλαινα*, 319 *ὅττι τάχιστον*, 5.17 *μηδὲ κάτοπτρον*. Unfortunately, the statistics collected by O'Neill (1942, 105–78) are of limited value, because he chose to treat appositives as independent words, even while admitting that their independence 'was very limited and that with the words that preceded or followed them they constituted *quasi units*', which were 'avoided in those verse-positions in which single words of the same metrical types were avoided' (pp. 109–10). He also chose to ignore elision. The further statistics compiled by Porter (1951, 3–63) can be assumed to suffer from the same drawback, since the author followed O'Neill's method. On appositives, see West (1982), 25–6, Fränkel (1968*a*), 142–7, Bulloch (1970), 260–3, and Devine and Stevens (1994), ch. 7.

[6] The third law forbids simultaneous word end after the third and fifth longs. This is infringed by *Hymn* 3.262, but not, as Meyer thought, by 6.91, where *ἀελίῳ ἔνι* coalesce. Meyer formulates further rules and tendencies in the course of his monograph. See also Bulloch (1970), 262, n. 5.

⏑–⏑ accounts only in part for Meyer's laws. Other word divisions are ruled out, so other factors are in play. Callimachus' overwhelming preference for placing amphibrachic words immediately before the trochaic caesura is, in some measure, explained by his preference for that caesura. According to West, 74% of his lines are thus articulated, while for *Hecale* alone, Hollis gives the proportion as 78%.[7] A word of the form ⏑–⏑ beginning in the first metron of a verse with trochaic caesura inevitably produces a sequence of three split bicipitia, as in *Hymn* 2.41, quoted above. Callimachus could not totally eliminate amphibrachic words, so he places them where they only produce two consecutive split bicipitia, while still avoiding even –⏑|⏑ –⏑|⏑ –| . . .

For anyone interested in the aesthetics of Greek verse, Callimachus' evident quest for supreme elegance makes his poetry a particularly rewarding subject of study. Hermann Fränkel's examination (1968*a*) of word-end and sense-pause in the hexameter[8] offers a sort of inverse view of Meyer's findings. It emerges that Callimachus' verses have a strong tendency to fall into four sections, as, for example, in *Hymn* 1.3:

–⏑⏑ –|⏑⏑ –⏑|⏑ –⏑⏑| –⏑⏑ ––
Πηλαγόνων ἐλατῆρα, δικασπόλον Οὐρανίδῃσι

or, with supplementary word-ends, *Hymn* 6.136:

–⏑|⏑ –|⏑⏑| –⏑|⏑ –|⏑⏑| –⏑|⏑ ––
φέρβε βόας, φέρε μᾶλα, φέρε στάχυν, οἶσε θερισμόν

It will be observed that the poet tends not to divide consecutive metra in the same way, so that each section has a different cadence: (1) –⏑⏑–, (2) ⏑⏑–⏑, (3) ⏑–⏑⏑, (4) –⏑⏑––.

If we look outside hexameter poetry for evidence of a degree of caution in admitting amphibrachic words in double-short metres, we find it in Lesbian poetry. The fragments of Alcaeus provide 42 alcaic decasyllables which are either complete, or near enough to

[7] West (1982), 153. Van Raalte (1986), p. 79 n. 3 gives 71·8%. For *Hecale*, see Hollis's edition (1990), 19.

[8] Fränkel (1968*a*), 142–7 saw the origin of the rhythmic articulation he had observed as historical, rather than aesthetic. But if that were so, why should it be more apparent in Callimachus than in Homer?

complete, to allow the pattern of word-end to be determined. None of these admits the division –⏑|⏑–⏑|⏑–⏑––. The nearest approach to that rhythm is Voigt 73 (*PLF* D 15) ὄττι μάλιστα σάλ[, where the break after ὄττι, if there is one, is very weak. Horace, too, keeps this rule. Out of his 317 decasyllables, only one breaks it, *C.* 1.26.12: *teque tuasque decet sorores.*[9] Among the sporadic decasyllables in the lyric of Sophocles and Euripides, I have found no example of the rhythm. Among 17 decasyllables in Aeschylus, I find only *Cho.* 385 χειρί· τοκεῦσι δ' ὅμως τελεῖται, where the strong pause after χειρί contrasts with the elision of δέ.[10]

Alcaeus' poems in other double-short metres offer, in theory, 62 opportunities to introduce amphibrachic words.[11] But in fact he admits just two such words, in consecutive lines of the same poem, Voigt 368 (*PLF* Z 45):

⏑⏑–⏑⏑|–⏑⏑–⏑|⏑–⏑|⏑––
––|–⏑⏑–|⏑⏑–⏑|⏑–⏑|⏑––
κέλομαί τινα τὸν χαρίεντα Μένωνα κάλεσσαι,
αἰ χρῆ συμποσίας ἐπόνασιν ἔμοιγε γένεσθαι

This is interesting, because the word division is dictated initially by the proper name, and is exactly replicated in the following line. The two lines also come close to rhyming: κάλεσσαι . . . γένεσθαι. Some special effect must surely be intended here, which we do not understand.

Sappho's preference is the same. Her poems in double-short rhythms offer 129 opportunities for amphibrachic words, but actually admit, at most, three: Voigt = *PLF* 44.16:

–– –⏑⏑–⏑|⏑–⏑|[⏑–⏑–
χῶρις δ' αὖ Περάμοιο θύγ[α]τρες[

and 17:

[9] Oddly enough, the previous colon (*hunc Lesbio* | *sacrare plectro*) contains Horace's only violation of another alcaic rule. See Page (1955), 323 with n. 2.

[10] For the tendency of the Attic dramatists to avoid amphibrachic words in anapaests, see Parker (1958), 87–9.

[11] For example, –⏑⏑–⏑⏑– offers one opportunity. I do not include initial double short, as in Voigt 368 (κέλομαί τινα . . .), because of the low probability of a verse beginning with an independent word scanning ⏑.

– – –⏑|⏑–⏑|⏑–[⏑⏑–⏑–
ἵππ[οις] δ' ἄνδρες ὕπαγον ὐπ' ἄρ[ματα

and, with elision, Voigt = *PLF* 48.1:

– – –⏑⏑–⏑|⏑–⏑|⏑–⏑–
ἦλθες, †καὶ† ἐπόησας, ἔγω δέ σ' ἐμαιόμαν

The next question, of course, is whether in general amphibrachic words form a significant part of Sappho's poetic vocabulary, and the answer is that they certainly do. There are 30 such words in the fragments of sapphic stanzas alone, and some 80 in all the fragments taken together, including only words which still scan ⏑–⏑ in their metrical context. Words found include *μάλιστα* (several times), feminine participles, such as *λίποισα, λάβοισα, ἔχοισα*, other parts of verbs (*πέπονθα, τέθαλε, γένοιτο*, etc.), combinations of noun or pronoun with appositive, like *ἔγω δέ, ἔχει με, τὸν ἄνδρα*. These examples illustrate effectively Sappho's ingenuity in avoiding amphibrachic words in dactylic-type rhythms, unless modified by elision, or otherwise.

It is worth offering one further illustration of the tendency to avoid –⏑|⏑–⏑|⏑– from another period and type of composition. The more substantial fragments of Bacchylides offer 578 possibilities, and, at most, 8 actual occurrences of amphibrachic words. That is 1·4%.

1.116 ⏑⏑– – –⏑|⏑–⏑|⏑– – –⏑–
Διὸς Εὐκλείου δὲ ἕκατι βαθύζωνον κόραν

Here, *ἕκατι* is closely associated with the preceding genitives.

5.28–30 – –⏑⏑–⏑⏑– – –⏑|⏑–⏑|⏑– –⏑– – –⏑–
λεπτότριχα σὺν ζεφύρου πνοιαῖσιν ἔθειραν ἀρίγνωτος
{μετ'} ἀνθρώποις ἰδεῖν

5.139 – –⏑|⏑–⏑|⏑– – –⏑–
βούλευσεν ὄλεθρον ἀτάρβακτος γυνά

11.99 – –⏑|⏑–⏑|⏑– – –⏑– – –⏑– –
κίκλῃ[σκε θύγατρ]α βοῶπιν, χεῖρας ἀντείνων πρὸς
αὐγάς

16 (15).2 –⏑|⏑–⏑|⏑–⏑⏑–
ὀλκ]άδ' ἔπεμψεν ἐμοὶ χρυσέαν

16 (15).25–6 –⏑|⏑–⏑|⏑–⏑⏑–⏑⏑–⏑⏑––
μῆτιν ἐπίφρον' ἐπεὶ πύθετ' ἀγγελίαν ταλαπενθέα

Elision.

19 (18).23–4 ⏑–⏑|⏑–⏑|⏑– ⏑ –⏑⏑–⏑⏑–
ἄκοιτον ἄϋπνον ἐόντα καλλικέραν δάμαλιν

Here, it is interesting to note that there are three amphibrachic words in succession, but only one divides consecutive double shorts.

Fr. *20 B (27).15
–⏑|⏑–⏑|⏑– – –⏑– –
νᾶες ἄγουσιν ἀπ' Αἰγύπτου μέγιστον

The *Epinicians* of Pindar provide 2,080 opportunities and 79 examples, or 3·8%. This is exactly the sort of distinction that one would expect to find between the two poets: a strong preference in the smooth and correct Bacchylides and a rather weaker preference in Pindar.[12] But Pindar's percentage still seems modest when one considers how ordinary are many of the words involved, e.g. ἑτοῖμος, ἔπειτα, μέγιστον, ὁμοῖα, κατ' οἶκον, ἀνήρ τις, παρ' ἀνδρί, ἐγὼ δέ, ἐμοὶ δέ, ἔθηκε, ἔδωκε, several cases of θυγάτηρ and γυνή, feminine participles, as in Sappho.

While not a complete survey, the material collected here suffices, I hope, to demonstrate that the rhythm . . . –⏑|⏑–⏑|⏑– . . . was distinctive enough in Greek to be admitted into verse only comparatively rarely, and that Dionysius genuinely heard something unusual in *Od.* 11.598, even if he failed to analyse his impression correctly. And we hear it too, although rendered in terms of stress. We are not dealing here with an embargo, like Porson's Law in the iambic trimeter and trochaic tetrameter, but with a negative preference, which hardens into a law for Horace and, most probably, Alcaeus, poets who repeated the same stanza form, and so developed a high degree of rhythmic refinement. The same preference is found in different

[12] Compare the treatment by the two poets of word-end after long anceps in dactylo-epitrite. See Parker (1966), 4–9.

poetic genres and dialects, including Lesbian Aeolic, with its distinctive system of accentuation. It applies not only to extended sequences in double-short rhythm like the dactylic hexameter, but to metres which admit no more than two double shorts in sequence, like the alcaic decasyllable and the D-phrase (–⏑⏑–⏑⏑–) in dactylo-epitrite. Onomatopoeia is a two-way process: the meaning suggests the sound, as well as the sound the meaning. The idea of a rock rolling down a hill no doubt played a part in convincing Dionysius that he was hearing an unusual rhythm. There is nothing to suggest that he noticed that the rhythm of 11.433 is almost identical.[13] But was he right in insisting on the simple impression of *speed*? It is hard to see how that could account for the tendency to avoid even as few as two consecutive divisions. In English, amphibrachic phrasing (with help from meaning, no doubt) can produce a bounding effect:

⏑ / ⏑ | ⏑ / ⏑ | ⏑ / ⏑ | ⏑ /
I galloped, Dirck galloped, we galloped all three.

Dale (1958), 34, with a surprising lack of caution, refers to the 'famous "bouncing" effect' of contiguous trochaic cuts in double-short rhythm in Greek.[14] G. S. Kirk (1966), 95–102 rightly questioned the idea of 'bouncing', but he was not looking beyond the dactylic hexameter.[15] In English verse, the regular ratio of two unstressed syllables to one stressed is far less common than double-short verse in Greek, and always tends to go galloping along ('The Assýrian came dówn like a wólf on the fóld . . . '). Quantitative verse is surely a different matter, and here I have to end in bathos. The question of exactly what Dionysius heard calls for an investigation of the perception of amphibrachic phrasing in quantitative rhythm beyond the scope of an ordinary student of Greek poetry.

[13] To Dionysius' way of thinking, there would have been just one difference: the double consonant after diphthong in *αἶσχος*. But that hardly seems enough to have made a serious difference to the hearer's perception of the line.

[14] In fact, I am probably to blame, at least in part, since, *audax iuventa*, I referred to the 'bouncing effect' of words of the form ⏑ – ⏑ in double-short metres in the article cited in n. 4 above, which was written in 1956 and, very kindly, mentioned by Dale in *Lustrum*, although it was not actually in print until after her official deadline of 1957.

[15] Note, however, that Kirk's statistics are based on O'Neill's, on which see above, n. 5.

21

What's in a Line? Papyrus Formats and Hephaestionic Formulae

Kiichiro Itsumi

In analysing lyric poetry generally one must be guided not by ancient colometry but strictly by objective internal criteria.

(M. L. West (1982), 33)

A detailed, up-to-date history [of the development of metrics in antiquity] would be a boon. But anyone who undertakes it faces a grave shortage of evidence for the most important periods.

(ibid. 28)

The Alcaic stanza was written in four lines, and was conceived as a four-verse unit, from the Alexandrian period to the middle of the twentieth century. Horace had been the paramount authority before the papyri were discovered, while Hephaestion gave theoretical support to this layout by providing metrical analysis.[1] All the Alcaeus papyri, moreover, present the Alcaic stanza in four lines. They were believed to provide a definitive guarantee of its four-line division.

However, the third verse can be in synaphea with the fourth.[2] The

[1] The text of Hephaestion relies on Consbruch, except citations from Sappho and Alcaeus. They follow the edition of Voigt, as do the ascriptions to each poet.

[2] Synaphaea is attested at Alcaeus 75.13 Voigt. The third line ends with *τυραννεύ-*. Unfortunately, the fourth line is missing. There may be two other instances: 73.2 and 73.6. In these, δ' is placed at the beginning of the fourth line, like Sappho 31.10 (between the first and second verses of the Sapphic stanza). Eliding δέ at the end of the verse may be an authorized exception of synaphea: cf. P. Maas (1929), §139; West (1982), 33.

separation of the fourth line from the third may not have been intrinsic. Professor West's illustration helps us to grasp the structure (1982, 33):

×–⏑–×–⏑⏑–⏑–||
×–⏑–×–⏑⏑–⏑–||
×–⏑–×–⏑–× : –⏑⏑–⏑⏑–⏑––||

The stanza consists of three verses of 'aaA' pattern, and, when the first or the second verse ('a') is expanded both forward and backward, it becomes the final verse ('A'). Once we prefer the logical clarity of this three-line analysis to uncritical obedience to the colometry of papyri, a different situation is conceivable.[3] Those producing papyrus texts may not have felt it necessary that the layout should exactly reproduce the metrical structure. It may have been devised primarily for convenience in reading and writing. If the stanzas were laid out in three lines, the third line would be much longer than the other two. Consequently the width of each column would be larger, and more space would be left blank on each papyrus sheet. A disproportionally long line would be neither reader-friendly nor economical. Even for scribes a shorter line would be preferable, for it saves them from transcriptional errors. Everyone who has experience of copying a poetic text realizes that a line which coincides with a word-end is easier to transcribe than a line in which a word is divided in the middle. If the third line were to be divided into two halves, the best and the most natural division would be after the ninth position as is traditional, because a word-end always falls there.

Another, more sceptical supposition is possible: the exact metrical structure had already become incomprehensible in the Hellenistic period. I should like to leave the question open. Whether Alexandrian scholarship correctly understood the metrical structure of the archaic lyrics or not, or in other words, whether the metrical structure was ignored on papyri deliberately or not, one thing is certain: Hephaestion, who found the four lines before him, had no doubts in accepting the four-line division and in analysing each of them as a

[3] I leave Hephaestion and Horace aside for the moment; Hephaestion will be discussed soon, and Horace in the final part of this paper.

metrically independent unit. That is, Hephaestion did not always correctly understand the metre.

Before we examine his analysis in detail, I will give some other examples on papyri which do not correctly reflect metrical structures.

1. The Sapphic stanza

Like the Alcaic stanza, this also is composed of three verses in an ‘aaA’ pattern:

–⏑–×–⏑⏑–⏑––||
–⏑–×–⏑⏑–⏑––||
–⏑–×–⏑⏑–⏑–× : –⏑⏑––||

The first and second verses are ‘verses’, or periods, in the modern sense since Boeckh. At the end of each, hiatus / *brevis in longo* may occur while word overlap is prohibited. On the other hand, a word may cross over the end of the third line into the fourth in the traditional layout (synartesis). This difference is ignored or not understood in the papyri. They always divide the verse after the eleventh position of the third line. The reason is simple: the shortened third line now appears equal to the first and second lines.

2. Alcaeus 130b Voigt (130 *PLF* lines 16–39) = P.Oxy. 2165 fr. 1 col. ii

The metrical structure is ascl || ascl || gl | ascl ||:

××–⏑⏑––⏑⏑–⏑–||
××–⏑⏑––⏑⏑–⏑–||
××–⏑⏑–⏑–
××–⏑⏑––⏑⏑–⏑–||

The layout on the papyrus is different. The third and the fourth lines are thus divided:

××–⏑⏑–⏑––
×–⏑⏑––⏑⏑–⏑–

This accords with word division. In all the repetitions word-end does not fall after the eighth position of the third line but after the ninth. According to the currently accepted interpretation, this is a manifestation of 'dovetailing'.[4] The third line and the fourth being united as one verse, the stanza as a whole again presents the pattern: 'aaA'. The combination of asclepiads and a glyconic is the same as fr. 5 Voigt (ascl || ascl || ascl || gl ||) though the arrangement is different and this poem is a truly four-verse stanza.

3. Alcaeus 140 Voigt (357 *PLF* + 140 + 203) = P.Oxy. 2295 fr. 1; P.Oxy. 2296 fr. 4
The metre of this poem is best articulated as gl | gl + ia ||:

–×–⏑⏑–⏑–
–×–⏑⏑–⏑–×–⏑–||

Synaphea occurs between the two glyconics at lines 4 and 6 (and 14, ἐπεί |). Lobel–Page prints these two lines together in one long line, disregarding the layout of the papyri. The fragments of the two papyri are not large and the left margin is deficient (like the right), but the horizontal arrangement of letters indicates that both of them lay out the two lines as

–×–⏑⏑–⏑––
×–⏑⏑–⏑–×–⏑–

4. Anacreon 346 *PMG* = P.Oxy. 2321
The metrical analysis of this poem is controversial. The papyrus seems to present ionic (anacreontic) metre, and some scholars accept this. But the first syllable does not fit this pattern:

–⏑⏑–⏑–⏑––
⏑⏑–⏑–⏑––
⏑⏑–⏑–⏑–⏑––

I prefer iambo-choriambic. Three cola are all overlapped in 'dovetailing':

–⏑⏑–⏑–⏑–
–⏑⏑–⏑–⏑–
–⏑⏑–⏑–⏑– ⏑––

[4] The term 'dovetailing' was invented by P. Maas (1962), §59, in an additional note. West gives it a detailed definition.

5. Pindar, *Paean* 9 = P.Oxy. 841, frr. 126–8 Snell–Maehler = A1 Rutherford

The papyrus establishes this arrangement for verses 3–5:

3 ⏑–⏑– –⏑⏑–⏑⏑–⏑⏑–⏑⏑|
4 –––⏑⏓–⏑⏑–⏑⏑|
5 ⏑–⏑⏑–⏑⏑–⏑⏑–|

To accept this layout as the authentic division of verses, one must suppose, like Snell, *brevis in longo* at the end of all the repetitions of both v. 3 and v. 4. It is theoretically not impossible, although highly unusual, for *brevis in longo* to occur at every repetition, but it is extraordinary for this to be repeated in two successive verses. Moreover at the fifth syllable of v. 4, instead of the blameless *καί*, the reading of the papyrus, an emendation *metri causa*, *ἄν* (Wilamowitz (1921), 490), has to be introduced to expel the long syllable which is in responsion with short. A century ago Housman diagnosed the error of the 'colometry' of this papyrus and proposed a characteristically punctilious solution ((1908), 12 = (1972), 769): 'It will be observed that this, the fourth line of the two strophes and antistrophes, always ends with a short syllable, which is never lengthened by position nor followed by hiatus; and that the end of the third line, wherever extant, obeys the same restriction. The fourth line therefore is apparently in synaphea with what precedes and follows, and *is merely a scribe's line, not a verse* (my italics). The division of the verse lies . . . where it is revealed by the syllaba anceps.'

6. Bacchylides Papyrus A

See L. P. E. Parker (2001).

Perhaps the most important and problematic papyrus in this respect is the Cologne Archilochus (P.Köln 58). This raises a question on asynarteta, and will be discussed below.

It is evident that concern for the reader's (and possibly also the scribe's) convenience sometimes overrides the exact metrical structure. Perhaps we may cite the following judgement from a quite different context in a recent article: 'Such dicola are usually printed with word-overlap. But there is no real need for such hyphenated division, given indentation understood as showing continuity' (Willink (2001), 73; his topic is a stasimon of *Antigone*, lines 604–5 =

615–16). Willink prefers the coincidence of line-end and word-end. He knows, of course, that the whole is one verse and that, if it is divided into two, the division entails 'dovetailing'; but he does not pursue such precision. Though it did not introduce indentation, Alexandrian scholarship may have thought the same as Willink. But Hephaestion did not. He believed that the divided lines were metrically meaningful. This is the next topic that requires discussion.

Hephaestion does not systematically treat the Alcaic stanza but mentions each line separately in more than one chapter. The Alcaic eleven-syllable, the first and the second lines in the traditional layout, is treated in §14 (*περὶ τῆς κατ' ἀντιπάθειαν μίξεως*), while the fourth, the Alcaic ten-syllable, in §7 (dactylic). The third, which is often called the Alcaic nine-syllable, is not mentioned anywhere in his book, but it is certain that he would have analysed it as iambic dimeter hypercatalectic. A verse which is equivalent to the Alcaic nine-syllable is cited as an example of hypercatalectic in §4 (*περὶ ἀποθέσεως μέτρων*).[5] Whatever the exact categorization may be, the four lines of the Alcaic make a metrical potpourri if we follow Hephaestion. His analysis is rejected even by the modern scholars who never doubt the four-line division itself; for example, Wilamowitz writes: 'Es bleibt aber die große Schwierigkeit, daß der Vers [= der alkaische Neunsilber] in der alkaischen Strophe in Synaphie mit dem Zehnsilber steht, und ich weiß eine befriedigende Deutung nicht zu geben. Hephästions Deutung 4, 4, iambisch-hyperkatalektisch, ist keine Erklärung, und sein Beleg bleibt unsicher, nicht weil er anonym ist, denn er muß alkmanisch sein [. . .], sondern weil er aus dem Zusammenhange gerissen ist' (1921, 413–14).

Unlike the Alcaic stanza, all the lines of the Sapphic are treated together by Hephaestion (§14). But this does not mean he grasps the essence of its metrical structure. For him the first three lines of the Sapphic are completely identical. They are all 'epichoriambic': trochaic + choriambic + iamb + *ἀδιάφορον*. According to his scheme the

[5] The transmitted text of this verse is heavily corrupt. Consbruch adopts the emendation of Wilamowitz who suggested that it belonged to Alcman: *εἶμ' ὧτε πυσσάκω λυθεῖσα*. Nothing is certain here. Bergk's classification as fr. lyr. adesp. has been followed, for example, by Page. It cannot be ruled out that this verse belonged to a poem of Alcaeus.

twelfth syllable is missing after the eleventh (catalexis in his sense) not only from the first and the second lines but from the third line. There can have been no occasion to listen to such an actual recitation as there used to be in the archaic period.

Besides the Alcaic and the Sapphic, I introduced above two other stanzas of Alcaeus (130b and 140 Voigt) to illustrate the failure of the papyri to represent exactly metrical structures. No line is cited from these poems by Hephaestion, nor are the two stanzas as a whole discussed. Nevertheless it is possible to guess how Hephaestion may have analysed each line of these stanzas. But before examining this, I should like to discuss another stanza of Alcaeus which reflects an interesting confusion on Hephaestion's part (70 Voigt; and possibly 117b Voigt too).

Alcaeus 70 is made up of two verses which are alternately repeated:

×–⏑–××–⏑⏑–⏑–||
××–⏑⏑––⏑⏑–⏑–||

Word-end always coincides with verse-end. Thus the papyrus (P.Oxy. 1234 fr. 2 col. I), unlike in 130b or 140, succeeds in reproducing the metrical structure. The latter verse is the asclepiad. Hephaestion's analysis of the asclepiad is 'antispastic trimeter acatalectic' (§10.3):

××–⏑|⏑––⏑|⏑–⏑–

This analysis is, of course, nonsense. Detailed refutation is unnecessary. What interests us is that his 'antispastic trimeter acatalectic' covers another verse, the pattern of which is different from the asclepiad. It is introduced in the same section of his book immediately after the asclepiad. The 'Alcaic twelve-syllable' is the name it is given. *τὸ δὲ ἀκατάληκτον τὸ μόνην τὴν τελευταίαν ἔχον ἰαμβικὴν καλεῖται Ἀσκληπιάδειον*, [examples], *τὸ δὲ μέσην μὲν ἔχον τὴν ἀντισπαστικήν, πρεπομένην κατὰ τὸν ἕτερον πόδα εἰς τὰ τέσσαρα τοῦ δισυλλάβου σχήματα* [i.e. ××], *ἑκατέρωθεν δὲ τὰς ἰαμβικάς, ὧν ἡ πρώτη καὶ ἀπὸ σπονδείου ἄρχεται* [i.e. ×–], *Ἀλκαϊκὸν καλεῖται δωδεκασύλλαβον*. We may extrapolate the following scheme for this 'Alcaic twelve-syllable':

×–⏑–|××–⏑|⏑–⏑–

This is identical with the first verse of Alcaeus 70. For us, it is most plausibly analysed as ia + gl, and this must be Hephaestion's own conclusion, for his description of the second and the third metra in total is the same as a glyconic (= 'antispastic dimeter acatalectic').

Hephaestion cites one verse as his illustration of this 'Alcaic twelve-syllable':

> *κόλπῳ σ' ἐδέξαντ' ἄγναι Χάριτες Κρόνῳ* (386 Voigt)
> – – ᴗ – – – – ᴗ ᴗ – ᴗ –

This text has not been found on papyri. As for the metrical scheme, none of the transmitted poems of Alcaeus is composed of ia + gl *κατὰ στίχον*. We do not know where Hephaestion found the verse above, but, judging from his usual habit, this is likely to be the first line of a poem, and if so, it may be followed by an asclepiad to make up a two-line stanza like 70 Voigt (as conjectured by Maas; cf. Voigt's apparatus). Perhaps this may be a reason why Hephaestion describes the asclepiad and the 'Alcaic twelve-syllable' (= ia + gl) successively in the same paragraph. He may even have wrongly assumed that both are variations of the same metre. But it is fair to note that, unlike Meillet (1923, 39) and some modern scholars, Hephaestion does not claim that these two verses are subsumed in the following form:

> ××××××– ᴗ ᴗ – ᴗ –||

Greek metre, at least in the period of recorded history, does not allow such an extravagant licence: see Itsumi (1982), 59–60.

There is a further confusion. Hephaestion elsewhere uses the same name, 'Alcaic twelve-syllable', for a different metrical form, 'epionic *a maiore* trimeter acatalectic' (§14 *περὶ κατ' ἀντιπάθειαν μίξεως*):

> *Ἰόπλοκ' ἄγνα μελλιχόμειδες ἄπφοι* (384 Voigt)
> ᴗ – ᴗ –| – – ᴗ ᴗ| – ᴗ – –

This verse appears to be a conflation of the first line of the Alcaic stanza and that of the Sapphic:

> × – ᴗ – × – ᴗ ᴗ – ᴗ – –

It may be written as iambic + hagesichorean, according to the nomenclature invented by West (1982, 30) and now firmly established. It is a rare verse (see Voigt, 'Conspectus metrorum', C2d Sappho and C2a Alcaeus), and, of course, structurally different from the other (ia + gl). I do not think Hephaestion was so muddled as to think that these two are the same. Probably the name 'Alcaic twelve-syllable' was already in circulation (καλεῖται/καλούμενον) to designate the two different entities. He may be careless, but not (one trusts) foolish.

We now go back again to the two poems discussed above (Alcaeus 130b and 140) and speculate how Hephaestion would analyse them. As already mentioned, although the metrical structure of 130b is ascl || ascl || gl | ascl ||, the papyrus divides the third verse in a different manner:

××–⏑⏑–⏑––
×–⏑⏑––⏑⏑–⏑–

The former half is usually called hipponactean by modern scholars. Hipponactean is wrongly postulated in Alcaeus 140 too:

–×–⏑⏑–⏑––
×–⏑⏑–⏑–×–⏑–

The name 'hipponactean' itself goes back to Hephaestion (§10.2).[6] But Hephaestion gives also another name, the Sapphic nine-syllable, to this colon. To be correct, of the two recorded names for this 'antispastic dimeter hypercatalectic' (as Hephaestion describes it), the first to be mentioned was the Sapphic nine-syllable. Hephaestion would have analysed the lines in question as the Sapphic nine-syllable rather than hipponactean. And how about the following cola? The cola which start with ×–⏑⏑ . . . are generally classified by Hephaestion into the class of ionic *a maiore* (§11). Neither of the two examples of Alcaeus above is listed there, but we find two examples each longer by an additional final syllable:

×–⏑⏑|––⏑⏑|–⏑–– (inc. auct. 16)
×–⏑⏑|–⏑–×|–⏑–– (inc. auct. 22)

Both are 'ionic *a maiore* trimeter acatalectic', and, according to Hephaestion, used by οἱ Αἰολεῖς. The former of them is, he writes,

[6] This nomenclature may have been wrong, for it is highly doubtful that Hipponax would have used an 'asymmetrical' (. . . –⏑⏑–⏑– . . .) phrase. West is suspicious of the ascription of the citation by Hephaestion to Hipponax (*175 *IEG*).

composed of two 'ionics' and a trochaic, while the latter is composed of an 'ionic' and two trochaics. Thus, it is reasonable to guess that Hephaestion would have analysed each of the two Alcaic lines above, the second of 130b and 140, as 'ionic *a maiore* trimeter catalectic'. Metrical potpourris, again, like the Alcaic stanza; but Hephaestion seems not to have worried.

That the line ××–⏑⏑–⏑–– is not called the Alcaic but the Sapphic nine-syllable suggests that Sappho used it somewhere. There is no clue to the source of Hephaestion's designation. So far we have not discovered any papyri of Sappho with the Sapphic nine-syllable. I should like to offer another hypothesis.

There are two possibilities. Sappho used it either *κατὰ στίχον* or in a small stanza (a third is conceivable but can be dismissed for the moment: a late book-poet found it in a stanza of Sappho and used it *κατὰ στίχον*). It is less likely that the Sapphic nine-syllable is stichic. Certainly Sappho was fond of composition *κατὰ στίχον*, but the stichic lines are longer than nine syllables. Two books of the Alexandrian edition of Sappho collect poems organized by stichic verses:

(book II) ××–⏑⏑–⏑⏑–⏑⏑–⏑–
(book III) ××–⏑⏑––⏑⏑––⏑⏑–⏑–

The verse in book II is, according to Hephaestion, an aeolic dactylic, and he calls it the Sapphic fourteen-syllable (§7.7; gl2d in Snell–West notation). The one in book III is what is now usually called the greater asclepiad (gl 2c). The name Hephaestion gives to it is the Sapphic sixteen-syllable (§10.6). Another stichic verse is the phalaecian (described by Hephaestion in §10.3):

××–⏑⏑–⏑–⏑––

This is again characteristically Sapphic: 'apud Sappho frequens est, cuius in quinto libro complures huius generis et continuati et dispersi leguntur' (Caesius Bassus; 230 Voigt). There is another verse which, Hephaestion writes (§11.5), is frequently used by Sappho. He calls it *Αἰολικόν*:

×–⏑⏑––⏑⏑––⏑⏑–⏑––

P.Oxy. 1787 (58 Voigt) supports the idea that this verse is used *κατὰ στίχον*.[7] I think that Lobel, Page, and Voigt are probably right to ascribe this verse to book IV. It is, in fact, the greater asclepiad whose first syllable is moved to the end of verse (hag 2c). Hephaestion cites more examples of stichic verses:

×–⏑⏑–⏑–⏑––	§11.3	154 Voigt	tel+ba (praxillean)
××–⏑⏑–⏑⏑–⏑–	§7.7	130 Voigt	gl^{d}
××–⏑⏑–⏑⏑––	§7.6	110 Voigt	pher^{d}
××–⏑⏑–⏑⏑–⏑⏑––	§7.6	115 Voigt	pher^{2d}
××–⏑⏑––⏑⏑––⏑⏑––	§10.4	140 Voigt	pher^{2c}

It should be noticed that these are all longer than nine syllables. It is more likely that the Sapphic nine-syllable is a line of a small stanza, like 94 (gl || gl || gl^{d} |||), 96 (cr+gl | gl | gl+ba |||), or 98 (gl || gl || gl +ba |||). My guess is that the Sapphic nine-syllable is followed by a line which starts with an anceps, like Alcaeus 130b or Alcaeus 140, or:

×–⏑⏑–⏑–⏑–– (cf. Sappho 96)

In other words, the Sapphic nine-syllable is virtually the glyconic plus a syllable which should stand at the beginning of the following colon, and these two cola are in synartesis. But, since word division always or very often falls after the ninth syllable, the Alexandrian edition presents the Sapphic nine-syllable separately. Hephaestion, or his predecessors, treats this line as a metrically meaningful unit and calls it the Sapphic nine-syllable.

I wrote above that the stichic verses of Sappho are longer than nine syllables. There are one or two exceptions. Sappho 168b Voigt can be analysed as a series of short verses, hagesichorean (×–⏑⏑–⏑––; eight syllables), *κατὰ στίχον*. However, Hephaestion combines two hagesichoreans into one line, which is thus comparable with the sixteen-syllable verse cited above (hag^{2c} = the metre of book IV (?) of Sappho), and classifies them together into 'ionic *a maiore* acatalectic tetrameter' (§11.5):

×–⏑⏑|–⏑–×|×–⏑⏑|–⏑–× (2 hag)
×–⏑⏑|––⏑⏑|––⏑⏑|–⏑–– (hag^{2c})

[7] Our knowledge of Sappho 58 and the metre in question is greatly increased by the recent discovery of a new Sappho papyrus (P.Köln Inv. 21351): see Gronewald and Daniel (2004*a*), (2004*b*).

This illuminates Hephaestion's understanding (rather, misunderstanding) of metre. At the same time it supports my guess about the 'origin' of the name of the Sapphic nine-syllable, because it suggests that the length of hagesichorean (eight syllables) seemed too short to be independently arranged *κατὰ στίχον*. Otherwise Hephaestion must have called hagesichorean 'the Sapphic eight-syllable'. Anyway, Sappho 168b is thus cited by Hephaestion:

> *Δέδυκε μὲν ἀ σελάννα καὶ Πληΐαδες· μέσαι δὲ*
> *νύκτες, παρὰ δ' ἔρχετ' ὤρα, ἔγω δὲ μόνα κατεύδω.*
> ×–⏑⏑|–⏑–×|×–⏑⏑|–⏑–×

Note the hiatus between *ὤρα* and *ἐγώ*. Also there is juxtaposition of two ancipitia between the second and the third 'metra', for, according to the analysis of Hephaestion, the second metron (and the fourth) is trochaic (the first and third are ionic *a maiore*).[8] Modern scholarship recognizes hiatus and the juxtaposition of ancipitia as indications of verse-end. Presumably the Alexandrian book may have laid out two verses in one line for economical or other reasons. However, the situation is differently interpreted by Hephaestion. It is a manifestation of his further ignorance as well: so-called asynarteta. The second case of presumably shorter stichic lines is, according to Hephaestion, really an example of asynarteta (Sappho 127). It is made up of two ithyphallica (§15.25), and the metrical context is totally uncertain:

> *Δεῦρο δηὖτε Μοῖσαι χρύσιον λίποισαι*
> –⏑–⏑––|–⏑–⏑––|

Now it is time to examine asynarteta. West's verdict on asynarteta is very simple and clear. In the section on the Epodes of Archilochus and Hipponax, he writes (1982, 43): 'when two short verses followed a longer line, they were written together in ancient books to make a line of matching length. Metricians who observed their independence called such lines *ἀσυνάρτητα*, "disconnected", though they failed to appreciate that the disconnection was of the same nature as that between periods written on different lines.' This verdict must have been written after the discovery of the Cologne Archilochus

[8] We do not know the nature of the last position of hagesichorean. It is either true long or anceps. It is also possible that some examples are long and others are anceps.

(P.Köln 58; 196a *IEG*). It is now well known that this papyrus lays out the 'epode' in distichs, despite hiatus / *brevis in longo* in the middle of the second verse in some lines:

– ⏖ – ⏖ – ⏖ – ⏖ – ⏑ ⏑ – – ||
– ⏑ ⏑ – ⏑ ⏑ – || × – ⏑ – × – ⏑ – ||

Hephaestion lists the same combination of these short verses, hem + 2 ia, under asynarteta (§15.9; the third asynarteton of Archilochus):

ἀλλά μ᾿ ὁ λυσιμέλης, ὦταῖρε, δάμναται πόθος.
– ⏑ ⏑ – ⏑ ⏑ – | – – ⏑ – ⏑ – ⏑ – |

This text is not found on the papyrus and may have belonged to another poem. Strictly speaking, it is uncertain whether the dactylic hexameter precedes it. But it is indisputable that Hephaestion would regard the second line of the Cologne Archilochus as an asynarteton: a verse made of two cola. Thus, only two explanations are logically possible. One is to follow West (above): Hephaestion 'failed to appreciate' that the hemiepes and the iambic dimeter 'were written together' on the papyrus 'to make a line of matching length' with the preceding dactylic hexameter. The alternative was proposed by Rossi (1976). He postulates an intermediate stage in the development of verse-end, 'something less than a verse-end but more than a simple diaeresis', for the border between the hemiepes and the iambic dimeter (215). In other words, we should admit that the definition of verse end accepted since Boeckh does not always have overriding validity.[9]

I think Rossi estimates Hephaestion undeservedly highly (I again leave aside Horace for the moment). Hephaestion, as is demonstrated above, tends naively to accept every line as we find it written on the papyri as a single, metrically meaningful unit. For him, a line is a line, and no more. At the same time West's verdict is not entirely precise (it is not his concern to define asynarteta strictly), because

[9] It was long before everyone accepted the definition of the verse end established by Boeckh (1811). As late as 1847 Hermann did not abandon the idea of asynarteta defined thus: '[versus] qui sicut placeret poetae nunc cohaerentibus numeris decurrerent, nunc ex duobus constarent non continuatis numeris ((1847), 7 = (1877), 115), and Tycho Mommsen (1864) occasionally resorts to asynarteta in Hermann's sense (for example, on Pindar, *Isthm.* 8 (his 7), lines 1 and 2).

Hephaestion covers more than he allows under the umbrella of asynarteta. For example, Hephaestion includes the following case among asynarteta (§15.8; the second asynarteton of Archilochus):

– ⏖ – ⏖ – ⏖ – ⏖ | – ⏑ – ⏑ – – |

There is no verse end in Boeckh's sense between two cola; in other words, the two cola are not a verse each.[10] Thus, the 'disconnection' in this line cannot be said to be 'of the same nature as that between periods written on different lines'. And this line does not follow, but precedes, another: an iambic trimeter catalectic (Archil. 188 *IEG*).

West's verdict is not applicable either, to the last of three examples of Archilochean asynarteta which Hephaestion cites (§15.2, 6; the first asynarteton of Archilochus):

Ἐρασμονίδη Χαρίλαε χρῆμά τοι γελοῖον
ἐρέω, πολὺ φίλταθ' ἑταίρων, τέρψεαι δ' ἀκούων.
× – ⏑ ⏑ – ⏑ ⏑ – – | – ⏑ – ⏑ – – |
(*or* × – ⏑ ⏑ – ⏑ ⏑ – × | – ⏑ – ⏑ – – |)[11]

This line is, or seems to be, stichic, and does not follow a longer line.

Hephaestion's definition of asynarteta is given in the first paragraph of §15: *Γίνεται δὲ καὶ ἀσυνάρτητα,* (1) *ὁπόταν δύο κῶλα* (2) *μὴ δυνάμενα ἀλλήλοις συναρτηθῆναι* (3) *μηδὲ ἕνωσιν ἔχειν* (4) *ἀντὶ ἑνὸς μόνου παραλαμβάνηται στίχου.* (1) and (4) are unambiguously clear, but (2) and (3) are not. First of all, does (3) really introduce a different condition from (2)? I am sceptical about this (see below) and think (3) explains (2) by using other expressions. But many do not agree. What is the difference? Rossi translates (2) 'which could not be knit together (i.e. different from each other)' and (3) 'which are not united (i.e. separated by word-end)'. Then, if we follow him strictly, *ἀσυνάρτητα* in Hephaestion's sense does not primarily mean 'disconnected cola' but 'different types of cola' (cf. his translation of

[10] I disregard the notorious line cited by Hephaestion, Archilochus fr. 190 *IEG καὶ βήσσας ὀρέων δυσπαιπάλους οἷος ἦν ἐπ' ἥβης*. West obelizes *δυσπαιπάλους* (presumably for a metrical reason).

[11] I take the final position of the first colon not as an anceps, but as a genuine long, as in the dactylic hexameter. This is only applicable to Archilochus, of course; similar verses of Cratinus and later poets are different (see below). Many think otherwise, but the difference is not essential at the moment.

συναρτηθῆναι). At the same time his definition of asynarteta is: (i) they are composed of two cola, and (ii) these cola are separated by word-end, but (iii) without the possibility of hiatus / *brevis in longo* (Rossi (1976), 207).

Van Ophuisen's translation yields an entirely different picture (1987, 137). According to him, (2) is 'which cannot be connected with each other', and (3) is, in this context, 'which cannot form a unity' (i.e. not belonging to one and the same metre). As for modern definitions, he virtually adds another to those given by Rossi: (iv) the first colon is always catalectic. However, as he admits, 'none of them applies to all the examples of asynartete metra Hephaestion provides'. Even his translation of (3) does not. The second line of the elegiac couplet (the so-called 'pentameter'), which is an asynarteton according to Hephaestion, is composed of the same metre. 'Pentameter' annoys Rossi too, because its two parts are both hemiepe and not different from each other, contrary to his interpretation of (2). Rossi tries to solve this difficulty by pointing out that a spondee does not replace a dactyl in the latter hemiepes. But this explanation is not applicable to other combinations in which the same phrase is repeated, such as two ithyphallica of Sappho 127, cited above.

I think modern scholarship has made a great effort to save Hephaestion, but in vain. He himself is not as strict as has been thought. It should not be forgotten that, according to Hephaestion, not only the Archilochean line, *Ἐρασμονίδη Χαρίλαε χρῆμά τοι γελοῖον*, is asynarteton but so too are the following lines of Cratinus (fr. 360.1–2 *PCG*), in which word division does not coincide with metrical division:

> *χαῖρ', ὦ μέγ' ἀχρειόγελως ὅμιλε τοῖς ἐπίβδαις,*
> ‒ ‒ ⏑ ⏑ ‒ ⏑ ⏑ ‒ | ⏑ ‒ ⏑ ‒ ⏑ ‒ ‒ |
> *τῆς ἡμετέρας σοφίας κριτὴς ἄριστε πάντων·*
> ‒ ‒ ⏑ ⏑ ‒ ⏑ ⏑ ‒ ⏑ ‒ | ⏑ ‒ ⏑ ‒ ‒ |

Are two cola separated by word-end? Not at all. But these are disconnected, Hephaestion would maintain. We are destined to be frustrated in seeking a good definition of asynarteta by examination of Hephaestion. Perhaps it would be better to search for his reasons for wishing to, and feeling obliged to, write a chapter on asynarteta.

Hephaestion seems to have introduced the idea 'asynarteta' when he encountered a line which was obviously difficult to divide into metra in a consistent manner, unlike the lines treated in the preceding chapters (§§7–14). The difficulty arises whenever a self-contained phrase, or part (colon), starts anew midway in the line. The first half of the Archilochean lines above, *Ἐρασμονίδη Χαρίλαε*, is, according to his analysis, anapaestic:

⏑–|⏑⏑–|⏑⏑–|–

But, after the long in the final metron, the trisyllabic dissection cannot be carried on further; the following part is, from his point of view, obviously quadrisyllabic (trochaic):

–⏑–⏑|––

In the two other Archilochean lines too, trisyllabic (dactylic) parts are followed by quadrisyllabic (trochaic or iambic) parts:

–⏑⏑|–⏑⏑|–⏑⏑|–⏑⏑| –⏑–⏑|––
–⏑⏑|–⏑⏑|– ––⏑–|⏑–⏑–

Moreover an odd syllable stands at the end of the former part in two of these three asynartetic lines. Thus, regular division into metra is impeded for two reasons; not only is consistency absent from the two parts (trisyllabic/quadrisyllabic) but 'catalexis' (in the Hephaestionic sense) occurs in the middle. It is noteworthy that the chapter on asynarteta is preceded by §14, in which the lines can be dissected into metra of equal length (i.e. quadrisyllabic), although these metra are not homogeneous: for example,

–⏑–×|–⏑⏑–|⏑–– 'epichoriambic trimeter catalectic'
(= the Sapphic eleven-syllable)
×–⏑–|×–⏑⏑|–⏑– 'epionic *a maiore* trimeter catalectic'
(= the Alcaic eleven-syllable)

It is not from the difference of metres or from the separation of two cola by word end that 'disconnection' (*ἀσυνάρτητα*) arises, but from the incapability of continuous, consistent dissection into metra. Asynarteton is, in a sense, the last resort of Hephaestion in order to analyse a line in which two independent parts are undeniably recognized in it.[12] This is my freer translation of his definition of asynarteta (cited above): 'Disconnections occur, whenever two parts, which cannot be connected with each other, and which lack consistency, are nevertheless written in the place of one line.'

It is now clear that we should deal separately with the following questions:

1. What kind of metre are the strophes (the so-called Epodes) of Archilochus?
2. What is the principle, if any, of the layout of the Alexandrian editions of Archilochus which Hephaestion is supposed to have read?
3. How did Hephaestion understand the Archilochean metre which was visualized in the Alexandrian edition?
4. To what extent are later poets different from Archilochus?

Question 3 has already been answered. The next to be tackled is Question 2. Two *a priori* principles seem to have been established:

(i) The length of a line must, in general, be equivalent to those common verses employed generally *κατὰ στίχον*; i.e. the dactylic hexameter, the trochaic tetrameter catalectic, or the iambic trimeter acatalectic or catalectic.

(ii) Archilochus' poetry must be either stichic or distichic. 'Epodes' are variations of the elegiac couplet (note that the so-called 'pentameter' is listed under asynarteta by Hephaestion). They are different from the three-line or four-line stanzas of Sappho or Alcaeus.

Thus, although

–⏑⏑–⏑⏑–||×–⏑–×–⏑–||

is made up of two verses, it is written as one line because (i) it matches the length of the dactylic hexameter, and (ii) it avoids creating a three-line stanza with the preceding dactylic hexameter. Conversely, the following is one verse by itself:

[12] More strictly, it is the last resort but one, because the chapter on asynarteta is followed by the final one, §16, where the first four syllables are, from Hephaestion's viewpoint, totally anomalous (polyschematists).

– ⏖ – ⏖ – ⏖ – ⏖ | – ⏑ – ⏑ – – ||

At the same time this line (i) is as long as the dactylic hexameter and, especially, the iambic trimeter catalectic which follows it, and (ii) also avoids creating a three-line stanza. The last case is different. I presume that there is verse end in the middle (see above):

× – ⏑ ⏑ – ⏑ ⏑ – – || – ⏑ – ⏑ – – ||

Each colon is a verse. But each is too short to be written as a single line in the edition of Archilochus. It is therefore written *κατὰ στίχον* as a whole.

Now back to Question 1. I propose that in the Epodes Archilochus created a new kind of verse by uniting dissected parts from the most common metres: the dactylic hexameter on one hand, and the iambic trimeter acatalectic or catalectic on the other.[13]

< (hem) >
< (4da) >
– ⏑ ⏑ – ⏑ ⏑ – | ⏑ | ⏑ – ⏑ ⏑ | – ⏑ ⏑ – – ||
< (erasm) >
< (2ia) >
× – ⏑ – × – ⏑ – | × – ⏑ – ||
< (ithyph) >
× – ⏑ – × | – ⏑ – ⏑ – – ||

There is a small piece of evidence to suggest that the phrase of the type *Ἐρασμονίδη Χαρίλαε* has its origin in the dactylic hexameter. Hephaestion writes that the double short in it can be replaced by a long and cites:

ἀστῶν δ' οἱ μὲν κατ' ὄπισθεν.
– – – – ⏑ ⏑ – – |

In the dactylo-epitrite of Pindar, Bacchylides, and tragedy, on the contrary, the double-short in so-called D (– ⏑ ⏑ – ⏑ ⏑ –) may not be

[13] Snell once proposed the same idea (1962, 31) with the following reservation in an attached note: 'Daß Archilochos das Hemiepes wirklich als Stück des Hexameters aufgefaßt hat, scheint mir . . . höchst wahrscheinlich. Die Frage, ob Archilochos das Hemiepes "richtig" aufgefaßt hat, ist damit natürlich nicht entschieden.' In the fourth edition this reservation is deleted.

contracted. This suggests that the Archilochean colon was different from D. Perhaps in adding an iambic (trochaic) element to the end of a hexameter opening, Archilochus aimed metrically at a mock-epic effect. I also suggest that, although it is not intended to be comical, the so-called encomiologus of Alcaeus cited by Hephaestion (§15.10) is of the same nature:

–⏑⏑–⏑⏑–|×–⏑–×|

The former is hemiepes. The latter is the first five positions of the iambic trimeter before the caesura (*pe*, according to West's notation). The dactylo-epitrite, especially as employed by Pindar and Bacchylides, is a late development. So too is the dicolon of Cratinus cited above. These forms replaced a true long by an anceps, and, more importantly, admitted the overlapping of the two parts over this 'link' anceps.

Before discussing Horace, it is necessary to survey quickly the poetic mainstream (the 'book poetry') of the Alexandrian period. These poems are basically stichic. If not, they are composed of a short, epode-type strophe, made up wholly or in part of stichic verses. Even the Alcaic or Sapphic stanza disappears. These forms are usefully collected by West (1982), 150–1. Book poets 'excavated', and freely combined, the verse forms of archaic monody. For example, Callimachus restored the 'choliambic' of Hipponax and used it either κατὰ στίχον, or in epodic forms (for example, with 2 ia in *Ia.* 5 = fr. 195 Pfeiffer). He also resumed the experiment originally conducted by Archebulus. The Archebulean is described at some length by Hephaestion (§8.9), taking examples from Callimachus (fr. 228 Pf.; P.Berol. 13417). Among Callimachus and his contemporaries, epigrams composed of 'exotic' metres were fashionable. Book 13 of the *Palatine Anthology* was based on a metrical handbook which collected examples of these.

Hephaestion's approach is fundamentally the same as that of these Alexandrians. He was particularly interested in stichic verses which were given special names, like the Archebulean. It is generally accepted that names such as glyconic have their origin in the poets who first used the verses in question κατὰ στίχον. It is needless to say that the metre itself was much older than the poet. But Hephaestion writes thus about glyconic: δίμετρον [sc. antispastic] δὲ ἀκατάληκτον *τὸ καλούμενον Γλυκώνειον, αὐτοῦ Γλύκωνος εὑρόντος αὐτό* (§10.2). In accordance with the traditional inclination of Greek intellectuals, he was keen to find a *πρῶτος εὑρέτης*.[14] Hephaestion's comment on the Sapphic stanza is suggestive (§14.1): *ἔστι δὲ καὶ παρ' Ἀλκαίῳ—καὶ ἄδηλον ὁποτέρου ἐστὶν εὕρημα.*

This is the situation in which Horace began studying Greek metre. He had to discover metrical 'rules' for himself. By examining closely the Alexandrian editions on his own, he searched out not only how verses (= lines) were arranged but also at which particular positions hiatus or word overlap occurred. He was keen to imitate every detail as he found it. He found hiatus / *brevis in longo* in the middle of the Archilochean asynarteta. So he imitated this. He found word overlap between the third line and the fourth of the Sapphic stanza. He imitated this too. Unfortunately, it escaped his notice that the third line was different from the first or the second. So he introduced hiatus between third and fourth. I believe Horace discovered all of these details by himself, without the aid of any handbooks. Hephaestion, who came after Horace, neglected such minutiae. It is evident who was cleverer. Horace can justly be proud of himself.[15]

[14] On this inclination see Kleingünther (1933).

[15] The title of this paper was proposed by Dr Neil McLynn, who corrected my English as well. I appreciate his kind assistance.

Other examples of the errors of the 'colometry' in the *Paeans* of Pindar will be discussed in my forthcoming book (Oxford, 2008).

22

Reconstructing Archetypes: A New Proposal and an Old Fallacy

Michael D. Reeve

In *Textkritik* (1927), Paul Maas's procedure for reconstructing an archetype involves the elimination first of witnesses that descend from others, then of readings that have no stemmatic weight. He gives each kind of elimination its own name: *eliminatio codicum descriptorum* (§4), *eliminatio lectionum singularium* (§8c). The distinction also explains a detail in the section where he introduces the latter: his list of the witnesses that may have *lectiones singulares* in his imaginary example does not include J, which has already been eliminated as a descendant of another extant witness, F (§8a). Similarly, when Martin West illustrates recension in a 'closed' tradition with a stemma in which F descends from B, he says 'we shall ignore F' before he embarks on the progressive elimination of variants (1973, 32–4); and Paolo Chiesa too retains both kinds of elimination (2002, 75–9).

As long as *eliminatio codicum descriptorum* is applied only to witnesses that descend from an extant ancestor, neither it nor Maas's distinction poses any problem of interpretation or coherence.[1] Understandably, therefore, Chiesa goes so far as to incorporate the restriction in his definition of *descriptus* (2002, 75–6). Before giving his example, however, Maas had embraced in *eliminatio codicum*

[1] I substitute 'ancestor' for Maas's *Vorlage* (§4), too narrow a term ('exemplar', 'model') in view of possible intermediaries, which he goes on to mention (§8i).

descriptorum any witness that descends from an ancestor 'that can be reconstructed without its help' (§4), and the clause is unusually obscure. Its obscurity is all the more vexing because it comes so early in the work.

In a commentary on *Textkritik* many times longer than the work itself (2003), Elio Montanari builds on the clause a different interpretation of the procedure that Maas prescribes—different, that is, from the one that I outlined in my opening paragraph. The reconstruction of an archetype, he argues, is tantamount to *eliminatio codicum descriptorum*, because one moves up the stemma from the bottom and eliminates witnesses at lower levels by reconstructing their ancestors (§§5.7, 13.2.2, 23.4.1, 25.5, 30.3.3, 31.3.1, 130.3). What Maas calls *eliminatio lectionum singularium* has no validity, he argues, except as a logical consequence of that *eliminatio codicum descriptorum* (§§25.5, 25.5.3, 30.3.4, 117.7.1).

Whether Montanari has interpreted Maas correctly I am inclined to doubt, but a full discussion would require a tedious parade of passages from *Textkritik* and might still reach no firm conclusion. One would need to examine, for instance, Maas's use of the term *Zeuge*, which on its first appearances (§§3, 4) suggests to me not 'witness either extant or reconstructed', as Montanari glosses it (§5.2.1), but 'extant witness'.[2] Furthermore, Montanari's way of dealing with Maas's omission of J from his list of the witnesses in his example strikes me as forced to the point of absurdity: he calls it 'a not altogether clear way of emphasizing that descendants of reconstructed witnesses are eliminated in just the same way as descendants of extant witnesses' (§25.5.1). On the other hand, the problematical clause about descent from a reconstructed witness may appear to support Montanari; in another context I have made a different suggestion about it (1989, 5–6), but nothing short of a copy annotated by Maas himself will ever show whether I was right or wrong. A way of reconciling Montanari's interpretation of Maas's *eliminatio* with mine would be to suppose that Maas began with the two kinds but in contemplating his imaginary example saw the correspondence between them and so went back and added the

[2] I thank Elio Montanari for an exchange of views on this point and others.

problematical clause without making the further adjustments that would have put his meaning beyond doubt.

To my mind, however, there is a more important question than what Maas intended: is Montanari right to argue that the two kinds of *eliminatio* collapse into one?

As Montanari does not illustrate his argument with any stemmata except by implication the one in Maas's example, I offer one, a reduced form of it:

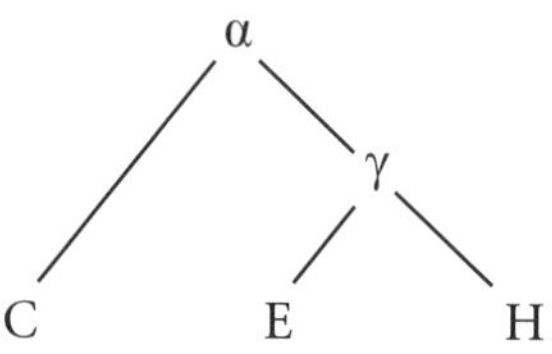

CEH have no authority against *α*. If, however, someone were to ask an editor 'can any of CEH be eliminated?', the answer would be not 'yes, all of them, because they all descend from *α*' but 'no' or 'only if we have *α*' or 'it depends on their readings'. Let *α* therefore have perished and CEH be given readings so that the editor has a task of reconstruction to carry out. Here are four stemmata that illustrate how readings in a passage might be distributed over the tradition:

(1)

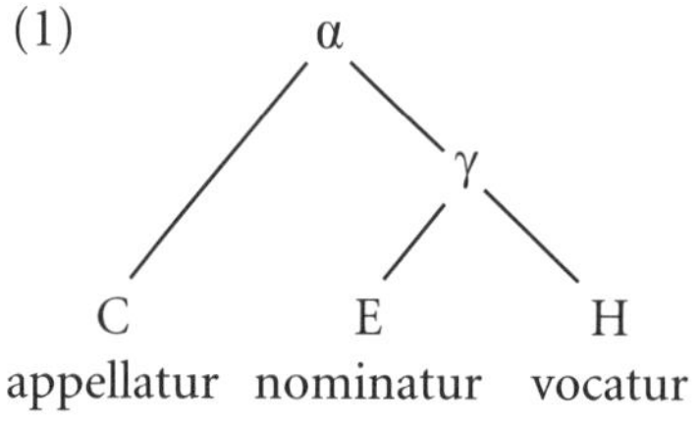

(2)

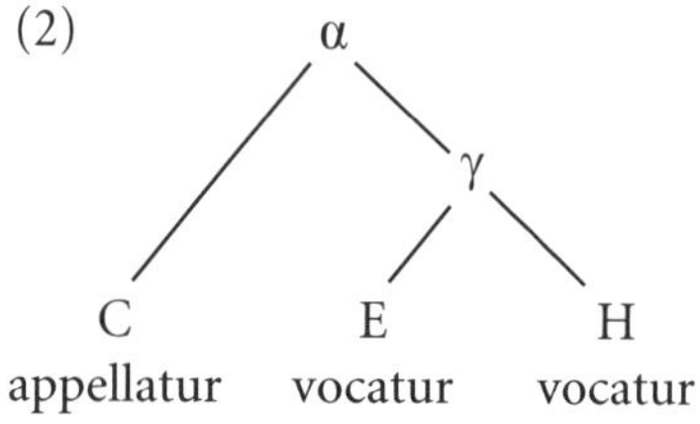

(3)

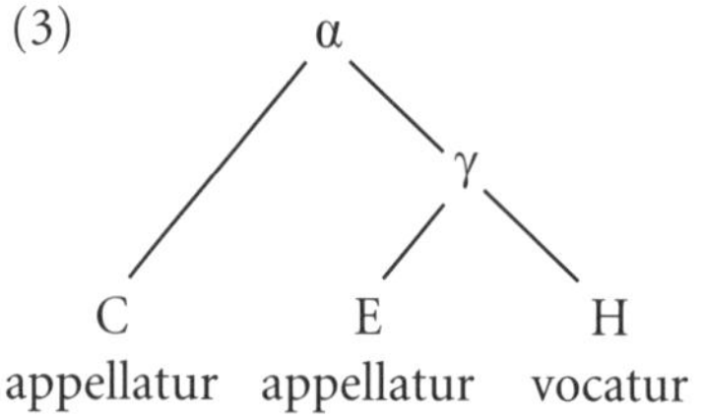

(4)

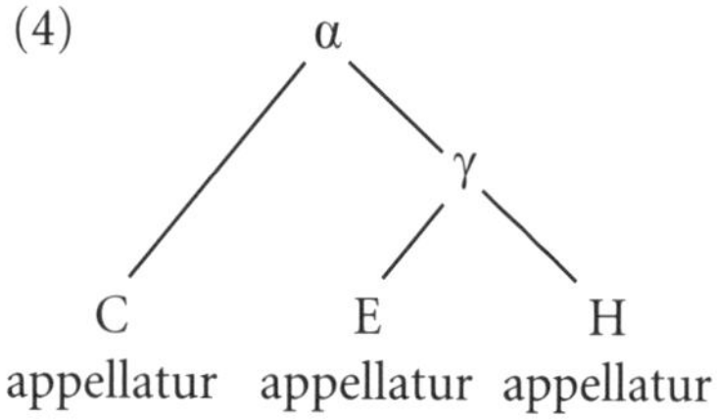

In (1) there is no purely stemmatic way of determining what reading γ or α had, so that no elimination is possible, whether of a reading or of a witness. In (2) γ plainly had *vocatur*, so that elimination is possible, whether of EH or their reading *vocatur* (*vocatur*, that is, as the reading of EH, not as a reading altogether). In (3) α and γ plainly had *appellatur*, so that elimination is again possible, not just of H or its reading *vocatur* but also of CγE or their reading *appellatur*. In (4) α and γ even more plainly had *appellatur*, so that elimination is possible yet again, whether of CγEH or their reading *appellatur*. (2)–(4), then, allow a kind of elimination, and whether one calls it *eliminatio codicum descriptorum* or *eliminatio lectionum singularium* does not matter. Whichever choice one makes, the elimination of witnesses that descend entirely from an extant ancestor is easily accommodated. I suggest this formulation: a witness can be eliminated wherever the reading of an ancestor is known. Witnesses that descend entirely from an extant ancestor will simply be an extreme case, in which the reading of an ancestor is known everywhere.

Actually it is hard to tell whether Montanari considered (4), but Maas seems to have ignored it, because he speaks of *Sonderlesungen* ('deviant readings', *lectiones singulares*). In much the same way, as Montanari points out (§25.1), he ignores the best evidence for the reading of β in his example, namely the agreement of ABC(D), which all descend separately from it (§8c). Any kind of elimination possible in (3), however, ought to be possible *a fortiori* in (4), just as the agreement of ABC(D) guarantees the reading of β *a fortiori* if the agreement of any two guarantees it. Maas's silence about (4) and about agreements of ABC(D) could therefore be used as an objection to Montanari's interpretation of his remarks on *eliminatio*.

In some respects, however, the analysis that I have given differs from Montanari's. Invoking Maas's problematical clause, which allows elimination of a witness if it descends entirely from an ancestor that can be reconstructed without its help, he would object that in (2) γ has not been reconstructed without the help of E or H, nor in (3)–(4) α without the help of C or γ; and only the elimination of H in (3) and of E or H in (4) would stand.[3] If this analysis has

[3] I have pointed out elsewhere (1989, 5) the embarrassment of having to choose a victim in configurations like (4) if one is felt to be needed.

advantages over mine in rigour or clarity, they elude me. On the contrary, Montanari draws a questionable conclusion from it. The contrast seen in (3)–(4) between the level immediately below the archetype, where neither C nor γ can ever be eliminated under his rules, and the level below that, where E or H sometimes can even though both are needed for defining γ, leads him to the generalization that in Maas's view no witness immediately below the archetype can ever be eliminated, however many there may be (§30.3.1–2). The generalization conflicts, however, not only with Maas's statement that in his example the reading of β can be deduced from agreement between any two of ABC(D) (§8c) but also with a later statement of Maas's that Montanari discusses (§117.7; he has to blame the conflict on Maas himself). In a stemma where two branches lead from the archetype and disagree, Maas noticed the contrast (§8e), and the reason for it is simply the absence by definition, at that level, of any witness that could resolve the disagreement in the way that C can between E and H or could in Maas's example between A and B. Where C and γ agree, the only reason for not granting that the reconstruction of α eliminates them is Maas's stipulation, in this context pointless, that the reconstruction must be done without their help.

I conclude that Montanari's analysis of *eliminatio*, whether or not it goes back to Maas himself, is an unsatisfactory compromise, in which he rightly fuses Maas's two kinds of *eliminatio*, yet by adhering to Maas's problematical clause misses a tidier way of doing so.

On the other hand, adopting as a rule of procedure the formulation that I suggested above, 'a witness can be eliminated wherever the reading of an ancestor is known', would have the drawback that H was eliminable in (2)–(4) but not in (1). Similarly, a formulation in which not witnesses but readings were eliminated would have the drawback that the same reading was eliminable when it occurred in one witness but not when it occurred in another. One can imagine the confusion that either way of speaking would cause. Furthermore, the category of witnesses that can be eliminated in their entirety is too useful to be treated merely as a special case of a wider category, because editors like to know which of the witnesses they can simply ignore. Naturally, before collation of what have been identified as witnesses, there can be no presumption either of dependence or of independence. When Montanari argues that unless one presumes independence one will be refusing to treat a witness as a witness and so voting for a police state in preference to the rule of law (§140.6), I concur only if he means no more than that any witness has a right to be collated.

Though I broadly agree, then, with Montanari's analysis of *eliminatio*, there are practical reasons why Maas's distinction between two kinds should be retained, *eliminatio codicum descriptorum* restricted to witnesses that descend from extant ancestors, and the problematical clause, at least if Montanari's interpretation is right, quietly forgotten.

* * *

In an attack on stemmatics, Enrico Flores devotes three of his five chapters to archetypes (1998, chapters iii–v).[4] Each of these three chapters includes a version of the same fallacious argument about conjunctive errors. Whether new or not in textual stemmatics (checking would be laborious), one version of the fallacy has an old and interesting analogue in another field.

Before tackling the fallacy itself, I must say how Flores understands 'archetype'. He begins by citing Maas's definition, 'the exemplar from which the first split began',[5] but takes it out of context (pp. 47–8). In context, as Montanari points out (§7.5.1–2), 'the first split' means the earliest of the splits revealed by analysis of the extant witnesses; but 'in reality' says Flores 'the first split or splits, a fact apparently too often forgotten, began from the moment when a text was written down and started to circulate and spread in a number of copies'. He therefore understands Maas's 'first' as the first from below, or in other words the first reached in the process of reconstruction from the extant witnesses; but since in this process many points of convergence may be reached before the archetype, he has to gloss 'the first' as 'the first before the extant tradition' (pp. 50–1).[6]

[4] He kindly sent me a copy. In my opinion, his most valuable point in the three chapters is his observation (pp. 77–9) that an error in a minuscule witness caused by misreading of capitals or uncials need not have come about, as editors tend to assume, when the text was transferred from one script to the other.

[5] Maas's wording is 'die Vorlage, bei der die erste Spaltung begann' (§5).

[6] In his review of Montanari's book (2003, 262), he ignores the need for the gloss when he repeats that he has always understood 'the first' as the first from below.

Equipped with this lopsided distinction between the first from above and the first from below, Flores goes on to allege that scholars have defined 'archetype' either from above as 'the oldest witness, a lost one, common to the whole manuscript tradition of a text' (presumably he means all the manuscripts that have ever existed) or 'the lost witness from which descend more or less immediately all the oldest witnesses that survive and the rest of the derivative manuscript tradition'. The second definition, as he says, is Maas's; but whose is the first? Quite apart from its poor wording (since a witness cannot be common to a tradition), what it defines is the original, unless the original is preserved or only its descendants count as witnesses. When Montanari says that for Maas the two definitions are equivalent (§7.5.5), how is he taking this first one?

Already, then, Flores's remarks about the meaning of 'archetype' betray misapprehension and confusion. Confusion persists when he tries to prove Maas's notion of 'archetype' incoherent, and it is in these attempts that he repeats in various forms a fallacious argument about conjunctive errors.

The simplest form occurs when he discusses the traditions of Aristotle's *Poetics* and Cicero's *Paradoxa* (pp. 68–74). In Gallavotti's stemma for the *Poetics* (essentially Kassel's), the Syriac translation of the tenth century shares errors with a hyparchetype β, from which the Greek manuscripts and the Latin translation of 1278 derive, and so an archetype α has been postulated.

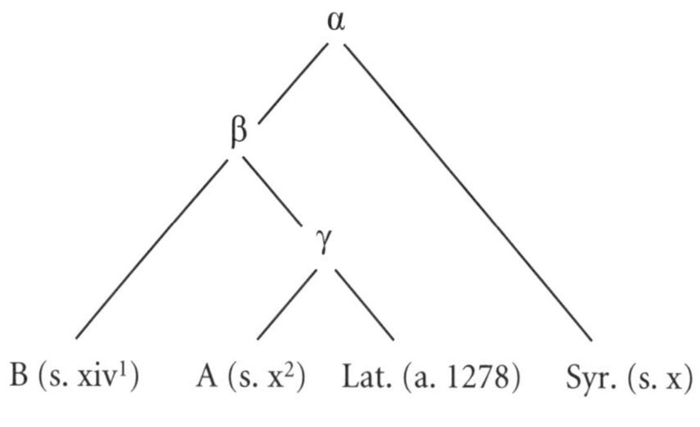

Flores argues that the errors in question could have reached the Syriac translation not from α but from a manuscript Λ that also had them (together, perhaps, with some of the errors hitherto blamed on the Syriac translation); and by the same argument he disposes of Gallavotti's hyparchetypes β and γ and Badalì's archetype for Cicero's *Paradoxa*. The argument amounts to this: the Syriac translation need not have acquired the errors that it shares with β through the latest ancestor that it shares with β. Alas, the proposition is self-contradictory. On whatever map of lost witnesses he chooses to place α, it has been defined as the latest common ancestor of β and the Syriac translation, and any further hypothesis that turns it into something else, such as not an ancestor of the Syriac translation at all, must be ruled out.

The argument owes such plausibility as it possesses to an ambiguity in expressions of potentiality. The archetype of Statius' *Silvae*, known as M, survives, and two manuscripts known as F and B were copied from it and therefore share its errors (Reeve (1977), 203, 206).[7] If one asks 'could B have got them from F?', there are two different questions that one might be asking: 'is it possible that B got them from F?', to which the answer is 'no' (F has significant errors absent from MB), and 'would it have been possible for B to get them from F?', to which the answer, on some level at least, is 'yes' (the scribe might have chosen F as his model rather than M). Perhaps it would have been possible for the Syriac translation to get the errors it shares with β from any number of manuscripts, but *ex hypothesi* it actually got them through α.

In a later passage, Flores sets out to show that the origin of conjunctive errors can be pushed back ever higher in the transmission, so high indeed that it may lie in the original (pp. 87–8). To that end he constructs an example in which three witnesses, ABC, share significant errors, xyz, 'which take one back to the archetype α'.

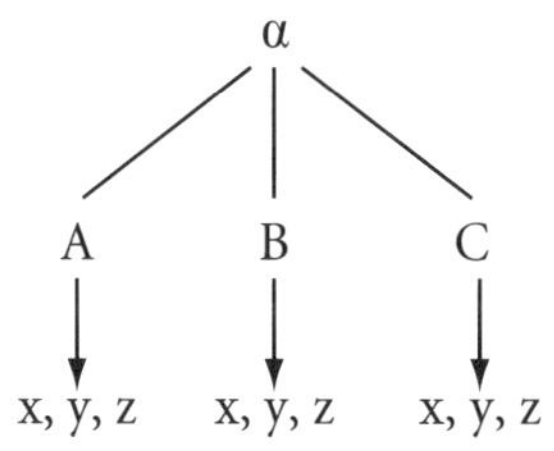

[7] I wanted a real example, and this was the first that came to mind.

For the moment he is using 'archetype' in a sense that he attributes to his opponents, 'witness without which ABC would not have existed'; and from the example he argues that α is not 'the only copy that survived, without which ABC would not exist'. Actually the conclusion follows immediately from the definition, because any ancestor of α, for instance the original, would satisfy it no less than α. Before I examine his argument, therefore, the definition must be tightened so that α is the *latest* witness without which ABC would not have existed. That is essentially how Maas defined 'archetype' and surely how most people define it;[8] and Flores too, since he is discussing one reconstructed witness, namely 'the archetype α', and not a line of reconstructed witnesses, presumably had that definition in mind.

His argument runs as follows: since all the ancestors of α as far back as a copy of the original could have had the error z, it may well be that ABC derive in various ways from that copy without any need to postulate an archetype. By definition, however, B (say) cannot have inherited any of the errors xyz from an ancestor of α down a line of tradition that did not pass through α; and if ABC derive in various ways from a copy of the original but not all through any later witness, then that copy of the original *was* α.

In the course of putting forward his fallacious argument, Flores comes close to exposing another fallacy. That z (say) is an error will be clear, he supposes, from the indirect tradition or from papyri, 'of the 2nd century AD, for instance', and 'the usual reasoning is that without α (more recent than the 2nd century AD on the evidence of the indirect tradition), which had the reading z and transmitted it to ABC, ABC could not have existed'. As he points out, however, z could have arisen in a copy of the original and the true reading have survived in a later descendant of another copy. Nevertheless, instead of concluding that α itself could perfectly well have been older than the indirect tradition or the second-century papyrus, he confines his remarks to the antiquity of z. The parenthesis 'more recent than the

[8] It was one of many definitions that I rejected in 'Archetypes' (1985), but my reason for rejecting it, that it rules out extant archetypes, is irrelevant here. I have since published a correction in '*Eliminatio*' (1989, n. 5) and an afterthought in 'Shared innovations' (1998, n. 87).

2nd century AD on the evidence of the indirect tradition' may even be an elaboration of his own rather than part of 'the usual reasoning'; at any rate, two pages earlier he had cited a reference of Alberti's to papyri of Herodotus that give better readings than the medieval manuscripts and had represented him as holding 'on good grounds' that since the papyri in question belong to the first three centuries AD 'it follows that the source of our two families must be placed after the 3rd century' (Alberti (1983), 194–5). I consider Alberti's argument fallacious. Maas (no less) committed the same fallacy when he inferred from Quintilian's discussion of *Ecl.* 4.62 that the reading unanimously attested by the manuscripts of Virgil, *cui . . . parentes*, did not yet exist in his day (§36); the fallacy has been exposed by Montanari (§89.1). This example leaves more room for debate, however, because Quintilian's knowledge of Virgil presumably went beyond a single copy.

Flores's third version of the fallacy about conjunctive errors occurs earlier in his book than the other two, but I take it last because he embeds it in a more complex argument (p. 54).[9] I do not feel sure that I have entirely grasped the argument,[10] but I will do my best to reproduce it, albeit with some phrases left in the original Italian. Though hypothetical again, xyz this time are not errors but manuscripts, and from an archetype θ they inherit the errors *abc*. Some of these errors, however, are older than others. The error *a* arose in the original and passed to all its descendants, θ included. The error *b* arose in a copy of the original called α and passed to β and any other copies of α that there may have been; it too reached θ. 'Ma θ' (and to this sentence he adds an exclamation mark) 'non è la somma delle serie complete' of all the manuscripts copied from the original, from α, from β, and so on. It derives ultimately from α, because it has the error *b*, but is wrongly imagined to be 'l'unico sopravvissuto di una serie sterminata di atti di copia'. If we move up the stemma from θ to α, we shall keep finding errors common to the whole tradition, but their number will gradually fall until in the original either none remain or only those that arose in it. The archetype, therefore, since

[9] I do not know whether it was this argument or something else on pp. 51–61 that convinced Montanari (§7.5.4).

[10] Giovanni Orlandi did me the favour of aiding my efforts.

it is always constructed 'dal basso e dalla tr. ms. conservatasi, come portatore degli errori comuni (o congiuntivi)', will always be a copy 'apparentemente unico', and he spaces out 'apparentemente' for emphasis. He goes on to call θ a constriction, the bottom of one funnel and the top of another inverted below it: the errors *abc* drop to the bottom of the upper funnel and by dispersing in the lower funnel reach xyz. The problem, he says, is that the constriction does not exist, because the errors in the upper funnel do not collect at the bottom but disperse. The apparent uniqueness of the archetype therefore results from the reductive logic of reconstructing a unique copy in reality non-existent 'as such' the further one moves up from the extant manuscripts to the original. 'That is the real explanation.'

I believe that the argument contains two fallacies, of which the one that I have been discussing is the first. It occurs in his remarks about moving up from the extant manuscripts to the original.

First one meets the archetype θ, which had the errors *abc*; but as one moves up through β and α to the original, *c* and *b* fall away until only *a* remains. The argument seems to be this: like θ, its ancestors β and α are reconstructed from below and therefore qualify for the name 'archetype', from which it follows that there was no single archetype θ. The fallacy, elementary again despite its complex setting, lies in not sticking to the original definition of 'archetype', namely 'latest common ancestor of xyz' or 'latest witness to which xyz owe the errors *abc*', but instead allowing β and α to count as archetypes even though *ex hypothesi* the oldest ancestor of xyz that can be reconstructed is θ, a descendant of β and α.

The second fallacy in the argument occurs when he introduces the image of the two funnels, which has been given memorable expression elsewhere (Reynolds (1983*a*), xiii):

It is probably true to say that the classical tradition as it expands and contracts in its course from Antiquity to the end of the Renaissance does conform to a basic pattern. In its crude and essential form it appears to the imagination to follow the traditional lines of the hourglass, which funnels down to a narrow middle and then bellies out again, or the simplified shape in which the female form is often represented—broad shoulders, tiny waist, full skirt. The vital statistics of the figure will vary considerably from text to text; but these diverse patterns, when superimposed one upon the other, should still produce a dominant shape. The slender waist is the most permanent feature, for the Dark Ages so constricted the flow of classical learning that for a time it was universally reduced to a trickle.

Flores transfers the image from history to stemmatic logic. For him θ could have been 'of the 9th century or the 3rd–5th', and what matters to him is its definition as a single manuscript, something narrower, that is, than the network of its earlier or later relatives. Now it may be that if one were to represent schematically, with the original at the top, the network of all the manuscripts that had ever had any of the errors *abc* up to the production of θ, it would look more like a pyramid than a funnel; but why should the extant manuscripts not all derive from a single point in the pyramid, especially if, by the time that the earliest of them was produced, attrition had turned the lower section of the pyramid into something more like a funnel? When Flores exclaims that θ is not the sum of all the manuscripts that had ever had any of the errors *abc*, who does he suppose holds that it is? Or is he demanding that it should be?

Though they differ in some respects, then, all three arguments contain versions of the same fallacy: shifting the definition of 'archetype'. In the second and third, he pushes the archetype further and further back in the tradition. That suits his own preference, because he regards what he takes to be Maas's archetype as so close in date to the extant witnesses that Maas leaves open 'a vast expanse between the archetype and the original text' (p. 50). In fact, however, it is precisely Maas's definition of 'archetype' that bridges part of the gap, because among extant witnesses Maas includes indirect evidence like quotations in ancient authors. As Montanari points out (§7.4.1), Flores simply overlooks an explicit statement of Maas's to that effect when he asserts that Maas excludes indirect evidence from his reconstruction.[11] When Maas discusses an imaginary stemma, he explains that A–J are 'manuscripts, printed editions, excerpts, paraphrases, citations, imitations, translations, etc.' (§8); similarly, his archetype loses that status if a witness independent of it supervenes in a section of the text (§16 last two paragraphs, §§24, 28), so that, for instance, the archetype in a passage of Plato's *Phaedrus* already

[11] In his review of Montanari's book (2003, 262), Flores shifts his ground by replying that he was concerned not with what Maas said but with the archetypes that the best editors had reconstructed by applying Maas's principles.

antedated Cicero when a papyrus of the 2nd century AD came to light (§37). Maas himself, then, accepted the consequence that the archetype changes when the witnesses change, and in my opinion a consequence of that consequence is the need to specify the witnesses that an archetype is the archetype of (Reeve (1985), 199, Montanari §55.3.4).[12] Flores's second and third arguments illustrate the same need.

Incidentally, it should not be thought that I am ignoring the possibility of contamination. Years ago I offered antistemmatists a more radical argument about contamination than any that Pasquali ever voiced, an argument that would make extant archetypes the only ones safe to discuss (1985, 199 n. 24).[13] A version of it could be applied to stemma (3) in the previous section:

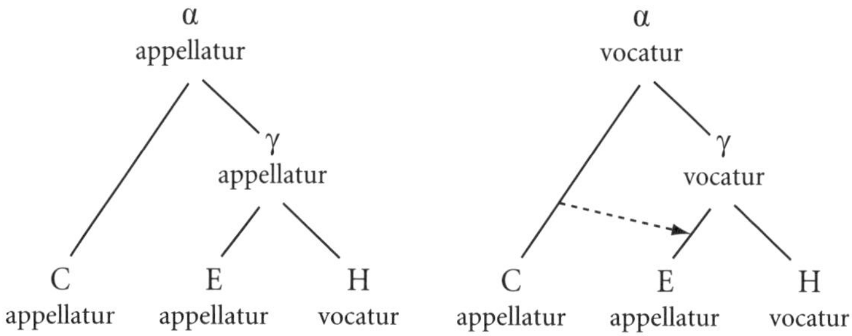

Variants among CEH that appear to have arisen in the first way could actually have arisen in the second. Elsewhere in his book, especially in the three chapters on archetypes, Flores stresses the problems that contamination poses for stemmatists, but all three of the arguments that I have examined here are put forward with no mention of it, and they seem designed to expose an even more fundamental flaw in the operations of stemmatists.

I said above that one version of the fallacy common to all three arguments has an old and interesting analogue. After linguists had

[12] In §8 Montanari rejects all departures from Maas's definition of 'archetype' and any extension from the latest common source of all extant witnesses to the latest common source of a specified number ('archetype of . . .').

[13] Montanari (§7.8) defends Maas's implicit restriction of 'archetype' to reconstructed witnesses; for 'extant archetype' he prefers 'secondary *codex unicus*' (§3.9.2).

defined a family of Indogermanic languages, August Schleicher drew a family tree of them ((1853), modified in (1860), 81) and later composed an Indogermanic fable (1868). Johannes Schmidt soon launched a famous assault on both the family tree and the fable ((1872), especially pp. 28–31)—not famous enough, however, to be mentioned in either of two attempts at bringing the fable into line with advances in Indogermanic research (Hirt and Arntz (1939), 113–15, Lehmann and Zgusta (1979)).[14] First he demolished Schleicher's Balto-Slavo-Germanic. Resemblances ignored by Schleicher, he argued, entailed families that cut across Schleicher's; whereas, for instance, Schleicher had associated Balto-Slavic with Germanic, and Greek with Italic, other features connected either Balto-Slavic or Greek with Indo-Iranian. Schleicher had therefore failed to show that Balto-Slavo-Germanic or Greco-Italic ever existed. Schmidt then assailed Indogermanic. In principle, the same kind of argument will carry the day; but if any two descendants of Indogermanic are independent of each other and the rest, then it can be reconstructed despite any contamination that may have taken place among the rest (I use 'contamination' as shorthand for any form of transmission other than descent). Schmidt therefore needed further arguments, and he used two. After conceding that some words and forms could safely be derived from a common ancestor, he proceeded to the harmless argument that reconstruction might lead only to a choice of possibilities. The same is true in any tradition, whether affected by contamination or not, and partial reconstruction is not misreconstruction. Furthermore, 'the poor supply of words that can be deduced with any degree of certainty' had worried Schleicher himself. Schmidt's other argument concerned Schleicher's reconstruction of *vividvantsvas* from Sanskrit *vidvatsu* and Greek εἰδόσι: the elements of *vividvantsvas* might all have existed at some time or other, but nothing proved that they ever coexisted. The argument resembles Flores's argument in the third passage discussed above, that the 'temporal stratification' of the errors *abc* makes θ a figment.

[14] In 'Shared innovations' (1998) I discussed the importance of Schleicher and Schmidt for the history of genealogical classification (pp. 464–9, 477–8, 483–4, 488–9, 502). Schleicher is also mentioned by Flores (1998), 66.

Was this argument of Schmidt's any better than Flores's? Schleicher's fable began with the title 'The sheep and the horses', and the word for 'and', an enclitic *ka*, was guaranteed, Schleicher said, by the agreement of Gothic, Sanskrit, Greek, and Latin. The sense of 'agreement' in which Greek τε agrees with Latin *que* immediately reveals a difference between manuscripts and languages: two extant manuscripts of the same classical text are never as unlike each other as two modern descendants of Indogermanic can be, for instance Italian and Czech, and before an agreement can be found between two languages rules of transformation usually need to be applied. Presumably, though, many of the rules that Schleicher accepted would also have been accepted by Schmidt. Schleicher did not say whether other words in the fable were guaranteed by the agreement, in this generous sense, of the same languages; but if they were, I do not see how they could fail to have coexisted with *ka*. Schmidt's objection therefore depends for its validity on one of three premises: that Schleicher made illogical inferences, that he did not always use the same stemma (perhaps because of gaps in the evidence), or that no stemma free from contamination was available for him to use. Without knowing more about the Indogermanic languages and Schleicher's methods of reconstruction, I cannot properly adjudicate. Provisionally, however, I declare in favour of Schleicher.

23

Critical Notes on the Greek Paroemiographers

Winfried Bühler

I

Σ Pl. *Resp.* 337a (p. 192 Greene)

ἤκουσα δέ, φησὶν ὁ Ταρραῖος,[1] *ἐγχωρίων λεγόντων ὅτι ἐν Σαρδόνι γίγνοιτο βοτάνη σελίνῳ παραπλήσιος, ἧς οἱ γευσάμενοι δοκοῦσι μὲν γέλωτι, σπασμῷ δὲ ἀποθνῄσκουσιν.*

Greene prints *γέλωτι*, the reading of the two manuscripts of the scholia. But the ending is clearly corrupt, by a wrong adaptation to the following dative *σπασμῷ*. Siebenkees (1798), 47 wrote *γελῶντες* instead, and was followed by C. F. Hermann (1851–3), vi. 133. This is better, but still not right. The correct reading is *γελᾶν*, written by Zen. Ath. 1.68 (cf. M. E. Miller (1868), 356), and also in *Prov. Bodl.* 833 (Gaisford (1836)).

II

Σ Pind. *Nem.* 7.155a (iii. 137.16 Drachmann)

The scholion on the last words of Pindar's seventh Nemean Ode (*ἅτε μαψυλάκας "Διὸς Κόρινθος"*[2]) begins: *Ἀλήτης {ἐλθὼν}*[3] *περὶ τῆς*

[1] Lucillus Tarrhaeus, collector of proverbs used by Zenobius.

[2] The proverb *Διὸς Κόρινθος* is first used by Pindar (*Nem.* 7.105) and explained by Zen. Ath. 1.66 and other paroemiographers.

[3] Deleted by Drachmann.

ἐν Κορίνθῳ βασιλείας προσῆλθε τῷ μαντείῳ τῷ ἐν Δωδώνῃ, ὅ ἐστι τοῦ Διός, καὶ ἔχρησεν[4] *αὐτῷ τότε κρατήσειν, ὅτε τις δῷ βῶλον γῆς.*

In the final clause *ὅτε* followed by the subjunctive *δῷ* is poetical: in prose, *ὅταν* would be necessary before a verb in the subjunctive.[5] I therefore conclude that the words *ὅτε τις δῷ βῶλον γῆς* are part of the oracle given to Aletes. In that case, *γῆς* cannot be the original reading for metrical reasons. Hence I assume that in the original text of the oracle the hexameter, of which *ὅτε τις δῷ βῶλον* was part, did not end in *γῆς*, but in *ἀρούρης*. Though I have not found another hexameter ending in *βῶλον ἀρούρης*, there are at least some similar combinations: Soph. *Aj.* 1286 *ὑγρᾶς ἀρούρας βῶλον*, Hom. *Il.* 21.232 *ἐρίβωλον ἄρουραν* and prov. Zen. vulg. 2.74 *βῶλος ἄρουραν* (also in other paroemiographers).

III

Σ Pind. *Nem.* 7.155*b* (iii. 138.17–139.1 Drachmann)

πέμπουσι . . . πρέσβεις οἱ Κορίνθιοι κατηγορήσοντας τῶν Μεγαρέων, οἳ προσελθόντες εἰς τὴν ἐκκλησίαν ἄλλα τε πολλὰ διεξῆλθον καὶ τέλος κτλ.

Drachmann informs the reader in the *apparatus criticus* in a short remark on *προσελθόντες* that a Platonic scholion (Euthyd. 292[e], p.123 Greene) has, together with the words *πρέσβεις . . . εἰς τὴν ἐκκλησίαν*, instead of *προσελθόντες* the compound *παρελθόντες*. Nevertheless, he retains *προσελθόντες* in the Pindar scholion. However, I have found in classical authors together with the words *εἰς τὴν ἐκκλησίαν* at least four other instances of *παρέρχεσθαι* and not *προσέρχεσθαι*: Aeschin. 3.95 *παρελθὼν εἰς τὴν ἐκκλησίαν λόγους διεξῆλθε*, ibid. 211 *παρελθόντα εἰς τὴν ἐκκλησίαν εἰπεῖν*, Dem. 21.162 *εἰς τὴν ἐπιοῦσαν ἐκκλησίαν . . . παρελθὼν κτλ.*, Xen. *Hell.* 1.7.11 *παρῆλθε δέ τις τὴν ἐκκλησίαν φάσκων κτλ.*

This was a technical term frequently used during the Athenian democracy. As I could not find any other example of *προσέρχεσθαι*

[4] Understand *τοῦτο* or *ὁ θεός*
[5] See K–G ii. 449 Anm. 4.

εἰς τὴν ἐκκλησίαν, I suppose that the scholiast to Plato wrote παρέρχεσθαι εἰς τὴν ἐκκλησίαν and that this was changed by a copyist to προσέρχεσθαι κτλ. I cannot absolutely exclude that in later times, when the Athenian democracy had long been abolished, no one in the same context said προσέρχεσθαι εἰς τὴν ἐκκλησίαν for παρέρχεσθαι κτλ. But Dio Cass. 38.16.6 παρῆλθεν ἐς τὴν ἐκκλησίαν suggests that the usage was long-lived.

IV

ὄνου παρακύψεως

Zen. Ath. 1.70, Zen. (vulg.) 5.39 = prov. Bodl. 740 and prov. Coisl. 371 in Gaisford (1836)

A

After the lemma and the remark that Menander had used the proverb ὄνου παρακύψεως in his Ἱέρεια,[6] Zen. Ath. loc. cit. continues: λέγουσι δὲ ὅτι κεραμεύς τις, οἱ δὲ ὅτι κοροπλάθος[7] ἔτρεφε πολλὰς (Zen. vulg.: ἔγραφε πολλοὺς falso Zen. Ath.) ὄρνιθας ἐν τῷ ἐργαστηρίῳ. ὄνος δὲ κτλ. But Zen. vulg. 5.39 has only the first derivation: λέγουσι δὲ ὅτι κεραμεύς τις ἔτρεψε πολλὰς ὄρνιθας ἐν τῷ ἐργαστηρίῳ. ὄνος δὲ κτλ. On the other hand, prov. Bod. 740 has no less than three alternatives: οἱ μέν φασιν ἐπὶ κεραμέως, οἱ δὲ ἐπὶ κουροπλάθου, ἄλλοι δὲ ἐφ' ἱστοῦ. ὀρνίθων γὰρ παρατρεφομένων κτλ.

I want to discuss here only one critical point. Gaisford writes ἱστοῦ in rec. B without any remark, and so does Leutsch in his notes on Zen. vulg. 5.39.[8] But as κεραμεύς and κο(υ)ροπλάθος are names of craftsmen, we must, I think, change ἱστοῦ into ἱστ<ουργ>οῦ. The fault may have happened by a *saut du même au même* from ου to οῦ. It should be said that ἱστουργός is a rather rare word: LSJ give only 2 examples, one of them Joseph. *Bell. Jud.* 1.479 ὅτι τὰς . . . μητέρας

[6] Fr. ap. scriptt. servat. 189 (*PCG* vi/2 p. 140).

[7] κοροπλάτης cod.: corr. Miller.

[8] Except that he wrote ἵστου (sic) with a wrong accent.

ἀπειλοῖεν οἱ περὶ Ἀλέξανδρον . . . ἱστουργοὺς ἅμα ταῖς δούλαις ποιήσειν.[9] At least ἱστουργία had already been used by Pl. *Symp.* 197b.

B

Coisl. 177 begins its explanation of the origin of this proverb with the words: ὀρνίθων γάρ τινων ἐν οἰκίᾳ τρεφομένων πολλῶν καὶ τῆς μὲν θύρας κεκλεισμένης οὔσης κτλ. The other paroemiographers which have this proverb do not include the word τινῶν in their otherwise identical or similar explanation of the proverb. It does not seem compatible with the following πολλῶν. But how did it come in? And why was it not deleted by Gaisford? Did the author of the Coislinian collection wrongly take ὄρνιθες to mean birds and, not knowing what kind of birds they were, pedantically add τινων? But in Attic ὄρνις usually means 'cock' (cf. LSJ s.v. iii 1) and not 'bird', and this must be the sense here. Gaisford, working as always in a hurry, should perhaps not be blamed for not seeing the difficulty. His text was repeated without any change by Leutsch and Schneidewin in *CPG* i. 136.

C

Zen. Ath. 1.70 and Zen. vulg. 5.39 say in the middle of the explanation ὄνος δὲ παριὼν . . . παρακύψας διὰ θυρίδος ἀνεσόβησε τὰς ὄρνιθας καὶ τὰ ἐν τῷ ἐργαστηρίῳ συνέτριψαν (Zen. vulg.: συνέτριψε Zen. Ath.) σκεύη. In place of καὶ τὰ . . . συνέτριψε σκεύη Leutsch on Zen. vulg. proposed either αἱ δὲ ἀναπτᾶσαι συνέτριψαν σκεύη or, with Zen. Ath. (and Suda o 397 = iii. 542.22 Adler), καὶ τὰ ἐν τῷ ἐργαστηρίῳ συνέτριψε σκεύη. But the latter cannot be right, because it is not the donkey itself, but birds that are frightened by it which smash the pottery. Leutsch's first interpretation is on the whole acceptable. I propose only a small change: to write instead of καὶ τὰ . . . συνέτριψε σκεύη: αἳ τὰ . . . συνέτριψαν σκεύη.

[9] Another appellation of this kind of craftsman was ὑφάντης (see Blümner (1912), 166).

D

Recensio Bodl. 740 Gaisford has at the end of its explication in all three manuscripts no fewer than three sentences beginning with the particle *τοίνυν*: *ὁ τοίνυν κύριος τοῦ ἐργαστηρίου εἰς κρίσιν εἰσάγει τὸν ὀνηλάτην. ἐρωτώμενος τοίνυν ἐκεῖνος, τίνος κρίνοιτο, ἔλεγεν "ὄνου παρακύψεως". εἴρηται τοίνυν* (sc. *ἡ παροιμία*) *ἐπὶ τῶν καταγελάστως συκοφαντουμένων*. Gaisford did not take offence at the clumsy triplication of this particle. But Zen. Ath. und Zen. vulg. have the variant—which is without doubt original—*ὁ τοίνυν κύριος ... ἐρωτώμενος δὲ ἐκεῖνος .... ἐπὶ τῶν καταγελάστως οὖν συκοφαντουμένων κτλ*.

V

Passio SS. Nicandri et Hermaei rescripta, Lackner (1980), 116 lines 56–8

Ταῦτα (sc. Nicandrum et Hermaeum Christianos comprehendendos et interficiendos esse) *ὁ ἀσεβὴς ἐκεῖνος Ἀλέξιος* (sc. magistratus urbis Myrae) *ἀναδιδάξας τὸν ἀσεβέστερον κόμητα Λιβάνιον καὶ τῆς μανίας αὐτοῦ τὴν τρυγίαν ἐπ' αὐτὸν* (sc. Libanium) *ἐκκενώσας* (cf. Psalm 74:9) *νικὴν κακὴν—τὸ τῆς παροιμίας—νενίκηκεν*.

Lackner (1980), 116 n. 22 confessed 'Für das angeblich sprichwörtliche *νίκην κακὴν νικᾶν* konnte ich keinen Beleg finden.' Nor do I know any, having in vain checked up all collections of Greek proverbs and also my personal notes on them.

I once thought of writing *Καδμείαν* instead of *κακὴν*, i.e. *νικὴν Καδμείαν νικᾶν*, comparing the widespead proverb *Καδμεία νίκη*, of which I have collected about fifty instances from Greek and Byzantine authors (Zen. Ath. 1.1 etc.). The lemma of the paroemiographers is always only *Καδμεία νίκη* (never *νίκη Καδμεία*), whereas the authors often add the verb *νικᾶν*, saying usually *Καδμείαν νίκην νικᾶν*, but also *νικᾶν νίκην Καδμείαν* (for instance Galen. *Difficil. respir.* 1.2 = vii. 760 Kühn). Never, as far as I know, do they say *νίκην Καδμείαν νικᾶν*.

I therefore had doubts about my conjecture and now tend to keep the transmitted reading. Looking around, I found at least one similar expression: Joseph. *Bell. Iud.* 1.540 (on King Herodes having collected together some men expected to condemn his two sons to death) ἔπειτα μηδενὸς ἀντιλέγοντος ἐποικτισάμενος, ὡς αὐτὸς ἁλίσκοιτο καὶ νικῶν νίκην πικρὰν κατὰ τῶν τέκνων, ἐπηρώτα τὴν γνώμην ἑκάστου. The expression is not called a παροιμία, but that seems to me doubtful even of the words κακὴν νίκην νικᾶν. It is rather a pointed expression taken by the author to be proverbial, explained by one author ἐπὶ τῶν ἐπὶ κακῷ νικώντων (Paus. Att. κ 1 = p. 188.1 Erbse), by another ἐπὶ τῶν κακῶς νικώντων (Maximus Planudes, *ap.* Lindstam (1919–20), 66 line 16).

VI

Pollux 9.100 (= ii. 175.19–23 Bethe)

καὶ μὴν καὶ Στησίχορος ἐκαλεῖτό τις παρὰ τοῖς ἀστραγαλίζουσιν ἀριθμός, ὃς ἐδήλου τὰ ὀκτώ· τὸν γὰρ ἐν Ἱμέρᾳ τοῦ ποιητοῦ (sc. Stesichori) τάφον ἐξ ὀκτὼ πάντων συντεθέντα πεποιηκέναι τὴν "πάντ' ὀκτώ" φασι παροιμίαν.

Thus the almost unanimous text of the manuscripts, except for some trivial errors which we can neglect here. But what does the first πάντων after ὀκτὼ mean in this context? Neither Bethe (1900–37) nor Hemsterhuys *et al.* (1706) comments on the problem. But the reading ἐξ ὀκτὼ πάντων is wrong. The correct reading is ἐξ ὀκτὼ γ ω ν ί ω ν, which is found in:

(i) Σ Arethae in Pl. *Lys.* 206e ἀστραγαλίζοντας (p. 456 Greene): λέγεται δέ τις ἐν αὐταῖς (sc. ταῖς πτώσεσι quattuor talorum) Στησίχορος καὶ ἑτέρα Εὐριπίδης, Στησίχορος μὲν ὁ σημαίνων τὴν ὀκτάδα, ἐπεὶ ὁ ἐν Ἱμέρᾳ (ἱέρᾳ cod.: correct. ex ii *infra*) τοῦ μελοποιοῦ τάφος ἐξ ὀκτὼ γωνίων συνέκειτο.

(ii) Eustath. in Hom. *Il.* 1289.59 (iv. 691.2–4 van der Valk): ἐλέγετο δέ τις ἐν αὐταῖς (sc. ταῖς πτώσεσι quattuor talorum) καὶ Στησίχορος, ὁ τὴν ὀκτάδα δηλαδὴ σημαίνων, ἐπεὶ ὁ ἐν Ἱμέρᾳ τῇ Σικελικῇ τάφος τοῦδε τοῦ μελοποιοῦ ἐξ ὀκτὼ γωνιῶν συνέκειτο.

(iii) Paus. att. fr. π 7 *πάντα ὀκτώ* (p. 203.13–16 Erbse (cf. Photius s.v. *πάντα ὀκτώ* ii. 378.24 Porson, Suda π 225 = iv. 23.13–17 Adler); de Stesichori sepulcro in Catania) . . . *τοῦ μνημείου ἔχοντος ὀκτὼ κίονας καὶ ὀκτὼ βαθμοὺς καὶ ὀκτὼ γωνίας.*

All three testimonies seem to go back to the lost work of Suetonius *Περὶ παιδιῶν*: cf. Taillardat (1967), 107 fr. 97 §22.

The change of *γωνίων* to *πάντων* in Pollux may be due to the following *πάντ' ὀκτώ* , which the scribe had perhaps already read and kept in his mind. Alternatively, the letters *ΓΩΝΙΩΝ* and *ΠΑΝΤΩΝ* can easily be confused.[10]

VII

Eustathius in Hom. *Od.* 1870.39–41 = ii. 208.42–5 Stallbaum (on Hom. *Od.* 19.465–6)

Eustathius gives the following comment on Odysseus' brief report to his parents of his wounding by the boar, when Homer had earlier given a much longer description (19.428–58):

συνελὼν . . . ἐν δυσὶν ἔπεσιν ἐκεῖνα τὰ πολλὰ ἔφη τὸ ὥς μιν θηρεύοντα ἤλασε σῦς καὶ ἑξῆς. οὕτω καὶ λάλος ὁ ἄνθρωπος †οὕτως† ὡσεὶ καὶ δωδωναΐζ†ω†ν χαλκ†εῖ†ον· καὶ αὖ πάλιν ἐν δέοντι σιγηλός, ὡς εἰ καὶ Πυθαγόρᾳ ἐφοίτησεν κτλ.

This is the text (without obeli) offered by the most recent edition of Eustathius' commentary on the *Odyssey* (Stallbaum (1825–6)). The two last faults have been recently corrected in passing by Trapp (2001), 429 s.v. *Δωδωναΐζω*: "*-ΐζων χαλκεῖον*[11] (sic pro *-ίζον χαλκίον*)". Both readings are so written in codex Marcianus 460, the probable autograph of Eustathius.[12] And shortly before these words *we have to read* *οὗτος* *instead of* *οὕτως*. I already had doubts about

[10] In passing, note that Stesichorus' tomb was not in Himera (*pace* Pollux, schol. Plat. and Eustath.) but in Catane (cf. e.g. S–S ɪ/1 472).

[11] *χαλκείον* inadvertently Trapp.

[12] Folio 209ʳ third last line. Cf. Formentin (1983), particularly 24. But there are some palaeographers—among them Jean Irigoin—who deny that this manuscript was written by Eustathius. It should be added that there is another manuscript of Eustathius' commentary on the *Odyssey* (Par. gr. 2702, s. xii) written by the same person who wrote Ven. 460, but less carefully; I did not consult this manuscript.

οὕτως[13] and was satisfied to see shortly before finishing this article, that *in the Marcianus not* οὕτως, *but* οὗτος *is written* (*sc.* Homer). This is without doubt the right reading, and is made public here for the first time.

Finally, in the same sentence there is still another peculiarity. I mean the word δωδωναΐζον instead of Δωδωναῖον. The normal form of this proverbial saying is τὸ Δωδωναῖον χαλκίον and not τὸ Δωδωναΐζον χαλκίον (cf. Zen. Ath. 1.2, Zen. vulg. 6.5 and many other paroemiographers, also Steph. Byz. s.v. Δωδώνη (p. 249 Meineke)). But there is more. There appears to be no other example of δωδωναΐζω / -ΐζων in Greek or Byzantine literature. Finally (which at first may seem decisive), Eustathius himself uses the normal form τὸ δωδωναῖον χαλκίον in four other places: (i) In *Il.* 335.46 (i. 524.24–5 van der Valk) ἐξ αὐτῆς (sc. τῆς Δωδώνης) τὸ παροιμιαζόμενον "δωδωναῖον χαλκίον" ἐπὶ τῶν πολυλόγων; (ii) In *Od.* 1760.55 δῆλον . . . ὡς ἐκ ταύτης (sc. Δωδώνης) καὶ τὸ παροιμιακὸν "Δωδωναῖον χαλκεῖον" (lege -ίον), περὶ οὗ Παυσανίας (sc. Atticista, δ 30 = p. 174 Erbse) φησίν, ὅτι κτλ. (iii) *Epist.* 43 p. 347 l.84 Tafel οὐκ ἄχαρις . . . λόγος, ὃς φιλεῖ καλὸν τὸ ὀλίγον καὶ πάντοτε. εἰ δὲ τὸ Δωδωναῖόν μοι περιφέρεις χαλκεῖον (lege -ίον), ἀλλὰ φλύαρος ἐκεῖνος ὁ ἦχος κτλ. (iv) *Comment. ad Dionys. Perieget.* 428 (*GGM* ii. 298.11) ἀπ' αὐτῆς (*sc.* τῆς Δωδώνης) καὶ τὸ Δωδωναῖον χαλκεῖον (lege -ίον) ἐπὶ τῶν πολυλόγων.[14]

But why then did Eustathius not use the normal form of our proverb as in *Od.* 1817.42? The answer is that the -ίζειν suffix, already common in Greek literature, was highly productive in the Byzantine period (see especially Debrunner (1917), 127–40, 'Die Verba auf -ίζειν').[15] Debrunner stresses (pp. 132 ff.) that 'Schallwörter sind bei -ίζειν . . . zahlreich wie τρίζειν . . ., κρίζειν . . . und Denominativa wie σαλπίζειν, κροταλίζειν und andere.' On p. 130 he quotes a verb ending in -ίζειν from Eustathius, πρωτεΐζειν ('"Πρωτεύς nachahmen" (Eustath.)'), without indicating its source: it is taken from *De emendanda vita monachica* 183 (p. 261.11 Tafel).

[13] Before looking up the Marcianus I had shown the reading οὕτως to a colleague who at first sight tended to keep the printed text.

[14] Cf. also Λόγος M *ap.* Wirth (2000), 209, 58 f. ἡ τῆς βασιλικῆς θερμότης πίστεως χαλκεῖον ἐχοάνευσε λάλον, where there is an allusion to our proverb (rightly recognized by the editor), from which the word Δωδωναῖον is absent.

[15] See also S–D i. 735 ff.

There are many more examples of verbs ending in -*ίζω* in Eustathius' *Opuscula*, of which I quote three: (i) *Op.* 19.33 (p. 165.54 Tafel) *ψευδόμεθα τὸ κλαίειν, ὅτε καὶ κροκοδειλίζομεν* (i.e. shed crocodile tears), *ἐφ' οἷς μὴ ἔχομεν κατεσθίειν ὁλοκλήρως τοὺς ἀδελφούς*, (ii) *Op.* 24.185 (p. 261.57 Tafel) *τὸ σιμωνίζειν* (i.e. Simonem [sc. Stylitam] imitari) *εἰς τάρταρον καθιέντι* (sc. *τῷ ἀρχιερεῖ*) *δι' ἀναθέματος*, (iii) *Op.* 25.71 (p. 289.89 Tafel) *ἐγένοντο ... γυναῖκες ... οἱ ἄνδρες οἱ δαυϊδίζοντες* (i.e. following David).

I therefore conclude that the unusual form *Δωδωναΐζον* has to be accepted. My little investigation has, against my own expectation, ended with the acceptance of an *ἅπαξ λεγόμενον* against possible doubts. In ancient and Byzantine texts a critical view is always necessary, but not every unusual expression is due to corruption.

24

Erasmus on Homer's Moly*

Rudolf Kassel

'Aristoteles philosophorum, ne Platone quidem iuxta M. Tullium excepto,[1] citra controversiam omnium doctissimus'—so Erasmus, in the preface to the 1531 Basle edition of Aristotle, informs his dedicatee John More[2]—'dicere solet, liberalium disciplinarum radices quidem subamaras esse, fructus vero dulcissimos.[3] Quod idem rectius, utpote poeta, significare videtur Homerus quum, depingens Moly, herbarum praestantissimam et adversus omne maleficiorum genus efficacissimam, ait eam radice nigra esse, sed flore lacteo candidoque.'[4] The assertion that Homer said the same thing as the Philosopher *rectius, utpote poeta*, must have caused many a reader to cudgel his brains in vain since the first edition. What Erasmus meant has been rendered unrecognizable by a misprinted letter: *tectius, utpote poeta*. Cf. *Ratio verae theolog.* LB v p. 85 F 'quod alibi dictum est tectius, alibi dilucidius refertur' and *Adag.* 1701 (ASD II 4 p. 151.

* Translated by Leofranc Holford-Strevens.

1 *De Fin.* 5. 7 'Aristoteles, quem excepto Platone haud scio an recte dixerim principem philosophorum.'

2 Cytowska (1974), 152 calls him 'den kleinen Sohn des Thomas Morus', but the *ornatissimus iuvenis* was about twenty-two years old (on him see Allen (1906–58), iv. 19). In what follows, the letters are cited by this edition; in citations of Erasmus' works LB as usual is the old Leiden edition by Johannes Clericus, ASD the new Amsterdam edition.

3 Incorporated by Erasmus into book 7 of his *Apophthegmata*, 'Aristoteles Stagirites 8' (LB IV p. 338 C). For the evidence see Searby (1998), §15, pp. 100 and 166–8.

4 *Epist.* 2432. 1–2, 12–17 Allen.

12) 'Eodem allusisse videtur [Plato], licet tectius, libro tertio [Legum].'[5]

The emended text transports Homer's magic herb into a context of allegorical interpretation in which one of the *Adagia* had already found a place for it (1835; ASD II 4 p. 236. 475): 'Qui e nuce nucleum esse vult, frangit nucem . . . Qui quaerit animi pabulum in arcanis litteris, scrutetur sub allegoriae involucro conditum mysterium . . . Nux enim foris tum dura est tum amara, intus suavissimum condit cibum. Huc referendum illud Homericum figmentum de moly herba, quam ait radicem quidem habere nigram, sed florem lacteum.' There follows a citation of Hom. *Od.* 10. 304–6 with a Latin translation.[6] *Involucrum*, like *integumentum*, was a stock term of allegorical exposition in the Middle Ages, as especially practised in the school of Chartres.[7] Both terms persisted in Erasmus' vocabulary to designate a 'veiling' or 'concealing' mode of presentation: thus *involucrum* also appears at *Adag.* 2932 (ASD II 6 p. 562. 289) 'sapientiam, quae variis involucris obtegitur apud priscos et alia atque alia specie proponitur, praesertim in divinis literis, quae tota ferme constat allegoriis',[8] *Epist.* 1304. 456 'figurarum involucris obtegere', *De misericord. Dom.* LB V p. 558 D 'erudita vetustas huiusmodi fabularum involucris [as in the myth of the Giants] aliquid significare voluit, quod ad hominum mores exprimendos pertinet'. It is found together with *integumentum* in the proem to the *Adagia*, ASD II 1 p. 46. 21: 'Donatus ac Diomedes . . . in omni paroemia requirere videntur involucrum aliquod, ut qui eam allegoriae speciem fecerint . . . Graecorum item quotquot sunt finitiones, aut sententiam ad vitam instituendam conducibilem aut metaphorae tectorium admiscent, quaedam utrunque cum altero coniungunt.' But a proverb like μηδὲν ἄγαν

[5] How easily *tectius* could become *rectius* can be seen from the corruption of *tecta* to *recta* in William Gager's *Dido*, cited by Jakobi (1988), 454 in reviewing an ill-executed modern edition.

[6] Cf. too *De dupl. cop. verb. ac rer.* ASD I 6 p. 236. 981. A somewhat forced connection of Moly with Platonic philosopher-kings is effected in *Epist.* 393.26 (dedication of *Institutio Principis Christiani* to Maximilian's grandson, the future Emperor Charles V).

[7] Kindermann (1998), 96–101; Junge (1999), 135; Zwierlein (1998), 45 and 52 = (2004), 43 and 50.

[8] In contrast to the 'nuda et aperta philosophiae praecepta' of *Adag.* 2901 (ASD II 6 p. 551. 5).

'nihil habet integumenti'. Here we also see the related term *tectorium*, which at *Enchiridion militis Christiani* LB v p. 29 B appears in the generalizing expression: 'litterae poetarum omnium, et ex philosophis Platonicorum, maxime vero Scripturae divinae . . . quae sub tectorio . . . numen claudunt'. To describe Orphic poetry Pico della Mirandola combines *involucrum* and *velamentum*, *Orat. de hom. dign.* p. 64 Buck 'Orpheus suorum dogmatum mysteria fabularum intexit involucris et poetico velamento dissimulavit.' The epithet *poetico* draws our attention back to Erasmus' *utpote poeta*. That this explanatory addition, 'seeing that he is a poet', 'as we expect of a poet', 'as is a poet's way', suits not *rectius* but *tectius* may also be demonstrated by a passage from Cristoforo Landino's exposition of Virgil in book 3 of his *Disputationes Camaldulenses*:[9] 'Quam quidem rem [the allegorical significance of Aeneas' wanderings] si non aperte ostendit, obscurius tamen, ut poetarum mos est, significat noster Virgilius' (p. 127. 21 Lohe). The final clarifying word, however, should go to an ancient author: Gellius 3. 2. 14 'ista autem omnia de dierum temporibus et finibus ad observationem discipulinamque iuris antiqui pertinentia cum in libris veterum inveniremus, non dubitabamus quin Vergilius quoque id ipsum ostenderit, non exposite atque aperte sed, ut hominem decuit poeticas res agentem, recondita et quasi operta veteris ritus significatione' [*Aen.* 5. 738–9].

[9] Zintzen (1985) = (2000), 401–26.

25

Homage to *G&R* 2nd ser. 11 (1964): 185–7 *or* The Sibyl Prophesies the Slaying of the Jabberwock

J. L. Lightfoot

ἀλλ᾽ ὁπόταν κατὰ γαῖαν ὅλαν μέγα σῆμα γένηται,
νὺξ ἔσται σκοτόεσσα πελώριος ἤματι μέσσῳ
ἀντολίης δύσεως τε μεσημβρίης τε καὶ ἄρκτου·
αὐτίκα καὶ κατὰ γῆν τε καὶ ὕδατος οἴδματα πόντου
ὀρφναίη πάντεσσι κακὴ καταχεύεται ἄχλυς,
καὶ ἁλινηχέα †τῶβ᾽† ἐν ἀβύσσῳ εἱλίξονται
Ταρτάρου ἀκαμάτου· καὶ εἰν βυθίοις †βορογώβοις†
ῥοχθήσει θορύβῳ ἁλὸς ἠχήεντα βέρεθρα.
αἰαῖ ἐγὼ δειλή, τί γενήσομαι ἤματι τῷδε,
ἡνίκ᾽ ὄφις βριαρὸς ἥξει καὶ πάντα ταράξει,
ὅς γε κεν ἀνθρώποισι καὶ ἀθανάτοισιν ἀνάσσοι
οὗ θ᾽ ἀριθμὸν λέξω καὶ τοὔνομα δηλώσαιμι·
οὔνομα γὰρ θῆρος μοῦνον δεκάδα σχήσειε
γράμματος ἀρχομένου, καὶ ἕνδεκα γράμματα πάντα
δηλώσει δείλοισι βροτοῖς, τετρασύλλαβος Ἄρης.
δήγματα φαρμακόεντα ποιῇ, σάρκας δέ τ᾽ ἀράξει,
καὶ φόβος ἔσται ἁπᾶσιν ὅθ᾽ ἥξῃ †βανδεροάρπαξ†
σκορπισμὸς δέ τε καὶ θάνατος καὶ κλαυθμὸς ἱκνεῖται.
δὴ τότε ἁγνὸς ἄναξ πάσης γῆς σκῆπτρα κρατήσων
ἥξει ῥομφαῖαν φορέων ἐπὶ αἰνοπέλωρον·
δηρὸν ζητήσει, δηρὸν δέ τε θῆρ᾽ ἀνιχνεύσει,
δηρὸν τηρήσει μιν †θουλγαίῳ† ἐνὶ δρυμῷ.

τῷ δὲ δοασσαμένῳ ὅ τι οἱ κεν κέρδιον εἴη
ὀξέα συρίζων τότε δὴ μετὰ ταῦτα φανεῖται
δεινὸς ὄφις φυσῶν πόλεμον καὶ κῆρα μέλαιναν
βαρβαρόφρων τε φλογὼψ πολυαίματος ἄφρονα λυσσῶν.
αὐτὰρ ἐπεὶ γυμνώσει ἀπὸ κολέου ξίφος ὄξυ,
Ἴσθι τότ' αἰνοδράκοντ', ὀλοὸν γένος, ἐγγὺς ὀλέθρου.
Αἰαῖ σοι, αἰαῖ τλῆμον, κατοδύρομαι οἰκτρῶς·
Βρασσομένης δέ τε γῆς ἔσται δουπήματα λυγρά
Βροντῆς τε στεροπῆς τε πυρός τ' ἀπὸ τοῖο πελώρου.
Ἔνθεν ἐπεσσύμενος ὃν λαιμὸν ἀπαμήσειε σιδήρῳ,
Ῥίψας ἐν γαίῃ βεβολημένον ὀξέι χαλκῷ
†Ϝορπαλ† ἐχιδνοφόνῳ, κεφαλὴν τ' ἀποδειροτόμησας
Οἴσει ἐπευξάμενος ἔτι θῦμον ἀποπνείουσαν.
Καὶ τότε αἰνοδράκοντι πεφήσεται λυγρὸς ὄλεθρος.
Καὶ τότε δὴ ζήσοντ' εὐφραινόμενοι ἐπὶ τούτῳ
Ἰοβόλον φοβερόν τε κατακτείναντι δάφοινον.
ὦ μακαριστός, ἐκεῖνον ὃς ἐς χρόνον ἔσσεται ἀνήρ,
πειραθεὶς κακότητος, ἵν' ὕστερον εὐφρανθείῃ.

6–7 cf. LXX Job 41:23–4 7 †βορογώβοις† locus desperatus 12–15 cf. Rev. 13:18 22 †θουλγαίῳ†: an ad *Θούλην γῆν* respicit?

ANMERKUNG

Das Versmaß strotzt vor Ungereimtheiten. Der Autor vernachlässigt Hiate und verlängert kurze Silben nach Belieben; ein Verstoß gegen die Herrmannsche Brücke findet sich in Vers 35. Die Aneignung homerischer und hesiodischer Verse erscheint schamlos: Wie dieser Graeculus der Waffe erlauben konnte, entweder aus Eisen oder scharfer Bronze zu sein (32–3), ist mir gänzlich unverständlich. Er verwendet Partikel als reine Füllwörter und erweist sich der Unterscheidung der Modi gegenüber als beinahe gleichgültig; ich neige dazu die Textstelle dem Zwielicht des Hellenismus zuzuschreiben.

Die Gematrie der Verse 12–15 entspricht Schülerniveau. Wenn der unsinnige Name "Jabberwocky" gemeint ist, worauf die Verwendung des Akrostichons der Verse 28–38 Hinweis gibt, kann die Zahl 10 allein durch die Annahme des ersten Buchstaben als konsonantisches Jod gebildet werden.

Die Textstelle war außerdem im Laufe ihrer Überlieferung nachhaltiger Verfälschung ausgesetzt. Zahlreiche Wörter sind durch völlige Unverständlichkeit gekennzeichnet. Dem *τῶβ'* in Vers 6 liegt höchstwahrscheinlich eine semitische Wurzel zugrunde. In Vers 34 scheint die Verderbnis unheilbar zu sein: War *ὅρπη* beabsichtigt (cf. Hesychius, *ο* 1307 *ὅρπη· σίδηρος, ἐν ᾧ τὸν ἐλέφαντα τύπτουσιν*)? Vergleiche auch *ἅρπη*, die Waffe, mit welcher Perseus die Gorgo enthaupten ließ (Pherekydes ap. Schol. Apoll. Rhod. iv.1515; Apoll. Bibl. ii 4.2).

Bibliography

Aarne A., and Thompson S. (1961), *The Types of the Folktale*[2] (Folklore Fellows Communications 184; Helsinki).

Abry, C. (2002), 'Omer m'a tuer . . . ou Moi-Même en personne', in Hurst and Létoublon (2002), 57–65.

Ackerman, R. (1974), 'Sir James G. Frazer and A. E. Housman: a relationship in letters', *GRBS* 15: 339–64.

Adams, J. N. (1982), *The Latin Sexual Vocabulary* (London).

—— (1983), 'Words for prostitute in Latin', *RhM* n.F. 126: 321–58.

Adler, A. (1928–38), *Suidae Lexicon* (Lexicographi Graeci 1; Leipzig).

Adrados, F. R. (1955), 'Nueva reconstrucción de los epodos de Archilochus', *Emerita* 23: 1–78.

—— (1964), 'El tema del aguila, de la epica acadia a Esquilo', *Emerita* 32: 267–82.

—— and Reverdin, O. (1984) (eds.), *La Fable* (Entretiens sur l'Antiquité Classique 30; Geneva).

Akurgal, E. (1962), 'The early period and the golden age of Ionia', *AJA* 66: 369–79.

Alberti, G. B. (1983), 'I papiri e l' "archetipo" di Erodoto', *Prometheus* 9: 193–6.

Alexiou, M. (1974), *The Ritual Lament in Greek Tradition* (Cambridge). [2nd ed. (2002) revised by D. Yatromanolakis and P. Roilos (Lanham, MD and Oxford)]

Allan, W. (2000), *The* Andromache *and Euripidean Tragedy* (Oxford).

—— (2001), *Euripides*: The Children of Heracles (Warminster).

Allen, J. T., and Italie, G. (1954), *A Concordance to Euripides* (Berkeley).

Allen, P. S. (1906–58), *Opus Epistolarum Des. Erasmi Roterodami* (Oxford).

Allison, D. C. (1993), *The New Moses: a Matthean Typology* (Minneapolis).

Aly, W. (1913), 'Die literarische Überlieferung des Prometheusmythos', *RhM* n.F. 68: 545–59. [= Heitsch (1966), 327–41]

Ameis, C. F., and Hentze, C. (1908), *Homers Ilias für den Schulgebrauch erklärt* vol. ii/2[4] (Leipzig).

—— (1913), *Homers Ilias für den Schulgebrauch erklärt* vol. i/1[7] (Leipzig).

Anderson, G. (2000), *Fairytales in the Ancient World* (London).

Armstrong, D., Fish, J., Johnston, P. A., and Skinner, M. B. (2004) (eds.), *Vergil, Philodemus, and the Augustans* (Austin).

Arnim, J. von (1893–6), *Dionis Prusaensis quem vocant Chrysostomum quae exstant omnia* (Berlin).

Arnott, W. G. (1996), *Alexis: the Fragments* (Cambridge).

Aro, S., and Whiting, R. M. (2000) (eds.), *The Heirs of Assyria: Proceedings of the Opening Symposium of the Assyrian and Babylonian Intellectual Heritage Project held in Tvärminne, Finland, October 8–11, 1998* (Melammu Symposia 1; Helsinki).

Asheri, D. (1988), *Erodoto: Le Storie.* Libro I (Milan).

Atherton, C. (1998) (ed.), *Monsters and Monstrosity in Greek and Roman Culture* (Nottingham Classical Literature Studies 6; Bari).

Auhagen, U. (1999), *Der Monolog bei Ovid* (Scripta Oralia 119; Tübingen).

Babbitt, F. C. (1927), *Plutarch: Moralia* I (Cambridge, MA and London).

Babut, D. (1969), *Plutarque et le Stoicisme* (Paris).

Bahntje, U. B. (1900), *Quaestiones Archilocheae* (diss. Göttingen).

Baier, T. (1999), 'Die Wandlung des epischen Erzählers. Apologe bei Homer, Vergil und Ovid', *Hermes* 127: 437–54.

Bain, D. M. (1991), 'Six Greek verbs of sexual congress (βινῶ, κινῶ, πυγίζω, ληκῶ, οἴφω, λαικάζω)', *CQ* NS 41: 51–77.

—— (1995), 'Farting or croaking or just noise? Sophocles, *Ichneutae* F 314.168 *TrGF* 4', *SIFC* 3rd ser. 13: 184–9.

—— (1999), 'The avoidance of euphemism. Basic language in Greek medical texts', in De Martino and Sommerstein (1999) (eds.), 259–91.

—— (forthcoming), 'Praefanda: the lexicography of ancient Greek aischrologia', in Thompson and Fraser (forthcoming).

Bakker, E. J., Jong, I. J. F. de, and Wees, H. van (2002) (eds.), *Brill's Companion to Herodotus* (Leiden, Boston, Cologne).

Bakker, W. F. (1966), *The Greek Imperative. An Investigation into the Aspectual Differences between Present and Aorist Imperatives in Greek Prayer from Homer up to the Present Day* (Amsterdam).

Baldassarre, I., and Pugliese Carratelli, G. (1990–2003) (eds.), *Pompei. Pitture e mosaici* (11 vols.; Rome).

Baldi, A. (1959), 'Strane analogie tra un antichissimo mito paleobabilonese e la trilogia di Oreste', *Aevum* 1–2: 145–7.

—— (1961), 'Tracce del mito di Etana in Archiloco ed Esopo', *Aevum* 35: 381–4.

Bannon, C. J. (1997), *The Brothers of Romulus: Fraternal Pietas in Roman Law, Literature, and Society* (Princeton).

Barlow, S. A. (1989), 'Stereotype and reversal in Euripides' *Medea*', *G&R* 2nd ser. 36: 158–71.

Barrett, C. K. (1998), *A Critical and Exegetical Commentary on the Acts of the Apostles* II (Edinburgh).

Barrett, W. S. (1964), *Euripides: Hippolytos* (Oxford).
Barr-Sharrar, B. (1982), 'Dionysos and the Derveni Krater', *Archaeology* 35: 13–19.
Baselt, B. (1978–86), *Händel-Handbuch* i–iii. *Thematisch-systematisches Verzeichnis* (Kassel, Tours, London, Basel).
Battezzato, L. (1995), *Il monologo nel teatro di Euripide* (Pisa).
Beare, F. W. (1981), *The Gospel according to Matthew. A Commentary* (Oxford).
Beeks, G. (1987), '"A club of composers": Handel, Pepusch and Arbuthnot at Cannons', in Sadie and Hicks (1987), 209–21.
Bekker, I. (1833), *Apollonii Sophistae Lexicon Homericum* (Berlin).
Belloni, L. (1988), *Eschilo: I Persiani* (Milan).
Bennett, A. (1998), *The Complete* Talking Heads (London).
Bennett, L. J., and Tyrrell, W. B. (1990), 'Sophocles' *Antigone* and funeral oratory', *AJP* 111: 441–56.
Bergk, T. (1882^{4}), *Poetae Lyrici Graeci* II (Leipzig).
Bernabé, A. (1996), *Poetarum Epicorum Graecorum Testimonia et Fragmenta, Pars* I^{2} (Stuttgart and Leipzig).
Bernhardy, G. (1857), *Theologumenorum Graecorum* (Programm Halle).
—— (1869), *Grundriß der griechischen Literatur* II/2^{2} (Halle).
Bers, V. (1974), *Enallage and Greek Style* (*Mnem.* Suppl. 29; Leiden).
Bethe, E. (1900–37), *Pollucis Onomasticon* (Lexicographi Graeci 9; Leipzig).
Bidez, I.(J.), and Cumont, F. (1922), *Imp. Caesaris Flavii Claudii Iuliani Epistulae Poemata Fragmenta Varia* (Paris).
Bierl, A., Calder, W. M. III, and Fowler, R. L. (1991), *The Prussian and the Poet: the Letters of Ulrich von Wilamowitz-Moellendorff to Gilbert Murray (1894–1930)* (Hildesheim).
Billault, A., and Buisson, A. (1994) (eds.), *Lucien de Samosate* (Lyon).
Binder, G. (1964), *Die Aussetzung des Königskindes, Kyros und Romulus* (Beiträge zur klassischen Philologie 10; Meisenheim am Glan).
—— (1997), review of Huys (1995), *Fabula* 38: 330–3.
Blanc, A., Lamberterie, C. de, and Perpillou, J.-L. (1997), 'Chronique d'Étymologie Grecque N° 2', *RPh* 3rd ser. 71: 147–79.
Blanckenhagen, P. H. von, and Alexander, C. (1962), *The Paintings from Boscotrecase* (Mitteilungen des Deutschen Archäologischen Instituts, Römische Abteilung, 6. Ergänzungsheft; Heidelberg).
Blumenthal, A. von (1922), *Die Schätzung des Archilochos im Altertume* (Stuttgart).
Blümner, H. (1912), *Technologie und Terminologie der Gewerbe und Künste bei Griechen und Römern. Erster Band*^{2} (Berlin and Leipzig).
Blundell, J. (1980), *Menander and the Monologue* (Hypomnemata 59; Göttingen).

Blundell, M. W. (1989), *Helping Friends and Harming Enemies: a Study in Sophocles and Greek Ethics* (Cambridge).
Boardman, J. (1998), *Early Greek Vase Painting* (London).
Bock, C. (1871), *De Baccharum Euripideae Prologo et Parodo: Particula Prior* (diss. Rostock).
Boeckh, A. (1811), *Pindari opera quae supersunt* I (Leipzig).
Boedeker, D. (1988), 'Protesilaos and the end of Herodotus' *Histories*', *Class. Ant.* 7: 30–42.
—— (2002), 'Epic heritage and mythical pattern in Herodotus', in Bakker *et al.* (2002), 97–116.
Bommelaer, J.-F. (1991), *Guide de Delphes: Le Site* (Paris).
Bonaria, M. (1955–6), *Mimorum Romanorum fragmenta* (Pubblicazioni dell'Istituto di filologia classica dell'Università di Genova 5; Genoa).
Bond, G. W. (1960), review of Lasserre and Bonnard (1958), *Gnomon* 32: 596–600.
—— (1981), *Euripides: Heracles* (Oxford).
Bossi, F. (1990), *Studi su Archiloco*² (Studi e commenti 8; Bari).
Bowie, A. M. (1981), review of J. Griffin, *Homer* and *Homer on Life and Death* (both Oxford 1980), *CR* NS 31: 157–9.
Bowie, E. L. (2002), 'Ionic *Iambus* and Attic *Komoidia*: father and daughter, or just cousins?', in Willi (2002), 33–50.
Bowra, C. M. (1940*a*), 'Sophocles on his own development', *AJP* 61: 385–401. [= (1953), 108–25]
—— (1940*b*), 'The fox and the hedgehog', *CQ* 34: 26–9.
—— (1953), *Problems in Greek Poetry* (Oxford).
Boyd, B. W. (2002) (ed.), *Brill's Companion to Ovid* (Leiden).
Brashear, W. (1975), 'Euripides' Bacchae 17–26', *ZPE* 19: 300–1.
Braun, E. (1994), *Lukian unter doppelter Anklage. Ein Kommentar* (Studien zur klassischen Philologie 85; Frankfurt am Main, Berlin, Bern, New York, Paris, Vienna).
Bremer, J. M., Erp Talman Kip, A. M. van, and Slings, S. R. (1987), *Some Recently Found Greek Poems* (*Mnem.* Suppl. 99; Leiden, New York, Copenhagen, Cologne).
—— and Handley, E. W. (1993) (eds.), *Aristophane* (Entretiens sur l'Antiquité Classique 38: Vandoeuvres and Geneva).
Bremmer, J. N., and Horsfall, N. M. (1987), *Roman Myth and Mythography* (*BICS* Suppl. 52; London).
Briggs, K. M. (1970), *A Dictionary of British Folk-Tales in the English Language. Part A: Folk Narrations* (London).
Brink, C. O. (1986), *English Classical Scholarship: Historical Reflections on Bentley, Porson, and Housman* (Cambridge and New York).

Broadhead, H. D. (1960), *The* Persae *of Aeschylus* (Cambridge).
—— (1968), *Tragica: Elucidations of Passages in Greek Tragedy* (Christchurch, N.Z.).
Brognanyi, B. (1979) (ed.), *Studies in Diachronic, Synchronic, and Typological Linguistics: Festschrift for Oswald Szemerényi on the Occasion of his 65th Birthday* (Amsterdam studies in the theory and history of linguistic science. Series IV, Current issues in linguistic theory 11.1–2; Amsterdam).
Bromwich, R. (1991), 'The *Tristan* of the Welsh', in Bromwich *et al.* (1991), 209–28.
—— Jarman, A. O. H., and Roberts, B. F. (1991) (eds.), *The Arthur of the Welsh: the Arthurian Legend in Medieval Welsh Literature* (Cardiff).
Brotherson, G., and Vollmer, G. (1987) (eds.), *Aesop in Mexico: die Fabeln des Aesop in aztekischer Sprache* (Veröffentlichungen des Ibero-Amerikanischen Instituts Preussischer Kulturbesitz Stimmen indianischer Völker 3; Berlin).
Brown, A. (1987), *Sophocles:* Antigone (Warminster).
Brown, C. J. (1996), 'In the Cyclops' cave: revenge and justice in *Odyssey* 9', *Mnemosyne* 4th ser. 49: 1–29.
Brown, R. E. (1993), *The Birth of the Messiah: a Commentary on the Infancy Narratives in Matthew and Luke*^{2} (London and Garden City, NY).
Bruhn, E. (1899), *Anhang zu Sophokles* (Berlin).
Brunck, R. F. P. (1772), *Analecta Veterum Poetarum Graecorum* (Strassburg).
Buchholtz, E. (1886), *Anthologie aus den Lyrikern der Griechen* (Leipzig).
Budelmann, F. (2000), *The Language of Sophocles: Communality, Communication and Involvement* (Cambridge).
Bulloch, A. W. (1970), 'A Callimachean refinement to the Greek hexameter', *CQ* NS 20: 258–68.
Burian, P. (1972), 'Supplication and hero cult in Sophocles' *Ajax*', *GRBS* 13: 151–6.
Burkert, W. (1984), *Die orientalisierende Epoche in der griechischen Religion und Literatur* (*SB Heidelberg* 1984.1; Heidelberg).
—— (1992), *The Orientalizing Revolution. Near Eastern Influence on Greek Culture in the Early Archaic Age* (transl. M. E. Pinder and W. Burkert; Cambridge, MA and London).
Burnett, A. (1997), *The Poems of A. E. Housman* (Oxford).
Burnett, A. P. (1973), '*Medea* and the tragedy of revenge', *CP* 68: 1–24.
—— (1983), *Three Archaic Poets: Archilochus, Alcaeus, Sappho* (London).
—— (1998), *Revenge in Attic and Later Tragedy* (Sather Classical Lectures 62; Berkeley, Los Angeles, London).
Bussler, E. (1887), *De sententiarum asyndeti usu Euripideo* (diss. Halle).

Buxton, R. G. A. (1980), 'Blindness and its limits: Sophocles and the logic of myth', *JHS* 100: 22–37.

Byron, G. (2003), *Dramatic Monologue* (London).

Calder, W. M. III (1979), 'Ulrich von Wilamowitz-Moellendorff on Sophocles: a letter to Sir Hubert Warren', *Cal. St. Class. Ant.* 12: 51–63.

—— (1988), [Correspondence], *LCM* 13: 160.

—— and Stern, J. (1970) (eds.), *Pindaros und Bakchylides* (Wege der Forschung 134; Darmstadt).

Cameron, A. (1995), *Callimachus and his Critics* (Princeton).

Carey, C. (1986), 'Archilochus and Lycambes', *CQ* NS 36: 60–7.

Cartledge, P. A. (1997), 'Deep plays: theatre as process in Greek life', in Easterling (1997*c*), 3–35.

Cavarzere, A. (1989), 'La *ΥΒΡΙΣ* delle Streghe (Archiloco in Orazio, Epodo 5.87ss.)', *Orpheus* 10: 117–20.

—— Aloni, A., and Barchiesi, A. (2001) (eds.), *Iambic Ideas: Essays on a Poetic Tradition from Ancient Greece to the late Roman Empire* (Lanham, MD).

Cazzaniga, I. (1959), 'La Laodice Priamide di Trifiodoro', *PP* 14: 321–36.

Chakravarty, U. (1997), *Indra and other Vedic deities: a Euhemeristic Study* (Contemporary Researches in Hindu Philosophy and Religion 8; New Delhi).

Chantraine, P. (1954), 'A propos de l'adverbe ionien λείως, λέως', *Glotta* 33: 25–36.

—— (1999), *Dictionnaire étymologique de la langue grecque. Histoire des mots*² (Paris).

Chantry, M. (1994), *Scholia in Aristophanem, Pars III. Scholia in Thesmophoriazusas, Ranas, Ecclesiazusas et Plutum; Fasc. IVa, continens scholia vetera in Aristophanis Plutum* (Groningen).

Chapouthier, F. (1973) (ed.), *Euripide* VI¹: *Oreste* (Paris).

Chiesa, P. (2002), *Elementi di critica testuale* (Testi e manuali per l'insegnamento universitario del latino 72; Bologna).

Christiansen, R. T. (1959), *Studies in Irish and Scandinavian Folktales* (Copenhagen).

Christodoulou, G. A. (1977), *Τὰ ἀρχαῖα σχόλια εἰς Αἴαντα τοῦ Σοφοκλέους* (Athens).

Clare, R. J. (1998), 'Representing monstrosity: Polyphemus in the *Odyssey*', in Atherton (1998), 1–17.

Clarke, M. L. (1937), *Richard Porson: A Biographical Essay* (Cambridge).

Clunies Ross, M. (1981), 'An interpretation of the myth of Thor's encounter with Geirrodr and his daughters', in Dronke *et al.* (1981), 370–91.

Cobet, C. G. (1878), *Collectanea Critica* (Leiden).

Cohoon, J. W., and Lamar Crosby, H. (1951), *Dio Chrysostom* III (London and Cambridge, MA).

Collins, B. J., Bachvarova, M., and Rutherford, I. (forthcoming) (eds.), *Anatolian Interfaces: Hittites, Greeks and Their Neighbors.*

Consbruch, M. (1906), *Hephaestionis Enchiridion* (Leipzig). [repr. Stuttgart, 1971]

Cook, A. B. (1914), *Zeus* vol. i (Cambridge).

Cornell, T. J. (1975), 'Aeneas and the twins: the development of the Roman foundation legend', *PCPS* NS 20: 1–32.

Corrêa, P. da Cunha (2001), 'The fox and the hedgehog', *Revista Phaos* 1: 81–92.

Couchoud, P.-L. (1928) (ed.), *Congrès d'histoire du Christianisme* (Paris and Amsterdam).

Cramer, J. A. (1839–41), *Anecdota Græca, e codd. Manuscriptis Bibliothecæ Regiæ Parisiensis* (Oxford). [reprinted Hildesheim, 1967]

Crawford, M. H. (1996), *Roman Statutes* (*BICS* Suppl. 64; London).

Croiset, A. (1880), *La Poésie de Pindare et les lois du lyrisme grec* (Paris).

Crooke, W. (1908), 'Some notes on Homeric folk-lore', *Folk-Lore* 19: 52–77, 153–89.

Csapo, E., and Slater, W. J. (1994), *The Context of Ancient Drama* (Ann Arbor).

Cunningham, I. C. (1971), *Herodas: Mimiambi* (Oxford).

Ćurčija-Prodanović, N. (1957), *Yugoslav Folk-Tales* (London).

Cytowska, M. (1974), 'Homer bei Erasmus', *Philologus* 118: 145–57.

Dale, A. M. (1958), 'Greek metric 1936–57', *Lustrum* 2: 5–51.

Dalfen, J. (1994–5), 'Die *ὕβρις* der Nachtigall. Zu der Fabel bei Hesiod (*Erga* 202–18) und zur griechischen Fabel im allgemeinen', *WS* 107–8: 157–77.

Dalley, S. (1989), *Myths from Mesopotamia. Creation, the Flood, Gilgamesh and Others* (Oxford).

Daly, L. W. (1961), 'Hesiod's fable', *TAPA* 92: 45–51.

D'Angour, A. (1997), 'How the dithyramb got its shape', *CQ* NS 47: 331–51.

Davies, J. K. (1971), *Athenian Propertied Families, 600–300* BC. (Oxford).

Davies, M. (1986), 'Alcaeus fr. 42', *Hermes* 114: 257–62.

—— (1987), 'The ancient Greeks on why mankind does not live for ever', *MH* 44: 65–75.

—— (1988), 'Stesichorus' *Geryoneis* and its folk-tale origins', *CQ* NS 38: 277–90.

—— (1997), 'Feasting and food in Homer: realism and stylisation', *Prometheus* 23: 97–107.

—— (2001), 'Homer and the fable', *Prometheus* 27: 193–210.
—— (2002), 'The folk-tale origins of the *Iliad* and the *Odyssey*', *WS* 115: 5–43.
—— (2003*a*), 'Heracles and Jonah', *SIFC* 4th ser. 1: 136–41.
—— (2003*b*), 'The Judgements of Paris and Solomon', *CQ* NS 53: 32–43.
—— (2004), 'Aristotle fr. 44 Rose: Midas and Silenus', *Mnemosyne* 4th ser. 57: 682–97.
Dawe, R. D. (1973), *Studies on the Text of Sophocles* vol. i (Leiden).
—— (1975–9^{1}, 1984–5^{2}, 1996^{3}), *Sophocles: Tragoediae* (Leipzig$^{1-2}$, Stuttgart and Leipzig^{3}).
—— (1982), *Sophocles: Oedipus Rex* (Cambridge)
—— (1998), '*ΕΙ ΚΑΙ ΤΡΙΤ' ΕΣΤΙ* . . . Editing Sophocles for the third time', in Most (1998), 111–22.
—— Diggle, J., and Easterling, P. E. (1978) (eds.), *Dionysiaca: Nine Studies in Greek Poetry by Former Pupils Presented to Sir Denys Page on his Seventieth Birthday* (Cambridge).
De Martino, F. (2003), 'Sofocle "stravagante"', in Sommerstein (2003), 435–64.
—— and Sommerstein, A. H. (1995) (eds.), *Lo spettacolo delle voci* (Bari).
—— (1999) (eds.), *Studi sull'eufemismo* (Bari).
De Stefani, A. (1909–20), *Etymologicum Gudianum quod vocatur* [*A–Z* only] (Leipzig). [reprinted Amsterdam, 1965]
Dean, W. (1959), *Handel's Dramatic Oratorios and Masques* (Oxford).
—— and Knapp, J. M. (1994), *Handel's Operas: 1704–1726*^{2} (Oxford).
Debrunner, A. (1917), *Griechische Wortbildungslehre* (Indogermanische Bibliothek 2.8; Heidelberg).
Decleva Caizzi, F. (1966), *Antisthenis Fragmenta* (Testi e documenti per lo studio dell'antichità 13; Milan and Varese).
Degani, E. (1993), 'Aristofane e la tradizione dell'invettiva personale in Greco', in Bremer and Handley (1993), 1–49.
—— and Burzacchini, G. (1977), *Lirici Greci* (Florence).
Denniston, J. D. (1939), *Euripides: Electra* (Oxford).
—— (1954), *The Greek Particles*^{2} (Oxford).
Depew, M., and Obbink, D. (2000) (eds.), *Matrices of Genre: Authors, Canons, and Society* (Cambridge, MA).
Des Places, E. (1983), *Eusèbe de Césarée: La préparation évangélique. Livres XII–XIII* (Paris).
Dettori, E. (2000), *Filita Grammatico* (Quaderni dei seminari romani di cultura greca 2; Rome).
Devereux, G. (1973), 'The self-blinding of Oedipus in Sophocles' *O.T.*', *JHS* 93: 36–49.

Devine, A. M., and Stevens, L. D. (1994), *The Prosody of Greek Speech* (New York and Oxford).

Dewald, C. (1997), 'Wanton kings, pickled heroes, and gnomic founding fathers: strategies of meaning at the end of Herodotus' *Histories*', in Roberts *et al.* (1997), 62–82.

Diehl, E. (1926^1, 1936^2, 1952^3), *Anthologia Lyrica Graeca* (Leipzig).

Diels, H. (1910), 'Orientalische Fabeln in griechischem Gewande', *Internationale Wochenschrift für Wissenschaft, Kunst und Technik* 4: col. 993–1002.

Dieteren, F., and Klock, E. (1990) (eds.), *Writing Women into History* (Amsterdam).

Diggle, J. (1967), '*Bacchae* 68–70', *CR* 17: 261–2. [= (1994*a*), 3–4]

—— (1969), 'Marginalia Euripidea', *PCPS* NS 15: 30–59. [= (1994*a*) 5–33]

—— (1970), *Euripides: Phaethon* (Cambridge Classical Texts and Commentaries 12; Cambridge).

—— (1972), 'Notes on the *Heraclidae* of Euripides', *CQ* NS 22: 241–5. [= (1994*a*), 51–8]

—— (1974), 'On the *Heracles* and *Ion* of Euripides', *PCPS* NS 20: 3–36. [= (1994*a*), 90–136]

—— (1981), *Studies on the Text of Euripides* (Oxford).

—— (1994*a*), *Euripidea: Collected Essays* (Oxford).

—— (1994*b*), *Euripidis Fabulae* vol. iii (Oxford).

—— (1996*a*), 'Epilegomena Phaethontea', *AC* 65: 189–99.

—— (1996*b*), 'P. Petrie 1.1–2: Euripides, *Antiope*', *PCPS* NS 42: 106–26.

—— (2004), 'Did Euripides plagiarise the *Medea* of Neophron?', *European Cultural Centre of Delphi. IX International Meeting on Ancient Greek Drama, on History and Myths, Symposium Proceedings* (Athens), 71–9.

Dijk, G. J. van (1997), *Ainoi, Logoi, Mythoi: Fables in Archaic, Classical, and Hellenistic Greek Literature with a Study of the Theory and Terminology of the Genre* (*Mnem.* Suppl. 166; Leiden).

Dilts, M. R. (1971), *Heraclidis Lembi Excerpta Politiarum* (*GRBS* Monographs 5; Durham, NC).

—— (1983–6), *Scholia Demosthenica* (Leipzig).

—— (1992), *Scholia in Aeschinem* (Stuttgart and Leipzig).

Di Marco, M., Palumbo Stracca, B. M., and Lelli, E. (2005) (eds.), *Posidippo e gli altri. Il poeta, il genere, il contesto culturale e letterario* (Appunti Romani di Filologia 6; Pisa and Rome).

Dindorf, W. (1825), *Scholia Graeca in Homeri Odysseam* (Oxford).

Dodds, E. R. (1940), 'Maenadism in the Bacchae', *HTR* 33: 155–76.

—— (1960), *Euripides: Bacchae*^{2} (1st ed. 1944; Oxford).

Döpp, S. (1991), 'Vergilrezeption in der ovidischen "Aeneis"', *RhM* n.F. 134: 327–46.

Domingo-Forasté, D. (1994), *Claudii Aeliani Epistulae et Fragmenta* (Stuttgart and Leipzig).

Donahue, J. R., and Harrington, D. J. (2002), *The Gospel of Mark* (Sacra Pagina 2; Collegeville, MN).

Donne, J. (1953), *The Sermons of John Donne* VI (ed. E. M. Simpson and G. R. Potter; Berkeley and Los Angeles).

Dornseiff, F. (1938), 'Zum homerischen Hermeshymnos', *RhM* n.F. 87: 80–4.

Dougherty, C., and Kurke, L. (2003) (eds.), *The Cultures within Ancient Greek Culture: Contact, Conflict, Collaboration* (Cambridge).

Dover, K. J. (1964), 'The poetry of Archilochus', in Reverdin (1964), 181–222. [= (1987), 97–121]

—— (1974), *Greek Popular Morality in the Time of Plato and Aristotle* (Oxford).

—— (1987), *Greek and the Greeks* (Oxford).

—— Griffin, J., Bowie, E. L., and West, M. L. (1980) (eds.), *Ancient Greek Literature* (Oxford).

Dowden, K. (1996), 'Homer's sense of text', *JHS* 116: 47–61.

—— (2004), 'The epic tradition in Greece', in Fowler (2004) (ed.), 188–205.

Drachmann, A. B. (1903–27), *Scholia vetera in Pindari carmina* (Leipzig). [reprinted Stuttgart 1997]

Dronke, U., Helgadóttir, G. P., Weber, G. W., and Bekker-Nielsen, H. (1981) (eds.), *Speculum Norroenum: Norse studies in memory of Gabriel Turville-Petre* (Odense).

Earp, F. R. (1944), *The Style of Sophocles* (Cambridge).

Easterling, P. E. (1977*a*), 'Character in Sophocles', *G&R* 2nd ser. 24: 121–9.

—— (1977*b*), 'The infanticide in Euripides' *Medea*', *YCS* 25: 177–91.

—— (1988), 'Tragedy and ritual', *Metis* 3: 87–109.

—— (1997*a*), 'Constructing the heroic', in Pelling (1997*b*), 21–37.

—— (1997*b*), 'From repertoire to canon', in Easterling (1997*c*), 211–27.

—— (1997*c*) (ed.), *The Cambridge Companion to Greek Tragedy* (Cambridge).

Ebeling, E. (1927), 'Die Babylonische Fabel und ihre Bedeutung für die Literaturgeschichte', *Mitteilungen der altorientalischen Geschichte* II/3 (Leipzig).

Edmonds, J. M. (1931), *Greek Elegy and Iambus* (London and Cambridge, MA).

Edwards, M. W. (1991), *The* Iliad*: A Commentary. Volume V:* Books 17–20 (Cambridge).

Eigler, U. (1988), *Monologische Redeformen bei Valerius Flaccus* (Beiträge zur Altertumswissenschaft 187; Frankfurt am Main).

Ellsworth, J. D. (1988), 'Ovid's "*Odyssey*": *Met.* 13,623–14,608', *Mnemosyne* 4th ser. 41: 333–40.

Erbse, H. (1949), *Untersuchungen zu den attizistischen Lexika* (Abhandlungen der deutschen Akademie der Wissenschaften zu Berlin, phil.-hist. Klasse, n. 2; Berlin).

—— (1969–87), *Scholia Graeca in Homeri Iliadem* (Berlin).

Eriksen, R. (1994) (ed.), *Contexts of Pre-Novel Narrative: the European Tradition* (Berlin and New York).

Ernout, A., and Meillet, A. (1959), *Dictionnaire étymologique de la langue latine*[4] (Paris).

Evjen, H. D. (1984) (ed.), *Mnemai: Classical Studies in Memory of Karl K. Hulley* (Chico, CA).

Fantham, E. (2004), *Ovid's* Metamorphoses (Oxford).

Fantuzzi, M., and Hunter, R. L. (2004), *Tradition and Innovation in Hellenistic Poetry* (Cambridge).

Farrell, J. (1992), 'Dialogue of genres in Ovid's "Lovesong of Polyphemus" (*Metamorphoses* 13.719–897)', *AJP* 113: 235–68.

Fauth, W. (1969), 'Kleinasiat. *ΟΥΠΙΣ* und *ΜΑΛΙΣ*', *Beiträge zur Namensforschung* n.F. 4: 148–71.

Fayer, C. (2005), *La familia romana* III (Rome).

Feder, J. G. H. (1765), *Amor Polyphemi ex Theocrito, Ovidio et Metastasio* (Erlangen).

Fenik, B. (1974), *Studies in the Odyssey* (*Hermes* Einzelschriften 30; Wiesbaden).

Ferrari, A. (1998) (ed.), *Filologia classica e filologia romanza: esperienze ecdotiche a confronto* (Incontri di studio 2; Spoleto).

Ferrari, F. (1983), *Ricerche sul testo di Sofocle* (Studi di lettere, storia e filosofia 34; Pisa).

Ferrer, D. (1990), *Virginia Woolf and the Madness of Language* (transl. G. Bennington and R. Bowlby; London and New York).

Fick, A. F. (1886, 1888), 'Die Sprachform der altionischen und altattischen Lyrik', *Beiträge zur Kunde der Indogermanischen Sprachen* 11: 242–72 and 13: 173–221.

Finglass, P. J. (2007), *Sophocles.* Electra (Cambridge Classical Texts and Commentaries 44; Cambridge).

Finnegan, R. (1977), *Oral Poetry. Its Nature, Significance and Social Context* (Cambridge).

Fish, J. (2004), 'Anger, Philodemus' good king, and the Helen episode of *Aeneid* 2.567–589: a new proof of authenticity from Herculaneum', in Armstrong *et al.* (2004), 111–38.

Fletcher, G. B. A. (1946), 'Supplements to the bibliography of Housman and other Housmanniana', *Durham University Journal* 38: 85–93.
Flores, E. (1998), *Elementi critici di critica del testo ed epistemologia* (Naples).
—— (2003), review of Montanari (2003), *Bollettino di Studi Latini* 34: 261–3.
Flower, M. A., and Marincola, J. (2002), *Herodotus: Histories. Book IX* (Cambridge).
Foley, H. (1989), 'Medea's divided self', *Class. Ant.* 8: 61–85.
—— (1995), 'Tragedy and democratic ideology: the case of Sophocles' *Antigone*', in Goff (1995), 131–50.
Fontenrose, J. (1959), *Python: a Study of Delphic Myth and its Origins* (Los Angeles).
—— (1978), *The Delphic Oracle* (Berkeley).
Formentin, M. (1983), 'La grafia di Eustazio di Tessalonica', *Bulletin della Badia Greca di Grottaferrata* NS 37: 19–51.
Forrest, W. G. (1960), 'Themistokles and Argos', *CQ* NS 10: 221–41.
Fortune, N. (1987) (ed.), *Music and Theatre: Essays in Honour of Winton Dean* (Cambridge).
Foster, B. R. (2005), *Before the Muses*[3] (Bethesda).
Fowler, D. P. (1989), 'First thoughts on closure: problems and perspectives', *MD* 22: 75–122. [= (2000), 239–83]
—— (1997), 'Second thoughts on closure', in Roberts *et al.* (1997), 3–22. [= (2000), 284–307].
—— (2000), *Roman Constructions. Readings in Postmodern Latin* (Oxford).
Fowler, P. G. (1997), 'Lucretian conclusions', in Roberts *et al.* (1997), 112–38.
Fowler, R. L. (2004) (ed.), *The Cambridge Companion to Homer* (Cambridge).
Fraenkel, E. D. M. (1932), 'Selbstmordwege', *Philologus* 87: 470–3. [= (1964), i. 465–8]
—— (1950), *Aeschylus: Agamemnon* (Oxford).
—— (1964), *Kleine Beiträge zur klassischen Philologie* (Rome).
Fränkel, H. (1962), *Dichtung und Philosophie des frühen Griechentums: eine Geschichte der griechischen Epik, Lyrik und Prosa bis zur Mitte des fünften Jahrhunderts* (Munich).
—— (1968*a*), 'Der homerische und der kallimachische Hexameter', *Wege und Formen frühgriechischen Denkens*[3] (Munich), 100–56. [Italian translation in M. Fantuzzi and R. Pretagostini (eds.), *Struttura e storia dell'esametro greco II* (Studi di metrica classica 10; Rome, 1996)]
—— (1968*b*), 'Eine Stileigenheit der frühgriechischen Literatur', *Wege und Formen frühgriechischen Denkens*[3] (Munich), 40–96.

Fränkel, H. (1975), *Early Greek Poetry and Philosophy* (transl. M. Hadas and J. Willis; Oxford).

Fraser, P. M. (1972), *Ptolemaic Alexandria* (Oxford).

Frazer, J. G. (1921), *Apollodorus:* Library (London and New York).

Frenschkowski, M. (1998), 'Traum und Traumdeutung im Matthäusevangelium. Einige Beobachtungen', *Jahrbuch für Antike und Christentum* 41: 45–64.

Friedrich, R. (1993), 'Medea *apolis*: on Euripides' dramatization of the crisis of the polis', in Sommerstein *et al.* (1993), 219–39.

Friedrich, W.-H. (1956), *Verwundung und Tod in der Ilias* (Göttingen). [English translation by J. G. Wright and P. Jones, *Wounding and Death in the* Iliad: *Homeric Techniques of Description* (London 2002)]

Fritz, K. von (1956), 'Das Proömium der Hesiodischen Theogonie', in Reinhardt *et al.* (1956), 29–45. [= Heitsch (1966), 295–315]

Funaioli H. (1907), *Grammaticae Romanae Fragmenta* (Leipzig). [reprinted Stuttgart, 1969]

Funke, G., Riethmüller, A., and Zwierlein, O. (1998), *Interpretation* (Akademie der Wissenschaften und der Literatur, Abhandlungen der Geistes- und Sozialwissenschaftlichen Klasse Nr. 6; Mainz).

Fusillo, M. (1997), 'How novels end: some patterns of closure in ancient narrative', in Roberts *et al.* (1997), 209–27.

Gaisford, T. (1814–20), *Poetae Minores Graeci* (Oxford).

—— (1836), *Paroemiographi Graeci* (Oxford). [reprinted Osnabrück 1972]

—— (1842), *Georgii Choerobosci dictata in Theodosii Canones, necnon Epimerismi in Psalmos, e cod. MSS.* (Oxford).

Garvie, A. F. (1969), *Aeschylus' Supplices: Play and Trilogy* (Cambridge). [reprinted Bristol, 2006]

—— (1978), 'Aeschylus' simple plots', in Dawe *et al.* (1978), 63–86.

—— (1986), *Aeschylus:* Choephori (Oxford).

—— (1994), *Homer:* Odyssey. *Books VI–VIII* (Cambridge).

—— (1998), *Sophocles:* Ajax (Warminster).

—— (1999), 'Text and dramatic interpretation in *Persae*', *Lexis* 17: 21–34.

Garzya, A. (2000), *Synésios de Cyrène: Correspondance* (Paris).

Gaster, T. H. (1969), *Myth, Legend and Custom in the Old Testament: a Comparative Study* (London).

Gellrich, M., 'Interpreting Greek tragedy', in Goff (1995), 38–58.

George, A. (2003), *The Babylonian Gilgamesh Epic. Introduction, Critical Edition and Cuneiform Texts* (Oxford).

Georgiadou, A., and Larmour, D. H. J. (1997), 'Lucian's vine-women (VH 1, 6–9) and Dio's Libyan women (Orat. 5)', *Mnemosyne* 4th ser. 50: 205–9.

Gera, D. L. (1993), *Xenophon's* Cyropaedia*: Style, Genre and Literary Technique* (Oxford).

Gerber, D. E. (1970), *Euterpe: An Anthology of Early Greek Lyric, Elegiac and Iambic Poetry* (Amsterdam).

—— (1978), 'The female breast in Greek erotic literature', *Arethusa* 11: 202–12.

—— (1999), *Greek Iambic Poetry. From the Seventh to the Fifth Centuries B.C.* (Cambridge, MA and London).

Gessel, B. H. L. van (1998), *Onomasticon of the Hittite Pantheon* (Handbook of Oriental Studies Section One. The Near and Middle East vol. 33; Leiden, New York, Cologne).

Ghali-Kahil, L. (1955), *Les Enlèvemenents et la retour d'Hélène dans les textes et les documents figurés* (Paris).

Gillies, M. M. (1928), *Apollonius Rhodius:* The Argonautica Book III (Cambridge).

Glick, W. (1973), *Henry D. Thoreau: Reform Papers* (Princeton).

Görgemanns, H. (1976), 'Rhetorik und Poetik im homerischen Hermeshymnus', in Görgemanns and Schmidt (1976), 113–28.

—— and Schmidt, E. A. (1976) (eds.), *Studien zum antiken Epos* (Meisenheim am Glan).

Goff, B. (1995) (ed.), *History, Tragedy, Theory: Dialogues on Athenian Drama* (Austin).

Golden, M. (1995), 'Baby talk and child language in ancient Greece', in De Martino and Sommerstein (1995), ii. 11–34.

Goldhill, S. D. (1987), 'The Great Dionysia and civic ideology', *JHS* 107: 58–76.

—— (1988), 'Battle narrative and politics in Aeschylus' *Persae*', *JHS* 108: 189–93.

Gordon, E. I. (1958), 'Sumerian animal proverbs and fables: collection Five', *Journal of Cuneiform Studies* 12: 1–21.

Gould, J. (1973), '*Hiketeia*', *JHS* 93, 74–103. [= (2001), 22–77 (with addenda)]

—— (1980), 'Law, custom and myth: aspects of the social position of women in Classical Athens', *JHS* 100: 38–59. [= (2001), 112–57]

—— (2001), *Myth, Ritual, Memory, and Exchange: Essays in Greek Literature and Culture* (Oxford).

Gow, A. S. F. (1936), *A. E. Housman: a Sketch together with a List of his Writings and Indexes to his Classical Papers* (Cambridge).

—— (1950), *Theocritus* (Cambridge).

Graf, E. (1889), *De Graecorum veterum re musica quaestionum capita duo* (diss. Marburg).

Grant, J. N. (1989) (ed.), *Editing Greek and Latin Texts. Papers given at the Twenty-Third Annual Conference on Editorial Problems, University of Toronto, 6–7 November 1987* (New York).

Graves, R. P. (1979), *A. E. Housman: the Scholar-Poet* (London).

Graziosi, M. T. (1990), 'Maffeo Vegio', *Enciclopedia Virgiliana* 5 (Rome), 468–9.

Greene, G.(W.) C. (1938) (ed.), *Scholia Platonica* (Philological Monographs published by the American Philological Association 8; Haverford).

Gregory, J. (2005) (ed.), *A Companion to Greek Tragedy* (Oxford).

Grethlein, J. (2003), *Asyl und Athen: die Konstruktion kollektiver Identität in der griechischen Tragödie* (Stuttgart).

Griffin, J. (1980), *Homer on Life and Death* (Oxford).

—— (1998), 'The social function of Attic tragedy', *CQ* NS 48: 39–61.

—— (1999*a*), 'Sophocles and the democratic city', in Griffin (1999*b*), 73–94.

—— (1999*b*) (ed.), *Sophocles Revisited: Essays Presented to Sir Hugh Lloyd-Jones* (Oxford).

Griffith, M. (1983), 'Personality in Hesiod', *Class. Ant.* 2: 37–65.

—— (1995), 'Brilliant dynasts: power and politics in the *Oresteia*', *Class. Ant.* 14: 62–129.

—— (1998), 'The king and eye: the role of the father in Greek tragedy', *PCPS* NS 44: 20–84.

—— (1999), *Sophocles:* Antigone (Cambridge).

—— and Mastronarde, D. J. (1990) (eds.), *Cabinet of the Muses: Essays on Classical and Comparative Literature in Honor of Thomas G. Rosenmeyer* (Atlanta).

Gronewald, M., and Daniel, R. W. (2004*a*), 'Ein neuer Sappho-Papyrus', *ZPE* 147: 1–8.

—— (2004*b*), 'Nachtrag zum neuen Sappho-Papyrus', *ZPE* 149: 1–4.

Groningen, B. A. van (1960), *La Composition littéraire archaïque grecque: procédés et réalisations*[2] (Nederlandse Akademie van Wetenschappen, Afd. Letterkunde N.R. 65.2: Amsterdam).

—— (1977), *Euphorion* (Amsterdam).

Grossardt, P. (2003), 'The title of Aeschylus' *Ostologoi*', *HSCP* 100: 155–8.

Grüninger, A. (1898), *De Euripidis Oreste ab histrionibus retractata* (diss. Basel).

Günther, H.-C. (1996*a*), *Exercitationes Sophocleae* (Hypomnemata 109; Göttingen).

—— (1996*b*), 'Zu dem Kölner Archilochospapyrus', *Lexis* 14: 61–99.

Gurney, O. R. (1990), *The Hittites*[2] (Harmondsworth).

Gusmani, R. (1964), *Lydisches Wörterbuch* (Heidelberg).

—— (1969), 'Sul samekh lidio', *Athenaeum* NS 47: 136–43.

Haas, V. (1994), *Geschichte der hethitischen Religion* (Leiden and New York).
Habisreitinger, J., Plath, R., and Ziegler, S. (1999) (eds.), *Gering und doch von Herzen. 25 indogermanistische Beiträge: Bernhard Forssman zum 65 Geburtstag* (Wiesbaden).
Haffter, H. (1957), 'Dem schwanken Zünglein lauschend wachte Cäsar dort', *MH* 14: 118–26.
Hägg, T. (1994), 'Orality, literacy, and the "readership" of the early Greek novel', in Eriksen (1994), 47–81.
Hahn, I. (1981), 'Aischylos und Themistokles: Bemerkungen zu den "Persern"', in E. G. Schmidt (1981), 173–86.
Hainsworth, J. B. (1980), 'Ancient Greek', in Hatto (1980), 20–47.
—— (1993), *The* Iliad*: a Commentary. Volume III:* Books 9–12 (Cambridge).
Haldane, J. A. (1965), 'Musical themes and imagery in Aeschylus', *JHS* 85: 33–41.
Hall, E. M. (1989), *Inventing the Barbarian: Greek Self-Definition through Tragedy* (Oxford).
—— (1993), 'Asia unmanned: images of victory in classical Athens', in Rich and Shipley (1993), 107–33.
—— (1996*a*), *Aeschylus:* Persians (Warminster).
—— (1996*b*), 'Is there a *polis* in Aristotle's *Poetics*?', in Silk (1996), 295–309.
—— (1997), 'The sociology of Athenian tragedy', in Easterling (1997*c*), 93–126.
Halliwell, S. (1980), 'Aristophanes' apprenticeship', *CQ* NS 30: 33–45. [= E. Segal (1996), 98–116]
Hammerstaedt, J. (1988), *Die Orakelkritik des Kynikers Oenomaus* (Beiträge zur klassischen Philologie 188; Frankfurt am Main).
Hammond, N. G. L. (1937), 'Diodorus' narrative of the Sacred War', *JHS* 57: 44–78.
Hangard, J. (1996), *Scholia in Aristophanem, Pars II. Scholia in Vespas, Pacem, Aves et Lysistratam; Fasc. IV, continens Scholia vetera et recentiora in Aristophanis Lysistratam* (Groningen).
Hansen, P. A. (2005) *Hesychii Alexandrini Lexicon. Volumen III. Π–Σ* (Sammlung griechischer und lateinischer Grammatiker 11/3; Berlin and New York).
Hanson, A. E. (1998), 'Galen: author and critic', in Most (1998), 22–53.
Hardie, P. R. (1993), *The Epic Successors of Virgil* (Cambridge).
—— (2002), *Ovid's Poetics of Illusion* (Cambridge).
Harmon, A. M. (1921), *Lucian* III (London and New York).
Harrauer, C. (2000), 'Die Tragödie der Glauke: Euripides, Medeia 1185–1202', *WS* 113: 31–52.

Harrison, S. J. (2000), *Apuleius. A Latin Sophist* (Oxford).
Harrison, T. (2000), *The Emptiness of Asia: Aeschylus'* Persians *and the History of the Fifth Century* (London).
—— (2002) (ed.), *Greeks and Barbarians* (Edinburgh).
Hatto, A. T. (1980) (ed.), *Traditions of Heroic and Epic poetry* 1: *The Traditions* (London).
Headlam, W. G. (1900), 'Upon Aeschylus—I.', *CR* 14: 106–19.
—— (1910), Agamemnon *of Aeschylus* (ed. A. C. Pearson) (Cambridge).
Heath, M. (1987), *The Poetics of Greek Tragedy* (London).
Heitsch, E. (1963*a*), 'Das Prometheus-Gedicht bei Hesiod', *RhM* n.F. 106: 1–15. [= (1966), 419–35]
—— (1963*b*), *Die griechischen Dichterfragmente der römischen Kaiserzeit* 1^2 (Göttingen).
—— (1966) (ed.), *Hesiod* (Wege der Forschung 44; Darmstadt).
—— (1968), 'Ilias B 557/8', *Hermes* 96: 641–60.
Helmbold, W. C. (1939), *Plutarch: Moralia* VI (Cambridge, MA and London).
Hemsterhuys, T. *et al.* (1706), *Julii Pollucis Onomasticum Graece & Latine* (Amsterdam).
Henderson, J. (1991*a*), 'Women and the Athenian dramatic festivals', *TAPA* 121: 133–44.
—— (1991*b*), *The Maculate Muse: Obscene Language in Attic Comedy*^{2} (New York and Oxford).
Henrichs, A. (1978), 'Greek Maenadism from Olympias to Messalina', *HSCP* 82: 121–60.
—— (1984), 'Male intruders among the maenads: the so-called male celebrant', in Evjen (1984), 69–91.
Henry, W. B. (2003), 'Contracted biceps in Pindar', *ZPE* 143: 11–16.
—— (2005), *Pindar's Nemeans: A Selection* (Sammlung wissenschaftlicher Commentare; Munich).
Herington, C. J. (1972), *The older Scholia on the Prometheus Bound* (*Mnem.* Suppl. 19; Leiden).
—— (1985), *Poetry into Drama: Early Tragedy and the Greek Poetic Tradition* (Sather Classical Lectures 49; Berkeley).
—— (1991), 'The closure of Herodotus' *Histories*', *ICS* 16: 149–60.
Hermann, C. F. (1851–3), *Platonis dialogi secundum Thrasylli tetralogias dispositi* (Leipzig).
Hermann, J. G. J. (1823), *Euripidis Bacchae* (Leipzig).
—— (1847), *Emendationes quinque carminum Olympiorum Pindari* (Leipzig). [= (1877), 110–28]
—— (1877), *Opuscula* VIII (Leipzig).

Herwerden, H. van (1868), *Analecta Critica ad Thucydidem, Lysiam, Sophoclem, Aristophanem et Comicorum Graecorum fragmenta* (Utrecht).

Hesk, J. (2003), *Sophocles:* Ajax (London).

Hester, D. A. (1971), 'Sophocles the unphilosophical: a study in the *Antigone*', *Mnemosyne* 4th ser. 24: 11–59.

Heubeck, A., West, S. R., and Hainsworth, J. B. (1988), *A Commentary on Homer's* Odyssey. *Volume I. Introduction and* Books I–VIII (Oxford).

Hiller, E. (1890), *Anthologia Lyrica Graeca sive Lyricorum Graecorum Veterum praeter Pindarum reliquiae potiores* (Leipzig).

Hirt, H., and Arntz, H. (1939), *Die Hauptprobleme der indogermanischen Sprachwissenschaft* (Sammlung kurzer Grammatiken germanischer Dialekte. Ergänzungsreihe 4; Halle).

Hirzel., R. (1907), 'Der Selbstmord', *Archiv für Religionswissenschaft* 11.

Höfer, O. (1909–10), 'Sandas, Sandes, Sandon', in Roscher (1884–1937), iv. 319–33.

Hoffmann, O. (1898), *Die griechischen Dialekte in ihrem historischen Zusammenhange* III: *Der ionische Dialekt* (Göttingen).

Hofmann, H. (1997) (ed.), *Groningen Colloquia on the Novel* 8 (Groningen).

—— (1999) (ed.), *Latin Fiction. The Latin Novel in Context* (London and New York).

Holland, R. (1926), 'Battos', *RhM* n.F. 75: 156–83.

Hollis, A. S. (1990), *Callimachus. Hecale* (Oxford).

—— (1997), 'The beginning of Callimachus' *Hecale*', *ZPE* 115: 55–6.

Holwerda, D. (1991), *Scholia in Aristophanem, Pars II. Scholia in Vespas, Pacem, Aves et Lysistratam; Fasc. III, continens Scholia vetera et recentiora in Aristophanis Aves* (Groningen).

Holzberg, N. (1996), *Ovid. Dichter und Werk*[2] (Munich).

Holzinger, K. von (1895), *Lykophron's* Alexandra (Leipzig).

Hooker, J. T. (1987), [Correspondence], *LCM* 12: 128.

Hooker, M. (1991), *A Commentary on the Gospel according to St Mark* (London).

Hopkinson, N. (2000), *Ovid:* Metamorphoses *XIII* (Cambridge).

Hordern, J. (2004), '*Cyclopea*', *CQ* NS 54: 285–92.

Hordern, J. C. (1999), 'The *Cyclops* of Philoxenus', *CQ* NS 49: 445–55.

—— (2002), *The Fragments of Timotheus of Miletus* (Oxford).

Horsfall, N. M. (2003), *Virgil:* Aeneid *11: a Commentary* (*Mnem.* Suppl. 244; Leiden).

Hose, M. (2003), 'Synesios und seine Briefe: Versuch der Analyse eines literarischen Entwurfs', *WJA* n.F. 27: 125–41.

Housman, A. E. (1888), '*ΣΩΦΡΟΝΗ*', *CR* 2: 242–5. [= (1972), i. 24–8]

Housman, A. E. (1901), 'Elucidations of Latin Poets, III', *CR* 15: 404–6. [= (1972), ii. 544–7]
—— (1908), 'On the Paeans of Pindar', *CR* 22: 8–12. [= (1972), ii. 763–9]
—— (1926), *M. Annaei Lucani belli civilis libri decem* (Oxford).
—— (1930), *M. Manilii Astronomicon Liber Quintus* (London).
—— (1931), *D. Iunii Juvenalis Saturae* (Cambridge).
—— (1972), *The Classical Papers of A. E. Housman* (ed. J. Diggle and F. R. D. Goodyear; Cambridge).
How, W. W., and Wells, J. (1912), *A Commentary on Herodotus* (Oxford).
Humphreys, S. C. (1983), *The Family, Women, and Death* (London).
Hunt, A. S., and Johnson, J. (1930), *Two Theocritus Papyri* (London).
Hunter, R. L. (1993), *The* Argonautica *of Apollonius. Literary Studies* (Cambridge).
—— (1999), *Theocritus: A Selection. Idylls 1, 3, 4, 6, 7, 10, 11 and 13* (Cambridge).
Hurst, A., and Létoublon, Fr. (2002) (eds.), *La Mythologie et l'*Odyssée*. Hommage à Gabriel Germain* (Recherches et rencontres: Publications de la Faculté des lettres de Genève 17; Geneva).
Hutchinson, G. O. (2001), *Greek Lyric Poetry: A Commentary on Selected Larger Pieces* (Oxford).
Hutter, M. (2003), 'Aspects of Luwian religion', in Melchert (2003), 211–80.
Huys, M. (1995), *The Tale of the Hero who was Exposed at Birth in Euripidean Tragedy: A Study of Motifs* (Symbolae Facultatis Litterarum Lovaniensis, ser. A vol. 20; Leuven).
Innes, D. C. (1972), 'Demetrius *On Style*', in Russell and Winterbottom (1972), 171–215.
Isager, S. (1998), '"The Pride of Halikarnassos". Editio princeps of an inscription from Salmakis', *ZPE* 123: 1–23.
Itsumi, K. (1982), 'The choriambic dimeter of Euripides', *CQ* NS 32: 59–74.
Jackson, J. (1955), *Marginalia Scaenica* (Oxford).
Jakobi, R. (1988), review of U. Baumann and M. Wissemann, *William Gagers Dido Tragoedia* (Bibliotheca Humanistica 1; Frankfurt am Main, Bern, New York), *Gnomon* 60: 453–5.
Jacoby, F. (1913), 'Herodot', *RE* Suppl. 2: 205–520.
Jacques, J.-M. (2002), *Nicandre* II (Paris).
Jamison, S. (forthcoming), *The Rig Veda between Two Worlds. Four Lectures at the Collège de France.* [delivered May 2004]
Janko, R. C. M. (1982), *Homer, Hesiod and the Hymns* (Cambridge).
Jebb, R. C. (1883[1], 1887[2]), *Sophocles. The Plays and Fragments. Part I: The* Oedipus Tyrannus (Cambridge).

Jebb, R. C. (1892), *Sophocles. The Plays and Fragments. Part V: The* Trachiniae (Cambridge).
—— (1894), *Sophocles. The Plays and Fragments. Part VI: The* Electra (Cambridge).
—— (1898), 'Notes on Bacchylides', *CR* 12: 123–33.
Jedrkiewicz, S. (1989), *Sapere e paradosso nell'Antichità: Esopo e la favola* (Rome).
Jenkyns, R. H. A. (1998), *Virgil's Experience: Nature and History; Times, Names and Places* (Oxford).
Jennings, V., and Katsaros, A. (forthcoming) (eds.), *Ion of Chios: Fragments of a Polymath.*
Jocelyn, H. D. (1980), 'A Greek indecency and its students: *ΛΑΙΚΑΖΕΙΝ*', *PCPS* NS 26: 12–66.
—— (1987*a*), review discussion of Brink (1986), *LCM* 12: 13–16, 29–32, 45–8, 61–4, 93–6, 106–12. [= (1988)]
—— (1987*b*) [Correspondence], *LCM* 12: 144.
—— (1988), *Philology and Education: a Review Discussion of C. O. Brink's* English classical scholarship: Historical Reflections on Bentley, Porson and Housman (Liverpool Classical Papers 1: Liverpool).
—— (1990), review of Naiditch (1988*a*), *LCM* 15: 58–63.
Jones, G. (1956), *Scandinavian Legends and Folk-tales* (Oxford and New York).
Jong, I. J. F. de (2001), *A Narratological Commentary on the* Odyssey (Cambridge).
—— (2004*a*), *Narrators and Focalizers: The Presentation of the Story in the* Iliad^2 (1st ed. 1987; Bristol).
—— (2004*b*), 'Introduction: narratological theory on narrators, narratees, and narrative', in de Jong, Nünlist, and Bowie (2004), 1–10.
—— (2004*c*), 'Homer', in de Jong, Nünlist, and Bowie (2004), 13–24.
—— Nünlist, R., and Bowie, A. M. (2004) (eds.), *Narrators, Narratees, and Narratives in Ancient Greek Literature* (*Mnem.* Suppl. 257; Leiden and Boston).
Jouan, F., and Van Looy, H. (2003), *Euripide: Tragédies* VIII/4 (Paris).
Jouanna, J. (2003), *Hippocrate: Oeuvres Complètes. Tome II, 2e partie. Airs – Eaux – Lieux*^{2} (Paris).
Junge, R. (1999), *Nicholas Trevet und die Octavia Praetexta. Editio Princeps des mittelalterlichen Kommentars und Untersuchungen zum pseudoseneca-nischen Drama* (Studien zur Geschichte und Kultur des Altertums n.F. 1. Reihe 14. Band; Paderborn, Munich, Vienna, Zürich).
Just, R. (1989), *Women in Athenian Law and Life* (London and New York).

Kahane, A., and Laird, A. (2001) (eds.), *A Companion to the Prologue of Apuleius'* Metamorphoses (Oxford).

Kaimakis, D. (1976), *Die Kyraniden* (Beiträge zur klassischen Philologie 76; Meisenheim am Glan).

Kakridis, J. T. (1930), 'Die Pelopssage bei Pindar', *Philologus* 85: 463–77. [= (1971), 55–68 = Calder and Stern (1970), 175–90]

—— (1971), *Μελετες και αρθρα. Τιμητικη προσφορα για τα εβδομηντα χρονια του συγγραφεα* (Thessaloniki).

Kallós, E. (1951–2), 'Gloses pour Archiloque', *Acta Antiqua* 1: 67–73.

Kamerbeek, J. C. (1953), 'Deux passages des Bacchantes d'Euripide', *Mnemosyne* 4th ser. 6: 192–7.

—— (1967), *The Plays of Sophocles: Commentaries. Part IV: The* Oedipus Tyrannus (Leiden).

—— (1974), *The Plays of Sophocles: Commentaries. Part V: The* Electra (Leiden).

Kannicht, R. (1969), *Euripides: Helena* (Heidelberg).

Kassel, R. (1954), *Quomodo quibus locis apud veteres scriptores Graecos infantes atque parvuli pueri inducantur describantur commemorentur* (diss. Mainz 1951; Meisenheim am Glan). [= (1991), 1–73]

—— (1976), 'Euripides Bakchen 23', *ZPE* 21: 35–6. [= (1991), 187–8]

—— (1991), *Kleine Schriften* (Berlin and New York).

Katz, J. T. (1999), '*Homeric Hymn to Hermes* 296: *τλήμονα γαστρὸς ἔριθον*', *CQ* NS 49: 315–19.

—— (forthcoming), 'The riddle of the *sp(h)ij-*: The Great Sphinx and her Indo-European background', in Peinault and Petit (forthcoming).

Kayano, S. (1985), *The Romance of the Bear God* (Tokyo).

Keller, O. (1963), *Die Antike Tierwelt* (Hildesheim). [reprint of Leipzig, 1909–13 ed.]

Kells, J. H. (1973), *Sophocles:* Electra (Cambridge).

Kenney, E. J. (1971), *Lucretius:* De Rerum Natura Book III (Cambridge).

—— (1977), *Lucretius* (*Greece & Rome* New Surveys in the Classics 11; Oxford).

—— (1989), 'Great Britain: Latin Philology', in *La Filologia Greca e Latina nel Secolo XX: Atti del Congresso Internazionale, Roma, Consiglio Nazionale delle Ricerche, 17–21 settembre 1984* (Biblioteca di studi antichi 56; Pisa), 619–49.

Kermode, F. (1967), *The Sense of an Ending* (London).

—— (1979), *The Genesis of Secrecy. On the Interpretation of Narrative* (Cambridge, MA).

Kindermann, U. (1998), *Einführung in die lateinische Literatur des mittelalterlichen Europa* (Tumhout).

Kirk, G. S. (1966), 'The structure of the Homeric hexameter', *YCS* 20: 75–152.
Klaerr, R., Philippon, A., and Sirinelli, J. (1989), *Plutarque: Oeuvres Morales* I/2 (Paris).
Kleingünther, A. (1933), *ΠΡΩΤΟΣ ΕΥΡΕΤΗΣ. Untersuchungen zur Geschichte einer Fragestellung* (Philol. Suppl. 26.1; Leipzig).
Knaack, G. (1888), 'Euphorionea', *Jahrbücher für classische Philologie* 137: 145–53.
Knox, B. M. W. (1961), 'The *Ajax* of Sophocles', *HSCP* 65: 1–37. [= (1979), 125–60]
—— (1977), 'The *Medea* of Euripides', *YCS* 25: 193–225. [= (1979), 295–322]
—— (1979), *Word and Action. Essays on the Ancient Theatre* (London and Baltimore).
Knox, P., and Foss, C. (1998) (eds.), *Style and Tradition. Studies in Honor of Wendell Clausen* (Beiträge zur Altertumskunde 92; Stuttgart and Leipzig).
Kock, T. (1893), 'Zu den Fragmenten der attischen Komike', *RhM* n.F. 48: 208–39.
Köhnken, A. (1971), *Die Funktion des Mythos bei Pindar: Interpretationen zu sechs Pindargedichten* (Untersuchungen zur antiken Literatur und Geschichte 12; Berlin).
Koettgen, L. (1914), *Quae ratio intercedat inter Indagatores fabulam Sophocleam et hymnum in Mercurium qui fertur Homericus* (diss. Bonn).
Konishi, H. (1987), 'Thucydides' *History* as a finished piece', *LCM* 12.1: 5–7.
Kopff, E. C. (1982), *Euripides: Bacchae* (Leipzig).
Kovacs, P. D. (1986), 'On Medea's great monologue (E. *Med.* 1021–80)', *CQ* NS 36: 343–52.
—— (1993), 'Zeus in Euripides' *Medea*', *AJP* 114: 45–70.
—— (2002*a*), *Euripides:* Helen, Phoenician Women, Orestes (Cambridge, MA).
—— (2002*b*), *Euripides:* Bacchae, Iphigenia at Aulis, Rhesus (Cambridge, MA).
—— (2003*a*), *Euripidea Tertia* (*Mnem.* Suppl. 240; Leiden).
—— (2003*b*), 'Toward a reconstruction of *Iphigenia Aulidensis*', *JHS* 123: 77–103.
—— (2005), 'Text and transmission', in Gregory (2005), 379–93.
Krappe, A. H. (1927), *Balor with the Evil Eye: Studies in Celtic and French Literature* (New York).
Krumbach, R., Pechstein, N., and Seidensticker, B. (1999), *Das griechische Satyrspiel* (Texte zur Forschung 72; Darmstadt).
Kühn, C. G. (1821–33), *Claudii Galeni Opera Omnia* (Leipzig).

Kühn, J., and Fleischer, U. (1989), *Index Hippocraticus* (Göttingen).
Kullmann, W. (1992), 'Das letzte Buch der *Odyssee*', in Müller (1992), 291–304.
Kurke, L. (1992), 'The politics of ἁβροσύνη in archaic Greece', *Class. Ant.* 11: 91–120.
Kurz, G. (1974), 'Humor bei Pindar?', in Reinhardt and Sallmann (1974), 5–25.
La Penna, A. (1964), 'Litteratura Esopica e litteratura Assiro-Babilonese I. Una favola di Archiloco e il poemetto di Etana', *RFIC* 92: 24–39.
Lackner, W. (1980), 'Eine unedierte Passion der Märtyrer Nikandros und Hermaios (BHG 2295)', *Jahrbuch der Österreichischen Byzantinistik* 29: 99–131.
Lacombrade, C. (1964), *L'Empereur Julien: Oeuvres Complètes. Tome* II, 2e *partie. Discours de Julien Empereur. Les Césars—Sur Hélios-Roi—Le Misopogon* (Paris).
Lada, I. (1993), '"Empathetic understanding": emotion and cognition in classical dramatic audience-response', *PCPS* NS 39: 94–140.
Laird, A. (2001), 'Paradox and transcendence: the prologue as the end', in Kahane and Laird (2001), 267–81.
Langdon, S. (1931), 'The legend of Etana and the eagle, or the epical poem "The city they hated"', *Babyloniaca* 12: 1–56.
Laroche, E. (1967), 'Comparaison du louvite et du lycien', *BSL* 62: 46–66.
—— (1973), 'Un syncrétisme gréco-anatolien: Sandas = Héraklès', in Simon (1973), 103–14.
Lasserre, F. (1950), *Les Épodes d'Archiloque* (Paris).
—— (1984), 'La fable en Grèce dans la poésie archaïque', in Adrados and Reverdin (1984), 61–104.
—— and Bonnard, A. (1958), *Archiloque. Fragments* (Paris).
Latacz, J. (1977), *Kampfparänese, Kampfdarstellung und Kampfwirklichkeit in der* Ilias, *bei Kallinos und Tyrtaios* (Munich).
—— (2000), *Homers Ilias, Gesamtkommentar* I (Munich).
—— (2003), *Homers Ilias, Gesamtkommentar* II (Munich).
Latte, K. (1953–66), *Hesychii Alexandrini Lexicon* [*A–O* only] (Copenhagen).
Lawson, J. C. (1934), 'Notes on Aeschylus, *Persae.* II', *CR* 48: 55–9.
Leach, E. W. (1988), *The Rhetoric of Space: Literary and Artistic Representations of Landscape in Republican and Augustan Rome* (Princeton).
Leaf, W. (1902), *The Iliad* II[2] (London).
Leeuwen, J. van (1890), 'Homerica IV. De caesura quae est post quartum trochaeum', *Mnemosyne* NS 18: 265–76.
Lefkowitz, M. R. (1981), *The Lives of the Greek Poets* (London).
—— (1986), *Women in Greek Myth* (London).

Lehmann, W. P., and Zgusta, L. (1979), 'Schleicher's fable after a century', in Brognanyi (1979), i. 455–66.

Lenz, F. W., and Behr, C. A. (1976–80), *P. Aelii Aristidis Opera quae exstant omnia* [1–16 only] (Leiden).

Lessing, G. E. (1790), *Leben des Sophokles*, cited from *G. E. Lessings Sämtliche Schriften* iii (ed. K. Lachmann; Stuttgart, 1892).

Levene, D. S. (1992), 'Sallust's *Jugurtha*: an "historical fragment"', *JRS* 82: 53–70.

Lewis, C. S. (1961), 'Four-letter words', *The Critical Quarterly* 3: 118–22

Liebel, I. (1812[1], 1818[2]), *Archilochi Reliquiae* (Leipzig).

Lightfoot, J. L. (1999), *Parthenius of Nicaea* (Oxford).

Lindstam, S. (1919–20), 'Senbyzantinska epimerismsamlingar och ordböcker', *Eranos* 19: 57–92.

Liou-Gille, B. (1980), *Cultes 'héroïques' romains: les fondateurs* (Paris).

Littleton, S. (1970), 'The "Kingship in Heaven" theme', in Puhvel (1970), 83–121.

Littré, É. (1839–61), *Oeuvres complètes d'Hippocrate* (Paris).

Livrea, E. (1970), 'L'*ainos* esiodeo', *GIF* 22: 1–20.

—— (2004), 'Un epigramma di Posidippo e il *Cyclops* di Filosseno di Citera', *ZPE* 146: 41–6.

Lloyd, G. E. R. (2003), *In the Grip of Disease. Studies in the Greek Imagination* (Oxford).

Lloyd, M. A. (1994), *Euripides: Andromache* (Warminster).

Lloyd-Jones, P. H. J. (1955), review of Bowra (1953), *JHS* 75: 158–9. [= (1990*b*), 362–6]

—— (1972), 'Tycho von Wilamowitz-Moellendorff on the dramatic technique of Sophocles', *CQ* NS 22: 214–28. [= (1982), 219–37 = (1990*a*), 401–18]

—— (1973), review of Housman (1972), *TLS* 9th February: 137–8. [= (1982), 182–7]

—— (1980), 'Euripides, Medea 1056–80', *Würzburger Jahrbücher* n.F. 6a: 51–9.

—— (1982), *Blood for the Ghosts: Classical Influences in the Nineteenth and Twentieth Centuries* (London).

—— (1988), [Correspondence], *LCM* 13: 128.

—— (1990*a*), *Greek Epic, Lyric and Tragedy: The Academic Papers of Sir Hugh Lloyd-Jones* (Oxford).

—— (1990*b*), *Greek Comedy, Hellenistic Literature, Greek Religion, and Miscellanea: the Academic Papers of Sir Hugh Lloyd-Jones* (Oxford).

—— (1994*a*), 'Notes on fragments of Sophocles', *SIFC* 3rd ser. 12: 129–48. [= (2005), 115–35]

Lloyd-Jones, P. H. J. (1994*b*), *Sophocles: Ajax, Electra, Oedipus Tyrannus* (Cambridge, MA and London).

—— (1996), *Sophocles: Fragments* (Cambridge, MA and London).

—— (1999), 'The Pride of Halicarnassus', *ZPE* 124: 1–14. [= (2005), 211–32]

—— (2005), *The Further Academic Papers of Sir Hugh Lloyd-Jones* (Oxford).

—— and Wilson, N. G. (1990), *Sophoclea: Studies on the Text of Sophocles* (Oxford).

—— (1992), *Sophoclis Fabulae* (Oxford). [revised impression of 1990 ed.]

—— (1997), *Sophocles: Second Thoughts* (Hypomnemata 100; Göttingen).

Long, A. A. (1968), *Language and Thought in Sophocles: A Study of Abstract Nouns and Poetic Technique* (University of London Classical Studies 6; London).

—— (1986), *Hellenistic Philosophy: Stoics, Epicureans, Sceptics*^{2} (1st ed. 1974; London).

Lopez Eire, A. (2003), 'Tragedy and satyr-drama: linguistic criteria', in Sommerstein (2003), 387–412.

Loraux, N. (1986), *The Invention of Athens: the Funeral Oration in the Classical City* (transl. A. Sheridan; Cambridge, MA and London).

Lord, A. B. (1960), *The Singer of Tales* (Cambridge, MA).

Lowe, N. J. (2000), *The Classical Plot and the Invention of Western Narrative* (Cambridge).

Luppe, W. (1995), 'ἀμφὶ εὐφρόνην und Weiteres zu den Archilochos-Papyrusfragment P. Oxy. XXII 2310, fr. 1', *Archiv für Papyrusforschung* 41: 20–3.

Maas, H. (1971), *The Letters of A. E. Housman* (London).

Maas, M., and Snyder, J. M. (1989), *Stringed Instruments of Ancient Greece* (New Haven).

Maas, P. (1927), *Textkritik* (Einleitung in die Altertumswissenschaft I.2; Leipzig, 1950^2, 1957^3) [the numbering of sections is the same in all editions]

—— (1929), *Griechische Metrik*^{2} (with addenda to 1st ed. 1923; Einleitung in die Altertumswissenschaft I/7; Leipzig and Berlin).

—— (1962), *Greek Metre* (transl. P. H. J. Lloyd-Jones; Oxford).

Macan, R. W. (1895), *Herodotus: the fourth, fifth, and sixth books* (London).

—— (1908), *Herodotus: the seventh, eighth, and ninth books* (London).

MacDowell, D. M. (2000), *Demosthenes: On the False Embassy (Oration 19)* (Oxford).

Macleod, C. W. (1982), 'Politics and the *Oresteia*', *JHS* 102: 124–44. [= (1983), 20–40]

—— (1983), *Collected Essays* (Oxford).

Maehler, H. (1982), *Die Lieder des Bakchylides. Erster Teil: Die Siegeslieder* (Leiden).
Magnelli, E. (1999), *Alexandri Aetoli Testimonia et Fragmenta* (Studi e Testi 15; Florence).
Mal-Maeder, D. van (1997), '*Lector, intende: laetaberis.* The enigma of the last book of Apuleius' *Metamorphoses*', in Hofmann (1997), 87–118.
Manuwald, B. (1983), 'Der Mord an den Kindern: Bemerkungen zu den Medea-Tragödien des Euripides und des Neophron', *WS* 17: 27–61.
March, J. (1991–3), 'Sophocles' *Ajax*: the death and burial of a hero', *BICS* 38: 1–36.
Marincola, J. (2005), 'Concluding narratives: looking to the end in classical historiography', *PLLS* 2: 285–319.
Marlow, A. N. (1955), 'A poet's scholarship: a study of Housman as a critic', *Proc. Leeds Philos. and Lit. Soc.* 7: 176–91.
Marquardt, I. (1884), *Claudii Galeni Pergameni scripta minora I* (Leipzig).
Marshall, I. H. (1978), *The Gospel of Luke: a Commentary on the Greek Text* (Exeter).
Martin, R. P. (2003), 'The pipes are brawling: conceptualizing musical performance in Athens', in Dougherty and Kurke (2003), 153–80.
Martini, E., and Sakolowski, P. (1986), *Mythographi Graeci* ii/1. *Parthenii Libellus Περὶ Ἐρωτικῶν Παθημάτων. Antonini Liberalis Μεταμορφωσέων Συναγωγή* (Leipzig).
Masson, O. (1952), review of Lasserre (1950), *Gnomon* 24: 310–16.
—— (1962), *Les Fragments du poète Hipponax* (Études et commentaires 43; Paris).
—— (1996), 'Nouvelles notes d'anthroponymie grecque XI', *ZPE* 110: 87–99. [= (2000), 243–55]
—— (2000), *Onomastica Graeca Selecta tome III* (Hautes études du monde gréco-romaine 28; Geneva).
Masters, J. (1992), *Poetry and Civil War in Lucan's* Bellum Civile (Cambridge).
Mastromarco, G. (1979), 'L'esordi "segreto" di Aristofane', *Quaderni di Storia* 10: 153–96.
Mastronarde, D. J. (1994), *Euripides: Phoenissae* (Cambridge).
Matchett, F. (2001), *Krsna: Lord or Avatara? The Relationship between Krsna and Visnu in the Context of the Avatara Myth as presented by the Harivamsa, the Visnupurana and the Bhagavatapurana* (Richmond).
Matthews, V. J. (1996), *Antimachus of Colophon* (Leiden, New York, Cologne).
Mayer, R. G. (1989), [Correspondence], *LCM* 14: 51.
Meillet, A. (1923), *Les Origines indo-européennes des mètres grecs* (Paris).

Meineke, A. (1849), *Stephani Byzantii Ethnicorum quae supersunt* (Berlin). [reprinted Graz 1958]

Meirvenne, B. van (1999), 'Puzzling over Plutarch. Traces of a Plutarchean Plato-study concerning *Lg.* 729a–c in *Adulat.* 32 (*Mor.* 71 B), *Coniug. Praec.* 46–47 (*Mor.* 144 F), and *Aet. Rom.* 33 (*Mor.* 272 C)', in Montes Cala *et al.* (1999), 527–40.

—— (2002), 'Plutarch on the healing powers of (a tricky) *παρρησία*. Observations in favour of a political reading of *de Adulatore et de Amico*?', in Stadter and van der Stockt (2002), 141–60.

Melchert, H. C. (1994), *Anatolian Historical Phonology* (Leiden Studies in Indo-European 3; Amsterdam and Atlanta).

—— (2002), 'The god Sanda in Lycia?', in Taracha, P. (2002), 241–52.

—— (2003) (ed.), *The Luwians* (Handbook of Oriental Studies Section One. The Near and Middle East vol. 68; Leiden and Boston).

—— (2004), *A Dictionary of the Lycian Language* (Ann Arbor and New York).

Menchi, S. S. (1980), *Erasmo da Rotterdam. Adagia: sei saggi politici in forma di proverbi* (Turin).

Merkelbach, R. (1962), *Roman und Mysterium in der Antike* (Berlin and Munich).

—— and West, M. L. (1974), 'Ein Archilochos-Papyrus', *ZPE* 14: 97–112.

Messi, M. (2000), 'Polifemo e Galatea: il *κῶμος* "imperfetto" di Teocrito, *Id.* VI e XI', *Acme* 53: 23–41.

Meuli, K. (1921), *Odyssee und Argonautika: Untersuchungen zur griechischen Sagengeschichte und zum Epos* (Berlin). [= (1975), ii. 593–676]

—— (1975), *Gesammelte Schriften* (Basel and Stuttgart).

Meyer, K. (1906), *The Triads of Ireland* (Royal Irish Academy Todd Lecture Series 18; Dublin).

Meyer, W. (1885), 'Zur Geschichte des griechischen und lateinischen Hexameters', *Kgl. Bayer. Akad. zu München, Sitzung. Philos.-philol. und hist. Cl.*, Heft VI (Munich), 979–1089.

Michelini, A. N. (1989), 'Neophron and Euripides' *Medeia* 1056–80', *TAPA* 119: 115–35.

Miller, D. A. (2000), *The Epic Hero* (Baltimore and London).

Miller, M. E. (1868), *Mélanges de littérature grecque* (Paris). [reprinted Amsterdam 1965]

Moles, J. (1996), 'Herodotus warns the Athenians', *PLLS* 9: 259–84.

—— (2002), 'Herodotus and Athens', in Bakker *et al.* (2002), 33–52.

Momigliano, A. (1942), 'Terra marique', *JRS* 32: 53–64.

—— (1945), 'The Locrian Maidens and the date of Lycophron's *Alexandra*', *CQ* 39: 53–64.

Mommsen, C. J. T. (1864), *Pindari Carmina* (Berlin).

Mondi, R. (1983), 'The Homeric Cyclopes: folktale, tradition, and theme', *TAPA* 113: 17–38.

Montanari, E. (2003), *La critica del testo secondo Paul Maas: testo e commento* (Strumenti e Studi NS 3; Florence).

Montes Cala, J. G., Sánchez Ortiz de Landaluce, M., and Gallé Cejudo, R. J. (1999) (eds.), *Plutarco, Dioniso y el Vino: actas del VI Simposio Espanol sobre Plutarco, Cádiz, 14–16 de mayo de 1998* (Madrid).

Montón Subias, S. (1990), 'Galateia', *LIMC* v/1: 1000–5.

Morgan, J. R. (1989), 'A sense of the ending: the conclusion of Heliodoros' *Aithiopika*', *TAPA* 119: 299–320.

—— and Stoneman, R. (1994) (eds.), *Greek Fiction: The Greek Novel in Context* (London and New York).

Morris, I. (1994) (ed.), *Classical Greece: Ancient Histories and Modern Archaeologies* (Cambridge).

Most, G. W. (1998) (ed.), *Editing Texts / Texte edieren* (Aporemata 2; Göttingen).

—— (2000), 'Generating genres: the idea of the tragic', in Depew and Obbink (2000) (eds.), 15–35.

—— (2005), *Doubting Thomas* (Cambridge, MA and London).

Müller, C. W. (1985), 'Die Archilochoslegende', *RhM* n.F. 128: 99–151.

Müller, R. J. (1992) (ed.), *Homerische Motiven. Beiträge zur Entstehung, Eigenart und Wirkung von Ilias und Odyssee* (Stuttgart).

Müller-Seidel, W. (1980), *Theodor Fontane. Soziale Romankunst in Deutschland*^{2} (Stuttgart).

Murray, G. G. A. (1902, 1904, 1909), *Euripidis Tragoediae* (Oxford).

—— (1924), *The Rise of the Greek Epic*^{3} (Oxford).

—— (1937^{1}, 1955^{2}), *Aeschyli septem quae supersunt Tragoediae* (Oxford).

—— (1940), *Aeschylus the Creator of Tragedy* (Oxford).

Myers, K. S. (1994), *Ovid's Causes: Cosmogony and Aetiology in the* Metamorphoses (Ann Arbor).

Nagle, B. R. (1988), 'A trio of love-triangles in Ovid's *Metamorphoses*', *Arethusa* 21: 75–98.

Naiditch, P. G. (1984), 'Dating errors in *The Classical Papers of A. E. Housman*', *American Notes and Queries* 22: 137–8.

—— (1988*a*), *A. E. Housman at University College, London: the Election of 1892* (Leiden, New York, Copenhagen, Cologne).

—— (1988*b*), 'Housman's knowledge of Greek', *LCM* 13: 142–4.

—— (1995), *Problems in the Life and Writings of A. E. Housman* (Beverly Hills).

Naiditch, P. G. (1998), 'Bibliography and the history of classical scholarship', *Echos du Monde Classique / Classical Views* 42: 645–62.

Nauck, A. (1848), *Aristophanis Byzantii Grammatici Alexandrini fragmenta* (Halle).

—— (1877), *Homeri Ilias* (Berlin).

Nelson, S. (1997), 'The justice of Zeus in Hesiod's fable of the hawk and the nightingale', *CJ* 92: 235–47.

Neumann, G. (1967), 'Der lykische Name der Athena', *Kadmos* 6: 80–7.

—— (1970), 'Beiträge zum lykischen IV', *Sprache* 16: 54–62.

—— (1979), 'Namen und Epiklesen lykischer Götter', in *Florilegium Anatolicum. Mélanges offerts à Emmanuel Laroche* (Paris), 259–71.

—— (1999), 'Zwei mykenische Personennamen', in Habisreitinger *et al.* (1999), 201–5.

Nickau, K. (1966), *Ammonii qui dicitur liber de adfinium vocabulorum differentia* (Leipzig).

—— (1977), *Untersuchungen zur textkritischen Methode des Zenodotos von Ephesos* (Untersuchungen zur antiken Literatur und Geschichte 16; Berlin).

Nieto Hernández, P. (2000), 'Back in the cave of the Cyclops', *AJP* 121: 345–66.

Nineham, D. (1968), *The Gospel of St Mark* (Pelican Gospel Commentaries; London).

Nøjgaard, M. (1984), 'La moralisation de la fable: d'Ésope à Romulus', in Adrados and Reverdin (1984), 225–52.

Norden, E. (1913), *Agnostos Theos* (Leipzig and Berlin).

—— (1924), *Die Geburt des Kindes* (Studien der Bibliothek Warburg 3; Leipzig).

Nörenberg, H.-W. (1973), 'Untersuchungen zum Schluss der *Περιήγησις τῆς Ἑλλάδος* des Pausanias', *Hermes* 101: 235–52.

Nussbaum, M. C. (1986), *The Fragility of Goodness: Luck and Ethics in Greek Tragedy and Philosophy* (Cambridge).

O'Hogain, D. (1988), *Fionn mac Cumhail: Images of the Celtic Hero* (Dublin).

O'Neill, E. G. (1942), 'The localization of metrical word-types in the Greek hexameter. Homer, Hesiod and the Alexandrians', *YCS* 8: 105–78.

Oberlies, T. (1998–9), *Die Religion des Rgveda* (Publications of the De Nobili Research Library 26–7; Vienna).

Oettinger, N. (1999), 'Das Ablaut des *i*-Kollektivums oder: idg. **méli-t* "Honig", gr. **ἄλφιτ-* "Gerste", heth. **péri* "Haus"', in Habisreitinger *et al.* (1999), 207–14.

Ong, W. J. (1982), *Orality and Literacy. The Technologizing of the Word* (London and New York).
Ophuisen, J. M. van (1987), *Hephaestion on Metre* (*Mnem.* Suppl. 100; Leiden).
Oranje, H. (1984), *Euripides' Bacchae: The Play and its Audience* (Leiden).
Osborne, R. G. (1988), 'Death revisited; death revised. The death of the artist in classical Greece', *Art History* 11: 1–16.
—— (1998), *Archaic and Classical Greek Art* (Oxford).
Otten, H. (1971), *Ein hethitisches Festritual* (Studien zu den Bogazkoy-Texten 13; Weisbaden).
Pack, R. A. (1963), *Artemidori Daldiani Onirocriticon Libri V* (Lepizig).
Page, D. L. (1934), *Actors' Interpolations in Greek Tragedy* (Oxford).
—— (1938), *Euripides:* Medea (Oxford).
—— (1942), *Greek Literary Papyri* I: *Poetry* (London and Cambridge, MA). [reprinted as *Select Papyri* III]
—— (1955), *Sappho and Alcaeus* (Oxford).
—— (1964), 'Archilochus and the oral tradition', in Reverdin (1964), 117–63.
—— (1972), *Aeschyli Tragoediae* (Oxford).
Page, N. (1983), *A. E. Housman: a Critical Biography* (London).
Palmieri, V. (1988), *Herennius Philo. De diversis verborum significationibus* (Naples).
Papaioannou, S. (2005), *Epic Succession and Dissension: Ovid,* Metamorphoses *13.623–14.582, and the Reinvention of the* Aeneid (Untersuchungen zur antiken Literatur und Geschichte 73; Berlin and New York).
Parke, H. W., and Wormell, D. E. W. (1956), *The Delphic Oracle* (Oxford).
Parker, L. P. E. (1958), 'Some observations on the incidence of word-end in anapaestic paroemiacs', *CQ* NS 8: 82–9.
—— (1966), 'Porson's Law extended', *CQ* NS 16: 1–26.
—— (1968), 'Split resolution in Greek dramatic lyric', *CQ* NS 18: 241–69.
—— (1997), *The Songs of Aristophanes* (Oxford).
—— (2001), 'Consilium et ratio? Papyrus A of Bacchylides and Alexandrian metrical scholarship', *CQ* NS 51: 23–52.
Parker, R. C. T. (1999), 'Through a glass darkly: Sophocles and the divine', in Griffin (1999*b*), 11–30.
Paton, W. R., Wegehaupt, I., and Pohlenz, M. (1974), *Plutarchi Moralia* I^2 (revised by H. Gärtner; 1st ed. 1925; Leipzig).
Pearson, A. C. (1924), *Sophoclis Fabulae* (Oxford).
Peinault, G.-J., and Petit, D. (forthcoming) (eds.), *Colloque de travail de la Societé des Études Indo-Européennes: langue poétique indo-européenne* (Paris).

Pelliccia, H. (1995), *Mind, Body, and Speech in Homer and Pindar* (Hypomnemata 107; Göttingen).
Pelling, C. B. R. (1997*a*), 'Aeschylus' *Persae* and history, in id. (1997*b*) (ed.), 1–19.
—— (1997*b*) (ed.), *Greek Tragedy and the Historian* (Oxford).
—— (forthcoming), 'Ion's *Epidemiai* and Plutarch's Ion', in Jennings and Katsaros (forthcoming).
Pérez Jiménez, A., García López, J., and Aguilar, R. M. (1999) (eds.), *Plutarco, Platón, y Aristóteles: Actas del V Congreso Internacional de la I.P.S. (Madrid-Cuenca, 4–7 de mayo de 1999)* (Madrid).
Pernot, L. (1994), 'Lucien et Dion de Pruse', in Billault and Buisson (1994), 109–16.
Perrotta, G. (1935), *Sofocle* (Messina and Milan). [reprinted Rome, 1963 and Florence, 1965]
Perry, B. E. (1952), *Aesopica* (Urbana).
—— (1965), *Babrius and Phaedrus* (Cambridge, MA and London).
Pervo, R. (1987), *Profit with Delight. The Literary Genre of the* Acts of the Apostles (Philadelphia).
Petrain, D. (2003), 'Homer, Theocritus and the Milan Posidippus (P.Mil.Vogl. VIII 309, col. III.28–41)', *CJ* 98: 359–88.
Pettazzoni, R. (1956), *The All-knowing God. Researches in Early Religion and Culture* (transl. H. J. Rose; London).
Pfeiffer, R. (1949), *Callimachus. Volumen 1. Fragmenta* (Oxford).
—— (1953), *Callimachus. Volumen II. Hymni et Epigrammata* (Oxford).
—— (1968), *History of Classical Scholarship. From the Beginnings to the End of the Hellenistic Age* (Oxford).
Pickard-Cambridge, A. W. (1988), *The Dramatic Festivals of Athens*^{2} (revised with a supplement by J. Gould and D. M. Lewis; Oxford).
Pinnoy, M. (1984), 'Plutarch's comment on Sophocles' style', *QUCC* NS 16: 159–64.
Pinsent, J. (1990), [Editorial comment], *LCM* 15: 1–2.
Platnauer, M. (1938), *Euripides:* Iphigenia in Tauris (Oxford).
Platt, A. (1898), 'Notes on Bacchylides', *CR* 12: 58–64.
—— (1910), 'Callimachus *Iambi* 162–170', *CQ* 4: 205.
Podlecki, A. J. (1984), *The Early Greek Poets and their Times* (Vancouver).
Pohlenz, M. (1937), *Herodot: der erste Geschichtsschreiber des Abendlandes* (Leipzig).
Pomeroy, S. B. (1975), *Goddesses, Whores, Wives and Slaves: Women in Classical Antiquity* (London).
Porson, R. (1822), *Φωτίου τοῦ Πατριάρχου Λεξέων Συναγωγή* (London).
Porter, H. N. (1951), 'The early Greek hexameter', *YCS* 12: 8–63.

Post, L. A. (1947), 'Aeschylean *onkos* in Sophocles and Aristotle', *TAPA* 78: 242–51.
Powell, J. U. (1919), 'On the new fragments of Greek poetry recently published at Berlin', *CR* 33: 91.
Prickard, A. O. (1879), *The Persae of Aeschylus* (London).
Propp, V. (1968), *The Morphology of the Folktale* (revised by L. A. Wagner; Austin, Texas, 1968). [Russian original Leningrad, 1928]
Puelma, M. (1972), 'Sänger und König', *MH* 29: 86–109.
Puhvel, J. (1970) (ed.), *Myth and Law among the Indo–Europeans: Studies in Indo-European Comparative Mythology* (Publications of the UCLA Center for the Study of Comparative Folklore and Mythology 1; Berkeley, Los Angeles, and London).
—— (1987), *Comparative Mythology* (Baltimore and London).
Raalte, M. van (1986), *Rhythm and Metre: Towards a Systematic Description of Greek Stichic Verse* (Studies in Greek and Latin linguistics 3; Assen and Wolfeboro, NH).
Radermacher, L. (1909), *Sophokles: Oidipus auf Kolonos* (Berlin).
—— (1931), *Der homerische Hermeshymnus* (Sb. Akad. der Wissenschaften in Wien, Ph.-hist. Klasse, 213.1; Vienna and Leipzig).
—— (1953), '*Πορδή*', *RE* 22/1: 235–40.
Raimondi, V. (2005), '*Αἰπολικὸς δύσερως* in Posidippo 19 A.-B.: un richiamo al Ciclope innamorato infelice di Theocr. *Idd.* 6 e 11', in Di Marco *et al.* (2005), 133–46.
Reeve, M. D. (1972), 'Euripides, *Medea* 1021–1080', *CQ* NS 22: 51–61.
—— (1977), 'Statius's *Silvae* in the fifteenth century', *CQ* NS 71: 202–25.
—— (1984), 'Tibullus 2.6', *Phoenix* 38: 235–9.
—— (1985), 'Archetypes', *Sileno* 11 [Miscellanea Barigazzi; published 1987]: 193–201.
—— (1989), '*Eliminatio codicum descriptorum*: a methodological problem', in Grant (1989), 1–35.
—— (1998), 'Shared innovations, dichotomies, and evolution', in Ferrari (1998), 445–505.
Rehm, R. (1994), *Marriage to Death: the Conflation of Wedding and Funeral Rituals in Greek Tragedy* (Princeton).
Reinhardt, K. (1948), 'Die Abenteuer der Odyssee', in *Von Werken und Formen. Vorträge und Aufsätze* (Godesberg), 52–162. [= (1960), 47–124]
—— (1960), *Tradition und Geist. Gesammelte Essays zur Dichtung* (Göttingen).
—— (1979), *Sophocles* (transl. H. Harvey and D. Harvey; German original 1933, 1941, and 1947; Oxford).
—— *et al.* (1956), *Festschrift Bruno Snell* (Munich).

Reinhardt, U., and Sallmann, K. (1974) (eds.), *Musa Iocosa: Arbeiten über Humor, Komik und Komödie. Andreas Thierfelder zum siebzigsten Geburtstag am 15. Juni 1973* (Hildesheim).

Repath, I. D. (2005), 'Achilles Tatius' *Leucippe and Cleitophon*: what happened next?', *CQ* NS 55: 250–65.

Reverdin, O. (1964) (ed.), *Archiloque* (Entretiens sur l'antiquité classique 10: Vandoeuvres and Geneva).

Revermann, M. (1999–2000), 'Euripides, tragedy and Macedon: some conditions of reception', *ICS* 24–5: 451–67.

Reynolds, L. D. (1983*a*), 'Introduction', in id. (1983*b*), xiii–xliii.

—— (1983*b*) (ed.), *Texts and Transmission: a Survey of the Latin Classics* (Oxford).

Rhodes, P. J. (2003), 'Nothing to do with democracy: Athenian drama and the *polis*', *JHS* 123: 104–19.

Rich, J., and Shipley, G. (1993) (eds.), *War and Society in the Greek World* (London).

Richards, G. (1941), *Housman, 1897–1936* (London).

Richardson, N. J. (1993), *The* Iliad*: a Commentary. Volume VI:* Books 21–24 (Cambridge).

—— (2003), Introduction to *The Homeric Hymns*, translated by J. Cashford (London).

Rieken, E. (1999), *Untersuchungen zur nominalen Stammbildung des Hethitischen* (Studien zu den Boğazköy-Texten 44; Wiesbaden).

Rijksbaron, A. (1991), *Grammatical Observations on Euripides' Bacchae* (Amsterdam Studies in Classical Philology 1; Amsterdam).

Risch, E. (1974), *Wortbildung der homerischen Sprache*^{2} (Berlin).

Rist, J. M. (1969), *Stoic Philosophy* (Cambridge).

Rivier, A. (1952), review of Lasserre (1950), *REG* 65: 464–68.

Roberts, D. H., Dunn, F. M., and Fowler, D. P. (1997) (eds.), *Classical Closure. Reading the End in Greek and Latin Literature* (Princeton).

Robertson, D. S. (1936), 'A. E. Housman', *CR* 50: 113–15.

—— (1949), 'Housman, Alfred Edward', *The Dictionary of National Biography 1931–1940* (London), 449–53.

Röhrich, L. (1974), *Märchen und Wirklichkeit*^{3} (Stuttgart).

—— (1991), *Folktale and Reality* (Bloomington, IN).

Roscher, W. H. (1884–1937) (ed.), *Ausführliches Lexikon der griechischen und römischen Mythologie* (Leipzig).

Rose, P. W. (1995), 'Historicising Sophocles' *Ajax*', in Goff (1995), 59–90.

Rose, V. (1886), *Aristotelis qui ferebantur librorum fragmenta* (Leipzig).

Rosen, R. M. (1988), *Old Comedy and the Iambographic Tradition* (Atlanta).

Rossi, L. E. (1976), 'Asynarteta from the archaic to the Alexandrian poets: on the authenticity of the New Archilochus', *Arethusa* 9: 207–29.

Roux, J. (1972), *Euripides: Les Bacchantes* II (Paris).

Russell, D. A. F. M. (1964), 'Longinus': *On the Sublime* (Oxford).

—— (1993), *Plutarch: Selected Essays and Dialogues* (Oxford).

—— and Wilson, N. G. (1981), *Menander Rhetor* (Oxford).

—— and Winterbottom, M. (1972), *Ancient Literary Criticism: the Principal Literary Texts in New Translations* (Oxford).

Rutherford, I. (2001), *Pindar's Paeans: a Reading of the Fragments with a Survey of the Genre* (Oxford).

Rutherford, R. B. (2005), *Classical Literature: a Concise History* (Oxford).

Sadie, S., and Hicks, A. (1987) (eds.), *Handel: Tercentenary Collection* (Basingstoke and London).

Saïd, S. (1984), 'Grecs et barbares dans les tragédies d'Euripide. La fin des différences?', *Ktema* 9 (1984): 27–53.

—— (2002), 'Greeks and barbarians in Euripides' tragedies: the end of differences?', in Harrison (2002), 62–100.

Saintyves, P. [= Nourri, E.] (1928), 'Le massacre des innocents ou la persécution de l'enfant prédestiné', in Couchoud (1928) (ed.), i. 229–72.

Sandbach, F. H. (1967), *Plutarchi Moralia Volumen VII* (Leipzig).

—— (1972^1, 1990^2), *Menandri Reliquiae Selectae* (Oxford).

Sandy, G. N. (1999), 'Apuleius' *Golden Ass*: from Miletus to Egypt', in Hofmann (1999), 81–102.

Sbardella, L. (2000), *Filita: Testimonianze e frammenti poetici* (Seminari Romani di Cultura Greca Quaderni 3; Rome).

Schade, G. (2001), 'Ovids Aeneis', *Hermes* 129: 525–32.

Schadewaldt, W. (1926), *Monolog und Selbstgespräch. Untersuchungen zur Formgeschichte der griechischen Tragödie* (Neue philologische Untersuchungen 2; Berlin).

—— (1975), *Homer Ilias. Neue Übertragung* (Frankfurt am Main).

Schake, J. (1968) (ed.), *Studien zur Sprachwissenschaft und Kulturkunde. Gedenkschrift für Wilhelm Brandenstein (1898–1967)* (Innsbrucker Beiträge zur Kulturwissenschaften 14; Innsbruck).

Scheer, E. (1881–1908), *Lycophronis Alexandra* (Berlin).

Schein, S. L. (1979), *The Iambic Trimeter in Aeschylus and Sophocles: a Study in Metrical Form* (Colombia Studies in the Classical Tradition 6; Leiden).

—— (1990), '*Philia* in Euripides' *Medea*', in Griffith and Mastronarde (1990), 57–73.

Scherer, A. (1964), 'Die Sprache des Archilochos', in Reverdin (1964), 87–116.

Schleicher, A. (1853), 'Die ersten Spaltungen des indogermanischen Urvolkes', *Allgemeine Monatsschrift für Wissenschaft und Literatur* 786–7.

—— (1860), *Die deutsche Sprache* (Stuttgart).

—— (1868), 'Eine fabel in indogermanischer ursprache', *Beiträge zur vergleichenden Sprachforschung* 5: 206–8.

Schmid, W., and Stählin, O. (1934), *Geschichte der griechischen Literatur* I/2 (Munich).

Schmidt, E. G. (1981) (ed.), *Aischylos und Pindar: Studien zu Werk und Nachwirkung* (Schriften zur Geschichte und Kultur der Antike 19; Berlin).

Schmidt, J. (1872), *Die verwandtschaftsverhältnisse der indogermanischen sprachen* (Weimar).

Schmidt, J.-U. (1999), 'Der Kindermord der fremden Kolcherin – ein tragischer Konflikt? Überlegungen zur *Medeia* des Euripides', *RhM* n.F. 142: 243–72.

—— (2003), 'Die Blendung des Kyklopen und der Zorn des Poseidon. Zum Problem der Rechtfertigung der Irrfahrten des Odysseus und ihrer Bedeutung für das Anliegen des Odysseedichters', *WS* 116: 5–42.

Schmidt, L. (1848), 'Lykophron', *RhM* n.F. 6: 135–7.

Schmitz, T. (1997), *Bildung und Macht: Zur sozialen und politischen Funktion der zweiten Sophistik in der griechischen Welt der Kaiserzeit* (Zetemata 97; Munich).

Schneider, R., and Uhlig, G. (1878–1910), *Apollonii Dyscoli quae supersunt* (Grammatici Graeci 1; Leipzig).

Schneidewin, F. W. (1838), *Delectus Poesis Graecorum Elegiacae, Iambicae, Melicae* (Göttingen).

Schröder, F. R. (1968), 'Der trunkene Dämon', in Schake (1968), 325–35.

Schroeder, F. M. (2002), 'Cyclopean superlatives', *Dionysius* 20: 9–22.

Schroeder, O. (1900), *Pindari carmina* (Leipzig).

Schürr, D. (1998), 'Kaunos in lykischen Inschriften', *Kadmos* 37: 151–2.

Schwabl, H. (1986), 'Zum Problem der Themenwahl in den homerischen Goetterhymnen', in Vaslef and Buschhausen (1986), 147–59.

Schwartz, E. (1887–91), *Scholia in Euripidem* (Berlin).

Seaford, R. A. S. (1984), *Euripides:* Cyclops (Oxford).

—— (1996), *Euripides: Bacchae* (Warminster).

—— (2000), 'The social function of Attic tragedy: a response to Jasper Griffin', *CQ* NS 50: 30–44.

Searby, D. M. (1998), *Aristotle in the Greek Gnomological Tradition* (Acta Universitatis Upsaliensis, Studia Graeca Upsaliensia 19; Uppsala).

Sebillot, P.-Y. (1968), *Le Folklore de la Bretagne* II (Paris).

Segal, C. P. (1981), *Tragedy and Civilization: an Interpretation of Sophocles* (Cambridge, MA and London).

—— (1995), *Sophocles' Tragic World: Divinity, Nature, Society* (Cambridge, MA and London).
—— (1996), 'Catharsis, audience, and closure in Greek tragedy', in Silk (1996), 149–72.
Segal, E. (1996) (ed.), *Oxford Readings in Aristophanes* (Oxford and New York).
Seidensticker, B. (1990), 'Euripides, *Medea* 1056–80, an interpolation?', in Griffith and Mastronarde (1990), 89–102.
Shackleton Bailey, D. R. (1962), 'Bentley and Horace', *Proc. Leeds Philos. and Lit. Soc.* 10: 105–15.
—— (1982), *A Profile of Horace* (London).
Shevoroshkin, V. (1967), *Lidijskij Jazyk* (Moscow).
Sidgwick, A. (1900), *Aeschyli Tragoediae* (Oxford).
Siebenkees, J. P. (1798), *Anecdota Graeca* (Nuremberg).
Sier, K. (1988), *Die lyrischen Partien der Choephoren des Aischylos* (Palingenesia 23; Stuttgart).
Silk, M. S. (1996) (ed.), *Tragedy and the Tragic: Greek Theatre and Beyond* (Oxford).
Simon, E. (1967), 'Boreas und Oreithyia auf dem silbernen Rhyton in Triest', *A & A* 13: 101–26.
Simon, M. (1973) (ed.), *Les Syncrétismes dans les religions grecque et romaine* (Paris).
Skutsch, F. (1909), 'Euphorion', *RE* 6: 1174–90.
Slater, W. J. (1969), *A Lexicon to Pindar* (Berlin and New York).
—— (1986), *Aristophanis Byzantii Fragmenta* (Sammlung griechischer und lateinischer Grammatiker 6; Berlin and New York).
Smith, B. H. (1968), *Poetic Closure. A Study of how Poems End* (Chicago and London).
Smith, R. (1995), *Handel's Oratorios and Eighteenth-Century Thought* (Cambridge).
Snell, B. (1961), *Bacchylidis Carmina cum Fragmentis* (Leipzig).
—— (1962), *Griechische Metrik*[3] (Gottingen).
—— and Maehler, H. (1975), *Pindarus: Pars II. Fragmenta* (Leipzig).
Snodgrass, A. M. (1998), *Homer and the Artists. Text and Picture in Early Greek Art* (Cambridge).
Söder, A. (1939), *Quellenuntersuchungen zum 1. Buch der Apollodorschen Bibliothek* (diss. Würzburg).
Solmsen, F. (1949), *Hesiod and Aeschylus* (Cornell Studies in Classical Philology 30; London and Ithaca, NY).
Solodow, J. B. (1988), *The World of Ovid's* Metamorphoses (Chapel Hill and London).

Sommer, F. (1930), in P. Kahle and F. Sommer, 'Die lydisch-aramäische Bilingue', *Kleinasiatische Forschungen* 1: 18–86.

Sommerstein, A. H. (1995), 'The anatomy of euphemism in Aristophanic comedy', in De Martino and Sommerstein (1995), 181–217.

—— (1997), 'The tragic audience, the *demos*, and the *Suppliants* of Aeschylus', in Pelling (1997*b*) (ed.), 63–79.

—— (2003) (ed.), *Shards from Kolonos: Studies in Sophoclean Fragments* (Le Rane Studi 34: Bari).

—— Halliwell, S., Henderson, J., and Zimmermann, B. (1993) (eds.), *Tragedy, Comedy and the Polis. Papers from the Greek Drama Conference Nottingham, 18–20 July 1990* (Le Rane Studi 11; Bari).

Sorum, C. E. (1982), 'The family in Sophocles' *Antigone* and *Electra*', *CW* 75: 201–11.

Soupault, R. (1971), *Breton Folktales* (transl. R. E. K. Meuss; London).

Sourvinou-Inwood, C. (1989), 'Assumptions and the creation of meaning: reading Sophocles' *Antigone*', *JHS* 109: 134–48.

—— (1990), 'Sophocles' Antigone as a "bad woman"', in Dieteren and Klock (1990) (eds.), 11–38.

Spanoudakis, K. (2002), *Philitas of Cos* (*Mnem.* Suppl. 229; Leiden).

Spengel, L. (1853–6), *Rhetores Graeci* (Leipzig).

Stadter, P. A., and van der Stockt, L. (2002) (eds.), *Sage and Emperor: Plutarch, Greek Intellectuals, and Roman Power in the Time of Trajan (98–117 AD)* (Symbolae Facultatis Litterarum Lovaniensis Series A 29; Leuven).

Stählin, O. (1905–34), *Clemens Alexandrinus* (Leipzig).

Stallbaum, G. (1825–6), *Commentarii ad Homeri Odysseam* (Leipzig). [Copy of the Rome 1549 ed.; reprinted Hildesheim 1960]

Starr, R. J. (1987), 'The circulation of literary texts in the Roman world', *CQ* NS 37: 213–23.

Steffen, V. (1960), *Sophokleous Ichneutai* (Warsaw).

Stephanopoulos, T. (1983), 'Drei alt-und neugriechishe Babywörter', *Glotta* 61: 12–15.

Stephens, S. A. and Winkler, J. J. (1995), *Ancient Greek Novels: the Fragments* (Princeton).

Stinton, T. C. W. (1975), '*Hamartia* in Aristotle and Greek tragedy', *CQ* NS 25: 221–54. [= (1990), 143–85]

—— (1990), *Collected Papers in Greek Tragedy* (Oxford).

Stockt, L. van der (1999*a*), 'Three Aristotles equal but one Plato: on a cluster of quotations in Plutarch', in Pérez Jiménez *et al.* (1999) (eds.), 127–40.

—— (1999*b*), 'A Plutarchan hypomnema on self-love', *AJP* 120: 575–99.

—— (2002), 'καρπὸς ἐκ φιλίας ἡγεμονικῆς (*Mor.* 814c): Plutarch's observations on the "old-boy network"', in Stadter and van der Stockt (2002), 115–40.

Subias-Konofal, V. (2004), 'L'eau et le rocher, ou le double portrait paradoxal du chant de Polyphème (*Métamorphoses* XIII, 789–869)', *REL* 82: 127–43.

Super, R. H. (1972), *Matthew Arnold, Essays Religious and Mixed* (Ann Arbor).

Swain, S. C. R. (1994), 'Dio and Lucian', in Morgan and Stoneman (1994), 166–80.

—— (1996), *Hellenism and Empire: Language, Classicism, and Power in the Greek World, AD 50–250* (Oxford).

Tafel, G. L. F. (1832), *Eustathii Metropolitae Thessalonicensis Opuscula* (Frankfurt am Main). [reprinted Amsterdam, 1964]

Taillardat, J. (1967), *Suétone: Περὶ βλασφημιῶν. Περὶ παιδιῶν* (Paris).

Taplin, O. P. (1986), 'Fifth-century tragedy and comedy: a synkrisis', *JHS* 106: 163–74. [≈ E. Segal (1996), 9–28]

—— (1992), *Homeric Soundings. The Shaping of the* Iliad (Oxford).

Taracha, P. (2002) (ed.), *Silva Anatolica. Anatolian studies presented to Maciej Popko on the occasion of his 65th birthday* (Warsaw).

Tarditi, G. (1968), *Archiloco* (Roma).

Tatum, J. (1989), *Xenophon's Imperial Fiction: On the Education of Cyrus* (Princeton).

Thompson, A., and Fraser, B. (forthcoming) (eds.), *Ancient Greek Lexicography* (London).

Thompson, D'A. W. (1936), *A Glossary of Greek Birds*² (London).

Tissol, G. (1990), 'Polyphemus and his audiences', *Syllecta Classica* 2: 45–58.

—— (2002), 'The House of Fame: Roman history and Augustan politics in *Metamorphoses* 11–15', in Boyd (2002), 305–35.

Touchefeu-Meynier, O. (1992*a*), 'Kyklops, Kyklopes', *LIMC* VI/1.154–9.

—— (1992*b*), 'Odysseus', *LIMC* VI/1.943–70.

—— (1997), 'Polyphemus I', *LIMC* VIII/1.1011–19.

Trapp, E. (2001), *Lexikon zur Byzantinischen Gräzität, 1. Band (A–K)*, (Österreichische Akademie der Wissenschaften, phil.-hist. Kl., Denkschriften 238, 250, 276, 203; Vienna).

Trencsényi-Waldapfel, I. (1959), 'Eine Aesopische Fabel und ihre Orientalischen Parallelen', *Acta Antiqua Academiae Scientiarum Hungaricae* 7: 317–27.

Treu, M. (1959), *Archilochos* (München).

Tronchet, G. (1998), *La Métamorphose à l'œuvre. Recherches sur la poétique d'Ovide dans les* Métamorphoses (Louvain-la-Neuve).

Trowell, B. (1987), '*Acis, Galatea and Polyphemus*: a "serenata a tre voci"?', in Fortune (1987), 31–93.
Tucker, T. G. (1892), 'Notes on Aeschylus', *CR* 6: 193.
Tyrrell, R. Y. (1887), 'Further note [sic] on Aristophanes, *Ranae* 1028', *CR* 1: 313.
—— (1892), *The Bacchae of Euripides* (London and New York).
—— (1897), *Sophoclis Tragoediae* (London).
Valk, M. van der (1971–87), *Eustathii Commentarii ad Homeri Iliadem pertinentes* (Leiden).
Vaslef, I., and Buschhausen, H. (1986) (eds.), *Classica et Mediaevalia: Studies in Honor of Joseph Szövérffy*, Washington and Leyden.
Verdenius, W. J. (1962), 'Notes on Euripides' Bacchae', *Mnemosyne* 4th ser. 15: 337–63.
—— (1980), 'Notes on the prologue of Euripides' *Bacchae*', *Mnemosyne* 4th ser. 33: 1–16.
—— (1981), 'Notes on the parodos of Euripides' *Bacchae*', *Mnemosyne* 4th ser. 34: 300–15.
—— (1985), *A Commentary on Hesiod, Works and Days, vv. 1–382* (*Mnem.* Suppl. 86; Leiden).
Verrall, A. W. (1889), *The* Agamemnon *of Aeschylus* (London).
Vian, F. (1952), *La Guerre des Géants: le mythe avant l'époque hellénistique* (Études et Commentaires 11; Paris).
—— (1974–81), *Apollonios de Rhodes* (Paris).
Vickers, B. (1973), *Towards Greek Tragedy: Drama, Myth, Society* (London and New York).
Visser, E. (1997), *Homers Katalog der Schiffe* (Stuttgart and Leipzig).
Voigt, E.-M. (1971), *Sappho et Alcaeus* (Amsterdam).
Von der Mühll, P. (1930), *Der Große Aias* (Basel). [= (1976), 435–72]
—— (1976), *Ausgewählte Kleine Schriften* (Schweizerische Beiträge zur Altertumswissenschaft Heft 12; Basel).
Vox, O. (1980), '*Πυγοστόλος*: una donna-uccello?', *Glotta* 58: 172–7.
Wachsmuth, C., and Hense, O. (1884–1912), *Ioannis Stobaei Anthologium* (Berlin).
Wackernagel, J. (1888), 'Miszellen zur griechischen Grammatik', *KZ* 29, 124–52. [= (1953–79), i. 627–55]
—— (1892), 'Über ein Gesetz der indogermanischen Wortstellung', *IF* 1: 333–436. [= (1953–79), i. 1–104]
—— (1916), *Sprachliche Untersuchungen zu Homer* (Forschungen zur griechischen und lateinischen Grammatik 4; Göttingen).
—— (1953–79), *Kleine Schriften* (Göttingen).
Walcot, P. (1966), *Hesiod and the Near East* (Cardiff).

Waldock, A. J. A. (1951), *Sophocles the Dramatist* (Cambridge).

Waszink, J. H. (1974), *Biene und Honig als Symbol des Dichters und der Dichtung in der griechisch-römischen Antike* (Rheinisch-Westfälische Akademie der Wissenschaften, Geisteswissenschaften: Vorträge 196; Opladen).

Waterfield, R., and Kidd, I. (1992), *Plutarch: Essays* (Harmondsworth).

Watkins, C. (1975), 'La famille indo-européenne de grec ὄρχις; linguistique, poétique et mythologique', *BSL* 70 (1975), 11–26. [= (1994), ii. 520–35]

—— (1985), 'Greek *menoináai*: a dead metaphor', *IJAL* 51 [Festschrift for Eric Pratt Hamp]: 614–18.

—— (1994), *Selected Writings* (Innsbrücker Beiträge zur Sprachwissenschaft 80; Innsbruck).

—— (1995), *How to Kill a Dragon: Aspects of Indo-European Poetics* (New York and Oxford).

—— (1998), 'Homer and Hittite Revisited', in Knox and Foss (1998), 201–11.

—— (2002), 'Homer and Hittite Revisited II', in Yener and Hoffner (2002), 167–76.

—— (forthcoming), '"Hermit Crabs", or new wine in old bottles. Anatolian and Hellenic connections from Homer and before to Antiochus I of Commagene and after', in Collins, Bachvarova, and Rutherford (forthcoming).

Watt, W. S. (1987), 'Housman's knowledge of Greek', *LCM* 12: 148.

Watts, A. W. (1963), *The Two Hands of God: the Myths of Polarity* (New York).

Webster, T. B. L. (1936[1], 1969[2]), *An Introduction to Sophocles* (Oxford[1]; London[2]).

Wecklein, N. (1888), *Äschylos Orestie* (Leipzig).

—— (1900), *Euripidis Orestes* (Leipzig).

Wedd, N. (1895), *Euripides: The Orestes* (Cambridge).

Wehrli, F. (1956), 'Hesiods Prometheus (Theogonie v. 507–616)', in *Navicula Chiloniensis: studia philologa Felici Jacoby professori Chiloniensi emerito octogenario oblata* (Leiden), 30–6. [= (1972), 50–5 = Heitsch (1966), 411–18]

—— (1969), *Die Schule des Aristoteles: Texte und Kommentar. Heft VII: Herakleides Pontikos* (Basel and Stuttgart).

—— (1972), *Theoria und Humanitas. Gesammelte Schriften zur antiken Gedankenwelt* (Zürich and Munich).

Weil, H. (1879), *Sept Tragédies d'Euripide* (Paris).

Wellhausen, J. (1903), *Das Evangelium Marci* (Berlin).

Wendel, C. T. E. (1914), *Scholia in Theocritum Vetera* (Leipzig).

—— (1935), *Scholia in Apollonium Rhodium Vetera* (Berlin).

Wessely, C. (1921), *Studien zur Paläographie und Papyruskunde* XX (Leipzig).
West, M. L. (1966*a*), *Hesiod:* Theogony (Oxford).
—— (1966*b*), 'Conjectures on 46 Greek Poets', *Philologus* 110: 147–68.
—— (1969), 'Three Greek baby-words', *Glotta* 47: 184–6.
—— (1973), *Textual Criticism and Editorial Technique* (Stuttgart).
—— (1974*a*), *Studies in Greek Elegy and Iambus* (Untersuchungen zur antiken Literatur und Geschichte 14; Berlin and New York).
—— (1974*b*), 'Ein wiedergefundenes Archilochos-Gedicht', *Poetica* 6: 468–512.
—— (1978), *Hesiod:* Works and Days (Oxford).
—— (1979), 'The parodos of the *Agamemnon*', *CQ* NS 29: 1–6.
—— (1980), 'Other early poetry', in Dover *et al.* (1980), 29–49.
—— (1982), *Greek Metre* (Oxford).
—— (1983*a*), *The Orphic Poems* (Oxford).
—— (1983*b*), 'Tragica VI', *BICS* 30: 63–82.
—— (1984), 'The ascription of fables to Aesop in archaic and classical Greece', in Adrados and Reverdin (1984), 105–36.
—— (1985*a*), *The Hesiodic Catalogue of Women. Its Nature, Structure and Origins* (Oxford).
—— (1985*b*), 'Ion of Chios', *BICS* 32: 71–8.
—— (1987), *Euripides:* Orestes (Warminster).
—— (1990), *Studies in Aeschylus* (Beiträge zur Altertumskunde 1; Stuttgart).
—— (1992), *Ancient Greek Music* (Oxford).
—— (1997), *The East Face of Helicon: West Asiatic Elements in Greek Poetry and Myth* (Oxford).
—— (1998), *Aeschylus: Tragoediae* (Stuttgart). [revised impression of 1990 ed.]
—— (1998–2000), *Homerus: Ilias* (Leipzig).
—— (2000), 'Fable and disputation', in Aro and Whiting (2000), 93–7.
—— (2001), *Studies in the Text and Transmission of the Iliad* (Munich and Leipzig).
—— (2003*a*), *Greek Epic Fragments from the Seventh to the Fifth Centuries B.C.* (Cambridge, MA and London).
—— (2003*b*), *Homeric Hymns, Homeric Apocrypha, Lives of Homer* (Cambridge, MA and London).
West, S. R. (1967), *The Ptolemaic Papyri of Homer* (Papyrologica Coloniensia 3: Cologne).
—— (1983), 'Notes on the text of Lycophron', *CQ* NS 33: 114–35.
—— (1984), 'Lycophron italicised', *JHS* 104: 127–51.
—— (1989), 'Laertes revisited', *PCPS* NS 35: 113–43.

—— (2001), 'Phoenix's antecedents: a note on *Iliad* 9', *SCI* 20: 1–15.
—— (2003), '*ΚΕΡΚΙΔΟΣ ΠΑΡΑΜΥΘΙΑ*? For whom did Chariton write?' *ZPE* 143: 63–9.
Whitley, J. (1994), 'Protoattic pottery: a contextual approach', in Morris (1994), 51–70.
Whitmarsh, T. (2005), *The Second Sophistic* (*Greece & Rome* New Surveys in the Classics 35: Oxford).
Wilamowitz-Moellendorff, T. von (1917), *Die dramatische Technik des Sophokles* (Philologische Untersuchungen 22; Berlin).
Wilamowitz-Moellendorff, U. von (1879), 'Parerga 1–27', *Hermes* 14: 161–86. [= (1935–72), iv. 1–23]
—— (1884), *Homerische Untersuchungen* (Berlin).
—— (1893), *Aristoteles und Athen* I (Berlin).
—— (1905), 'Lesefrüchte 92–116', *Hermes* 40: 116–53. [= (1935–72), iv. 169–207]
—— (1906), *Die Textgeschichte der griechischen Bukoliker* (Berlin).
—— (1914), *Aischylos: Interpretationen* (Berlin).
—— (1921), *Griechische Verskunst* (Berlin).
—— (1923), *Griechische Tragödien Übersetzt* IV (Berlin).
—— (1924*a*), 'Lesefrüchte 181–192', *Hermes* 59: 249–73. [= (1935–72), iv. 343–67]
—— (1924*b*), review of Pearson (1924), *DLZ* 45: 2315–18. [= (1935–72), i. 461–3]
—— (1926*a*), 'Die Verklärung Christi', *Reden und Vorträge* II[4] (Berlin), 280–93.
—— (1926*b*), 'Lesefrüchte 203–217', *Hermes* 61: 277–303. [= (1935–72), iv. 404–30]
—— (1935–72), *Kleine Schriften* (Berlin and Amsterdam).
Wilkins, J. (1993), *Euripides:* Heraclidae (Oxford).
Willi, A. (2002) (ed.), *The Language of Greek Comedy* (Oxford).
—— (2003), 'New language for a New Comedy: a linguistic approach to Aristophanes, *Plutus*', *PCPS* NS 49: 40–73.
Williams, R. J. (1956), 'The literary history of a Mesopotamian fable', *Phoenix* 10: 70–7.
Willink, C. W. (1966), 'Some problems of text and interpretation in the *Bacchae*. I.', *CQ* NS 16: 27–50.
—— (1989), *Euripides:* Orestes (Oxford). [revised impression of 1986 ed.]
Willink, C. W. (2001), 'Critical studies in the cantica of Sophocles: I. Antigone', *CQ* NS 51: 65–89.

Wilson, J. V. K. (1985), *The Legend of Etana: a New Edition* (Warminster).
Wilson, N. G. (1983), *Scholars of Byzantium* (London).
Windszus, W. (1991), *Georg Friedrich Händel. Acis and Galatea (1. Fassung), HWV 49a*, Hallische Händel-Ausgabe, I/9/1 (Kassel, New York).
Winkler, J. J. (1985), *Auctor & Actor. A Narratological Reading of Apuleius'* Golden Ass (Berkeley and Los Angeles).
Winnington-Ingram, R. P. (1980), *Sophocles: an Interpretation* (Cambridge).
Wirth, P. (2000), *Eustathii Thessalonicensis opera minora: magnam partem inedita* (Corpus fontium historiae Byzantinae, Series Berolinensis 32; Berlin and New York).
Worthington, I. (1990), 'The ending of Euripides' "Medea"', *Hermes* 118: 502–5.
Wyss, B. (1935), *Antimachi Colophonii Reliquiae* (Berlin).
Wyttenbach, D. (1795–1830), *Plutarchi Moralia* (Oxford).
Yener, K. A., and Hoffner, H. A. (2002) (eds.), *Recent Developments in Hittite Archaeology and History. Papers in Memory of Hans G. Güterbock* (Winona Lake, IN).
Zadorojnyi, A. (forthcoming): '*ὥσπερ ἐν ἐνόπτρῳ*: the rhetoric and philosophy of Plutarch's mirrors', to appear in a collection on *Synkrisis in Plutarch's Lives* edited by N. Humble and A. Powell.
Zintzen, C. (1985), 'Zur Aeneis-Interpretation des Cristoforo Landino', *Mittellateinische Jahrbuch* 20: 193–215. [= (2000), 401–26]
—— (2000), *Athen, Rom, Florenz: ausgewählte kleine Schriften* (Hildesheim, Zürich and New York).
Zwierlein, O. (1998), 'Interpretation in Antike und Mittelalter', in Funke *et al.* (1998). [= (2004), 29–51]
—— (2004), *Lucubrationes Philologae. Band 2: Antike und Mittelalter* (Untersuchungen zur antiken Literatur und Geschichte; Berlin and New York).

Index Locorum

Index of Greek Words

General Index